ISBN 978-1-5285-8752-5
PIBN 10925660

This book is a reproduction of an important historical work. Forgotten Books uses
state-of-the-art technology to digitally reconstruct the work, preserving the original format
whilst repairing imperfections present in the aged copy. In rare cases, an imperfection in
the original, such as a blemish or missing page, may be replicated in our edition. We do,
however, repair the vast majority of imperfections successfully; any imperfections that
remain are intentionally left to preserve the state of such historical works.

1 MONTH OF
FREE
READING

at

www.ForgottenBooks.com

By purchasing this book you are
eligible for one month membership to
ForgottenBooks.com, giving you
unlimited access to our entire
collection of over 1,000,000 titles via
our web site and mobile apps.

To claim your free month visit:

www.forgottenbooks.com/free925660

English
Français
Deutsche
Italiano
Español
Português

www.forgottenbooks.com

Mythology Photography **Fiction**
Fishing Christianity **Art** Cooking
Essays Buddhism Freemasonry
Medicine **Biology** Music **Ancient**
Egypt Evolution Carpentry Physics
Dance Geology **Mathematics** Fitness
Shakespeare **Folklore** Yoga Marketing
Confidence Immortality Biographies
Poetry **Psychology** Witchcraft
Electronics Chemistry History **Law**
Accounting **Philosophy** Anthropology
Alchemy Drama Quantum Mechanics
Atheism Sexual Health **Ancient History**
Entrepreneurship Languages Sport
Paleontology Needlework Islam
Metaphysics Investment Archaeology
Parenting Statistics Criminology
Motivational

REPORTS OF CASES

DETERMINED IN

THE DISTRICT COURTS OF APPEAL

OF THE

STATE OF CALIFORNIA

C. P. POMEROY

REPORTER

RANDOLPH V. WHITING

ASSISTANT REPORTER

VOLUME 31

SAN FRANCISCO

BANCROFT-WHITNEY COMPANY

1917

San Francisco
The Filmer Brothers Electrotype Company
Typographers and Stereotypers

DISTRICT COURTS OF APPEAL.

(iii)

TABLE OF CASES—VOL. 31.

CASES APPROVED, DISAPPROVED, CRITICISED, AND DISTINGUISHED.

TABLE OF CASES CITED—VOL. 31.

CITATIONS—VOL. 31.

CALIFORNIA.
CONSTITUTION.

STATUTES.

CODE OF CIVIL PROCEDURE.

CODE OF CIVIL PROCEDURE—Continued.

CIVIL CODE.

PENAL CODE.

SECTION	PAGE	SECTION	PAGE
22	433, 438	960	369
182	460, 462	971	363
195	488	1070	369
211	5	1111	779, 782, 794
270a	736	1191	353, 354
288a	793	1202	353, 354
460	420	1203	353
503	363	1247	520, 521, 522
508	363, 364, 366, 367	1248	522
628f	240	1253	730
809	368	1329	799
950	794	1382	354
951	368	1425	199, 200, 201, 203, 204
954	369		

POLITICAL CODE.

SECTION	PAGE	SECTION	PAGE
433	26	1771	351, 352
472	8	1775	351
654–691	9	3731	272, 273
663	10, 25	3753	529, 530
664	10	3785	60
666	23	3788	59, 60, 61, 62, 63
667	10	3817	59, 60, 61
669	10	4013	392
671	24, 27, 28	4017	392, 393
682	23, 26	4018	392
691	9	4041	800
1543	352	4290	23, 25, 26, 27, 28
1565	351, 352	4300g	799
1617	142, 143	4307	799

IDAHO.

Rev. Code, sec. 5220. Judgment.................................. 752
Rev. Code, secs. 5223, 5224. Judgment 753

IOWA.

Code, sec. 1789. Life Insurance................................. 177

UNITED STATES.

Rev. Stats., sec. 5234. Receivers of National Banks..........708, 709

REPORTS OF CASES

DETERMINED IN

THE DISTRICT COURTS OF APPEAL

OF THE

STATE OF CALIFORNIA.

[Crim. No. 339. Third Appellate District.—June 22, 1916.]

THE PEOPLE, Respondent, v. ALBERT FRANCIS FERRARA, Appellant.

CRIMINAL LAW—ROBBERY—EVIDENCE—REGISTRATION AT HOTEL UNDER OTHER THAN TRUE NAME—VERBAL PROOF BY WITNESS.—In a prosecution for the crime of robbery, it is not error to permit a witness, who went with the defendant on the night of the commission of the crime to an adjoining town, to testify that they went to a hotel and that the defendant registered under a name other than his true name.

ID.—STATEMENTS OF DEFENDANT AT PRELIMINARY EXAMINATION—PROOF BY REPORTER—REFERENCE TO NOTES NOT FILED.—In such a prosecution there is no error in allowing the phonographic reporter who acted at the preliminary examination to refer to his original notes to enable him to testify as to certain statements made by the defendant at such hearing, notwithstanding such notes had not been filed.

ID. — CONTRADICTORY TESTIMONY — CONSIDERATION BY JURY—INSTRUCTION.—An instruction that contradictory testimony is admissible only for the purpose of impeaching the credibility of a witness and that the jury might not consider it as evidence of the truth of such statements, is properly refused.

ID.—GUILT OF DEFENDANT—TAKING OF PROPERTY BY FORCE AND FEAR—USE OF DISJUNCTIVE—INSTRUCTION.—An instruction that if the jury found that the taking of the money was accomplished by means of "force or fear," they could find a verdict of guilty, is not erroneous, notwithstanding that the information charged that the taking was accomplished by means of force *and* fear.

31 Cal. App.—1

APPEAL from a judgment of the Superior Court of San Joaquin County, and from an order denying a new trial. C. W. Norton, Judge.

The facts are stated in the opinion of the court.

Cross & Lynch, for Appellant.

U. S. Webb, Attorney-General, and J. Charles Jones, Deputy Attorney-General, for Respondent.

ELLISON, J., *pro tem.*—The defendant has been convicted of the crime of robbery and sentenced to imprisonment for the term of fifteen years. He prosecutes this appeal from the judgment and order denying his motion for a new trial.

In view of the youth of the defendant and the judgment rendered the record has been examined with great care, the result of which is that no reversible error has been found. In fact, the trial seems to have been conducted with unusual care and regard for the defendant's rights. Many points are made by appellant for a reversal, and they will be given such consideration as seems proper.

It is claimed that the *corpus delicti* was not proved. A brief narrative of the salient facts of the case will show that this position is not well taken.

The prosecuting witness, Duffy, came from Merced to Stockton on the afternoon of the second day of September, 1915, arriving there about 4 o'clock, and went to a saloon kept by a man named Grohmans. There he met the defendant and they had several drinks. At about 4:30 P. M. Duffy, in company with the defendant, left the saloon and went to the boat landing for the purpose of taking a boat to San Francisco. The defendant bought a boat ticket for himself and one for Duffy. The officers at the boat landing refused to let Duffy go on the boat because of his intoxicated condition and took up his ticket, returning to him the price thereof, one dollar. The two then returned to the Grohmans saloon and were there informed that a Southern Pacific train would leave for San Francisco at about 7 o'clock. The two walked to the Southern Pacific depot and when they reached it learned that the train they expected to take had gone; they were told that a Santa Fe train would leave at about 8:30. The

defendant told Duffy he knew the way to the Santa Fe depot
and they started to walk there, the defendant taking the
lead. When they were within about 150 yards of the Santa
Fe depot the defendant said: "Give me a smoke." While
sitting there on the side of the railroad track, smoking, a
man came along with a lantern and the defendant asked him
what time the train would leave and defendant told Duffy
he said about 9 o'clock. (It seems Duffy is somewhat deaf.)
Shortly after this man left the defendant attracted Duffy's
attention to something up the track and when Duffy turned
his head the defendant struck him just back of the ear. Duffy
jumped up and the defendant struck him again between the
eyes and once on the hand. After Duffy had been thus struck
he felt "everything going—everything kind of commenced to
get dark for me." Duffy testified that after this he had a
faint recollection of defendant going through his pockets.
After some time Duffy regained consciousness and managed,
after several efforts, to get to his feet. The defendant was
gone and Duffy did not see him again until after his arrest.
Duffy testified that when he was struck by the defendant he
had in his pocket about $28; that when he came to his money
was all gone—there was none in his pockets. He testified that
just before he left Modesto he got two checks which he cashed,
one for $30 and one for $12.50, and then detailed, as best
he could, what he spent from that time until he was struck,
and figured he had about $28 left. There was much other
testimony in the case, among which were statements of the
defendant to the officers, which were manifestly false, but the
above recital is sufficient for the purpose of noticing the points
relied upon for a reversal.

It is claimed that the proof is insufficient to show that the
money alleged to have been taken was the property of the
complaining witness. But the evidence that Duffy got two
checks in Modesto, had them cashed, and that the money in
his pocket at the time he was struck was a part of the proceeds
of these checks, is sufficient to show that the money was his
property.

The evidence is amply sufficient to justify the jury in finding that it was taken from his person by force or fear. The
evidence was sufficient to justify a conviction of the defendant. It is claimed that certain statements of the accused
were given in evidence before the *corpus delicti* had been

proved. None was admitted before the complaining witness
had testified to the facts above recited.

It is claimed that the court erred in allowing verbal proof
of the contents of a certain hotel register. A witness, James
Farley, testified that on the night of the alleged robbery the
defendant went with him in an auto to the town of Tracy.
He testified that at the hotel in Tracy to which they went
and spent the night the defendant wrote something on the
hotel register. He did not write the name Ferrara, but witness did not know what name he did write. This testimony
was objected to on the ground that the hotel register was the
best evidence of its contents. The witness was testifying to
an act of the defendant witnessed by him. The witness did
not know what particular name he signed on the register,
and it was immaterial. The material thing was that he
signed a name other than his own or, to put it another way,
that he registered but did not write his own name. We think
this was primary evidence of the fact and that the act was
material.

Nor was there any error in allowing in evidence the statements of third persons. The record shows that witness Cor-
lett, over objection, testified that when prosecuting witness
and defendant were standing at the bar, close together, defendant stated that he had a couple of packages—was going
away on the train—but did not know where they were located.
Witness told defendant to "go down the street and see if
you can locate the packages," and defendant said "all right.
So they went together and come back with the packages."
We see nothing in this of which the defendant can complain.
He heard the conversation and statements and acted upon
them.

During the trial the phonographic reporter, who acted as
such at the preliminary examination, was sworn and asked
if the defendant at such hearing made certain statements,
and to enable him to answer was requested to and did get
his original notes of such examination. Objection was made
to the use of the notes upon the ground that "they had not
been filed." The reporter was directed to file his notes and
the objection was overruled. In this we perceive no error.
The witness was present at the examination and made notes
of the testimony, and was using them as a basis for the testimony he was giving. He had a right to refresh his memory

from such notes, and if he had no independent recollection
of what the defendant testified to, he could read his notes
of the testimony. In thus using his notes he stood in no different position from any other person who might have been
present and made notes of what the defendant said. (Code
Civ. Proc., sec. 2047.)   If it had been sought to use the transcript of the notes as a deposition, the questions raised by
counsel might require fuller consideration.

It was not necessary to fix time, place, and circumstances
of alleged statements made by defendant by questioning him
thereon before proving such statements. His declarations
and statements were original evidence against him, and the
rules as to impeachment of witnesses did not apply.

The court refused to give the following instruction asked
by the defendant: "The jury is instructed that contradictory
testimony is admissible only for the purpose of impeaching
the credibility of the witness, and you may not consider it as
evidence of the truth of such statements." This instruction
was properly refused. The evidence of the prosecuting witness (to illustrate) was contradictory of the testimony of the
defendant, but it was evidence of the truth of the facts he
testified to and was to be so considered by the jury. Counsel
evidently had in mind the rule as to proof of statements made
by a witness at other times contradicting his testimony given
at the trial. If so, he was unfortunate in expressing the rule.

The court instructed the jury that they could find a verdict
of guilty if the taking of the money was "accomplished by
means of force or fear used upon or against the said John
Duffy by the said defendant, or by said defendant putting
said John Duffy in fear." Counsel claim that the instruction
was erroneous, in that it used the disjunctive "or" instead
of the conjunctive "and" between the words "force" and
"fear." The instruction as to this feature of it is in the language of the statute (Pen. Code, sec. 211), wherein it is provided: "Robbery is the felonious taking of personal property
in the possession of another, from his person or immediate
presence, and against his will, accomplished by means of force
or fear." But, while the statute is thus worded, counsel takes
the position that as the information alleged that the taking was
accomplished by means of force and fear, "force and fear"
were words descriptive of the manner in which the offense was
committed and had to be proved as alleged. The instruction

as given was a correct statement of the law, and while it was alleged that *fear and force* were the means used, the offense was complete if either was proved as the means by which the taking was accomplished.

We find no error in the record and the judgment and order are affirmed.

Chipman, P. J., and Hart, J., concurred.

A petition for a rehearing of this cause was denied by the district court of appeal on July 22, 1916, and a petition to have the cause heard in the supreme court, after judgment in the district court of appeal, was denied by the supreme court on August 21, 1916.

———————

[Civ. No. 1630. First Appellate District.—June 26, 1916.]

MILTON T. U'REN, Respondent, v. STATE BOARD OF CONTROL et al., Appellants.

STATE CONSERVATION COMMISSION—COMPILATION OF LAWS—EMPLOYMENT OF ATTORNEY AT LAW—ASSENT OF ATTORNEY-GENERAL NOT REQUIRED.—The State Conservation Commission, under the provisions of the act creating such commission (Stats. 1911, p. 822), is not required to procure the assent of the attorney-general as provided by section 472 of the Political Code, as a condition to its employment of an attorney at law to compile the laws of the different nations, the federal government and the states of the Union affecting conservation, for the use of such commission, as such services are in the main clerical in character and possible of performance by other than a licensed attorney at law.

ID.—CLAIM FOR SALARY—MANDAMUS TO AUDIT DEMAND—FORM AND MANNER OF PRESENTATION.—In a proceeding in *mandamus* to compel the State Board of Control to audit and allow the claim of such attorney for his salary for a certain month, it cannot be urged in defense that the claim therefor was not presented in the form and manner provided by law, where the same was presented in the same form and manner in which the salary claims for previous months had been presented under the rules of the board and upon which it had acted approvingly.

ID.—EMPLOYEES OF COMMISSION—APPROVAL OF SALARY CLAIMS—POWERS OF STATE BOARD OF CONTROL.—Under the act creating the

State Conservation Commission and authorizing it to employ for
the purposes for which the commission was created such expert,
technical, professional, and clerical assistants "upon such terms as
it may deem proper," and setting apart a specific fund for the
payment of such obligations as the commission might thus create,
the approval of a claim for such services by the commission is
final, and the functions of the State Board of Control relative
thereto are merely those of an auditing body, with no discretion
or control over the amount for which the claim should be allowed.

ID.—AUDITING OF CLAIMS—MANDAMUS.—Where one official board or
body is given authority by statute to create an obligation against
a specific fund in the state treasury, and another official board or
body is intrusted with the powers of an auditor in respect to
claims generally against the state, the powers and duties of the
latter in respect to such claims may be controlled by the courts
and compelled by writs of mandate.

ID.—AUDITING OF CLAIM FOR SERVICES FOR COMMISSION—MANDAMUS—
CONSENT OF STATE NOT REQUIRED.—The principle that the state
cannot be sued without its consent has no application to a proceeding in *mandamus* to compel the State Board of Control to audit
a claim for services rendered to the State Conservation Commission.

APPEAL from a judgment of the Superior Court of the
City and County of San Francisco. James M. Seawell, Judge.

The facts are stated in the opinion of the court.

U. S. Webb, Attorney-General, Robert W. Harrison, Deputy
Attorney-General, and Sullivan, Sullivan & Theo. J. Roche,
for Appellants.

Fred. J. Goble, and U'Ren & Beard, for Respondent.

RICHARDS, J.—This is an appeal from a judgment ordering the issuance of a writ of mandate directed to the defendants, the State Board of Control, and also the members of
said board, requiring them to audit and allow the claim of
the plaintiff against the state treasury for the sum of two
hundred dollars for his salary as an employee of the California
State Conservation Commission for the month of July, 1912.
Concerning the facts of the case there is no material dispute.
The plaintiff, who is an attorney at law, was employed on or
about July 1, 1911, by the California State Conservation Commission under the provisions of an act creating said commission (Stats. 1911, p. 822), by the terms of which it was au-

thorized to employ, for the purposes for which it was created,
·"such expert, technical, professional and clerical assistants,
and upon such terms as it may deem proper.'' The particular
service which the plaintiff was employed to perform was ''to
compile for the use of said State Conservation Commission
the laws of the different nations, the federal government and
the states of the Union affecting conservation generally.''
The plaintiff proceeded under such employment to do such
work, and continued therein up to August 1, 1912. The
salary claims for the intervening months up to July 1, 1912,
were presented to and audited and approved by the board of
control without objection, but when on July 30, 1912, his
salary claim for July was presented in the same form and
manner in which his salary claims for previous months had
been presented and allowed, it was refused allowance by the
board of control, which action on the part of said last-named
board led to this application for a writ of mandate to the
superior court, which upon hearing was directed to be issued,
whereupon the defendants took and now prosecute this appeal.

There are two contentions of the appellants which may be
disposed of upon the threshold. The first is that the plaintiff
being an attorney at law, and the services being in the nature
of legal services, he could not be legally employed by the conservation commission without first having obtained the written consent so to do from the attorney-general under the express provisions of section 472 of the Political Code, which
consent was not in fact obtained. We are of the opinion that
this section of the Political Code has no application to the
case at bar nor to the plaintiff's employment. While it is
true that the plaintiff was and is an attorney at law, and
while it is true that the services which he was engaged to perform were of such a nature as might best be performed by
one skilled in knowledge of the law, still they were not such
services as were strictly professional in their nature or as only
a licensed attorney at law could perform, but, on the contrary,
were in the main clerical in character, which the plaintiff or
anyone else with his ability could well have performed without the possession of the title or license of an attorney at law.
This being so, we hold with plaintiff that compliance with section 472 of the Political Code was not a prerequisite to the
plaintiff's employment.

The next contention of the appellant is that the claim of
the plaintiff was properly rejected, for the reason that it was
not presented in the form and manner provided by law. We
find no merit in this contention, for the reasons that it is conceded that the claim was made out and verified and presented
in the same form and method which had been pursued for
several previous months under the rules of the state board of
control and upon which it had theretofore acted approvingly.
If in this instance such board intended to require a different
form or method of verifying and presenting this particular
claim, it should have based its rejection of it upon that ground,
and permitted plaintiff to remedy whatever defects in form
existed, and not having done this, it cannot be heard upon
application for a writ of mandate to urge for the first time
mere formal defects in the presentation of the plaintiff's
claim.

This brings us to the main question involved in this appeal,
which is as to the scope of the powers with which the board
of control is invested in the matter of the allowance and rejection of claims on the state treasury in payment for services rendered to other boards and commissions of the state
within the sphere of their respective functions, and for which
they are by the several acts of their creation invested with the
power to contract upon such terms as they may deem proper.

It is the contention of the appellant that its powers in this
respect are absolute, and that with its discretion in the allowance or rejection of any claim against the state treasury the
courts have not the right or power to interfere. We cannot
give our support to this contention. The State Board of Control was created under the provisions of the act of 1911 embracing sections 654 to 691 of the Political Code (Stats. 1911,
p. 590), which act repealed all prior statutes relating to the
creation, powers, and duties of prior auditing and examining boards, of which the State Board of Control was to be the
successor. The powers and duties of this board were more
ample and varied under the act of their creation than those
of prior commissions or boards exercising similar functions
had been; but in the matter of its relation to the various kinds
of claims upon the state treasury, these are classified, and the
powers and duties of the board with respect to them are set
forth in the following sections of the Political Code:

"Sec. 663. Claims against state. Every claim against the state for which an appropriation has been made or for which a state fund is available, must be presented to the board for its scrutiny before being paid. The board may for cause postpone action upon a claim for not exceeding one month.

"Sec. 664. Any person having a claim against the state for which an appropriation has been made, may present the same to the board in the form of an account or petition and the secretary of the board must date, number and file such claim. The board must allow or reject the same within thirty days. The concurrence of two members of the board shall be required to approve and allow any claim against the state in whole or in part."

"Sec. 667. If no appropriation has been made, or if no fund is available for the payment of any claim against the state, the settlement of which is provided by law, or if an appropriation or fund has been exhausted, such claim must be presented to the board which shall audit the same and if approved by at least a majority vote thereof it shall, with the sanction of the governor, be transmitted to the legislature with a brief statement of the reasons for such approval."

"Sec. 669. Any person having a claim against the state, the settlement of which is not otherwise provided for by law, must present the same to the board at least four months before the meeting of the legislature, accompanied by a statement showing the facts constituting the claim, verified in the same manner as complaints in civil actions. Before finally passing upon any such claim, notice of the time and place of hearing must be mailed to the claimant at least fifteen days prior to the date set for final action. At the time designated the board must proceed to examine and adjust such claims. It may hear evidence in support of or against them and, with the sanction of the governor, report to the legislature such facts and recommendations concerning them as may be proper. In making such recommendations the board may state and use any official or personal knowledge which any member thereof may have touching such claims."

An examination of these sections of the Political Code will show that there are two classes of claims which come within the purview of the State Board of Control. These are, first, claims for which an appropriation has been made or for which a state fund is available, and, second, claims for which no appropriation has been made, or for which for any reason no fund is available. The claim in question in the instant case comes within the first of these classes. The plaintiff was employed by the California State Conservation Commission to do certain work within the scope of its functions and at the fixed monthly sum for salary, for which his claim was presented to the State Board of Control, the conservation commission having already approved said claim. The purposes for which the State Board of Control was created, and the powers with which it was invested, are, so far as may be discoverable from the terms of the statutes, in no very essential sense different from those governing the creation and defining the powers and duties of the state board of examiners, the final predecessor of the board of control. In the early case of *Lawrence* v. *Booth*, 46 Cal. 187, it was held that as to that class of claims against the state treasury of which the power of creation and propriety as to amount were matters intrusted to the discretion of other departments of the state government, the functions of the state board of examiners were merely those of an auditing body, with power to pass upon the regularity in form of the claim, but with no discretion nor control over the amount for which the claim should be allowed. In the comparatively recent case of *Sullivan* v. *Gage*, 145 Cal. 759, [79 Pac. 537], the case of *Lawrence* v. *Booth* was commented upon, and the distinction clearly drawn between those classes of claims with reference to which the validity of the action of the official, body, or board creating the obligation, or its amount, were not called into question, and those classes of claims wherein the validity of the order creating them was in controversy; and as to the former the views of the court in the case of *Lawrence* v. *Booth* were upheld.

In the instant case the power and authority of the conservation commission to employ the expert, professional, and clerical services of the plaintiff in the course of, and for the purpose of, carrying into effect the objects of its creation, has not been and cannot seriously be called into question. Having the power to enter into the contract of employment ''upon such terms as it might deem proper'' (Stats. 1911, p. 823), and having had set apart a specific fund in the state treasury for the payment of such obligations as it might thus create, it must follow that the approval of the plaintiff's claim as evidenced by the requisition of the conservation commission upon

the state treasury for the payment thereof constituted the
final determination as to the validity and propriety of the
obligation, and hence that the powers of the board of control
in respect to said claim were limited to those of an auditing
body passing only upon the sufficiency in form of the plaintiff's demand.

The doctrine is well settled in numerous cases that where
one official, board, or body is given authority by statute to
create an obligation against a specific fund in the state
treasury, and another official, board, or body is intrusted with
the powers of an auditor in respect to claims generally against
the state, the powers and duties of the latter in respect to such
claims may be controlled by the courts and compelled by writs
of mandate. (*Lewis* v. *Colgan*, 115 Cal. 529, [47 Pac. 357];
Scott v. *Boyle*, 164 Cal. 321, [128 Pac. 941], and cases cited.)

In the closing brief of appellant it is earnestly and elaborately contended that since as a fundamental proposition the
state cannot be sued without its consent, and since this action
is in the nature of a suit to compel the payment of money to
plaintiff by the state, that it cannot therefore be maintained.
But to our minds this principle has no application to the instant case. This is not in form or substance an action against
the state to determine a contested claim against its treasury.
The state has already by the act of its legislature set apart a
specific fund for the payment of such obligations as the conservation commission had power to create; and the state has
also by legislative act invested said conservation commission
with the express power to create this specific obligation
through its employment of the plaintiff to assist in carrying
into effect the objects of its existence. The state is thus in
a position of having assented to this claim; and this is an action or proceeding merely to compel the official auditor in the
form of the board of control to perform a duty expressly enjoined upon it by law.

We can perceive no reason why the action of the trial court
was not proper in directing the issuance of the writ.

Judgment affirmed.

Lennon, P. J., and Kerrigan, J., concurred.

A petition to have the cause heard in the supreme court,
after judgment in the district court of appeal, was denied by
the supreme court on August 25, 1916.

[Civ. No. 1822. First Appellate District.—June 27, 1916.]

EDWARD C. GOLDNER. Respondent, v. WM. CRANE SPENCER et al., Defendants; THOS. E. CURRAN, Administrator, etc., Appellant.

MORTGAGE—FRAUD ON CREDITORS OF MORTGAGOR—INSUFFICIENCY OF EVIDENCE—DECISION ON FORMER APPEAL CONCLUSIVE.—In the second trial of an action for the foreclosure of a mortgage, where the court had before it practically the same evidence which was before it upon the first trial and also before the supreme court upon the first appeal, the decision of the supreme court upon such appeal as to the insufficiency of the evidence to support the defense set up by a judgment creditor of the mortgagor that such mortgage was executed with intent to defraud creditors is conclusive upon the second appeal.

ID.—RELEASE OF FRACTIONAL ACRE FROM MORTGAGE—ERRONEOUS FINDING—RIGHTS OF REDEMPTIONER NOT PREJUDICED—RELEASED PORTION WITHOUT VALUE.—A judgment creditor of the mortgagor, entitled to be a redemptioner of the property to be sold under the decree of foreclosure and sale, is not injured by an erroneous finding that a small fraction of an acre had been released from the operation and effect of the mortgage, where it is expressly found that such fraction of land was of practically no value.

APPEAL from a judgment of the Superior Court of the City and County of San Francisco, and from an order denying a new trial. John E. Richards, Judge presiding.

The facts are stated in the opinion of the court.

Henry N. Beatty, Francis Dunn, and Thomas E. Curran, for Appellant.

L. W. Lovey, and Walter E. Dorn, for Plaintiff and Respondent.

Walter H. Robinson, for Defendants and Respondents.

KERRIGAN, J.—This is an appeal by the defendant, Thos. E. Curran, as administrator of the estate of Elizabeth Cullen, deceased, from a judgment in plaintiff's favor, and from an order denying said defendant's motion for a new trial. The facts of the case as disclosed by the record are these: In the month of November, 1904, the defendant, William Crane Spencer, borrowed the sum of three thousand dollars from Elizabeth Cullen, giving his promissory note therefor. In the month of December of the same year he received the additional sum of seven thousand dollars, which he was to invest for her. Mrs. Cullen died in the year 1906, and the defendant, Thos. E. Curran, was appointed her administrator with the will annexed, and in that capacity brought an action against William Crane Spencer to recover both the money he had borrowed and the sum which had been intrusted to him. In that action judgment was rendered in favor of the administrator for the sum of $10,946.46, with interest and costs, on March 22, 1908. A transcript of this judgment was recorded in the county of Placer on the sixth day of April, 1908, and it then became a lien upon whatever interest said Spencer then had in the property lying in said county and being the subject of the present action.

In the meantime, and in the early part of the year 1907, William Crane Spencer had gone to Paris, France, and there and during that year had executed his note and mortgage for the sum of twenty-one thousand dollars covering the Placer County property to Edward C. Goldner, plaintiff in this action, who was a half-brother of Spencer, and a resident of Paris. The mortgage was recorded in the county of Placer on March 16, 1908, prior to the recordation there of the transcript of the judgment obtained by Curran. The present action to foreclose said mortgage was commenced in the month of September, 1909, in the county of Placer. The defendant Curran appeared in said action and set up the issue of fraud in the transaction between the plaintiff Goldner and William Crane Spencer, invalidating said note and mortgage, or at least subordinating the same to the Curran judgment. The trial court found upon this issue in Curran's favor, but upon appeal to the supreme court this finding was held to be unsupported by sufficient evidence and the judgment was reversed. The case is reported in *Goldner* v. *Spencer*, 163 Cal. 317, [125 Pac. 347]. The cause was then transferred to the city and county of San Francisco for a second trial, and from the judgment therein rendered in the plaintiff's favor, and from the order denying a new trial, the defendant Curran prosecutes this appeal.

The first contention made by the appellant Curran is that the evidence is insufficient to sustain the judgment against his contention upon the issue of fraud. It is conceded, however, that the trial court upon the second trial of the cause had before it practically the same evidence which was before the trial court of Placer County upon the first trial of the cause, and also before the supreme court upon the first appeal. This being so, we are bound by the views expressed by the supreme court as to the weight, sufficiency, and effect of this evidence upon the form~r appeal, and, as we have seen, the supreme court has held such evidence insufficient to sustain the issue tendered by the defendant Curran as to the fraudulent character of the transaction between the plaintiff Edward C. Goldner and William Crane Spencer. No further comment upon this phase of the present appeal is necessary than merely to call attention to the language of the supreme court upon the former appeal. (*Goldner* v. *Spencer,* 163 Cal. 317, [125 Pac. 347].)

The next contention of the appellant is that the court in its findings upon the second trial of the cause committed an error in finding that a certain small, irregular portion of the premises in question amounting to less than one-third of an acre, and separated from the balance of the tract by a turn in the county road, had been released from the operation and effect of the Goldner mortgage, when in fact there was no evidence of such release. The injury which the defendant Curran claims to have suffered from this alleged error is that, having sold the interest of said Spencer in the entire tract upon an execution issued upon the Curran judgment, and having become the purchaser thereof by said sale, he has thereby become entitled to be a redemptioner of the property to be sold under the decree of foreclosure and sale in the present action, and that since the court has erroneously found that this small fraction of an acre has been released from the effect of said mortgage and sale, his burden as a redemptioner has been thereby increased as to the balance of the property. While the record appears to be wanting in the evidence of the release of this small piece of land sufficient to sustain this particular finding of the court, it does appear that the court has expressly found that this fraction of an acre of land is of practically no value. There is enough evidence in the record to sustain this finding, and this being so, the court's

error in finding the fact of its release from the effect of the
Goldner mortgage and sale was an error without injury to
the appellant, and was therefore not sufficiently material to
justify a reversal of the case.

There are no other material contentions of the appellant
upon this appeal which are not disposed of in the decision of
the former appeal.

Judgment and order affirmed.

Lennon, P. J., and Richards, J., concurred.

A petition to have the cause heard in the supreme court,
after judgment in the district court of appeal, was denied by
the supreme court on August 25, 1916.

[Civ. No. 1754. First Appellate District.—June 28, 1916.]

LOUISA R. FREITAS, Respondent, v. MANUEL F. FREITAS, JR., et al., Appellants.

LIFE INSURANCE—ACTION BETWEEN CONFLICTING CLAIMANTS—PAY
MENT INTO COURT—PLEADING.—Where, in an action between conflicting claimants to the amount called for in a policy of life
insurance, the insurer does not defend the action but deposits the
money in court subject to a determination of such conflicting
claims, it becomes immaterial as to whether the complaint states
a cause of action against such insurer.

ID.—ACTION ON POLICY—RIGHTS UNDER ANTENUPTIAL AGREEMENT—
SUFFICIENCY OF COMPLAINT.—The complaint in such an action is
sufficient as between the conflicting claimants, where it is alleged
that the plaintiff was induced to marry the insured by an antenuptial
agreement, wherein he promised the plaintiff that if she would
marry him he would make her the beneficiary of the policy, and
that upon his marriage with the intent of performing his agreement he caused the plaintiff to be named as beneficiary and delivered the policy to her, and thereafter secured possession thereof
and without her knowledge or consent substituted the defendants
as beneficiaries.

ID.—ANTENUPTIAL AGREEMENT—REDUCTION TO WRITING—NONESSENTIAL
AVERMENT—PRESUMPTION.—The complaint in such an action is
not subject to general demurrer for failure to allege that the

antenuptial agreement was reduced to writing, as such agreement, as a matter of pleading, will be presumed to be in writing.

ID.—EXECUTION OF ANTENUPTIAL AGREEMENT—WRITING NOT ESSENTIAL. Such an antenuptial agreement is not required to be in writing where the same became fully executed by the act of the insured in procuring his wife to be designated as the beneficiary of the policy.

ID.—STATUTE OF FRAUDS—EXECUTED ORAL AGREEMENT.—The statute of frauds has no application to executed oral agreements.

APPEAL from a judgment of the Superior Court of Alameda County. Wm. H. Waste, Judge.

The facts are stated in the opinion of the court.

Louis B. Diavila, and Jos. P. Lucey, for Appellants.

Rose & Silverstein, for Respondent.

THE COURT.—The plaintiff in this case is the widow of Manuel T. Freitas, deceased. The defendants, Manuel F. Freitas, Jr., Mary Freitas Lopez, Francisco Freitas, and Anna Freitas Nula are the children of said deceased by a former marriage. The defendant Unica Portugueza de Estada da California is a beneficiary corporation. The complaint in substance alleged, and the trial court in effect found, that the plaintiff was induced to marry Manuel T. Freitas, since deceased, by an antenuptial agreement, wherein he promised the plaintiff that if she would marry him he would make her the beneficiary of a policy of life insurance in the sum of one thousand dollars which he then held and which had been issued to him by the corporation defendant. Upon his marriage to the plaintiff Freitas, with the intent and purpose of performing his antenuptial promise, caused the plaintiff to be named as the beneficiary in the policy of insurance, and thereupon delivered the same to her. Subsequently he secured possession of the policy and, without the consent or knowledge of the plaintiff, caused the children above mentioned to be substituted as beneficiaries, and they were the beneficiaries named in the policy at the time of his death.

The corporation defendant did not defend against the action, but deposited in court the amount called for in the policy subject to a determination of the conflicting claims of the plaintiff and the other defendants.

Judgment was rendered for the plaintiff, from which the individual defendants alone have appealed.

The demurrer of these last-named defendants to the complaint was rightly overruled. Having paid the fund in controversy into court, the corporation defendant in effect waived any defense it might have had against either or both of the conflicting claimants; and being apparently satisfied with the lower court's adjudication of the controversy, it is of no consequence whether or not the complaint stated a cause of action against the corporation. (*Jory* v. *Supreme Council etc.,* 105 Cal. 20, [45 Am. St. Rep. 17, 26 L. R. A. 733, 38 Pac. 524]; *Adams* v. *Grand Lodge,* 105 Cal. 321, [45 Am. St. Rep. 45, 38 Pac. 914]; *Hoeft* v. *Supreme Lodge,* 113 Cal. 91, [33 L. R. A. 174, 45 Pac. 185]; *Supreme Council* v. *Murphy,* 65 N. J. Eq. 60, [55 Atl. 507, 509].)

The complaint as between the plaintiff and the appealing defendants stated a cause of action. The case of *Gagossian* v. *Arakelian,* 9 Cal. App. 571, [99 Pac. 1113], has no application to the facts of the present case. Here the cause of action relied upon proceeded upon the theory that the plaintiff had acquired an equitable right to the sum secured by the policy of insurance which the insured could not defeat by any act of his, and which the individual defendants as mere voluntary beneficiaries possessing no equities could not deny. That such a right may be acquired under the facts pleaded here, and will when established receive recognition and protection at the hands of a court of equity, is settled in this state. (*Adams* v. *Grand Lodge, supra; Jory* v. *Supreme Council, supra.*)

The complaint states a cause of action notwithstanding the fact that the antenuptial agreement pleaded was not alleged to have been reduced to writing as required by section 1624 of the Civil Code, and section 1973 of the Code of Civil Procedure. As a matter of pleading, the agreement was presumed to be in writing.

The evidence supports the findings, and the findings support the judgment. While the evidence shows, and the court in effect found, that the antenuptial agreement was not expressed in writing, nevertheless the evidence further shows, and the court found, that in keeping with his agreement and the consideration of the plaintiff's marriage to him, Freitas, the insured, procured her to be designated as the beneficiary

of the sum secured by the policy of insurance. The antenuptial contract thereby became fully executed (*Supreme
Lodge* v. *Ferrell*, 83 Kan. 491, [33 L. R. A. (N. S.) 777, 112
Pac. 155]) and it is settled law that the statute of frauds
has no application to an executed oral agreement (*Bates* v.
Babcock, 95 Cal. 479, 488, [29 Am. St. Rep. 133, 16 L. R. A.
745, 30 Pac. 605]).

The judgment appealed from is affirmed.

A petition to have the cause heard in the supreme court,
after judgment in the district court of appeal, was denied by
the supreme court on August 25, 1916.

[Civ. No. 1755.   First Appellate District.—June 28, 1916.]

LOUISA R. FREITAS, Respondent, v. MANUEL F. FREITAS, JR., et al., Appellants.

LIFE INSURANCE—ACTION TO RECOVER AMOUNT OF POLICY—CLAIM
UNDER ANTENUPTIAL AGREEMENT—PAYMENT TO SUBSTITUTED BENE-
FICIARIES—PLEADING—SUFFICIENCY OF COMPLAINT.—In an action
to recover the amount called for by a policy of insurance, the complaint states a cause of action where it is alleged that the plaintiff
was made the beneficiary of the policy under the terms of an
antenuptial agreement, and that the insured after delivering the
policy to the plaintiff secured possession thereof and without her
knowledge or consent substituted the defendants as beneficiaries,
notwithstanding that the insurer had paid the amount of the policy
to the defendants prior to the commencement of the action.

ID.—ACTION FOR MONEY HAD AND RECEIVED—LACK OF CONTRACTUAL
PRIVITY—WHEN MAINTAINABLE.—An action for money had and
received may be successfully maintained even though not founded
upon allegations showing an express privity of contract between
the parties, upon the theory that if one of the parties has received
money due and owing to the other under circumstances which make
it his duty to surrender the money to the rightful owner, the law
will imply the promise to do so, and thereby create the requisite
contractual privity.

APPEAL from a judgment of the Superior Court of Alameda County. Wm. H. Waste, Judge.

The facts are stated in the opinion of the court.

Louis B. Diavila, and Jos. P. Lucey, for Appellants.

Rose & Silverstein, for Respondent.

THE COURT.—Save in one particular the facts in this
case, as shown by the pleadings and proof, are in their essential features substantially the same as those pleaded and
proven in the case of *Freitas* v. *Freitas, ante,* p. 16, [159
Pac. 611], No. 1754, this day decided, the present case being
different only in the particular that the beneficial society in
which the deceased was insured had upon the death of the
deceased paid to the defendants the sum of one thousand five
hundred dollars, called for by the policy of insurance. As a
consequence the society was not made a party defendant.
Judgment went for the plaintiff, from which the defendants
severally appeal upon the grounds that the complaint does
not state a cause of action, and that the findings do not support the judgment.

Here, as in the case above mentioned, the plaintiff's cause
of action proceeded upon the theory that the plaintiff had
acquired a superior equitable title to the sum in suit; and, for
the reasons stated in said case numbered 1754, and upon the
authority of the cases therein cited, we are of the opinion
that the facts pleaded in the present case are sufficient to constitute a cause of action against the defendants, who were
alleged and shown to be mere voluntary beneficiaries. True it
is, as counsel for the defendants contend, that the plaintiff's
cause of action pleaded savors strongly of an action for money
had and received. Such an action, however, may be successfully maintained even though not founded upon allegations
showing an express privity of contract between the parties.
This is so upon the theory that if one of the parties has
received money due and owing to the other under circumstances which make it his duty to surrender the money to
the rightful owner, the law will imply the promise to do so,
and thereby create the requisite contractual privity. (*Commissioners* v. *Bloomington,* 253 Ill. 164, [Ann. Cas. 1913A,
477, 97 N. E. 280]; *Kreutz* v. *Livingston,* 15 Cal. 344; *Colusa
Co.* v. *Glenn County,* 117 Cal. 434, [49 Pac. 457]; *Whittle*
v. *Whittle,* 5 Cal. App. 696, [91 Pac. 170].)

It is conceded that the evidence supports the findings; and if we be correct in the conclusion that the fac s stated in the complaint show a cause of action, then it follows that the findings, which are in substantial accord with the allegations of the complaint, support the judgment.

The point made concerning the invalidity of the ante-nuptial contract, and the consequences claimed to flow therefrom, was also made in the case previously decided and therein determined adversely to the contention of the defendants. It need not therefore be again adverted to.

The judgment appealed from is affirmed.

A petition to have the cause heard in the supreme court, after judgment in the district court of appeal, was denied by the supreme court on August 25, 1916.

[Civ. No. 2052. Second Appellate District.—June 28, 1916.]

W. A. HAMMEL, Appellant, v. JOHN FRANCIS NEYLAN et al., etc., Respondents.

PUBLIC OFFICERS—SERVICES OF SHERIFF IN CONVEYING PRISONERS—UNWARRANTED DISALLOWANCE OF CLAIM BY BOARD OF CONTROL—OVERCHARGE FOR PREVIOUS SERVICES.—The State Board of Control is without power to refuse to allow the claim of the sheriff of a county for services rendered and expenses necessarily incurred in conveying persons adjudged by the superior court to be committed to state prisons and other state institutions, on the ground that such official was indebted to the state in a certain amount for similar services rendered in previous years which he had received and which was in excess of that to which he was justly and legally entitled.

ID.—SERVICES IN CONVEYING PERSONS TO STATE INSTITUTIONS—ALLOWANCE OF CLAIM BY STATE BOARD OF CONTROL.—Under the provisions of section 4290 of the Political Code, the sheriff of a county is entitled to receive and retain for his own use the sum of five dollars per diem for conveying prisoners to and from the state prisons, and for conveying persons to and from insane asylums, together with all expenses necessarily incurred therewith, subject only to the condition that his claim therefor is properly presented to the State Board of Control, as provided by section 663 of the Political Code, for its scrutiny, which scrutiny and examination is limited by such provision to an inquiry as to whether such officer has ren-

dered the services set forth in his claim and whether the amount
claimed for expenses was necessarily incurred in the performance
thereof.

ID.—REFUSAL TO ALLOW CLAIM—REMEDY OF CLAIMANT.—Upon the refusal of the board of control to allow such a claim upon the ground
of overcharges made in previous years, the remedy of the claimant
is *mandamus*, and not by appeal to the legislature, as under the
provisions of section 671 of the Political Code the latter remedy
is only applicable where the board finds that the services were not
performed or the expenses not incurred.

ID.—MANDAMUS—ABUSE OF DISCRETION—ENFORCEMENT OF PARTICULAR
ACTION.—While it is the general rule that where an officer, board,
or tribunal is vested with power to determine a question upon
which a right depends, *mandamus* will not lie to control the discretion of such officer, board, or tribunal in the determination
thereof, nevertheless the writ will lie to correct abuses of discretion, and to force a particular action by the inferior tribunal
or officer, when the law clearly establishes the petitioner's right
to such action.

APPEAL from a judgment of the Superior Court of Los
Angeles County.   John W. Shenk, Judge.

The facts are stated in the opinion of the court.

Leon F. Moss, for Appellant.

U. S. Webb, Attorney-General, Robert M. Clarke, Deputy
Attorney-General, and John F. Neylan, for Respondents.

SHAW, J.—Plaintiff filed his petition in the superior court
of Los Angeles County praying for a writ of mandate against
the State Board of Control and members thereof, commanding it and them to allow and approve certain claims, the
aggregate amount of which was the sum of $2,199.26, pre-
sented by him as sheriff of said county against the state for
services rendered by him as such sheriff in the month of
December, 1914, and expenses necessarily incurred in conveying persons, adjudged by the superior court of said county
to be committed, to state prisons and other state institutions.
Defendants answered alleging, among other things, that on
January 21, 1914, they, in the performance of the duty imposed upon them by law, discovered, determined, and adjudged that petitioner was indebted to the state of California in the sum of $2,199.26, paid to and received by him as

sheriff from the state of California upon claims presented
during the years 1911, 1912, and 1913, for alleged services
and necessary expenses incurred by him as such official for
conveying prisoners to state institutions, which claims were,
to the extent of $2,199.26, in excess of that to which he was
justly and legally entitled, and the allowance of which by
said board was obtained by means of fraudulent representations made with intent to deceive and defraud, and which did
deceive and defraud, these defendants and the state of California; that petitioner has refused to recognize such payments
as being in excess of the sum to which he was entitled during
said years of 1911, 1912, and 1913, or repay the same, although demand had been made therefor by respondents upon
an itemized list of said alleged overcharges delivered to petitioner; that by reason of such fact respondents claim the right
to withhold from petitioner, to the extent of $2,199.26, the
allowance and payment of other claims due him under section
4290 of the Political Code. The answer further alleged that
"respondents deny that petitioner has no plain, speedy, and
adequate remedy in the ordinary course of law for the enforcement of right in the premises, and allege that petitioner
has no rights in the premises or as claimed and alleged by him
in his petition for writ of mandate herein; that said petition
does not state facts sufficient to constitute a cause of action
against these respondents or any or either of them, or against
the state of California, nor does said petition state facts
sufficient to entitle petitioner to the relief sought therein, nor
to any relief." And further alleged "that this honorable
court has no jurisdiction of the subject matter set forth in
said petition, nor to grant the plaintiff the relief sought
therein."

Attached to each of the nine claims so presented and showing the action of respondents had thereon and reasons therefor, as required by section 666 of the Political Code, was a
statement as follows:

"Office of State Board of Control.
"Sacramento, Cal., Feb. 2, 1915.

"The annexed account for 207.85/100 two hundred seven &
85/100 presented by Wm. A. Hammel for transportation of
prisoners to Folsom is rejected and disallowed under section
666, Political Code of the state of California, and Sec. 682
of the Political Code of the state of California, for the reason

that said claimant is now indebted to the state of California
in the sum of $2,199.26, moneys by him had and received for
the use and benefit of the said state of California, prior to
the date hereof, all of which said claimant has heretofore
refused and does now refuse to repay to the state despite
demand made of him for such repayment.''

It must be conceded, upon admitted allegations of the petition, stipulations made, and uncontroverted evidence offered
by petitioner, that the claims in question were found and
determined by the board of control to be properly made out
and presented in full compliance with the law and the rules
governing the same as adopted by said board, and no question is raised as to the truth and correctness thereof or petitioner's right to have the same allowed, save and except that
respondents assert, without offering any proof thereof, that
petitioner is indebted to the state for the collection of overcharges for services rendered and expenditures made during
the years 1911, 1912, and 1913, claims for which had at the
time been duly approved and allowed by said board of control, warrants issued therefor by the controller and paid in
usual course.

Upon trial, and after petitioner had introduced his evidence, the respondents, without offering any evidence, moved
the court to dismiss the petition and said proceeding upon
the ground ''that this court has no jurisdiction of the subject matter set forth in said petition, nor to grant to petitioner the relief sought therein; and that this court has no
jurisdiction of the parties respondent to this proceeding; that
the petition does not state facts sufficient to constitute a cause
of action against these respondents or any or either of them,
or against the state of California; nor does said petition state
facts sufficient to entitle petitioner to the relief therein
sought, nor to any relief.'' The court made an order granting the motion, and caused a judgment to be entered dismissing the proceeding, from which petitioner prosecutes this
appeal.

In support of the court's ruling, respondents insist, first,
that the State Board of Control in acting upon claims presented for its allowance is vested with judicial powers, and
having in its discretion refused to allow the claims, *mandamus*
will not lie to compel other action than that taken; second,
that under the provisions of section 671 of the Political Code

petitioner's remedy, if aggrieved by the action of the board, was an appeal to the legislature.

As to the first proposition, it is undoubtedly the general rule that where an officer, board, or tribunal is vested with power to determine a question upon which a right depends, *mandamus* will not lie to control the discretion of such officer, board, or tribunal in the determination thereof. (*Inglin* v. *Hoppin*, 156 Cal. 483, [105 Pac. 582].) Nevertheless, as stated in the above-entitled case: "The above cases [cited in the opinion] abundantly show that *mandamus* will lie to correct abuses of discretion, and will lie to force a particular action by the inferior tribunal or officer, when the law clearly establishes the petitioner's right to such action"; or, we may add, where in determining the matter confided to such board its discretion has been controlled by a consideration of questions not relating to the subject involved, and therefore not properly within its discretion (26 Cyc. 161); or, as stated in *State* v. *Stutsman*, 24 N. D. 68, [Ann. Cas. 1914D, 776, 139 N. W. 83], "where the discretion is made to turn upon matters which, under the law, should not be considered." And this we conceive to be the vice of respondents' position.

Section 4290 of the Political Code provides: "The sheriff shall be entitled to receive and retain for his own use, five dollars *per diem* for conveying prisoners to and from the state prisons, and for conveying persons to and from the insane asylums, or other state institutions, not otherwise provided for by law; also, all expenses necessarily incurred in conveying insane persons to and from the insane asylums, and in conveying persons to and from the state prisons, or other state institutions, which *per diem* and expenses shall be allowed by the board of examiners and collected from the state." Under this provision the sheriff is entitled to collect and receive from the state for the services specified five dollars per day and expenses necessarily incurred in the performance thereof, subject only to the condition that his claim therefor is properly presented, as here done, to the board of control, as provided in section 663 of the Political Code, for its scrutiny, which scrutiny and examination under the provision quoted is limited to an inquiry as to whether the sheriff has rendered the services set forth in his claim and whether the amount claimed for expenses was necessarily incurred in such performance; and upon a finding favorable to claimant.

then, as provided by section 4290, the board of control has no discretion other than to allow such *"per diem* and expenses." (*Hensley* v. *Superior Court,* 111 Cal. 541, [44 Pac. 232].) Since as to such claims the right to scrutinize is thus limited, it must follow that the board may not refuse to allow a claim concededly correct and properly presented, upon grounds other than those specified; that is, where it finds the services were not performed or the expenses not necessarily incurred. (*Lawrence* v. *Booth,* 46 Cal. 187.) The mere assertion, such as here made, that the claimant is indebted to the state, whether by reason of his having theretofore wrongfully obtained its funds or negligently operated a motor car as a result of which state property was damaged, furnishes no reason for disallowing his claim, for the reason that under the statute it is not made to depend upon a determination of such questions. Therefore, if it be conceded the petitioner as such sheriff was indebted to the state on account of other dealings, such fact is no ground for disallowing the claims presented for services rendered and expenses incurred by him for and on behalf of the state.

While under section 682 the board is vested with powers of supervision over matters concerning the financial and business policies of the state and may institute investigations and proceedings to conserve the interests thereof, no power, however, is vested in it to institute or maintain actions for the recovery of funds due the state. Such powers of supervision and investigation so given it under section 682 must, in a case of the character here involved, be exercised subject to and controlled by the provisions of section 4290.

Moreover, in regularly approving and allowing the claims presented by Hammel for services and expenses rendered and incurred during the years 1911, 1912, and 1913, for which warrants had been issued and paid, the board of control, to a limited extent, acted judicially in exercising the powers of investigation vested in it, and its decision in such matter was final and conclusive so far as a collateral attack thereon is concerned. (Black on Judgments, sec. 532; *Sullivan* v. *Gage,* 145 Cal. 759, 766, [79 Pac. 537]; *Cahill* v. *Colgan,* 3 Cal. Unrep. 622, [31 Pac. 614].) Conceding that the controller might in a proper case (sec. 433, Pol. Code), where it was made to appear that a claimant had by fraud obtained moneys of the state, institute an action to recover the same, no such power is vested in the board of control. And if it has no power to institute such action, it is likewise wanting in power to interpose, as a defense in a proceeding for *mandamus*, a counterclaim based upon such alleged fraud.

Coming now to the second proposition which, as shown by the record, is that upon which the trial court based its judgment and order that the proceeding be dismissed. Section 671 of the Political Code provides that "Any person interested, who is aggrieved by the disapproval of a claim by the board, may appeal from the decision to the legislature of the state, by filing with the board a notice thereof, and upon the receipt of such notice the board must transmit the demand and all the papers accompanying the same, with a statement of the evidence taken before it, to the legislature." Respondents insist and the court held that by virtue of this provision, and conceding, as found by the board of control, that petitioner had performed services the *per diem* for which and expenses necessarily incurred in connection therewith, as fixed by section 4290 of the Political Code, amounted to the sum of $2,199.26, which claims therefor the board refused to allow for the alleged reason that he had theretofore, in other dealings had with the state, fraudulently obtained a sum of money in amount equal to such claims, his remedy, and only remedy, was an appeal to the legislature. We cannot consent to this proposition. Had the board found that petitioner had not performed the services claimed, or found the expenses incurred in the performance thereof were unnecessary, then, upon its determination of the question so confided to it, petitioner's only remedy would be an appeal to the legislature to pass a law for his relief, since in the absence of such facts the allowance of his claim would be clearly unauthorized. As said by the learned trial judge, the legislature has the right to fix the conditions upon which state funds will be paid out. By section 4290 it has prescribed such conditions, and the board of control has, as stated, found that those conditions were complied with by petitioner, but disallowed the claims upon grounds other than those prescribed. Hence, on an appeal to the legislature it would be called upon, not to review the questions as to whether petitioner had complied with the conditions upon which it had directed the board of control to allow the claims, but whether petitioner had been guilty of the alleged fraud with which he is charged by the board

of control. Except as to the Senate when sitting as a court
of impeachment (sec. 1, art. VI, Const.), the legislature possesses no judicial power, and hence could not try the question
as to whether or not petitioner had, as claimed, by means of
fraud looted the state treasury. Nor by such provision was
it ever intended that this subordinate agency of the state,
vested with limited powers, should ignore the plain import of
the language used in section 4290, thus leaving one aggrieved
by its unwarranted action with no remedy or redress other
than to appeal to, that is, petition (Magna Charta, and sec.
10, art. I, State Constitution) the legislature for the enactment of another law in effect declaring that it (the legislature) meant and intended just what was said in section 4290
of the Political Code. To so apply the provision of section
671 would not only place the State Board of Control above
the law, but lead to an absurdity. One may readily conceive
of claims presented to the board where its disallowance thereof
would be final, leaving the claimant with no remedy other
than to petition the legislature for relief. To such cases only
the provision must be held applicable. Where, however, the
legislature has, as here, provided that a sheriff shall for services designated receive a *per diem* of five dollars, together
with the expenses necessarily incurred in the performance of
such services, and directed that the board of control shall
allow claims therefor, it leaves to the board no discretion other
than to allow such claims upon finding facts the existence of
which is made the only condition upon which such allowance
is directed by the legislature, and the absence thereof the only
ground for refusal to allow the same. For such refusal in a
proper case an appeal to the legislature provides no adequate
remedy. The allowance under the circumstances is one "spe-
cially enjoined" by law upon respondents, and for its refusal
to perform the act so enjoined a writ of mandate lies to compel such performance. (Code Civ. Proc., sec. 1085; *Lawrence
v. Booth*, 46 Cal. 187; *Sullivan v. Gage*, 145 Cal. 759, [79 Pac.
537].)

The judgment is reversed.

Conrey, P. J., and James, J., concurred.

A petition to have the cause heard in the supreme court,
after judgment in the district court of appeal, was denied by
the supreme court on August 25, 1916.

[Civ. No. 1590.   First Appellate District.—June 30, 1916.]

GEORGENIA E. CLARK, Respondent, v. Q. E. HOTLE, Appellant.

ACTION ON PROMISSORY NOTE—COUNTERCLAIM FOR MONEY ADVANCED—
CONFLICTING EVIDENCE—FINDINGS CONCLUSIVE.—In an action on a
promissory note, where the defendant set up a counterclaim based
on the claim that defendant had paid a certain joint note of himself and plaintiff's assignor, the proceeds of which had been used
by the latter for his personal use instead of on a joint enterprise,
the finding of the trial court against the counterclaim, based upon
conflicting evidence, is conclusive on appeal.

APPEAL from a judgment of the Superior Court of
Alameda County.   William H. Waste, Judge.

The facts are stated in the opinion of the court.

Ezra W. Decoto, for Appellant.

Carleton Gray, A. F. St. Sure, and St. Sure, Rose & Cal-
laghan, for Respondent.

THE COURT.—This is an appeal from the judgment in
favor of plaintiff and against defendant in an action on a
promissory note.

The defendant does not deny that he executed and delivered
the note to plaintiff's assignor, one S. J. Norris, as alleged in
the complaint, but he sets forth in his answer a counterclaim
for a certain amount.   The court found against this defense;
and the sole question presented by the record is as to whether
or not the evidence supports that finding.

After the making of the note and before its maturity Norris,
the payee thereof, and the defendant borrowed from the First
National Bank of Oroville one thousand dollars, giving the
bank their joint note for that sum, the proceeds by agreement
being placed to the personal account of Norris.   At the time
of this transaction defendant and Norris had entered into a
tentative agreement concerning some development work of
the Feather River Canal Company's property, under the terms
of which Hotle was to make certain monthly advances.   This
agreement was subsequently reduced to writing and signed by

the parties. According to the testimony of Hotle the money borrowed from the bank was for the personal account of Norris, and when the note became due Norris refused to pay it; that Hotle thereupon took it up, and that Norris refused to allow him credit therefor upon the amount to be advanced under their Feather River Canal Company contract.

Norris, on the other hand, testified that the one thousand dollars borrowed from the bank and placed to his personal account was used and paid out, as intended by both parties, for the account of the Feather River Canal Company, and that the defendant was given credit therefor.

The surrounding circumstances tend strongly to support the testimony of Norris; but in any event there is a substantial conflict in the evidence, in view of which the settled law is that the finding of the trial court must stand.

Judgment affirmed.

[Civ. No. 1789. First Appellate District.—July 5, 1916.]

W. H. BONE, Appellant, v. H. V. TRAFTON, Respondent.

ATTACHMENT—DEFECTIVE AFFIDAVIT ON UNDERTAKING—AMENDMENT.— An undertaking on attachment to which is attached an affidavit of justification of sureties which by inadvertence fails to state whether the sureties are freeholders or householders is subject to amendment, and when amended it has the effect of validating the proceeding from its inception.

ID.—FILING OF NEW UNDERTAKING — FIRST ATTACHMENT NOT ABANDONED—INTERVENING CHATTEL MORTGAGE—LACK OF PRIORITY.—The filing of a new affidavit and undertaking on attachment and the procuring thereon of a new writ of attachment to correct the omission in the original affidavit accompanying the undertaking to state whether or not the sureties were freeholders or householders, does not constitute an abandonment of the original or first attachment, so as to permit a chattel mortgage executed between the issuance of the two writs to become a first lien, where the attached property was held by the sheriff at all times under the first attachment.

APPEAL from a judgment of the Superior Court of Santa Cruz County. Benjamin K. Knight, Judge.

The facts are stated in the opinion of the court.

Edward J. Kelly, for Appellant.

George P. Burke, for Respondent.

THE COURT.—This is an appeal from the judgment. In this case the trial court prepared an opinion, which correctly sets forth the facts and the law applicable thereto, and which, omitting what is said touching one point not necessary, we think, to a disposition of the case, we adopt as follows:

In this action plaintiff seeks to recover damages from the defendant, as sheriff, for the alleged wrongful sale of personal property under a writ of attachment, without having first tendered to plaintiff the amount of a chattel mortgage owned by plaintiff, and which plaintiff claims antedated said writ of attachment.

The decision in the case involves a question of law based upon the following facts, which are undisputed, viz.: On October 7, 1914, in an action filed in this court (the superior court of the county of Santa Cruz), entitled, "*Arbanasin v. Radovan,*" Radovan was sued for $370, and costs, alleged to be due for merchandise sold to him by assignor of Arbanasin. On the day the action was filed an affidavit and undertaking for attachment were also filed, and the writ of attachment was issued and placed in the hands of the sheriff for service. The writ was levied by the sheriff upon personal property, the title to which, so far as this action was concerned, was vested in Radovan free from encumbrance. On October 16, 1914, nine days subsequent to the levying of the attachment, Radovan executed and delivered to the plaintiff in this action, W. H. Bone, a chattel mortgage for $630 covering the attached property. The mortgage was duly recorded on October 17, 1914. Thereafter, on the same day, Radovan filed a notice of motion that he would, on October 23d, move the court to discharge the attachment, on the ground "that the undertaking required by law before the writ should issue was not accompanied by the affidavit of the sureties thereon and therein that they were freeholders or householders within this state." Thereafter, to wit, on October 19, 1914, Arbanasin made and filed another affidavit and undertaking on attachment, and had issued thereon another writ of attachment, which was also placed in the hands of the sheriff for service. On October 23d, the day on which the motion to discharge

the attachment was heard, Arbanasin presented to the court
an application and asked permission to file a third undertaking, amending the undertaking filed on October 7th, and he
based his application upon an affidavit in which, among other
things, it was stated that the defect in the first undertaking
was the omission of the word "free" or "house" in the blank
space before the word "holder" in the affidavit of justification
of sureties attached to said undertaking, and was "a mere
unintentional oversight on the part of the officer or notary
taking such affidavit." The court thereupon, on said twenty-
third day of October, 1914, allowed the amended undertaking
to be filed, and denied the motion to discharge the attachment. No appeal was taken from the order of the court in
this respect, and it became final. The plaintiff Bone now
claims that the act of Arbanasin in filing the second affidavit
and undertaking on October 19th, and having procured
thereon a new writ of attachment, all of which was done before the court permitted the filing of the amended undertaking, constituted a total abandonment of the original or first
attachment, and that thereby the mortgage lien of Bone became and was a first lien.

The defect in the affidavit was amendable (*Tyson* v. *Rein-
ecke*, 25 Cal. App. 696, 700, [145 Pac. 153], *Peterson* v. *Beggs*,
26 Cal. App. 760, [148 Pac. 541], *Jones* v. *Leadville*, 10 Colo.
464, [17 Pac. 272]), and there is ample authority holding that
where a statute permits the correction of an original undertaking, or the substitution of a new one, it has the effect of
validating the proceeding from its inception. (*Griffith* v. *Milwaukee Harvester Co.*, 92 Iowa, 634, [54 Am. St. Rep. 573,
61 N. W. 243]; 3 Standard Ency. of Pro., p. 460; *McCraw* v.
Welch, 2 Colo. 284; *State Bank* v. *Morris*, 13 Iowa, 136; *Pierse*
v. *Miles*, 5 Mont. 549, [6 Pac. 347]; *Langstaff* v. *Miles*, 5 Mont.
554, [6 Pac. 356]; Drake on Attachment, sec. 148.) Accordingly, in the present case, under the broad terms of section 558
of the Code of Civil Procedure, it must be assumed that at
all times subsequent to the filing of the first undertaking there
was a valid attachment unless, as claimed by the plaintiff, the
first attachment was abandoned by the filing of the new affidavit and undertaking. In the case at bar the evidence shows
without contradiction that the sheriff levied upon, at all times
held possession of, and finally sold the personal property by
virtue of the first attachment; and the sheriff in thus holding

and selling the property did not attempt to levy the second attachment at all but entirely ignored it.   There was no evidence that Arbanasin or the sheriff intended to abandon the first attachment.   In order to prevail, it was incumbent upon the plaintiff to make such proof, and having failed to do so, judgment was properly rendered against him.   The authorities support this view.   (*Stephens* v. *Mansfield*, 11 Cal. 363; *Marquart* v. *Bradford*, 43 Cal. 526–529; *Wood* v. *Etiwanda Water Co.*, 147 Cal. 228, 234, [81 Pac. 512]; *Utt* v. *Frey*, 106 Cal. 392–397, [39 Pac. 807]; 1 Words and Phrases, p. 4.) In the case of *Wright* v. *Westheimer*, 3 Idaho, 232 (2 Idaho, 962), [35 Am. St. Rep. 269, 28 Pac. 430], the facts are almost identical with the facts of the case at bar.   In that case an attachment was levied upon real estate.   That was an action to quiet title to land by removing a cloud therefrom caused by the issuance and levy of certain attachments.   Subsequently a second attachment was obtained by the same plaintiff and levied by the sheriff upon the same property.   Defendant claimed, among other grounds, that the act of procuring the second attachment operated as an abandonment of the first. The court said: "The appellant alleges in the complaint that the levy of the first writ was abandoned by reason of the issuance of the second writ and levying it upon the identical property on which the first writ was levied.   The respondents by their answer deny the abandonment of the levy of the first writ, and state in their answer the reason for procuring the issuance of the second writ as follows: 'The said plaintiff having at that time come into more open and notorious assertion of rights and ownership in the said real estate, the defendants herein caused a new writ to issue, as provided by law, and procured the same to be levied on all the interest the said D. D. Wright then had in said real estate.'   The abandonment of the first writ made an issue in the pleadings, the burden resting on the plaintiff.   The record contains no evidence of abandonment.   It is, however, contended that the abandonment was established by the issuance of the second writ, and the levying of the same upon the identical parcel of land on which the first writ had been levied.   The answer to this is that the respondents denied any intention of abandoning the lien secured by the first writ, and aver that they procured the issuance of the second writ as a precautionary measure only. The law does not presume or favor abandonments. The issue having been made by the pleadings, it was incumbent upon the appellant to establish the fact of abandonment, which he failed to do."

Judgment affirmed.

[Civ. No. 2070.   Second Appellate District.—July 5, 1916.]

S. O. LONG, Petitioner, v. SUPERIOR COURT OF THE COUNTY OF SAN DIEGO et al., Respondents.

JUSTICE'S COURT APPEAL — DISMISSAL — LACK OF DILIGENCE.—The provision of section 583 of the Code of Civil Procedure that an action shall be dismissed by the court in which the same shall have been commenced, or to which it may be transferred on motion of the defendant, unless brought to trial within five years after the defendant has filed his answer, does not apply to actions pending in the superior court on appeal thereto from a justice's court, but the court possesses inherent power in its discretion to make an order of dismissal.

APPLICATION for a Writ of Review originally made to the District Court of Appeal for the Second Appellate District.

The facts are stated in the opinion of the court.

W. A. Martin, and F. J. Trude, for Petitioner.

W. P. Cary, for Respondents.

SHAW, J.—Pursuant to a writ of review issued out of this court, the superior court of San Diego County through its clerk has made a return of the transcript and record of the proceedings had and taken by respondents in a certain case entitled *"T. P. Banta v. S. O. Long,"* from which it appears that on November 6, 1905, a judgment was rendered in favor of the plaintiff therein by the recorder's court of Imperial township (then a part of San Diego County), from which the defendant, who is petitioner here, on November 7, 1905, perfected an appeal upon questions of both law and fact to the superior court of San Diego County. No further proceeding was taken by either party to said action until June 7, 1915, at which time defendant therein, pursuant to notice given, moved the court to dismiss the same upon the grounds, first, that the action had not been prosecuted with diligence; second, that it had not been brought to trial by plaintiff within five years after defendant had filed his answer therein, as required by section 583 of the Code of Civil Procedure. The court denied the motion and proceeded to a trial of the case, as a result of which judgment went for plaintiff.

The contention of petitioner is that upon the facts stated, the court had no jurisdiction other than to make an order granting his motion to dismiss the action.

The sole point involved is whether the provision of section 583 of the Code of Civil Procedure, providing that an action shall be dismissed by the court in which the same shall have been commenced, or to which it may be transferred on motion of the defendant, unless brought to trial within five years after the defendant has filed his answer, applies to actions transferred to the superior court on appeal from a recorder's or justice's court. This question was involved in the case of *Pistolesi* v. *Superior Court*, 26 Cal. App. 403, [147 Pac. 104]. There the petitioner applied for a writ of mandate to compel the superior court to dismiss the action upon facts identical with those here presented. The court held that section 583 of the Code of Civil Procedure did not apply to actions pending in the superior court on appeal thereto from a justice's court, and that while the court possessed inherent power in its discretion to make an order of dismissal, it could not be compelled to do so. To what is said in the opinion in that case, we may add that the case is not brought strictly within the provisions of the statute, since it appears that defendant filed his answer in the justice's court, and upon the issues so joined a trial was had. We regard the case above cited as determinative of the question presented, and upon the authority thereof the proceedings of the superior court in the action of *T. P. Banta* v. *S. O. Long*, made the subject of this review, are affirmed.

Conrey, P. J., and James, J., concurred.

A petition to have the cause heard in the supreme court, after judgment in the district court of appeal, was denied by the supreme court on August 31, 1916.

[Civ. No. 1840.   First Appellate District.—July 6, 1916.]

JAMES W. HAGAN, Respondent, v. EMMA J. HAGAN, Appellant.

TRUST—CONVEYANCE BY HUSBAND TO WIFE—CONFLICTING EVIDENCE— FINDINGS CONCLUSIVE.—In an action by a husband for a decree that his wife holds title to certain real property, conveyed by him to her by gift deed, in trust for his use and benefit, findings based upon conflicting evidence that the wife held an undivided one-half interest in a certain piece of the property in litigation for the use and benefit of plaintiff, but that plaintiff had made a gift of the other property to defendant, cannot be disturbed on appeal.

APPEAL from a judgment of the Superior Court of Santa Clara County.   J. R. Welch, Judge.

The facts are stated in the opinion of the court.

Morrison, Dunne & Brobeck, and R. L. McWilliams, for Appellant.

Milton L. Schmitt, for Respondent.

RICHARDS, J.—This is an appeal from that portion of a judgment which is in plaintiff's favor in an action wherein the plaintiff seeks a decree that the defendant, his wife, holds the title to several certain pieces of real estate in the counties of Santa Clara, San Diego, and Kern in trust for the plaintiff's use and benefit.   The trial court held that the properties in Santa Clara and San Diego Counties were the sole and separate property of the defendant by virtue of certain deeds of gift from the plaintiff to her, but that as to the Kern County property, which the plaintiff had also transferred to the defendant by a conveyance in the form of a deed of gift, she took and held an undivided one-half of the same in trust for the plaintiff's use.   It is from this latter portion of the judgment of the lower court that the defendant has appealed.

Practically the only question presented for the consideration of this court is whether the evidence is sufficient to sustain the findings and judgment of the trial court as to the property involved in this appeal.

There are certain undisputed facts which may be first recited. The plaintiff and defendant were married in the city of New York in the year 1887. The plaintiff had been married before and had three daughters. At the time of his second marriage he was forty-five years of age, while the defendant was then but twenty-five years old, and was a schoolteacher, with a salary of from $40 to $50 a month, but with no other income or property. The plaintiff had been for several years a traveling salesman for a large jewelry house, in which he had an interest, and was earning from fifteen thousand dollars to twenty thousand dollars a year. At the time of his marriage he was the owner of some personal and real property, including the Kern County ranch, consisting of about 640 acres of land, which was at that time, however, believed to be of comparatively small value. The married life of plaintiff and defendant was for many years a happy and congenial one. He was a fond, trustful, and doting husband, and she a faithful helpmeet, traveling with him, looking after the details of his financial affairs, collecting his earnings and depositing them in various banks, and drawing upon them and upon his account with his firm at her own pleasure and without any question on her husband's part. At Christmas in 1888, being in Santa Clara County, he bought a lot in San José and gave it to his wife for a Christmas present. In the following year he executed and delivered to her a deed of gift to the Kern County lands. In December, 1890, being in San Diego, he bought, at the suggestion of a mutual friend, the San Diego lot, and gave it also to her for a Christmas present. In the year 1900 he acquired and conveyed to her lands in Tacoma, Washington, by like deed of gift; in fact, the plaintiff at various times conveyed to his wife all of his real estate which he owned before marriage and all that he acquired afterward; and he also practically placed in her control all of his earnings and personal property. He also had his life insured in her favor in sums amounting to thirteen thousand dollars, some of the policies of which have matured and their amounts become available to her. In the meantime the plaintiff had grown old, and had lost his position and earlier earning capacity and been otherwise unfortunate in certain business ventures. In the year 1911 the plaintiff and defendant quarreled over some trifling financial matter, and the difficulty then occasioned presently involved the whole question of their property rights. The defendant claimed all of the property which had been given into her hands as her own, and left the plaintiff penniless and practically dependent upon his daughters for support. Thereupon the plaintiff commenced this action to have a trust in his favor declared as to the California property rights.

Thus far the evidence in the case is practically undisputed; and the trial court upon this state of the record was entirely justified in finding that the plaintiff had presented the defendant outright with the title to the Santa Clara and San Diego lots; but as to the Kern County property, the testimony of the plaintiff and of the defendant is in sharp conflict as to the real purpose of the purported gift, the plaintiff testifying that his intention in placing the title to said property in the name of his wife was simply for their mutual protection in view of the perils incident to his nomadic life, and as an assurance of a means of livelihood for them both in their old age; and he also testified to numerous incidents tending to illustrate his claim that they both considered and spoke of it as their common property. The plaintiff is supported in his testimony by the testimony of his three daughters and their husbands as to similar illustrative conversations and incidents occurring between the parties. On the other hand, the defendant testifies that at all times the conveyance of the Kern County property to her was intended and considered to be a gift absolute investing her with the whole title to the property; and in this she also is in a measure supported by the testimony of her relatives and friends.

If the trial court believed, as it was entitled to do, the testimony offered by and on behalf of the plaintiff in preference to that presented by and on behalf of the defendant, we make no question but what a sufficiently clear and convincing case was made justifying the court's decree that the defendant had received and held at least an undivided one-half of the Kern County property for the plaintiff's use and benefit; and the trial court having so decreed upon evidence of such character and conflict, this court will not under well-settled rules disturb the findings and judgment of the lower tribunal.

Judgment affirmed.

Lennon, P. J., and Kerrigan, J., concurred.

[Civ. No. 1975.   Second Appellate District.—July 6, 1916.]

CITY OF LOS ANGELES (a Municipal Corporation), Appellant, v. ROSCOE E. MOORE et al., Respondents.

JOHN GRIFFIN JOHNSTON, Cross-complainant and Respondent, v. CITY OF LOS ANGELES (a Municipal Corporation), Appellant; O. B. CARTER, Respondent.

EMINENT DOMAIN — OWNERSHIP — FORMER ADJUDICATION — EVIDENCE— ADMISSIBILITY OF JUDGMENT-ROLL AND FINDINGS—ESTOPPEL.—In an action by a city to condemn land for the purpose of widening a thoroughfare, where defendant pleaded a former adjudication as to the title of the land between the city and his predecessor, the judgment-roll and findings in the former action are admissible in evidence, although uncertain as to the identity of the land, where the pleadings admitted that the precise tract involved was in dispute in the former action, the judgment not being so ambiguous as to be void; and the former judgment estops the plaintiff in the second action.

APPEAL from a judgment of the Superior Court of Los Angeles County, and from an order denying a new trial. Frank G. Finlayson, Judge.

The facts are stated in the opinion of the court.

Albert Lee Stephens, City Attorney, and Myron Westover, Deputy City Attorney, for Appellant.

Carter, Kirby & Henderson, Charles Lantz, and Davis, Lantz & Wood, for Respondents.

JAMES, J.—This action was brought by the city of Los Angeles to condemn two certain strips of land lying on either side of Avenue 20, for the purpose of widening that thoroughfare. The only question to be considered on this appeal concerns the matter of the ownership of one parcel of land affected by the condemnation. The city of Los Angeles, the plaintiff, claimed that it was the owner of this parcel; the trial court, however, determined that the title was in respondent Carter. Carter, by his answer made to the complaint, pleaded a former adjudication as to this precise parcel of

land, had in an action in which his predecessor in interest
was the plaintiff and the city of Los Angeles a defendant.
Carter maintained, in which contention he was sustained by
the trial judge, that by the judgment in the action last referred to, the municipality was estopped from again litigat-
ing the question of title. In the action, the judgment in
which Carter pleaded in bar, and which we will hereafter refer
to as the Fox case, the plaintiff there sought to quiet his title
to a lot which he designated as lot 8 of the additional subdivision of the Hamilton Tract, as per map thereof recorded
in Book 28, at page 96, Miscellaneous Records of Los Angeles
County. The judgment followed the description of the land
as contained in the complaint. By reference to the map mentioned, it is found that, while the northerly, easterly, and
southerly boundary lines are distinctly marked by continuous
black lines, the westerly side of the lot, instead of there being a boundary line marked in like manner as on the other
sides, shows two dotted lines extending between the prolonga-
tion of the northerly and southerly boundary lines of the lot,
and which dotted lines inclose a wedge-shaped parcel varying
from about fifty feet at one end to about thirty or thirty-five
feet at the other. It is this wedge-shaped piece of ground that
the city claimed in this action to be the owner of. Precisely
stated, the city's claim is that the judgment rendered in the
Fox case, by referring to the map of the Hamilton Tract for
a description of the property affected, did not accurately
describe any certain property, and that because of such
ambiguity the judgment could not be aided by any extraneous
evidence and could not be pleaded as a bar in estoppel of the
right of the city to here again assert title. The city objected
to evidence offered by Carter of the judgment-roll in the Fox
case, and also to the stenographic reporter's record of the
testimony of a surveyor who was called upon to identify the
small parcel in dispute in the Fox case. The judgment in the
Fox case was not so ambiguous as to be void. It referred to
the map of the tract as recorded, which map did, it is true,
leave clouded in some uncertainty the exact location of the
southerly boundary line of lot 8. Nevertheless, as between
Fox and the city of Los Angeles, it was admitted in the pleadings in that case that the precise tract of land which is involved here was in dispute, and that it was included within lot
8 as shown on the recorded map. The city in the Fox case

affirmatively alleged that the wedge-shaped tract of land was a part of lot 8, and the court found in that case that the plaintiff Fox was the owner of all of lot 8 and that the city was not the owner of that portion of it to which title was especially alleged as being in the city. The Fox suit brought directly in issue the matter of title to the small parcel of land, and the city admitting in that action that the parcel was contained within lot 8, should be estopped from afterward asserting that the judgment in the Fox case adjudicating the fee title to be in Fox and that the city had no interest in the land, did not settle that question. There was no appeal taken in the Fox case and no effort made, so far as appears, to have that judgment revised in any way. We think that the pleadings and findings in the Fox case were proper to be introduced in evidence in this action in order to illustrate the issues presented in that suit. (*Graves* v. *Hebbron*, 125 Cal. 400, [58 Pac. 12].) On the question of estoppel, the case of *People* v. *Holladay*, 93 Cal. 241, [27 Am. St. Rep. 186, 29 Pac. 54], is in point.

The appeal taken herein was both from the judgment and from an order denying a motion for a new trial.

The judgment and order are affirmed.

Conrey, P. J., and Shaw, J., concurred.

[Civ. No. 1977. Second Appellate District.—July 6, 1916.]

CITY OF LOS ANGELES (a Municipal Corporation), Respondent, v. ROSCOE E. MOORE et al., Defendants.

JOHN GRIFFIN JOHNSTON, Cross-complainant and Appellant, v. CITY OF LOS ANGELES (a Municipal Corporation), Cross-defendant and Respondent; O. B. CARTER, Cross-defendant and Respondent.

EMINENT DOMAIN—WIDENING OF CITY THOROUGHFARE—OWNERSHIP OF LAND—BURDEN OF PROOF.—In this action brought by the city of Los Angeles to condemn, for the purpose of widening a certain thoroughfare therein, an irregular plot of ground aligning a portion of the northeasterly boundary of lands patented to the city, and to which the appellant claimed ownership as devisee under the will of a grantee of the city to a large tract of land, which was claimed to include the plot in question, it is held that by reason of the inaccuracies appearing in the surveys of the engineers who gave testimony for the appellant as to the monuments and lines of the land described in the deed of appellant's testate, the appellant had failed to sustain the burden of proof that the plot in dispute was included in the deed.

ID.—REPAYMENT OF SEWER ASSESSMENT—REDEMPTION FROM EXECUTION SALE—RIGHT TO REIMBURSEMENT.—The appellant in such action is not entitled, as a condition to a determination against his ownership of the property, to be repaid the amount of a sewer assessment, which he paid upon redeeming the property from an execution sale had on a judgment against him.

APPEAL from a judgment of the Superior Court of Los Angeles County, and from an order denying a new trial. Frank G. Finlayson, Judge.

The facts are stated in the opinion of the court.

Charles Lantz, and Davis, Lantz & Wood, for Cross-complainant and Appellant.

Albert Lee Stephens, City Attorney, C. D. Pillsbury and Myron Westover, Deputy City Attorneys, for Plaintiff, Cross-defendant and Respondent.

Carter, Kirby & Henderson, for Cross-defendant and Respondent O. B. Carter.

JAMES, J.—This is an appeal taken by John Griffin Johnston, against whom judgment was entered and an order made denying his motion for a new trial. The appeal calls into question the correctness of the decision of the trial judge, wherein it was determined that said appellant had no interest in an irregular plot of ground aligning Avenue 20 in the city of Los Angeles, which the city by condemnation seeks to take for the purpose of widening that thoroughfare. The trial judge determined title to be in defendant O. B. Carter. That determination on the separate appeal of the city of Los Angeles taken to this court was affirmed in an opinion filed this day, *ante*, p. 39, [159 Pac. 872] (Civil No. 1975).

The land in question aligns a portion of the northwesterly boundary of lands patented to the city of Los Angeles. By deed made in 1863, the city of Los Angeles conveyed to John

S. Griffin and J. C. Welsh a large tract of land embracing more than two thousand acres. It was stipulated at the trial that the title to all of this land and the land in dispute was vested in the city of Los Angeles immediately prior to the making of the deed mentioned. Welsh subsequently conveyed to Griffin and Griffin later to one Hamilton, who subdivided the land so obtained into "Hamilton's Subdivision" and "Hamilton's Additional Subdivision." Appellant Johnston, as the devisee under the will of John S. Griffin, claimed that the plot of land in dispute was included in the deed to Griffin and Welsh from the city, and was not included in the deed made by Griffin to Hamilton; hence, that it was distributed to him under the will in the estate of Griffin. Under the stipulation made, in effect that the title was in the city unless divested by the Griffin-Welsh deed, appellant at the trial assumed the burden of establishing that the land was located within the boundaries of the large tract conveyed to Griffin and Welsh. In order to establish the northwesterly boundaries of the plot so conveyed, it was necessary to locate the original patent boundary of the city. This boundary, as surveyed and described in the patent, starting from the northwest city patent corner, pursued a meandering course southwesterly to a point made by the junction of the Los Angeles River with the Arroyo Seco. From this point, called Station 35, the line proceeded in a northwesterly meandering course, following the bed of the Los Angeles River. Station 36, being the one immediately northwesterly of the point Station 35, was described as being at the edge of the water of the river. The river for some distance in that locality is confined on the west by a chain of hills composed in the main of a shale or rock formation. In the Griffin-Welsh deed the southerly corner of the land described was located at a monument marked by a mound of stones, the location of which the testimony showed was well known to old residents and its location was by the testimony accurately fixed at the trial. The testimony of the surveyors, who attempted to trace the lines of the Griffin-Welsh land, showed that the monument mentioned at the southerly corner of the property was disregarded. The testimony also showed that had the location of this monument been taken as a starting point and the line run northerly, the land in dispute would have been thrown without the parcel conveyed to Griffin and Welsh. The inaccuracy of the lines of these surveyors was also illustrated in the testi-

mony by showing that, assuming the points taken by them to
correctly locate stations on the northwesterly city patent line,
by turning the angle at the point Station 35 at the south and
starting northwesterly according to the angle and call of the
patent description, Station 36 would not have been located in
the edge of the stream of the Los Angeles River, but would
have been thrown on the hillside to an elevation of seventy-
three feet above the present river-bed.   The testimony showed
very conclusively that the bank of the river on the west was of
rocky formation, and therefore could have been affected but
little in the course of years by the current of the water.   These
inaccuracies appearing in the surveys of the engineers who
gave testimony for appellant, the trial judge held that the burden of showing that the title of the city had been divested by
the Griffin-Welsh deed had not been sustained.   In this conclusion we agree.   It is said that defendant Carter cannot
raise the question that the land was not so included in the
Griffin-Welsh deed, because he affirmed in his answer that the
land was so included.   It is true that in one of the defenses set
out Carter did make that allegation, but he expressly abandoned and disclaimed that contention at the trial, and hence
we think that allegation cannot be viewed as an admission of
the fact contended for.   The maps made by the city covering
the lands of Griffin Subdivision show recognition of the "Se-
pulveda Corner," that being the point marked by the mound of
stones hereinbefore referred to at the south line of the Griffin
tract.   Defendant Carter introduced in evidence, as declarations against interest, sworn statements made to the city assessor by John S. Griffin for eight different years, the first being for 1883 and the last for 1898, which statements purported
to set forth all of the land owned by Griffin in the city of Los
Angeles, and none of these statements described any of the
land in dispute.   It was not error to allow in evidence the decree in an action to quiet title brought by one Fox against the
city of Los Angeles, which was introduced by Carter.   That
action is described in the opinion treating of the appeal of the
city as against Carter.   It was competent evidence against the
city, and if not relevant to the issues as between Johnston and
Carter, could have no prejudicial effect, in view of the conclusion as indicated that Johnston did not sustain the burden of
proof that the land in dispute was within the plot described in
the Griffin-Welsh deed.

Finally, it is claimed on the part of appellant Johnston that a determination in favor of the title of Carter should only be made upon a condition for the repayment to Johnston of the sum of $284.85, which amount, prior to the trial in the action, had been assessed against the property to cover municipal sewer improvements.   The payment of the claim arose in this way: There was a judgment in the superior court in a separate matter against Johnston and others amounting to the sum of $1,053.10, which Carter became the owner of by purchase. Carter caused an execution to be issued upon this judgment and a levy and sale made against any interest which Johnston might have in the land in dispute.   At this sale Carter caused such interest to be struck off to the nominal party who was acting for him, for the sum of five hundred dollars, which was credited upon the judgment.   The sewer assessments becoming payable, Carter caused these to be paid, and notified the sheriff that if Johnston made redemption under the execution sale, that these sewer assessments should be included in the redemption charge.   A mortgagee of Johnston redeemed, paying the five hundred dollars and also the $284.85 required for sewer improvements.   It is the latter amount that Johnston claims the court should have required by its judgment to be repaid to him.   We think this contention is without merit.   If Johnston, as is here determined, had no interest in the property, he was not, nor was his mortgagee, required to redeem, and if they had refused to do so, the result would have been that Johnston would have had a credit of five hundred dollars on the judgment entered against him.   Having chosen to redeem, speculating upon it being determined that he had some interest in the property which had been made the subject of the execution sale, he, in our view, was a voluntary actor, and a court of equity in such an action as this would not lend him aid in the direction of recovery for the sewer assessments paid.   This was not a case where Carter as the moving party sought to have cleared away a cloud caused by a sale or assessment against his property; the title in him as it is now determined was clear of any such lien, real or apparent.

Our conclusion is that the evidence fully sustains the judgment as made by the trial court; that no errors appear which warrant a new trial being granted to appellant.

The judgment and order are affirmed.

Conrey, P. J., and Shaw, J., concurred.

[Civ. No. 1582.   Third Appellate District.—July 6, 1916.]

EMIGH-WINCHELL HARDWARE COMPANY (a Corporation), Appellant, v. AMOS PYLMAN et al., Respondents.

MECHANICS' LIENS — EQUITABLE JURISDICTION — APPEAL.—A mechanic's lien is of equitable cognizance, although created by law; and an appeal in an action to foreclose the same lies to the supreme court.

APPEAL from a judgment of the Superior Court of Yolo County.   W. A. Anderson, Judge.

The facts are stated in the opinion of the court.

Devlin & Devlin, for Appellant.

White, Miller, Needham & Harber, for Respondents.

THE COURT.—This is an action to foreclose a mechanic's lien and to bring about a sale of the premises should it be necessary to enforce the payment as claimed.

It was said in *Weldon* v. *Superior Court*, 138 Cal. 427, [71 Pac. 502]: "The action, so far as it sought to foreclose the lien against the premises, was unquestionably an equitable suit." In *Goldtree* v. *City of San Diego*, 8 Cal. App. 505, [97 Pac. 216], citing that case, it was said: "The contention that the lien is not of equitable cognizance because created by law cannot be considered.   Such a distinction would destroy all equitable jurisdiction to carry out the provisions of the code.   The remedy for the enforcement of the lien is clearly an equitable one."

The jurisdiction is in the supreme court (Const., sec. 4, art. VI), and the case is therefore transferred to that court.

[Civ. No. 1492.   Third Appellate District.—July 6, 1916.]

E. A. MAJORS, Appellant, v. MARK A. GIRDNER, Respondent.

CORPORATION—SALE OF STOCK—NATURE OF TRANSACTION.—The acceptance by a corporation of a promissory note given in payment for its stock upon the agreement that the corporation will issue the stock and deliver it to the purchaser upon the execution and delivery of the note, constitutes a present sale of the stock, and the stock becomes *ipso facto* the property of the purchaser, notwithstanding the certificate therefor is not issued and delivered.

ID.—CERTIFICATE OF STOCK—EVIDENCE OF OWNERSHIP.—A certificate of stock of a corporation is only the evidence of the ownership thereof, and merely constitutes proof of property which may exist without it.

ID.—RESCISSION OF SALE—FRAUD—PLEADING—OFFER OF RESTORATION OF STOCK—ESSENTIAL AVERMENT.—In an action by the assignee of a corporation to recover on a promissory note, assigned to the plaintiff for the purpose of collection only, and accepted by the corporation for the purchase price of stock, where the answer asks for affirmative relief by way of a rescission of the contract of sale upon the grounds of fraud and misrepresentation, and the surrender and cancellation of the note for want of consideration by reason of such fraud, it is essential that the answer by appropriate averment show an offer to restore the stock, notwithstanding the certificate therefor has not been issued.

ID.—FRAUD OF CORPORATION—INSUFFICIENCY OF EVIDENCE.—The failure of a corporation to keep its agreement, upon a purchase of its stock, that it will contemporaneously with the execution and delivery of the promissory note of the purchaser given therefor, issue the stock to the purchaser, and the failure to keep its agreement to sell the stock upon his demand at a price in advance of that paid therefor, does not involve such misrepresentation and fraud as will work a rescission of the contract of sale, but is merely a breach of the covenants of the contract.

APPEAL from a judgment of the Superior Court of Sonoma County, and from an order denying a new trial. Emmet Seawell, Judge.

The facts are stated in the opinion of the court.

E. J. Dole, for Appellant.

L. G. Scott, for Respondent.

HART, J.—The action is on a promissory note for the
sum of $350, which, it is alleged, was made and delivered by
the defendant to the Pacific Coast Securities Company, a corporation (for brevity to be hereinafter referred to as "the
corporation"), and after such execution and delivery, assigned by the original payee to the plaintiff, "who is now the
lawful owner and holder thereof."

The answer admits the execution and delivery of the note
as alleged in the complaint, but asserts that the instrument
was procured from the defendant by the corporation above
named through misrepresentation and fraud.

The gist of the charges of fraud set out in the answer may
thus summarily be stated: That the corporation, through its
duly accredited agents, called upon the defendant and offered
him the stock of the corporation at the price of $15 per share,
the par value of which was $10 per share; that said agents
guaranteed and warranted said stock to be of the value at
least of $15 per share; that at said time, as an inducement
to the defendant to buy said stock, said agents entered into
an agreement in writing, whereby they bound the corporation "to extend the time of payment of note to suit applicant
for stock and to resell stock for $20, if so desired, by Janu-
ary 15, 1914," said agreement being signed by "E. H.
McConkey, by Clements & Harold, agent." The further
representations were made, so the answer states, that said stock
"was very valuable," that the same could be turned and sold
at any time for $15 per share, and that the corporation was
in a flourishing condition and was financially sound. It is
alleged that each and all of said representations were made
for the purpose of inducing the defendant to purchase said
stock, and that they were false and fraudulent, made with
the intent to deceive the defendant and to persuade him to
buy the stock; that said stock was not at said time of any
real market value, that there were no prospects of the same
being of any material market value, and that it was not then
"worth $10 per share or any other amount, and that said
corporation never intended to resell the same for $20 per share
or $15 per share or $10 per share or for any other amount
so far as said corporation had any knowledge"; that said
corporation "was not in a money-getting and flourishing
financial condition at the time or at any other time." It is
alleged that the defendant believed the representations so

made, and was thus deceived and misled into purchasing, and
did purchase, twenty-five shares of said stock, "which he
would not otherwise have purchased."

It is further charged that the corporation represented and
agreed that, upon the execution and delivery by the defendant to it of the note in suit, it would at once and without
delay issue to said defendant twenty-five shares of its stock
which would, as it was then represented was true of other
stock of the same kind, earn and return dividends of not less
than seven per cent per annum, "which was the only consideration for the execution of said note to said corporation,
and that this was the only consideration ever to be given or
paid for said promissory note, but defendant alleges that said
corporation did not execute and deliver or issue stock to
defendant or in his name or in any other person's name for
him, and did never deliver to said defendant any certificate
of stock, or thing at all, and there was nothing whatever
given for said promissory note and the same was without consideration and has been at all times without consideration."
These facts, it is declared, were not discovered by the defendant until the time at which he applied for a renewal of the
note so as to extend the time for the payment thereof, when,
upon giving the renewal note and at the same time paying
to the corporation $25 in cash as and for principal and pay-
ing the interest accrued upon the original note, he asked what
had become of the corporate stock certificate which the corporation had agreed to issue to him, and that he was then
told and assured that the certificate for the twenty-five shares
of stock had been issued as agreed upon, "which statement was
false, and said corporation and the officers and members
thereof knew that the same was false and untrue"; that "said
stock was not then nor had it ever at any time been issued
to defendant." It is averred, in effect, that but for the false
representation then made as to the issuance of said stock and
the further false representations as to the value of said stock
and the flourishing and sound financial condition of the corporation, the defendant would not have made and delivered
to the corporation the renewal note in lieu of the original
note or paid to the corporation the sum of $25 on the prin-
cipal and the accrued interest on the original note.

The "separate and further defense" set up in the fourth
paragraph involves, in effect, along with some conclusions

of the pleader, an iteration, substantially, of the allegations of the preceding paragraphs of the answer. It is to the
effect that all the agreements, etc., between the corporation and
the defendant "were *purely executory,* in that the matters
and things and agreements on the part of said corporation
were never performed and were matters precedent to the
issuance of said note and notes, in that said corporation was,
as per the stipulations, to execute and deliver to defendant the
certificate of stock . . . before said note or notes were to be
delivered or to take effect, and said corporation was to place
defendant in a position that he should be protected and guaranteed that the stock would and should be of the guaranteed
value of $15 per share, and in that said stock should mean
while be drawing dividends, none of which matters and things
were done or performed by said corporation, and *the defendant had the right to rescind the same at any time,* and did rescind the same in writing before the bringing of this action
and before the acquisition or possession thereof by plaintiff
herein, all of which matters and things plaintiff well knew
before the taking over of said note by him," etc.

The efficacy of the answer in the statement of a defense to
the action was not challenged by demurrer.

The cause was tried by a jury and a verdict returned in
favor of the defendant. Judgment was entered accordingly.

The plaintiff appeals from the judgment and the order
denying him a new trial.

In the outset, it is proper to state that no claim is here
made that the plaintiff is an innocent purchaser of the note
for value. On the contrary, it is conceded that the plaintiff
is acting solely in this action for the corporation, the original
payee, and that the note was assigned to him for the purpose
of collection only.

The point is made for the first time in this court that the
answer does not state facts sufficient to constitute a defense
to the cause of action pleaded by the plaintiff.

One of the objections specifically made against the answer
is that the defendant, who asks for affirmative relief by way
of a rescission of the contract of sale upon the ground of fraud
and the surrendering up and cancellation of the note in suit
for want of consideration therefor by reason of such fraud,
has not by appropriate or other averment in his answer offered to restore the stock which he alleges he purchased from

the corporation. The point is well taken. The transaction between the corporation and the defendant constituted, according to the history thereof as it is explained by the answer, an executed contract of sale, and the stock became the property of the defendant upon the consummation of that transaction, notwithstanding that the certificate for the stock was not, so the answer declares, issued and delivered to the defendant. (*Mason* v. *Lievre*, 145 Cal. 514, [78 Pac. 1040].) A certificate for the stock of a corporation is only the evidence of the ownership thereof, or, as the cases put the proposition, it merely constitutes proof of property which may exist without it. (*Mitchell* v. *Beckman*, 64 Cal. 117, [28 Pac. 110], and cases therein cited.) In that case, it is among other things said: "When the corporation has agreed that a person shall be entitled to a certain number of shares in its capital, to be paid for in a manner agreed upon, and that person has agreed to take and pay for them accordingly, he becomes their owner by a valid contract made upon a valuable consideration." In this case, according to the answer, the defendant made application for the purchase of the stock, and the same was approved by the corporation by accepting the note of the defendant in payment therefor. This, as stated, constituted a sale (Civ. Code, sec. 1721, *Johnson* v. *Dixon Farms Co.*, 29 Cal. App. 52, [155 Pac. 134] ; 35 Cyc. 25), and thereupon the title to or ownership of the stock *ipso facto* vested in the defendant.

It is a settled rule in equity and expressly affirmed by legislative fiat (Civ. Code, sec. 1691, subd. 2) that in an action for rescission the party seeking the remedy "must restore to the other party everything of value which he has received from him under the contract," etc. While there are in the answer some vague and indefinite allegations intended to disclose that the stock was not of the value it was represented to be by the agents of the corporation, there is no allegation in the defendant's pleading that it is wholly valueless. If it was of some value (and it may be assumed that it was, it being property), it was the duty of the defendant, as a prerequisite to his right to a rescission of the contract on the ground of fraud, to restore or offer to restore by appropriate and sufficient averment in his answer the stock to the plaintiff or to the corporation, for whose benefit the plaintiff is admittedly suing (*Kelley* v. *Owens*, 120 Cal. 502, [52 Pac. 797]), and to do this it was not requisite, as we have already shown, that he should have previously had issued to him or had in his possession the certificate for the stock, which is, as suggested, the mere physical evidence of the interest he owned in the capital stock of the corporation.

The answer, as a pleading seeking affirmative relief, is in other respects by no means an exemplar in pleading. But, taken in its entirety, we are able to say that the allegations of fraud on the part of the corporation in the transaction eventuating in the sale of the stock are sufficient in substance for the purpose for which they were intended to place the answer, as a pleading looking for affirmative relief, beyond the reach of a general demurrer.

But, notwithstanding the defectiveness of the answer, the case appears to have been tried by the plaintiff upon the theory that the defendant's pleading was sufficient in all respects, no objection whatever having been made by the plaintiff to the evidence offered by the defendant in support of the charge of fraud as set forth in his answer. Even if it be true, however, that, by failing to demur to the answer and to object to evidence offered in support of the allegations thereof, the plaintiff waived restoration of the stock by the defendant, and that the case was tried by the plaintiff upon the theory that the defendant had, in the matter of pleading, gone as far as required in an action for rescission, still the evidence falls far short of supporting the verdict.

The defendant's was the only oral testimony offered and received in his behalf, and, since the plaintiff presented no evidence from which even the remotest inference of fraud on the part of the corporation in the transaction may be drawn, it necessarily follows that the jury predicated their verdict wholly upon the testimony of the defendant. The facts of the transaction will, therefore, be taken from his version thereof, and as so taken may briefly be stated as follows:

On the twenty-second day of October, 1913, the defendant made an application to the corporation for twenty-five shares of its capital stock for $15 per share. The application was in printed form, presumably the form regularly used by the company for that purpose, and the same was signed by the defendant. At the same time that said application was executed and delivered to the agents of the corporation, Messrs. Clement & Harold, by whom the transaction was conducted for the corporation, the defendant as in payment for said stock made and delivered to said agents his promissory note for the sum of $375, payable on the fifteenth day of January, 1914. For this note a receipt was delivered to the defendant, the same being signed: "E. H. McConkey (vice-president and manager of the corporation), by Clement & Harold, agents." Among other things, said receipt contained the following agreement on the part of the corporation: "We agree to extend time of payment on note to suit applicant for stock and to re-sell stock for $20, if desired, by January 15, 1914."

The defendant, some time before the fifteenth day of January, 1914, made a demand upon or request of the corporation to sell the stock in accordance with the above agreement. The corporation did not sell the stock. On or about January 15, 1914, the defendant gave the corporation a renewal note for the original one (page 25, Transcript), and, on the nineteenth day of that month, the corporation, through its secretary, W. B. Slade, forwarded the original note to the defendant, with the following letter: "Enclosed you will find your old note for $375, due on January 15, 1914, marked 'canceled.'" On the fifteenth day of May, 1914, the defendant paid the corporation the accrued interest and the sum of $25 on the principal of the note previously given, and asked for and was granted a further extension of time for the payment of the balance of said note, giving in lieu thereof the note in suit for the sum of $250. Said note was dated on the day of its execution and delivery (May 15, 1914), and made payable four months after date, or on the sixteenth day of September, 1914.

On the eleventh day of September, 1914, the defendant addressed to McConkey, manager of the corporation, the following letter: "It will be necessary for you to extend the time on my note to Oct. 15, 1914, as I have no funds at present, but expect to cash some securities before that time to pay same with. I have explained to the lady in the office, as she can tell you."

On September 5, 1914, (ten days prior to the date of the maturity of the note in suit), the defendant received from the corporation a duly executed certificate for the twenty-five shares of stock purchased by him.

The defendant testified: That, when the matter of the sale
and purchase of the stock was under negotiation between him
and the agents of the corporation, the said agents "represented that they had the agency for the California State Life
Insurance Company, that they was reselling all of their business for them. As I had stock in the California State Life
Insurance Company, I took a chance. They represented that
the dividends were enormous and that the dividends were
already earned; they had the money to pay the dividends.
. . . After representing that they had the agency for the California State Life, and as I knew that they were doing a big
business, and representing that the dividends were earned,
they had them there to pay, and that if I didn't want the
stock that they would resell it on the fifteenth day of January.
Q. Now, you are speaking about this stock in the Pacific Securities Company? A. Yes, sir. Q. This was the stock that
these agents tried to sell you? A. Yes, sir."

The defendant, after so testifying, further said that the
reason he renewed the note on the several occasions referred
to above was because he was told that the stock had been
issued to him, although he had not received the certificate
therefor. He declared that the agreement was that the certificate would be issued and dated at the time of the delivery
of the original note, and that he would, therefore, be entitled
to any dividends earned by the stock from that time on; that,
as a matter of fact, the certificate was not issued until nearly
a year after he had bought the stock, and that he would, as
a consequence, lose the dividends, if any accrued upon the
stock, for the entire time during which he believed he was
the owner of it. On cross-examination, however, the defendant testified that the reason he renewed the note as indicated
was because he did not have ready money with which to take
the note up.

The above is the sum of the testimony upon which the jury
founded their verdict.

Nowhere is there any testimony to be found in the record
that the corporation was not financially sound or not doing
a business profitable to its stockholders. Nor did the defendant testify or show by any other testimony or proof that the
capital stock of the corporation was not of the value that it
was represented to be by the corporation's agents. And there

is absolutely no proof whatever that the stock purchased by the defendant was not dividend earning property.

As to the representations made by the corporation's agents to the defendant at the time the stock was purchased by the latter, it is difficult to say from the testimony of the defendant whether, in making said representations, the agents were referring to the California State Life Insurance Company and its stock or to Securities Company and its stock, In any event, the testimony of the defendant, as it is presented in this record, is that he personally knew that the stock to which said agents were referring and as to which the representations mentioned were made was of great value and profitable to the stockholders.

But, when boiled down to its actual purport, the real gist of the defendant's complaint against the transaction involved herein, as the same is gathered from his testimony, is that he has been defrauded of the dividends to which he was entitled on his stock, because the corporation failed to keep its alleged agreement that, contemporaneously with the delivery to it of the original note, it would issue and deliver to the defendant a certificate for the twenty-five shares of stock purchased by him, and, furthermore, that he suffered injury because it failed to keep its agreement to sell said stock for him, upon his demand, at a price in advance of that paid by him therefor, by January 15, 1914. It is very obvious that these omissions on the part of the corporation do not involve such misrepresentation or fraud as will work a rescission of the contract of sale. Indeed, they cannot be said to involve misrepresentation at all. They amounted to a mere breach of certain covenants of the contract. As above stated, the stock purchased by the defendant became his property the moment that the sale was completed, and the certificate amounted only to tangible proof of such ownership. He was, of course, entitled to a certificate showing his ownership of the stock, but the failure of the corporation to issue and deliver it to him could not have the effect of vitiating the contract of sale or impairing his title to the stock. It was, as above suggested, merely the violation by the corporation of an obligation which the defendant by appropriate legal proceedings could have compelled it to discharge.

As to the point involving failure by the corporation to resell the stock, it is perfectly clear that, even if that were

a legitimate ground upon which rescission of the sale could
be worked, the defendant, having made a payment on the
original note and given a new note for the balance subsequent
to the expiration of the time within which he was authorized
to require the corporation to resell his stock, thereby waived
that covenant or, at any rate, is by that act estopped from
setting up the breach thereof as against the honesty and good
faith of the transaction culminating in the making of the
note in dispute or as against the legal integrity of the note
itself.

Our conclusion is that the proofs utterly fail to disclose
fraud on the part of the plaintiff in the transaction involved
herein, and that if the stock of the defendant earned dividends during the period of time intervening between the date
of the purchase thereof and the date of the issuance and
delivery to the defendant of the certificate for said stock for
which the corporation has not accounted or which it has not
paid to the defendant, the latter should have set up the
amount of such dividends as a setoff or counterclaim to the
note in suit. This was the only recourse left to him under
the facts of the transaction as he himself has detailed them
in this case.

The judgment and the order are reversed, with directions
to the court below to grant the defendant leave, if he may
elect to take that course, so to amend his answer as to plead
therein any counterclaim available to him by reason of the
stock dividends claimed by him.

Chipman, P. J., and Ellison, J., *pro tem.*, concurred.

[CIV. No. 1552. Third Appellate District.—July 6, 1916.]

C. CURTIN et al., Petitioners, v. W. S. KINGSBURY, etc., Respondent.

SCHOOL LANDS—REDEMPTION FROM DELINQUENT TAX SALES—FAILURE TO PAY INTEREST—EFFECT OF ACT OF MAY 14, 1915.—Purchasers of school lands sold to the state for delinquent taxes in the year 1907, and for which a deed to the state was made in the year 1912, are not entitled to redeem, where they did not, prior to the going into effect of the act of May 14, 1915 (Stats. 1915, p. 605), providing that "the unsold portions of the sixteenth and thirty-sixth sections of school lands . . . shall be sold at public auction by the surveyor-general," make a payment of all interest due and unpaid on the land as required by section 3788 of the Political Code under the amendment of March 2, 1909 (Stats. 1909, p. 122), along with their payment of the taxes, penalties, and accruing costs.

ID.—STATUS OF DEFAULTING PURCHASERS — RESTORATION—COMPLIANCE WITH EXISTING LAWS.—Upon a sale made to the state of school lands for nonpayment of taxes followed by a deed to the state therefor, all rights of defaulting purchasers in such lands are extinguished, and the only method by which they can be restored to their former rights is by compliance with the law existing at the time of making application for such restoration.

ID.—CONDITIONS TO RESTORATION — RIGHT OF STATE TO IMPOSE.—The state under such circumstances has the right, as the absolute owner of the lands, to dictate the terms upon which they may be repurchased by the original or a new purchaser, or the conditions upon which the owners or purchasers or their assigns may be restored to their original state or title.

ID.—PAYMENT OF INTEREST AS CONDITION TO REDEMPTION—REASONABLENESS OF METHOD.—The method provided by the amendment of 1909 to section 3788 of the Political Code (repealed by the act of 1915) of enforcing payment of interest as a condition to the repurchase or redemption of school lands sold for nonpayment of taxes is not more burdensome than the former method of foreclosure.

APPLICATION for a Writ of Mandate originally made to the District Court of Appeal for the Third Appellate District, to compel the surveyor-general to issue a certificate of purchase of school lands.

The facts are stated in the opinion of the court.

W. H. Larew, and Jos. Barcroft, for Petitioners.

U. S. Webb, Attorney-General, and Robert T. McKisick, Deputy Attorney-General, for Respondent.

CHIPMAN, P. J.—Mandate. It appears by the petition that, on November 19, 1901, the state of California issued its certificate of purchase to one J. Frank Miller for all of section 36, township 9 south, range 19 east, M. D. B. & M., in Madera County, for which he paid twenty per cent of the purchase price of $1.25 per acre, said land being "only fit for grazing purposes"; that there remained due to the state one dollar per acre, or $640, with interest at seven per cent per annum; that, in 1904, said Miller assigned said certificate of purchase to plaintiff Curtin and W. C. Hensley, who "entered into the possession of said land and became and were the sole owners thereof, subject only to the paramount title of the state." On February 21, 1910, said Hensley died and thereupon petitioner R. C. Jay was appointed and now is administrator of his estate. On June 22, 1907, the land in controversy was sold to the state for nonpayment of taxes, followed by a deed to the state dated July 16, 1912. On June 13, 1913, petitioner Curtin applied for and received from the auditor of Madera County an estimate of the amount necessary to redeem said land from tax sale, and, on the same day, paid to the treasurer of said county the amount of said estimate, together with other delinquent taxes on the land, which "redemption was duly recorded, and it was noted upon the recorded certificate and the recorded tax deed that the land was redeemed"; on September 10, 1915, at the request of petitioners, the auditor and treasurer furnished them "a statement of all interest then due and unpaid on said" land, and petitioners paid to the treasurer the amount shown by said statement. It is then alleged that the certificate of sale issued to said Miller has been lost, and that the defendant refuses to accept from the treasurer of Madera County the amounts paid by petitioners and refuses to issue a new certificate of purchase in lieu of the lost one. It is alleged, upon information and belief, that there are no claims adverse to petitioners to said land. There is also an allegation "that no foreclosure for nonpayment of interest ever was had or attempted in the matter of the delinquency in payment of interest as provided in the Political Code or at all; that the certificate of purchase remains uncanceled by any foreclosure.'' The prayer is for an alternative writ of mandate directing defendant to receive the moneys tendered by petitioners and to issue a new certificate of purchase in lieu of the lost one.

The issue presented is raised by a general demurrer filed by respondent to the petition.

By an act approved May 14, 1915 (Stats. 1915, p. 605), which, for convenience, will hereinafter be referred to as chapter 389, it was provided that "the unsold portions of the sixteenth and thirty-sixth sections of school lands . . . shall be sold at public auction by the surveyor-general.'' It is the contention of respondent that "under this method all applications to purchase school lands at a fixed statutory price are abolished. Nobody can apply to purchase lands of the character described in the act. Intending purchasers must attend the sale at the time and place stated in the notice of sale and there bid in open competition against any and all other persons who desire to acquire the land,'' and respondent maintains that "this act conflicts with the provisions of section 3788 of the Political Code *in toto,* and with so much of section 3817 as affects school lands''; that "under the law as it stood when the sale was made the sole remedy of the delinquent purchaser was to repurchase the land within six months from that date''; that the delinquent purchaser had no vested right to redeem the property, his only right being a preference given him to repurchase within six months; and that this privilege was withdrawn by chapter 389, *supra.*

Petitioners' reply to the above contention that "the state may diminish the penalties, extend the time for redemption or lessen the burden upon the delinquent taxpayer, but the state cannot increase the penalties, shorten the time for redemption, or add further penalties, burdens, and conditions of redemption, after the date of sale to the state,'' and "none of the statutes relied upon by the defendant purport to be retroactive.''

The method prescribed by section 3817 of the Political Code in 1883 for the redemption of school lands sold for delinquent taxes applied only to purchasers who had paid "the full amount of one dollar and twenty-five cents per acre.'' (Stats. 1883, p. 23.) This section remained unchanged until

1895, when it was made to apply to purchasers "when the full amount of the purchase price of one dollar and twenty-five cents per acre has not been paid, except where the deed to the state, provided for in section three thousand seven hundred and eighty-five, has been filed with the surveyor-general." (Stats. 1895, pp. 308–340.) By this act there were many changes made in the sections of the Political Code relating to the sale, redemption, and disposition of lands sold for delinquent taxes. School lands were made subject to the act and were referred to in sections 3785 and 3788 as well as in section 3817. By section 3785 it was provided that where the full price for the land has not been paid and where the tax deed to the state has been forwarded by the county recorder to the surveyor-general, "the state shall dispose of such lands in the manner provided in section three thousand seven hundred and eighty-eight." Section 3788 provided that in such case "the said lands shall again become subject to entry and sale, in the same manner, and subject to the same conditions, as apply to other state lands of like character, except that the former possessors or owners of the land thus deeded to the state, their heirs or assigns, shall be preferred purchasers thereof for the period of six months after the deeds are filed with the surveyor-general." It was required of the intending purchaser that as a condition to his purchase he should pay, in addition to the price of the land, all delinquent taxes, penalties, costs, and accrued costs prior to and subsequent to the date of sale to the state. The sections of the Political Code as amended by the act of 1895 was the law of 1901, when the purchase was made by plaintiffs' assignor. By that act (sec. 3788, Pol. Code) the right given to the purchaser whose land had been sold to the state for delinquent taxes was not to redeem, as was the right given by the act of 1883, but was a right to become a purchaser in preference to any other person if, when application was made, there was no other conflicting application. His rights were no greater than those of any other purchaser, except that he was a preferred purchaser for a limited period.

We have seen that the taxes became delinquent and the land was sold to the state in 1907 and a deed made to the state in 1912, which was duly filed with the surveyor-general. Had no other statute intervened, plaintiffs' right would have been that of a preferred purchaser and not of a redemptioner.

Section 3817 was amended in 1897, 1901, and 1905, but not affecting that part of the section referring to school lands. In 1909 the legislature added to the section the following: "and an application has been filed therefor in that office." This act was passed February 22, 1909, and took effect sixty days thereafter. (Stats. 1909, p. 42.) At the same session, on March 2, 1909, section 3788 was also amended, retaining the provision making the former possessor or owner of the lands sold a preferred purchaser for a period of six months after the filing of the deed in the office of the surveyor-general. And it was further provided: "That the former possessors or owners of said land thus deeded to the state, their heirs or assigns, shall have the right to be restored to their former state and title (at any time either during the said period of six months above referred to, or afterward, and before application for said land is made and filed with the surveyor-general by any other person) upon paying to the county treasurer"—1. A sum equivalent to the taxes, penalties, and accruing costs; 2. All delinquent taxes, penalties, and costs which have accrued upon such lands subsequent to the date of the certificate of purchase under which the former possessors or owner, or their heirs or assigns, claimed title to said lands; 3. Also all unpaid interest up to the first day of January following the day when he shall make payment to the county treasurer. (Stats. 1909, p. 122.)

The payments made by plaintiffs to the county treasurer, as appears from the petition, seem to have been made as redemptioners, whereas, whatever right they had was given to them by the statute as preferred purchasers. It is perhaps immaterial whether these payments were made as redemptioners or as purchasers if they were sufficient to comply with the law applicable when the payments were made. Now, the sale to the state for delinquent taxes extinguished all rights of plaintiffs to the lands subject to the right of redemption during the five years' period and before the deed passes the legal title to the state. Such sale vests the equitable and the deed the legal title of the land in the state. (*Santa Barbara County* v. *Savings & Loan Soc.*, 137 Cal. 463, 465, [70 Pac. 457].) As against the state the property owner at the end of five years has forfeited all rights to the property, except the privilege accorded him by the statute of redeeming it at any time before the state actually enters, sells, or disposes of it. (*Baird* v. *Monroe,* 150 Cal. 560, 567, [89 Pac. 352].) The state had the power to say upon what terms and in what manner the title thus vested in the state might be divested. It could have denied all right to redeem or to purchase.

In 1907, when the land was sold for delinquent taxes, plaintiffs' right under the amendments to the Political Code by the act of 1895 was that of a preferred purchaser for the period of six months after the deed is filed with the surveyor-general. (Pol. Code, sec. 3788.) They did not avail themselves of that right, and it was lost to them. By the acts of 1909 the state offered to restore them "to their former state and title" upon conditions more favorable than were given by the act of 1895, for they were allowed to comply with the statute as preferred purchasers within six months, and were to be restored to their title at any time before another application was made for the same land, and upon terms no different than were imposed by the act of 1895, except that the payment of interest upon the unpaid purchase price was required to be paid. As this was an obligation attached to the original contract, its payment cannot be regarded as an additional burden. But whether it was or not, we think the state had the right, as the absolute owner of the land under the tax deed, to dictate the terms upon which it might be repurchased by the original or a new purchaser, or the conditions upon which the purchasers or owners or their assigns might be restored to their original state and title.

The payments made by the plaintiffs to the county treasurer were made June 13, 1913, at which time no other application had been made to purchase the land, but the payment did not include interest, and no interest was then paid or tendered, and, on September 10, 1915, they again attempted to redeem from delinquent tax sale by paying the then accrued taxes, penalties, and costs, and they also paid to the auditor and treasurer of Madera County "all interest then due and unpaid on said land."

It appears from the petition that, on July 15, 1915, the surveyor-general advised petitioners that said land could be redeemed under section 3788 of the Political Code, but also advised petitioners of the act of 1915, S. B. 906, chapter 389 (copy of which was inclosed in the letter of advice), stating that said "act became effective August 8, 1915, superseding

section 3788 of the Political Code," and that, in the opinion
of the surveyor-general, "all land that had been sold to the
state for nonpayment of taxes wherein the tax deed was filed
in this office, would be subject to sale under the provisions
of said S. B. 906. Inasmuch as the land was not redeemed
on or before August 8, 1915, this office considers [describing
the land] to be vacant state land and subject to sale under
the provisions of S. B. 906." Petitioners were, therefore,
fully aware of the attitude of the state, and that they were
required to make payment on or before August 8, 1915, in
order to preserve their rights. This they did not do.

The act of 1915 provided: "Section 1. The unsold portions of the sixteenth and thirty-sixth sections of school lands
. . . shall be sold at public auction by the surveyor-general.
. . . Sec. 3. Those parts of all acts in conflict with this act
are hereby repealed." (Stats. 1915, p. 605.) Without question, section 3788 of the Political Code is in conflict with this
act and is thereby repealed so far as it provided a different
method for the disposition of school land.

We do not think petitioners had any vested right which
was violated by the act of 1915. The absolute title to the
land, as we have said, vested in the state by the tax deed,
and the state could provide any method it chose for the subsequent disposition of the land, and could at any time change
such method without impairing the right of any applicant to
purchase who had not complied with the then existing law.

Petitioners claim that "the penalty provided by law for
the nonpayment of interest is foreclosure, whereby the principal paid upon the purchase price becomes forfeited and the
certificates canceled upon foreclosure and not otherwise."
And it is hence contended that as there has been no such
foreclosure, petitioners were not required to pay accrued interest as a condition to the repurchase or redemption of the
land, and that it was a violation of their contract to require
such payment.

It was held in the recent case of *Aikins* v. *Kingsbury*, 170
Cal. 674, [151 Pac. 145], that "the method of procedure by
the act of 1867–68, for terminating the right of a defaulting
purchaser of school lands purchased under that act was not
exclusive, and he may not complain of a different method of
procedure subsequently established by the state for accomplishing that end which did not impose upon him more bur-

densome conditions than the former.'' (Syllabus.) As above suggested, we do not think the method of enforcing payment of interest by making it a condition for repurchase or redemption where the land is sold for nonpayment of delinquent taxes, is any more burdensome than to enforce payment by foreclosure. Certainly it is less expensive and less annoying to the intending purchaser or redemptioner. But aside from this consideration, we think, as already pointed out, the sale to the state for nonpayment of taxes culminating in a deed to the state extinguished all rights of petitioners, and that they thereafter could be restored to their former or any rights only by compliance with the law existing at the time they might apply for such restoration.

The writ is denied.

Hart, J., and Ellison, J., *pro tem.*, concurred.

A petition to have the cause heard in the supreme court, after judgment in the district court of appeal, was denied by the supreme court on September 1, 1916.

[Civ. No. 1794.   First Appellate District.—July 7, 1916.]

UNION TRUST COMPANY OF SAN FRANCISCO (a Corporation), Administrator, etc., Appellant, v. PACIFIC TELEPHONE & TELEGRAPH COMPANY (a Corporation), Respondent.

ESTATES OF DECEASED PERSONS—SURRENDER OF STOCK IN LOCAL CORPORATION TO FOREIGN EXECUTOR — RECOVERY BY SUBSEQUENTLY APPOINTED LOCAL ADMINISTRATOR.—The voluntary surrender by a domestic corporation of stock therein owned by a resident of another state at the time of his death to the foreign domiciliary executor of the deceased, and subsequently to the rightful devisee under the will, prior to any local ancillary administration, constitutes a good defense to an action for the stock brought by the local ancillary administrator against the corporation.

ID.—PERSONAL PROPERTY OUTSIDE OF STATE—TAKING OF POSSESSION BY LOCAL ADMINISTRATOR.—Although the executor or administrator of the domicile cannot maintain a suit in another state to recover personal property or collect a debt due the estate, yet he may take possession of such property peaceably without suit, or collect a debt if voluntarily paid, and if there is no opposing administration in the state where the property was situated, its courts will recognize his title as rightful, and protect it as fully as if he had taken out letters of administration there; and the voluntary payment of the debt by such debtor under such circumstances would be good, and constitute a defense to a suit by an ancillary administrator subsequently appointed.

APPEAL from a judgment of the Superior Court of the City and County of San Francisco.   Daniel C. Deasy, Judge.

The facts are stated in the opinion of the court.

Heller, Powers & Ehrman, for Appellant.

Pillsbury, Madison & Sutro, for Respondent.

LENNON, P. J.—This is an appeal from a judgment in favor of the defendant.   The facts as set forth in the brief of appellant are conceded to be correctly stated, and, so far as they are material to the questions of law involved, are as follows: David R. Downer died in the state of New Jersey on March 1, 1911, being then a resident of that state.   Thereafter his will was admitted to probate in the courts of New Jersey having jurisdiction of his estate.   A part of the property of the estate of the decedent consisted of fifteen shares of preferred capital stock of the defendant corporation, valued at one thousand five hundred dollars.   The defendant's office and principal place of business was and is in the city and county of San Francisco.   At the time of the death of the decedent the certificates of stock in question were in his possession in the state of New Jersey, and came into the possession of the executor named in his will, who thereafter as such executor surrendered the certificates of said stock to the defendant, which transferred the shares of stock on its books to said executor and issued to him a new certificate for the same.   Thereafter the said executor duly indorsed and transferred said stock to Edith A. Barnes, one of the devisees under the will of said decedent, who subsequently surrendered the same to the defendant, which thereupon issued to Edith A. Barnes a new certificate for the stock in question.   On July

31 Cal. App.—5

29, 1913, the courts of New Jersey approved the final accounts
and acts of the executor in said estate. Thereafter an exem-
plified copy of the will of said decedent was admitted to probate by the superior court of the city and county of San
Francisco, and ancillary letters of administration with the
will annexed issued to the plaintiff, which thereupon demanded of the defendant that it issue to plaintiff, as such
ancillary administrator with the will annexed, a certificate for
the fifteen shares in question, and this demand being refused,
brought this action against the defendant for the possession
of said stock.

The trial court from the foregoing facts found in favor of
the defendant and entered its judgment accordingly, and
from that judgment the plaintiff prosecutes this appeal.

The sole question presented for determination upon this
appeal is as to whether the delivery by the defendant of the
shares of stock in question to the foreign administrator of the
decedent, and also to his devisee entitled thereto, in the absence of prior ancillary administration, and the appointment
of the plaintiff as administrator with the will annexed in this
state, constitutes a good defense to this action by such ancillary administrator to recover said stock. The appellant
chiefly relies for its right to such recovery upon the case of
Murphy v. *Crouse*, 135 Cal. 14, [87 Am. St. Rep. 90, 66 Pac.
971], as approved in the cases of *Richards* v. *Blaisdell*, 12 Cal.
App. 101, [106 Pac. 732], and *McDougald* v. *Low*, 164 Cal.
107, [127 Pac. 1027]. It is pointed out on behalf of the respondent that the case of *Murphy* v. *Crouse* involved a controversy between the domiciliary administrator of a foreign
state and the ancillary administrator appointed here as to
which had the better right to the possession of the personal
property of the decedent; and that in such a case the respondent concedes that the local ancillary administrator has the
better right, but insists that such is not the situation in the
case at bar, and in support of such insistence directs our attention to the early case of *Brown* v. *San Francisco Gaslight Co.*,
58 Cal. 426, wherein it was held that in the absence of local
ancillary administration the foreign administrator of a decedent was entitled to a transfer of the stock of a nonresident
decedent in a California corporation without taking out letters
here; and that the case of *Brown* v. *San Francisco Gaslight
Co.* was considered and distinguished in the case of *Murphy*

v. Crouse upon the very ground contended for by the respondent here; and that the two later cases above cited do not undertake to lay down a contrary rule. Our attention has not been called by the appellant to any case in this or other jurisdictions declaring a different rule to that invoked in the case of *Brown* v *San Francisco Gaslight Co.;* but, on the contrary, the respondent cites a large number of cases from other states wherein the principle for which it contends has found adoption, and in many of which the facts are identical with those of the instant case—notably the cases of *Luce* v. *Manchester & L. R. R. Co.,* 63 N. H. 588, [3 Atl. 618]; *Hutchins* v. *State Bank,* 12 Met. (Mass.) 421; *In re Cape May etc. Co.,* 51 N. J. L. 78, [16 Atl. 191]; *Putnam* v. *Pitney,* (*In re Washburn's Estate*), 45 Minn. 242, [11 L. R. A. 41, 47 N. W. 790]. The principle invoked in these cases has been well set forth in the one last mentioned, wherein the court says: ''The modern decisions have so far drifted away from former narrow views as to hold almost universally that although the executor or administrator of the domicile cannot maintain a suit in another state to recover personal property or collect a debt due the estate, yet he may take possession of such property peaceably without suit, or collect a debt if voluntarily paid; and that if there is no opposing administration in the state where the property was situated, its courts will recognize his title as rightful, and protect it as fully as if he had taken out letters of administration there; and also that the voluntary payment of the debt by such debtor under such circumstances would be good, and constitute a defense to a suit by an ancillary administrator subsequently appointed.''

We think the foregoing embodies a correct statement of the principle declared in the case of *Brown* v. *San Francisco Gaslight Co.,* 58 Cal. 426, and that the cases of *Murphy* v. *Crouse,* 135 Cal. 14, [87 Am. St. Rep. 90, 66 Pac. 971], *Richards* v. *Blaisdell,* 12 Cal. App. 101, [106 Pac. 732], and *McDougald* v. *Low,* 164 Cal. 107, [127 Pac. 1027], are not to be understood as departing from it, or as applicable to cases of the voluntary delivery of the stock of a local corporation to a foreign domiciliary administrator prior to any local ancillary administration, or to cases involving no rights arising out of the inheritance tax laws, or out of the claims of local creditors; and that the defendant herein, having voluntarily surrendered the possession of the stock in question to the foreign domiciliary executor of the decedent, and subsequently to the rightful devisee under his will prior to any local ancillary administration, has by proof of so doing established a good defense to this action.

Judgment affirmed.

Kerrigan, J., and Richards, J., concurred.

A petition for a rehearing of this cause was denied by the district court of appeal on August 5, 1916, and a petition to have the cause heard in the supreme court, after judgment in the district court of appeal, was denied by the supreme court on September 5, 1916.

———————

[Civ. No. 1982.   Second Appellate District.—July 7, 1916.]

JOHN G. LYNCH et al., Respondents, v. BEKINS VAN & STORAGE COMPANY (a Corporation), Appellant.

WAREHOUSE—LOSS OF STORED GOODS BY FIRE—STORAGE IN FIREPROOF WAREHOUSE—EXPRESS CONTRACT—EXISTENCE OF IMPLIED CONTRACT IMMATERIAL.—Upon an appeal from a judgment in an action against a warehouse-keeper for the loss of stored goods by fire, the judgment must be sustained irrespective of whether an implied contract arose that the goods were to be stored in a fireproof warehouse, where the evidence amply sustains the finding that there was an express contract to that effect.

ID.—EVIDENCE OF EXPRESS CONTRACT—ADVERTISEMENTS AND PRINTED MATTER.—The admission of evidence showing representations by advertisements and printed matter, to the effect that the defendant had at its disposal fireproof warehouses and offered to customers to furnish storage of that kind, is without error, as it tends to corroborate the evidence of the plaintiff as to the express contract made and found by the court.

ID.—DIFFERENCES IN PRICES BETWEEN FIREPROOF AND NONFIREPROOF STORAGE.—The practice or habit of the defendant in charging a different price for storage, according to whether or not it was fireproof, is not admissible, in the absence of knowledge by plaintiffs of such fact prior to the contract of storage.

ID.—CHARACTER OF STORAGE—BOOK ENTRIES OF DEFENDANT—SELF-SERVING DECLARATIONS.—The entry made by defendant's agent in its order book at the time of the giving of the order to it for storage, not having been seen or known of by the plaintiff when the transac-

tion was closed, is self-serving, and not admissible to corroborate its
evidence, consisting of the positive statement of its agent, contradicting plaintiff, that nothing was said in the conversation about fireproof
storage, and that the contract was for nonfireproof storage.

ID.—CUSTOM AS TO LIMITATION OF LIABILITY—LACK OF KNOWLEDGE OF
    PLAINTIFFS—PROOF INADMISSIBLE.—In the absence of any misrepre-
    sentation made by plaintiffs as to the character of the stored goods,
    or that they refused upon demand to truly state that character, a
    general custom among warehousemen to insert in their receipts a pro-
    vision limiting their liability for loss by fire to $50 per package, or
    one of refusing to accept antiques and jewelry of great value, is
    inadmissible.

ID.—IMPEACHMENT OF DEFENDANT'S AGENT—ADVERTISEMENTS.—Defend-
    ant's advertisement of ability to furnish fireproof storage, though
    unknown to plaintiffs, is admissible, for the purpose of contradicting
    defendant's agent's testimony that nothing was said about storage in
    a fireproof building.

APPEAL from a judgment of the Superior Court of Los
Angeles County.   Frank G. Finlayson, Judge.

The facts are stated in the opinion of the court.

Collier & Clark, and Jones & Evans, for Appellant.

Williams, Goudge & Chandler, for Respondents.

JAMES, J.—Plaintiffs in this case were awarded judgment for the sum of $11,376, as the value of certain household
goods, antique articles, bric-a-brac, etc., which had been delivered into the charge of defendant as a warehouse-keeper.
The merchandise had been transported from an eastern point
to Los Angeles by a corporation, conducted as an adjunct
to the defendant, although separate in its operation and management.   On the arrival of the merchandise in Los Angeles
plaintiffs visited the office of the defendant and there, through
the agent of defendant, arranged for the storage of the goods.
The merchandise was taken in charge by the defendant and
stored in a warehouse near the railway station, but before
a receipt therefor had been delivered to the plaintiffs a fire
occurred which destroyed the warehouse and its contents,
including the property of plaintiffs.   The warehouse in which
the property was stored, as has already appeared, was not
fireproof.   Plaintiffs in suing to recover the value of their

property alleged that an express contract had been made with them, that the storage should be in a fireproof warehouse; second, that irrespective of the express verbal contract, defendant had, by numerous advertisements which had come to the attention of plaintiffs, represented that the storage furnished by it was fireproof, and that the plaintiffs relied upon such representations; and nothing having been said by any agent of the defendant to the contrary, by the storage of the goods with defendant, plaintiffs contended that an implied contract arose that the merchandise was to be protected in a fireproof building. Both of these contentions were sustained by the trial judge, although the further claim that the fire occurred through the negligence of the defendant was decided against the plaintiffs. An appeal was taken from the judgment.

The trial judge having determined that there was an express contract for the furnishing of fireproof storage, and the record disclosing evidence amply sufficient to sustain that finding, the judgment should be affirmed unless alleged errors pointed out in the admission and rejection of testimony are found to be meritorious. We think it unnecessary to go into any discussion of the question as to whether the implied contract arose by reason of the printed representations made by defendant as to the character of storage furnished by it. On the part of the plaintiffs the testimony showed that when the order was given to the defendant to store the goods of the plaintiffs, inquiry was made on the part of the plaintiffs of the person in charge of defendant's office as to whether the storage would be "fireproof," to which the defendant's agent replied, "Oh, yes." The plaintiffs were strangers in the city of Los Angeles and were not acquainted with the buildings used by the defendant for warehouse purposes. It seems that the defendant had a fireproof storehouse under its control, which was at a greater distance from the railroad tracks than the nonfireproof building in which the goods were stored. It is admitted that the defendant was able to and could furnish, when required, storage which by reason of the character of the building would furnish absolute protection against fire. The admission of evidence showing representations by advertisements and printed matter, to the effect that the defendant had at its disposal fireproof warehouses and offered to customers to furnish storage of that kind, was without error, as it tended to corroborate the evidence given by plaintiffs as to the express contract made and found by the court. That it also tended to furnish a basis for an implied contract, we need not discuss for the reasons already given.

It is claimed on the part of appellant that the court erred in rejecting the evidence of an entry made in the defendant's order book at the time of the giving of the order. This entry was made by the agent of defendant and it was offered as corroborative evidence tending to sustain defendant's contention that the contract was for nonfireproof storage. It was not claimed that the plaintiffs saw this entry or had any knowledge thereof at the time the transaction was closed. Such a declaration would be purely self-serving and incompetent to be introduced in evidence. It was not claimed that defendant's agent, when she testified, needed to refer to the order as a memorandum refreshing her recollection, for she testified very positively that nothing was said in the conversation to the effect that the storage to be furnished should be fireproof.

It is claimed again that the court erred in rejecting evidence as to the difference between the prices charged by the defendant for fireproof and nonfireproof storage. It is not contended that any knowledge of such difference had been conveyed to the plaintiffs prior to the making of the contract for storage, and, so far as they were concerned, this practice or habit of the defendant was a secret matter which could not in any way affect the contract. Defendant was allowed to show by its employee that the charge as made against the plaintiffs for the storage of their goods was a charge customarily made by it for nonfireproof storage. This evidence, no doubt, was considered by the trial judge in making up his conclusion of fact as to the existence of the express contract, the correctness of which conclusion we have no right to here consider—it must be deemed to be the fact. There was no error committed by the court in rejecting evidence offered by the defendant to prove a general custom among warehousemen to insert in warehouse receipts a provision limiting their liability for loss by fire to $50 per package, or a custom of refusing to accept antiques and jewelry of great value. Such a custom undisclosed to plaintiffs, as it was, could not have been considered to their detriment in the trial of the issues presented. There is no claim that there was any misrepresentation made by the plaintiffs as to the character of their goods, or that they refused upon demand to truly state that character. It is also contended that as to some of the evidence of representations by advertisements, there was no proof that the plaintiffs saw or relied upon such statements, and that the court for that reason should not have received the evidence. The evidence objected to under this head consisted of a calendar upon which was printed an advertisement that defendant was able to provide fireproof storage. It was objected that as the plaintiffs had not seen this calendar at the time they gave their order for storage, it furnished no evidence in support of their cause of action because they could not have relied upon such representations. The trial judge limited the effect of this evidence and admitted it for a proper purpose when he said: "They cannot claim that they relied upon the advertisement unless they saw it. They did not see it. They are not offering this in evidence to prove that they relied upon this, but to show that at that time the person representing the company with whom they were dealing knew that her company advertised that it had a fireproof building. That being so, there being one fireproof building and one that was not, it may legitimately be argued that if nothing was said about it being a fireproof building, she would naturally have said, 'We have one which is fireproof and one which is not; which do you want?' On the other hand, if the plaintiff did contract for a fireproof building, there would be no occasion for saying that, or for calling their attention to the fact that there was one fireproof building and one which was not, because if they had contracted for it and this witness knew it, she would either order the goods to be sent to the building which was fireproof or else notify them of not doing so. In other words, the advertisement of the fireproof warehouse is a circumstance that has some tendency to contradict her present testimony, to show that her recollection is not accurate; that is, that there is to some extent an inconsistency between her saying that there was no contract for a fireproof warehouse, and her knowledge that there was an advertisement that there was a fireproof warehouse." Mr. Collier (for the defendant): "I see the purpose which the court presents." The Court: "That is the purpose for which it may be admitted. I presume that is the reason running through counsel's mind."

The brevity of this opinion may not seem commensurate with the voluminous record and briefs filed in this cause, but to our minds the appeal is entitled to no more extended consideration than has been given to it. The trial court, by its determination that an express contract had been made for fireproof storage, determined the whole case, except as the defendant might be able to show that there was error committed at the trial. We think that none of the contentions for error is of merit, and that the judgment should be affirmed.

The judgment is affirmed.

Conrey, P. J., and Shaw, J., concurred.

[Civ. No. 1761. First Appellate District.—July 10, 1916.]

E. WILLIAMS, Respondent, v. PARROTT & COMPANY (a Corporation), Appellant.

CONTRACT—SALE OF PORTION OF SALMON PACK ON COMMISSION—SUBSEQUENT NEGOTIATIONS FOR HANDLING OF ENTIRE PACK—EFFECT OF TERMINATION OF NEGOTIATIONS.—An optional agreement entered into between a corporation engaged in the business of packing salmon and a brokerage corporation, whereby the former agreed to deliver to the latter five thousand one hundred cases of certain kinds of canned salmon of the pack of the year 1909, to be sold by the latter at what is conventionally termed the opening price for the pack of that year, thereafter and before delivery to be named, and to be communicated by the former to the latter, and to be by the latter confirmed and assented to within five days after such communication, the latter to receive a brokerage of five per cent upon its sales, is not canceled by negotiations entered into in the early part of the year following the date of the agreement for the handling of the whole pack of the year, amounting to some fifty thousand cases, and the subsequent writing of a letter, referring to the letters by dates containing the proposition as to the handling of the entire pack, and declining the business, as such optional agreement and the subsequent negotiations were separate contracts, and the refusal to make delivery of the cases called for by such agreement constituted a breach of contract.

APPEAL from a judgment of the Superior Court of the City and County of San Francisco, and from an order denying a new trial. John L. Childs, Judge presiding.

The facts are stated in the opinion of the court.

J. Early Craig, for Appellant.

Chickering & Gregory, for Respondent.

KERRIGAN, J.—This is an appeal from the judgment and from an order denying the defendant's motion for a new trial.

The action was brought by plaintiff for sums alleged to be due from the defendant to the assignor of plaintiff, the Apex Fish Company, for a consignment of canned salmon which defendant had sold for the account of said fish company, which was a corporation engaged in the business of packing salmon having its principal place of business in the state of Washington. Defendant in its answer admitted itself to be accountable for the moneys received from the transaction set forth in plaintiff's complaint, but set up a counterclaim for $1,034, and denied liability for anything in exce s of the difference between that sum and plaintiff's demand, and which difference it paid.

The facts of the case were stipulated to except when consisting of letters, which were introduced in evidence.

The counterclaim was based on the following facts: On October 7, 1908, the Apex Fish Company entered into an optional agreement with defendant, whereby the former agreed to deliver to the defendant five thousand one hundred cases of certain kinds of canned salmon of the pack of the year 1909, to be sold by the defendant at what is conventionally termed the opening price for the pack of that year, thereafter and before delivery to be named, and to be communicated by the fish company to the defendant, and to be by the defendant confirmed and assented to within five days after the same had been communicated to it. Defendant was to receive a brokerage of five per cent upon its sales of the five thousand one hundred cases.

Thereafter, in the month of December, 1908, the defendant entered into six optional contracts with different persons for the sale of these goods, subject to approval of opening price of the year 1909 when named. The "opening price" was annually fixed by certain large packers in the early fall, and it was the custom of packers to notify those holding contracts for salmon of the naming of the opening price. The six contracts referred to were accepted by the Apex Fish Company.

In the early part of the year 1909 the company entered into negotiations with the defendant for the handling by the latter of the whole of its 1909 pack of salmon, amounting to some fifty thousand cases. These negotiations were terminated on May 12, 1909, when the defendant wrote the Apex Fish Company a letter, in which it stated, referring to the company's offer to allow the defendant to handle its entire pack for 1909, that after duly considering the matter "we have concluded that it is best to decline the business, which we do, thanking you for your offer and the courtesies extended." Subsequent to the writing of this letter the opening price was named. The fish company gave to the defendant no notice thereof, but immediately upon learning of it the defendant telegraphed to its representative, who was then in Washington, to confirm to the Apex Fish Company the opening price on its behalf. Its representative did so, and requested delivery of the five thousand one hundred cases agreed to be delivered under the contract of October 7, 1908. The fish company refused to make the delivery, taking the position that the contract was canceled by the fact of the negotiations for the entire pack of 1909 and their termination in the spring of that year. This was the view adopted by the trial court, which rendered its judgment accordingly in favor of the plaintiff in the sum of $1,034, with interest and costs.

We are of the opinion that the contention of the defendant must be sustained that the contract of October 7, 1908, between the Apex Fish Company and the defendant, and the subsequent negotiations relative to the entire pack of salmon for the year 1909, were separate transactions, and that the letter of May 12, 1909, written by the defendant, declining the business, referring as it did to the letters by dates containing the proposition, had reference to the latter negotiations alone, and did not operate as a cancellation of the earlier contract. Accordingly it must be considered that the refusal of the Apex Fish Company to deliver the five thousand one hundred cases of salmon when defendant confirmed the opening price constituted a breach of contract, for which the defendant is entitled to recover, and that the conclusion reached by the court that the contract of October 7, 1908, was canceled in May, 1909, is not supported by the evidence, and that its judgment based on such conclusion cannot stand.

The judgment and order are reversed.

Lennon, P. J., and Richards, J., concurred.

A petition to have the cause heard in the supreme court, after judgment in the district court of appeal, was denied by the supreme court on September 7, 1916.

[Civ. No. 1774. First Appellate District.—July 11, 1916.]

JAMES McNEIL et al., Respondents, v. F. L. KREDO et al., Appellants.

ACTION TO RECOVER MONEY—EXECUTORY CONTRACT TO PURCHASE LAND—RESCISSION—PLEADING.—A complaint to recover a certain sum of money paid under an executory contract for the purchase of land states a cause of action where it alleges that the defendants without cause repudiated the contract, declared it canceled, and denied to plaintiffs any right or interest thereunder, as, this being true, plaintiffs were relieved from the obligation of further performance on their contract and were privileged to accept defendants' renunciation of the contract as a rescission of the same.

ID.—RESTORATION OF CONSIDERATION.—In the absence of a special demurrer, such a complaint is sufficiently certain in its allegations to the effect that plaintiffs had not received and retained by virtue of the contract anything of value from the defendants, and it was not essential to the statement of a cause of action to allege that the plaintiff had placed or had offered to place defendants *in statu quo* before electing to accept defendants' alleged rescission of the contract.

ID.—PLEADING AND PROOF—PARTNERSHIP OBLIGATION—INDIVIDUAL LIABILITY.—The allegation of the complaint that the contract in controversy was a partnership obligation does not preclude proof of the fact that it was the individual obligation of one of the defendants.

APPEAL from a judgment of the Superior Court of the City and County of San Francisco, and from an order denying a new trial. E. P. Shortall, Judge.

The facts are stated in the opinion of the court.

A. M. De Vall, for Appellants.

E. B. Mering, for Respondents.

THE COURT.—The defendants herein were sued individually and as copartners. The appeal is from the judgment entered in favor of the plaintiffs and against the defendant F. L. Kredo individually, and from an order denying him a new trial.

The action was for the recovery of the sum of $980 alleged to have been paid to the defendants pursuant to the terms of an executory contract for the purchase and sale of certain ranch property situate in the county of Mendocino. The plaintiff's complaint proceeded upon the theory that subsequent to the payment of the sum sued for, and without default by the plaintiffs, the defendants repudiated the contract and elected to rescind the same. Upon the trial of the case it developed in evidence that the contract in controversy was not a partnership obligation and that it had been executed only by and between the plaintiffs and the defendant F. L. Kredo individually. Accordingly a nonsuit was granted to the defendant H. F. Kredo and the partnership.

The complaint states a cause of action. It in effect alleged that the defendants without cause repudiated the contract, declared it canceled, and denied to plaintiffs any right or interest thereunder. This being so, the plaintiffs were relieved from the obligation of further performance on their part and were privileged to consider and accept the defendant's renunciation of the contract as a rescission of the same. (*Liver* v. *Mills*, 155 Cal. 459, 463, [101 Pac. 299]; *Simmons* v. *Sweeney*, 13 Cal. App. 283, 289, [109 Pac. 265]; *Seals* v. *Davis*, 25 Cal. App. 68, [142 Pac. 905].) In the absence of a special demurrer the complaint is sufficiently certain in its allegations to the effect that the plaintiffs had not received and retained, by virtue of the contract, anything of value from the defendants. Consequently it was not essential to the statement of a cause of action to allege that the plaintiff had placed or had offered to place the defendants *in statu quo* before electing to accept the defendant's alleged rescission of the contract. The allegation of the complaint that the contract in controversy was a partnership obligation did not preclude proof of the fact that it was the individual obligation of the defendant F. L. Kredo. (Code Civ. Proc., sec. 578; *Grangers' Union* v. *Ashe*, 12 Cal. App. 757, [108 Pac. 533].)

The evidence, in our opinion, sustains the findings of the trial court as to the making of the contract, its performance by the plaintiffs, the sums paid by them thereunder, and its repudiation and rescission by the defendants. The findings support the judgment. Standing alone, finding No. 6 may, as a result of a clerical misprision, be somewhat uncertain, but when considered and construed with the context of the findings as a whole, their numerical order and general arrangement, it is fairly certain that finding No. 6 refers to paragraph 6 of the complaint.

This disposes of all of the points made in support of the appeal which we deem worthy of discussion.

The judgment and the order appealed from are affirmed.

A petition for a rehearing of this cause was denied by the district court of appeal on August 10, 1916, and a petition to have the cause heard in the supreme court after judgment in the district court of appeal, was denied by the supreme court on September 7, 1916.

[Civ. No. 2073. Second Appellate District.—July 11, 1916.]

MATTHEW BAILEY, Petitioner, v. SUPERIOR COURT OF THE COUNTY OF KERN and MILTON T. FARMER, Judge Thereof, Respondents.

MANDAMUS—ACTION TO COMPEL SHERIFF TO DELIVER PERSONAL PROPERTY—EXECUTION NOT STAYED.—An order of the superior court requiring a sheriff to take into his possession and deliver to the petitioner certain personal property and documents is not stayed by the mere fact of perfecting an appeal from the judgment therein, under the alternative method of appeal, without giving the stay bond provided in section 943 of the Code of Civil Procedure.

ID.—DUTY OF SHERIFF TO COMPLY WITH ORDER—ABILITY TO COMPLY—PROPERTY HELD BY THIRD PARTY.—It is the duty of a sheriff to comply with a judgment against him commanding him to take possession of and deliver to petitioner certain personal property, where the judgment has not been reversed or set aside and no stay bond

given; and whether the defendant can comply with the order by
reason of the fact that the property is in the possession of another
can only be determined by the court upon the showing made by him
in response to a citation to show cause why he should not be punished
for contempt for failure so to do.

ID.—JUDGMENT AGAINST HOLDER OF PROPERTY—STAY BOND ON APPEAL.
The fact that another party having possession of the property in
question has appealed from a judgment against it for its recovery
and given a stay bond on appeal is not a matter for consideration
in the proceedings against the sheriff.

APPLICATION originally made to the District Court of
Appeal for the Second Appellate District for a Writ of Mandate to direct the Superior Court of Kern County to issue a
citation against the sheriff to show cause why he should not
be punished for contempt of court for refusing to obey a
Writ of Mandate.

The facts are stated in the opinion of the court.

E. L. Foster, George E. Whitaker, Charles A. Barnhart,
Sullivan & Sullivan and Theo. J. Roche, Leon E. Morris, and
Robert M. Clarke, for Petitioner.

Wiley & Lambert, and C. E. Arnold, for Respondents.

SHAW, J.—Original application to this court for a writ
of mandate.

It appears that the petitioner, Matthew Bailey, as plaintiff, filed a petition in the superior court of Kern County,
wherein Thomas A. Baker was made respondent, praying
judgment that a writ of mandate be issued directed to Baker,
as sheriff of Kern County, requiring him to deliver to petitioner certain personal property and documents in the petition fully described. Upon trial of said proceeding, judgment was rendered for the plaintiff, in accordance with which
a peremptory writ of mandate was issued commanding Baker,
as such sheriff, to immediately take into his possession the
personal property and documents described therein and deliver the same to Matthew Bailey, the petitioner for said writ;
that Baker refused to comply with the writ upon the ground
that he had appealed from the judgment. Thereupon petitioner presented to the court an affidavit setting forth the
fact of Baker's refusal to comply with the order of court.

and upon which he prayed that a citation be issued by respondent requiring Baker to appear and show cause why he should not be punished for contempt of court in so refusing to obey the writ of mandate. The court refused to issue such citation; whereupon petitioner has applied to this court for a writ of mandate to be directed to the respondent herein, requiring it to issue the citation to Baker as prayed for. In response to the alternative writ of mandate granted by this court directed to the respondent requiring it to show cause why it should not issue the citation prayed for by petitioner in the proceeding against Baker, respondent has made return, assigning as grounds for its refusal, first, the fact that Baker, adopting the alternative method of appeal as provided in sections 941a, 941b, and 941c of the Code of Civil Procedure, has perfected an appeal from the judgment wherein said writ of mandate was issued; and, second, that the defendant in a certain action for claim and delivery of the personal property and documents involved, brought by defendant against the Security Trust Company, and wherein judgment was rendered in favor of Bailey, has appealed therefrom, giving a stay bond as provided in section 943 of the Code of Civil Procedure.

It is conceded that Baker in perfecting his appeal gave no undertaking or bond whatsoever, and the sole question presented is whether or not the order made requiring Baker to take into his possession and deliver to petitioner the personal property and documents involved is stayed by the mere fact of perfecting an appeal from the judgment therein without giving the stay bond provided for in section 943 of the Code of Civil Procedure. This section provides: "If the judgment or order appealed from direct the . . . delivery of documents or personal property, the execution of the judgment or order cannot be stayed by appeal, unless the things required to be assigned or delivered be placed in the custody of such officer or receiver as the court may appoint, or unless an undertaking be entered into on the part of the appellant, with at least two sureties, and in such amount as the court, or a judge thereof, may direct, to the effect that the appellant will obey the order of the appellate court upon the appeal." The order requiring Baker, as such sheriff, to deliver the documents and personal property to petitioner brings it clearly within the provisions of the section quoted. No bond or undertaking was given, and hence the enforcement of the order was not stayed by the taking of an appeal therefrom. The perfecting of the appeal, whether taken pursuant to the alternative method in which no undertaking on appeal is required, or taken pursuant to sections 939, 940, and 941 of the Code of Civil Procedure, the last of which sections provides that an undertaking in the sum of three hundred dollars shall be filed, does not operate as a stay of execution where the judgment or order is one designated in sections 942 and 945, inclusive, of the Code of Civil Procedure. Thus, where an appeal from a judgment or order directing the payment of money is perfected under either method, it does not effect a stay of execution unless a written undertaking be executed on the part of the appellant in double the amount named in the judgment; and so where an appeal is taken from an order or judgment directing the delivery of personal property or documents, then, as provided in said section 943, an undertaking must be given in order to stay the enforcement thereof. (See *Ex parte Clancy*, 90 Cal. 553, [27 Pac. 411]; *Doudell v. Shoo*, 159 Cal. 448, [114 Pac. 579]; *United States Fidelity etc. Co.* v. *More*, 155 Cal. 415, [101 Pac. 302].)   In support of its contention respondent relies upon the cases of *Palache v. Hunt*, 64 Cal. 473, [2 Pac. 245], and *Ballagh v. Superior Court*, 25 Cal. App. 149, [142 Pac. 1123]. In those cases, however, respondent was not required to deliver personal property or documents, and therefore the facts were not such as to bring the cases within the provisions of section 943, nor of any other provision of the code requiring a stay bond to be given.

Neither is the fact that the Security Trust Company has given a stay bond for a judgment rendered against it a matter for consideration in this proceeding. The judgment here is against Baker, and until reversed or set aside, since no stay bond was given, it is clearly his duty to comply with the order; and whether or not the order is one with which he can comply can only be determined by the court upon the showing made by him in response to a citation to show cause why he should not be punished for contempt for failure so to do.

In the absence of any stay bond given, plaintiff is entitled to the processes of the court to enforce the order made, which, until reversed or stay bond given, stands as a valid judgment to be enforced by the processes of the court to which petitioner is entitled for the purpose of having a judicial determination of the question as to whether Baker can perform the acts as ordered. Assuming the property to be held by another, there is nothing to show that such other would not on demand deliver it to Baker as sheriff, or that he has made any effort to obtain possession of it. At all events, no legal reason whatever is presented here showing why Baker should not comply with the order, from which it follows that the trial court respondent here should issue the citation, and upon a hearing determine whether he be in contempt for disobedience of the order.

The alternative writ heretofore issued directing respondent to issue the citation as prayed for by petitioner is made peremptory.

Conrey, P. J., and James, J., concurred.

[Civ. No. 2122.   Second Appellate District.—July 14, 1916.]

S. H. PETERS, Petitioner, v. SUPERIOR COURT OF THE COUNTY OF SAN BERNARDINO and J. W. CURTIS, Judge Thereof, Respondents.

JUSTICE'S COURT APPEAL—BOND ON—JUSTIFICATION OF SURETIES—FAILURE TO GIVE NOTICE OF TIME OF JUSTIFICATION—DISMISSAL.—Where the sureties on a bond on appeal from a justice's court appear and justify without any notice being given to the opposite party, and without circumstances excusing the justification after the time prescribed by law, the bond is ineffectual, and the appeal must be dismissed.

APPLICATION originally made to the District Court of Appeal for the Second Appellate District for a Writ of Certiorari to review an order of the Superior Court of San Bernardino County denying a motion to dismiss an appeal from the Justice's Court.

The facts are stated in the opinion of the court.

W. T. Craig, H. R. Archibald, and A. Henderson Stockton, for Petitioner.

A. S. Maloney, for Respondents.

JAMES, J.—*Certiorari* to review proceedings had on a motion made to dismiss an appeal taken to the superior court of the county of San Bernardino from the justice's court of Colton township. In the justice's court action this petitioner was the plaintiff and secured judgment against A. Crowell and H. C. Crowell. The defendants in that action appealed. The motion made by the petitioner in the superior court was to dismiss the appeal taken by the Crowells, because the sureties on the undertaking on appeal had failed to justify upon notice to the plaintiff after exception had been taken to their sufficiency. The superior court denied the motion. We have before us the record of the proceedings and evidence heard by the superior court on which the motion was determined. It appears by the uncontradicted evidence that after the appeal was taken, and on the tenth day of January, 1916, the attorneys for the plaintiff in the justice's court action, whose offices were in the city of Los Angeles, received through the mails a copy of the notice of appeal and a copy of the bond given on appeal, with request that they acknowledge service on the notice of appeal and return the same to the justice. The attorneys for the plaintiff thereupon wrote to the attorney for the defendants-appellants, whose office was in the city of San Bernardino, acknowledging receipt of the notice of appeal and bond, and informing said attorney that they had accepted service of the notice of appeal and returned the same to the justice of the peace, at the same time inclosing a notice of exception to the sureties on the undertaking. This letter, it was admitted, was received by the attorney addressed on January 12th. The notice of exception to sureties was filed with the justice on January 14th. In another letter received in San Bernardino on January 12th, the plaintiff's attorneys stated to the opposing counsel: "Kindly give me as much notice as possible of the date of justification of sureties." To this letter a reply was made to the effect that the hearing of the justification of sureties would be taken up some time later in the month. On the 14th of January the San Bernardino counsel received from the plaintiff's counsel a letter in which he was advised that the plaintiff would insist upon the sureties justifying strictly in accordance with law; that is, within five days from the date of the exception. No notice of any justification was given, but on the 18th of January the sureties appeared before the justice and justified.

In excuse for not having given a notice to the plaintiff as to
the time when the sureties would appear for justification,
counsel for the defendants and for the respondent here set
out in his affidavit made to the superior court, "that from
the fourteenth day of January, 1916, to the nineteenth day of
January, 1916, a great amount of rain fell, causing floods and
stopping traffic on all railroads, so that affiant was unable
to mail notice of date of justification of sureties to the plaintiff and his attorneys; that affiant sought to communicate
by telephone with Los Angeles, where plaintiff and plaintiff's
attorneys reside, but was unable to do so on account of the
severity of the storm and rainfall; that the said sureties justified before J. B. Hanna, Justice of the Peace of Colton
Township, on the eighteenth day of January, 1916; said sureties residing in the city of San Bernardino, were compelled
to go to Colton on a switch engine on said day, being the
only manner in which they could reach Colton on account
of the severity of the rainfall." It therefore appears that the
justification of the sureties was made wholly without any
notice being given to the opposite party. So far as the service of the various notices is to be considered, we think that
the parties are not entitled to raise any question as to the
sufficiency of such service now, as they at the time adopted
that service as sufficient and proceeded to act upon it. If
circumstances existed which would excuse the appealing parties for holding the justification after the time prescribed by
law, such facts are not disclosed, for it appears that no notice
was attempted to be given at all; that the sureties did not
justify upon notice either within or after the expiration of
five days from the date of receipt of the notice of exception.
The statement that traffic was delayed by reason of storms,
and telephone connection with Los Angeles (where the opposing counsel resided) cut off, would not excuse the appellants
from at least depositing in the mails a notice of the date when
the sureties would justify; and further, it does not appear
but that by some other means of communication, telegraph
or messenger, such notice might have been given and in time.
The justification of the sureties taking place without notice,
of course it must be considered the same as though no justification at all was had. As we have pointed out, there was
no attempt made to have the sureties justify upon notice at
any time after the exception was taken to their sufficiency;

in other words, plaintiff was never afforded an opportunity
to be present, as he was entitled to, at the time the sureties
appeared for justification.   The undertaking on appeal, upon
failure of the sureties to justify upon notice to the adverse
party, became ineffectual for any purpose, and the appeal
must necessarily be considered as though no undertaking had
been given.   Such is the express provision of section 978a
of the Code of Civil Procedure.

The order of the superior court denying petitioner's motion
to dismiss the appeal in the justice's court action herein
in the certified record referred to is annulled; petitioner to
have his costs.

Conrey, P. J., and Shaw, J., concurred.

A petition to have the cause heard in the supreme court,
after judgment in the district court of appeal, was denied
by the supreme court on September 11, 1916.

[Civ. No. 1514.   Third Appellate District.—July 14, 1916.]

S. W. WINSOR, Respondent, v. SILICA BRICK COMPANY (a Corporation), Appellant.

ACTION FOR DAMAGES — BREACH OF CONTRACT OF EMPLOYMENT — DISCHARGE FROM SERVICE—PLEADING—INSUFFICIENT COMPLAINT.—In an
action for the recovery of damages for the breach of a contract,
wherein the plaintiff assigned to the defendant certain leases and
contracts for the removal of earth and clay materials to be used in
the manufacture of brick and other articles, and agreed to give his
entire time and attention to the business of the defendant for a
period of years, in consideration of the delivery to him of certain
shares of the capital stock of the defendant and the agreement to
employ him for the said period at a stated monthly salary, the complaint fails to state a cause of action for damages for the alleged
violation of the terms of the contract in so far as the wrongful dismissal of the plaintiff by the defendant is alleged, where the only
averment charging such dismissal is that the defendant refused "to
perform the contract any longer or further or in whole or in part
or to any extent," and still so refuses, and that the plaintiff has
been prevented from performing the contract in any respect or at

all by reason of the "aforesaid refusal and continued refusal of said defendant."

ID.—DISCHARGE OF PLAINTIFF—INSUFFICIENCY OF EVIDENCE.—A letter written by the defendant to the plaintiff stating that the former "hereby releases you from any further services in its behalf. This will enable you to seek employment elsewhere," does not constitute a clear and unequivocal act of dismissal, and is not sufficient to support a finding of a discharge, when read in connection with the uncontradicted testimony of the secretary of the defendant as to a statement made by the plaintiff a few days before the receipt of the letter that he had an opportunity to obtain employment elsewhere if the defendant would release him from the contract.

ID.—PREVENTION OF PERFORMANCE — INSUFFICIENCY OF EVIDENCE.—In the absence of evidence of any affirmative act on the part of the plaintiff after the receipt of such letter showing a willingness upon his part to proceed with the contract, the allegation in such complaint that the defendant prevented the plaintiff from proceeding with the performance of the contract is not sustained.

APPEAL from an order of the Superior Court of Sacramento County denying a new trial. Peter J. Shields, Judge.

The facts are stated in the opinion of the court.

A. L. Shinn, and C. L. Shinn, for Appellant.

Charles O. Busick, and O. G. Hopkins, for Respondent.

HART, J.—This action was brought by the plaintiff for the recovery of damages for the breach of a contract between him and the defendant.

A trial by jury was had, verdict for plaintiff in the sum of seven thousand three hundred dollars returned, and judgment entered in accordance therewith.

The defendant moved for a new trial. The court made an order denying the motion, and this appeal is from said order.

The contract, for the alleged breach of which the plaintiff seeks damages through this action, was made and entered into by and between the plaintiff and the defendant on the twenty-sixth day of July, 1910. It is set out in full in the complaint. It recites and covenants that the plaintiff, party of the first part, has agreed to assign and has assigned to the party of the second part, the defendant, all his right, title, etc., in and to certain leases and contracts for the removal of earth and clay materials to be used in the manufacture of brick and other articles, "and has agreed to give his entire time and attention to the business of the party of the second part for a period of five years"; that in consideration therefor the defendant has given said plaintiff thirty thousand shares of its capital stock and agreed to employ the plaintiff for the term of five years at a monthly salary of two hundred dollars as a minimum, "and an additional amount equal to five per cent of the net profits of the party of the second part over and above the first twenty-eight thousand dollars of net profits each year." The plaintiff was not only to give his exclusive time and attention to the manufacture of brick and "such other articles as the defendant may elect" and in the performance of such service was to work at such place or places as the defendant might direct, putting in such service the best of his ability and knowledge in brick manufacture, but he was also to deliver to the defendant "all formulae known and used by him for the manufacture of such articles as the party of the second part may desire to manufacture, and that said formulae shall be entered upon the books of the party of the second part and shall become the property of the party of the second part during said five years." Besides some other provisions of the contract which it is not necessary specifically to refer to here, it is further agreed by the plaintiff that "during said five years he will not engage in any other business in the state of California, nor advise or assist in any manner any person or corporation that manufactures or sells articles similar to any articles manufactured by the party of the second part."

The complaint is in two counts—the one for damages for the alleged violation of the terms of the contract by the wrongful dismissal of the plaintiff by the defendant from its service, and the other for damages for the alleged failure of the defendant to pay to the plaintiff the five per cent on the net profits of the corporation over and above the first twenty-eight thousand dollars of the net profits of the concern, which profits, it is alleged, amounted in the aggregate for the year ending with the discharge of the defendant to the sum of eight thousand dollars, the total amount for which judgment is asked being the sum of seventeen thousand two hundred dollars. It may here be stated that no evidence was offered or received in support of the averments of the second count,

and the same may, therefore, be dismissed without further
notice.

The complaint avers that, upon the making of the contract,
the plaintiff entered upon the performance of the terms
thereof so far as it related to him and "began the discharge
of his duties thereunder and thereafter continued such performance and to discharge said duties" until on or about the
twentieth day of September, 1911, when said defendant, without the consent and against the will of the plaintiff, "refused
to perform said contract any longer or further in whole or
in part, to any extent, or at all, and still so refuses; that this
plaintiff was then and there and has ever since been and still
is ready and willing to perform said contract fully and in all
respects on his part and ever since said twentieth day of
September, 1911, *he has been prevented from performing said
contract in any respect or at all, by reason of the aforesaid
refusal and continued refusal of the defendant.*"

The defendant filed an answer and a cross-complaint. In
the former, in addition to making specific denials of the averments of the complaint, after admitting, however, the making of the contract referred to, it set up a special defense,
alleging that, after the plaintiff entered upon the discharge
of his duties under said contract, it was ascertained by the
defendant that the plaintiff was surreptitiously receiving commissions from persons upon sales by such persons of machinery and other supplies to the defendant for its use in its
business, and that the plaintiff had not accounted to the defendant for the commissions so received; that thereupon
negotiations were had between the plaintiff and the defendant
looking to the cancellation of said contract, which negotiations
led to an agreement between the parties on or about the
eighteenth day of September, 1911, canceling and annulling
said contract in consideration of the payment by the defendant to the plaintiff of the sum of $125, the same to be in full
satisfaction of all claims against said defendant; that of
the sum so agreed to be paid the plaintiff, the defendant
paid him the sum of $88.90.

The cross-complaint charges that, solely by and through
willful and fraudulent misrepresentations relative to the
value of the leases transferred to the corporation and to the
ability and experience of the plaintiff as a manufacturer of
brick and other articles made out of clay, the defendant was

induced to enter into the contract which is the basis of this action.

As there is no evidence in the record bearing upon the charges so made, further consideration thereof is not necessary.

Although, as stated, the case was tried by a jury, the court nevertheless made specific findings against the defendant and in favor of the plaintiff upon all the vital matters presented by the pleadings. These findings, in view of the submission of the issues of fact to a jury, were manifestly unnecessary.

We think the complaint fails to make out a case for damages for a breach of the contract upon the part of the defendant. It will be noted that in paragraph 4 of that pleading it is alleged that the defendant refused "to perform the contract any longer or further or in whole or in part or to any extent," and still so refuses, and that the plaintiff has been prevented from performing the contract in any respect or at all by reason of the "aforesaid refusal and continued refusal of said defendant." This is the only averment in the complaint which it may be claimed charges that the plaintiff was discharged, and it is clear that it falls far short of being a direct allegation that the plaintiff was discharged from the employment of the defendant. It is not inconceivable or even improbable that an employer might, for reasons sufficient to himself, be of the opinion that it would be better for him or his business to refuse to allow an employee, under a contract with him (the employer) for personal services, to continue his labors, and still expect and intend to remain faithful to his obligation to pay such employee his compensation, as called for by the contract, as it became due. The most that can be said of the complaint is that, since the twentieth day of September, 1911, the defendant had prevented the plaintiff from performing any work. This is not an averment that, at that time, or at any other time, the defendant discharged the plaintiff and refused any longer to be bound by its contract. It might perhaps be an averment that the corporation had refused to pay the plaintiff his monthly salary, but for this violation of the contract he would have an action for the salary due, and nothing else. He quite clearly cannot maintain an action for compensation unearned without a direct averment of discharge from employment.

The point thus considered, although necessarily raised by
the demurrer, is not discussed or touched upon by counsel
for the appellant in their briefs; and, while we believe it to
be sufficient to warrant a reversal of the judgment, we shall
for the reason that respondent was given no opportunity to
answer or discuss the point, and for the further reason that,
in our opinion, the judgment cannot justly be upheld upon a
consideration of the record even upon the assumption that
the complaint does state a cause of action for a breach of the
contract, further consider the record and the points to which
the counsel for both sides solely address their attention and
the discussion in their respective briefs.

Two points are made by the defendant against the legal sta-
bility of the verdict, viz.: 1. That the alleged discharge of
the plaintiff from the service of the corporation, having been
the act of the secretary of said corporation, and such act
not appearing to have been authorized by the corporation
itself, was the exercise of a power not within the scope of the
authority of the secretary. It is hence argued that the attempted discharge was none at all either in law or in fact.
2. That the evidence does not support the implied finding of
the jury that the secretary discharged the defendant.

We are of the opinion that the last stated point must be
sustained, and it will not be necessary, therefore, to consider
the point first above stated.

The plaintiff's version of the transaction which, he claims,
resulted in his dismissal from the service of the corporation,
is, in substance, as follows: That on the seventeenth day of
September—about fourteen months after he entered upon the
performance of his part of the contract pleaded in the complaint—he received the following letter, signed by J. P.
Dargitz, secretary of the corporation, said letter being dated
at Sacramento, September 16, 1911: "By request of the
Board of Directors, you will please report at this office before
returning to the plant."

In obedience to the request so made, the plaintiff called at
the office of the corporation, in the Oschner Building, Sacramento, and there met Dargitz. What occurred between the
plaintiff and Dargitz at that interview may best be told in the
former's own language as a witness: "I saw Mr. Dargitz. I
came in and addressed him as I usually did, 'How do you
do?' and I was in very much need of some money, I never

had been paid up while I worked with them. I told him I had
to have some money, my creditors were pressing me, I could
not get any more credit, and he shook his head, he said, 'We
have no money.' He took out a bank-book, showed me a
check-book with a little red line on it, he claimed they had
overdrawn their account in a Sacramento bank where they
had deposited, where they had done their business, the Sacramento Valley Trust Company, I believe. He got up and
motioned me to go out in the anteroom, and I followed him
out there. He closed the door, he says, 'Winsor,' he says,
'I am very sorry, but we have no money any more, and we
will have to let you go.' And I says 'I am very sorry, I got
to get my money,—don't I get any money here?' He says,
'We have not got it, but I can give—I will give you some
money, if you will release that contract.' I said, 'Let's
see your money.' He said, 'Well, I will have to get it from
Mr. Pierce; excuse me a moment.' He opened the door, went
into the room, came out with a typewritten sheet, and said,
'If you will sign that I will get the money from Mr. Pierce.'
I read the document over and it was an agreement that I was
to relinquish all claims and release the Silica Brick Company
for the sum of $125. I told Mr. Dargitz that I could not
sign it. He said, 'I can get that amount through the cour-
tesy of Mr. Pierce.' I said, 'I will think it over,' and walked
out of the office and never went back. I never had any conversation with him concerning the cancellation or surrender
of the contract at any time after that or before.''

A few days thereafter, the plaintiff received from Dargitz
the following letter, which was dated at Sacramento, September 20, 1911: ''As per your agreement with me, Monday, the
18th, I am now ready to hand you check and settle contract.
*The company hereby releases you from any further services
in its behalf. This will enable you to seek employment elsewhere.*''

The plaintiff further testified that at one time he was a
member of the defendant's board of directors; that he had
received from the corporation thirty thousand shares of its
capital stock; that the plant was ''shut down'' for a while
during the course of his directorship, but resumed operations
thereafter; that again it stopped operations, and at this time
he was no longer a director; that when it ''shut down'' on
the last occasion it seemed to him ''that the plant was not

going to reopen again." He testified: "I have been willing
and ready at all times since the execution of this contract
to comply with the terms of the contract."

The plaintiff himself was the only witness who gave testimony in his own behalf, and the foregoing constitutes a fair
résumé of the only testimony offered and received upon the
question of his alleged discharge by the defendant.

As explanatory of the language of the letter last above presented herein, Dargitz testified that, in the conversation referred to by the plaintiff in his testimony, the important part
of which is given above, the plaintiff said to the witness that
he "was very anxious to know what was going to be done out
there" (referring to the plant); that he (plaintiff) "had
been laboring under uncertainties so long that he wanted to
have some definite idea what was going to be done, and he
wanted me to tell him what condition the company was in,
and whether the thing was going ahead. I told him that it
was very doubtful, that the company never had been financed
and was not financed then and heavily indebted. *He said
that he had an opportunity to get a good position with
N. Clark & Sons in Alameda,* and if this thing was not going
to go pretty quick, that he wanted to take advantage of that
position, and that he would like to quit if this was still uncertain. I replied that my candid and confidential advice to
him would be to accept that position, as this was still very
uncertain; and he wanted to know *if the company would release him,* and I said I thought they would."

The testimony so given by Dargitz was not in any manner
or degree contradicted by the plaintiff, although he was recalled to the witness-stand in rebuttal after Dargitz gave
said testimony.

It is very apparent that the letter addressed by Dargitz to
the plaintiff under date of September 20, 1911, is not so
phrased as to constitute it a clear and an unequivocal act of
dismissal. Upon its face it is capable of the construction that
by it the defendant did not intend peremptorily to discharge
the plaintiff, but intended it to mean simply this: that the
company was willing to release the plaintiff from his obligations under the contract, and so afford him an opportunity to
secure employment elsewhere, it being left to the plaintiff to
elect whether he would or would not accept the release. This,
we say, is a meaning which may reasonably be attached to the

letter when construed according to its face or without reference to matters extrinsic thereto. But, when construed by
the light of the testimony of Dargitz and even that of the
plaintiff himself, it becomes absolutely certain that the meaning and intent of the letter is as it is so given. The latter
testified, it will be remembered, that, after Dargitz proposed
to him that the company would pay him the sum of $125 in
consideration of the cancellation of the contract, he finally
replied: "I will think it over," and thereupon he left the
company's office and did not return. This reply, together
with the fact, to which the plaintiff himself testified, that
the plant was closed down and "seemed that it was not going
to reopen again," was reasonably sufficient to justify Dargitz
in at least believing that the proposition so made was not or
would not be wholly unsatisfactory to the plaintiff, and that
one of the objects which the latter was then seeking to accomplish was to secure release from the obligations of the
contract.

If, however, there still remains some reason for doubting
what the true intention of the company was in addressing
said letter to the plaintiff, then a consideration of the testimony of Dargitz (and there is no substantial reason why in
this connection that portion of his testimony explaining the
language and the purpose of the letter should not be
considered, since it was not contradicted), will well-nigh conclusively show that the letter was not intended as a
peremptory dismissal of the plaintiff from the service of the
company, but merely to release him from the burdens of the
contract so that he might be given free and full opportunity
to seek and accept other employment. Dargitz testified, as
we have shown, that, in the conversation with the plaintiff on
the 18th of September, or three or four days prior to the
receipt of the letter in question by the plaintiff, the latter
declared that he then had an opportunity to obtain employment with a firm in Alameda and asked Dargitz if he (the
latter) thought the company would release him (plaintiff)
from the contract, and that Dargitz replied that he thought
it would. Thus it is very clear that Dargitz had reason to say
to the plaintiff that he was released from his contract with
the company without being actuated by any motive or intention of discharging the plaintiff and so abandoning the contract. That Dargitz, when writing the letter, had in mind

the previous conversation with the plaintiff regarding the
question whether the company would be willing to release
the latter from the obligations of the contract, is plainly evidenced by the suggestion in said letter—"This will enable
you to seek employment elsewhere."

In considering Dargitz' testimony for the purpose of
ascertaining the intent and scope of the letter, we have not
been unmindful of the rule that it must be assumed, as a
general proposition, that the evidence introduced by the van-
quished party in opposition to that upon which the verdict
has been founded was, for sufficient reasons, repudiated or
disregarded by the jury. In this instance, however, there are
several considerations which will justify an appellate court
in taking into account, in passing upon the question whether
the jury were warranted in reaching the verdict returned,
the testimony of the party by whom the issue has been lost.
First among these is the fact, as before suggested, that the
testimony of Dargitz or the verity thereof was not directly or
expressly contradicted by the plaintiff. The second is that
the testimony of Dargitz has every appearance of being probable, since it explains why he uses in the letter language indicating that the company was willing to *release* the plaintiff
from and not itself abandon the contract or peremptorily
discharge the plaintiff, regardless of its obligation to give
him employment for the full term of five years at the stipulated salary. As seen, Dargitz, in explaining why he addressed the letter to the plaintiff in the language in which it
was phrased, testified that the latter in effect stated to him
in the conversation previously had between them that he
could secure employment with N. Clark & Sons of Alameda,
if the company would release him from any further obligation of proceeding with the performance of the contract on
his part. The fact that Dargitz, in his testimony, named
the firm by which the plaintiff declared to him that he had
an opportunity to be employed is significant, inasmuch as the
plaintiff, having been recalled to the witness-stand after the
defendant had rested its case, had absolutely nothing to say
about N. Clark & Sons, not denying that he referred to said
firm in his conversation with Dargitz, a denial which undoubtedly he would not have neglected to make had the fact
been a mere figment of the latter's mind or without foundation.

But, whatever might have been the intent and purpose of the letter, it must readily be apparent upon a reading of the letter that it was so vague and uncertain in that regard as not to have justified the plaintiff, without making further investigation to ascertain its real import, in treating it as an unconditional and peremptory dismissal.

While the complaint alleges that the plaintiff was willing and ready to perform the contract in all respects, but that he was *prevented from so doing* by the acts and conduct of the defendant, there is absolutely no testimony in the record that he presented himself to the defendant and offered to perform his part of the contract after the receipt of the letter of September 20, 1911. On the contrary, he himself testified that he never had any conversation with Dargitz, "concerning the cancellation or surrender of the contract at any time" after the conversation which was had just previously to the receipt of said letter. Nor is there any testimony, other than whatever in that direction may be extracted from the letter itself, that the defendant prevented the plaintiff from proceeding with the execution of the terms of the contract on his part. It is true that he testified, as he pleaded, that he was ready and willing at all times to carry out his part of the agreement, but we think that he ought to have shown that he unequivocally manifested to the defendant such readiness and willingness. In other words, we think that, since the letter announcing his release from the contract did not involve a clear and an unequivocal act of dismissal, he should have shown that by some affirmative act on his part that he manifested to the company that he did not acquiesce in the proposition contained in the letter and did not desire to be released from the contract. This he could have done by presenting himself to the defendant as ready and willing to proceed with the performance of the contract. (*Olmstead* v. *Bach*, 78 Md. 132, [44 Am. St. Rep. 273, 275, 22 L. R. A. 74, 27 Atl. 501].) Of course, if, after so presenting himself and offering to go on with his work, the plaintiff had been prevented by the defendant from proceeding, with an intention in the latter not to pay him the stipulated salary, he then would have been entitled to bring his action for a breach of the contract, as it would be a useless and futile act to continue so to present himself and offer to proceed with the performance of the contract after the defendant had positively refused to permit him to do so. (*De Camp* v. *Hewitt,* 11 Rob. (La.) 290, [43 Am. Dec. 204].) Or, if the act of the defendant had constituted a clear, unequivocal, and unconditional and peremptory discharge of the plaintiff, then, perhaps, the latter need not have presented himself and offered to continue with the performance of the contract, such dismissal being itself a sufficient prevention of the performance of the contract by the defendant.

Our conclusion is, however, that, under the peculiar circumstances of this case, the plaintiff did not do all that was required of him to entitle him to institute and maintain an action for his compensation under the terms of the contract for the whole of the unexpired term thereof. Indeed, assuming that the complaint states a cause of action, we believe that the plaintiff has failed to sustain the allegations thereof, inasmuch as there is no substantial evidence, either express or constructive, or, to state it in the strict language of the law of evidence, either direct or inferential, to support the averment that the defendant *prevented* the plaintiff from proceeding with the performance of the contract on his part.

It is hardly necessary to suggest that, in the consideration of the points upon which we feel impelled to reverse the case, we have assumed without deciding that the secretary of the corporation, Dargitz, was duly vested with authority to discharge the plaintiff.

The order appealed from is reversed.

Chipman, P. J., and Ellison, J., *pro tem.*, concurred.

[Civ. No. 2068.   Second Appellate District.—July 20, 1916.]

JOHN B. COX, Petitioner, v. WILLIAM C. JEROME, as Auditor of the County of Orange, Respondent.

JUSTICES OF THE PEACE — COMPENSATION — INCREASE DURING TERM OF OFFICE—CONSTRUCTION OF CONSTITUTION.—Justices of the peace of townships are included in the officers referred to in section 9 of article XI of the state constitution, which forbids an increase in the compensation paid to them during their terms of office.

ID.—COUNTY GOVERNMENTS—CREATION OF TOWNSHIPS.—The legislature is required, under section 4 of article XI of the constitution, to establish a system of county governments which shall be uniform throughout the state, and under this section the legislature may provide for township organization, but no such township organization has been established, although the legislature from time to time, by various general laws and statutes known as county government acts, has provided for a uniform government of the counties and subdivisions therein, but the townships mentioned in such acts have no governmental machinery or officers so distinct from the county as to identify such townships as being possessed of functions designed to be possessed by "township organization" referred to in section 4 of article XI of the constitution.

APPLICATION originally made to the District Court of Appeal for the Second Appellate District for a Writ of Mandate to compel the Auditor of Orange County to issue his warrant for services performed by the Justice of the Peace of Santa Ana Township.

The facts are stated in the opinion of the court.

N. D. Meyer, A. W. Rutan, and R. Y. Williams, for Petitioner.

L. A. West, A. E. Koepsel, and Walter Eden, for Respondent.

JAMES, J.—Petition for writ of mandate to require respondent, as auditor of the county of Orange, to issue to petitioner certain warrants upon the treasury of the county, in payment of money which it is alleged is due to petitioner for official services performed as justice of the peace of Santa Ana township. An answer was filed raising issues of law only, and the matter has been submitted for decision.

At the time petitioner assumed office in January, 1915, the law provided that justices of the peace should receive from the county for services rendered in criminal cases the sum of $75 per month. On the eighth day of August, 1915, an enactment of the legislature [Stats. 1915, p. 1032] became of effect which provided that in counties of the fourteenth class and in townships having a population of fifteen thousand or over, the justices of the peace should receive for services rendered in criminal cases the sum of one hundred dollars per month. The township in which petitioner was acting was found by the census taken to contain over fifteen thousand inhabitants, and his claim was thereafter made for compensation at the increased rate. The vital question presented is as to whether, under the constitutional prohibition against increase of compensation during the term of office of certain officials, petitioner shall have the benefit of the larger amount for his services in criminal cases. Section 9 of article XI of the constitution provides as follows: "The compensation of any county, city, town, or municipal officer shall not be increased after his election or during his term of office. . . . " It is argued that a township justice of the peace is neither a county, city, town, nor municipal officer, and that therefore there is no constitutional restraint placed upon the legislature to increase the compensation of such justice at any time. The legislature is required, under the direction of section 4 of article XI of the constitution, to establish a system of county governments which shall be uniform throughout the state. It is in that section also provided that the legislature may provide for township organization. But no township organization, within the meaning of the section referred to, has been established. While the legislature has from time to time, by various general laws and statutes known as county government acts, provided for a uniform government of the counties and subdivisions therein, it has been held that the townships mentioned in such acts have no governmental machinery or officers so distinct from the county as to identify such townships as being possessed of functions designed to be possessed by "township organization," referred to in section 4 of article XI above cited. In *Ex parte Wall*, 48 Cal. 279, [17 Am. Rep. 425], it was held that the legislature did not, when they divided the county into townships, create "town govern

ments." It was there said: "The townships have neither
been given personality nor any other of the attributes of a
corporation; no official has been named empowered to call
the inhabitants or voters together for the purposes of consultation and joint action; no act has been passed providing
for any presiding officer, or regulating the mode of conducting business, or of declaring the result of the action of the
inhabitants or voters when assembled. . . . " It would
then appear that in the classification of township justices of
the peace, these officials either must be referred to as officers
of the county, or become some species of state officers. Under
the constitution as it is now written justices of the peace are
not specifically mentioned as belonging to the judicial department of the state; such judicial power is declared to consist
of the Senate, the supreme court, district courts of appeal,
superior courts, "and such inferior courts as the legislature
may establish in any incorporated city or town, township,
county, or city and county." In the case of *People* v. *Cobb*,
133 Cal. 74, [65 Pac. 325], the question as to whether a city
justice of the peace was a city or a county officer was discussed, and while not given precise definition in the decision,
the court there said: "It may be admitted that city justices
of the peace do not come, or at least do not altogether come,
within the category of county or township officers; but it is
equally clear that they do not come altogether within that
of city officers. They cannot, therefore, strictly speaking,
be said to be either county officers or city officers, for that
would imply that they were exclusively such; but without
much impropriety they may be said to be either. More accurately speaking, they, as well as county justices, form part
of the judicial system of the state. . . . It does not follow,
however, from the peculiar nature of their offices, that justices of the peace or other judicial officers do not constitute
part of county or city governments." This decision also
affirms the propriety of including provisions affecting justices of the peace in the county government acts. In reason,
at least, there would seem to be no sound basis for declaring
that township justices of the peace were not intended to be
affected by the provisions of section 9, article XI, of the constitution in the matter of increasing their compensation during their terms of office. The legislature has not seen fit
to provide for separate township government. The court

intimates in the Cobb case, *supra,* that a city justice of the peace possesses in some measure qualities of a county officer. In cases in which the question as to the right to increase the compensation of justices or constables was involved, and there have been several, it has never been denied that the provisions of section 9 of article XI affect these officers, and the supreme court has so assumed, without any suggestion that the subject was open for debate. We refer to *Smith* v. *Mathews,* 155 Cal. 752, [103 Pac. 199], and *Crockett* v. *Mathews,* 157 Cal. 153, [106 Pac. 575].

We are not disposed to discuss other questions presented by counsel for respondent in opposition to the prayer of the petition. Our conclusion is that petitioner, as justice of the peace of Santa Ana township, is one of the officers mentioned in the constitutional provision cited, which forbids an increase in the compensation paid to him during his term of office.

The prayer for a peremptory writ is denied.

Conrey, P. J., and Shaw, J., concurred.

A petition to have the cause heard in the supreme court, after judgment in the district court of appeal, was denied by the supreme court on September 18, 1916.

[Civ. No. 1832. Second Appellate District.—July 21, 1916.]

CITY OF LOS ANGELES (a Municipal Corporation), Respondent, v. LOS ANGELES PACIFIC COMPANY (a Corporation) et al., Appellants; MARTHA J. AYLESWORTH et al., Defendants.

EMINENT DOMAIN — PUBLIC PARK — POWER POLE LINE AND PROPOSED SUBWAY RIGHTS OF ELECTRIC RAILROAD COMPANY—PROTECTION FROM CONDEMNATION—DUTY OF COURT.—In an action brought by a municipal corporation to condemn a large tract of land for the purposes of a public park, where there is included in such tract certain parcels belonging to an electric railway company and used by it for the purposes of a power pole line and certain other parcels which the company had acquired for the purpose of constructing and operating a subway, it is the duty of the court to determine as a matter of fact, both as to the pole line and the subway parcels, whether they had been dedicated to a public use, upon which issue the burden of proof is on the defendant, and if either or both of them were devoted to a public use, then the court should determine as a matter of fact whether that and the proposed park use were consistent, upon which issue the burden of proof is on the plaintiff, and if the respective uses are not in fact wholly inconsistent, then it is the further duty of the court to fix the terms and conditions of condemnation by the city, and the manner and extent of use of the property "for each of such purposes."

Id.—Taking of Property Already Devoted to Public Use—Construction of Statutes.—The statutes contemplate the taking of private property for public use, and also that property already devoted to public use may be taken for a more necessary public use, but that in the latter case where the proposed new use is also consistent with the existing public use, the two rights shall be exercised in common, under the terms and conditions appropriate to the case.

Id.—Taking of Property for Park Purposes — Determination of Legislative Body of Municipality—How Far Conclusive—Construction of Park and Playground Act and Code.—The general rule which is found in section 1241 of the Code of Civil Procedure and in the Park and Playground Act (Stats. 1909, p. 1066 et seq.), and which authorizes the legislative body of a city to finally determine that the public necessity and convenience require that certain land be condemned for park purposes, is modified by subdivision 4 of section 1240 of such code, enacted to meet the specifically designated case where it is proposed to condemn land already subject to an existing public use; and under such a situation, while the court will recognize as final the determination of the legislative body that the taking of the land is necessary for public use, it is required also to recognize the existing public use, and to provide for the terms and conditions upon which the existing use may continue, if in fact the two uses are capable of coexisting on the same premises.

Id.—Los Angeles Charter — Use of Part of Park for Power Pole Line.—The provision of section 119b of the charter of the city of Los Angeles, that all property located therein which has been or may be set apart or dedicated for the use of the public as a park or parks shall forever remain inviolate to the use of the public for such purpose, means no more than that when land has been acquired by the city for park uses, such land shall not thereafter be appropriated to other uses, and does not prevent such city from acquiring land for park purposes, subject to the use thereof for another purpose to which it has been dedicated, where the two uses are consistent and capable of existing together.

Id.—Lands Occupied for Power Pole Line Purposes—Public Use.— The use of land occupied by an electric railway company for pole line purposes is a public use.

Id.—Lands Acquired for Subway — Noncompletion — Public Use.— Parcels of land purchased and held by an electric railway company for the purpose of constructing therein a subway are devoted to a public use, notwithstanding that all parcels necessary to the construction of such subway had not been obtained, where about ninety per cent of the parcels had been acquired and it is shown to be the intention of the company to complete the enterprise.

ID.—AMOUNT OF COMPENSATION—ACCRUED TAXES AT TIME OF AWARD.— In awarding damages in an action in eminent domain, section 1249 of the Code of Civil Procedure excludes all consideration other than the value of the property at the date of the issuance of the summons in the action, and therefore no award is permissible for taxes and assessments not accrued at the time of the award.

ID.—EASEMENT FOR POLE LINE—RIGHT TO COMPENSATION FOR TAKING.— An easement over land for a power pole line acquired by a street railroad corporation is a substantial property right, the value of which should be accounted for by any other party seeking to enforce a superior right of eminent domain upon the same premises; and the owners of the fee are not entitled to all the compensation to be allowed for the taking of the land, if the right of way is to be included in the condemnation without any reservation of further right of use by the company.

APPEAL from a judgment of the Superior Court of Los Angeles County, and from an order denying a new trial. Lewis R. Works, Judge.

The facts are stated in the opinion of the court.

Frank Karr, R. C. Gortner, and A. W. Ashburn, Jr., for Appellants.

Albert Lee Stephens, City Attorney, and Charles S. Burnell, Assistant City Attorney, for Respondent.

CONREY, P. J.—Appeal from interlocutory judgment of condemnation and from an order denying motion for new trial.

This action was brought for the condemnation of a large tract of land within the city of Los Angeles for the purpose of a projected public park, commonly known as "Silver Lake Park." The action was brought after and pursuant to proceedings by the city council of the city of Los Angeles, which said proceedings were had in accordance with the provisions of the "Park and Playground Act of 1909" (found at page 1066 et seq., Stats. 1909). Included with the land sought to be condemned were certain parcels belonging to appellants herein and designated as parcels 43, 46, 86, 87, 92, 93, and 94; also a certain other parcel of land claimed by the defendant railway company as belonging to it by virtue of dedication to public use and occupied by it for pole line purposes, which parcel is not separately described in the complaint, but is described in the answer and amendment to answer of appellants, and was at the trial of this action designated, for convenience, as parcel 46½. Parcels Nos. 86, 87, 92, 93, and 94 stand of record in the name of the Los Angeles Pacific Land Company, but that company holds the same as trustee for the Pacific Electric Railway Company, the land company having been formed as a matter of convenience in holding lands for the railway company, and all of the money for the purchase of said lands having been advanced by the railway company, which owns all of the stock of the land company. The Los Angeles Pacific Company is merely the predecessor of the Pacific Electric Railway Company, and has been absorbed into the latter company by a consolidation under section 473 of the Civil Code. Parcels 43, 46, and 46½ are, and at the time of the commencement of this action, on January 18, 1913, were, being used for the purposes of a high tension electric power transmission line extending from defendant's Olive substation on Sunset Boulevard, across the proposed parkway in a general southwesterly direction. This pole line carries fifteen thousand volts of electricity, which form the chief supply of energy for the operation of defendant's cars over its western division, which includes all of Hollywood, Beverly, Sawtelle, Santa Monica, and several other west coast beaches. Parcels 87, 93, and 94 were prior to the commencement of this action acquired for the purpose of constructing and operating an electric railroad subway from defendant's Hill Street station, Los Angeles, to its Vineyard station at the westerly city limits. The subway has not been actually constructed, and the court found that these parcels of land, which form but part of a long strip of land, acquired and held as a right of way for electric railroad subway purposes, had not been devoted to public use.

Parcels 86 and 92, it is admitted, have never been devoted to public use, and with respect to those parcels no complaint is made by appellants which will require separate consideration.

The court refused to reserve in its judgment any electric railroad power pole line or subway rights to these defendants or to limit the plaintiff's taking to an estate subject to the existing pole line and subway rights. The lands are by the judgment condemned in fee, and in effect it requires the elimination of the power pole line and subway from the parkway district. The court also denied the defendant any award for the taking of pole line parcel 46½. The court, while it made allowances to defendants for certain taxes and assessments which accrued since the commencement of this action, refused to provide for payment to defendants of other taxes and assessments which may be levied upon the condemned lands before the entry of final judgment and payment of awards.

Among the principal points which appellants urge upon this appeal are the following:

1. That the court erred in refusing to preserve to defendants their existing electric railroad power pole line and subway rights in parcels 43, 46, 46½, 87, 93, and 94.

2. That the court erred in refusing to make allowance for accruing taxes and assessments as requested by defendants.

3. That an award should have been made for the taking of pole line parcel 46½.

Also, that the court failed to find upon important issues of fact, and that certain material findings fail of support in the evidence.

An issue as to consistency between the proposed park use and the existing uses claimed by appellants, and of the right to a reservation of the right of common user, was raised by the answer, which besides denying the necessity of taking the whole or any part of the land for park purposes, also set forth the existing public uses to which the lands of defendants had been devoted by them, and alleged damages which will accrue to portions not sought to be condemned, unless such reservation of the right of common user be allowed. This issue is not met by the findings, except by finding that "it is necessary that the plaintiff take and condemn for public use" the described land. It is also found, in effect, that the subway parcels are not devoted to public use. There is no specific finding that the taking of an unqualified fee is necessary for the purpose for which the plaintiff is condemning, but the court, as a conclusion of law, holds "that the plaintiff is entitled to an interlocutory judgment adjudging that . . . said property be condemned in fee to the use of the plaintiff for public park purposes." In the absence of qualification, this must mean an absolute, unconditional fee, ever free from all rights on the part of the defendants to use the premises for either electric railroad, power pole line, or subway purposes.

Appellants contend, and it is not denied, that the court treated this question as a question of law and not as one of fact. The court deemed itself bound by the decision of the city council to take the fee of the lands described in the ordinance of intention, because the legislature, in the court's opinion, had delegated to the city council the determination of the question of what lands should be taken and what estate therein should be taken for park or playground purposes, and assumed that that determination was, under the park act, final, and deprived the court of any power whatever to pass upon these questions which appellants say are delegated to the court under sections 1240 and 1247a of the Code of Civil Procedure. The court treated it as a question of necessity, and determined the case upon a solution of the question of whether the council's decision is conclusive as to the necessity of taking any particular land for a given improvement, and the necessity of taking the entire estate in the land.

The "Park and Playground Act of 1909," in section 7 thereof, referring to condemnation of land for park purposes, reads as follows: "The complaint shall set forth, or state the effect of, the ordinance of intention, and the ordinance ordering the improvement, but need not set up any other proceedings had before the bringing of the action. Said ordinances shall be conclusive evidence, in such action, of the public necessity of the proposed improvement." As stated in the complaint and found by the court, the city council by its ordinance, adopted by a vote of more than two-thirds of its members, declared that the public interest and convenience required that the described lands be acquired for park purposes, and that for that purpose it is necessary that the plaintiff take and condemn for public use the said lands; and the court, relying upon that ordinance, and without other evidence showing the necessity for the taking, made its findings as we have stated.

Section 5 of the Park and Playground Act provides for a condemnation action to be brought, pursuant to direction therefor by the city council; and section 6 declares that "said action shall in all respects be subject to and governed by such provisions of the Code of Civil Procedure now existing, or that may be hereafter adopted as may be applicable thereto, except in the particulars otherwise provided for in this act." The procedure in condemnation is outlined in the title on Eminent Domain, section 1237 et seq. of the Code of Civil Procedure. Section 1241, as in force in January, 1913, when this action was commenced, provides that "Before property can be taken, it must appear: . . . 2. That the taking is necessary to such use." By an amendment in force on August 10, 1913 (before this action came on for trial), the following addition was made to subdivision 2 of that section: "*Provided,* when the legislative body of a county, city and county, or an incorporated city or town, shall, by resolution or ordinance, adopted by vote of two-thirds of all its members, have found and determined that the public interest and necessity require the acquisition, construction or completion, by such county, city and county, or incorporated city or town, of any proposed public utility, or any public improvement, and that the property described in such resolution or ordinance is necessary therefor, such resolution or ordinance shall be conclusive evidence; (a) of the public necessity of such proposed public utility or public improvement; (b) that such property is necessary therefor, and (c) that such proposed public utility or public improvement is planned or located in the manner which will be most compatible with the greatest public good, and the least private injury; *provided,* that said resolution or ordinance shall not be such conclusive evidence in the case of the taking by any county, city and county, or incorporated city or town, of property located outside of the territorial limits thereof."

Section 1240 of the Code of Civil Procedure, as in force in January, 1913 [Stats. 1911, p. 620], provides that "The private property which may be taken under this title includes: . . . 4. Property appropriated to public use; but such property shall not be taken unless for a more necessary public use than that to which it has already been appropriated; *provided,* that where any such property has been so appropriated by any individual, firm or private corporation, the

use thereof for a public street or highway of a municipal
corporation, or the use thereof by a municipal corporation
for the same public purpose to which it has been so appropriated, shall be deemed more necessary uses than the public
use to which such property has been already appropriated;
*and provided, further, that where property already appro-
priated to a public use* or purpose, by any person, firm or
private corporation, *is sought to be taken by a municipal corporation, for another public use or purpose, which is consistent with the continuance of the use of such property or
some portion thereof for such existing purpose,* to the same
extent as such property is then used, or to a less or modified
extent, *then the right to use such property for such proposed
public purpose, in common with such other use or purpose,*
either as then existing, or to a less or modified extent, *may
be taken by such municipal corporation, and the court may
fix the terms and conditions upon which such property may
be so taken, and the manner and extent of the use thereof
for each of such public purposes, and may order the removal
or relocation of any structures or improvements therein or
thereon, so far as may be required by such such common use.''*
By amendment in force August 10, 1913, said subdivision 4
was amended to read as follows: ''Property appropriated to
public use; but such property shall not be taken unless for a
more necessary public use than that to which it has already
been appropriated; *provided,* that where any such property
has been so appropriated by any individual, firm or private
corporation, the use thereof for a public street or highway of
a county, city and county, or incorporated city or town or the
use thereof by a county, city and county, or any incorporated
city or town or municipal water district, for the same public
purpose to which it has been so appropriated, or for any other
public purpose, shall be deemed more necessary uses than
the public use to which such property has already been appropriated; *and provided, further,* that where property already
appropriated to a public use or purpose by any person, firm
or private corporation, is sought to be taken by a county,
city and county, incorporated city or town, or municipal water
district, for another public use or purpose, which is consistent with the continuance of the use of such property or
some portion thereof for such existing purpose, to the same
extent as such property is then used, or to a less or modified

extent, then the right to use such property for such proposed public purpose, in common with such other use or purpose, either as then existing, or to a less or modified extent, may be taken by such county, city and county, incorporated city or town, or municipal water district, and the court may fix the terms and conditions upon which such property may be so taken, and the manner and extent of the use thereof for each of such public purposes, and may order the removal or relocation of any structures or improvements therein or thereon, so far as may be required by such common use. But property appropriated to the use of any county, city and county, incorporated city or town or municipal water district, may not be taken by any other county, city and county, incorporated city or town, or municipal water district while such property is so appropriated and used for the public purposes for which it has been so appropriated.'' Section 1247a of the Code of Civil Procedure reads as follows: ''The court shall also have power to regulate and determine the place and manner of removing or relocating structures or improvements, or of enjoying the common use mentioned in the fourth subdivision of section 1240.''

No one here denies that the power to finally determine the necessity of taking specified property for a public use may be delegated to a city council. The questions now at issue are to be settled by reading the Park and Playground Act together with the code provisions applicable to the case, and thereby ascertaining the legislative will. The statutes contemplate the taking of private property for public use. They also contemplate that property already devoted to a public use may be taken for a more necessary public use. They further contemplate that where it is proposed to take for public use property already devoted to a public use, and where the proposed new use is also consistent with the existing public use, the two rights shall be exercised in common, under the terms and conditions appropriate to the case. To meet this particular situation, section 1240 of the Code of Civil Procedure, in subdivision 4 thereof, authorizes the court in its decree of condemnation, to ''fix the terms and conditions upon which such property may be so taken, and the manner and extent of the use thereof for each of such public purposes.'' In the comparative construction of statutes, they are to be harmonized as fully as may be, so as to give them complete

and reasonable effect.   An apt means to this end is obtained
by permitting a statute, applicable to a particular class of
facts, to operate as a modification of statutes of broad and
general scope.   So here we may assume that the general rule
as found in section 1241 of the Code of Civil Procedure and
in the Park and Playground Act authorizes the city council,
in an ordinance like that here in question, to finally determine
that the public necessity and convenience require that certain
described land be condemned for park purposes.   But this
general rule is modified by subdivision 4 of section 1240, enacted to meet the specifically designated case where it is proposed to condemn land already subject to an existing public
use.   In this particular situation, while the court, under the
above assumption, will recognize as final the determination of
the council that the taking of the land is necessary for the
proposed use, it is required also to recognize the existing public use, and to provide for the terms and conditions upon
which the existing use may continue, if in fact the two uses
are capable of coexisting on the same premises.   It is not
uncommon to have railroads in parks, and their presence has
been so regulated that they aided in making the parks acces-
sible, without interfering with safe administration of both of
those public uses.   (*People* v. *Park and Ocean R. R. Co.*, 76
Cal. 156, [18 Pac. 141].)   Respondent's counsel argue that
these principles can have no application in this case, because
the use for which the city seeks to take the property is not,
and under the law cannot be, consistent with the existing use
of the property.   They say that the use of the property either
for the purpose of maintaining a pole line thereover or a subway thereunder is not, and as a matter of law cannot be,
consistent with its use for park purposes, since the organic
law governing the city of Los Angeles prohibits the use of
park lands for any other purpose whatsoever.   The property
sought to be condemned in this action is sought to be taken
for the purpose of a public park and for no other purpose,
and the charter of the city of Los Angeles provides: "All
lands and real property located in the city of Los Angeles
which have been heretofore, or which may be hereafter, set
apart or dedicated for the use of the public as a public park
or parks, shall forever remain to the use of the public as such
park or parks, inviolate, and no part of said lands or real
property shall ever be used or occupied for any other pur-

pose.'' (Charter of the City of Los Angeles, sec. 119b, Stats. 1911, p. 2113.)

Under this provision, it is contended that the city has no power to permit the use of any part of a public park for the maintenance of a power line or of a railroad, either above, on, or below the surface of the ground; that the use of park lands for such purposes would be unlawful, and the city would not have the power to condemn land for park purposes subject to a use prohibited by the charter; therefore, they say, it follows that the use which the city intends to make of the land sought to be taken is not, and under the law cannot be, consistent with the continuance in use of such land for pole line purposes, or for the projected subway, and neither the court, the city council, nor any other tribunal would have the power to find or declare that the use of the land for park purposes was consistent with its use for any other purpose, and for these reasons that the court was not only not required to pass upon the question of consistency, but was without any power whatsoever to do so.

In response to the above contention we may observe, by the way, that the ordinance upon which respondent relies does except from condemnation certain railroad rights of way located within the limits of the proposed park, and those exceptions are carried into the judgment of condemnation. It is also worthy of note that the pole line and the right of way for a subway pertain to a railroad which extends beyond the city limits and is under state control. If respondent's theory of the case is to be accepted, it will follow that a state or interstate railway, having established rights of way, tracks, and depots within the city, may be excluded from the city by virtue of a city ordinance ordering that the lands thus occupied shall be taken and included within a city park, and the courts must obey such legislative mandate by condemning the property, without the right to make any inquiry as to the consistency of the public uses, or to prescribe conditions under which the several uses may coexist. Under the statutes to which we have referred, we do not perceive that any such extraordinary limitations have been drawn around the judicial power as vested in the courts. And giving to the above-quoted section of the city charter its full effect in any case to which, within the limits of the state constitution, it may be applied, it means no more than that when land has been acquired by the city for park uses, such land shall not thereafter be appropriated to other uses.

Respondent's counsel insist that the use of the land occupied by appellants for pole line purposes is not a public use, because the power is furnished only to the railway company and not to the general public. They rely upon authorities which they claim in support of the proposition that a power pole line furnishing electric power to operate the cars of a railway company is not a part of the railroad or a necessary adjunct thereto, in aid of which such company would be entitled to exercise the power of eminent domain. Conspicuous among the decisions to which they refer is *Re Condemnation of Land by Rhode Island Suburban Ry. Co.*, 22 R. I. 455, [52 L. R. A. 879, 48 Atl. 590]. The action was one wherein the railway company sought to condemn a lot for a powerhouse, to generate electricity for its lines of road, for coal pockets for the storage of coal, and for a conduit to carry water from the river to the engine. The supreme court of Rhode Island set aside the judgment in favor of petitioner and ordered a new trial. The court conceded that it is not always necessary that the public use be direct and obvious. "There is a class of cases where the public does not use the land itself, and yet the public necessity is so direct and obvious as to imply a public use. Such, for example, are cases of taking land for engine-houses, car-houses, and repair-shops on steam railroads. These buildings must necessarily be contiguous to the railroad, and, while the public may not use the buildings as such, yet they are of such a character that, without them, the public could not adequately use the railroad itself. They are in fact a part of the railroad. In some cases land for the storage of wood and coal for steam railroads has been held to be taken for a public use. In all of these cases, however, a particular location is made necessary, because of the requirements of the steam railroads." The court was of the opinion that these considerations do not apply to an electric railroad, since in the latter case there is a wide area of location and consequent freedom of choice, as contrasted with the imperative necessity which is usually found on steam railroads for a particular location. "Neither is it of interest to the public whether the cars are run by trolley or by storage batteries. The company is not limited to a particular location for a power-house, for coal pockets, or for a water supply." The foregoing decision was discussed in *Rockingham County Light & Power Co.* v. *Hobbs,* 72 N. H. 531, [66 L. R. A. 581, 58 Atl. 46], where that court expressed a different view of the matter, and pointed out the reason why greater freedom of choice of location in the case of an electric road does not interfere with the element of necessity in determining the right of condemnation. "It is probable that in many cases the establishment and operation of electric railways for the accommodation of the public will depend upon the possibility of generating or collecting electricity at a low cost. A water-power, or a port at which coal may be landed from sea-going vessels directly into the coal pockets of a power-house, will render it possible to furnish electric railway facilities for public use at points situated many miles distant from the water-power or port, that could not otherwise be furnished at all, or, at least, without much greater cost to the public. In such cases the imperativeness of the necessity attaches to the freedom of choice as to location, rather than to the proximity of a particular location to the railroad line. If land adjoining an electric railway may be taken for a power-house—as to which there can be no doubt—no good reason is apparent why land at a distance may not be taken if the public good so requires. Of course, if land located at a distance may be taken for a power-house, *it must follow that necessary land, or rights in land, may be taken for constructing and maintaining a line of wires between the power-house and the railway.*" Without entering into a discussion of the lines of decision illustrated above—there being apparently no California decision directly meeting the specific case—we are of the opinion that the power pole lines in question here are devoted to a public use as part of the railway system operated by the Pacific Electric Railway Company. In their principal essentials, electric railroads now have the same legal *status* as steam railroads. (Civ. Code, sec. 465a.)

Section 465 of the Civil Code says: "Every railroad corporation has power: . . . 3. To purchase, . . . hold and use all such real estate and other property as may be absolutely necessary for the construction and maintenance of such railroads, and for all stations, depots and other purposes necessary to successfully work and conduct the business of the road;

"4. To lay out its road . . . and to construct and maintain the same, . . . with such appendages and adjuncts as may be necessary for the convenient use of the same;

"7. To purchase lands . . . to be used in the construction and maintenance of its road, and all necessary appendages and adjuncts, or acquire them in the manner provided in title seven, part three, Code of Civil Procedure, for the condemnation of lands."

Since, as we have concluded, parcels 43, 46, and 46½ have been dedicated to public use, it becomes the duty of the court to determine, as a matter of fact, the issue raised as to the consistency or inconsistency of that use with the proposed park use. If the respective uses are not in fact wholly inconsistent, then it was the further duty of the court to fix the terms and conditions of condemnation by the city, and the manner and extent of use of the property "for each of such purposes."

The same result would follow as to the so-called subway parcels, if in fact they were devoted to public use as subways of the railroad prior to the commencement of proceedings by the city for the creation of the proposed park. As to each of these parcels, the finding of fact, based upon undisputed evidence, is that the land was purchased and is held by the defendant Los Angeles Pacific Land Company "for a special and peculiar purpose and use, to wit, for the purpose of constructing therein, thereunder and over, and in and along its lands extending from a point in the vicinity of Fourth and Hill Streets in the city of Los Angeles, in a general westerly and southerly direction through said parcel to the westerly city limits of the city of Los Angeles and beyond to a point of connection in the railroad of the Pacific Electric Railway Company at or near Vineyard station, a railroad to be operated through a subway; but in this connection the court finds the fact to be that said land was not at the commencement of this action and is not now, and never has been, used for such purposes; and further, that said defendant has not acquired either the fee to or easements or rights of way under or over, or any other interests in, such entire strip of land between said terminal points as would be necessary in order to enable it to construct and operate such railroad, nor has it acquired any franchise so to do." Although the title to the parcels in question is held in the name of the land com-

pany, the consideration therefor was paid by the railway company, and the land is held for its use for the purpose stated
in the findings. The entire expenditures made by the defendant in purchasing the property required by it for the proposed subway exceeded two millions of dollars, and there is
a great public need for a subway, to relieve the congestion
of traffic on the street surfaces of the city. The enterprise,
although delayed, has not been, in any sense of the word,
abandoned by the railway company. About ninety per cent
of the right of way therefor has been acquired. All of this
is shown by uncontradicted evidence. The judgment of the
court below, in its relation to the matter of the subway, proceeds upon the theory that, under the facts found, these parcels were not already devoted to public use, but should be
treated as private property.

"It is property appropriated to public use, which is . . .
protected from condemnation except 'for a more necessary
public use'; and as to lands owned by defendant, but which
have not been thus appropriated, *and are not likely in the
future to be needed* for the existing public use, the inhibition
does not apply." (*Southern Pac. R. R. Co.* v. *Southern Cal.
Ry. Co.*, 111 Cal. 221, [43 Pac. 602].) In that case it was
clear that the strip of land sought to be condemned—although
located within the limits of a tract acquired by defendant as
part of its right of way—was not in use by the defendant and
would not probably be needed for railroad purposes. The
defendant had completed its road upon adjacent land, and
had ample room thereon for its business. We are plainly
left to infer that if the execution of its plans had been merely
unfinished, and if the orderly completion of the work under
those plans had required that defendant use for railroad purposes the land sought to be condemned for the use of the
plaintiff, the claimed prior devotion thereof to public use by
the defendant would have been sustained. From the findings
quoted above, it seems that the court, in determining that
the parcels in question have not been appropriated to a public
use, placed its principal stress upon the facts that appellants
have not yet acquired title to all of the property necessary
to complete the strip over which they expect to construct the
proposed lines, and have not obtained any franchise allowing
the road to be constructed across the streets which intersect
the strip. We cannot subscribe to the doctrine that no part

of a right of way may be considered as having been devoted
to the public use for which it has been acquired, until all of
the right of way has been acquired. That rule would place
unreasonable and unnecessary obstacles in the way of such
enterprises. It is sufficient that a corporation in charge of
a public use, in the due prosecution of its enterprise, has lawfully obtained for that use property necessary therefor, with
a reasonable prospect that the work will be carried to completion. And the prior ownership of a franchise relating to
street crossings is not essential to the right to condemn, or to
hold for the proposed use, other portions of the right of way.
(*Tuolumne Water etc. Co.* v. *Frederick,* 13 Cal. App. 498,
[110 Pac. 134].)

It is our opinion that the court in its findings should have
determined as a matter of fact, both as to the pole line and
the subway parcels, whether they had been devoted to a public
use, and that upon this issue the burden of proof was upon
the defendants. If either of them was devoted to a public
use, then the court should have determined as a matter of
fact whether that and the proposed use were consistent, and
on this issue the burden of proof was upon the plaintiff to
show that the uses were not consistent and that they were not
on any reasonably possible terms capable of continuing together on the parcels sought to be condemned. The general
principle that the state will not exercise the power of eminent
domain any further than the necessity of the public requires
is recognized by the provisions of the code to which we have
referred. Therefore, after the defendants in a case like this
have shown that their land is devoted to a public use for which
the right of condemnation might be exercised in their behalf,
they are protected from destructive interference unless the
city can establish by sufficient evidence that in fact the use
for park purposes cannot coexist with continued use of the
property by the defendants.

Appellants claim that the court in making its interlocutory
judgment erred in refusing to reserve this action for further
orders covering the matter of taxes and assessments accrued
subsequent to the commencement of the action and levied by
the city of Los Angeles. In accordance with the findings of
fact, the court allowed to the defendants certain sums covering the values of the parcels of land to be condemned, of which
it was specified that certain portions of the aggregate sums

represented taxes and assessments which became liens upon said parcels subsequent to the filing of this action and which the defendants have paid or owe. The defendants requested that the interlocutory judgment contain a provision reserving the case for further consideration in order that the respective defendants may receive, in addition to the awards therein provided for, the amount of any and all taxes and assessments upon parcels of land owned by them respectively which shall have been levied or accrued or become a lien upon said premises at the time of payment of the awards herein. With this request the court did not comply, and we think that the refusal was justified. In section 1249 of the Code of Civil Procedure it is provided that for the purpose of assessing compensation and damages (when, as in this case, the issue is tried within one year after the date of commencement of the action), "the right thereof shall be deemed to have accrued at the date of the issuance of summons and its actual value at that date shall be the measure of compensation for all property to be actually taken. . . . If an order be made letting the plaintiff into possession, as provided in section 1254, the compensation and damages awarded shall draw lawful interest from the date of such order. . . . " Section 1254 states the conditions under which, pending an appeal from the judgment, a plaintiff who has paid into court, for the defendant, the required sums, may take possession of and use the property until the final conclusion of the litigation. The property is not taken, so as to interfere with the defendants' ownership of their property, until the compensation is made to, or paid into court for, the owner. These facts draw a line of distinction between the case in hand and the New York decisions relied upon by appellants. (*In re Mayor etc. of the City of New York*, 40 App. Div. 281, [58 N. Y. Supp. 58]; *In re Morris Avenue in the City of New York*, 118 App. Div. 117, [103 N. Y. Supp. 180].) Those cases arose under statutes whereby the actual appropriation of property occurred at a time prior to the ascertainment of the amount of damages to be paid. Manifestly, the defendants could not be charged with subsequent taxes against property which they had ceased to own. Therefore, the city was not permitted to retain, out of the award made in the condemnation proceedings, the amount of such tax assessments. Section 1249 of the Code of Civil Procedure, "excludes all consideration of other than the value of the property at the date of the issuance of the summons in the action." (*City of Los Angeles v. Gager*, 10 Cal. App. 378, [102 Pac. 17].)

It is next claimed that the court erred in refusing to make an award to defendant Pacific Electric Railway Company for the taking of power pole line parcel 46½. Respondent replies that in fact the term "Parcel 46½" was not used to designate any parcel of land sought to be taken, but was a term adopted merely for convenience, to indicate that portion of the pole line which had been built across certain parcels designated by appropriate numbers and which were all owned by defendants other than these appellants, and awards were made to the owners for the taking thereof. To this appellants reply that the bill of exceptions is stipulated to contain all of the evidence in the case and a full and true copy "of all of the judgment-roll, except the pleadings of defendants other than the above-named defendants, which said pleadings of said other defendants do not relate to or in any manner affect the rights of the above-named defendants-appellants herein and have no bearing upon the issues raised by the said defendants-appellants in the superior court"; and appellants say that there is no evidence to the effect that there is or was any other owner of parcel 46½ or any interest therein, except the Pacific Electric Railway Company, who was in occupation of the same under claim of dedication and who was devoting the same to public use; that the evidence is absolutely all one way on this point, and that therefore the court erred in failing to award to appellants the value of the right of way. While it does appear in the findings and judgment that the court found that this land belonged to other defendants and did award to other defendants sums for the taking thereof, appellants claim that under this bill of exceptions, which contains all of the evidence in the cause, that those findings and those awards were entirely without the support of any evidence. In the answer of defendants they describe the so-called power pole line parcel 46½, allege their ownership thereof and devotion thereof to public use, and further say "that said parcels of land constitute a part of a right of way for said transmission power line, as an adjunct to the railroad of the defendant, and if said parcels of land are taken without reserving to these defendants the right to hereafter maintain and operate said high power transmission line, this defendant and said remaining portion of said lands will be damaged in the sum of one million dollars; that the defendant Pacific Electric Railway Company now owns, and has for many years heretofore owned and been in possession of, a right of way through" certain lands, describing the same in detail. Testimony was introduced by the defendants showing the facts with reference to the dedication of the land to public use and the acquirement of title to a perpetual pole line easement by the Pacific Electric Railway Company. Basing their argument upon the facts thus shown, appellants contend that the owner of the land, by permitting the railway company to enter thereon and establish its public use, thereby dedicated the land to public use so that the title to the land, so far as necessary to that public use, passed to the company; that is, a perpetual easement; that the defendant has therefore a title to this power pole line easement by dedication, and not by adverse possession. It has been held in the case of public service corporations that when it appears that, although the entry was originally without right, the owner permitted the corporation to make an entry on his land and complete and construct works for which his land was appropriated, and failed to bring an action until after public interests, by reason of the construction, have intervened, the right of the owner to maintain ejectment is denied and he is remitted to an action for damages alone. (*Gurnsey* v. *Northern California Power Co.*, 160 Cal. 699, 709, [36 L. R. A. (N. S.) 185, 117 Pac. 906].) It follows, say appellants, that they are entitled to compensation for the taking of this land, although their title was an easement only.

To the foregoing the respondent replies that the answer contains only an allegation of ownership by the defendants of a right of way over the land (Tr., fols. 477–493). Respondent denies that the testimony shows a dedication thereof to public use and the acquiring of title to a perpetual or any pole line easement. This argument seems to be based upon the previous argument that the use of a pole line for the purposes described is not a public use. It is admitted by respondent that the testimony shows the construction of the pole line and its use for transmission of power to the railway company, but respondent says this does not prove that any title to an easement has been acquired. (Respondent's Brief, p. 163 et seq.) "Not only did they fail to introduce any testimony to that end, but even had they done so, the finding of the court that the title to the land embraced in the parcels traversed by this portion of the pole line was in other parties, was equivalent to a finding against the contention of these appellants."

We are inclined to the view that *Gurnsey* v. *Northern California Power Co.*, 160 Cal. 699, [36 L. R. A. (N. S.) 185, 117 Pac. 906], recognizes that under the circumstances there stated the easement acquired by the corporation became a substantial property right, the value of which would have to be accounted for by any other party seeking to enforce a superior right of eminent domain upon the same premises. The owners of the fee, therefore, are not entitled to all of the compensation to be allowed for the taking of the land, if the right of way is to be included in the condemnation without any reservation of further right of use thereof by the defendants.

It is deemed unnecessary to review in detail the several other claims by appellants that the findings do not cover all of the issues raised by the answer, and that the evidence is insufficient to support certain findings. Assuming that upon another trial the court will apply to the case the principles which we have endeavored to make clear in this decision, it is not to be expected that the findings then made will omit any necessary fact or leave room for doubt as to their meaning.

The judgment and order are reversed.

James, J., and Shaw, J., concurred.

[Civ. No. 1462. Second Appellate District.—July 22, 1916.]

SECURITY LIFE INSURANCE COMPANY OF AMERICA (a Corporation), Appellant, v. LENA M. SCOTT BOOMS et al., Respondents.

LIFE INSURANCE—ILLNESS OF INSURED BETWEEN DATE OF APPLICATION AND DELIVERY OF POLICY—LACK OF KNOWLEDGE BY INSURER—CANCELLATION OF POLICY.—A life insurance company is entitled to have a policy of insurance canceled upon tender of the amount of premium paid, where the applicant for the policy between the date of her application and the time of acceptance of the application and date of the delivery of the policy had an attack of typhoid fever, and the company was without knowledge or notice of such illness until after the delivery of the policy.

ID.—APPLICATION FOR LIFE INSURANCE—CHANGES IN PHYSICAL CONDI-
TION PENDING NEGOTIATIONS — DUTY OF APPLICANT.—The obligation
rests upon an applicant for life insurance to disclose such changes
in his physical condition as occur pending the negotiations as would
influence the judgment of the company as to the advisability of accepting the risk.

ID.—REPRESENTATIONS IN APPLICATION—TIME.—The representations contained in an application for insurance must be presumed to refer to
the time of the completion of the contract of insurance.

APPEAL from a judgment of the Superior Court of
Orange County. W. H. Thomas, Judge.

The facts are stated in the opinion of the court.

C. R. Allen, and B. E. Tarver, for Appellant.

Head & Marks, for Respondents.

CONREY, P. J.—On or about October 12, 1910, Mary L.
Young made application to appellant for an insurance policy
upon her life, to be issued in favor of her daughter, Lena M.
Scott, who is the respondent, Lena M. Scott Booms. In that
application she agreed that the statements therein made by
her were full, complete, and true, and should in the absence
of fraud be deemed representations and not warranties. It
was further agreed therein that the policy should not take
effect until acceptance of the application and payment of the
first premium. Payment of the first premium was completed
and the policy was delivered on the eighteenth day of November, 1910. The application contained answers to questions asking whether the applicant had theretofore had any
of certain named diseases, the list not including typhoid fever.
The following question was: "Have you had any illness, disease, or injury other than as stated by you above?" to which
a negative answer was returned. In February, 1911, Mrs.
Young was afflicted with appendicitis, and after an operation
therefor she died. On or about the third day of November,
1910, Mrs. Young became ill with typhoid fever. The disease ran its course in about ten or twelve days, and she was
substantially recovered therefrom on the eighteenth day of
November. The evidence does not show that the appendicitis
was in any way consequent upon the typhoid fever, and we
shall assume that the two diseases were entirely separate and

disconnected. After proof of death of Mary L. Young had been made in connection with respondent's claim on the policy, the plaintiff commenced this action to obtain cancellation of the policy, basing its demand upon the allegation that at the time said application for insurance was accepted by the plaintiff, and also at the time when the premium was paid and the policy delivered, Mary L. Young was not in good health, but was then and there seriously ill. It was further alleged that immediately upon being informed of the condition of the said Mary L Young's health and illness as above stated, which was not until after the death of said Mary L. Young, the plaintiff tendered to the defendant the amount of the premium paid and demanded return of the policy for cancellation, which demand was refused. By her answer respondent denied said allegations as to illness of Mrs. Young; denied that the plaintiff did not learn of Mrs. Young's illness until on or about the twenty-third day of November, 1911, but alleged that plaintiff was fully advised of such illness during the time thereof, to wit, between the third and eleventh days of November, 1910; alleged that such illness existed only between the third and eleventh days of November, 1910. The defendant filed a cross-complaint, seeking to recover judgment on the policy, to which an answer was filed setting up the same facts as were alleged in the complaint. Judgment was entered to the effect that the plaintiff recover nothing on its complaint, and also was in favor of the defendant as demanded in her cross-complaint. The court's findings of fact state that Mary L. Young was in good health from the tenth day of October, 1910, until the third or fourth day of November, 1910, and that she was in good health on the eighteenth day of November, 1910; also that the application for insurance was accepted on the first day of November, 1910, and that the policy was delivered and the premium paid on the eighteenth day of that month.

The findings are silent concerning the question as to plaintiff's knowledge of any illness of the assured during said month of November. The evidence shows that no information came to the corporation concerning that illness until after the death of Mrs. Young, unless such information is shown by the disputed evidence that the agent who received and forwarded the application and who delivered the policy and collected the premium, visited the house of the assured during her said illness early in November, 1910. It was further agreed that the acceptance of the application should be by the company at its executive office in Chicago, Illinois, and the policy named certain officers who alone should have power to make or modify the contract or make any promise or representation concerning the same. Assuming only for the purpose of the argument that the company would have been bound by knowledge of said agent concerning the illness in question, it follows that appellant was entitled to a finding upon this issue of fact, and we must determine the remaining question in the case as if the finding had been in favor of the plaintiff; that is, that the plaintiff was without knowledge or notice of Mrs. Young's illness until after the delivery of the policy and after the death of the assured.

"The completion of the contract of insurance is the time to which a representation must be presumed to refer." (Civ. Code, sec. 2577.) "It is well settled that the obligation rests upon an applicant for life insurance to disclose such changes in his physical condition as occur pending the negotiation as would influence the judgment of the company as to the advisability of accepting the risk." (*Thompson* v. *Travelers' Ins. Co.*, 13 N. D. 44, [101 N. W. 900].) The decisions generally are to the same effect. (See note in 8 L. R. A. (N. S.), p. 983.) Since, in accordance with the section of the Civil Code quoted above, the representations contained in the application must in this case be deemed to refer to the time when the premium was paid and the policy delivered, it follows that the assured at that time represented that she had not had any of the diseases to which she returned a negative answer and had not had any illness or disease other than as specifically stated by her. To say that these representations may be ignored in the instance of a person who receives a life insurance policy immediately following upon an attack of typhoid fever, would be to deny one of the most important rights of the contracting party. The inherent probability that the plaintiff would have hesitated to issue a policy upon the life of Mrs. Young at that particular time, raises to very substantial importance its right to have been informed of the facts.

The appeal is from the judgment, and the judgment is reversed.

James, J., and Shaw, J., concurred.

[Civ. No. 1986.   Second Appellate District.—July 22, 1916.]

I. W. GLEASON et al., Appellants, v. C. J. PROUD, Respondent.

CONTRACT—TRUTH OF REPRESENTATIONS—RELIANCE UPON.—A contracting party is entitled to rely on the express statement of an existing fact, the truth of which is known to the opposite party and unknown to him, as the basis of a mutual agreement, and he is under no obligation to investigate and verify the statements to the truth of which the other party to the contract, with full means of knowledge, has deliberately pledged his faith.

ID.—EXCHANGE OF REAL PROPERTY FOR BONDS—VALUE OF BONDS—LACK OF MISREPRESENTATION AS TO VALUE.—Such principles, however, are inapplicable to an action to rescind a contract of exchange of real property for bonds of a corporation, on the ground of misrepresentation as to the value of the bonds, where the agent of the defendant furnished the plaintiff with all the information that his principal and himself had concerning the value of the bonds, which consisted of letters written by third parties, and requested the plaintiff to investigate the writers of the letters.

APPEAL from a judgment of the Superior Court of Los Angeles County, and from an order denying a new trial. J. P. Wood, Judge.

The facts are stated in the opinion of the court.

Harold A. Gilman, Tanner, Taft & Odell, and Tanner, Odell, Odell & Taft, for Appellants.

Victor T. Watkins, Thorpe & Hanna, Joseph Musgrove, and Charles W. Lyon, for Respondent.

CONREY, P. J.—This is an action to enforce an alleged right of rescission of a contract and exchange of property between plaintiffs and defendant. The plaintiffs appeal from the judgment and from an order denying their motion for a new trial.

The alleged misrepresentations relate to bonds of the Bisbee Light & Power Company, an Arizona corporation, which were transferred by defendant to plaintiff I. W. Gleason as the principal part of the consideration given by Proud for the property conveyed to him by Gleason. The transaction took place in September and October, 1908. Respondent Proud had acquired these bonds a few weeks before that time by transfer from A. W. McPherson and W. F. Nordholt in consideration of real property conveyed to them by Proud. In that transaction one H. A. Landwehr had acted as an agent for Proud, and in that way had acquired some knowledge concerning the Bisbee bonds and Proud's ownership thereof.

In the original complaint filed in this action it was alleged that the defendant made certain representations of fact upon which the plaintiffs relied, and that such representations were false; also, that the defendant concealed certain material facts which, if they had been known to plaintiffs, would have caused the plaintiffs to refuse to enter into the contract. At the trial the evidence wholly failed to establish any intentional misrepresentations or concealments of fact made by the defendant or his agent. Without abandoning their claim that the representations complained of were known by the defendant and his agents to be false, the plaintiffs at the trial further amended their complaint by alleging that the defendant was not, nor were his agents, warranted in making said assertions or statements by the information they possessed when the same were made, although they may have believed them to be true. Presumably this amendment was made to bring the case within the terms of the definition of actual fraud contained in section 1572 of the Civil Code, whereby actual fraud consists of certain acts and circumstances, one of which is "the positive assertion, in a manner not warranted by the information of the person making it, of that which is not true, though he believes it to be true."

The plaintiffs do not base their action upon any representations made personally by the defendant. Their claim is that Landwehr was Proud's agent, and that Landwehr made or caused to be made the representations upon which they relied. On this appeal it is contended that the court erred in sustaining objections to questions asked of the witness Landwehr designed to show the fact of his agency by proving declarations made by him as to the person for whom he was acting; also, that the court erred in holding that there was not sufficient evidence to show that Landwehr was the agent of Proud, and in refusing to permit evidence to be introduced relating to the untruthfulness of the representations which he made or caused to be made.

In view of our conclusion upon another phase of the case, hereafter to be stated, it will not be necessary to discuss these alleged errors; and for the purposes of the argument we shall assume, without deciding, that Landwehr was the agent of Proud, and that the facts which the plaintiffs sought to prove to be untrue were in fact untrue. For if Landwehr, acting on behalf of the defendant, did not make the representations complained of, or did not cause the plaintiffs to rely upon any representations as coming from him or vouched for by him, then plaintiffs cannot maintain this action. There is no substantial conflict in the evidence in this case. The defendant was content to submit the case upon the testimony of the plaintiffs and their witnesses.

When respondent was negotiating the exchange by which he acquired the Bisbee bonds, the parties with whom he was transacting that business furnished him two letters purporting to state facts concerning the Bisbee bonds and their value. These letters were dated August 27, 1908, were addressed to H. A. Landwehr, one of them was signed by A. W. McPherson, and the other by Bank of Santa Monica, per H. J. Englebrecht, cashier. In the course of the negotiations leading to the transaction involved in the present action, Landwehr delivered these letters to Mr. Gleason and Mr. Gleason, besides reading those letters, had personal interviews with Mr. Englebrecht and also with Mr. Nordholt. These letters contained all of the information that Landwehr or the defendant Proud had concerning the bonds, and it is upon the falsity of the statement of facts therein contained that the plaintiffs rely. To ascertain the circumstances under which these letters were received by Gleason, we will take his own testimony: "At the time when Mr. Landwehr gave those letters, he said that they were the letters that had been delivered to him in connection with this deal between Mr. Proud and McPherson and Nordholt, describing the bonds in that deal. He asked me to go down and have a talk with Mr. Englebrecht. . . . These letters were written to Mr. Landwehr in connection with that deal, less than a month before. The letters themselves show that that was the purpose." Again he testified, referring to Landwehr, as follows: "I don't think he said anything about knowing anything about the bonds himself. I don't remember that he said that this was the information he had on it; he said this was the information he did have. I don't think

he said that was all the information he had.   He did not profess to know anything about it himself; as a matter of fact,
he did not tell me to investigate for myself.   *He told me to
investigate these men."*   Again he said: "Mr. Proud made
no representations except through his agents, the persons that
I have spoken of, Mr. Landwehr and the other parties that
made the representations that induced me to make a trade of
my property.   The letters and the statements of McPherson
and Nordholt induced me to part with my property to Mr.
Proud.   If it had not been for those letters, I would never
have parted with the property."   And again: "He did not
profess to know anything superior to the evidence that he
had put up to me.   That was far superior to anything he
might have.   I did not consider any opinion that he might
have.   He had an opinion.   He said he thought that it was
all right.   He did not say that he based his information upon
anything other than the representations that he had from
these men who wrote the letters.   I believe he gave me all
the information he had."

It will be noted that Landwehr did not make any positive
assertions with respect to the facts contained in those letters,
and did not even vouch for the writers of the letters.   He
advised appellants to investigate the men who wrote the
letters, and appellants acted upon that advice.   Being acquainted with Mr. Bittinger, an officer in the First National
Bank of Los Angeles, appellant I. W. Gleason inquired of Mr.
Bittinger, asking if he knew Mr. Englebrecht and if he could
rely upon a letter of that kind; to which Mr. Bittinger replied
that he did know Englebrecht and he was a good fellow, and
Bittinger did not think he would write a letter of that kind
unless he knew the facts contained in it to be true.   It was
after receiving that assurance that appellant went to see Mr.
Englebrecht, and in conversation with him obtained further
statements favorable to the bonds.   We entirely agree with
counsel for appellants in their contention that a contracting
party is entitled to rely on the express statement of an existing fact, the truth of which is known to the opposite party
and unknown to him, as the basis of a mutual agreement;
and that he is under no obligation to investigate and verify
the statements to the truth of which the other party to the
contract, with full means of knowledge, has deliberately
pledged his faith.   (*Spreckels* v. *Gorrill,* 152 Cal. 383, 395,

[92 Pac. 1011].) But the facts of this case are not such as to make those principles applicable here. There is a total absence of express statement or positive assertion of the alleged untrue facts by Landwehr. There is a further total absence of relationship between respondent and the writers of those letters, or of any voucher for the reliability of those persons either by the respondent or his agent, such as would be necessary before making the respondent responsible for their statements.

Without regard to other questions discussed in the briefs, it thus clearly appears upon the record that plaintiffs are not entitled to recover.

The judgment and order are affirmed.

James, J., and Shaw, J., concurred.

A petition for a rehearing of this cause was denied by the district court of appeal on August 21, 1916, and a petition to have the cause heard in the supreme court, after judgment in the district court of appeal, was denied by the supreme court on September 18, 1916.

[Civ. No. 1989. Second Appellate District.—July 22, 1916.]

WILLIAM J. TEMPLE, Appellant, v. GEORGE B. GORDON, Respondent.

PRELIMINARY INJUNCTION—DISCRETION—APPEAL.—The granting of a preliminary injunction is not a matter of right, but the application is addressed to the sound discretion of the court, which is to be exercised according to the circumstances of the particular case; and its action upon such application will not be reviewed in the appellate court unless it shall clearly appear that there was an abuse of its discretion.

ID.—SIMILARITY OF BREAD WRAPPERS—DENIAL OF PRELIMINARY INJUNCTION—DISCRETION NOT ABUSED.—Upon this appeal from an order denying a motion for a preliminary injunction restraining the defendant from using a certain wrapper upon bread manufactured and sold by him, on the ground of its similarity to the wrapper used by the plaintiff, it is held that in view of the nature of the relief demanded, and of the conflicting evidence which came before the superior court upon the order to show cause, it cannot be said that the plaintiff's right to such injunction was conclusively established, or that the court abused its discretion in denying the motion.

APPEAL from an order of the Superior Court of Los Angeles County dissolving a restraining order and denying a motion for a preliminary injunction. John M. York, Judge.

The facts are stated in the opinion of the court.

Joseph F. Westall, and Henry T. Hazard, for Appellant.

Jones & Weller, for Respondent.

CONREY, P. J.—This is an appeal by the plaintiff from an order dissolving a restraining order and denying plaintiff's motion for a preliminary injunction. The application for the order was heard upon the complaint, and affidavits produced on both sides.

For about two years prior to defendant's acts of which the plaintiff complains plaintiff was engaged in manufacturing and selling a certain kind of bread, to which he gave the name of "Faultless" bread. In June, 1913, he caused to be registered as belonging to him the trademark and trade name "Faultless" as applied to that product, and obtained a certificate thereof from the Secretary of State of the state of California. In selling his bread thereafter he was accustomed to have each loaf wrapped in a certain kind of paper upon which was printed:

"FAULTLESS
BREAD
MADE BY
OCCIDENTAL BAKERY
Brdy. 4770   Los Angeles   A-5020."

These words and figures were printed in dark blue ink in a certain distinctive form. He advertised extensively his product under said trade name and built up a valuable business in the sale of the described bread. The plaintiff charged that thereafter the defendant, with intent to deceive and defraud the public and to injure and defraud the plaintiff, caused to be put up in similar packages a kind of bread sold by him, copying the general design, color of ink, etc., and

caused the bread to be sold in a nearly similar wrapper to
that of the plaintiff, on which he placed the following printed
matter:

"PEERLESS

PURITY   QUALITY

PEERLESS
BREAD
MADE BY
GORDON BREAD CO.

South 4797   Los Angeles."

Samples of these wrappers are attached as exhibits to the complaint and are found in the transcript on appeal. The affidavits which accompanied the complaint were made by drivers
of bread wagons for the plaintiff and contain statements of
fact tending to show a similarity in appearance of the articles
as placed on the market by the defendant to those sold by the
plaintiff; tending also to show that some persons were deceived thereby, and that the bread sold by the defendant was
inferior in weight and quality, but that nevertheless it was
competing successfully with plaintiff's bread in the various
establishments where bread was sold in the city of Los Angeles, and that plaintiff's business was being injured thereby.
In response to the order to show cause the defendant presented to the court affidavits of himself and of several drivers
of his delivery wagons and of several grocers who had been
selling bread purchased from the plaintiff as well as from the
defendant. The defendant denied many of the important
allegations of the complaint. Among other things, the defendant stated in his affidavit and the accompanying affidavits
stated matters tending to show that it was not true that by
reason of close similarity of the names "Faultless" and
"Peerless," or of the wrappers and packages as sold by the
defendant, the public could be or was misled or imposed upon;
that the defendant had been engaged in the manufacture and
selling of bread in the city of Los Angeles for at least five
years prior to the commencement of this action; that the wrappers used by him did not nor did he intend by them to imitate
the plaintiff's trademark or label.

On the hearing of this motion it was not necessary for the
court, in order to warrant a denial of the order asked for by
plaintiff, to pass upon the merits of the case. The court may
have concluded that the essential facts were so clearly in dis-

pute and the right of plaintiff to any relief so much in doubt under the showing made, that it would decline to grant any injunction at all until a trial on the merits. "The granting of a preliminary injunction is not a matter of right, but the application is addressed to the sound discretion of the court, which is to be exercised according to the circumstances of the particular case; and its action upon such application will not be reviewed in the appellate court unless it shall clearly appear that there was an abuse of its discretion." (*Santa Cruz Fair Building Assn.* v. *Grant,* 104 Cal. 306, [37 Pac. 1034].)

The plaintiff's case does not appear to be based upon any claim of exclusive right by reason of a trademark, since the trademark as registered by him relates only to the name or quality of the thing sold. (Civ. Code, sec. 991.) The claims asserted by him are based upon "the principle that in the interest of fair commercial dealing courts of equity, where one has been first in the field doing business under a given name, will protect that person to the extent of making competitors use reasonable precautions to prevent deceit and fraud upon the public and upon the business first in the field." (*Dunston* v. *Los Angeles Van etc. Co.,* 165 Cal. 89, 94, [131 Pac. 115, 117].) The relief rests upon the deceit or fraud which the later comer into the business field is practicing upon the earlier comer and upon the public. In view of the nature of the relief demanded, and in view of the conflicting evidence which came before the superior court under the order to show cause, we are unable to say that the plaintiff's right to a temporary injunction was conclusively established, or that the court abused its discretion in denying the motion.

The order appealed from is affirmed.

James, J., and Shaw, J., concurred.

[Civ. No. 1411.   Third Appellate District.—July 22, 1916.]

PACIFIC COAST DRIED FRUIT COMPANY (a Corporation), Appellant, v. CHARLES SHERIFFS et al., Doing Business Under the Firm Name of the Sheriffs Brothers Company, Respondents.

SALE OF PRUNE CROP—ACTION FOR BALANCE DUE—OWNERSHIP—EVIDENCE —PLAINTIFF NOT REAL PARTY IN INTEREST.—Where, in an action to recover a sum of money alleged to be the balance due on a contract for the sale of a crop of dried prunes, the case was tried and decided upon the sole theory that the plaintiff was not the real party in interest, by reason of the fact that the prunes were owned by the individual lessee of the ranch upon which they were grown, and not by the plaintiff corporation, which such lessee organized and of which he owned all the capital stock, except a few shares issued for the working purposes of the corporation, the judgment will not be disturbed upon appeal, even though the evidence upon the question of such ownership was not in conflict, where such evidence was of a character that the trial court was warranted in discrediting it.

ID.—EVIDENCE—REJECTION OF TESTIMONY—RIGHT OF TRIAL COURT.—It is within the legal province or discretion of the trial court to reject *in toto* the testimony of any witness, but such rejection must not be arbitrary.

APPEAL from a judgment of the Superior Court of Sonoma County.   Thos. C. Denny, Judge.

The facts are stated in the opinion of the court.

R. L. Thompson, and T. J. Butts, for Appellant.

T. J. Geary, for Respondents.

HART, J.—The plaintiff appeals from a judgment rendered and entered against it and in favor of the defendants.

The action is for the recovery of the sum of $1,887.12, alleged to be the balance due from the defendants to the plaintiff on a contract of sale made and entered into between the parties on the twenty-ninth day of September, 1913, whereby, it is alleged, the plaintiff sold and delivered to the defendants 132,878 pounds of dried prunes, at the agreed price of one hundred dollars per ton for the first ten tons thereof and $120 per ton for the balance thereof.

The undisputed facts are: That one H. W. Eberling was, in the year 1913, and for several years prior thereto, the lessee of the prune orchard known as the "Leak Ranch," situated on Mark West Creek, in Sonoma County. He also, in the year 1913, was the lessee of another prune orchard, in said county, known as the Gibbons Ranch. On the first day of May, 1913, the said Eberling entered into a written contract with the California Fruit Canners' Association, whereby he agreed to sell and deliver to said association from forty to fifty tons of dried prunes, grown on the Leak and Gibbons ranches, at "3 cent base," said prunes to be delivered on board of cars at a station called Fulton, in Sonoma County. The consummation of said contract of sale was made dependent upon the happening of certain conditions pertaining to quality of fruit as dried. Upon the execution of said contract, the California Fruit Canners' Association paid said Eberling the sum of five hundred dollars, in two different checks made payable to Eberling, one for two hundred dollars and the other for three hundred dollars. Thereafter, and before the prunes or any portion thereof were delivered, the canners' association paid Eberling the additional sum of two hundred dollars, making a total payment of seven hundred dollars.

On the fifteenth day of August, 1913, the following contract was mutually entered into by Eberling Bros. and the defendants:

"In consideration of the sum of one dollar by each to the other paid, the receipt of which is hereby acknowledged, Eberling Bros. has this day sold, and Sheriffs Brothers Company of Healdsburg, Cal., have this day bought my crop of Dried French and Sugar prunes grown on what is known as Leak and Givins ranches Est 100 tons more or less.

10 tons @ $100.00 per ton
Balance @ $120.00 " "

"It is hereby expressly agreed that said fruit shall be delivered in first class order, all of which is to be of choice merchantable quality, thoroughly cured and well dried.

"Any wet or rain damaged stock is to be weighed back, or taken at a reduced price as may be agreed upon.

"To be delivered at on board cars Mark West.

"Terms—Cash on delivery.

"SELLER EBERLING BROS.,

"SHERIFFS BROTHERS COMPANY,

"By CHAS. SHERIFFS."

These further facts are also undisputed: That, subject to the conditions of the foregoing contract, viz., that the prunes so bargained for should "be delivered in first class order, all of which are to be of choice, merchantable quality, thoroughly cured and well dried," etc., the defendants bought the crop of prunes on the ranches in said contract named, estimated at one hundred tons, at the rate of one hundred dollars per ton for the first ten tons and $120 per ton for the remainder, the fruit to be delivered on board the cars at the railroad station at Mark West, in Sonoma County; that all the prunes, except the two cars in dispute here, were so delivered to the defendants and received by them at Healdsburg, in said county; that all the prunes were, prior to the commencement of this action, paid for except the last two cars, which are involved in this action and which amounted in money to the sum herein sued for; that, when the said last two cars reached Healdsburg, the place of consignment, the California Canners' Association seized and took possession of them in an action brought by it in claim and delivery, said association claiming to be the owner of said prunes by virtue of its contract with H. W. Eberling, above mentioned herein; that H. W. Eberling had, prior to the seizure by the canners' association of the two cars of prunes as above indicated, delivered to the said association nine or ten tons of prunes, which amounted to more in money than the sum of seven hundred dollars which was advanced to said Eberling by the canners' association.

The appellant expressly admits these facts: That H. W. Eberling was the lessee of the Leak and Gibbons ranches, and owned half the prune crops grown thereon; that H. W. Eberling entered into the contract, above referred to, with the canners' association for the sale of the prunes in controversy in this action; that, after the making of the contract between the canners' association and H. W. Eberling, and before the making of the contract between Eberling Bros. and the defendants, the plaintiff was incorporated. The disputed fact in the case and upon which the decision of the controversy is made to hinge is whether the fruit in question was sold to the plaintiff by Eberling prior to the making of the contract with the defendants.

The plaintiff contends that the determination of the ultimate issue presented here is whether the contract between Eberling and the canners' association is merely executory or constituted a sale. "If it was a sale," proceeds the plaintiff, "then the title passed to the canners' company and Eberling could not thereafter convey the fruit to the Pacific Coast Dried Fruit Company. And if the canners' fruit was shipped to Sheriffs Bros. at Healdsburg, the canners' company had a right to replevin it." On the other hand, continues the plaintiff, "if said contract was executory and Eberling had until the fifteenth day of October, 1913, in which to fulfill it, and he did not fulfill his contract by that time, the California Canners' Association had an action for damages against H. W. Eberling, but it had no title to the fruit, and the sale of the fruit to the Pacific Coast Dried Fruit Company was valid, as was the sale to Sheriffs Bros."

Counsel for the appellant then proceeded to show that the contract referred to was executory, and that, therefore, the canners' association did not, and could not, acquire title to the fruit until the same was delivered to and accepted by it.

The case, however, was tried and decided upon the sole theory that the defendants never entered into any contract with the plaintiff whereby the latter agreed or promised to sell and deliver to them any prunes, that said plaintiff, as a matter of fact, never did sell and deliver to the defendants any prunes, and that said plaintiff is not the real party in interest in this action (sec. 367, Code Civ. Proc.); that it cannot, therefore, maintain this action, and is not entitled to any judgment of any kind or character against the defendants. Upon this theory of the case, it is manifestly unimportant whether the contract between Eberling and the canners' association constituted a sale or a mere agreement to sell.

The court made no other findings than the following: "1. That the plaintiff did not, on or about September 29, 1913, or on any other date or at any time, sell or deliver to the defendants . . . at Healdsburg . . . or any other place . . . any quantity of prunes; 2. That the defendants . . . did not at any time or place agree or promise to pay to the plaintiff any price for any prunes and that defendants . . . did not at any time or place enter into any contract with the plaintiff for the purchase from plaintiff of any quantity of dried prunes; 3. That the defendants . . . have not paid to the plaintiff the sum of $5,885.56 or any sum of money whatever on account of any dried prunes received by the defendants

. . . from the plaintiff; 4. That there is nothing due from the defendants . . . to the plaintiff on any account.''

Thus it will be observed that, as stated, the whole theory of the case as it was tried by the defendants and decided by the court was that the plaintiff was not the real party in interest, and the sole question here is, therefore, whether the above findings derive sufficient support from the evidence.

We cannot say that the decision was not justified.

The contract upon which this action is founded was, as is above shown, between Eberling Bros. and Sheriffs Bros. The prunes referred to in said contract were those produced or to be produced on the Leak and Gibbons ranches, of which H. W. Eberling, who conducted the negotiations culminating in the contract, was the lessee. In that contract it is expressly provided that the Sheriffs Bros. were to receive, for the prices therein specified, "*my* crop of Dried French and Sugar prunes grown on what is known as the Leach (Leak) and Givins (Gibbons) ranches.''

Charles Sheriffs testified that, in the course of his negotiations with H. W. Eberling for the purchase of said prunes, no word was ever uttered or suggestion made or intimated that the Pacific Coast Dried Fruit Company had any interest, direct or remote, in said prunes or the contract into which he was about to enter with Eberling Bros. for the purchase of the same. Indeed, he testified that, having heard prior to the time he began negotiations for the purchase of the prunes that the Eberlings had formed a company called the "Pacific Dried Fruit Company,'' he asked H. W. Eberling, just before the contract was executed, why he did not sell his crop of prunes to his own company (referring to plaintiff), and that Eberling replied that he did not desire to take that course, that the fruit belonged to him (Eberling) and that "he wanted to sell it on the outside for the best price he could get for it.'' The witness further testified that, when making payments for prunes delivered to him under said contract, he invariably did so by drawing his checks in the name and favor of H. W. Eberling, the latter having requested him to make his checks out in that manner.

On the other hand, the plaintiff presented some testimony which raised an apparent conflict in the evidence upon the question whether it at any time became the owner of the prunes in question or whether said prunes were transferred

to it by Eberling before the making of the contract to which
the defendants are parties. H. W. Eberling testified that he
transferred his 1913 crop of prunes to the plaintiff prior to
the making of the contract between Eberling Bros. and Sheriffs
Bros. The consideration for the transfer, he said, was the
issuance to him by the plaintiff of three hundred shares of
its stock. He never received any cash from the plaintiff for
the transfer. The minutes of a meeting of the board of directors of the plaintiff, held July 21, 1913, were introduced
in evidence and disclosed that, upon motion of Director C. W.
Eberling, "the property of Harry W. Eberling, known as
Eberling Bros., viz: 100 tons of prunes, valued at $10,000.00,
with the packing house, cannery and other equipment, and
cash to the value of $6,000.00, together with his good will,
accepted by the company and that the secretary be instructed
to issue 336 shares of the company's stock in respect thereof."
The foregoing action, the minutes further show, was subsequently ratified by Directors H. W. Eberling, C. W. Eberling, and J. T. Lyons, and acknowledgment of receipt of
stock issued by the plaintiff (to whom it does not appear)
was also noted in said minutes. There were also introduced
what purported to be the minutes of a meeting of the board
of directors, held on August 7, 1913, which tended to show
that the corporation, by said board, had invested H. W. Eberling with authority "to sell the whole or any part of the
prunes that he put into this corporation as one of his assets
and which are grown on his ranch at Fulton, Sonoma County,
and to receive payment therefor. And, moreover, he is hereby
authorized to use such moneys as he may receive in payment
therefor in such a way as may seem fit and to the best interests of said corporation in the discharge of its obligations."

The foregoing is, substantially, about all the testimony the
object of which was to show ownership of the prunes in the
plaintiff.

As stated, there is *apparently* a conflict in the evidence upon
the question of the ownership of the prunes involved in this
action. Whether, however, in reality, there was a conflict,
was a question for the determination of the trial court. If
that court concluded, as with perfect propriety we may assume
that it did, that the testimony introduced by the plaintiff
upon that question was wholly unbelievable, and so entirely
discredited and disregarded it, then there was no actual con-

flict, for the situation in that case would be the same as if the plaintiff had introduced no proof whatsoever upon the subject.

That it is within the legal province or discretion of the trial court to reject *in toto* the testimony of any witness is a proposition so obvious under our system and so often confirmed by the courts that its statement is all that should be necessary to certify its soundness. In the very nature of the case this should be the rule. It was announced in the earliest history of the jurisprudence of the state and has never been varied from. In *Blankman* v. *Vallejo*, 15 Cal. 639, 646, the very learned Mr. Justice Baldwin, with the sanction of the court, said: "We do not understand that the credulity of a court must necessarily correspond with the vigor and positiveness with which a witness swears. A court may reject the most positive testimony, though the witness be not discredited by direct testimony impeaching him or contradicting his statements. The inherent improbability of a statement may deny to it all claims to belief." (See, also, *County of Sonoma* v. *Stofen*, 125 Cal. 32, 35, [57 Pac. 681]; *People* v. *Milner*, 122 Cal. 171, 179, 180, [54 Pac. 833]; *Clark* v. *Tulare Lake Dredging Co.*, 14 Cal. App. 414, 432, 433, [112 Pac. 564].)

It is unnecessary to say, of course, that neither a trial court nor a jury may arbitrarily reject the testimony of a witness. There must be a sufficient legal reason for its rejection or discretion is abused. But, unless the action of a trial court or jury in repudiating testimony given before it appears to be inherently erroneous or upon its face as involving an arbitrary disregard of such testimony, an appeal court must assume and, indeed, presume, that upon sufficient reasons the testimony was deemed to be wanting in verity, and, therefore, without probative or evidentiary force or value.

While it does not rest upon this court to search for and develop the specific reason or reasons by which the trial court was led into the rejection of the testimony presented by the plaintiff, we may, nevertheless, properly call attention to some considerations disclosed by the record which, upon their face at least, might well lead to the conviction that the testimony so brought into the case was entitled to no weight or possessed no persuasive force. In the first place, it is to be observed, in this connection, that the prunes in question were shipped to Sheriffs Bros. by and in the name of "Eberling Bros.," and that, when the fruit was seized by the canners' association under the writ of replevin, H. W. Eberling alone fought the case apparently for and in behalf of himself, and, according to his own admissions on the witness-stand, at no time after the fruit was so taken possession of did he say or represent or pretend in that action or otherwise that the prunes were the property of the plaintiff, until about the time of the commencement of this action.   In the second place, it is to be noted that the contract with the canners' association was made prior to the incorporation of the plaintiff and prior to the execution of the contract between Eberling Bros. and the defendants.   It will further be noted that the latter contract called for better prices and profits for and on the prunes than H. W. Eberling agreed to sell the prunes at and would have obtained under the contract with the canners' association.   Thus it is manifest that it would have been greatly to the financial advantage of H. W. Eberling to have delivered the prunes in question to the Sheriffs Bros. under the latter's contract than to have delivered them to the canners' association under its contract.   And it by no means involves a far-fetched proposition to venture, upon the record as it appears here, that the reason which inspired Eberling to attempt to make it appear that the plaintiff and not he was the real party to the contract with the defendants was this: that, if it could be shown that the fruit was *delivered* by the plaintiff to the defendants, under the latter's contract, when said fruit was placed in the cars for shipment at Mark West, the seizure of the prunes by the canners' association, which confessedly had had no dealings with the plaintiff, would involve a matter which concerned no other person than the Sheriffs —that is to say, the fruit having been delivered to them *by the plaintiff* according to their contract, the title thereto had vested in the defendants before the seizure, and that it was, therefore, the latter's duty and no concern of the plaintiff, which was under no obligation of any kind or character to the canners' association, to see that the association restored the fruit to their possession.   However that may be, the considerations to which we have above referred, we repeat, are, at least upon their face, sufficient justly to generate distrust in the asseverations of H. W. Eberling that the prunes in question were the property of the plaintiff and in the good faith of the purported transfer of the fruit to said plaintiff

by H. W. Eberling, as the minutes of its board of directors
introduced in evidence in this case purport to attest. And
if, upon those considerations, the trial court felt constrained
to discredit the testimony presented by the plaintiff upon the
question of ownership and so disregarded entirely said testimony, we cannot say that the court, in so doing, was not
justified or abused its discretion in that respect.

Thus we have reviewed the record as it is presented to us,
and, while thus we have been led to the conclusion that the
findings of the court that the defendants never at any time
had any transaction whatever with the plaintiff and are not
indebted to the plaintiff in any sum on account of the prunes
in question are amply supported and that said findings support the judgment, it must be conceded that the sole defense
relied upon by the defendants, as indicated, and the theory
upon which the cause was decided, which theory necessarily
followed from the nature of said defense, are extremely
technical; for H. W. Eberling was, according to the testimony,
practically the corporation plaintiff itself. He organized it
and owned all the capital stock thereof, with the exception of
a few shares issued for the working purposes of the corporation, and the money, property, and assets transferred to it
by him—indeed, the whole of its assets—had constituted his
own individual property. If he had made out a clear case of
indebtedness to him or the corporation for the prunes in question, we might, under the circumstances thus pointed out, be
justified in reversing the judgment. As shown, however,
technically, plaintiff was not the owner of the prunes in question according to the court's findings, which are fortified by
sufficient evidence, and is, therefore, not the real party in
interest in this action; but, more than this, it is very clear
from the record that apparently the court could have further
found, as certainly it should have found, if the face value
of the testimony presented by the defendants may be accepted
as the correct test of its probative force, and thus have disposed of the case upon its merits against the plaintiff, that
H. W. Eberling did agree in writing to sell the prunes in
dispute to the canners' association prior to the incorporation
of the plaintiff and prior to the making of the contract with
the defendants; that while the prunes were still on a "siding"
at the Mark West railway station, H. W. Eberling assured an
agent of the canners' association that they were there to be

consigned to that association in pursuance of the terms of its contract with "Eberling Bros."; that the assurance so made to the said agent was false and designed to mislead the canners' association as to the disposition which Eberling really intended to make of the prunes; that, as a matter of fact, he at all times intended to ship them to Sheriffs Bros., to whom he had agreed to sell them at prices in advance of those specified in the contract with the association; that he did consign them to the defendants; that the canners' association, having learned of the duplicity, brought suit to obtain possession of the prunes, did, in fact, secure possession of and retained them, and presumably paid Eberling the prices for them stipulated in its contract; that, as a consequence of the act of the association in taking possession of the prunes, the defendants did not then, nor did they ever, get actual possession of the fruit; that H. W. Eberling treated the action by the association as of his and not as of the concern of the defendants, and, accordingly, himself fought the case for and on behalf of himself; that, on the seventeenth day of December, 1913, almost three months after the association brought its claim and delivery action for the purpose of obtaining possession of the prunes, H. W. Eberling, upon being paid by the defendants the sum of $327.57, executed and delivered to them a receipt therefor acknowledging payment "in full for all fruits delivered by Eberling Bros."; that, at the time of the delivery of said receipt, Eberling said nothing about an indebtedness due him from the defendants on account of the prunes in question, and that he made no claim against the defendants on that account until long after the delivery of said receipt. In view of all these facts, we think it is very clear that justice demands that the judgment, though resting on a technical defense, should be affirmed, and it is so ordered.

Chipman, P. J., and Ellison, J., *pro tem.*, concurred.

[Civ. No. 1955. Second Appellate District.—July 24, 1916.]

GWYNN E. HOPKINS, Respondent, v. CHARLES L. SANDERSON et al., Appellants.

SCHOOL LAW—OFFER OF EMPLOYMENT OF LIBRARIAN—FAILURE TO ACCEPT IN TIME—SECTION 1617, POLITICAL CODE.—Even though section 1617 of the Political Code, providing that "any teacher who shall fail to signify his acceptance [of a school position] within twenty days after such election, shall be deemed to have declined the same," be held not to apply to the position of librarian, it is within the right of the board of trustees of a school district to require one seeking such position to give notice of acceptance within the time provided by said section, and where the board in its offer of such position requires acceptance to be made within twenty days, under the belief that said section applies, but the applicant fails to accept within said time, there is no employment, and no salary can be recovered.

ID.—OFFER OF EMPLOYMENT—EVIDENCE.—Where a written notice of the employment of a party as librarian of a school district stated that it was given under section 1617 of the California school code, and that an acceptance was required under said section within twenty days, and that failure to comply with such provision rendered the position vacant, it was sufficiently made to appear that the employment was conditional upon acceptance within the time prescribed, although no demand was made for the production of the original notice, where the president of the school board, without objection, was permitted to testify that the board of trustees elected the plaintiff with the proviso outlined in the notice.

APPEAL from a judgment of the Superior Court of Los Angeles County. Charles Wellborn, Judge.

The facts are stated in the opinion of the court.

A. J. Hill, County Counsel, Hugh Gordon, Deputy County Counsel, and Frederick W. Smith, for Appellants.

M. P. Hopkins, for Respondent.

JAMES, J.—The plaintiff herein was awarded in the trial court a writ of mandate to compel the payment to her of certain money which she alleged was due her for three months' services as librarian for the Whittier Union High School District. She alleges that she was employed by the board of trustees of said district on the fourth day of June, 1915. This employment was denied on the part of the defendants, and it was alleged affirmatively that there had been an offer made to the plaintiff to employ her in the capacity of librarian, said offer being made with the express condition that notice of acceptance should be furnished within twenty days, and that no such notice was furnished within said time. On behalf of the plaintiff there was introduced in evidence a minute record of the board of trustees of a meeting held on June 4, 1915, wherein the employment of various persons as teachers and in other capacities was recorded, the plaintiff being one of the number mentioned in that minute. Upon this proof plaintiff rested as having made out a *prima facie* case. In the answer a copy of the document which it was alleged had been sent to the plaintiff, notifying her of her employment as librarian, was set out. An affidavit contradicting the genuineness and due execution of the instrument was filed, raising an issue as to that matter. That notice contained the following provision: "This notice is in conformity with section 1617 of the California School Code. An acceptance of same is required under provisions of same section, within twenty days. Failure to comply with such provision renders the position vacant." The original notice was not introduced in evidence. When the defendants sought to prove by an officer of the school board that the notice as alleged had been sent to the plaintiff, it was objected that no demand had been made for the production of the original, and that secondary evidence to establish the fact was not proper to be received. There was considerable argument had at the trial upon the question raised by the objection. However, without objection, the president of the school board was permitted to testify that the board of trustees elected the plaintiff with the proviso as outlined in a notice which was sent to her,—that ratification or acceptance by the employee must be signed and returned within twenty days, or the office would become vacant. It was, therefore, sufficiently made to appear that the employment of the petitioner as made by the board at its meeting of June 4, 1915, was conditional upon notice of acceptance being received within twenty days thereafter. As we have before stated, it was not contended that there was any such acceptance within the time provided; in fact, the express testimony showed that the plaintiff did not attempt to comply with the requirement until after the twenty days had expired.

The board then refused to consider her acceptance as being within time and refused to certify to her employment. It is said that the offer of employment requiring acceptance within twenty days only applied to teachers, citing section 1617 of the Political Code. That section in its provisions relating to the acceptance of school positions does refer only to teachers when it declares: "provided, further, that any teacher who shall fail to signify his acceptance within twenty days after such election shall be deemed to have declined the same. . . . " The trial judge seems to have agreed with this contention when he found that the employment of the petitioner was completed at the time of the meeting of the board of trustees. In support of such determination the argument is that as the board of trustees was not required in the case of employees other than teachers to demand that notice of acceptance be given within twenty days, the engagement of such other employees would be complete at the time of the adoption of the resolution selecting them. We are not in accord with the trial court in this conclusion. It was undoubtedly within the right of the board of trustees to require a notice of acceptance to be given on the part of the person proposed to be employed; and whether the section of the school law referred to required it or not, it was without question the belief of the board that the section did so require it, and it was their intent when the notice of selection was sent to the plaintiff that the employment should not be completed until the plaintiff had notified the board that she would accept their offer. If such a condition were wholly unauthorized, then where the board did make the condition it would follow, not that the contract of employment was completed at the time the resolution was adopted, but that there was no employment, as it was wholly without the intent of the board at that time so to make it complete. We think the trial judge was in error as to his conclusion, and that the plaintiff, not having accepted the position offered to her within the time limited, was not entitled to the salary attached to the position.

The judgment is reversed.

Conrey, P. J., and Shaw, J., concurred.

[Civ. No. 2032. Second Appellate District.—July 24, 1916.]

In the Matter of the Application for the Disbarment of WILSON H. SOALE, an Attorney at Law.

Attorney at Law—Disbarment Proceeding—Violation of Confidence of Client—Sufficiency of Evidence.—In this proceeding for the disbarment of an attorney at law for violating his oath in certain transactions involving the property of a client, it is held that on the record the court was justified in determining that the accused violated such oath, that the client reposed confidence in him, and that he abused such confidence.

Id.—Judgment of Suspension—Time—Contingent upon Payment of Claim of Accuser.—A judgment suspending an attorney at law for one year "and thereafter until the claim of the accuser is fully paid," is warranted, if the amount is ascertained, but is too uncertain to be enforced, except as to the stated period of one year, where the corporate stock wrongfully purchased by the attorney with the money of his client is not shown to be wholly worthless, and the amount lost thereby is not determined.

Id.—Suspension of Attorney for Unlimited Period.—In a disbarment proceeding an attorney may be suspended for a period not necessarily limited as a fixed and determinate period of time, but for an uncertain time, subject to the right of the accused to relieve himself therefrom by making restitution of a stated amount of money which he had improperly obtained by means of his misconduct.

APPEAL from a judgment of the Superior Court of Los Angeles County disbarring an attorney at law from practice. Fred H. Taft, Judge.

The facts are stated in the opinion of the court.

Gray, Barker & Bowen, Wheaton A. Gray, and Bennett & Carey, for Appellant.

Schweitzer & Hutton, for Respondent.

CONREY, P. J.—The Los Angeles Bar Association filed in the superior court of Los Angeles County an accusation verified by the oath of one Grace A. Hilborn, charging that Wilson H. Soale had violated his oath as an attorney and counselor at law by the commission of certain acts therein described. An answer was filed denying the facts alleged as showing defendant's misconduct. After trial of the issues thus presented the court found that all of the allegations of the accusation are true, and it was ordered "that the accused, Wilson H. Soale, be deprived of the right to practice as an attorney at law in the state of California for one year from date hereof, and thereafter until the claim of the accuser, Grace A. Hilborn, against said accused is fully paid." From this judgment he appeals.

In September, 1909, and thereafter during the occurrence of the transactions involved in this case, Mr. Soale, as a member of the firm of Soale & Crump, was engaged in practice as an attorney and counselor at law in the city of Pasadena, California. At the beginning of these transactions the lady now known as Grace A. Hilborn was Grace Hilborn Jenkins, the wife of one Jenkins. In September, 1909, Mrs. Jenkins went into the office of Soale & Crump and entered into a discussion with Mr. Soale concerning her business affairs and her property. As a result of that discussion, as she was expecting to be absent from Los Angeles County for some time, Mrs. Jenkins executed to Mr. Soale and Mr. Crump, as copartners, a general power of attorney, which, among other things, authorized them to convey real property for her and in her name. According to her testimony this was done pursuant to a suggestion by Mr. Soale that she would do well to let them care for the property and look out for it for her. Acting under this employment and authority, an exchange of property was negotiated by which, in return for five acres of land owned by Mrs. Jenkins near Alhambra, she acquired one thousand dollars and a house and lot in Pasadena, which we will designate as the Summit Avenue property. The matters complained of in this proceeding relate to an additional transaction in which Mrs. Jenkins received four thousand shares of stock of a corporation called the Automatic Car Coupler Company, in exchange for the Summit Avenue property.

In January, 1910, Mrs. Jenkins consulted Mr. Soale about obtaining a divorce from her husband, and an agreement was made as to the amount of the fee to be paid to Soale & Crump for their services in that matter. Such is the effect of the testimony of Mrs. Jenkins. The complaint in the divorce action was not filed until some months after the first consultation, and it was during that interval that the transactions occurred which are the subject of the complaint herein.

The Automatic Car Coupler Company appears to have been incorporated in the early part of the year 1909, with a capital stock of fifty thousand shares of the par value of one dollar each. It was organized in Pasadena, and its principal business grew out of an automatic car coupler invention which was transferred to the corporation in return for certain shares of the stock. At the same time shares of treasury stock were sold at ten cents per share, and from time to time during the year 1909 the price was advanced by resolution of the directors of the corporation until they had raised it to par for sales by the company. Mr. Soale was one of the early stockholders. He owned four thousand shares of stock acquired at ten cents per share. Soale & Crump also owned one thousand shares of stock. The four thousand shares belonging to Mr. Soale are the same shares that were transferred to Mrs. Jenkins in exchange for the Summit Avenue property, and under the circumstances to which we shall refer. In November, 1909, Mr. Soale caused the four thousand shares to be transferred to his son-in-law, Lewis Sprague, and left the new certificate with Mrs. Sprague for her husband. Soale received no consideration for this transfer.

Dr. D. T. Bentley, a retired physician residing in Pasadena, was engaged in the real estate business. He was acquainted with Mr. Soale and occasionally consulted him in regard to legal matters. Mr. Soale informed him that Mrs. Jenkins wanted to trade her Summit Avenue property for stock. Thereupon Dr. Bentley called upon Mrs. Jenkins and entered into negotiations with her for the transfer of her property to Sprague in exchange for the four thousand shares which were represented as the property of Sprague. Thereupon Mrs. Jenkins called upon Mr. Soale and told him of Dr. Bentley's proposition, and that she had told Dr. Bentley that she would do just exactly as Mr. Soale said, and asked him if he knew anything about the automatic car coupler stock. Soale replied that he had stock in the company; that he was surprised that any stock had been offered for sale; that it was a splendid company, had five hundred dollars in the treasury, and that she would be very lucky to get it. He said: "I have stock in it myself, so I can watch and care for it for you just exactly and take care of it for you. You leave it to me." A few days later she called at the office and Mr. Soale told her that the deed was made out and ready for her to sign and the certificate of stock ordered. She signed the deed and he handed her the certificate. The terms of the transaction were that in exchange for the stock, received at a valuation of four thousand dollars, Mrs. Jenkins transferred the Summit Avenue property at a valuation of five thousand dollars, but subject to a two thousand dollar mortgage, and in addition thereto paid one thousand dollars. This one thousand dollars was paid by checks to the order of Sprague, indorsed by him, and the proceeds received by Soale. The only way in which Mr. Soale paid over the money to Sprague was by using it in payment of bills incurred for the support of Sprague and his family. It seems that Sprague had never been able to support his family, and that Mr. Soale was in the habit of contributing largely to the support of that family by paying its bills along with his own.

During these negotiations Mr. Soale stated to Mrs. Jenkins that he had been looking this thing up, and Lewis Sprague was a man about town who wanted a home and was willing to trade, but did not tell her, and she did not know until long afterward, that Sprague was Soale's son-in-law, or that any financial or business relations existed between Soale and Sprague. Immediately after the Summit Avenue property was conveyed to Sprague, Mr. Soale placed that property in the hands of real estate agents for sale. In placing the property with B. O. Kendall Company, as agents, he gave a price of five thousand dollars, and stated that "it is a snap and will not be on the market long until it is sold." The deed by which Mrs. Jenkins conveyed the Summit Avenue property to Lewis Sprague was executed on the second day of March, 1910, and recorded July 28, 1910. On the same day, and immediately following the record of that deed, there was recorded another conveyance executed July 26, 1910, whereby Lewis Sprague and his wife conveyed the same property to Wilson H. Soale. A few months later Mr. Soale conveyed the Summit Avenue property to a purchaser subject to the existing two thousand dollar mortgage, and received a further consideration of two thousand dollars. He testified that this two thousand dollars went to Sprague, his son-in-law; but he further stated that this was done by paying bills amounting to two thousand dollars and a great deal more for the sustenance of his son-in-law and his family. They were paid with Soale's checks. "That is the way the business was carried on most of the time they were married. I was disbursing agent for the whole family and they brought the bills to me.''

Dr. Bentley claimed a commission for negotiating the trade in which he acted as agent. When Mrs. Jenkins informed Mr. Soale that Bentley wanted to charge her a commission, Mr. Soale said: "Never mind; you leave it all to me. I will see Bentley and see what can be done. You leave it all for me." Later he told her that he had managed to get Dr. Bentley down to $50, and she paid that amount through Soale to Bentley. Soale paid Bentley an additional sum of $150 out of the one thousand dollars obtained from Mrs. Jenkins in the trade, but did not inform Mrs. Jenkins, and she did not know that anything was being paid to Bentley other that the $50 paid as above stated.

Many of the facts given in the foregoing statement were denied by appellant in his testimony, but are supported by other evidence. We give them as the facts in the case because the court found that all of the allegations stated in the accusation are true, and it is necessarily implied that the court found these facts in accordance with the testimony of the accusing witness and against the testimony of appellant. Under the well-established rule, a court of appeal must assume the facts to be as found by the trial court when those facts find support in the evidence, notwithstanding other evidence to the contrary.

Aside from their contention that some of the facts above stated are not supported by the evidence, counsel for appellant insist that there is no evidence to support the implied finding that the shares of stock transferred to Mrs. Jenkins were not substantially worth four thousand dollars, or one dollar per share, as they were assumed to be in making the exchange. They further contend that, even if appellant defrauded Mrs. Jenkins in the transaction, he was not in that transaction acting as an attorney at law, and could not be said to have violated his oath and duty as an attorney at law by anything that he did therein. Finally they say that the court exceeded its authority in rendering the judgment, which not only ordered that the accused be deprived of the right to practice as an attorney at law in the state of California for one year from the date thereof, but further deprived him of that right "until the claim of the accuser, Grace A. Hilborn, against said accused is fully paid."

Aside from the patent rights transferred to it and possibly a small sum of money in the treasury, the only asset of the Automatic Car Coupler Company in March, 1910, seems to have been a certain contract dated November 1, 1909, made between that corporation and the Electric Traction Supply Company, a Missouri corporation, by which the latter company was given the exclusive right to manufacture and sell the said patented automatic couplings within the United States of America. Certain obligations were entered into by the Missouri company for the payment of royalties, and a minimum amount was named for a series of years commencing with the year beginning November 1, 1910. It was not shown that any business has ever been transacted under that contract or any income received therefrom. Prior to March, 1910, the Automatic Car Coupler Company had manufactured a limited number of car couplers, which had been given or loaned to certain railway corporations, evidently for advertising purposes. It is stated in the testimony of Mrs. Jenkins that when she consulted Mr. Soale about the proposed exchange involved in this case, he said that the Automatic Car Coupler Company stock was well worth a dollar per share, and perhaps more. He also told her of the contract with the Electric Traction Supply Company, and said that on account of this contract the stock would be as good as six per cent from the 1st of November, 1910; but he also gave her a copy of the contract and she took it away with her. On behalf of the accuser only one witness was questioned about the value of the Automatic Car Coupler Company's stock, and he did not claim to know anything about its value. Over defendant's objection this witness, J. W. Dubbs, was permitted to say that when he bought stock in the company about one year before March, 1910, he bought it from the company and paid ten cents a share. At the close of the case for the prosecution, defendant's counsel moved for a nonsuit, but as it was in general terms and did not specify any particular defect in the evidence, that motion should be disregarded. (*Coffey v. Greenfield*, 62 Cal. 602, 608; *Schroeder v. Mauzy*, 16 Cal. App. 443, 450, [118 Pac. 459].) The defendant introduced much evidence to support his claim that the market value of stock in this company was equal to or in excess of the par value, and it is our duty to consider all of the evidence and determine whether as a whole the evidence is sufficient to sus-

tain the implied finding against defendant on this branch of
the case; for notwithstanding testimony to the contrary, the
finding must be sustained if the record contains evidence
which by itself would be sufficient to support such finding.
We will refer to defendant's witnesses in the order of the
references to their testimony in the brief of his counsel. Karl
Elliott was the secretary of the corporation. He knew of
sales made early in 1910 at one dollar per share, and one
sale at one dollar and twenty-five cents per share. The first
stock sold by the company was at ten cents a share, the next
price was twenty-five cents a share, next fifty cents a share,
and late in 1909, eighty cents a share. After that the asked
price was one dollar, but no sales made by the company at
that price.

Frank R. Bonny was president of the corporation. His
regular occupation was that of a conductor in the freight department of an electric railroad. He said that he knew the
value of the Automatic stock in March, 1910, and that it was
one dollar and twelve and one-half cents per share. He sold
two hundred shares of his stock at that time and at that price.
It was much sought after, and still worth one dollar per share
even down to the date of the trial in April, 1913. He knew
of other sales as follows: one thousand shares sold in August,
1909, by the corporation, at eighty cents; four hundred shares
sold in August, 1909, by the corporation, at eighty cents; two
hundred shares sold in December, 1909, at one dollar, by the
witness to Mr. Heiss; five hundred shares sold by the witness
in November, 1909, at one dollar per share; two hundred and
fifty shares bought by the witness July 15, 1910, at one dollar and twenty-five cents per share; three thousand eight hundred shares bought July 1, 1910, by Mr. Goode, at one dollar
per share; three thousand four hundred shares bought in
March, 1911, by Mr. Goode at one dollar per share. The
principal part of Mr. Bonny's stock consisted of ten thousand
shares issued to him by the company in return for the patent
rights which he transferred to it in March, 1909. He had
a few other small transactions in the stock besides those above
noted. The following occurred on his cross-examination: "Q.
Did you ever place any of this on the public market for sale?
A. No, sir. Q. Do you know whether any of it ever was
placed on the market for sale? A. I don't know. Q. All
the sales were among your own people and your associates,

were they not? A. It was. Q. Officers of the corporation
and their associates; all of it was made that way? A. Yes.''

E. S. Goode became a stockholder in this corporation in
April, 1910, when he purchased between eleven thousand and
twelve thousand shares at one dollar per share. While he
asserted that he would not now take less than that amount
for his stock, he did not claim that he knew at any time what
the stock was worth in the market. On cross-examination
this witness admitted that after purchasing the stock in question he made an assignment for the benefit of his creditors
and did not list this property as part of his assets. ''I bought
the stock in my name and transferred it to my wife and
nephew, except fifty shares stood in my name. . . . I was trying to buy a controlling interest in the company. Would do
it to-day if I could get it.''

The defendant, Wilson H. Soale, testifying about the stock
transferred to Mrs. Jenkins, was asked: ''Is that stock worth
any money now?'' to which he replied: ''Certainly; it is
worth more than it was traded for.'' C. M. Gruell, a shipping
clerk, testified that the stock was quoted at from one dollar
to one dollar and thirteen cents in the early part of 1910.
Cross-examination developed that he had very little actual
knowledge of the subject. C. H. Wills testified that the
market value of the stock in the early part of 1910 was eighty
cents per share. He had bought some of the stock from the
company when it was ten cents per share, and later sold
some to Mr. Bonny at one dollar per share. F. H. Norwood,
the original patentee of the automatic car coupler, testified
that the value of the stock in March, 1910, was eighty cents
per share; that shortly before that time he sold some stock
to Mr. Bonny at one dollar per share. Norwood also testified
that he received ten thousand shares of the stock in consideration of the transfer of his patent rights to the company.
Whether he and Bonny received ten thousand shares each
for the transfer of separate patents, or received that number
of shares jointly for a joint transfer of patents, does not
clearly appear. Frank L. Heiss, clothing merchant, testified
that the value of this stock on the market in February and
March, 1910, was one dollar per share. He bought his stock
from Bonny at that price and knew of other sales at the same
price.

On this record was the court justified in determining that
the accused violated his oath and his duties as an attorney
and counselor at law? One of the stipulations in the statutory
oath is that the person admitted will faithfully discharge the
duties of an attorney and counselor at law to the best of his
knowledge and ability. One of these duties requires the attorney and counselor "to maintain inviolate the confidence
... of his client." (Code Civ. Proc., sec. 282, subd. 5.) In
order to support the charges here, it must have appeared that
Mrs. Jenkins was Mr. Soale's client, that she reposed confidence in him as a counselor at law, and that he violated that
confidence. On behalf of the accused it is contended that in
connection with the exchange of Mrs. Jenkins' Summit Avenue
property for corporation stock, he was not acting in his capacity as an attorney, "because in its nature the act complained
of was a personal business transaction requiring no skill of
attorney and no knowledge or understanding of law." The
causes for which an attorney may be removed or suspended
are stated in section 287 of the Code of Civil Procedure. Under that section as amended in 1911 this defense could not be
maintained; but if the nature of the facts is such as claimed
by the accused, that would be a good defense against charges
based, as these are, upon transactions occurring in the year
1910. Thus, in the case of *In re Collins,* 147 Cal. 8, 12, [81
Pac. 220], where it clearly appeared that the acts complained
of were not done by the respondent in his professional capacity
or in connection with any matters in which his duties as
an attorney were involved, it was held that "to the extent
that an attorney may be disbarred for causes which affect
his moral integrity in dealings with others of a purely personal character, and transacted in his private capacity, the
statute has provided that it shall be done by the court only
when he has been convicted of a felony, or of a misdemeanor
involving moral turpitude." It is our opinion, however, that
in these transactions Mrs. Jenkins reposed confidence in Mr.
Soale as a counselor at law. The evidence does not indicate
that he was engaged in business as an agent or broker or
maintained his office for any purpose other than in the course
of his profession as an attorney and counselor. She went
to him in that office and called upon him for advice and
assistance in the conduct of her business affairs, without any
notice or suggestion that in accepting the employment he was

representing her in any way other than in his professional
capacity. The occupation of a lawyer is not confined to appearances for parties in actions in courts of justice. A very
large part of the professional work done by them consists in
advice given to clients for the general purpose of aiding
them in the conduct of their business affairs. At the time
of these transactions Mrs. Jenkins was consulting Mr. Soale
concerning a proposed action at law, and it appears that she
consulted him about her other business affairs indiscriminately and without any attempted classification of the transactions as being partly within and partly without the scope
of his professional business. She was entitled to believe that
she was under his care as a counselor employed by her. The
fact that in this particular transaction he did not enter any
fee charges against her does not change the situation at all,
for he was entitled to charge such fees if he so desired. We
conclude, therefore, that she did repose confidence in him as
her counselor at law, and the only remaining question is as
to whether or not he maintained inviolate that confidence.
The phrase, "maintain inviolate the confidence," as contained
in section 282 of the Code of Civil Procedure, is not confined
merely to noncommunication of facts learned in the course
of professional employment; for the section separately imposes the duty to "preserve the secrets of his client."

Appellant contends that under the evidence in this case it
appears that he did not intend to wrong Mrs. Jenkins or to
defraud her in any way in the trade, and that even if false
representations and concealments occurred which are chargeable against him, no cause of action has been established,
since the stock was in fact worth the four thousand dollars
which it cost her. Some of the circumstances involved, to
which we have referred, tend to show that the accused secretly
treated as his own property which, by his advice and pursuant to a plan conceived by him, she was induced to transfer
to a third person without knowledge of the fact that in reality
her property was passing into appellant's hands. The court
was entitled to believe, and did believe, these to be the facts;
and this being so, the conclusion is clearly warranted that
he considered the transaction as one favorable to himself,
and to which he believed that she would not consent if she
had known his real interest therein. Under these circumstances, it should be determined that a lawyer is violating

the confidence of his client, even though in its ultimate result the transaction does not lead to a substantial financial loss on the part of the client. In order to sustain an accusation in a disbarment proceeding in a case of this character, it is not necessary to establish all of the facts with reference to the ultimate loss on the part of the client which might be necessary in an action brought by her against him for damages on account of the alleged deceit.

Our conclusions, as above stated, are sufficient to require us to sustain a judgment removing or suspending the accused from the right to practice his profession. We have to consider further only the claim that the court exceeded its authority by rendering an indefinite and uncertain judgment suspending the accused not only for one year from the date of the judgment, but also "thereafter until the claim of the accuser, Grace A. Hilborn, against said accused is fully paid." The court found that all of the allegations of the accusation are true. One of those allegations was that the four thousand shares of stock were worthless. It was also alleged, and the evidence shows without question, that the value parted with by the accuser amounted to four thousand dollars. It was held by the supreme court of California in the only decision which covers the question that in a disbarment proceeding the accused might be suspended for a period not necessarily limited as a fixed and determinate period of time, but could be for an uncertain time, subject to the right of the accused to relieve himself therefrom by making restitution of a stated amount of money which he had improperly obtained by means of his professional misconduct. (*In re Tyler*, 78 Cal. 307, [12 Am. St. Rep. 55, 20 Pac. 674].) In that case the record showed the amount as established by another judgment, and the judgment of suspension was not subject to attack by reason of any uncertainty in the amount which the accused was required to restore. Following that decision, we think the judgment in the case at bar should be sustained in the form in which it was entered, unless it requires to be modified on account of uncertainty in its statement of the amount of the claim of the accuser. If the evidence is sufficient to show that the stock was worthless, that amount would be four thousand dollars, with interest. The record herein shows that at some time the accuser obtained a judgment against Soale by reason of these same transactions, but that judgment

is not before the court and we do not know either its date
or the amount to be recovered as specified therein. We think
that the evidence in this case is insufficient to prove that the
stock was worthless. That being so, the amount of the claim
referred to in the judgment is not ascertained, and the above-
quoted final clause thereof is too uncertain to be capable of
enforcement.

It is ordered that the judgment herein be modified by striking therefrom the words, ''and thereafter until the claim of
the accuser, Grace A. Hilborn, against said accused is fully
paid.'' As thus modified the judgment is affirmed.

James, J., and Shaw, J., concurred.

─────────

[Civ. No. 1482. Third Appellate District.—July 26, 1916.]

S. E. SLADE LUMBER COMPANY (a Corporation), Respondent, v. OSCOE E. DERBY et al., Appellants.

FRAUD—TRANSFER OF CORPORATE STOCK—INTENT TO DEFRAUD CREDITORS
—SUPPORT OF FINDING.—In an action by a judgment creditor to
have a transfer of corporate stock made by a husband to his wife
declared void on the ground that the transfer was made without
consideration and at a time when the defendant was indebted to the
plaintiff and to others in a large amount, a finding that the gift was
made with intent to delay and defraud creditors is supported by
evidence that the defendant owned one-third of the stock of the
corporation, that the year before the transfer the corporation lost
one-third of the amount for which it was capitalized, and that the
defendant, fully aware of the financial condition of the corporation, a few months before the transfer offered to plaintiff all his
stock if plaintiff would assume his liabilities thereon.

ID.—TRANSFER WITH INTENT TO DEFRAUD—INSOLVENCY IMMATERIAL.—
A solvent person may transfer property with intent to hinder his
creditors, as well as one who is insolvent.

ID.—EVIDENCE OF FRAUD.—The question whether a conveyance is in fraud
of the rights of a creditor is one of fact, and it can only be inferred
in most cases from all the attending facts and circumstances.

ID.—JUDGMENT AND EXECUTION—ADMISSION IN EVIDENCE.—In an action
by a judgment creditor to set aside a transfer on the ground of
fraud, it is not error to admit in evidence the judgment, and writs
of execution in the action in which the judgment was obtained, as it

is necessary to enable such a creditor to maintain the action for
him to show that he was a judgment creditor and that he had exhausted his legal remedies to obtain satisfaction of the judgment.

Id.—Admission of Evidence—Liberal Rule.—In an action to set aside
transfers on the ground of fraud, great latitude should be allowed
in the admission of circumstantial evidence, and objections to questions on the ground of irrelevancy are not favored.

APPEAL from a judgment of the Superior Court of Alameda County, and from an order denying a new trial. William H. Waste, Judge.

The facts are stated in the opinion of the court.

Oliver Ellsworth, and Snook & Church, for Appellants.

Corbett & Selby, and Fitzgerald, Abbott & Beardsley, for
Respondent.

ELLISON, J., *pro tem.*—The plaintiff, as a judgment creditor of the defendant, Oscoe E. Derby, brought this suit in
equity to have declared void a transfer of 99 shares of the
capital stock of the Derby Estate Company (a corporation),
made by said Oscoe E. Derby to his wife, the defendant Mary
L. Derby. As grounds for the relief asked the plaintiff
alleged that said transfer was made without consideration,
at a time when the defendant Oscoe was indebted to the plaintiff in a large amount, and to others; that the gift of the
shares of stock in said corporation was made by said defendant
Oscoe to his wife for the purpose of and with the intent to
hinder and defraud his creditors and particularly this plaintiff, in contemplation of insolvency and while the said defendant was insolvent. The findings of the trial court were in
accordance with the allegations of the complaint, and a decree
was given and made declaring said transfer to be void as to
the plaintiff creditor, and said 99 shares of the capital stock
of the Derby Estate Company subject to the payment of the
plaintiff's judgment. The appeal is from the judgment and
also from an order denying a motion for a new trial. For
brevity, the defendant Oscoe E. Derby will be referred to
as the defendant.

The principal point relied upon by appellants for a reversal
is the claim made that the findings of the court are not supported by the evidence. The record is quite large, and it is

impossible, in an opinion of reasonable length, to review all the testimony. The following salient facts may be stated in narrative form and give a general impression of the situation: In the year 1883 one E. M. Derby, the father of the defendant, died. After the settlement of his estate in the probate court, and in the year 1890, his heirs formed the corporation, Derby Estate Company, to take over and manage all the property of the estate of E. M. Derby except his interest in the lumber business. To it was transferred all the estate property with the above exception, and the stock of the corporation, six hundred shares, was issued as follows: three hundred shares to Nancy M. Derby, widow of the deceased; one hundred shares to the defendant, a son of the deceased; one hundred shares to Augustus B. Derby, a son of deceased; ninety-five shares to Lizzie D. Harmon, a daughter of deceased, and five shares to her husband, A. K. P. Harmon.

At the time of his death E. M. Derby was engaged in the lumber business with one G. H. Payne, and the business was conducted after his death by his family and said Payne, until December 13, 1891, at which time the E. M. Derby & Co. corporation was formed and all the property and assets connected with the lumber business transferred to it. The six hundred shares capital stock of the last-named corporation were issued to the following persons: two hundred shares to O. E. Derby; 201 shares to A. B. Derby; 197 shares to George H. Payne; one share to Nancy M. Derby and one share to Lizzie D. Harmon, the stock having a par value of one hundred dollars per share and the capital stock being sixty thousand dollars. George H. Payne died at some date prior to January, 1909.

After the creation of the E. M. Derby & Co. corporation, it conducted a large lumber business in Alameda County. In the course of its business it bought much lumber from the plaintiff and from E. J. Dodge Co., a corporation. The purchases from the plaintiff from January 25, 1907, to January 13, 1909, amounted to $96,196.02, and during the same period payments were made from time to time which left a balance due the plaintiff on the last-named date of about seventy-two thousand dollars, and after that date lumber was sold by the plaintiff to said corporation amounting to $10,689.09. The

defendant was legally liable as a stockholder for the payment
of one-third of this indebtedness. He testified that he was
aware of his stockholder's liability. The witness, George
T. Klink, an accountant appointed by the court to investigate
the condition of E. M. Derby & Co.'s affairs, presented an
itemized statement which showed that the corporation in its
business transactions had been losing, recently, large sums
of money. His report showed that during the year 1908 there
was an actual loss of at least as much as twenty-two thousand
dollars, and in addition to this there was written off the books,
uncollectible notes, $10,914.79, and fourteen thousand dollars
of accounts deemed worthless. These notes and accounts
were the accumulations of several years. The result of this
witness' investigations was that, on January 13, 1909, the
E. M. Derby & Co. corporation had assets of the total value
of $187,781.76 and liabilities amounting to $177,598.76, leaving a book excess of assets of only about eleven thousand
dollars. Counsel, in trying to show on the one side that the
corporation was solvent and on the other that it was insolvent, have presented other figures which it would be necessary
to consider if we were at this point endeavoring to show
solvency or insolvency. But as, for present purposes, we
are only presenting figures to show that the corporation had
a large indebtedness as compared with its assets, the above
figures are sufficient for the purpose.

On January 13, 1909, the defendant made a gift to his wife,
the other defendant, of his 99 shares of the corporate stock of
the Derby Estate Company, being the shares of stock involved
in this litigation. The evidence shows it had a value of about
twenty-five thousand dollars. Prior to that time, and on the
sixteenth day of November, 1908, the defendant gave to
plaintiff a written option by which he offered to transfer to
plaintiff all his stock in the E. M. Derby & Co. corporation
in consideration that plaintiff would assume all of his liabilities entailed by the stock—"The idea of the above proposition being that myself and brother will be willing to release
all claims to our holdings in E. M. Derby & Co. if you will
assume all liabilities thereof." On May 24, 1909, the defendant transferred all his stock in the E. M. Derby & Co. to Miss
G. V. Rose, a stenographer in the office of his attorney. This
transfer was made without consideration—a gift.

January 15, 1909, the defendant deeded to his mother real estate worth eight thousand dollars, and she, on the same day, conveyed it to the Derby Estate Company. By these two deeds and the previous transfer of defendant's stock in the Derby Estate Company to his wife she got the full benefit of the transfer of the real estate.

August 11, 1909, the E. M. Derby & Co. transferred all its real and personal property to J. F. Carlston and Oliver Ellsworth, in trust for its creditors. September 8, 1909, all the real estate of E. M. Derby & Co. and of the defendant was attached on claims held by Central Bank and Rogers, amounting to fifty-five thousand dollars, and sold under execution. The defendant, in addition to his stockholder's liability in E. M. Derby & Co. had indorsed notes for said company amounting to fifty-five thousand dollars, and was individually liable thereon. He also owed his sister, Mrs. Harmon, twelve thousand dollars, secured by mortgage on certain real estate. He also owed one-third of an indebtedness of the E. M. Derby Co. to E. J. Dodge Co. of $10,770.40, his proportion thereof being $3,569.12. After the transfer of all of the assets of the E. M. Derby & Co. to J. F. Carlston and Oliver Ellsworth, trustees in trust for the creditors of the corporation made, as above stated, on August 11, 1909, the plaintiff received from said trustees different sums of money which were credited on the indebtedness of E. M. Derby & Co. to it. These payments, together with other money secured between January 13, 1909, and August 11, 1909, reduced the indebtedness of E. M. Derby & Co. to the plaintiff to $36,187.21. On April 13, 1910, the plaintiff brought an action against the defendant to recover, upon his stockholder's liability, his proportion of the above indebtedness, and, on July 29, 1910, secured a judgment therein against the defendant for the sum of $12,358.40. On May 10, 1910, the plaintiff having obtained an assignment to it of the claim of E. J. Dodge Co. against E. M. Derby & Co., brought an action against the defendant to recover judgment against him for his proportion thereof as a stockholder, and, on July 29, 1910, recovered a judgment against him for $3,671.09. Upon these two judgments last mentioned the plaintiff brings this suit as a judgment creditor to set aside the transfer of the 99 shares of stock of E. M. Derby Estate Company by defendant to his wife. The figures here-

inbefore given may not in all cases be wholly accurate but they
are sufficiently accurate for present purposes.

The foregoing statement does not contain a recital of all
the facts proved tending to support plaintiff's case. In fair-
ness to the defendant, it should be stated that on the trial
he gave more or less plausible reasons and explanations for
the various transfers of property made by him, but the trial
judge was at liberty not to accept them at their face value,
and evidently did not.

We think this bare recital of the history of events, with
the inferences that may legitimately and properly be drawn
therefrom, show that the court had ample justification for its
finding that the gift of the 99 shares of stock was made with
intent to hinder and delay the creditors of defendant in collecting their debts. In fact, it is difficult to see what other
conclusion could properly be reached.

The defendant owned one-third of the stock of a corporation engaged in the active business of buying and selling
lumber. It was losing money rapidly, the year before the
stock was transferred to his wife having lost twenty thousand
dollars, or one-third of the amount for which it was capitalized. The defendant was fully aware of the condition of the
company. It was, as counsel express it, a "sinking ship,"
and defendant fully realized and appreciated the situation—
so much so that, in November, 1908, he offered, in connection
with his brother, to transfer to the plaintiff all his stock in
the corporation if plaintiff would assume all of his liabilities
entailed by the stock. One witness testified that, in addition
to the transfer of all his stock to get released from his stockholder's liability, the defendant and his brother also offered
to transfer to plaintiff their personal real estate holdings,
valued at thirty-eight thousand dollars. This was denied by
defendant but, for aught we know, the court may have believed the witness. This conduct shows exactly what the
defendant believed to be the condition of the company, and
gives an insight, and a clear one, into his state of mind and
desires. Not having made the suggested deal with the plaintiff, in January, 1909, he gave to his wife the stock in dispute.
Next he deeded to his mother certain real estate without consideration, and next made a stenographer in the office of his
attorney a present of all of his stock in the E. M. Derby &
Co.; and all these things were being done when he was largely

indebted as herein indicated.   But one inference can be properly drawn from this conduct.

We deem it unnecessary to go into a close mathematical calculation to figure out on a close margin whether the defendant at the time of the transfer might have had a small excess of assets above his liabilities.   A solvent person may transfer property with intent to hinder his creditors, as well as one who is insolvent.   "It is obvious, therefore, that the question upon which the case must turn is whether the conveyance is in fraud of the rights of the plaintiff as a creditor. This, under our statute, is a question of fact (Civ. Code, sec. 3442), that is to say, a question of intent."   (*Knox* v. *Blanckenburg*, 28 Cal. App. 301, [152 Pac. 62].)   It is not often that direct proof of fraud can be obtained.   People do not in such cases proclaim their intent.   It can only be inferred in most cases from all the attending facts, circumstances, and conditions and by ascribing to the conduct of people those motives which would ordinarily be the motives of others doing like things under like circumstances.

Appellant assigns as error the admission in evidence of judgment, writs, and execution in the suit brought by plaintiff to obtain the judgment, the foundation of the suit.   To enable the plaintiff to maintain this suit it was necessary for him to show that he was a judgment creditor and that he had exhausted his legal remedies to obtain satisfaction of his judgment.   Some other objections are raised as to the admission of testimony, but as most of them had a bearing upon the question of insolvency, they need not be further considered.   In this class of cases a wide latitude is permissible.   "In litigations of the class under consideration, great latitude should undoubtedly be allowed in regard to the admission of circumstantial evidence for the purpose of proving participation in manifest fraud.   Objections to testimony as irrelevant are not favored in such cases, since the force of circumstances depends so much upon their number and connection.   The evidence should be permitted to take a wide range, as in most cases fraud is predicated on circumstances, and not upon direct proof."   (*Bush & Mallett Co.* v. *Helbing*, 134 Cal. 676, [66 Pac. 967].)

We are of the opinion that the finding of the court that said 99 shares of stock were transferred by the defendant to his wife in fraud of the rights of his creditors, and especially of the plaintiff, is sustained by the evidence.   Finding no reversible error, the judgment and order are affirmed.

Chipman, P. J., and Hart, J., concurred.

A petition to have the cause heard in the supreme court, after judgment in the district court of appeal, was denied by the supreme court on September 21, 1916.

[Civ. No. 1540.   Third Appellate District.—July 26, 1916.]

G. W. WIGLEY, Petitioner, v. SOUTH SAN JOAQUIN IRRIGATION DISTRICT et al., Respondents.

PUBLIC OFFICERS — RECALL — IRRIGATION DISTRICT OFFICERS — ACT OF 1911—CONSTITUTIONALITY OF.—The act of 1911 providing that the holder of any elective office of any irrigation district may be removed or recalled at any time by the electors does not violate section 18 of article IV or section 1 of article XXIII of the constitution, and is valid.

ID.—POWER OF LEGISLATURE—CONSTRUCTION OF SECTION 18, ARTICLE IV, AND SECTION 1, ARTICLE XXIII, OF CONSTITUTION.—Prior to the adoption of the constitutional provisions upon the subject, the legislature had the power, under its general legislative authority, to pass acts for the recall of public officers; and neither section 18 of article IV nor section 1 of article XXIII of the constitution can be construed to have taken that power from it.

ID.—CONSTRUCTION OF CONSTITUTION — RESTRICTION OF LEGISLATIVE POWERS.—The constitution of this state is not to be considered as a grant of power, but rather as a restriction upon the powers of the legislature, and it is competent for the legislature to exercise all powers not forbidden by the constitution of the state, or delegated to the general government, or prohibited by the constitution of the United States.

APPLICATION originally made to the District Court of Appeal for the Third Appellate District for a Writ of Mandate against the Board of Directors of South San Joaquin Irrigation District, commanding it to call an election for the recall of one of its members.

The facts are stated in the opinion of the court.

Clary & Louttit, for Petitioner.

L. L. Dennitt, for Respondents.

ELLISON, J., *pro tem.*—This is an application for a writ
of mandate to the board of directors of the South San Joaquin
Irrigation District, commanding it to call an election for the
recall of one of its members.

The application for the writ shows that the recall petition
presented to said board conformed in all respects to the provisions of an act of the legislature as found in the statutes
of the extra session of 1911, at page 135. This act provides:
"The holder of any elective office of any irrigation district
may be removed or recalled at any time by the electors."

Counsel for the board of directors take the position that
the legislature, in passing the above act and extending the
recall to officers of an irrigation district, acted in violation
of certain provisions of the state constitution and exceeded
its powers. This conclusion is attempted to be sustained by
a reference to section 18 of article IV of the constitution,
and to section 1 of article XXIII. Section 18 provides for
the removal of certain officers, such as governor, judges, etc.,
by impeachment, and concludes with this sentence: "All other
civil officers shall be tried for misdemeanor in office in such
manner as the legislature may provide," and section 1 of
article XXIII provides for the recall of certain specified
officers, viz., for the recall of elective officers of counties,
cities and counties, and cities and towns of the state, but does
not in express terms provide for the recall of district officers.
Considering these two sections of the constitution, counsel's
position may be stated as follows: Since the constitution does
not provide for the recall of district officers but does provide
that they may be removed from office after a trial and conviction of misdemeanor in office, it follows that the latter
provision is exclusive, and the legislature has no power to
pass any act for their removal other than an act to provide
for their removal for cause. The argument challenges the
power of the state legislature to pass the act of 1911. It must
be considered, however, that, in the absence of section 1,
article XXIII, of the state constitution, the legislature would

have plenary power to pass laws providing for the recall of public officers. This results from the nature and form of our state government. As was said in *Sheehan* v. *Scott*, 145 Cal. 684, [79 Pac. 350]: "The express declaration in section 1, article IV, of the constitution of this state, that 'The legislative power of the state shall be vested in a Senate and Assembly,' includes all the legislative power of the state whose exercise is not expressly prohibited to the legislature, or conferred upon some other body. In the face of this declaration there can be no implication of the absence or nonexistence of such power, but whoever would claim that the power does not exist in any particular case, or has been improperly exercised, must point out the provision of the constitution which has taken it away or forbidden its exercise. 'The constitution of this state is not to be considered as a grant of power but rather as a restriction upon the powers of the legislature, and it is competent for the legislature to exercise all powers not forbidden by the constitution of the state, or delegated to the general government, or prohibited by the constitution of the United States.' (*People* v. *Coleman*, 4 Cal. 46, [60 Am. Dec. 581].)"

Prior to the enactment of section 1, article XXIII, of the constitution, it was conceded, if not directly decided, that the legislature had the power to pass acts for the recall of public officers. Thus, in *Conn* v. *City Council*, 17 Cal. App. 717, [121 Pac. 719], the record in that case disclosed that the charter of the city of Richmond was adopted at a time when there were no recall provisions in the state constitution. The charter expressly provided for the recall of all elective city officers. It was held in that case that the charter provision as to recall of the elective officers of the city was valid, and within the power of the people of the city to make and within the power of the legislature to approve. The charter, when approved by the legislature, became a law of the state in the same sense that the act of 1911 is a law of the state. We have here, then, a decision holding that the legislature did not need any constitutional grant to give it power to pass an act for the recall of public officers.

2. In the same case it was said: "Manifestly the tenure of office, and the method of removing an elected city official, are purely municipal affairs, which in no sense conflict with the constitutional provisions relating to the tenure of office

or the removal by impeachment of state officers. Similar recall provisions, as applied to administrative officers, have been upheld and declared not to be in conflict with either state or federal constitution in other jurisdictions, where the points of attack were identical with the arguments advanced here."

In *Good* v. *Common Council*, 5 Cal. App. 269, [90 Pac. 46], it is said: "A case of 'removal for just cause' in this sense implies some misconduct upon the part of the officer, or imputes to him some violation of the law. Under such circumstances it is necessary that the charges against him shall be based upon some refusal to obey or intention to violate the law prescribing his duties. There are often such penalties attached to proceedings for the removal of officers 'for cause shown' that they are and should be carefully guarded from abuse (*Croly* v. *Sacramento*, 119 Cal. 234, [51 Pac. 323]); but as to the right to the office as against the people, it is a well-recognized rule that the agency may be terminated at any time by the sovereign power without reason given. (*Matter of Carter*, 141 Cal. 319, [74 Pac. 997].)"

We conclude that section 18 of article IV, providing that officers may be tried for misdemeanors in office in such manner as the legislature may prescribe, does not deprive the legislature of power to provide for the recall of public officers by the electorate.

3. As section 1 of article XXIII of the constitution is not, nor was it intended to be, a *grant* of power to the legislature, so it will not be held to take from the legislature the power it already had to pass acts for the removal of public officers, unless such intent clearly appears and is the reasonable conclusion to be drawn from the language used. It contains no language prohibiting the legislature from passing such acts. "There can be no implication of the nonexistence of such power, but whoever would claim that the power does not exist in any particular case, must point out the provision of the constitution which has taken it away or forbidden its exercise." (*Sheehan* v. *Scott*, 145 Cal. 686, [79 Pac. 351].)

Our conclusion is that the act of 1911 is not in conflict with any constitutional provision, and is a valid exercise of legislative power. The demurrer to the petition for a writ of mandate is overruled. Let a writ of mandate issue directed to the board of trustees of the South San Joaquin Irrigation

District, commanding it to call the election asked for in the
recall petition on file with it.

Chipman, P. J., and Hart, J., concurred.

A petition to have the cause heard in the supreme court,
after judgment in the district court of appeal, was denied
by the supreme court on September 21, 1916.

[Crim. No. 497. Second Appellate District.—July 27, 1916.]

THE PEOPLE, Respondent, v. JACK LETOILE, Appellant.

CRIMINAL LAW—INCEST—ACCOMPLICE—LACK OF CORROBORATION—EVI-
    DENCE — IMPROPER ADMISSION OF. — In a prosecution for incest
    charged against a father and alleged to have been committed with
    his eldest daughter, a conviction cannot be sustained where the
    only corroboration of the prosecuting witness, who consented to
    the acts charged and was therefore an accomplice, was the testimony
    of the younger sister, admitted over the objection of the defense,
    who was called by the prosecution as a witness in rebuttal to testify
    as to trouble between herself and her father about the time of
    his arrest, and asked by the district attorney whether or not she
    had trouble with him with regard to his acts of sexual intimacy
    with her, which question was answered in the affirmative, as evi-
    dence of similar acts with a person other than the one named in
    the information in such a case is not admissible; nor was such
    evidence admissible as rebuttal testimony, on the theory that the
    defendant had opened the door for it by testifying that he had
    had trouble with his two daughters on the subject of their staying
    out late at night, the latter testimony having been adduced upon
    cross-examination and under adverse rulings upon his objections
    thereto, in which he stated that he had not had any trouble with his
    daughters.

ID.—TRIAL BEHIND CLOSED DOORS—VIOLATION OF CONSTITUTION.—While
    the court has the right to regulate the admission of the public to
    the courtroom in the trial of a criminal case in any appropriate
    manner in order to prevent overcrowding or disorder, the right does
    not exist to wholly exclude the public, as under article I, section 13,
    of the constitution of this state the party accused in a criminal
    prosecution is given the right to a public trial.

APPEAL from a judgment of the Superior Court of Los
Angeles County, and from an order denying a new trial.
Gavin W. Craig, Judge.

The facts are stated in the opinion of the court.

Guy Eddie, for Appellant.

U. S. Webb, Attorney-General, and Robert M. Clarke, Deputy Attorney-General, for Respondent.

CONREY, P. J.—Defendant was convicted and sentenced to imprisonment for the crime of incest committed with his eldest daughter. His appeal is from the judgment and from an order denying his motion for a new trial.

Testimony directly supporting the charge was given by the prosecuting witness, the daughter of the defendant. It was claimed by the defendant that according to her own testimony she had consented to the acts constituting the ground of complaint, and that she being therefore an accomplice, the conviction cannot be sustained without corroborative evidence tending to connect the defendant with the commission of the offense.

The only corroborative evidence found in the record is contained in the testimony of Mary Letoile, a sister of the prosecuting witness, Lucy Letoile, which testimony was admitted over objections thereto. This witness was called by the prosecution as a witness in rebuttal, and was questioned about trouble between herself and her father at about the time of his arrest. This question was asked by the district attorney: "About that time and for some time previous thereto, had you had trouble with him with regard to his acts of sexual intimacy with you?" After an objection had been made and overruled, she answered that question in the affirmative. Evidence was thus placed before the jury not only by the prosecuting witness that the defendant had committed the crime of incest with her, but also by the daughter Mary that defendant had committed a like crime with her. Unless this was corroboration of Lucy's testimony respecting the offense charged in this action, there is no corroboration in the record. The jury may have believed Lucy's testimony as to the defendant's acts, but that those acts were done with her consent and that she was an accomplice therein; and in that event their verdict was necessarily based also upon the testimony of Mary, which tended to show the defendant's disposition to commit that kind of a crime by showing that he had com-

mitted such a crime with a person other than the one named
in the information. The decisions in this state are uniform
to the effect that such evidence in prosecutions for crimes
of this class is not admissible. (*People* v. *Bowen*, 49 Cal. 654;
People v. *Stewart*, 85 Cal. 174, [24 Pac. 722]; *People* v.
Elliott, 119 Cal. 593, [51 Pac. 955].)

It is suggested, however, that the testimony was properly
admitted in rebuttal, in that the defendant had opened the
door therefor by testifying that he had had trouble with his
daughters Lucy and Mary because of their staying out late
at night against his wishes, and that that was the only trouble
he ever had with his daughters. Examination of the record
does not support this view of the defendant's testimony. In
order to show animus of the prosecuting witness against him,
the defendant testified that he had had trouble with Lucy,
and incidentally further testified that he had trouble with both
Lucy and Mary, on the subject of their staying out late at
night. It was only upon cross-examination and under adverse
rulings upon his objections thereto that the defendant stated
that he had not had any other trouble with his daughters.
As to the daughter Mary, this was immaterial to the case.
She had not been a witness and therefore had given no testimony for or against the defendant. In *People* v. *Turco*, 29
Cal. App. 608, [156 Pac. 1001], we had occasion to examine
the authorities bearing upon the limits of the right of cross-
examination of a defendant in a criminal case, and the limits
of the right to introduce rebuttal testimony based upon facts
elicited by such cross-examination. The principle was recognized that the people have the right on the cross-examination
of a defendant to draw out anything which will tend to contradict or modify his testimony given on his direct examination,
and that such testimony of the defendant may be met by
testimony in rebuttal. In the present case, however, we do
not think that the circumstances shown by the record are
such as to warrant the application of the rule stated. The
testimony of the witness Mary Letoile, to which we have referred, should have been excluded.

At the beginning of the trial in this case the court made
an order, which was thereafter enforced, requiring all persons
other than those directly connected with the trial to withdraw
from the courtroom, and tried the case "behind closed doors."

We do not doubt the right of the court to regulate the admission of the public to the courtroom in any appropriate manner in order to prevent overcrowding or disorder, but the right does not exist to wholly exclude the public. Under article I, section 13, of the constitution of this state, the party accused in a criminal prosecution is given the right to a public trial. Referring to a similar order made in *People* v. *Hartman*, 103 Cal. 242, [42 Am. St. Rep. 108, 37 Pac. 153], the supreme court said: "This was a novel procedure, and has no justification in the law of modern times. We know of no case decided in this country supporting the course of procedure here pursued. It is in direct violation of that provision of the constitution which says that a party accused of crime has a right to a public trial." No objection was made by or on behalf of the defendant to this course of procedure by the court, and the point is made for the first time on this appeal. In view of our conclusions upon the first question discussed herein, it seems unnecessary to base our decision upon the proposition that the defendant was deprived of his right to a public trial. (See, also, *People* v. *Swafford*, 65 Cal. 223, [3 Pac. 809], and the comment thereon in 103 Cal. 245, [42 Am. St. Rep. 108, 37 Pac. 153].)

The judgment and order are reversed.

James, J., and Shaw, J., concurred.

[Crim. No. 490. Second Appellate District.—July 27, 1916.]

THE PEOPLE, Respondent, v. TONY VISCONTI, Appellant.

CRIMINAL LAW—ASSAULT WITH DEADLY WEAPON WITH INTENT TO MUR-DER—DEFENSE OF ALIBI—INSTRUCTION.—In a prosecution for assault with a deadly weapon with intent to murder, where the evidence of the prosecution made out a *prima facie* case, and the defendant offered evidence in support of his claim of an alibi, it was error for the court to refuse to instruct the jury, upon defendant's request, that in making the proof of an alibi defendant was not obliged to establish that defense by a preponderance of evidence or beyond a reasonable doubt, but that it was sufficient to entitle him to a verdict of not guilty if the proof raised in the minds of

the jury a reasonable doubt as to the presence of the defendant
at the place where the crime was alleged to have been committed
and at the time referred to in the information; nor did the fact that
the court gave a general instruction to the effect that the jury
must believe beyond a reasonable doubt that the defendant committed the crime before they could convict him, relieve the failure
to give said instruction from prejudice.

APPEAL from a judgment of the Superior Court of Riverside County, and from an order denying a new trial.
Charles Munroe, Judge presiding.

The facts are stated in the opinion of the court.

Ford & Nelson, for Appellant.

U. S. Webb, Attorney-General, and Robert M. Clarke,
Deputy Attorney-General, for Respondent.

JAMES, J.—Defendant was charged with the crime of
assault with a deadly weapon with intent to murder. He was
found guilty as charged, and has taken an appeal from a judgment of imprisonment, as well as from an order denying his
motion for a new trial.

The complaining witness gave testimony identifying the
defendant as being the man who entered her house in the
night-time and who struck her with a gun after she had
attempted to shoot him. It appeared that the man with whom
the encounter was had entered the house of the prosecutrix
with burglarious intent. The prosecuting witness positively
identified defendant as being the perpetrator of the crime;
she testified that there was some light in the house—perhaps
a lantern—but she was not sure about that. The defendant
denied that he was the person who had assaulted the prosecutrix, and introduced his wife and another witness who
gave testimony in corroboration of his claim that he was not
at the house of the prosecutrix on the night charged, but was
at another place some distance away. In view of the testimony offered for the purpose of establishing an alibi, the
defendant asked the court to give an instruction by which
the jury was to be informed that in making the proof of an
alibi the defendant was not obliged to establish that defense
by a preponderance of evidence or beyond a reasonable doubt,
but that it was sufficient to entitle him to a verdict of not

guilty if the proof raised in the minds of the jury a reasonable
doubt as to the presence of the defendant at the place where
the crime was alleged to have been committed and at the
time referred to in the information.   The court refused to
give this instruction, or any instruction upon the matter of
the defense of an alibi.   It seems to be conceded, as it must,
that the instruction as proposed was pertinent and proper;
but the contention is made that inasmuch as the trial judge
did instruct the jury that they must believe beyond a reasonable doubt that defendant committed the crime, no prejudice
would arise by reason of the failure to instruct directly upon
the matter of the alibi proof.   The instruction of the court
which was given was general, and stated in substance that
before conviction could be had it was incumbent upon the
prosecution to prove beyond a reasonable doubt all of the matters alleged in the information.   We think that defendant was
entitled to have some particular and specific instruction given
touching the matter of his defense of an alibi.   It is said
in our decisions that the matter of alibi proof is not strictly
"a defense."   However, in the American & English Encyclo
pedia of Law, as cited in the case referred to below, this
expression is made: "The true doctrine seems to be that
where the state has established a *prima facie* case, and the
defendant relies upon the defense of alibi, the burden is upon
him to prove it, not beyond a reasonable doubt, nor by a
preponderance of the evidence, but by such evidence, and to
such a degree of certainty, as will, when the whole evidence
is considered, create and leave in the mind of the jury a reasonable doubt of the guilt of the accused."   (*People* v.
Winters, 125 Cal. 325, [57 Pac. 1067].)   It may well have
been that the testimony introduced by the prosecution did
make out to the minds of the jury and beyond a reasonable
doubt *prima facie* the guilt of the accused.   Yet if upon the
evidence offered by him tending to show that at the time
in question he was not at the place, nor where he could have
committed the crime, a reasonable doubt was created in the
minds of the jury, such doubt of course would avail the defendant and entitle him to an acquittal.   The quantity and
variety of evidence and the quality of proof which would be
sufficient to raise such doubt where an alibi was sought to be
proven are proper and pertinent subjects for an instruction
to the jury, and we think were within the right of defendant

to insist upon. There are no decisions in this state directly
upon the point presented, but in a similar state of the law
the Oklahoma court has decided in agreement with appellant's
contention. (*Courtney* v. *State*, 10 Okl. Cr. 589, [140 Pac.
163].) We are of opinion that the error in refusing to give
the offered instruction was prejudicial, and that defendant
is entitled to a new trial.

The judgment and order are reversed.

Conrey, P. J., and Shaw, J., concurred.

A petition to have the cause heard in the supreme court,
after judgment in the district court of appeal, was denied by
the supreme court on September 25, 1916, and the following
opinion then rendered thereon:

THE COURT.—The application for a hearing in this court
after decision by the district court of appeal of the second
appellate district is denied.

In denying the application we deem it proper to say that
we are not to be understood as intimating that the refusal
to give such an instruction as was refused in this case would
in all cases be deemed by us sufficient cause for reversal.
Especially is this true in view of the provisions of section 4½
of article VI of the constitution.

In denying the application for hearing in this court we
assume that the district court of appeal concluded, in view
of the circumstances of this particular case as shown by the
record, that the refusal of the trial court to permit the requested instruction operated substantially to the prejudice
of the defendant.

[Civ. No. 2078. Second Appellate District.—July 29, 1916.]

IVA L. GARRETT, Plaintiff, Cross-defendant and Appellant, v. WILLIAM EDWARD GARRETT, a Minor, Cross-defendant and Respondent; BANKERS LIFE COMPANY (a Corporation), Defendant and Cross-complainant.

APPEAL — MOTION TO DISMISS — INSUFFICIENT NOTICE OF MOTION.—A notice of motion to dismiss an appeal on the ground that the appellant had failed to furnish the requisite papers is insufficient where such notice fails to point out and designate the particular papers necessary to the consideration of the appeal which are claimed to have been omitted from the record.

ID.—LIFE INSURANCE LAW—CHANGE OF BENEFICIARY—CONSENT OF INSURER—VOID BY-LAW.—A by-law of a life insurance company providing that a change in the beneficiary named in the certificate of membership "shall not be binding until the consent of the association shall be indorsed on the said certificate of membership" must be disregarded as of no force or effect, where it is inconsistent with and restrictive of the right given by the laws of the state under which said company was created to an insured to change his beneficiary at pleasure.

ID.—FILING OF COPY OF INDORSEMENT CHANGING BENEFICIARY—PRESENTATION OF ORIGINAL—SUFFICIENT COMPLIANCE WITH BY-LAW.—A by-law of a life insurance company providing that a copy of the indorsement on the certificate of membership changing the beneficiary and signed by the member shall be filed with the company is sufficiently complied with where the original was presented to the company.

ID.—CHANGE OF BENEFICIARY—WHEN EFFECTED.—Where the holder of a life insurance certificate has the right to change the beneficiary named therein at his pleasure, and makes indorsement of the change upon his certificate in the manner and form required by a by-law of the company, and forwards the same to the company, which received it the day before his death, the change is effectually made, notwithstanding his death occurs before the change is indorsed by the company upon his certificate.

ID.—STAY OF EXECUTION—RUNNING OF PERIOD OF LIMITATION.—An order staying execution of a judgment made on the day a judgment is rendered runs from that date, and not from the date of the entry of the judgment.

ID.—REVERSAL OF JUDGMENT—RESTORATION OF AMOUNT.—A party obtaining through a judgment before reversal any advantage or benefit must restore the amount he got to the other party after the reversal.

APPEAL from a judgment of the Superior Court of Los Angeles County. Louis W. Myers, Judge.

The facts are stated in the opinion of the court.

Robert L. Hubbard, for Appellant.

Charles S. Peery, and William Ellis Lady, for Respondent.

SHAW, J.—This is a contest waged between the widow and minor son of Edward E. Garrett, deceased, each claiming certain money due as insurance upon his life, and which money the insurance company had paid into court to abide the result of the litigation.

The respondent William Edward Garrett, pursuant to notice thereof, presents a motion to dismiss the appeal. As grounds therefor the notice specifies the following: First, that the appellant has not perfected said appeal in the manner required by law and the rules of the above-entitled court; second, that appellant has not filed in the above-entitled court, within the time allowed by law or otherwise, or at all, the requisite papers on appeal from the judgment herein, from which said judgment said appellant has attempted to or has taken an appeal; third, that the pretended stipulation contained on page 82 of appellant's transcript was never signed by nor agreed to by the attorneys for cross-defendant and respondent William Edward Garrett, or either of them; fourth, for other and further reasons apparent upon the appellant's transcript of record.

Section 1010 of the Code of Civil Procedure provides that the notice of a motion must state the *grounds* upon which it will be made. Section 954 of the Code of Civil Procedure provides that, "If the appellant fails to furnish the requisite papers, the appeal *may* be dismissed." Respondent in his notice does not pretend to designate or point out what papers requisite to a consideration of the appeal are omitted from the record, and it is impossible to determine from the notice wherein appellant has failed to perfect her appeal, or wherein she has failed to file the requisite papers on appeal, or what further reasons *apparent* upon the record respondent refers to as grounds for the motion. The provision of the section last quoted is similar to that contained in section 556 of the Code of Civil Procedure, which provides that a writ of attach-

ment may be discharged when improperly or irregularly
issued. It has been held, however, that a notice to discharge
a writ of attachment "because the said writ was improperly
issued" is insufficient in failing to specify the particular
grounds therefor. Says Judge Field, in discussing the sufficiency of a notice of motion in the case of *Freeborn* v. *Glazer*,
10 Cal. 337: The provision that the attachment may be discharged on the ground that the writ was improperly issued,
"does not obviate the necessity of specifying the particular
points of irregularity upon which the motion will be made.
It is only a provision that whenever the writ is improperly
issued, that fact will authorize the application for its discharge. It is like a great variety of provisions indicating the
general ground or reason upon which parties may proceed,
or the action of the court may be based, and which are never
held to obviate the necessity of specifying the points of objection upon which the moving party will rely." To the same
effect is *Donnelly* v. *Strueven*, 63 Cal. 182, and *Loucks* v.
Edmondson, 18 Cal. 203. While these cases involved motions
for the discharge of writs of attachment upon the ground
that they were improperly and irregularly issued, the principle upon which they were decided is likewise applicable to
the provision contained in section 954, to the effect that an
appeal may be dismissed if appellant fails to furnish the
requisite papers. The notice of motion to dismiss should
point out and designate the particular papers claimed by respondent to have been omitted from the record. In our
opinion, the notice of the motion is insufficient under section
1010, *supra*, in that it fails to apprise appellant of the grounds
of the motion. It is true that the proposed stipulation as to
the correctness of the record was not signed by respondent's
attorneys; but, as appears from the record, it was certified
by the clerk.

Respondent insists that the notice of appeal was not properly served. As appears from the record, respondent's attorney resided in San Francisco and appellant's attorney in Los
Angeles. The notice of appeal was served by mail; and while
the transcript discloses the filing of the notice with the clerk,
it does not show service thereof. An affidavit presented, however, covers this omission by showing proper service by mail.
(*Estate of Stratton*, 112 Cal. 513, [44 Pac. 1028]; *Warren* v.
Hopkins, 110 Cal. 506, [42 Pac. 986].) There is no merit

in respondent's contention that Peery, his attorney, had associated with him W. E. Lady, an attorney in Los Angeles, upon whom the service of the notice of appeal should have been made. Lady, as shown by the record, appeared, not as attorney for respondent, who was represented by Charles S. Peery, but as attorney for the Bankers Life Company, and also in another suit wherein the minor son of deceased was contesting his will. This, however, did not constitute him attorney of record for respondent, and his acts, statements, and conduct, as shown by affidavits filed, were of a character well calculated to raise serious doubt in the mind of appellant as to his position in the case. Under these circumstances, and conceding that he did act with Peery, appellant very properly served the notice of appeal upon the latter, as to whom there was no question of his being attorney of record for respondent. Moreover, conceding Mr. Lady, who resided in Los Angeles, to be also an attorney of record for respondent, we find nothing in section 1012 of the Code of Civil Procedure prohibiting service by mail upon Mr. Peery. The service was equally effective made upon either attorney.

As appears from the findings made and undisputed facts alleged in the pleadings, the Bankers Life Company, a corporation having its principal place of business in Des Moines, Iowa, and created under the laws of that state as a life insurance company, did, in June, 1903, issue to Edward E. Garrett two certificates of membership in said Bankers Life Company, by each of which, upon the death of the assured, it agreed to pay to Emma L. Garrett, the then wife of said Edward E. Garrett and named in said certificates of membership as the beneficiary therein, the sum of two thousand dollars. Some time after the issuance of said certificates of membership, Edward E. Garrett and Emma L. Garrett, his wife, named as beneficiary therein, were divorced. Whereupon the insured, as he concededly had the right to do, changed the beneficiary named in said certificates, substituting for his divorced wife his son, William Edward Garrett, respondent herein. At a later date Edward E. Garrett married Iva L. Garrett, plaintiff herein, and thereafter, on March 10, 1914, he duly executed and indorsed upon each of said certificates of membership the following: "I, Edward E. Garrett, holder of the within certificates Nos. 130461-2, hereby revoke all directions by me heretofore made as to the disposition of the

benefit accruing thereunder, and now direct that said benefit
shall be paid to Iva L. Garrett, bearing to me the relation
of wife." The certificates so indorsed were duly forwarded
to the Bankers Life Company at Des Moines, Iowa, and received by said company on March 14, 1914, and on March 16,
1914, there was indorsed upon each of said certificates the
following, to wit: "Consented to and acknowledged March
16, 1914. Bankers Life Company, R. W. B." On March
15, 1914, after the receipt by said Bankers Life Company of
said certificates of membership, together with the indorsements made thereon by Edward E. Garrett, he died. As
found by the court, the law of Iowa touching the right of an
assured to change the beneficiary in such certificates is found
in section 1789 of the Iowa code, and is as follows: "The beneficiary named in the certificate may be changed at any time
at the pleasure of the assured, as may be provided for in the
articles or by-laws, but no certificate issued for the benefit
of a wife or children shall be thus changed so as to become
payable to the creditors." The court also found that by the
by-laws of the company it was provided that "Any member
may, with the consent of the association, make a change in
the beneficiary in his certificate without requiring the consent
of such beneficiary. The change proposed shall be indorsed
on the certificate of membership, and signed by the member,
and shall not be binding until the consent of the association
shall be indorsed on the said certificate of membership; a
copy of such indorsement signed by the member, and filed
with the association." Further findings are, that said Edward
E. Garrett did not at any time make or cause to be made
a copy of said proposed change of beneficiary, nor file with
the Bankers Life Company a copy of said proposed change
which was indorsed upon the certificates, and that the approval
of such proposed change by said Bankers Life Company was
made after the death of said Edward E. Garrett and in
ignorance of the death of said Edward E. Garrett; that pursuant to the order of court said Bankers Life Company paid
into court the sum of $4,074 for the benefit of the parties
entitled thereto. And as a conclusion of law found that
said attempted change of beneficiary was not completed and
the beneficiary named in said certificates was not changed
from said William Edward Garrett to the said Iva L. Gar-

rett, and that William Edward Garrett was the beneficiary in and entitled to all the proceeds and benefits of the said certificates. Upon these facts the court erroneously, in our opinion, rendered judgment in favor of defendant William Edward Garrett, from which plaintiff appeals.

In the absence of anything to the contrary shown, we must presume that the right of the Bankers Life Company to make by-laws is governed by the laws of Iowa, with which they must not be inconsistent. (Cal. Civ. Code, sec. 301.) The Iowa statute, the existence of which is found by the court, provides that the insured may, not *"with the consent of the association,"* as provided in the by-laws, but *"at his pleasure,"* change the beneficiary named in the certificates. To thus restrict the right and make it subject to the consent of the company, without which such change could not be made, would, in effect, nullify and destroy the statutory provision. As we construe the statute, the provision that a change may be made *"at the pleasure"* of the insured, "as may be provided for in the . . . by-laws," refers to the mode or means adopted by the company for effecting the change, which in this case appears to be by an indorsement upon the certificates expressing the intention of the insured. The rules adopted therefor by the company must be reasonable and not restrictive of the right given by the statute to the holder of the certificates. That part of the by-law providing that a change in the beneficiary named in the certificate, "shall not be binding until the consent of the association shall be indorsed on said certificate," being inconsistent with and restrictive of the right given by the general laws of Iowa, must be disregarded as of no force or effect. Conceding that the provision of the by-laws that "a copy of such indorsement, signed by the member and filed with the association," was not, as found by the court, complied with, nevertheless the original so presented to the association was equally as effective for the purpose to be subserved, which was notice and data for its records, as the copy thereof could have been. Indeed, it appears that the company, on March 16th, in returning the certificates, stated, "copies have been made for our records," thus waiving the requirement, as it might do. (*Marsh* v. *American Legion of Honor,* 149 Mass. 517, [4 L. R. A. 382, 21 N. E. 1070]; *St. Louis Police Relief Assn.* v. *Tierney,* 116

Mo. App. 447, [91 S. W. 968]; *Hall* v. *Allen*, 75 Miss. 175, [65 Am. St. Rep. 601, 22 South. 4].) To construe the provision otherwise would, in our opinion, be giving weight to the shadow rather than to the substance.

Moreover, equity regards that as done which ought to have been done (1 Pomeroy's Equity Jurisprudence, sec. 364), and the insured having the right at his pleasure to change the beneficiary named in the certificates, and having made the indorsement upon the certificates in the manner and form required by the association, and forwarded the same to the company, which, as found, received them on March 14th, the day before his death, he had done all in his power to change the beneficiary, and his death following such change, notice of which was brought home to the company prior to his death, was sufficient to and did constitute an effectual change in the beneficiary named. (*Supreme Conclave Royal Adelphia* v. *Cappella*, 41 Fed. 1; *John Hancock Mut. Life Ins. Co.* v. *White*, 20 R. I. 457, [40 Atl. 5]; *Luhrs* v. *Luhrs*, 123 N. Y. 367, [20 Am. St. Rep. 754, 9 L. R. A. 534, 25 N. E. 388].) In *Heydorf* v. *Conrack*, 7 Kan. App. 202, [52 Pac. 700], it is said: "Where a holder of a certificate in a mutual benefit society desires to change the beneficiary therein, and does all that he is required to do by the by-laws of the society, and then dies before the change is completed, a court of equity will decree the payment of the money the same as if the desired change had been fully completed in the lifetime of the assured." See, also, *Hirschl* v. *Clark*, 81 Iowa, 200, [9 L. R. A. 841, 47 N. W. 78], and *Supreme Lodge* v. *Price*, 27 Cal. App. 607, [150 Pac. 803], to the effect that where the intended change is brought home to the association during the life of the insured, the beneficiary so designated by him is entitled to recover.

In our opinion, the findings clearly show that the insured in his lifetime changed the beneficiary named in the certificates, substituting for William Edward Garrett his wife, Iva L. Garrett, notice of which fact was brought to the notice of the company prior to his death, in a manner which substantially complied with all legal requirements; that his right to change the beneficiary was not subject to and did not depend upon the consent of the company; that if it did so depend, the company must be deemed to have assented thereto upon receipt of the certificates upon which such change was

indorsed and signed by the insured, and the fact that such
consent of the company was not indorsed thereon until after
his death was, under the circumstances, immaterial.

As stated, the Bankers Life Company paid into court the
fund which constituted the subject of the litigation. On December 12, 1915, the court rendered its decision and judgment in the matter, awarding the money involved to William
Edward Garrett, and on the same day the court made an order
staying execution for a period of ten days. Judgment was
entered on December 15, 1915. On December 23, 1915, the
following order was made by the court:

"It appearing that the above mentioned sum of $4,074 is
now justly due and payable to said William Edward Garrett,
I hereby order that it be paid to him by the Treasurer of Los
Angeles County, California, and the County Auditor of said
county is hereby ordered to allow this demand upon the Treasurer of said county for said sum of $4,074, in favor of said
William Edward Garrett in payment thereof, less any moneys
paid or due as city and county taxes on said fund. Dated
this 23rd day of December, 1915.

"LOUIS W. MYERS, Judge."

Upon this order, made without the knowledge of appellant
or her attorney, and other steps duly taken as required in
withdrawing money from the county treasury in such cases,
the money was paid over to the guardian of said minor. On
December 24, 1915, plaintiff and appellant served her notice
of appeal herein, followed in due time by the filing of the
requisite undertaking. Thereafter, upon the application of
the plaintiff to the court, it made an order vacating and setting aside its former order upon the ground that it had been
made through inadvertence. No steps, however, were taken
by appellant in the trial court to have said fund restored to
the county treasury. But she has presented to this court a
motion for an order directing the minor, William Edward
Garrett, and his guardian, and also Charles S. Peery and
W. E. Lady, both individually and as attorneys for William
Edward Garrett, to restore and repay into the county treasury
of Los Angeles County the sum of $4,074, being the amount of
money deposited with the clerk of the superior court by the
Bankers Life Company to abide the result of this action and
so withdrawn pursuant to the order of court above set out;

and also requiring said parties to show cause why they should not be adjudged guilty of contempt for having applied for said order and, pursuant thereto, withdrawn said money from the treasury of Los Angeles County.

The contention of appellant is that the order staying execution did not begin to run until the entry of judgment on December 15th. This for the reason that prior to such time no execution could have issued. Such, in our opinion, is not the legal effect of the order. As we construe it, the ten-day order staying execution commenced to run from its date, to wit, December 12th, and expired on December 22d. On December 23d, when the order for the withdrawal of the funds and payment thereof to William Edward Garrett was made, no appeal had been taken and the time of the stay of execution had expired; hence the court had authority to make the order upon which the money was withdrawn and applied in payment of an existing judgment as to which at the time no appeal had been perfected. In our opinion, the fact that the court, after the money had been paid over in satisfaction of the judgment, vacated and set aside the order upon which it was paid could not vest this court with jurisdiction to order the restoration of the fund. The rule in such cases, as we understand it, is "that a party obtaining through a judgment before reversal any advantage or benefit must restore the amount he got to the other party after the reversal." (*Reynolds* v. *Harris*, 14 Cal. 680, [76 Am. Dec. 459] ; sec. 957, Code Civ. Proc.; *Bank of United States* v. *Bank of Washington*, 6 Pet. 19, [8 L. Ed. 299]. See, also, *Patterson* v. *Keeney*, 165 Cal. 465, [Ann. Cas. 1914D, 232, 132 Pac. 1043].) But conceding without deciding that the trial court could have ordered the fund restored, no such order was made.

Our conclusion is that the respondent's motion to dismiss the appeal should be denied; that appellant's motion to have the fund restored and to cite the parties to show cause why they should not be adjudged guilty of contempt for applying for the order pursuant to which the fund was paid should likewise be denied; that the judgment appealed from should be reversed and the trial court instructed to enter judgment upon the findings for the plaintiff and cross-defendant Iva L. Garrett; all of which is so ordered.

Conrey, P. J., and James, J., concurred.

A petition for a rehearing of this cause was denied by the district court of appeal on August 28, 1916, and a petition to have the cause heard in the supreme court, after judgment in the district court of appeal, was denied by the supreme court on September 25, 1916.

[Civ. No. 1996. Second Appellate District.—July 29, 1916.]

F. A. BRODE et al., Appellants, v. S. A. D. CLARK, Respondent.

APPEAL—GENERAL ORDER GRANTING NEW TRIAL—CONFLICTING EVIDENCE. Where the evidence is conflicting as to material matters, an order granting a new trial will be affirmed on appeal, notwithstanding the written order of court contains a statement of what purports to be the reasons influencing the court in granting the motion, where the order is such as to require it to be treated as a general one, the court not having expressly limited it to definite grounds, and the grounds of motion having included the one of the insufficiency of the evidence.

APPEAL from an order of the Superior Court of Los Angeles County granting a new trial. J. P. Wood, Judge.

The facts are stated in the opinion of the court.

P. W. Thomson, for Appellants.

Hammack & Hammack, for Respondent.

JAMES, J.—This appeal is taken from an order granting to the defendant a new trial. The notice of appeal specifies that the appeal was taken from an order entered on the eleventh day of September, 1913. There appears not to have been any formal minute order entered, but the court filed a written order which, after directing that a new trial be granted, set out certain argument, evidently the opinion of the court, upon one question of law involved in the case. The motion for a new trial was made upon various grounds, including that of the insufficiency of the evidence to sustain the findings of the court. It appears that there was contradictory evidence as to certain issues presented. Notwithstanding

that the written order of court contains a statement of what
purports to be the reasons influencing the court in granting the motion, we think the order must be treated as a general one, and that it must be assumed in that case that the
court, not having expressly limited its order to other definite
grounds, may have granted the motion because of the insufficiency of the evidence. The evidence presenting a conflict
as to material matters, this court has no function to review
the action of the trial judge.

The ground might also be urged, although we find no suggestion of it here on behalf of respondent, that the notice of
appeal does not on its face, by specifying the eleventh day
of September, 1913, as the date of the entry of the order granting a new trial, point to the order as shown by the record
which appears to have been filed on October 20, 1913. However, for the reasons first stated, the order should be affirmed.

The order is affirmed.

Conrey, P. J., and Shaw, J., concurred.

[Civ. No. 1507.   Third Appellate District.—July 31, 1916.]

REBECCA BROWN, Respondent, v. D. J. CANTY,
Appellant.

APPEAL—JUDGMENT-ROLL—ORDERS NOT INCORPORATED IN BILL OF EX-
CEPTIONS—REVIEW NOT PERMITTED.—Upon an appeal taken from a
judgment in an action to quiet title upon the judgment-roll without
any bill of exceptions or statement of the case, the appellate court
can only consider such papers and orders as are declared by the
code to constitute a part of the judgment-roll, notwithstanding
included in the transcript there are certain exhibits and orders
upon which reliance is made for a reversal of the judgment.

APPEAL from a judgment of the Superior Court of Fresno
County. George E. Church, Judge.

The facts are stated in the opinion of the court.

E. A. Williams, for Appellant.

Burns & Watkins, for Respondent.

ELLISON, J., *pro tem.*—Plaintiff brought this action to
quiet her title to a quarter-section of land in Fresno County.

Her complaint alleged facts showing the legal title to the land
to be in her.   The defendant, for answer, denied plaintiff's
title.   He then alleged a certain contract entered into between
him and certain other parties, viz., J. E. Hughes, T. E. Braly,
and W. J. Hotchkiss, the result of which was that Hotchkiss
had purchased the land described in the complaint from the
state of California, but had the state make its deed to one
Barthold, in trust for said Hotchkiss and this defendant; that
plaintiff had full knowledge of defendant's interest in said
land at the time she purchased it from Hotchkiss, to whom
Barthold had deeded it.   He alleged his interest in the land
was an undivided four-tenths, and that notwithstanding plaintiff had knowledge of his claim and interest, she obtained a
deed from said Hotchkiss and said Barthold conveying to her
said quarter-section of land.   Judgment went for the plaintiff
and the defendant appeals from the judgment without any bill
of exceptions or statement.

The complaint states a cause of action and the findings support the judgment.

The only points relied upon for a reversal are: (1) That
defendant having introduced in evidence a *lis pendens* filed
in an action entitled *Canty* v. *Hotchkiss* stating defendant's
right therein to this same land, (2) this was notice to Mrs.
Brown and to the court that defendant claimed an interest
in the land and that the plaintiff knew of his claim when
she bought the land from Hotchkiss; and this all being true,
(3) the court erred in denying defendant's motion to compel
Hotchkiss and Barthold to intervene herein in order that the
judgment might bind all parties interested in the land, and
(4) that no valid judgment could be entered without their
presence.   But, unfortunately for appellant, the court is unable upon this record to consider any of these suggested matters.   Upon this appeal we may only consider such papers
and orders as are declared by the code to constitute a part
of the judgment-roll.   None of the evidence introduced upon
the trial by either party is a part of the judgment-roll.
Therefore, we do not know what evidence the plaintiff introduced, we do not know that defendant introduced the *lis pendens* referred to nor that he made any proof of the existence
of the contract set up in his answer, nor that he made any
motion for an order that Hotchkiss and Barthold be compelled
to intervene (see Code Civ. Proc., sec. 387), nor that the court

denied any such motion. It is true there are certain exhibits and orders printed in the transcript, but they have no place therein, not being any part of the judgment-roll.

This is so thoroughly settled that a citation of authority is unnecessary, but one case will be referred to. In *Pedrorena v. Hotchkiss*, 95 Cal. 636, 638, [30 Pac. 787, 788], it is said: "There are two minute orders printed in the transcript, from one of which it appears that the default was set aside and defendant allowed to answer upon certain stated conditions, and from the other, that the answer filed was stricken out, because defendant had failed to comply with the conditions upon which the default was set aside, and he was permitted to answer. The statute does not make these minute orders part of the judgment-roll. (Code Civ. Proc., sec. 670.) They are. therefore, improperly in the record—there being no bill of exceptions—and we cannot notice the points attempted to be made in regard to them."

The judgment is affirmed.

Chipman, P. J., and Hart, J., concurred.

[Civ. No. 1517. Third Appellate District.—July 31, 1916.]

THOMAS THOMSEN, Respondent, v. IDA AMELIA THOMSEN, Appellant.

DIVORCE—ASSIGNMENT OF COMMUNITY PROPERTY—DISCRETION.—In actions for divorce on the ground of adultery or extreme cruelty, subdivision 1 of section 146 of the Civil Code confers upon the trial court a wide latitude for the exercise of its judgment and discretion in assigning the community property to the respective parties, and in every case it will be presumed that such discretion has been wisely and properly exercised.

ID.—CRUELTY OF WIFE—AWARD OF MORE THAN ONE-HALF OF COMMUNITY PROPERTY TO HUSBAND—DISCRETION NOT ABUSED.—In an action for divorce wherein the decree is granted to the husband on the ground of extreme cruelty, there is no abuse of discretion in awarding to the husband more than one-half of the community property, notwithstanding the wife has been a hard-working woman and by her efforts has assisted in accumulating the property, as her cruelty must be taken into consideration in making the award.

ID.—ANTENUPTIAL HOLDINGS OF HUSBAND—CONSIDERATION IN AWARDING COMMUNITY PROPERTY.—Where a divorce is granted to the husband on the ground of the wife's cruelty, it is proper to take into consideration, in awarding the community property, the antenuptial holdings of the husband used by him after marriage and intermingled with the common holdings, notwithstanding such separate holdings cannot be traced into any specific piece of property.

ID.—AWARD OF PROPERTY IN SEVERALTY TO ONE SPOUSE.—In awarding the community property, the court may consider all of the property as one asset or fund, composed of separate units, and award all of designated and described pieces of property to one party, instead of an undivided interest in all.

APPEAL from a judgment of the Superior Court of San Joaquin County. Frank H. Smith, Judge.

The facts are stated in the opinion of the court.

Light & Crane, and Gordon A. Stewart, for Appellant.

Arthur L. Levinsky, for Respondent.

ELLISON, J., *pro tem.*—In this action the trial court granted an interlocutory decree of divorce to the plaintiff on the ground of defendant's cruelty and made a decree adjusting the property rights of the parties. Upon this appeal the defendant claims that in the decree too much of the property was awarded to the plaintiff.

A brief narrative of some facts disclosed by the record will be sufficient to present the point raised. The plaintiff and defendant intermarried in 1876. At the time of this marriage the plaintiff was possessed of some property. By hard work, economy, and thrift their worldly possessions have increased until at the time of the trial they owned real and personal property as follows:

A tract of land containing about 60 acres, valued
at ....$ 5,100
Another of about 60 acres valued at............ 3,780
Another of about 40 acres valued at............ 3,400
And other tracts aggregating 408 acres, valued
at 34,680
                                              _____
                                              $48,960
Stock, crops, and farming implements.......... 10,000
                                              _____
    Total $58,960
And their indebtedness amounted to about.......$2,500

By its decree the court awarded to the plaintiff 107 acres of the land, and the balance of the real estate was ordered divided equally between the parties, and also the growing crops and all personal property and money. It was also decreed that all indebtedness should be paid equally by them.

Counsel for appellant seems to be satisfied with this division of the property with the exception that he claims that his client should have been awarded one-half of the 107 acres of land, and that all of it should not have been awarded to the plaintiff.

Subdivision 1 of section 146 of the Civil Code provides: "If the decree be rendered on the ground of adultery, or extreme cruelty, the community property shall be assigned to the respective parties in such proportions as the court, from all the facts of the case, and the condition of the parties, may deem just." This code section confers upon the trial court a wide latitude for the exercise of its judgment and discretion, and in every case it will be presumed that such discretion has been wisely and properly exercised. It has been said that it is the duty of the court to award to the innocent party more than one-half of the community property when the divorce is granted for cruelty. Thus, in *Eslinger* v. *Eslinger*, 47 Cal. 62, 64, it is said: "Section 146 of the Civil Code required that the community property shall be equally divided between the parties; but the next section makes an exception to the general rule by providing that if the divorce be granted on the ground of adultery or extreme cruelty, the guilty party shall receive only such portion as the court shall deem just under the facts of the case. The inference is that in the excepted cases the injured party is to receive, as a general rule, more than one-half of the property, and as much more as the court shall deem just. Under the circumstances of this case, we think the court ought to have awarded to the wife three-fourths of the community property."

1. Counsel states that, as the evidence shows the defendant has been a hard-working woman and by her efforts assisted in accumulating the property, she should have been awarded at least one-half of all of it. But this feature of the case is not controlling. Many cases arise wherein all the property has been accumulated entirely by the efforts of the husband, unaided by the wife's labor, and wherein, upon a divorce being granted to the wife upon the ground of the husband's

cruelty, she has been awarded much more than one-half of the common property. In such cases, one of the circumstances the court must take into consideration and give due weight to is the important fact that one spouse has been cruel to the other, which cruelty has resulted in disrupting the home and marriage ties.

2. In finding No. XIV the court finds that at the time of the plaintiff's marriage to the defendant he had five hundred dollars on deposit in bank; that there was due to him from one Hansen one thousand two hundred dollars, which was afterward collected; that he owned 175 stands of bees, some of which he sold for $250; two wagons and horse, worth two hundred dollars; 65 acres of land, which he subsequently sold for one thousand dollars. (While the findings do not total these figures, it is proper to state that they aggregate $3,150.) The court finds that all of said sums of money and property were used by the plaintiff after the marriage in the purchase of real estate and farming implements, and that by reason of the use of said money and property and by reason of work and labor done and performed by both spouses, all the lands described in the findings were bought.''

It is apparent from the record that the court felt that it could not trace with sufficient accuracy any of the plaintiff's antenuptial holdings into any specific piece of property now owned by the plaintiff so as to declare it to be his separate property; yet it did consider the fact that plaintiff had this property at the time of his marriage and that it and its increase were intermingled in the common holdings, a circumstance to be considered by it in making a fair and equitable division of the property. With this in mind, and without deciding that any specific piece of land was separate property, the court awarded to the plaintiff the 107 acres of land in severalty. We discover no error or abuse of discretion in so holding and acting. Nor was the amount thus awarded to plaintiff in severalty large in comparison with the total value of the estate. In appellant's brief it is stated that the entire property of the parties had a value of about $58,156, and that the 107 acres awarded to the plaintiff were worth $9,560. It thus appears that, by the decree, the plaintiff was awarded $33,858 and the defendant $24,298; or, reduced to a percentage basis, the plaintiff was awarded about fifty-eight per cent and the defendant forty-two per cent of the entire holdings.

The court has found that the antenuptial holdings of plaintiff were used in acquiring this property and were of the value of $3,150. Allowing interest on this fund for forty years at four per cent, compounded annually (which is certainly low enough), and it would now amount to $15,330.50. With all these facts before it the court was fully justified in disposing of the property as it did, and appellant has no just grounds of complaint.

3. Appellant takes the position that the court must divide the community property in some proportion between the spouses, that the code so provides, and it has no authority to award all of the 107 acres to the plaintiff, as such act was not a division. In adjusting the property rights of the parties the court may consider all the common property as one asset or fund, composed of separate units, and can often more equitably settle and adjust matters by giving all of designated and described pieces of property to one party than by awarding to each an undivided interest in all. We know of no principle of law or practice that would forbid such a course of action. The court is no more bound to award to each spouse an undivided interest in each piece of land than it is to award to each an undivided interest in each cow or horse.

The judgment is affirmed.

Chipman, P. J., and Hart, J., concurred.

[Civ. No. 1513. Third Appellate District.—July 31, 1916.]

ANNIE GALLO, Respondent, v. A. GALLO, Appellant.

ADVERSE POSSESSION—OWNERSHIP OF ADJOINING PATENTED LANDS—INCLOSURE OF BOTH HOLDINGS—LEASING FOR GRAZING PURPOSES—INSUFFICIENT PROOF OF TITLE.—Where two brothers owned adjoining quarter-sections of patented land of little value, and neither lived nor resided upon the land covered by his patent for any long period after obtaining it, and neither had lived on any part of the half section for many years, the fact that one of the brothers inclosed both holdings with a wire fence, and leased the land for short periods for grazing purposes unknown to the other brother, is insufficient to sustain a claim to the whole tract by adverse possession.

ID.—HOSTILE CHARACTER OF HOLDING—ESSENTIAL ELEMENT.—In order
to make out an adverse possession sufficient to constitute a defense
under the statute of limitations, the owner must be notified in some
way that the possession is hostile to his claim.

ID.—PAYMENT OF TAXES—REDEMPTION FROM TAX SALES—INSUFFICIENT
COMPLIANCE WITH STATUTE.—The payment of taxes required as an
element of adverse possession is not complied with by the redemption of the land from tax sales.

APPEAL from a judgment of the Superior Court of Tulare
County. J. A. Allen, Judge.

The facts are stated in the opinion of the court.

Webster, Webster & Blewett, and Farnsworth & McClure,
for Appellant.

A. H. Ashley, and Power & McFadzean, for Respondent.

ELLISON, J., *pro tem.*—Plaintiff brought this action to
quiet her title to the northeast quarter of a certain section
of land situated in Tulare County, and obtained judgment as
prayed for. The defendant appeals.

On the trial the plaintiff introduced as evidence of her title
to the quarter-section a patent from the United States to her
husband, Giacomo Gallo, dated August 9, 1897, and a deed
from the latter to her, of August 12, 1911, conveying the land.

The defendant (who is a brother of said Giacomo Gallo)
as a defense alleged that he had obtained title to the land by
adverse possession, and made no other claim.

Upon this appeal the defendant insists that the findings of
the court to the effect that he had not acquired title by adverse
possession are not sustained by the evidence, and this is the
only question presented.

The record shows that, at about the time plaintiff's grantor
obtained his patent for the northeast quarter of the section,
the defendant obtained a patent for the northwest quarter
of the same section. Evidently the land was considered of
little value at the time. Neither brother lived nor resided
upon the land covered by his patent for any long period after
obtaining it, and neither has lived on any part of the half
section for many years. (The plaintiff's quarter-section ad-
joins the defendant's on the east, and the two constitute the
north half of the section.) The defendant testified that he

built a fence on the east side of the land in dispute about 1903 and during the same year inclosed the half section. The fence was of posts and three wires. When he first built the fence he leased the half section to one Goodale for two years at a rental of nine dollars per year. "He agreed to pay the taxes and build the fence." He pastured some cattle on it for two years. At some date, not stated, defendant leased the half section to a man, whose name he cannot recall, under a verbal lease for five years. He paid the rent, $40, for one year and no more, and defendant does not know how long he was on the land, but never saw him after the first year. In 1911 he leased the land to one Howard for five years under a written lease. This action was begun in October, 1912. The defendant never resided on the land in dispute and never made any use of it except as above stated. The land is in Tulare County and plaintiff's grantor, during all this time, lived in Stockton, and defendant testified his brother never knew he was leasing the land. He also testified that he had the whole half section assessed to himself, and paid all taxes on it for at least fifteen years. The evidence as to the payment of taxes is that they went delinquent in 1905 and that no taxes were paid in 1906, 1907, and 1908 until 1909, when the defendant redeemed the land from tax sales.

The witness, John Gallo, testified that, in the year 1908, the defendant told his father (the husband of plaintiff) that he wanted some money for taxes and his father laughed and said to him: "What rents are you getting from the land?" He said: "Not much." So father said to him: "If you will pay all the taxes, what is left you can keep for your troubles."

It is very clear to us that the defendant did not sustain his plea of adverse possession. The elements required to make out an adverse possession sufficient to constitute a defense under the statute of limitations are clearly stated in *Unger* v. *Mooney*, 63 Cal. 595, [49 Am. Rep. 100], and need not here be repeated. In said case it is said: "The adverse character of the possession must in every case be manifested to the owner. The owner must be notified, in some way, that the possession is hostile to his claim, or the statute does not operate on his right. As was said in the case cited in 84 N. Y., per Andrews, J., [*Trustees of East Hampton* v. *Kirk*, 84 N. Y. 215, 38 Am. Rep. 505], 'the object of the statute defining the acts essential to constitute an adverse possession is, that the

real owner may, by unequivocal acts of disseizor, have notice
of the hostile claim and be thereby called upon to assert
his legal title.' Hence, an open and notorious occupation
with hostile intent is a necessary constituent of an adverse
holding.''

The defendant did not personally occupy the land. No one
nor all of the persons to whom he leased it ever occupied it
for any five consecutive years.

The record does not show that taxes were paid for any one
period of five years. Under the decisions construing subdivision 2 of section 325 of the Code of Civil Procedure, it is
held that redeeming land from tax sales is not the payment
of taxes contemplated by the law as an element of adverse
possession. "If it [the payment of taxes] is an element in
the adverse possession tending to show good faith, certainly
during those years in which the taxes have not been paid the
possession lacks an essential element required in the statute.
During all the years in which the delinquency was allowed,
the true owner might forbear suit because of his knowledge
that the person in possession had not paid taxes, thereby indicating that he was not holding adversely.'' (*McDonald* v.
McCoy, 121 Cal. 73, [53 Pac. 427].)

The relationship of the parties has a bearing and may well
be considered. Two brothers owning adjoining land of little
value—far from where they are residing—used only for grazing stock; one brother puts a wire fence around both holdings
and leases it for short periods. Such act from a stranger,
owning no adjoining land, would have far greater significance
as showing a hostile holding, than when being done by a
brother owning the adjoining land.

In considering the case on appeal, it will be presumed that
all testimony introduced at the trial tending to support the
findings of the trial court was accepted by it as true. The testimony of John Gallo, above referred to, wherein he states
that, in 1908, the defendant asked his father for money for
taxes and the latter said to him: "If you will pay the taxes,
what is left you can keep for your troubles,'' is sufficient in
itself to negative all inferences of an adverse and hostile holding, and clearly sufficient to show that plaintiff's grantor was
not advised of any hostile claims, but rather points to an understanding between brothers for their mutual benefit. (See
Note v. *Hall* 28 Cal. App. 361, [152 Pac. 436].) Consider-

ing the family relationship of the parties, the language used by the district court of appeal in *Glowner* v. *De Alvarez*, 10 Cal. App. 196, [101 Pac. 433], seems not inappropriate for quotation in this connection: "There are no equities in favor of a party seeking by adverse holding to acquire the property of another."

The judgment is clearly right, and is affirmed.

Chipman, P. J., and Hart, J., concurred.

———————

[Civ. No. 2100. Second Appellate District.—August 1, 1916.]

FLETCHER COLLECTION AGENCY (a Corporation), Petitioner, v. SUPERIOR COURT OF LOS ANGELES COUNTY et al., Respondents.

JUSTICE'S COURT APPEAL—MOTION TO DISMISS—FAILURE OF SURETIES TO JUSTIFY—SERVICE OF NOTICE OF JUSTIFICATION.—Upon a motion made to dismiss a justice's court appeal upon the ground that the sureties on the undertaking on appeal did not justify in the manner and form required by law, the decision of the superior court upon conflicting affidavits as to when the notice of justification of the sureties was served, is not subject to review in the appellate court upon *certiorari* proceedings.

ID.—WAIVER OF JUSTIFICATION—FAILURE TO APPEAR.—Justification of sureties on an undertaking given on a justice's court appeal is waived where the party excepting to the sufficiency of the sureties fails to appear at the time and place mentioned in the notice of justification.

ID.—FILING OF NEW UNDERTAKING—PRIMA FACIE JUSTIFICATION.—The filing of a new undertaking on the day fixed for the justification of sureties, which has attached to it the requisite affidavit sworn to before the justice, establishes a *prima facie* justification.

ID.—APPEAL UPON QUESTION OF LAW—RECORD—STATEMENT OF GROUNDS. Jurisdiction of a justice's court appeal taken on questions of law alone is not lost by reason of the omission to include in the statement on appeal the grounds upon which the party appealing intended to rely.

APPLICATION for a Writ of Review originally made to the District Court of Appeal for the Second Appellate District to review an order of the Superior Court of Los Angeles County refusing to dismiss a Justice's Court appeal.

The facts are stated in the opinion of the court.

George P. Cook, for Petitioner.

Frank A. McDonald, for Respondents.

CONREY, P. J.—On application of the petitioner a writ of review was issued herein, to determine whether the defendant superior court has regularly pursued its authority in refusing to dismiss an appeal from the justice's court, in an action wherein the petitioner was plaintiff and Frank A. McDonald et al. were defendants. The facts are shown by the return filed herein.

After judgment in the justice's court, the defendants in that action filed notice of appeal on questions of law and filed their undertaking on appeal. On November 17, 1915, the plaintiff filed exceptions to the sureties on the appeal bond. On November 22, 1915, before 1 o'clock P. M., appellants served on the plaintiff a notice "that defendants will justify the sureties on the new appeal bond filed by them in the above-entitled case, and you will take further notice that defendants will file a new appeal bond in the above-entitled action on the 22d day of November, 1915, at the hour of 4:30 P. M., in Department F of the above-entitled court, at the courthouse in the city of Los Angeles, Cal." The plaintiff and its attorneys did not appear in the justice's court at the time specified. The justice's docket is silent as to justification by the sureties or as to any appearances by either party before the justice's court at the time specified in the notice of justification of sureties. But the undertaking filed on that day contains the statutory form of affidavit on an undertaking, with a certificate showing that it was subscribed and sworn to before the justice of the peace on that same day, November 22, 1915, and an indorsement was made thereon showing the filing of the undertaking on that day.

The papers on appeal having been duly transmitted to the superior court and filed therein, the plaintiff gave notice of motion to dismiss the appeal upon the grounds:

"1. That the sureties on the undertaking on appeal heretofore filed by said defendants did not justify in the manner and form required by law and in accordance with the provisions of section 978 of the Code of Civil Procedure.

"2. That the statement on appeal filed by said defendants does not state any grounds of appeal, as required by section 975 of the Code of Civil Procedure."

The motion was based upon the papers on file and affidavits. The affidavits were for the purpose of showing, and tended to show, that the notice of justification of sureties was not served until the next morning after the time for justification as specified in the notice.   Counter-affidavits were filed positively affirming that the notice was served between 12 and 1 o'clock on the twenty-second day of November.   For the purpose of determining the questions raised as to its jurisdiction to entertain the appeal, the superior court considered these conflicting affidavits, and determined that the notice was served on the 22d at the hour named in the appellants' affidavits.   Therefore, as to that disputed fact we consider ourselves obliged to adopt the conclusion of the superior court.

On these facts respondents claim that the failure of the party excepting to the sufficiency of the sureties to appear at the time and place mentioned in the notice of justification was a waiver of such justification, and that the affidavit of the sureties before the justice, as shown on the undertaking itself, wherein they made oath that they were residents and householders and respectively worth the sum specified in the undertaking, etc., establishes a *prima facie* justification, and that nothing further was required under the circumstances here shown.   We think that this contention should be sustained. It is directly supported by the decision in *Bank of Escondido* v. *Superior Court*, 106 Cal. 43, [39 Pac. 211], and in *Budd* v. *Superior Court*, 14 Cal. App. 256, [111 Pac. 628].

The other ground upon which petitioner rests his contention that the superior court exceeded its jurisdiction is that the statement on appeal does not contain the grounds upon which the parties appealing intended to rely, as required by section 975 of the Code of Civil Procedure.   Assuming the statement to be insufficient as specified, it does not result that thereby the court was deprived of its appellate jurisdiction over the case.   (*Rauer's Law & Collection Co.* v. *Superior Court*, 26 Cal. App. 289, [152 Pac. 957].)

The order of the superior court refusing to dismiss the appeal is affirmed.

James, J., and Shaw, J., concurred.

[Crim. No. 363.   Third Appellate District.—August 1, 1916.]

In the Matter of the Application of YEE KIM MAH, for a Writ of Habeas Corpus.

CITY OF SACRAMENTO — MISDEMEANORS COMMITTED WITHIN CORPORATE LIMITS—JURISDICTION.—The several justices' courts of the county of Sacramento have jurisdiction over all misdemeanors enumerated by the general laws of the state committed within the municipal limits of the city of Sacramento, as well as those committed outside of such limits and within the territorial boundaries of the county of Sacramento.

ID.—JURISDICTION OF MISDEMEANORS—WHITNEY ACT—EFFECT OF CODE AMENDMENT—REPEAL OF ACT AS TO SACRAMENTO.—The provisions of the "Whitney Act" (Stats. 1885, p. 213), giving to police courts of cities having a population of over thirty thousand and under one hundred thousand inhabitants exclusive jurisdiction of all misdemeanors punishable by fine or imprisonment, or both by such fine and imprisonment, committed within the limits of such cities, if ever applicable at any time to the city of Sacramento, have been, so far as such city is concerned, repealed or superseded by the enactment of section 1425 of the Penal Code, in the year 1905 (Stats. 1905, p. 705), which provides, among other things, that justices' courts shall have jurisdiction of all misdemeanors committed within their respective counties punishable by fine not exceeding five hundred dollars, or imprisonment not exceeding six months, or by both such fine and imprisonment.

ID.—JURISDICTION OF POLICE COURT OF SACRAMENTO—EFFECT OF CHARTER.—The provisions of sections 162 and 164 of the freeholders' charter of the city of Sacramento, approved in 1911 (Stats. Ex. Sess. 1911, p. 305), establishing a police court in such city and giving it jurisdiction "of all misdemeanors enumerated by the general laws or by ordinances of the city and of all other crimes cognizable by justices' courts and courts of justices of the peace and police courts under the constitution and laws of the state of California," do not confer upon the police court so established *exclusive* jurisdiction of all simple misdemeanors committed under the general laws of the state within the limits of such city, but give it concurrent jurisdiction with the justices' courts of the county of Sacramento.

APPLICATION for a Writ of Habeas Corpus originally made to the District Court of Appeal for the Third Appellate District.

The facts are stated in the opinion of the court.

John Q. Brown, for Petitioner.

Lee Gebhart, Hugh B. Bradford, and S. J. Otis, for Respondent.

HART, J.—In the justice's court of Riverside township, in the county of Sacramento, the petitioner was charged with and convicted of a misdemeanor growing out of the violation by him of the legislative act entitled "An act to regulate the sale of poisons," etc., and, claiming that the judgment of conviction is void because the court before which he was tried was without jurisdiction to try the action against him, he seeks his release from the custody of the sheriff of Sacramento County, by whom he is now being detained by authority of the said judgment of conviction and sentence thereupon imposed upon him, through the writ of *habeas corpus*.

In the outset it may be observed that, although the act of the violation of certain of whose provisions the petitioner was adjudged guilty prescribes penalties for the first and second convictions thereunder which are within the jurisdiction of justices' or police courts to impose, yet, for a third conviction of the same person for the violation of the provisions thereof, the punishment prescribed is by imprisonment in the state prison for not less than one year and not more than five years. It hence follows that, where a person is charged with the violation of the provisions of said act, together with two previous convictions thereunder, jurisdiction to try the person so offending is in the superior court. (*People* v. *Sacramento Butchers' Protective Assn.*, 12 Cal. App. 471, 478, [107 Pac. 712].) It is, however, conceded by the petitioner that the conviction of which he here complains was of what is popularly termed a simple or "high-grade" misdemeanor of which justices' and police courts have jurisdiction, and this concession necessarily carries with it the further concession that he was not charged with and convicted of a violation of the provisions of the statute with two prior convictions thereunder.

The point made by the petitioner, however, results from the following facts: That, as the petition shows and the demurrer interposed thereto by the respondent admits, the crime of which he was convicted was committed within the limits of the city and the judicial township of Sacramento, said township being coextensive, territorially, with the municipal limits of said city; that Riverside township, in the county of Sacramento, in which the petitioner was charged with, tried for, and convicted of the offense for which he is now being restrained of his liberty, is not embraced within or a part of the city of Sacramento. In other words, and in brief, the petition shows that the crime of which the petitioner stands convicted was committed within the municipal limits of the city of Sacramento, and that he was charged, prosecuted, and convicted in a judicial township territorially independent of and distinct from the said city and township. It is the contention that under the terms of the so-called Whitney Act (Stats. 1885, p. 213), the police court of the city of Sacramento has sole and exclusive jurisdiction of all misdemeanors punishable by fine or imprisonment, or by both such fine and imprisonment, committed within the limits of said city, and that, therefore, a justice's court whose township or territorial jurisdiction is outside or not embraced within the limits of said city cannot legally acquire or exercise jurisdiction of misdemeanors so committed. It follows, so the argument goes, that the conviction of the petitioner in the justice's court of Riverside township is *coram non judice* and void.

The "Whitney Act," section 1, provides: "The judicial power of every city having thirty thousand and under one hundred thousand inhabitants, shall be vested in a police court to be held therein by the city justices, or one of them, to be designated by the mayor, but either of said justices may hold such court without such designation, and it is hereby made the duty of said city justices, in addition to the duties now required of them by law, to hold said police courts.

"Sec. 2. The police courts shall have exclusive jurisdiction of the following public offenses committed in the city: First, petit larceny; Second, assault or battery, not charged to have been committed upon a public officer in the discharge of official duty, or with intent to kill; Third, breaches of the peace, riots, affrays, committing willful injury to property, *and all misdemeanors punishable by fine or imprisonment, or by both such fine and imprisonment;* Fourth, of proceedings respecting vagrants, lewd, or disorderly persons."

The third section invests said court with "exclusive jurisdiction of all proceedings for a violation of any ordinance of said city, both civil and criminal, and of an action for the

collection of any license required by any ordinance of said
city." Said court is also authorized by said act to hear and
conduct the preliminary examination of charges of which the
superior court has jurisdiction, and to commit the offenders
to trial in said last-mentioned court.

The argument advanced in support of the position that
from the foregoing provisions of the "Whitney Act" the city
of Sacramento, as a municipal corporation, derives all the
judicial power with which it is invested, is, so it is asserted
and contended, that the census of the year 1910 disclosed that
said city had acquired a population of over thirty thousand
inhabitants, but still contained less than one hundred thousand inhabitants, and that said city, therefore, after the said
census was taken and upon the official declaration thereof,
was automatically shifted into a class which brought it within
the scope of the "Whitney Act" with respect to its judicial
power; that said city is still a city having a population of
over thirty thousand and under one hundred thousand inhabitants, and still subject to the provisions of the "Whitney
Act" regulating the power and jurisdiction of the police
courts in cities of that class.

Varying legislation respecting justices' and police courts,
their power and jurisdiction, has, from time to time, been
enacted since the adoption of the codes in 1872; but, in deciding the question submitted in this proceeding, it is not necessary to review said legislation or enter into a detailed examination of the changes and amendments so made in the law
with respect to those courts. It is sufficient if we find, as we
think we have correctly found, that the provisions of the
"Whitney Act," even if at any time they were applicable to
the city of Sacramento, have been, in so far as they affected
the question of the jurisdiction of the police court of said
city, superseded by legislation enacted subsequently to the
passage of said act.

The legislature of 1905 (Stats. 1905, p. 705) added a new
section to the Penal Code, numbered 1425, which is now a part
of said code, and which prescribes and regulates the jurisdiction of justices' courts in criminal cases. It is by said section
provided, among other things, that said courts shall have jurisdiction of "all misdemeanors punishable by fine not exceeding five hundred dollars, or imprisonment not exceeding six
months, or by both such fine and imprisonment," committed

within their respective counties. That section, or the precise provisions thereof, were embraced within section 115 of the Code of Civil Procedure (see Deering's Pocket Edition, Code Civ. Proc., of year 1906) ; but the legislature, doubtless viewing the subject matter of said section as coming strictly and hence more appropriately within the purview, nature, and purpose of the Penal Code, adopted said section into and as a part of the latter code in the year 1905, as stated. In 1907, the legislature, at its regular session, in furtherance of its manifest object of making the provisions of the section a part of the criminal law system of our state, repealed section 115 of the Code of Civil Procedure. (Stats. 1907, p. 682.)

While it is true, as seen, that the provisions of section 1425 of the Penal Code were, as section 115 of the Code of Civil Procedure, a part of the law of the state and no doubt governed in the matter of the jurisdiction of justices' courts (unless they were or had been superseded by some subsequent enactment) prior to and at the time said section 1425 of the Penal Code was enacted, it is also obviously true that the enactment of said last-mentioned section constituted and involved an act of new and independent legislation, or an act no different, in a legal sense, from any other legislative act involving legislation upon a subject upon which there had theretofore been no legislation by the legislature. The legislature, in other words, in enacting section 1425, put an entirely new section into the Penal Code, notwithstanding that the identical section had been and then was the law of the state expressed in the form of a section of another of the four codes. And in so enacting said section, the legislature gave vent to its latest utterance or expression upon the subject to which the section relates. The effect of the enactment of the section was, therefore, to repeal at least so much of the provisions of the "Whitney Act" as pretended or purported to vest in the police court of the city of Sacramento "exclusive jurisdiction of . . . all misdemeanors punishable by fine or imprisonment, or by both such fine and imprisonment," committed in said city, assuming only for the purposes of this case that by the provisions of the Whitney Act the power and jurisdiction of the police court of said city had theretofore been governed and regulated. This is only to say that section 1425 of the Penal Code is now the law which is controlling in the matter of the jurisdiction of justices' courts, and that, unless that section runs counter to some subsequent legislation upon the subject, those courts have jurisdiction of any of the offenses therein enumerated committed anywhere within their respective counties. It follows, of course, subject, however, to the qualification that so much of section 1425 as confers such jurisdiction has not, since its enactment, been repealed either exp.essly or by necessary implication, that it was within the lawful jurisdiction of the justice's court of Riverside township to try the petitioner for the misdemeanor charged to have been committed by him within the limits of the city of Sacramento, said township being, as seen, as is the city of Sacramento, within the county of Sacramento.

The only legislation to which our attention has been directed or which we have in mind purporting to prescribe the powers and jurisdiction of the police court of the city of Sacramento, and which has been had since the enactment of section 1425 of the Penal Code, is to be found among the provisions of the freeholders' charter of the city of Sacramento, approved by the legislature at its extra session in the year 1911. (Stats. & Amdts. to the Codes, Ex. Sess. 1911, p. 305.) But the provisions of said charter relating to the powers and jurisdiction of the police court of said city are in no manner or degree repugnant to or inconsistent with the powers and jurisdiction of justices' courts as conferred by section 1425 of the Penal Code. And we think it is very plain that the judicial scheme established by said charter was intended to and does supersede or take the place of any previously established scheme for a police court for said city.

Article XII of the charter of said city contains, among other provisions, the following: "Sec. 162. There is hereby constituted a police court in and for the city of Sacramento. . . . Sec. 164. Said police court shall have jurisdiction: 1. Of all misdemeanors enumerated by the general laws or by ordinances of the city and of all other crimes cognizable by justices' courts and courts of justices of the peace and police courts under the constitution and laws of the state of California. . . . 3. Of the examination and commitment of persons charged with the commission of any offense that may be prosecuted by indictment or information; 4. Such other criminal jurisdiction as is, or may hereafter be, conferred by law upon police courts, justices' courts, or justices of the peace. . . . "

202 MATTER OF APPLICATION OF YEE KIM MAH. [31 Cal. App.

The validity of said article of the said charter is not questioned here, nor could it be successfully. The authority for the establishment of police courts by freeholders' charters is in section 8½ of article XI of the constitution. That authority was first conferred by the people through the constitution by an amendment added to that instrument in the year 1896. (Sec. 8½, art. XI.) Prior to the adoption of that amendment courts could not be established by a freeholders' charter, or by a mere concurrent resolution, the means whereby the state legislative body approves such a charter. (*Ex parte Sparks*, 120 Cal. 395, [52 Pac. 715].) Parenthetically, it may be stated that the said amendment has since been added to by other amendments adopted by the people, which, however, in no way affect the question submitted here.

By the provisions, then, of the charter of the city of Sacramento we must be guided in determining the powers and jurisdiction of the police court of said city, and whether the jurisdiction so conferred is made exclusive as to all misdemeanors cognizable by justices' courts committed within the borders of said city. Under cardinal canons of construction, the article in said charter creating and establishing a police court in said city supersedes or necessarily repeals, so far as the city of Sacramento is concerned, any provisions of any previous section purporting to confer jurisdiction upon said court.

It is very clear that the provisions of said charter setting up a police court in said city do not pretend, nor can they reasonably be construed to have been intended, to confer upon the court so established *exclusive* jurisdiction of all simple misdemeanors committed within the limits of said city. The word "exclusive" is nowhere used in those provisions. It is obvious to our minds that the most that was intended by those provisions of the charter, so far as are concerned misdemeanors committed under the general laws of the state, is that the police court of said city shall have concurrent jurisdiction with the justices' courts of the county of such misdemeanors when they are committed within the limits of said city. This clearly appears to be true from the language of the first subdivision of section 164, viz.: "Said police court shall have jurisdiction of all misdemeanors enumerated by the general laws of the state . . . and *of all other crimes cognizable by justices' courts and courts of justices of the peace*," clearly meaning, not that thus the several justices' courts of the county of Sacramento shall not exercise the jurisdiction over misdemeanors committed anywhere within the territorial boundaries of the county of Sacramento, including, of course, the city of Sacramento, as provided by section 1425 of the Penal Code, but that, as stated, the police court may also exercise, along with the justices' courts of the county acting upon the authority of the mentioned section of the Penal Code, jurisdiction over "all misdemeanors enumerated by the general laws of the state" committed within the limits of said city. We can perceive no reasonable ground upon which any other construction can be given the provisions of the charter under consideration.

It will not, of course, be doubted that but for that particular provision of the Sacramento city charter which gives to the police court its jurisdiction over misdemeanors under the general laws, or a like provision in some general law of the state, the police court of said city would not have jurisdiction over such misdemeanors or of "other crimes cognizable by justices' courts," whatever those "other crimes" might be if not coming within the category of misdemeanors; for the powers and jurisdiction of a police court proceed from special legislative grant only, and when a statute or a charter, legally sanctioned by the legislature, undertakes to establish such a court and to grant to it the requisite powers and jurisdiction for its limited purposes, such court's powers and jurisdiction must be measured by and remain within the terms of the grant.

Our conclusion is, as must be manifest from the views herein expressed, that, if the Whitney Act ever applied to the police court of the city of Sacramento, its provisions, so far as they purport to give that court exclusive jurisdiction of misdemeanors punishable by fine not exceeding five hundred dollars or imprisonment not exceeding six months, or by both such fine and imprisonment, committed within the limits of the city of Sacramento, have been, so far as said city is concerned, repealed or superseded by the more recent legislative mandate on that subject as expressed in section 1425 of the Penal Code; that, moreover, said provisions have been superseded by the provisions of the freeholders' charter of said city, adopted and approved in the year 1911, establishing a police court therein and prescribing and regulating its powers and jurisdiction, and that said charter provisions are

not in conflict with or repugnant to any provision of section
1425 of the Penal Code. It follows, of course, that the justice's court of Riverside township did not transcend its lawful
authority and jurisdiction in taking cognizance of and trying
the case made against the petitioner by the complaint charging
him with a misdemeanor under the general law of the state.

Accordingly, the demurrer to the petition is sustained, the
writ discharged, and the petitioner remanded.

Chipman, P. J., concurred.

[Civ. No. 1465.   Third Appellate District.—August 8, 1916.]

BRYAN ELEVATOR COMPANY (a Corporation), Respondent, v. HERBERT E. LAW, Appellant.

CONTRACT—INSTALLATION OF ELEVATOR PLANT—UNSATISFACTORY CON-
TROLLING DEVICES—UNWARRANTED REMOVAL OF ENTIRE PLANT BY
OWNER.—Under the terms of a contract for the construction and
installation of an elevator plant and service in a building, the
owner is not justified in removing the machines installed under
the contract on the ground that the controlling devices furnished
for the elevators were unsatisfactory, and in installing a particular
type of controllers, which could not be purchased without also
purchasing the machine itself, where the construction of the plant
was in every other way satisfactory to the owner, and it is shown
that other controlling devices were obtainable in the open market
which could be used with the installed machines and purchased independent of the machines themselves.

ID.—SATISFACTORY PERFORMANCE OF CONTRACT—WHAT CONSTITUTES.—
Where a contract requires work to be done to the satisfaction of
the person contracting therefor, only such performance is required
as is satisfactory to the mind of a reasonable person.

APPEAL from a judgment of the Superior Court of the
City and County of San Francisco, and from an order denying a new trial. B. V. Sargent, Judge presiding.

The facts are stated in the opinion of the court.

Edgar C. Chapman, for Appellant.

Thomas, Beedy & Lanagan, for Respondent.

CHIPMAN, P. J.—In the first count of the complaint plaintiff seeks to recover the sum of sixteen thousand dollars upon a written contract entered into by plaintiff and defendant, January 20, 1905, for the construction and installation of an elevator plant and service by plaintiff for the Monadnock Building, San Francisco. The second count was for necessary repairs to the elevators, elevator equipments, and elevator hatchways in said building of the alleged value of $4,604.33. The third count is for elevator parts and supplies alleged to have been sold and delivered to defendant by plaintiff, for which defendant agreed to pay the sum of $2,053.10. Plaintiff had judgment on the first count for the sum of $13,375, with interest from May 1, 1908. The findings and judgment on the second and third counts were in favor of defendant.

Both parties appeal from the judgment. Defendant's appeal is presented in this record and plaintiff's appeal on the same transcript is presented in No. 1466. Defendant also appeals from the order denying his motion for a new trial. The cause was tried by the court without a jury. The issues tried may be understood from the findings of facts by the court:

"II. That thereafter and on or about the 1st day of September, 1905, the said plaintiff entered upon and commenced the installation of said elevators, and proceeded with said installation as rapidly as the unfinished condition of said building would permit. That on or about the 18th day of April, 1906, and prior to the completion of the installation of said elevators, said building was injured and almost completely destroyed by earthquake and fire; that by reason of the damage suffered by said building, through said earthquake and fire, plaintiff was unable to continue with the performance of its said agreement for a long time thereafter; that as soon as said building was sufficiently repaired to make the work of installation of said elevators possible, the plaintiff continued the work of such installation; that plaintiff at all times, in good faith proceeded with the performance of the obligations imposed upon it by said agreement and furnished the materials and performed the labor required of it by said contract and honestly and faithfully performed said contract and completed the performance thereof on or about the 1st day of May, 1908, except as regards the controlling devices furnished by said plaintiff on the five passenger elevators which were not satisfactory to defendant and on account of which said defendant declined to accept the same and removed them from the building, and in this behalf the court finds: That said controlling devices did not operate satisfactorily and defendant was justified in rejecting the same and in removing them from said building and putting in other controlling devices. The court also finds that although said defendant declined to accept the said controlling devices as furnished by plaintiff and was justified in removing them from said building and in putting in other controlling devices, said plaintiff substantially performed the said contract.

"III. That the agreement hereinabove referred to was completed by said plaintiff on or about the 1st day of May, 1908, except that the defendant was not satisfied with the controllers on the said five passenger elevators and declined to accept the said controllers. That the length of time in completing said agreement by the said plaintiff was no greater than the amount of time said plaintiff was prevented from performing by the neglect of the said defendant in completing said building and by the earthquake and fire above referred to.

"IV. That in all regards, other than as above set forth, the plaintiff duly and faithfully performed all the conditions of said agreement above referred to on its part to be performed according to the terms of said agreement; that said plaintiff completely installed and equipped the elevators referred to in the said agreement in accordance with the plans and specifications attached to said agreement and made a part thereof, with the exception that the said defendant was not satisfied with said passenger elevator controllers or the elevator machines connected therewith and he declined to accept the same and removed all of said controllers and all of said elevator machines from said building and replaced the same with other elevator controllers and other elevator machines and installed said last mentioned controllers and machines in said building.

"That the reasonable market value of said elevator controllers and elevator machines so installed by said defendant was and is the sum of $15,156.00; and in this connection the court finds that the reasonable market value of said controllers so installed by defendant was and is the sum of $2625.00.

"But the court finds that defendant was not justified in rejecting the elevator machines so furnished by plaintiff or any of them and was not justified in installing other elevator machines in place of them, and that said defendant could and did replace said controllers with controllers of a design, workmanship and efficiency satisfactory to him for the sum of $525.00 each or a total sum of $2625.00. . . .

"VI.   That the sum of $21,375.00 is the reasonable value of the work done and the materials furnished by plaintiff in installing elevator machines and equipment for the defendant in said Monadnock Building, and the reasonable value of the materials furnished and accepted and the installation work accepted and used by defendant and that said defendant has paid plaintiff the sum of $8,000.00 and has suffered damages on account of plaintiff's failure to furnish controlling devices satisfactory to him in the sum of $2625.00; and that, after deducting from the contract price the said payment of $8,000.00 and the sum of $2625.00 to indemnify and compensate the defendant for the damages so suffered by him, there is now due, owing and unpaid from said defendant to said plaintiff the sum of $13,375.00, together with interest thereon at the rate of 7% per annum from the 1st day of May, 1908. . . .

"And as conclusions of law from the foregoing facts, the court finds the plaintiff is entitled to judgment against the said defendant for the sum of $13,375.00, together with interest on said sum from the 1st day of May, 1908, at the rate of 7% per annum, amounting to $4228.72, and for its costs of suit herein expended."

Plaintiff was properly to install, furnishing all the labor and materials therefor, four passenger elevators and one passenger elevator and safe lifter, and to alter the old passenger elevator then in use in the Bishop Building into a freight elevator, and to install two hydraulic ram sidewalk elevators, together with a flashlight signal system in accordance with certain plans and specifications made by Meyer & O'Brien, who were the architects of said building and of said work.

So far as this appeal reaches, the only dispute we are to settle relates to the installation of the five passenger elevators. And as to these the objection raised by defendant was to the unsatisfactory operation of the electrical controllers.

On November 5, 1906, defendant wrote plaintiff as follows: "In conformity with the provisions of our contract for elevators in the Monadnock Building, I advise you that the controlling devices are unsatisfactory and in my judgment inadequate for the requirements and therefore request that the control be replaced by that used by the Otis Elevator Co." Plaintiff replied, on November 9th, saying: "We cannot at this time accept a decision as to the controllers in the Monadnock Building, because in no case are those controllers complete and such as the design of the apparatus which we are to give you contemplates. Moreover as the writer explained to you sometime ago the present controllers are operating under conditions which are in no way a proper test of them, and further that the completion of the controllers is delayed purposely by us in order to keep machines in operation until the balance of the plant is ready to run, when the present controllers can be put into the condition which it is intended that they should be. The work on the permanent controllers is progressing as rapidly as circumstances will permit, and when completed and the present controllers finished and put in proper condition you will have no cause for complaint regarding them."

On June 5, 1907, defendant's manager, Mr. Huntington, wrote plaintiff as follows: "As Mr. Law has already notified you, we wish the controllers on the elevators now in the Monadnock Building changed to the Otis Elevator Company's controller. You may place it first on No. 2 elevator, and we will try it out."

The matter drifted along, the correspondence and the testimony showing that each party attributed to the other party the alleged failure of the controllers to give proper service, until, October 15, 1907, we find that plaintiff wrote defendant as follows: "Since writing to you yesterday we learn that you are taking our machines out of the Monadnock Bldg., and to this we make the most emphatic protest. We demand that we be allowed to demonstrate that these engines are all right by having them put entirely in our charge for sufficient time to prove our claims. All we ask of you is to have doors put on the engine room and have both your employees and all outsiders kept out of it. As our contract at the Monadnock Bldg. is not completed, we desire to know from you at once whether we shall go ahead with this final work! Awaiting your immediate reply, we remain." Defendant replied, on October 17th: "We have no objection to your completing your contract on the Monadnock Building in so far as it relates to the freight elevator in the back of the building and the two hydraulic ram sidewalk elevators." On November 29, 1907, defendant wrote plaintiff as follows: "We have taken out the passenger elevators from the Monadnock Building, and they are now in the basement. What disposition do you desire made of them by us?" On December 3d, plaintiff replied to this letter, stating: "We have turned the same over to our attorneys."

It does not appear at what date defendant removed the plaintiff's machines, but Mr. Robbins, manager of Otis Elevator Company, testified that the first bill rendered by his company was dated October 12, 1907, "and that was not made until after the Otis machines were put in the building—after they were put in, the machines which they substituted were removed. I don't just remember the date when that was done." As we understand the evidence, the Otis machines were taken to the building about October 12, 1907, the plaintiff's controllers and machines were then removed from their settings and the Otis machines and controllers put in their place.

Defendant states in his brief: "The court found that the real defect in the elevator plant was in the controller, and we think it was justified in reaching this conclusion." The correspondence as well as the testimony shows that the construction of the elevators, the machinery and appliances used in operating the plant, except the controllers, were entirely satisfactory to defendant. The contract did not specify any particular type of controller, though doubtless plaintiff contemplated putting in the one it manufactured. The provision of the contract was: "The contractor agrees that the elevator service going by the machines shall be continuous and that the control of the car shall be positive and the operation of elevators shall give satisfaction in every particular. In the event that the elevator machine or the controlling device proves unsatisfactory or inadequate to requirements, the contractor shall replace the machinery or controlling device with other machinery and control satisfactory to the owner. In the event of any dispute of the efficiency of any part of the

elevator machinery or control, the decision of the owner is
to be final and conclusive.''

It appeared from the testimony that the controller was so
far independent in its construction that a controller of the
Otis or any other design than the Bryan controller could be
substituted and the engines and other machinery connected
with and required in operating the completed elevator remain
undisturbed. The court found and the evidence was that
the Otis controllers had a value each of $525, and the five in-
stalled, $2,625.

The court found that the reasonable value of all the work
done and materials furnished by plaintiff in installing elevators and equipment, "and the reasonable value of the
materials furnished and accepted and the installation work
accepted and used by defendant," was $21,375, from which
the court deducted the payment of eight thousand dollars, and
the value of the five Otis controllers, $2,625, leaving due
plaintiff $13,375.

The portion of the findings to which defendant now objects
is the following: "That defendant was not justified in rejecting the elevator machines so furnished by plaintiff or any
part of them, and was not justified in installing other elevator
machines in place of them and that said defendant could
and did replace said controllers with controllers of a design,
workmanship and efficiency satisfactory to him, for the sum
of $525.00 each, or a total sum of $2625.00.'' Defendant's
position is thus stated in his opening brief: "These findings
which we have just quoted cannot be harmonized in any way,
for if under the evidence defendant was justified in rejecting
the controllers, he was equally justified in rejecting the
machines; not because the machines were defective in any
particular, but because it was impossible to buy any controllers that could be used with these machines. The only
proper controllers on the market were those manufactured
by the Otis Elevator Company, and these could not be had,
as we have pointed out, without the purchase of the Otis
Elevator machines. It follows, therefore, that as Mr. Law
was compelled to pay $15,156 for the Otis elevator controllers
and machines, that he is entitled to deduct that amount from
the contract price.''

The testimony was that the Otis Elevator Company would
not sell its controllers to plaintiff or to defendant without

also selling its machines to go with them. Witness Greenbaum, a mechanical engineer and president of plaintiff company at the time the contract was made and up to 1909, was
asked whether there were high-speed controllers in the market
other than the Otis controller, and answered: "I believe one
particularly was the Cutler-Hammer; another was the one
sold by the Scheurman people, from whom I did buy one;
there were quite a number of different style high-speed controllers at that time. There was a firm in Baltimore whose
name I can't remember at the present time; and one in
Chicago, and these firms made a specialty of making controllers and nothing else. They were not elevator men at
all in any sense of the word. They simply make controller
machinery, and in that machinery they make elevator controllers. Q. And they would send those controls to anybody
who made application? A. Yes, sir." On cross-examination
he testified that these controllers were all manufactured in
the east and the manufacturers had no agency here; that he
did not "tell Mr. Law anything about them," and that he
did not believe them any better controls than his own.

The testimony was that, during all the time and up to the
day it learned its machines were being removed, plaintiff
was endeavoring to bring its elevators up to a standard of
efficiency which would be reasonably satisfactory to defendant,
and during all this time there was a constant controversy
between the parties as to the way the elevators were being
run by defendant's employees, plaintiff complaining that
they were careless and inattentive to their duties in not properly caring for the machinery and in not properly operating
the elevators; defendant contending that this was not true,
and pointing out specific defects. And, finally, without previous notice of his intention so to do, defendant removed the
machines and controllers and substituted Otis machines and
controllers, and notified plaintiff to take its property away,
which plaintiff did, under an agreement that in doing so
the rights of neither party should be prejudiced. Witness
Greenbaum testified on cross-examination as follows: "Q.
What became of the machines after they were taken out?
A. They were taken across the bay and stored. Q. Taken
across the bay by yourself? A. We took them over there.
Q. Where did you store them? A. In the Van Emon elevator
plant. Q. What use was made of them subsequently? A. I

junked them. Q. Was there anything the matter with the
machinery? A. No; not that I know of. Q. Then why was
they junked? A. Because they were second-hand machines,
and you can't sell second-hand machines, particularly what
you call high-speed second-hand machines, to be installed in
the building again. People won't take them.'' He testified
that the reasonable value of the materials put in by plaintiff
and removed from the building by defendant was ten thousand
five hundred dollars—that is, the value of the controllers
and engines and ropes or cables; "thirteen thousand five hundred dollars was the reasonable value of the work we furnished and left in the building at the time our machines were
taken out, and that material and that construction were used
by Mr. Law when he put in the new machines.''

The inquiry seems to us to be narrowed to the question,
Was defendant justified in substituting entirely new machines
and controllers, entailing a loss to plaintiff of the machines
and controllers installed by it? The court made no specific
finding of the value of these machines and controllers, but
it found the value of all the work done and machinery furnished to be $21,375, from which it deducted the payment
made, eight thousand dollars, and the value of the controllers
furnished by defendant, $2,625. The court found that de-
fendant was justified in putting in the Otis controller, but
in view of the testimony that a controller of other design
could have been put in without removing plaintiff's machines,
it found that the cost of these controllers, $525 each, was the
limit of defendant's damage. And this narrows the inquiry
still further to the single question, Was the plaintiff properly
chargeable also with the cost of the Otis machines, which was
$12,530?

What was the right with which the contract clothed defendant? It is not necessary to discuss the question as applicable
to what defendant did in the present case. He decided that
the Bryan controller was not satisfactory, and the evidence
and the finding of the court sustained him in his decision.
Neither is it necessary to discuss his right to have an Otis
controller, for he got it and the court allowed him the cost
of it. It is claimed, however, that because he was obliged
to take and pay for the Otis machines in order to get the
Otis controller, defendant was within his rights in removing
plaintiff's machines, although he had made no objection to

them, and requiring plaintiff to pay for them. In support
of this claim reliance is placed upon the case of *Singerly* v.
Thayer, 108 Pa. St. 291, [56 Am. Rep. 207]. In that case
Thayer made the following proposition to Singerly: "I proposed to put my patent hydraulic hoist in your new building
on Chestnut Street (including a duplex pump worth eight
hundred dollars) according to verbal specifications given by
your architect, for two thousand three hundred dollars, warranted satisfactory in every respect." Plaintiff in error accepted this proposition and the elevator was substantially
finished, but proved unsatisfactory. He therefore declined
to accept it, and gave notice that he desired it to be removed.
This Thayer refused to do, and thereupon "Singerly took
it down and holds it subject to the order of Thayer, who
brought the suit, claiming the contract price." In comment-
ing upon the contract the court said: "The proposition was
made to induce him [Singerly] to purchase a kind of elevator
not in general use. The fair inference is that he desired to
procure one that would be satisfactory to himself. The manifest import and meaning of the language used is that it should
be satisfactory to him. . . . He did not agree to accept what
might be satisfactory to others, but what was satisfactory to
himself. This was a fact which the contractor gave him
the right to decide. . . . To justify a refusal to accept the
elevator on the ground that it is not satisfactory, the objection
should be made in good faith." The court found from the
evidence, though conflicting as to the efficient working of the
elevator, that it was sufficient "to show the plaintiff in error
acted in good faith and not in mere caprice in refusing to
accept it."

As we shall presently see, the authorities do not agree with
the rule here stated—that it is sufficient if the purchaser "acts
in good faith and not in mere caprice." It will be observed
that in the case cited the contract was for the purchase of an
entire machine. In the present case the contract recognized
two distinct parts—the machines and the controllers. In the
case cited the hoist was regarded as a novelty in design, and
the objection was to the working of the entire machine, which
may have influenced the decision. It is possible the opinion
would have been different had Singerly objected only to the
duplex pump, which could have been supplied in the open
market if the one furnished had been objected to. In the

case here the specifications carefully described all the various
parts of the elevators which were to be furnished constituting
the plant, the controllers being separately described. "The
rule very generally adopted," as was stated in *Dodge* v.
Kimball, 203 Mass. 364, [133 Am. St. Rep. 302, 89 N. E.
542], "is that, to entitle the plaintiff to recover, he needs to
show only that he proceeded in good faith in an effort to perform the contract, and that the result was a substantial performance of it, although there may be various imperfections
or omissions that call for a considerable diminution of the
contract price. The reason for this construction of such contracts is in part the difficulty of attaining perfection in the
quality of the materials and workmanship, and of entirely
correcting the effect of a slight inadvertence, and the injustice of allowing the owner to retain without compensation
the benefit of a costly building upon his real estate, that is
substantially, but not exactly, such as he agreed to pay for.
In none of the courts of this country, so far as we know, is
the contractor left remediless under conditions like those
above stated. The recovery permitted is generally upon the
basis of the contract, with a deduction for the difference between the value of the substantial performance shown and
the complete performance which would be paid for at the
contract price." (*Harlan* v. *Stufflebeem*, 87 Cal. 508, [25
Pac. 686] ; *Seebach* v. *Kuhn*, 9 Cal. App. 485, [99 Pac. 723] ;
Hall v. *Clark*, 7 Cal. App. 609, [95 Pac. 382].) In *Shepard*
v. *Mills*, 173 Ill. 223, [50 N. E. 709], the contract was for
the building of a heating apparatus. Among other things,
the court said: "A literal compliance with such contracts is
not necessary to a recovery, but it will be sufficient that there
has been an honest and faithful performance of the contract
in all its material and substantial particulars, and no omission
on essential points, or willful departures from the contract;
and mere technical or unimportant omissions will not defeat
a recovery of the contract price, less any damages, however,
requisite to indemnify the owner." (*Otis Elevator Co.* v.
Flanders Realty Co., 244 Pa. St. 186, [90 Atl. 624] ; Page
on Contracts, sec. 1387.) The evidence showed an honest and
faithful endeavor to install an efficient controller. It is true
this part of the elevator can hardly be said to be of slight
importance, and an omission to supply a controller reasonably satisfactory would not have fallen within the category

of a slight deviation. But, slight or otherwise, the failure of the controllers first placed by plaintiff to prove themselves efficient was met and the cost allowed to defendant; in other words, the defendant got what he demanded and for the damage he was indemnified. If the cases cited do not apply strictly, the principle underlying them would seem to be applicable. We think, without doubt, had the Otis people allowed their controller to be used without compelling the purchase of their machines, defendant would have no ground of complaint.

The rule, as we understand it, found in *Singerly* v. *Thayer, supra,* that where the contract requires work to be done to the satisfaction of the person contracting for the work, his rejection of it cannot be called in question "if he acted in good faith and not in mere caprice in refusing to accept it," we think is too broad and not in harmony with the generally accepted rule. It was said in *Gladding, McBean & Co.* v. *Montgomery,* 20 Cal. App. 276, 279, [128 Pac. 790]: "A stipulation in a contract to perform to the satisfaction of one of the parties only calls for such performance as should be satisfactory to a reasonable person." (Citing cases.) In *Keeler* v. *Clifford,* 165 Ill. 544, [46 N. E. 248], the action was to recover for certain grading and leveling done under a contract which provided that all grading was to be done to the satisfaction of said Keeler. The court said: "Where a contract is required to be done to the satisfaction of one of the parties, the meaning necessarily is that it must be done in a manner satisfactory to the mind of a reasonable man. The plain construction of the contract in this regard is that the work was to be completed in accordance with the contract, in such a manner that appellant, as a reasonable man, ought to be satisfied with it." (*Hawkins* v. *Graham,* 149 Mass. 284, [14 Am. St. Rep. 422, 21 N. E. 312]; *Richison* v. *Mead,* 11 S. D. 639, [80 N. W. 131], and cases cited in the opinion.)

Under the rule contended for by appellant it would be difficult, if not impossible, to show that the party was not acting in good faith, and his right to say he was not satisfied would be practically arbitrary, excluding all question of its exercise being reasonable or unreasonable.

In the present case appellant not only refused to be satisfied unless Otis controllers were used, but he claimed the right to exercise this refusal, knowing that these controllers could not be obtained without purchasing machines, at great cost, which were not essential to their use. He at no time requested plaintiff to obtain controllers other than the Otis controllers, several of which were obtainable in the open market. Without previous notice to plaintiff, or its consent, he removed plaintiff's machines and controllers and installed the Otis machines and controllers. Under the existing circumstances we think it would be unreasonable to hold that the contract permitted him to exercise what was little short of an arbitrary power.

The judgment and the order appealed from are affirmed.

Hart, J., and Ellison, J., *pro tem.*, concurred.

A petition to have the cause heard in the supreme court, after judgment in the district court of appeal, was denied by the supreme court on October 5, 1916.

[Civ. No. 1466.   Third Appellate District.—August 8, 1916.]

BRYAN ELEVATOR COMPANY (a Corporation), Appellant, v. HERBERT E. LAW, Respondent.

CONTRACT—INSTALLATION OF ELEVATOR PLANT—PURCHASE OF OLD MACHINERY—LIABILITY FOR LOSS.—Under the terms of a contract for the construction and installation of an elevator plant and service, which provided, among other things, that the owner of the building agreed to sell for the sum of one dollar in hand paid to the contractor all old elevator machinery, the contractor must sustain the loss thereof, where it removed the machinery to its shops, and it was there destroyed by fire, notwithstanding the contractor made a reduction in its bid in the contract of a certain sum on account of such old machinery, which was to be reinstalled and used as a freight elevator in the building in question.

APPEAL from a judgment of the Superior Court of the City and County of San Francisco. B. V. Sargent, Judge presiding.

The facts are stated in the opinion of the court.

Thomas, Beedy & Lanagan, for Appellant.

Edgar C. Chapman, for Respondent.

CHIPMAN, P. J.—The appeal in this case is from the third cause of action set forth in the complaint. The transcript appears to be in all respects the same as the same case, No. 1465, this day decided, *ante*, p. 204, [160 Pac. 170]. Why plaintiff's appeal was not urged in that case instead of making it the subject of a different number does not appear and is perhaps immaterial.

As a cause of action it is alleged that "plaintiff sold and delivered to defendant, at his request, certain goods, to wit, elevator parts and supplies," for which defendant agreed to pay the sum of $2,053.10. The claim of plaintiff is that it is entitled to recover the sum of $2,053.10, in addition to what it claimed in the first cause of action, which was disposed of in the case numbered 1465, for certain parts of the old elevator machinery formerly in the Bishop Building, and that when it was destroyed by the disaster of April 18, 1906, it belonged to defendant and the loss was his. Among the provisions of the contract was the following: "The owner agrees to sell for the sum of $1.00 here in hand paid to the contractor all old elevator machinery now installed in the Bishop Block, situated as described heretofore and hereby acknowledges and constitutes this his receipt for same." Plaintiff took possession of this machinery and removed it to its shops, where it was when destroyed. We think it clear that the title to the machinery was in plaintiff when it was destroyed, and we find nothing in the contract that would fix the loss upon defendant by such casualty. Indeed, the provision intended to cover losses by act of God would seem to relieve defendant from such loss. It is true that Mr. Greenbaum, president of plaintiff company, testified that because of having received this old machinery which was to be altered and reinstalled in the Monadnock Building, plaintiff reduced its bid in the contract one thousand six hundred dollars, "for the privilege of using that freight machine for installation in the building." But if it was the property of plaintiff when destroyed, the use which plaintiff intended to make of it is immaterial. We cannot see that the loss was the less to it than it would have been had it purchased the machinery from some other person.

Plaintiff's claim is that the parts thus lost it had to supply, for which defendant should pay. The court, in its ninth finding, recites the facts and finds, "that there is not now due, owing, and unpaid from the defendant to the plaintiff the sum of $2,053.10 or any part thereof."

We think the finding supported by the evidence and the judgment is therefore affirmed.

Hart, J., and Ellison, J., *pro tem.*, concurred.

———

[Civ. No. 1520. Third Appellate District.—August 8, 1916.]

ROY E. ARUNDELL, Respondent, v. AMERICAN OIL FIELDS COMPANY (a Corporation), Appellant.

Evidence—Proof of Fact by Inference.—Direct evidence of a fact in dispute is not required in all cases, as the law recognizes the force of indirect evidence which tends to establish such fact by proving another, which, though not in itself conclusive, affords an inference or presumption of the existence of the fact in dispute.

Id.—Negligence—Proof by Indirect Evidence.—Negligence, like any other fact, may be inferred from a preponderance of the evidence, whether it be circumstantial or direct, and the plaintiff is not required to prove his case beyond a reasonable doubt.

Id.—Injury to Tool-dresser on Oil Derrick—Falling of Improperly Hoisted Casing-pipe—Inference of Negligence.—In an action for damages for personal injuries sustained by a tool-dresser in a derrick for drilling an oil well from the falling upon his hand of a joint of casing-pipe which he and the driller in charge were endeavoring to hoist from the well, the negligence of the defendant is sufficiently proven by evidence that the driller adopted a plan of handling the pipe, which was testified to by experts as unsafe, and by not using the elevators provided for the purpose.

Id.—Master and Servant—Risks of Injury Assumed by Servant.—The ordinary risks which a servant assumes as incidental to his employment are such as may not be avoided by the exercise of reasonable care by the master or by his servant who is superior to the injured servant.

Id.—Instruction—Sympathies and Prejudices of Jury—Proper Refusal.—An instruction to the effect that the jury should not be governed by sympathy but by the evidence, and that in considering the evidence the jury should not be influenced by the fact that the plaintiff is a laboring man and the defendant a corporation, is properly refused.

APPEAL from a judgment of the Superior Court of Kern County, and from an order denying a new trial. J. W. Mahon, Judge.

The facts are stated in the opinion of the court.

Olin Wellborn, Jr., and George E. Whitaker, for Appellant.

Shepard & Alm, and J. R. Dorsey, for Respondent.

CHIPMAN, P. J.—Judgment for ten thousand dollars followed the verdict of a jury as damages suffered by plaintiff for the loss of his right hand while in defendant's employ. The appeal is from the judgment and from the order denying defendant's motion for a new trial.

In 1910 plaintiff, then twenty-three years of age, worked for defendant for about six months, receiving $3.50 per day and board, including Sundays. He had had some previous experience in the oil fields, being employed principally as a "roustabout." For some weeks previous to November 15, 1910, he had been employed by defendant as a "tool-dresser," and was working in that capacity on that date. He commenced work at midnight, the accident occurring at about 4:30 o'clock in the morning. The only other person at work on the derrick at the time was one A. F. Mellen, designated as a "driller."

Plaintiff's testimony as to what he was doing and the cause of the accident was as follows: "I was jarring on a pipe, running the spear to the bottom of the pipe, and jarring it up trying to free the pipe to get it loose in the well—it was froze. The well was somewhere in the neighborhood of two thousand feet deep. A spear is a contrivance you put on the tools, the same as you do a bit, then you can go down into the casing and take hold of it. The string of tools was about forty feet long. It may be a little more with the spear. I continued jarring on the pipe two or three hours. After I was through jarring I pulled on the casing, trying to pull it loose. I got it partly loose, then I parted the pipe; it was hard to tell where. By 'parting the pipe,' I mean pulled it in two. I next tried to take the spear out of the hole. I didn't succeed, because the top joint was crimped near the top, and the spear would not come through. We had to take the joint out and get it out of the road—the top joint. I unscrewed it. In the first place Mellen and I had to unscrew this joint loose from the rest of the pipe. We both helped to do it. After that was done I put a rope on the pipe and Mellen pulled it up in the derrick. If I remember right, I mentioned the fact about using elevators, I said that to Mr. Mellen. He said, 'No,' to use the rope. I tied the rope on with a timber hitch just below the collar, probably six or eight inches, maybe a foot. The collar is about six inches wide. The rope was about an inch or a little more thick. It was a strand out of a drilling cable, about ten feet long. After tying the rope to the pipe I hooked it on to the block-hook. It had an eye in it. Block-hook is what they generally use for handling casing, the one that is permanently in the casing block. I slung the eye of the rope over that hook in the casing block. Mr. Mellen pulled the casing up in the derrick with the casing block by means of the engine and apparatus. At the time he was at the throttle. You can reach it from the derrick floor. This happened about 4 or 5 in the morning. It was dark. I could see about twenty foot in the derrick; above that I could not distinguish anything. After Mellen had hoisted that pipe I pulled the tools up and took that spear out. I lifted the tools just high enough so that I could take the spear off. It was on the lower end. The spear got above the floor. Mellen told me to elevate the tools at that time. Mellen had not got around to helping me yet. I put on the wrenches to break the joint. It would not take me but a few minutes to loosen that joint. When I removed it the tools were naturally moving around to a certain extent; jarring them, rather. They were practically perpendicular all the time but they would swing. I did not lower or elevate them. We didn't get the spear loose. This joint of pipe fell and caught my hand. I had my hand on the spear at the time. I just started to steady the tools to put on the wrench. The pipe dropped down around the tools. It struck me back of the thumb joint on the wrist. It removed my thumb, two fingers, and part of the others. The pipe was six and five-eighths inches in diameter. It weighed,

I think, twenty pounds to the foot. It was fourteen or fifteen feet long. . . . They amputated the hand at the wrist in the hospital.''

Defendant makes the following points against the validity of the judgment: 1. Insufficiency of the evidence to show how the accident happened; 2. Contributory negligence; 3. Plaintiff assumed the risks of the employment; 4. Plaintiff was not injured by the negligent act of an employee ''having the right to control or direct the services'' of plaintiff; 5. Errors occurring at the trial.

Plaintiff's testimony above given conveys some notion of how the accident happened, but it becomes necessary to inquire further into the particulars and plaintiff's relation to the work in hand. Much testimony was given explanatory of the relative duties of the driller and the tool-dresser in a derrick for drilling an oil well. Witness Crites, who was superintendent of the Peerless Oil Company in the Kern River field, and had been in the oil business continuously since 1896, ''in the operating department, drilling wells, etc.,'' and was ''familiar with the custom and manner of performing work in and around derricks,'' testified: ''The driller is a man that has charge of the tools, and you look to him, of course, to do that part of the work. The tool-dresser's business is to help the driller. If there is a boiler, he takes care of the boiler; keeps the fire up and keeps water in the boiler, and attends to the work in and around the rig that the driller requires of him; dressing bits, helping him in all sorts of ways around the derrick. The tool-dresser has certain duties which are strictly his duties, and the driller has certain other duties which are strictly his duties. As to the general work, the driller is boss of the rig and directs the work in and around the derrick. In the performance of work that requires both the tool-dresser and the driller to lend a hand, the driller directs the work. Attending to the boiler is one of the routine duties that the tool-dresser is supposed to do. If he wants any help, he usually asks the driller to help him. In the actual work of sinking a well, handling the tools, hoisting the casing, and such matters, the driller directs that work. The driller controls the derrick, directs the tool-dresser in and about his work in the derrick.'' Other witnesses described the driller as ''the man that does the work inside and does the directing of it. He is supposed to be boss when he is on tower." ("Tower" means the same as "shift" in other mining operations, and in plaintiff's case was from midnight until noon.)

Witness Harry Arundell, who was "lease drilling superintendent" of defendant company, testified to the duties of the tool-dresser and driller. "The tool-dresser's duties are to fire and look after the boiler, take care of the engine and assist the driller around the rig, under the driller's orders. He works under the driller's orders entirely; the driller in a derrick has, in a way, a right to control and direct the services of the tool-dresser at his work. All the tool-dresser's work is generally under his supervision. He has to do the work to the driller's satisfaction. The meaning of 'tool-dresser' is dressing and sharpening tools. . . . In this line of work it is necessary to use a timber hitch almost every day around a drilling rig, particularly hoisting pipe. If a timber hitch is properly tied with a dry rope, it would not permit a pipe to slip from the rope and fall; it could be tied with a wet rope so that it can't slip. A wet rope would be stiff and hard to use, and would not draw down tight, and would have a tendency to open up if the weight was taken off of it. . . . The scope of the duties of driller and tool-dresser are understood by them usually so that they can work without much said. Ordinary work, sometimes very little spoken; ordinarily each knows his duty and goes ahead and does it. It was the duty of the tool-dresser to step to the throttle when the tools started up, and to run the engine while the tools are hoisted out. Custom made it the duty of the driller to be at the throttle when the pipe was hoisted. It is the tool-dresser's duty, under the driller's supervision, to fasten the hoisting block and hook to the pipe."

It is not necessary to quote further from the testimony as to the relative duties of the driller and tool-dresser. There is but little difference between the testimony of plaintiff and defendant on this point, and there is substantial agreement that the driller is the directing head of the work in the derrick and controls the movements of the tool-dresser.

A. F. Mellen was the driller in charge of the work when the accident occurred. He and plaintiff were the only persons present. His deposition was taken by defendant and was introduced by plaintiff and read in evidence. As to the accident he testified: "It is a kind of a mystery how the joint of pipe happened to fall. In raising the pipe to strip the tools through it while taking off the spear the pipe fell—fell from up in the derrick. We pulled it up there with a block and tackle, the casing-block—I did. It was fastened to a sling made of rope. Arundell fastened the rope to the piece of pipe that fell. It was his duty. He knew how to fasten it. Nobody directed him how to fasten it. As a rule, we generally kept the block and tackle on the hook all the time. It is a tool-dresser's place to put that on; it is almost always carried on the hook. The elevators generally hang on them. The elevators are used to put in a long string of pipe; and the sling is used for a small article. As a general thing, they were both of them hanging on the same hook. I don't know whether they were on that night—as a rule, they were on. I hoisted the pipe up with an engine. I ran the engine. . . . I could not say how high I hoisted it. All that I had to go by was the lines. I figured on hoisting it to the blocks at the top of the derrick—probably forty feet. Arundell hooked it on. I could see for myself that the pipe was unscrewed when I hoisted. . . . The rope was put on after the pipe was unscrewed. While Arundell was putting the rope on it I was at the engine. After I helped to unscrew it I went to the engine and told him to let the blocks down while he connected with the rope. I saw when he got the rope finally connected. When the rope was on I hoisted it. I could see for myself it was ready to be hoisted. I could not say definitely how high I hoisted it; I figured on how much line I had. I went by the coils on the shaft. I took the blocks to the top of the derrick, at least forty feet from the bottom of the floor. I had a way of ascertaining whether it was at the top or not. It could not have been from the top six or eight feet. I don't know just exactly. . . . It was dark at the time I hoisted it. I didn't look up to see." It appeared that the derrick was lighted by four incandescent globes of sixteen-candle power and so placed under the roof of the derrick that they cast no light in the open space above the roof into which the pipe was hoisted. The roof was about twenty feet above the floor. The witness, continuing, testified: "I don't know how the pipe happened to get loose from the rope that Arundell fastened it to. The rope didn't come down with the pipe; it stayed on the hook. When we took Arundell to the doctor, the rope was hanging on to the hook with the timber hitch still in it; that showed it slipped—showed the pipes slipped out of it. . . . I am sure the pipe slipped down the rope; the rope was still on the block and the timber hitch was still in it when I came back; that was after 7 o'clock. Arundell was hurt between 4 and 5. . . . When I hoisted the string of tools up I didn't hear any blow or jar as if it had hit up there. I didn't feel any indication of the tools hitting the pipe when I ran the engine. It seems like you could have felt such a thing. The only thing I could figure on why the pipe slipped through the rope and came down, it must have become loosened—picked it up on the tools. That was a theory; I have no knowledge. . . . When you can see in the daylight it is the tool-dresser's duty to watch for that. In the dark he could not see. . . . The man at the throttle who is hoisting it could not see it at the same time he was performing his duty at the engine there—it is impossible. . . . The man at the engine could not see anything in the top of the derrick. On the night in question I hoisted this block to the top of the derrick as far as I could possibly do. I had six or eight feet more to run—I mean I could hoist it further. . . . I don't think it was possible to escape my attention, if it had been so adjusted that there was danger of it slipping out; at that distance it seemed all right. The rope knot was on the side away from me. I could see the turns of the rope on the pipe next to me." He testified that after he had hoisted the pipe he set the brake to hold it with the calf-wheel and then pulled up the tools preparatory to taking it off the spear. "While I was letting it back again so the spear would not have to drop far it stuck a little, enough to turn a twist in the rope two or three times when Arundell started to take it off. Of course, while he was doing that, I was letting it down with the brake. When I got it down two or three inches of the floor I went to the tools myself, and had just got hold of them with my hands when I heard this racket; that was all there was to it." On cross-examination he testified that when Arundell tied "that knot around the pipe it was pretty close to the collar; he tied it two or three inches. The collar is about six inches; it was eight or nine inches from the top. We lifted three or four joints of pipe with the same knot. It didn't show any tendency at that time to slip." He testified that "the closer you get to the collar the better it is, as they most always slip some; and for that reason it is better to tie as close to the collar as you can.''

Plaintiff testified further: ''At the time this accident happened it had been raining—everything was wet and slippery. There is always an opening in the center of the roof of the derrick. Of course, directly under the roof would not much water fall. The roof came to a peak, like this [illustrating], about three or three and a half feet opening clear across the derrick the full width of the rig from front to bacᶦ·. The roof covers each side; leaves the center open. . . . I didn't have anything to say about how the hoisting of this pipe and the removing of the spear was to be done. All told, I had worked in and around oil well derricks approximately five or six months. No similar state of circumstances arose in my experience during that time. It was the first time that I ever had exactly that kind of work to do, and it became necessary to remove a joint of casing out of the well in order to remove the spear. I personally tied the knot by means of which that particular pipe was hoisted. I tied a timber hitch. [Witness illustrates.] I tied a safe knot; I tied it in the usual manner. I had been experienced in tying knots of that kind ever since I had been working in the oil business. The tying of that knot is a frequent occurrence; use those knots every day. I could not say how high that pipe was hoisted by Mr. Mellen, because it went up where there was no light. It was none of my business to pay any attention to that. . . . There were no lights above the roof. The roof is about twenty feet high above the floor, I judge. . . . During the daytime or daylight I could have seen the position of the pipe, and the man who hoisted it could see; not after night. He could in the daytime by stepping out just a little. He could still hold the throttle and look up to the top of the derrick.'' On cross-examination he testified that he had worked there for four months and was fit for the work he was expected to do, although he ''was not what you call an experienced man in particular''; that ''the string of tools would be about forty feet from where the cable joins the rope-socket down to the bottom of the spear.'' A working model of a derrick in operation was brought into court by defendant and used in the examination of witnesses. Plaintiff was called upon to and did illustrate by this model with much particularity how he and Mellen conducted the work before and up to the time of the accident. Not having the model before us, we are deprived to considerable extent of the advantage enjoyed by the jury. There was testimony of several witnesses to the effect that it would have been the proper thing to do, and safer, to have hoisted the pipe with the elevators. Plaintiff testified: "The elevators which I had been using when I broke the pipe ['by "broke" we understand is meant unscrewing it] were set aside on the derrick floor. The elevator block was hanging somewhere in the derrick. I got that down far enough to hook the rope into it; then I pulled the pipe up in the derrick. After I hooked one end of the rope to the hook, one end was already on the casing, I tied the rope to the casing—that is the timber hitch I refer to in my testimony." He then described how he hoisted the tools high enough to get at the spear which was at the lower end—"high enough to unscrew it. The next step was to take the spear off. . . . When I was proceeding to unscrew the spear there, the joint of pipe that was held in the air dropped. The rope that held it did not break; the rope did not break loose from the hook; the rope remained aloft and the pipe came down. . . . Mellen was presumably at the throttle during the lifting of the pipe. . . . I knew my duties and went ahead with the performance of them; Mellen knew his duties and went ahead with the performance of his." On redirect he testified: "I mean by saying I knew my duties, as I testified a moment ago, that I knew my duties as tool-dresser; that is, when I was told to do anything I knew how to go around and do it. . . . I don't know of my own knowledge that the pipe slipped through the knot; I know by what Mellen said afterward. If I remember right, I asked before I tied this rope around there if we should not use the elevators—something to that effect. I did not have any particular reason for that, only I just took it that that would be the best way in doing it. He told me to use the rope." On recross: "Q. Did Mellen give you any directions about the tying of that knot, or any advice or any suggestions or anything, or did you know? A. I knew what knot to use." His attention was called to testimony he had given, as we understand, in a deposition: "Q. Did the pipe go clear down or was it stopped by the piece of rope with the eye in it which was fastened to it? A. It dropped through the knot. Q. It did not break the rope, then? A. No, sir. Q. But it slipped down there

through the knot which you had tied around it and came
through it? A. Yes, sir. Q. How did you ascertain that?
A. Because it could not possibly happen without—that is, it
could not have slipped through the knot without the pipe was
raised and the weight was taken off the pipe to let the knot
become slack. Q. How did you know that the knot was slack?
A. The pipe could not have slipped through it without it did.
Q. Could not the rope break? A. The rope did not break.
Q. Did the rope remain hanging on the block-hook? A. Yes,
sir. Q. So that your theory of the manner in which the
accident happened is that the tools were hoisted in such a
way that they lifted the pipe enough to shake the rope loose
from it sufficiently to let it drop down through the knot?
A. Yes, sir. Q. You believe that is the way the accident happened? A. Yes, sir.''

Expert witnesses were called by plaintiff to explain what
they regarded as the proper and safe way to remove a spear
from the tools under circumstances such as existed in the
present case. Witness T. Phillips, a driller of many years'
experience, testified: "I was running the opposite tower the
day Mr. Arundell was injured. There are two towers—the
morning tower (from noon to midnight) and the afternoon
tower (from midnight to noon). . . . Assuming that the top
joint was crimped, so that the spear would not pass through
it, and assuming that I wanted to remove the spear from the
lower end of the tools, the only way to go about it is to bring
that spear up and take it off. I would take off the top joint
of pipe and take it off. I would hoist it that high, probably
[demonstrates with model]. I would only hoist it above
the floor here high enough so that I could break this joint.
About there is where I would put the casing [demonstrating].
I would suspend the casing about at that point, with the
brake on the calf-wheel; it would not be over three or four
feet. . . . I would break it and take the spear off, then let
the casing down and pull the tools out through it, . . . and
after you get your tools out there is nothing in the way of
putting the pipe anywhere you want to. I would take the
elevator rather than use a one-inch manila rope to hoist it
with. I think it would be more safe; with that rope there is
a chance of slipping. Where the elevators are fastened on
to the casing there is not much chance in the matter. If I
merely hoisted it up that distance, there is a chance of the

rope slipping; there is always a chance if the rope is wet; there is a chance for it to slip. It was raining that night; it had been raining when I went off tower. I don't think it is safe to hoist that pipe a greater distance than that under any circumstances—not with a hitch on, because, you see, if that rope is wet there is a chance for it to slip—anything loosens it up it is liable to slip through and you once loosen it and it won't take hold again. It would not be apt to slip without anything interfering with if it it was properly tied. There would have to be something to interfere with it if it was drawn up by a knot properly tied. . . . Up that high it is pretty close to the center of the derrick or to the pipe. Of course, there is a chance for it to swing over and catch." Given the circumstances in this case of the pipe hoisted up toward the top of the derrick and that the tools were hoisted out of the well so as to reach the spear to take it off, and in attempting to take it off the pipe fell, he testified: "I would say that there is only one chance to cause the pipe to fall. If the knot was properly tied, the only chance would be catching the tools on to this pipe and raising it up and lifting the weight off the rope. The tools were approximately forty-five feet in length. A pipe being hoisted in that manner, assuming it to be a fourteen-foot pipe with a rope, say eight or ten feet, that would have to get very near to the top to clear it from the tools." Referring to the manner the pipe was hoisted and its height in the derrick, he testified: "I should think it would be carelessness in a man to hoist it up where it was."

Other witnesses expressed similar opinion, though one or more testified that the upper joint of pipe should be unscrewed and drawn up a few feet above the floor of the derrick— three or four feet—and the tools then drawn up through the pipe and the spear taken off at this opening in the pipe. The tools could then be drawn up through the pipe and disposed of, the pipe screwed on again and let down into its place or laid aside if faulty. But all agreed that the pipe need not and should not be raised but a few feet above the floor.

Witness Cox testified: "If I should hoist it [the pipe] up that way and then afterward hoisted the tools up so as to get at the spear; assuming that it was dark and I could [not] see any distance above the top of the roof there, I would not really know when I had that pipe in a safe place—I suppose it would be guesswork. I would not guess at it, I would not pull it up there; if I did I would use the elevators. If I did pull it up with a rope, it is liable to fall—to come in contact with some part of the rig that you could not see or something, and the rope might slip. If you hoisted the tools in order to get at that, in order to get at the spear, assuming the tools were about forty feet in length, the rope-socket would not likely pass through the pipe without catching on the bottom of the pipe. If the pipe was tied up by means of a rope—a sling—there would not be much chance to pull it up without hitting the bottom of the pipe. The pipe would not hang perpendicular; in my opinion, the tools would probably catch on the side of it. The chances are that would have an effect on the knot or rope, it would loosen up your knot; if your rope was wet or stiff, or a new rope, it would give you slack on your rope.''

Witness Nangle, having explained the process of taking off the spear and removing the tools under the circumstances here, testified: ''I would raise the joint by means of an elevator. It is safer. I would not raise that joint of pipe above the roof; I would not consider it safe to do that.''

Witness Hutchings testified: ''I would not think it was equally safe to hoist that pipe way up to the top of the derrick out of the reach of the tools and then hoist the tools— not in my experience I would not.'' Speaking of the rope as attached in the present case and the pipe hoisted up as described, he testified: ''It would not slip unless the tools caught it and raised it up and loosened the hitch. The timber hitch will hold the pipe safely, I suppose, if there is not anything to interfere with it. . . . You see, the tools are liable to catch on this joint here [indicating on model], and raise it up, and it will unhook the rope up there, if he was using a rope— raises that joint [indicating]; it would not be apt to unhook if he used the elevator. [Witness demonstrates pulling tools up, showing how they would catch on the pipe.] If the pipe was lifted in that manner, it would loosen timber hitch. . . . This pipe is bound to hang out of the perpendicular. The tools would catch on the bottom of the pipe and raise that up, and it will loosen that knot; then, when they drop back, of course, it will slip—bound to slip. If this rope was a one-inch manila rope, and wet at the time, it would make a lot of difference on the holding qualities of the rope, it would be stiff, would not draw down tight; you could not make that knot as safe, it would not draw down as hard on the pipe, and would be more easily loosened, if anything raised the pipe and slackened the pull on the rope. If it was a manila rope and not a cotton rope, it would make a lot of difference—it is stiffer and won't draw down like this one. [Referring to sample piece of cotton rope in the courtroom.]"

Witness McManus testified: "I would not lift a pipe to the top of a derrick by means of a rope tied in a timber hitch. I would consider it careless on the part of a man who did that, as long as he had an elevator there to handle it."

Witness Harry Arundell testified: "Q. If, under the circumstances just stated, the driller hoisted the pipe to a great distance up in the derrick, up near the top, would you consider that a safe manner of proceeding or not? A. I would consider it dangerous to hoist anything to the top of the derrick by a rope, unless great care is taken. There would be danger of getting tangled up and falling, the knot slipping or becoming untied."

The height of the derrick is not certainly given by any witness. Witness Phillips thought it eighty-two feet; witness Harry Arundell stated that the standard derrick was eighty-two to eighty-four feet from below the crown-block to the ground. "The bottom of the casing-block, the hook, would be about ten feet under the crown; that would be about seventy-two feet up." Witness Phillips thought the tools were about forty-five feet long.

Expert witnesses called by defendant testified that a timber hitch, if properly tied, as the evidence showed was the case here, would not slip even though interfered with while holding up a pipe, for example, by the tools when elevated. But on this point the evidence is decidedly conflicting, as will be seen from the testimony introduced by plaintiff. There was sufficient evidence to justify the jury in finding that Mellen, who, for the time, represented the authority and responsibility of defendant, was guilty of negligence in raising the pipe so far above the roof of the derrick that the rope by which it was held suspended could not be seen, and leaving the pipe thus suspended at a height where the tools when elevated would interfere with it. Mellen was not at all certain to what height he lifted the pipe. He testified that "all he had to go by was the lines"; that "he could not say how high he hoisted

it. I figured on how much line I had. I went by the coils
on the shaft. . . . I figured on hoisting it to the blocks at the
top of the derrick—probably forty feet.'' In view of the testimony that it was not necessary to take the obvious risk of
hoisting the pipe into a space of darkness and that in taking
this unnecessary course care was not observed to make sure
that the tools when elevated would not interfere with it, and
that if this happened, it was almost certain that the knot
would become loosened and the pipe slip through it, the jury
might well have inferred the negligence of defendant to have
been the proximate cause of the accident. The principles
enunciated in the cases cited by defendant, that negligence
will not be presumed merely from injury shown, or from facts
unexplained that an accident has occurred, and that the burden of proof was on plaintiff to show defendant's negligence,
need not be gainsaid. But the law does not require in all
cases direct evidence of a fact in dispute. The law recognizes the force of indirect evidence which tends to establish
such fact by proving another which, though not in itself conclusive, affords an inference or presumption of the existence
of the fact in dispute. (Code Civ. Proc., sec. 1832.) An inference is a deduction which the reason of a jury makes from
the facts proved (Code Civ. Proc., sec. 1958); but an inference must be founded upon fact legally proved. (Code Civ.
Proc., sec. 1960.) The testimony showed that Mellen adopted
a plan of handling the tools and pipe, which the witnesses
testified was unsafe, by hoisting the pipe into a dark space
where the timber knot by which it was held could not be seen,
or any tendency of its slipping be observed, and by not using
the elevators which would have held the pipe in perfect security. This was his initial act of negligence, and it was followed by another step, testified to as unsafe, which was to
elevate the tools without being assured that they would not
interfere with the pipe, knowing, as he must be presumed to
have known as a competent driller, that such interference
might loosen the knot holding the pipe and permit the pipe
to slip through. One or more of defendant's witnesses testified, and it is urged in argument, that the danger was not increased by the height to which the pipe was hoisted, for had
it been raised but five or six feet and had fallen, it would as
surely have injured plaintiff. This suggestion ignores the
fact that had the pipe been raised but a few feet from the

floor, both plaintiff and Mellen could have observed any tendency of the pipe to slip, and, besides, there would in that case have been no tools hovering around the pipe and endangering the security of the knot in the rope. Defendant contends that the testimony shows a clear space between the tools and the lower end of the pipe, and hence the impossibility of the tools having had anything to do with the pipe's slipping through the rope. This contention is grounded on the assumption that Mellen hoisted the pipe to the top of the derrick, a fact not deducible from Mellen's testimony, the only witness who had any knowledge on the subject. The estimates given of the inside height of the derrick, the length of the tools and pipe, and the pieces of rope and the blocks used on each would leave but a small, if any, margin of space between the tools and pipe. Mellen said he hoisted the pipe probably forty feet; again, that he did not know how high he hoisted it; again, that it was a few feet from the top; again, that he had only the lines to go by or the coils on the shaft, but he did not say he counted the coils or examined his line. If he hoisted the pipe only forty feet, it would not have cleared the tools, for they were forty-five feet long, as Phillips testified. And this witness, who worked on this same derrick as driller, testified that the pipe "would have to get very near to the top to clear it from the tools." Defendant further suggests that the evidence is as consistent with the theory that the rope was carelessly tied by plaintiff as that the pipe was raised and the rope loosened by the tools. This suggestion derives no force from the testimony, for both plaintiff and Mellen testified that plaintiff tied a proper timber hitch, and the testimony of many witnesses was that a timber hitch properly tied is safe and not likely to loosen its grip. We think the evidence was fairly responsive to the issues presented by the complaint and answer, and that there was sufficient evidence to justify the jury in attributing the injury to defendant's negligence.

It is contended that the injury to plaintiff was caused by an assumed risk. In support of this contention it is claimed that plaintiff "had the same opportunity of observing the situation as Mellen had"; that "he was in as good a position as Mellen to notice the danger and risk of the business"; that it is not charged that the appliances furnished were not adequate and the place a safe one in which to work or that Mellen was an unskillful driller. Under these circumstances it is urged that plaintiff's injury "was the result of an accident happening in the ordinary course of the business in which he was employed and the risk of which he assumed as one of the hazards of his employment." The rule is relied on as stated by Labatt: "That a servant assumes all the ordinary risks which are incidental to his employment," and that, "unless the plaintiff can adduce evidence which tends fairly to show that the injured person, by reason of his want of experience or his tender years, was not chargeable with that comprehension of the risk which, in the absence of such evidence, he is presumed to have possessed." (1 Labatt on Master and Servant, p. 2102.) Conceding the correctness of the rule, as it existed when the accident happened, that "the servant assumes all the ordinary risks which are incidental to his employment," the question is, What is meant by the term, "ordinary risks"? It certainly is not meant that the servant assumes all risks of injury that may result in the ordinary course of his employment, for the master, under such a rule, would never be held liable. We take it the ordinary risks which the servant assumes are such as may not be avoided by the exercise of reasonable care by the master or by his servant who is superior to the injured servant. It cannot be said that plaintiff and Mellen stood upon an equal footing or that plaintiff's opportunities of observing what Mellen was doing and how he was doing it were equal. Plaintiff could not know nor could he be presumed to have anticipated the possibility or probability of Mellen's not having hoisted the pipe sufficiently far to clear the tools. Plaintiff was in no situation to observe what Mellen was doing or how he was doing it. He was at his post of duty endeavoring to "break" the spear, ignorant of his position of danger caused by Mellen's carelessness and negligence. By the exercise of ordinary care on Mellen's part the accident would not have happened.

Appellant contends that plaintiff tied the timber hitch, raised the tools and moved the tools after they were raised, and hence if the tools caused the rope on the casing to be loosened, it was caused by plaintiff's negligence and he cannot recover. The testimony was that Mellen hoisted the pipe to a place above the roof and set his brake. Under Mellen's orders, and with his assistance, plaintiff hoisted the tools high enough above the floor to allow him and Mellen to remove the spear. Mellen testified: "I pulled the tools up and prepared to take the spear out. . . . We pulled the tools up to the joint in the pipe, about even with the floor." What plaintiff did in the matter was done under Mellen's orders, with his personal assistance, and without any knowledge or comprehension of the dangerous position of the pipe, and it seems to us the jury were justified in finding that he acted as a reasonably prudent and cautious man would have acted under the circumstances. The accident did not happen by reason of hoisting the tools too far—they were raised only sufficiently high to admit of removing the spear. The cause of the accident, as the evidence warranted the jury in finding, was that the pipe was not hoisted high enough. Of course, it was incumbent upon plaintiff to exercise his senses and reasoning faculties, and whether he did so in the present case was to be determined by the jury taking into account all the attending circumstances. The accident cannot be traced to any act of plaintiff which was not performed in the line of his duty or directly ordered to be done by his superior. We do not think defendant sustained the burden of proving contributory negligence of plaintiff as the cause of his injury.

The point urged that plaintiff "was not injured by the negligent act of an employee of defendant having the right to direct and control his services," we think cannot be maintained. Section 1970 of the Civil Code provides that the "employer shall be liable for such injury when the same results from the wrongful act, neglect or default . . . of a person employed by such employer having the right to control or direct the services of such employee injured." It seems to us the testimony of both plaintiff and defendant showed very clearly that the work in and around an oil-well derrick is under the direct control of the driller. In the absence of the superintendent his authority is supreme. It is by virtue of this authority given by custom to the driller that he has the *right* to exercise it. One of defendant's witnesses, himself president or vice-president of several oil companies, testified: "In removing a pipe from the well, as in this case, in determining what was to be done with the top joint of casing, the driller would tell the tool-dresser what they were going to do, and that if the tool-dresser should say, 'No, I don't think that should be done,' the superintendent on the lease would get another tool-dresser, if I was the driller." We have called attention, in the earlier part of this opinion, to sufficient testimony to show that Mellen had the right and exercised it to direct plaintiff in his work.

Error is claimed in the court's not allowing defendant to prove by witness Munzer the condition of the weather in Kern County at the time of the accident. It had been shown by plaintiff that it was raining the night of the accident, and the purpose of the offered evidence was not so much to dispute a fact of no great importance in the case as it was "in determining which party spoke the truth." The report offered was made up by the Kern County Land Company at Bakersfield from reports sent in by superintendents of farms in various part of the county. These reports were telephoned to the telephone operator in the office; he reported them to the stenographer, and she "makes the proper record of it." It was a purported copy of this record that was offered. Aside from its nonofficial and hearsay character, the reports from the Kern County Land Company's farms would not disprove that it rained at the oil well in question. The ruling was not error.

Error is claimed in giving the following instruction: "Presumptive or circumstantial evidence is admissible in civil cases. When direct evidence cannot be produced, minds will form their judgments on circumstances. So in this case it is not necessary that the plaintiff produce direct evidence as to what caused the casing, mentioned in this case, to fall, if any casing did fall, but such cause may be inferred from all of the circumstances in the case." It is contended that "a jury is not permitted to infer the negligence of a defendant from circumstances unless they are strong enough and convincing enough to exclude every other reasonable hypothesis than that of negligence." We have already referred to the law that the fact of negligence may be proved by indirect as well as by direct evidence. (*Jones* v. *Leonardt*, 10 Cal. App. 284, [101 Pac. 811]; Code Civ. Proc., sec. 1832.) Negligence, like any other fact, may be inferred from a preponderance of the evidence, whether it be circumstantial or direct, and plaintiff is not required to prove his case beyond a reasonable doubt. The instruction, fairly considered, merely told the jury that they were at liberty to determine the question of defendant's negligence from evidence other than direct proof of the cause of the accident.

The court refused the instruction, requested by defendant, to the effect that the jury should not be governed by sympathy but by the evidence, and that in considering the evidence the jury should not be influenced by the fact that plaintiff is a laboring man and defendant a corporation. A jury sworn to try the case and a true verdict render upon the evidence must be presumed to have obeyed their oath, and, unless it should appear that they were influenced by sympathy or prejudice and not by the evidence, we must presume that their verdict was based upon the evidence. Nothing in the record tends to show that the jury acted out of sympathy for plaintiff or through prejudice against defendant.

An instruction asked by defendant was refused in which the jury were told that plaintiff could not recover "unless they find he has a preponderance of evidence supporting the following propositions: First, that the plaintiff was not at the time of the accident guilty of any failure to exercise ordinary care for his own safety which approximately contributed to his injury; second, that the defendant was guilty of negligence in the manner charged in the complaint; third, that such negligence was the proximate or direct cause of the plaintiff's injuries in question"; and that if plaintiff has failed to sustain by evidence these propositions or any one of them, he cannot recover. The first subdivision of this instruction is in effect an instruction that the burden is upon plaintiff to show by a preponderance of the evidence that he was not guilty of contributory negligence. For one who fails to exercise ordinary care for his own safety, and he is injured in consequence thereof, certainly contributes thereto. But this issue was presented by defendant, and upon it rested the burden of establishing it by a preponderance of evidence and not upon plaintiff to prove the negative of that issue. That it was necessary for plaintiff to show that defendant was guilty of the negligence charged and that such negligence was the proximate cause of plaintiff's injuries, is undoubtedly true. Defendant was entitled to these instructions, and plaintiff claims they were elsewhere given in the charge, which is not denied, but defendant contends that "if counsel wished these instructions to be considered, they should have incorporated them in the record. Not having done so, they cannot now rely upon them to show no error was committed by the refusal of the lower court to give the instructions." The transcript does not purport to contain all the instructions, and it is apparent that it does not. Error must be shown, and if equivalent instructions, though not in the same language, were given, no error was committed. If no such instructions were given, it was defendant's duty so to show. We have seen that the evidence was sufficient to justify the jury in finding the fact that defendant was guilty of negligence as charged and as the issues were tried, and that such negligence was the proximate or direct cause of plaintiff's injuries. Under such circumstances defendant was not prejudiced by the ruling of the court.

Instructions, given by the court, numbered 12 and 15, are criticised, for the reason that by No. 12 "the jury were told that dangerous appliances or a danger in the work did not bar the right of the plaintiff to recover unless the employee 'fully understood, comprehended, and appreciated' the danger"; and that in No. 15 the instruction "assumes the existence of facts not in evidence." Instruction numbered 12 is the statement of the law as found in section 1970 of the Civil Code, and read in its entirety is not error, and if not applicable we cannot see that it could have been prejudicial. Instruction numbered 15 appears to us to have been drawn with strict adherence to evidence admitted at the trial. It does not assume the existence of any facts. It stated: "If you believe from evidence that," etc.

We have given the case such attention as its importance seems to have demanded, and, finding no prejudicial error in the record, the judgment and order are affirmed.

Hart, J., and Ellison, J., *pro tem.*, concurred.

[Crim. No. 364.   Third Appellate District.—August 9, 1916.]

In the Matter of the Application of CHARLES CENCININO for a Writ of Habeas Corpus.

FISH AND GAME—POWER OF LEGISLATURE—CONSTITUTIONAL LAW.—By the adoption in the year 1902 of section 25½ of article IV of the constitution, providing that the legislature may provide for the division of the state into fish and game districts and may enact such laws for the protection of fish and game therein as it may deem appropriate to the respective districts, the people expressly vested in the legislature of the state the sole and exclusive power over and control of legislation relating to the fish and game of the state, and withdrew from the local subdivisions of the state whatever power they might have previously exercised over such subject under section 11 of article XI of the constitution, which grants to counties, cities, towns, and townships of the state the right to make and enforce within their respective limits all such local, police, sanitary, and other regulations as are not in conflict with general laws.

ID.—CONSTITUTIONAL PROVISION MANDATORY.—The provisions of section 25½ of article IV of the constitution are mandatory, notwithstanding the use therein of the word "may."

ID.—STATUTORY CONSTRUCTION—PERMISSIVE LANGUAGE.—Where the purpose of the law is to clothe public officers with power to be exercised for the benefit of the public, language which is permissive in form is to be construed as peremptory.

ID.—WITHDRAWAL OF POLICE POWER.—The people may at any time legally withdraw from local authorities the power of police or any portion thereof which they have by their constitution granted to such authorities.

APPLICATION for a Writ of Habeas Corpus originally made to the District Court of Appeal for the Third Appellate District.

The facts are stated in the opinion of the court.

J. J. Carin, and Leon E. Prescott, for Petitioner.

HART, J.—The petition alleges that the petitioner is illegally held in restraint of his personal liberty by the sheriff of Humboldt County, and the return of that officer shows that he detains and is detaining the petitioner in custody under the authority of a warrant of arrest issued out of the justice's court of Trinidad township, said county, upon a complaint charging the petitioner with the violation of the provisions of Ordinance No. 118, passed by the board of supervisors of Humboldt County on the sixteenth day of November, 1912, and which, by virtue of a provision therein contained, went into effect on the third day of December, 1912.

Said ordinance reads in part as follows:

"Section I.   It shall be unlawful at any time to offer for shipment, ship, transport or receive for shipment or transportation from the County of Humboldt, State of California, to any place outside of said County of Humboldt, State of California, any crabs caught in or taken from any of the waters within the limits of the said County of Humboldt, State of California.

"Section II.   It shall be unlawful at any time to offer for shipment, ship, transport or receive for shipment or transportation from the County of Humboldt, State of California, to any place outside of said County of Humboldt, State of California, any clams of any kind or character produced or taken from any ground, waters, or territory within the limits of said County of Humboldt, State of California.

"Section III.   Every person who shall violate any of the provisions of this ordinance shall be guilty of a misdemeanor and upon conviction thereof shall be punished by a fine not exceeding five hundred dollars or by imprisonment in the County Jail not exceeding six months or by both such fine and imprisonment."

The ordinance declares that the true intent and purpose thereof is "solely to secure the better protection of the crabs and clams in the public waters and grounds within the County of Humboldt, State of California, and not for the regulation of the business of dealing in crabs and clams."

The petitioner, in support of his claim that his restraint is illegal, makes this point: That, by the adoption, in the year 1902, of section 25½ of article IV of the constitution (see Stats. 1901, p. 948), the people expressly vested in the legislature of the state the sole and exclusive power over and control of legislation relating to the fish and game of the state. Manifestly, the effect of that construction of said provision is to exclude the legislative bodies of local political subdivisions of the state from any power or right to legislate with respect to those subjects.   If this be a sound position, it follows, of course, that the ordinance whose provisions the petitioner has been charged with violating relates to a subject not within the legislative competence of the board of supervisors of Humboldt County, is therefore void, and, as a necessary consequence, under or upon the purported ordinance no complaint stating a public offense can be formulated.

The section of the constitution in question reads as follows: "The legislature may provide for the division of the state into fish and game districts, and may enact such laws for the protection of fish and game therein as it may deem appropriate to the respective districts."

The legislature of 1911 (Stats. 1911, p. 425), in pursuance of the authority vested in it by that provision of the constitution, passed an act whereby it divided the state into six fish and game districts. By said act the first district was made to embrace, among several other counties, the county of Humboldt. At its session in the year 1915, however (Stats. 1915, p. 589), the legislature repealed said act and passed in lieu thereof another act, by the provisions of which the state was divided into twenty-nine fish and game districts. By this law that part of Humboldt County constituting Humboldt Bay was placed in districts Nos. 8 and 9. At the same session the legislature enacted section 628f of the Penal Code (Stats. 1915, p. 112), which, among other provisions, contains an inhibition, on pain of punishment as for a misdemeanor, the shipment or offer for shipment or receipt for shipment or transportation any species of crab taken in fish and game districts 8 and 9.

The ordinance under which the petitioner has been proceeded against includes, in its inhibitions and penalty, all of Humboldt County, covering, therefore, those portions of Humboldt Bay which form parts of fish and game districts 8 and 9.

The authority vested in the legislature by section 25½ of article IV of the constitution to divide the state into districts for the purposes of legislation affecting fish and game was undoubtedly inspired by the fact, based upon experience in that direction, that, owing to the varied conditions with respect to fish and game existing in different parts of the state, no uniform legislation justly applicable and appropriate to the whole state and the diversified conditions therein existing as to game and fish was practicable or feasible. Regulations necessary and appropriate in one part of the state might be wholly unnecessary and, indeed, unjust, and, therefore, inappropriate in other parts thereof. This is the only rational explanation of the scheme with respect to the matter of taking fish out of the waters of the state and hunting for game contemplated by the above provision of the constitution. And experience has demonstrated the necessity and efficacy of that scheme. Prior to the adoption of that amendment, it was within the competence of the boards of supervisors of the several counties to regulate the matter of taking and hunting fish and game within their respective territorial jurisdictions. These local regulations were often harsh and unjust, and sometimes inadequate to the proper protection of fish and game, the object of all such legislation merely being to provide against their ultimate extinction, which would inevitably result from an absence of proper legal restraint upon their destruction, or, in other words, to provide ample opportunity for their propagation in a degree commensurate with their nature in that respect. And to accomplish this highly important end the people finally conceived that the whole subject could be the better and more justly treated by legislation wholly in the control of the state legislature and such as is authorized by the provision of the constitution above quoted herein. So, in considering said provision, keeping in mind the reasons thus suggested as the animating cause of the adoption thereof, and at the same time keeping in view the nature or character of the power with which the legislature is thus invested the conclusion seems to be inevitable that, by said provision, it was intended, as the petitioner contends is true, to clothe the state legislature with sole and exclusive control and power, so far as legislation is concerned, over the fish and game of the state, and, therefore, to take from local political subdivisions of the state any right which they might have had prior to the adoption of said provision of the constitution legislatively to deal with or regulate the matter of pursuing fish and game. Therefore, our opinion is that the language of section 25½ is mandatory and not merely permissive, as the use of the auxiliary verb "may" as among the operative words of the provision might, upon first blush, imply.

The word "may" as used in a statute or constitution is often interpreted to mean "shall" or "must." Such interpretation always depends largely, if not altogether, on the object sought to be accomplished by the law in which that word is used. It seems to be the uniform rule that, where the purpose of the law is to clothe public officers with power to be exercised for the benefit of third persons, or for the public at large—that is, where the public interest or private right requires that the thing should be done—then the language, though permissive in form, is peremptory. As was said by the supreme court of the United States in *Supervisors* v. *United States,* 4 Wall. 436, [18 L. Ed. 419], construing a statute of the state of Illinois similarly phrased to the provision in question here: "What they [public officers] are employed to do for a third person, the law requires shall be done. The power is given, not for their benefit, but for his. It is given as a remedy to those entitled to invoke its aid." (See, also, *Hayes* v. *County of Los Angeles,* 99 Cal. 74, [33 Pac. 766].)

But the provision of the constitution in question has been given by our own courts a construction in accord with the views above expressed. (*Ex parte Prindle,* 7 Cal. Unrep. 223, [94 Pac. 871].) In that case, which was decided by the district court of appeal of the second district, so much is said which has a direct bearing upon the question before us here that it would extend this opinion to an unreasonable length to attempt to reproduce herein all that is contained therein which is forcibly pertinent to this case. It will suffice to say that the court in that case held that the provision of the constitution under consideration is mandatory, notwithstanding the employment of the word "may" therein.

In the case of *In re Cole,* 12 Cal. App. 290, [107 Pac. 581], while not necessary therein to decide the question, this court, nevertheless, in considering the effect of s ction 25½ of article IV of the constitution, strongly intimated that its language and terms were mandatory. The court had under consideration an ordinance of Sonoma County prohibiting the catching of fish in rivers, streams, or sloughs in said county. The ordinance considered in that case was regularly passed by the board of supervisors previous to the adoption into article IV of the constitution section 25½, and the court held that, as the ordinance involved a valid act at the time of its enactment, and, as the constitutional provision was prospective and not retroactive in its operation, said provision could not be held, in view of article XXII of the constitution, to have effected a repeal of said ordinance or impaired its validity in any respect. The court, however, used this significant language: "The most that could be urged by the petitioners is that the power to regulate the pursuit of fish and game had been taken away from the board of supervisors and given exclusively to the legislature."

In considering the question before us, we have not been unmindful of the fact that by section 11 of article XI of the constitution, the people have granted to the counties, cities, towns, and townships of the state the right to make and enforce, within their respective limits, "all such local, police, sanitary, and other regulations as are not in conflict with general laws." Nor are we antagonistic to the proposition that, although fish and game constitute the property of the people of the state in their collective capacity, the matter of the regulation of the pursuit of fish and game is within the police power (*Ex parte Maier*, 103 Cal. 476, [42 Am. St. Rep. 129, 37 Pac. 402]), and that it would be within the competence of local legislative boards to regulate that matter under the power granted to them by said section 11 of article XI in the absence of any limitation placed by the people upon the exercise by them of said power, and so long as such legislation did not contravene any general law of the state. But, as has been shown, and as is clearly manifest, the power of local boards to regulate or legislate upon the subjects of fish and game has been withdrawn by the people by their expression in section 25½ of the constitution and subsequent to the delegation by them of the power which such local authorities may exercise under section 11 of article XI.

That the people may, at any time, legally withdraw from local authorities the power of police or any portion thereof which they have by their constitution granted to such authorities, is a proposition far beyond the realm of all debate. The police power, like the right of eminent domain, is an attribute of sovereignty. In this country it resides or inheres in the sovereignty of the states, and sovereignty, which means all the power inherent in a commonwealth, is, generally, exercised by the state itself, but it is so exercised because, only, the power has been delegated to it by the people of the state, in whom, primarily, it resides. It therefore follows as a matter of course that the people may delegate or grant that power to any competent authority, to be exercised exclusively or concurrently with some other authority or to a limited extent, with the residue of the power or its ultimate control in some other body or authority, or in the people themselves. In the case of the fish and game of the state, the people have, as seen, withdrawn or taken from counties, cities, and towns whatever power they might have exercised over those subjects by virtue of section 11 of article XI of the constitution. This they had the right to do, and in doing it still left to counties, etc., plenary power to make and enforce proper and necessary police regulations upon a variety of subjects coming within the scope and purview of the power of police. It follows that there cannot be justly claimed to exist any inconsistency or repugnancy between section 11 of article XI and section 25½ of article IV. It is true, as has been suggested, that the legislature might not have exercised the authority vested in it by section 25½ of article IV, and it is equally true that had it failed to do so, it could not be compelled by any known legal process to legislate upon the subject of fish and game. But this does not mean that the exclusive power to regulate the pursuit of fish and game is not still in that body under that provision of the constitution, or that counties and cities, etc., may regulate the matter on the failure of the legislature to exercise the right and power so conferred upon it. It is, under the terms of the constitutional provision, solely for the legislature to determine when and how the taking of fish and the killing of game shall be regulated, as well as to determine what portions of the state shall be included within fish and game districts and what portions shall be excluded therefrom and not subject to any regulations upon those subjects.

We conclude from the reasons herein stated that counties, cities, towns, and townships are no longer authorized to legislate upon or in any manner or degree interfere in the matter of the pursuit of fish and game; that, consequently, Ordinance No. 118 of Humboldt County, under and by virtue of the provisions of which it is sought to prosecute and punish the petitioner, is void, and that his arrest and restraint are, therefore, illegal.

The petitioner is accordingly discharged.

Ellison, J., *pro tem.*, concurred.

[Civ. No. 1426.   Third Appellate District.—August 14, 1916.]

JOHN M. BOSCUS et al., Copartners, Respondents, v. CHARLES H. WALDMANN et al., Appellants.

MECHANIC'S LIEN—FORECLOSURE—PLEADING—DATE OF COMPLETION OF BUILDING—SUFFICIENCY OF COMPLAINT.—In an action to foreclose a mechanic's lien, an allegation that the building was completed "on or about" a specified date, which date was less than thirty days before the alleged date of the filing of the claim of lien, is sufficient to warrant proof of the exact date of completion.

ID.—COMPLETION OF CONTRACT—SUFFICIENCY OF AVERMENT.—An allegation in such an action that the building was completed according to the terms of the contract sufficiently shows that the contract was completed.

ID.—BUILDING CONTRACT — OMISSION TO FILE BOND — LIABILITY OF OWNER.—Under section 1183 of the Code of Civil Procedure, as amended in 1911, it is the duty of the owner to exact from the contractor a bond and file the same in the office of the county recorder, if he would restrict his liability to laborers, materialmen, or subcontractors for their claims to the contract price, and where he fails to make such exaction, there is then imposed upon him the penalty of paying all liens to the extent of the value of the work done and materials furnished.

ID.—COMPLETION OF BUILDING BY OCCUPATION — OMISSION TO FILE NOTICE—ESTOPPEL.—The owner of a building is estopped from claiming that the lien of a claimant other than the original contractor was not filed within thirty days after occupation of the building, where no notice of such occupation was filed, as the requirement of section 1187 of the Code of Civil Procedure as to the filing of notice of completion applies as well to the statutory completion of a building by occupation, acceptance, or cessation of labor, as to actual completion.

APPEAL from a judgment of the Superior Court of the City and County of San Francisco.   Marcel E. Cerf, Judge.

The facts are stated in the opinion of the court.

Alexander D. Keyes, for Appellants.

A. P. Dessouslavy, and P. A. Bergerot, for Respondents.

HART, J.—This is an action of foreclosure under the mechanic's lien law.

On the eleventh day of April, 1912, the appellants, the Waldmanns, and the defendant, Marcuse, entered into an agreement in writing whereby the latter agreed to erect upon certain real property of the first named parties, situated in the city of San Francisco, a three-story frame building for the sum of $18,915, which sum was to be paid in certain specified installments at specified times, the last installment ($4,728.75) being made payable thirty-five days after the completion of said building. Said contract was filed for record in the office of the county recorder of the city and county of San Francisco on said eleventh day of April, 1912, but there was not filed with said contract before the work was commenced, or at any other time, the bond provided by section 1183 of the Code of Civil Procedure, or any bond whatever.

Immediately after the eleventh day of April, 1912, the defendant, Felix Marcuse, commenced the erection of said building upon the real property described in the complaint, in pursuance of the terms of said contract between him and the Waldmanns, and the complaint alleges that he completed the same "on or about October 26, 1912; that no notice of the completion of said building or contract was ever filed in the office of the county recorder of said city and county of San Francisco; that all the terms and conditions of said contract to be by said Felix Marcuse kept and performed have been by him duly kept and performed." It is averred that of the contract price for said building not more than the sum of ten thousand dollars has been paid by the Waldmanns to said Marcuse, and that "there ever since has remained and still remains due and unpaid from defendants [the Waldmanns] . . . to said Felix Marcuse, under said contract, and for said extra work and materials, a sum exceeding $10,000.00."

On the sixth day of May, 1912, said Marcuse, as such contractor, entered into an agreement with the plaintiffs by which the latter undertook and promised to do all the plumbing work for said building and to install the steam-heating plant and the radiators therein, in accordance with the plans and specifications adopted by the Waldmanns and said Marcuse, said plans and specifications being attached to and forming a part of the contract for the erection of the building; that plaintiffs by said agreement agreed to furnish all the materials and necessary labor, to commence said work at once, to prosecute the same without delay, and to have said work finished as soon as possible; that said Marcuse agreed to pay the plaintiffs therefor $2,190, as follows: seventy-five per cent of the work done as the same should progress, and the remaining twenty-five per cent thirty-five days after the completion of the building.

It is alleged that, during the course of the erection of the building, the plaintiffs, at the request of said Marcuse, performed certain extra work and furnished certain extra materials. The various and several items of extra work and materials so performed and furnished are separately set out and described in the complaint, and the total amount thereof, stated in money, is $315.65. There are eleven of these items of extra work performed and extra materials furnished, and the complaint alleges that as to the first six items of such extras in the order in which they are set forth in that pleading, the prices therefor were fixed and agreed upon between plaintiffs and the said Marcuse; that as to the remaining five items thereof, no price was fixed or agreed upon for the same, but that the amounts claimed for the said last five items constitute the reasonable value thereof. It is alleged that no time within which said extra work was to be done was fixed or agreed upon, except that it was agreed that the same was to be done during the course of the erection of the building and as soon as possible, and that no time was fixed for the payment to the plaintiffs for said extra work; "that plaintiffs have further performed all the conditions of said agreement of May 6, 1912, to be by them performed; that said extra work was agreed to be done and was actually done, and that said extra materials were furnished to be used and were actually used in the construction of said building." It is further averred that all said extra work was done and the extra materials were furnished by the plaintiffs upon the order of said Marcuse and with the consent of the said defendants, Charles H. and Nellie V. Waldmann; "that the said price of $2,190 is and was the reasonable value of the work provided by the said agreement of May 6, 1912, to be done by plaintiffs."

It is alleged that the sum of $750 only has been paid on the price fixed in the agreement of May 6, 1912, and that nothing has been paid the plaintiffs on account of the extras aforesaid, and that, with the sum due on account of said extras added to the balance remaining unpaid and due under the said written agreement of May 6, 1912, there is now due the plaintiffs from the appellants the total sum of $1,755.65.

The complaint is in two counts. The first alleges that the plaintiffs on the nineteenth day of November, 1912 (admitted by all the parties to have been the 20th instead of the 19th of November as alleged), filed their claim of lien, duly verified, in the office of the county recorder of the city and county of San Francisco. In the second count it is alleged: "That, on November 30, 1912, defendants, Charles H. Waldmann and Nellie V. Waldmann, filed for record in the office of the county recorder of said city and county of San Francisco their notice wherein it was stated that a cessation of labor on said building had occurred October 26, 1912, and that, on November 25, 1912, there had been a cessation of labor for thirty days; that on December 10, 1912, plaintiffs, for the purpose of securing a lien for the amount due them as aforesaid, filed in said recorder's office their claim of lien, duly verified by the oath of John M. Boscus, one of said plaintiffs," etc.

A demurrer on both general and special grounds interposed by the defendants Waldmann was overruled, and said defendants thereupon answered the complaint specifically denying all the averments of the same, with the exception, however, of paragraph VI thereof, relating to the extra work done and the extra materials furnished by the plaintiffs, and as to said extras they admitted that they were done and furnished by the plaintiffs, but, it is alleged, upon an express agreement that there would be no extra charges therefor, some of them merely involving the correction of work which was called for by the building contract but which was defectively executed.

As separate and distinct defenses the answer in substance alleges: 1. That the plaintiffs ceased to labor and ceased to furnish materials in the construction of said building prior to the eighth day of October, 1912, and that the claim of lien set forth in each of the causes of action declared upon was filed for record more than thirty days after the plaintiffs ceased to labor and ceased to furnish materials to be used in the construction of said building; 2. That the defendants Waldmann, as owners, began the occupation and use of said building on the seventeenth day of October, 1912, "and that the claims of lien of the said plaintiffs were filed more than thirty days after such occupation and use commenced, to-wit,

on the 20th day of November, 1912, and on the 10th day of
November, 1912, respectively, and were, therefore, filed for
record after the time allowed by law and these defendants
allege that such occupation and use by these defendants as
such owners was open, notorious and continuous.''

Finally, answering both causes of action relied upon by the
plaintiffs, the answer points out the requirements as to plumbing prescribed by the specifications, and then charges that the
plaintiffs failed to comply with those requirements in a number of specifically mentioned material particulars.

The court's findings are in substance as follows: That the
building, except as to certain trivial imperfections, involving
items, aggregating, in money, the sum of $17, for which credit
was allowed the appellants, was completed by Marcuse ''on
or about October 26, 1912, and subsequent to October 20,
1912''; that, barring the trivial imperfection referred to in
the construction of said building, all the terms and conditions of the contract to be by said Marcuse kept and performed have been by him duly kept and performed; ''that
ever since on or about October 20, 1912, there remained, and
now remains, due and unpaid from defendants Charles H.
Waldmann and Nellie V. Waldmann to said Marcuse under
said contract a sum exceeding $6,500.'' It is further found
that all the terms of the contract of May 6, 1912, between
Marcuse, as agent of the defendants, and the plaintiffs,
whereby the latter were to do the plumbing work in and upon
said building, and provide the labor and materials therefor,
were duly performed by the plaintiffs, and that the latter
performed the extra work and furnished the extra materials
alleged in the complaint and above referred to, the said agreement of May 6, 1912, and the extra work all being executed
and performed according to the specifications forming part
of the building contract. It is also found ''that, on October
17, 1912, defendants Charles H. Waldmann and Nellie V.
Waldmann entered into, and ever since have been in, the
actual and exclusive use and occupation of said building.''

It was alleged in the answer and, as seen, admitted to be
true by counsel for both parties, that the first claim of lien by
the plaintiffs was filed on the twentieth day of November,
1912, and not on the nineteenth day of November, 1912, as
the complaint alleges.

It was also admitted by the appellants that no notice of
completion of the building was ever filed by them, but that
(so the plaintiffs allege and admit) a notice of cessation of
labor was filed on November 30, 1912, stating that, on November 25, 1912, there had been a cessation of labor for thirty
days.

It is alleged by the complaint and not denied by the answer
that the bond mentioned in section 1183 of the Code of Civil
Procedure was not filed with the original contract in the office
of the county recorder, and thus the failure to file such bond
was admitted.

Upon the findings and the admissions mentioned the court
entered its decree, awarding the plaintiff the sum of $1,738.65,
or the sum of $1,755.65 minus the said sum of $17 allowed for
the "trivial imperfection," decreed that the plaintiffs were
entitled to a lien on the real property described in the complaint and the building thereon and a foreclosure thereof, and
a sale of said property at public auction to satisfy their claim.

The Waldmanns have appealed from said judgment under
the alternative method.

The findings and the judgment are, as is obvious, based
upon the first count of the complaint—that is, the decree, in
accordance with the findings, adjudged the plaintiffs to be
entitled to the lien and the benefits thereof filed on the twentieth day of November, 1912, upon the theory that the building was completed on the twenty-sixth day of October, 1912.

The contract between the plaintiffs and the original contractor, Marcuse, was made and filed and the work performed
and the materials furnished thereunder after the existing law
providing for the enforcement of mechanics' and laborers'
liens was passed by the legislature of 1911, and hence by the
provisions of that law must the questions presented by this
appeal be tested.

The complaint, which is not to be indorsed as a perfect
pleading in a case of this character, is nevertheless sufficient,
and states a cause of action in the first count, upon which the
judgment is based. We shall not consider all the objections
to which it is urged that it is amenable. One of these objections may be noticed, however. It is that the allegation that
the building was completed according to the terms of the contract "on or about October 26, 1912," and that the claim of

lien was filed on the nineteenth day of November, 1912, is too
indefinite, and is not equivalent to the statement that completion took place within thirty days before November 19,
1912. (Citing *Cohn* v. *Wright*, 89 Cal. 86, [26 Pac. 643].)
The case cited has reference particularly to a finding in the
criticised language of the complaint. We think, however,
that the language may and should be held sufficient in a complaint in a case of this character to warrant proof of the
exact date, and that no substantial injury to the appellants
could have followed from the ruling on the demurrer, so far
as that language of the pleading is concerned. It is further
insisted that the complaint was defective, in that it alleged
that the *building* rather than the *contract* was completed.
The complaint, as we have seen, declares that the building
was completed *according to the terms of the contract,* and
this sufficiently showed that the contract was completed, assuming that there is any substantial merit to the distinction
sought to be drawn by appellants. We think the court made
no error in overruling the demurrer.

The most important objection to the judgment, however, is
that certain of the vital findings upon which it is founded are
not supported by the evidence, and this involves the principal question around which the controversy submitted here
revolves and upon which its solution hinges, viz., whether the
plaintiffs filed their claim of lien—that of November 20,
1912—within the time prescribed by the statute; and, furthermore, whether said finding is sufficiently definite to constitute a clear and distinct finding of the fact to which it is
addressed. The appellants also attack the finding respecting
the extra work and materials above spoken of.

Section 1183 provides for a lien in favor of all persons for
labor performed upon or for material used in the construction of any building, etc., for the value of the labor so done
and the materials so furnished. This provision is only de-
claratory of the right expressly guaranteed by our constitution to artisans, mechanics, laborers, and materialmen to a
lien upon property upon which they have bestowed labor and
materials in the improvement thereof or the erection of a
building thereon. (Const., art. XX, sec. 15.) The same section, however, further provides that any person having charge
of the construction, etc., of the building or other improve-

ment, "shall be held to be the agent of the owner for the purposes of this chapter," thus binding the owner to any subcontracts with other persons in the construction or repair of the building or other improvements, provided, of course, such subcontracts are within the scope or the terms, conditions, and specifications of the original contract. A bond (heretofore referred to) is also provided by this section. It is the duty of the owner to exact this from the contractor and file the same in the office of the county recorder with the contract if he would restrict his liability to laborers and materialmen or subcontractors for their claims to the contract price. If he fails to require such bond to be executed and filed and none is filed, there is then imposed upon him "the penalty of paying all the liens to the extent of the value of the work done and materials furnished." (*Roystone Co.* v. *Darling,* 171 Cal. 526, [154 Pac. 15].)

But the provisions with which the principal question here is concerned are in section 1187. Said section, among other things, provides that "every person save the original contractor claiming the benefit of this chapter, within thirty days after he has ceased to labor or has ceased to furnish materials, or both; or at his option, within thirty days after the completion of the original contract, if any, under which he was employed, must file for record with the county recorder . . . a claim of lien containing," then follows a specification of the facts which the lien must contain and recite. Said section proceeds: "Any trivial imperfection in the said work, or in the completion of any contract by any lien claimant, or in the construction of any building, improvement or structure, or of the alteration, addition to, or repair thereof, shall not be deemed such a lack of completion as to prevent the filing of any lien; and, in all cases, any of the following shall be deemed equivalent to a completion for all the purposes of this chapter: the occupation or use of a building . . . by the owner, or his representative; or the acceptance by said owner or said agent, of said building . . . or cessation from labor for thirty days upon any contract or upon any building . . . ; the filing of the notice hereinafter provided for. The owner may within ten days after completion of any contract, or within forty days after cessation from labor thereon, file for record in the office of the county recorder . . . a notice setting forth the date when the same was completed, or on which cessation from labor occurred, together with his name and the nature of his title, and a description of the property sufficient for identification, which notice shall be verified by himself or some other person on his behalf. . . . In case such notice be not so filed then the said owner and all persons deraigning title from or claiming any interest through him shall be estopped in any proceedings for the foreclosure of any lien provided for in this chapter from maintaining any defense therein based on the ground that said lien was not filed within the time provided in this chapter; provided, that all claims of lien must be filed within ninety days after the completion of any building," etc.

It is not contended, nor could it be successfully, that under section 1187 a lien claimant, other than the original contractor, may not file his lien within thirty days after the happening of any one of two events, viz.: 1. After he has ceased to labor or ceased to furnish materials, as the case may be, or both, if he has both performed the labor and furnished the materials; 2. After the completion of the original contract. The appellants do contend, however, that the plaintiffs should have filed their lien within thirty days after the seventeenth day of October, 1912, the date upon which it is found by the court that the Waldmanns, owners of the property, entered into the occupation of the building. The argument is that a lien claimant, other than the original contractor, must file his claim of lien, within thirty days after the first act constituting a completion of the building, whether it be an actual or only a statutory completion, and that if he fails to do so, then his right to a lien is lost. To be more explicit, the argument is: That, if a completion is effected, either by occupation or a cessation from labor or by acceptance, the time for the filing of the lien begins to run on that day, and the claimant cannot then claim the right to file his lien within thirty days after the building has actually been completed, if such actual completion occurs on a date subsequent to the completion by occupation or by acceptance or by cessation from labor, as the case may be.

In reply to the proposition so advanced, the plaintiffs say that, even if it be true that in this case the occupation and use of the building constituted a statutory or constructive and not an actual completion of the building, the defendants were, nevertheless, required to file the notice of completion required by section 1187, and, having failed to file such notice, they are now estopped, under the terms of said section, from maintaining any defense in this action "based on the ground that said lien was not filed within the time provided in this chapter." The defendants argue, however, that the provision with regard to the notice of completion to be given applies solely to an actual completion and not to the statutory or constructive completion.

In the case of *Roystone Co.* v. *Darling*, 171 Cal. 526, [154 Pac. 15], the supreme court, for the first time because it was the first case calling for it, elaborately reviewed the lien law of 1911, which constitutes a general revision of the law theretofore existing upon that subject in this state. In that case, through Mr. Justice Shaw, the scope, the intent, and the meaning of the several provisions of that statute were thoroughly explored and lucidly exposed and explained. The question as to the application of the requirement of the statute that notice shall be given of the completion of the building to the several events constituting the equivalents of completion, when actual completion has not been effected, did not arise in that case. And, since the amendment of section 1897 (Stats. 1897, p. 202), whereby, for the first time, provision for notices of completion and cessation from labor were incorporated into that section, the proposition has been touched upon in but one case, *Meyer* v. *City Street Improvement Co.*, 164 Cal. 645, 648, [130 Pac. 215], which was decided before the revision of 1911, whereby, however, no change was made in respect of the requirement of notices prescribed by the 1897 amendment. In that case the court uses language strongly intimating, if not directly deciding, that notices should be filed in all cases. The precise language of the court is: "The first paragraph requires a notice of completion to be filed by the owner *in every case in which a lien may be filed under section 1183.*"

And no sound reason has been suggested in the briefs, and none has occurred to us, for holding that the requirement as to notice was not intended as well to apply to the statutory completion of a building as to the actual completion thereof. "The words 'shall be equivalent to a completion' mean shall be equal in legal effect to a completion; that is, shall be treated for the purpose of filing a lien, as an actual completion." (*Kerckhoff-Cuzner Mill & Lumber Co.* v. *Olmstead,* 85 Cal. 80, 84, [24 Pac. 648].) The object of the statute in requiring notice to be given in any case is not only to prevent the filing of premature liens, and thus the unseasonable and unnecessary embarrassment of the property of the owner, but, principally, to protect the claimant from losing his right to a lien or suffering it to lapse by default, due to his want of knowledge of some sort of the date on which the time within which he is required to file his lien has commenced to run, so that he may preserve and have the benefit of the remedy granted to him by the constitution. The legislature certainly could not have intended that lien claimants, in the cases of statutory completion, other than those where the owner is required to file a notice, should be compelled to exercise constant vigil over the movements of the owner to see whether he had commenced occupation of the building or had accepted it before its actual completion. Indeed, it would be impossible for the claimant to know whether occupation before actual completion had taken place, since, clearly, "occupation" within the meaning of the statute involves not a question of fact alone, but also a question of law. An owner, for reasons of convenience, might enter into the occupation of a building while it is still in course of completion, with the understanding that it is not then to be accepted and that the work of completion shall be proceeded with. Hence, occupation is a question of law to be determined upon the circumstances under which it occurs. The argument that, following out to its logical conclusion that the provision as to notice applies to all the events constituting a constructive completion, would lead to the absurdity of requiring notice to be given of the filing of the notice of the completion of a contract or of the cessation from labor, is far-fetched and fallacious. The notice of the completion of the building, or of the cessation from labor, is itself notice of the event. The effect of filing a notice of the completion of a building in the office of the county recorder is, it is true, only to give constructive notice of that fact, but it is the legal and common method for giving such notice, and by it parties whose rights in the subject to which the notice relates are affected are, according to the legislative judgment, the more likely to obtain actual knowledge of the facts which the notice must contain. But, whether they do or do not acquire actual knowledge of the fact or facts which the notice must contain, there should be, as a matter of public policy, some legal foundation for charging them with notice, which cannot be done where the act as to which some kind of notice should be had is left to the capriciously exercised option of an individual.

It follows from the views thus ventured that, conceding it to be true that lien claimants must file their claims of lien within thirty days after the happening of the first act which constitutes a completion, whether the same be actual or statutory, or, in other words, that they cannot exercise the option of filing their liens within thirty days after any one of several events of completion which have occurred on different dates, the plaintiffs were not bound by the fact of the occupation of the building on the 17th of October, assuming that such occupation amounted to the completion of the building within the contemplation of the statute in such case. They, in other words, could not be charged with notice of such completion, and even if they had been shown to have had actual knowledge of the fact, the defendants, under the express and mandatory terms of the statute, would have been estopped from basing any defense against the assertion of their right to the lien on the ground of the failure to file the same within time.

It further follows from the views above expressed that the finding that "on October 17, 1912, defendants, Charles H. Waldmann and Nellie V. Waldmann, entered into, and ever since have been in the actual and exclusive use and occupation of said building," was wholly unnecessary, and indeed, supererogatory, and is, therefore, immaterial, assuming that the finding was intended to declare as a fact that the building or contract had been constructively completed by occupation.

The lien upon which the plaintiffs rely, however, has reference to the actual completion of the building on the twenty-sixth day of October, 1912. This lien, as we have seen, was filed on the twentieth day of November, 1912, and is the lien pleaded in the first count of the complaint and the one to which the court found the plaintiffs to be entitled.

As above stated, it is contended by the appellants that the evidence does not support the finding that the building was actually completed on the twenty-sixth day of October, 1912. The record does not support the contention.

The defendant, C. H. Waldmann, testified that the last work done on the building was by the painter on the twenty-sixth day of October, 1912. On that day he did some work of painting on the house. It required him about two hours to do the work. This work was done, it is to be assumed, in pursuance of the building contract or the specifications attached thereto as a part thereof. The court was justified from this testimony in finding, as it did, that the building was completed on the twenty-sixth day of October. So long as the work performed was called for by the contract and essential to the completion of the building, the extent of the work or the length of time required to do it is wholly immaterial, for in such case the last stroke of the painter's brush marked the time of the completion. It may be true that if, when the lien was filed and it was sought to enforce it through a judicial decree, the two hours' work of the painter was still unfinished, and such work constituted all that was necessary to complete the building according to the terms and conditions of the contract and specifications, the omission to do that work might justly be treated as a "trivial imperfection" in the work of completion; but this argues nothing against the proposition above stated that the finishing of the work of painting marked the date of the actual completion of the building, said work being all that was necessary actually to complete it.

But there is some other testimony, or, strictly speaking, an admission by the appellants, which tends to support the finding that the building was actually completed on the twenty-sixth day of October. The complaint, in the second cause of action therein stated, alleges that the appellants, on the thirtieth day of November, 1912, filed for record in the office of the county recorder of the city and county of San Francisco their notice "wherein it was stated that a cessation of labor on said building had occurred October 26, 1912," etc. This averment is not denied by the answer, and it therefore stands in the record as an admitted fact. It matters not what the purpose of the filing of said notice by appellants or the pleading of the fact by the plaintiffs was; the fact is consistent with and supports the finding that the building was actually completed on October 26th, and it constituted a fact in the case which it was competent and proper for the court to consider in reaching a conclusion upon the question of actual completion.

But it is further insisted, with respect to the finding of actual completion, that it constitutes no finding at all upon that question, inasmuch as the finding does not definitely fix the date upon which the actual completion occurred. The finding is, as seen, that the building "was duly completed and constructed, except for a trivial imperfection in such construction, by Felix Marcuse, according to the terms of the contract . . . on or about October 26, 1912, and subsequent to October 20, 1912."

The finding would ordinarily be held to be rather indefinite and perhaps would, standing alone, be insufficient to support the judgment. But, as has been shown, the appellants admitted that there was a cessation from labor on October 26th, and this admission must be viewed as a part of the findings. And viewed as a part of the findings and considered with the finding above referred to, it becomes reasonably clear and certain from the findings that the actual completion of the building occurred on the twenty-sixth day of October. But we think that the phrase "on or about" should be held to mean either the day mentioned or a day in very near proximity thereto. It cannot reasonably be held to mean, in other words, if not the day designated, a day ten, fifteen, or twenty days therefrom. Ordinarily, it is understood to refer to a day or two before or subsequent to the day specifically named. The lien of the plaintiffs was filed on the twentieth day of November, 1912; the finding declares that the building was completed subsequent to the twentieth day of October, and "on or about" or within a day or two of the twenty-sixth day of October. In this view, the finding makes it reasonably clear and definite that the lien was filed within thirty days after the completion of the building.

The next objection is that the finding as to the extra work done and extra materials furnished by the plaintiffs, and as to the reasonableness of the value of the same, does not derive sufficient support from the evidence.

We cannot, at the expense of extending this opinion beyond its present length, reproduce herein testimony or the

substance thereof which we think sustains the finding referred
to. It must suffice for us to say that we have carefully examined the testimony and therefrom have been convinced
that the court was amply justified in making said finding.

There are no other points requiring special notice.

The judgment is affirmed.

Chipman, P. J., and Ellison, J., *pro tem.*, concurred.

A petition to have the cause heard in the supreme court,
after judgment in the district court of appeal, was denied by
the supreme court on October 12, 1916.

[Civ. No. 1826.   First Appellate District.—August 15, 1916.]

GEORGE SELLERS, Appellant, v. SOLWAY LAND COM-
PANY (a Corporation), et al., Defendants; BALFOUR,
GUTHRIE & CO. (a Copartnership), et al., Respond-
ents.

REAL ESTATE BROKERS — ORAL AGREEMENT TO SHARE COMMISSIONS —
STATUTE OF FRAUDS — SECTION 1624, SUBDIVISION 6, CIVIL CODE. —
The provision of subdivision 6 of section 1624 of the Civil Code
was only designed to protect owners of real estate against unfounded
claims of brokers, and does not extend to agreements between
brokers to co-operate in making sales for a share of the commissions.

ID. — CONTRACT BETWEEN REAL ESTATE BROKERS — AGREEMENT TO PAY
SPECIFIC COMPENSATION—AUTHORITY TO EXECUTE CONTRACT—WRIT-
ING ESSENTIAL.—A contract made by the manager of the land and
loan department of a real estate partnership agreeing to pay a
second broker a specific amount of money for the procuring of a
purchaser for land for the sale of which the copartnership were the
agents, is void, where the authority of the person signing the contract on behalf of the partnership is not in writing.

ID.—ACTION ON CONTRACT — PLEA OF STATUTE OF FRAUDS — KNOWLEDGE
OF RENDITION OF SERVICES—LACK OF ESTOPPEL.—In an action to
recover upon such a contract the copartnership is not estopped from
setting up the statute of frauds, by reason of the fact that it knowingly held the signer of the contract out to the world as having the
authority he assumed, and of its knowledge that such employee was
dealing with the plaintiff, and had performed services under the

invalid contract, where it also appears that the sale was made without knowledge that the plaintiff was interested other than by a verbal notification made some time previously that he was endeavoring to sell the land to the purchasers.

APPEAL from a judgment of the Superior Court of the City and County of San Francisco. A. E. Graupner, Judge.

The facts are stated in the opinion of the court.

J. E. Rodgers, A. F. Bray, and Sterling Carr, for Appellant.

McCutchen, Olney & Willard, and J. M. Mannon, Jr., for Respondents.

LENNON, P. J.—In this action the plaintiff sued the defendants for the sum of $6,250, alleged to be due as a commission upon the sale of a large ranch in Contra Costa County, the complaint alleging that said sale was made through the efforts of the plaintiff under the contract hereafter set out. The land was the property of the defendant Solway Land Company, and was being managed and handled by the defendants Balfour, Guthrie & Co., a copartnership, consisting of a number of individuals, some of whom are named as defendants, and upon the sale referred to the copartnership received a commission of two and one half per cent upon its sale price of one hundred and thirty thousand dollars, to wit, the sum of $3,250, as compensation for the care of the ranch during a certain period and for its sale. The agency of the defendants, Balfour, Guthrie & Co., was, however, unknown to the plaintiff, and the complaint charges them as owners. At the conclusion of the evidence a motion of defendant Solway Land Company to dismiss as to it was granted, and no question is raised as to the correctness of the court's action in this regard. Hereafter in this opinion the term "defendants" will refer only to Balfour, Guthrie & Co.

The negotiations between the plaintiff and the defendants for his contract were conducted by him with one R. F. McLeod, an employee of the defendants and the manager of a department of their business known as the land and loan

department. The contract was signed by McLeod on behalf
of the defendants and is in the following terms:

"San Francisco, 22nd Sept., 1909.

"Mr. Geo. Sellers,
  "Oakley, Cal.

"Dear Sir:

"Replying to your letter of 21st inst., the price we are
asking for the Solway ranch is $125,000, including stock and
implements and interest in the pumping plant. We would
be willing to accept one-half cash and carry the balance at
6% net for a reasonable time. We will pay 5% commission
on the above price to the party effecting a sale.

"You are no doubt aware that part of the ranch is rented
to Japanese for potatoes, etc., and possession of same cannot
be given until expiry of the lease this fall.

"Yours truly,
"BALFOUR, GUTHRIE & Co.
"Per (Signed) R. F. McLEOD.

"P. S.—There is about 1700 acres altogether."

(It may be said parenthetically that at the time of the sale
the price of the property had been increased.)

It is an established fact in the case, and not disputed, that
the authority from the defendants to McLeod to enter into
this contract was not conferred in writing. The action having been dismissed as to the defendant Solway Land Company, the remaining defendants at the conclusion of the
trial moved that the jury be directed to return a verdict in
their favor, upon the ground of the lack of written authority
to McLeod, section 2309 of the Civil Code requiring that an
authorization to an agent to enter into a contract required
to be in writing must itself be evidenced by a written instrument. This motion was also granted, and the jury thereupon returned its verdict in favor of the defendants. From
the judgment entered thereon the plaintiff takes this appeal.

In support of his appeal plaintiff urges that the court
erred in directing the jury to find in defendants' favor for
two principal reasons, viz., first, that the plaintiff's contract
being one between broker and broker, is not governed by
section 1624, subdivision 6, of the Civil Code, and that therefore McLeod's authority to enter into it was not required
to be in writing; and, second, even if the contract sued upon

be one that is governed by said section, the conduct of the defendants in reference thereto estops them from availing themselves of the bar of the statute.

The authorities in this state holding that an oral contract between brokers whereby one employs or secures the co-operation of another to sell real estate is valid and enforceable, may be roughly divided into three classes. The first class comprises cases where the brokers' agreement was purely and simply one of partnership, such as *Coward* v. *Clanton*, 79 Cal. 23, [21 Pac. 359], *Gorham* v. *Heiman*, 90 Cal. 346, [27 Pac. 289], *Bates* v. *Babcock*, 95 Cal. 479, [29 Am. St. Rep. 133, 16 L. R. A. 745, 30 Pac. 605], and *Baker* v. *Thompson*, 14 Cal. App. 175, [111 Pac. 373]; the second comprises cases where the agreement of the brokers was to divide between them, either equally or in a stated proportion, a commission or compensation to be received by one of them from the owner of the land to be sold, such as *Casey* v. *Richards*, 10 Cal. App. 57, [101 Pac. 36], *Hageman* v. *O'Brien*, 24 Cal. App. 270, [141 Pac. 33]·, *Reynolds* v. *Jackson*, 25 Cal. App. 490, [144 Pac. 305], *Hellings* v. *Wright*, 29 Cal. App. 649, [156 Pac. 365], *Jenkins* v. *Locke-Paddon Co.*, 30 Cal. App. 52, [157 Pac. 537]; and the third class consists of cases, two in number, in which one broker, having a contract from the owner to sell real property, has agreed with a second broker to pay him for his services either in procuring a buyer for the property or assisting in that end—those cases being *Saunders* v. *Yoakum*, 12 Cal. App. 543, [107 Pac. 1007], and *Johnston* v. *Porter*, 21 Cal. App. 97, [131 Pac. 69].

In the case at bar the contract, as we have seen, is one to pay a specific amount, viz., five per cent on the purchase price, for the procuring of a purchaser, and would fall within the last-named classification and be governed by the authority of those cases, unless it contains elements differentiating it from them and making inapplicable the rule therein followed.

The leading case in this state upon the question is *Gorham* v. *Heiman*, 90 Cal. 358, [27 Pac. 289], and which has been cited in practically every decision upon the subject which has since been rendered. The agreement there was between brokers to co-operate in the selling of a mine and to divide commissions, and the court referring thereto used this language: "Counsel seem to rely on section 1624 of the Civil Code, subdivision 6. But clearly that provision was only designed to protect owners of real estate against unfounded claims of brokers. It does not extend to agreements between brokers to co-operate in making sales for a share of the commissions." It will be seen upon examination that all the cases in the first and second classification made above dealt with agreements between brokers to co-operate in the common object of procuring a purchaser for real property, and come squarely within the authority of *Gorham* v. *Heiman*.

With regard to the remaining two cases, it appears that in *Saunders* v. *Yoakum, supra*, "defendant agreed with plaintiff that if he would procure a purchaser for any or all of the property, he would pay to the plaintiff a commission in the event of a sale." Plaintiff performed his agreement, and the defendant received a commission of one thousand two hundred dollars, and refused to pay plaintiff for his services. The latter thereupon brought suit, and recovered four hundred dollars as the value thereof. Upon appeal the contention of the defendant that the contract was void because not in writing was overruled upon the authority of the leading case above cited, the court construing the agreement to be one between brokers to co-operate in making a sale for a share of the commission, and referring to the services of the plaintiff as being rendered "in assisting the defendant to earn his commission."

In the second case—*Johnston* v. *Porter et al.*—it appears that Johnston, the plaintiff, introduced the purchaser of the property to the defendant Morey, who was acting as the agent of the owner, and also assisted in conducting the negotiations which resulted in a sale. Morey orally agreed to compensate Johnston for his services. Upon the conclusion of the sale Morey received a commission of $2,250, out of which he offered to pay Johnston $250. Johnston being dissatisfied with the amount tendered by Morey, brought suit upon the oral agreement for the reasonable value of his services. The court allowed a recovery of one thousand five hundred dollars out of $2,250 received by Morey. Upon appeal the judgment was sustained, this court construing the agreement between Morey and Johnston as being one between two brokers to co-operate in the sale of real estate, using this language: "Subdivision 6 of section 1624 of the

Civil Code, which declares an agreement authorizing or
employing an agent or broker to sell real estate for a compensation or commission to be invalid unless reduced to
writing, was designed only for the protection of real estate
owners against the unfounded claims of brokers; and it was
never intended to be applied to contracts between brokers
co-operating in the sale of real property and agreeing to
share commissions earned as the result of such sale,'' citing
Gorham v. *Heiman, supra.*

If it be the law in this state, as stated in *Gorham* v. *Heiman,* that the section of the code under consideration ''was
only designed to protect owners of real estate against unfounded claims of brokers,'' then the authorization to the
employee of the defendants McLeod did not need to be in
writing. But, as was said in the later case of *Aldis* v.
Schleicher, 9 Cal. App. 372, [99 Pac. 526], that section is
''equally applicable to any contract whereby one, whether
owner or not, employs another to effect a sale of real estate,
and agrees unconditionally to pay a stipulated sum for the
performance of such services.''

It will be observed that in *Gorham* v. *Heiman,* in which
the rule was first laid down that the provisions of subdivision 6 of section 1624 of the Civil Code apply only to
contracts between the owners of real estate and brokers, the
contract there being considered was literally an agreement
between brokers, dealing with each other as such, to unite
their efforts in the disposal of a mine, and to divide the
compensation to be earned in the event of success, and that
there was no employment by one of the other. Evidently
such a contract was one of partnership, and did not come
within the terms of the section, whether the legislative intent in enacting it was merely to protect owners of real
estate or its scope was much broader. As already pointed
out, the cases following *Gorham* v. *Heiman,* with the exception of the two noted, all dealt with agreements between
brokers to divide commissions to be received as the result
of their joint efforts; and even in those two, while the agreement as to the compensation of the complaining broker was
more in the nature of a direct promise by the other to compensate him for services already or thereafter to be rendered, it is still apparent that they dealt with each other
as agents, that they were both interested in the result of their

common efforts, and that the compensation agreed to be paid, or allowed by the court, was a part only of the compensation of the employing broker, thus preserving in some degree the idea of co-operation between broker and broker for a division of the fee, and enabling the court in its desire to prevent the defeat of an equitable claim to construe the agreement as one for the division between brokers of a compensation jointly earned.

In the case at bar there is no such partnership between the brokers, nor any agreement to divide compensation, and no effort on the part of the plaintiff to obtain a division of the commission received by the defendants. On the contrary, the amount sued for is almost double the sum which the employing brokers received as their compensation for the care of the property and its sale. There was, moreover, no knowledge on the part of the broker employed that his employers were in fact agents, and the contract is one of employment for a specific compensation. In the complaint the employing brokers are charged as the owners of the property; and it was only during the progress of the trial that the plaintiff discovered that they were not such owners, and when such discovery was made there was no amendment of the complaint requested. If we hold this case not to come within the provisions of section 1624 of the Civil Code, we must ignore the careful insistence to be discerned in the cases upon the existence of a partnership, or of an agreement to divide commissions, or of the existence of a fund received by one broker in which the second broker may be allotted a share—and lay down the rule that all these things are immaterial, and that a direct contract of employment to sell real estate for a specific compensation is invalid if made by the owner of the property with a broker, but is valid if made between two brokers—contrary to the rule declared in *Aldis* v. *Schleicher,* 9 Cal. App. 372, [99 Pac. 526], and which appears to us to be plainly applicable to the case at bar.

We are, therefore, constrained to hold that the plaintiff neither by the allegations of his complaint nor his proof upon the trial brought his case within the authority of those holding that a contract between brokers to co-operate in the sale of real estate for a division of the compensation to be thereby earned is valid and enforceable although not in writing. The first contention of the appellant must accordingly be disallowed.

The second contention of the appellant is that even if the contract sued upon be one that is required to be in writing, the conduct of the defendants in reference thereto estops them from availing themselves of the bar of the statute for three reasons, viz., first, because the defendants knowingly held McLeod out to the world as having the authority he assumed; second, because the defendants knew that McLeod was dealing with the plaintiff; and, third, because the defendants accepted the benefits of McLeod's acts.

The principle of estoppel is one of equity; and whether in a given case the facts and circumstances shown are sufficient to create it is a question for the court.

It is also well settled that estoppels are not favored, their effect being to prevent the truth being shown.

The facts on which the plaintiff's plea of estoppel is based are, briefly, that McLeod was the manager of the department of the defendants' business known as the land and loan department; that as such manager he answered all correspondence addressed to the defendants on matters relating to that department; that he had authority, though not in writing, to consult and deal with agents in regard to a sale of the defendants' land; that a contract similar to the one given to the plaintiff was subsequently entered into by him on behalf of the defendants with a person other than the plaintiff; that the efforts of the plaintiff to sell the ranch were known to McLeod and to the foreman and superintendent of the ranch. which the plaintiff visited a number of times in the company of prospective buyers; that plaintiff expended money in advertising the ranch in his endeavor to procure a purchaser, and, finally, that the persons to whom the ranch was sold were first interested in its purchase by the plaintiff, who sent them to McLeod for the purpose of arranging terms and closing up the transaction, but without advising McLeod that he had done so.

It further appears, however, that the negotiations were conducted by the purchasers with McLeod, and that nothing was said by them concerning the plaintiff's participation in the matter, and that the sale was made to them without knowledge on the part of McLeod that the plaintiff was interested in it other than a verbal notification made some time previously that he was endeavoring to sell the land to these people.

We are of the opinion that the court correctly held that the above facts were insufficient to constitute an estoppel as against the plea of the statute of frauds.

It has long been held in this state that an agent having sold real property under a contract of employment invalid because not in writing can recover neither upon the contract nor upon *quantum meruit.* (*McCarthy* v. *Loupe,* 62 Cal. 299; *Myres* v. *Surrhyne,* 67 Cal. 657, [8 Pac. 523]; *Zeimer* v. *Antisell,* 75 Cal. 509, [17 Pac. 642]; *McPhail* v. *Buell,* 87 Cal. 115, [25 Pac. 266]; *Shanklin* v. *Hall,* 100 Cal. 26, [34 Pac. 636]; *McGeary* v. *Satchwell,* 129 Cal. 389, [62 Pac. 58]; *Jamison* v. *Hyde,* 141 Cal. 109 [74 Pac. 695].)   Although in these cases no question of estoppel is considered, they offer a strong analogy to the case at bar, for all the facts present here and claimed by the plaintiff to constitute an estoppel were necessarily present in those cases, viz., an invalid employment, knowledge of its invalidity, knowledge of rendition of services under the contract, and acceptance of the benefits arising from the performance of the contract by the agent.   The statute of frauds, however, was held to bar the agent's recovery.

In the case of *McRae* v. *Ross,* 170 Cal. 74, [148 Pac. 215], the question of estoppel under circumstances somewhat similar to those in the case at bar was considered.   In that case a ranch in Solano County had been sold.   A. T. Ross and three other respondents (sisters and brother of A. T. Ross) were owners.   McRae claimed to have found the purchaser, and relied upon a broker's note from A. T. Ross alone.   There was no written authority from the other respondents to A. T. Ross, but McRae claimed that they had held him out as their agent and that they were estopped from raising the defense of the statute of frauds, particularly Civil Code, section 2309. This alleged holding out (one of the elements claimed in the estoppel in the case at bar) consisted of statements claimed to have been made to McRae by the respondents to the effect that A. T. Ross was authorized to act for them, and that he was in charge of the ranch.   It was held that there was no estoppel, the court saying (Mr. Justice Sloss writing the opinion): "It is clear that the findings in favor of the defendants Raymond H. Ross, Mabel I. Ross and Mrs. Henry

are in accord with the undisputed evidence. A contract for
the sale of real estate, or for the employment of a broker to
sell real estate, must be in writing. (Civ. Code, sec. 1624;
Code Civ. Proc., sec. 1973.) None of these three defendants
ever made any written contract with plaintiff, or even had
any written communication with him. Plaintiff attempted to
show that each of them had referred him to a brother, their
codefendant, Albert T. Ross, as the person in charge of the
ranch. But the testimony was that Albert did not have any
written authority to bind them, and this was necessary to empower him to make a contract on their behalf to sell real estate
or employ an agent to sell it. (Civ. Code, sec. 2309.) Even
if the making of the oral statements had been shown without
contradiction—which is not the case—such statements would
not have bound these defendants. There is no ground for
the contention that the alleged declarations raised an estoppel
against the three defendants. To so hold would be to destroy
the statutory requirement that authority to sell real estate
must be in writing.''

The appellant strongly relies on the case of *Seymour v. Oel-
richs*, 156 Cal. 782, [134 Am. St. Rep. 154, 106 Pac. 88]. In
that case the plaintiff Seymour sued for damages for breach
of a contract of employment, his employment to cover a period
of ten years. The contract was not in writing, and, therefore, void under the statute of frauds. The claim of estoppel
was based upon the ground that the defendants when negotiating for his employment promised him a written contract,
and had induced him, in order to permit him to accept the
employment, to resign a life position carrying a good salary
with a right to a pension upon retirement. Through circumstances arising subsequent to his entering upon his employment the written contract was not given to Seymour, and,
after rendering services under the verbal contract for a
period of three years, he was dismissed. In holding the defendants estopped to set up the statute of frauds the supreme
court laid emphasis upon the fact that it was not because of
the rendition of services under the contract that the estoppel
was allowed, but because of the change of position suffered by
the plaintiff through having resigned a lucrative position—
and which he could not now regain—in order to accept the
employment. It was held that it would be a fraud upon the
plaintiff if the defendants, after having induced him to resign

from his position upon the promise of a ten year written contract, and having failed to reduce the contract to writing, were permitted to set up the invalidity of the oral contract to defeat recovery. The court emphasized the fact that the plaintiff was not helped by the performance of services. On this subject it says: "Under this claim the fact of part performance by plaintiff plays no part whatever. . . . Plaintiff's case in this regard would be just as strong if after his resignation he had been prevented by defendants from beginning to perform."

Thus far we have considered the question of estoppel only so far as it is affected by the evidence offered by the plaintiff; but since plaintiff's claim is based upon the alleged holding out by the defendants of their employee McLeod as having authority to enter into the contract; upon their knowledge of the plaintiff's activity in the performance of the contract, and upon their accepting the benefit of the results of his labors, we think it plain that the court, in considering whether the estoppel claimed had been established, was bound to consider all of the evidence offered upon those matters, whether by the plaintiff or the defendants. In that view of the case the plaintiff's position becomes still more untenable, for the defendants offered evidence tending to show that the plaintiff's contract has expired long before the sale took place, that he had been warned to desist from his efforts to sell the ranch, and that the plaintiff recognized by his acts that his contract was no longer in effect; and that even if the sale of the property was made to persons who were first interested in it by the plaintiff, the latter was guilty of gross negligence in failing to report to the defendants that he had brought the property to the attention of its ultimate buyers, thus allowing the defendants to deal with them in ignorance of their liability to pay to the plaintiff a commission. These facts would have a strong bearing upon the question of whether the defendants received any benefit from the contract made by this agent, and consequently upon the potency of the plaintiff's appeal to the equitable jurisdiction of the court for the application of the principle of estoppel in his favor.

There is no merit in the final point urged by the appellant that the court having at the conclusion of the plaintiff's case denied defendants' motion for a nonsuit, the invalidity of the contract and the facts adduced by the plaintiff in support of his plea of estoppel at that time appearing, it was error to subsequently grant the motion of the defendants to direct the jury to return a verdict in their favor.

For the foregoing reason the judgment is affirmed.

Richards, J., and Kerrigan, J., concurred.

A petition for a rehearing of this cause was denied by the district court of appeal on September 14, 1916, and a petition to have the cause heard in the supreme court, after judgment in the district court of appeal, was denied by the supreme court on October 12, 1916.

[Civ. No. 1813. First Appellate District.—August 23, 1916.]

PEOPLE'S WATER COMPANY (a Corporation), Respondent, v. HARRY BOROMEO et al., Appellants.

EJECTMENT — FINDINGS — LACK OF INCONSISTENCY. — In an action in ejectment, wherein the plaintiff alleges seisin or right of possession in itself for the period of five years last past, and also alleges possession on the part of the defendants at the time of the commencement of the action, and the answer of the defendants denies the plaintiff's possession and right of possession for the period claimed, and alleges that the defendants have been in the adverse possession of the premises for more than twelve years, there is no inconsistency between the finding of the plaintiff's seisin within five years and of the defendants' adverse possession for the period of twelve years prior to the filing of the complaint, nor is the latter finding sufficient to bar the plaintiff's recovery under section 318 of the Code of Civil Procedure, where it is also found that the defendants had not paid the taxes for the requisite years.

ID.—FAILURE TO PAY TAXES—INVALIDITY OF ASSESSMENTS—BURDEN OF PROOF.—Where in such an action it is admitted that the taxes levied and assessed for the years in question were not paid, and it is contended that the assessments were invalid, the burden is upon the defendants to show such invalidity.

ID. — COMPUTATION AND ENTRY OF TAXES BY AUDITOR — OMISSION NOT FATAL.—A tax assessment is not invalid by reason of the failure of the county auditor to comply with section 3731 of the Political Code, which requires him, after receiving from the state board of equalization a statement of whatever changes have been ordered by said board in the assessment-book of the county, and after making the corresponding changes, if any, in said assessment-book, to then compute and enter in a separate money column in the assessment-book the respective sums to be paid as a tax on the property, and segregate and place in their proper columns of the book the respective amounts due in installments, as such work is no part of the levy, but is merely a step in the process of the collection of taxes.

APPEAL from a judgment of the Superior Court of Alameda County.   Everett J. Brown, Judge.

The facts are stated in the opinion of the court.

Milton Shepardson, and L. A. Kottinger, for Appellants.

Tom Bradley, and Harry E. Leach, for Respondent.

THE COURT.—This is an appeal from a judgment in an action of ejectment. The plaintiff alleges seisin or right of possession in itself for the period of five years last past, and also alleges possession on the part of the defendants at the time of the commencement of the action. The answer of the defendants denies the plaintiff's possession and right of possession for the period claimed, and alleges that the defendants have been in the adverse possession of the premises for more than twelve years. The trial court found in favor of the plaintiff's seisin during the past five years, but also found that the defendants had been in the open, notorious, exclusive, and uninterrupted possession of the premises during the period from 1901 up to March 22, 1912, the date of the filing of the complaint. The court, however, found that the taxes had been duly levied and assessed upon said premises for the years 1903, 1904, 1907, 1909, and 1911, which had not been paid by the defendants or any of them, or by any person on their behalf; and thereupon found as a conclusion of law that the plaintiff was entitled to the possession of the premises in question.

The appellants contend that the finding by the court of the plaintiff's seisin within five years and of the defendants' adverse possession for the period of twelve years prior to the filing of the complaint are inconsistent, and also contends that the latter finding by the court is sufficient to bar the plaintiff's recovery under section 318 of the Code of Civil Procedure. There is no merit in either of these contentions.

The seisin which the plaintiff had in the premises at the time of the commencement of the action and for the period of four years immediately preceding that date was merely the right of possession which could only be destroyed by the ripening of the defendants' title by adverse possession through their compliance with all of the legal requirements, including the payment of taxes necessary to produce that result; section 318 of the Code of Civil Procedure is to be read in connection with sections 322, 323, and 325 of the same code, which set forth the legal prerequisites of the creation of such a title by adverse possession as would defeat the plaintiff's seisin in law.

The final and only substantial contention involved in this appeal arises out of the appellants' admission that the taxes levied and assessed upon the premises for the years above set forth were not paid by them, but their insistence that said taxes were not legally assessed or levied, and hence that they were not bound to pay them. This contention is based upon a number of alleged irregularities in the levy and assessment of the taxes for said years, but in the closing brief of appellants these are finally refined down to the single contention that section 3731 of the Political Code was not complied with by the officials charged with the duty of making a proper and legal levy and assessment of the taxes to be charged against the premises in question.

In this section of the Political Code the county auditor, after receiving from the state board of equalization a statement of whatever changes have been ordered by said board in the assessment-book of the county, and after making the corresponding changes, if any, in said assessment-book, must then compute and enter in a separate money column in the assessment-book the respective sums to be paid as a tax on the property, and segregate and place in their proper columns of the book the respective amounts due in installments. The record shows that this duty was not performed by the auditor in respect to the property and for the years in question; but the respondent insists, and we think correctly, that this work of the auditor as required by the foregoing section of the Political Code is no part of the levy and assessment of the taxes, but is merely a step in the process of their collection. The terms "levied" and "assessed" employed in section 325 of the Code of Civil Procedure in relation to taxes have been considered to have reference to the act of the board of supervisors in making the levy and of the asses or in making the assessment, and have no reference to the acts of the auditor in making the computations and carrying out the columns and segregating installments required by section 3731 of the Political Code. (*Allen* v. *McKay,* 120 Cal. 332, [52 Pac. 828] ; *Waterhouse* v. *Clatsop,* 50 Or. 176, [91 Pac. 1083].)

The argument of the appellants that every step in the process of making up the assessment-roll is *strictissimi juris,* and must be complied with to the letter before a valid obligation to pay taxes is imposed upon the property owner, while no doubt true in its application to the proceeding leading up to a valid levy and assessment of the tax, has not been held to apply with the same degree of strictness to the mere ministerial acts of the clerk of the board of supervisors and of the auditor in making the affidavits and carrying out the computations after the taxes have been duly levied and assessed. (*Steele* v. *San Luis Obispo County,* 152 Cal. 785, [93 Pac. 1020].)

The plaintiff having introduced in evidence the assessment-rolls for the years in question, showing that taxes were levied and assessed upon the property, the burden was then cast upon the defendants to show that these levies and assessments were not valid in order to entitle them to claim the benefit of the sections of the code relating to title by adverse possession. In our opinion they have not sustained this burden, and it follows that the trial court was not in error in its conclusion of law that the plaintiff was entitled to possession of the premises in dispute.

Judgment affirmed.

A petition for a rehearing of this cause was denied by the district court of appeal on September 22, 1916, and a petition to have the cause heard in the supreme court, after judgment in the district court of appeal, was denied by the supreme court on October 20, 1916.

[Civ. No. 1501. Third Appellate District.—August 25, 1916.]

PACIFIC MANUFACTURING COMPANY (a Corporation) et al., Respondents, v. R. A. PERRY et al., Appellants.

BUILDING CONTRACT—ABANDONMENT BY CONTRACTOR—AMOUNT APPLICABLE TO LIENS—RULE PRIOR TO REVISORY ACT OF 1911.—Under the mechanic's lien statutes as they existed prior to the Revisory Act of 1911 (Stats. 1911, p. 1313), where a valid building contract was executed and filed and the work thereunder abandoned by the contractor before completion, the amount of the contract price applicable to the liens of other persons than the contractor was to be determined in accordance with section 1200 of the Code of Civil Procedure, and in determining such amount allowance was required to be made for the cost of completing the building.

ID.—DEVIATIONS FROM PLANS—ADDED COST OF BUILDING—RIGHT OF CONTRACTOR—VALIDITY OF CONTRACT.—A building contract is not rendered void by reason of alterations in the plans adding materially to the cost of the building, where the contract was recorded and expressly provided that should the owner at any time during the progress of the building request any alterations, deviations, additions, or omissions from said contract, specifications, or plans, he should be at liberty to do so, and the same should in no way affect or make void the contract, but would be added to or deducted from the amount of said contract price, as the case might be, by a fair and reasonable valuation.

ID.—NOTICE OF NONRESPONSIBILITY—WHEN NOT REQUIRED.—An owner of a building is not required to give notice of nonresponsibility, as provided by section 1192 of the Code of Civil Procedure, in a case where there is a valid recorded contract made on her behalf and with her knowledge and consent, as the contract is the measure of her liability.

APPEAL from a judgment of the Superior Court of Alameda County, and from an order denying a new trial. William H. Waste, Judge.

The facts are stated in the opinion of the court.

Snook & Church, and C. Irving Wright, for Appellants.

W. B. Rinehart, C. L. Colvin, Ezra W. Decoto, and Robert B. Gaylord, for Respondents.

CHIPMAN, P. J.—The action is to foreclose laborers' and materialmen's liens for work performed and materials furnished in the construction of a residence and garage in the city of Oakland. With the action by Pacific Manufacturing Company were consolidated ten other actions. The following findings of fact were made by the court:

That defendant R. A. Perry was the reputed owner, defendant Winifred A. Perry the real owner, of the premises; that on June 10, 1910, the said R. A. Perry and defendant Magneson entered into a written contract whereby the latter agreed "to construct and complete certain buildings, to wit, a certain brick veneered and frame residence and garage appurtenant thereto upon the above-described land and premises and to furnish the labor and materials" therefor, according to certain plans, drawings, and specifications, which said plans, drawings, and specifications were attached to and made part of said contract, and the same was duly recorded on June 13, 1910; that the agreed price for said work and materials was $23,567, payable in progressive installments, the sum of six thousand dollars to be paid thirty-five days after the date of acceptance by architect and owner. Among other provisions, the contract contained the following:

"Third. Should the owner at any time during the progress of said buildings, request any alterations, deviations, additions or omissions from said contract, specifications, or plans, he shall be at liberty to do so, and the same shall in no way affect or make void the contract, but will be added to or deducted from the amount of said contract price, as the case may be, by a fair and reasonable valuation.

"Fourth: Should the contractor at any time, during the progress of said work, refuse or neglect to supply a sufficiency of materials or workmen, the owner shall have the power to provide materials and workmen (after three days' notice in writing given) to finish the said works, and the expenses shall be deducted from the amount of said contract price.

"Ninth: No extras will be allowed except agreed on in writing at time of making same, and signed by both interested parties.

"Tenth: It is hereby agreed by both interested parties that the said party of the second part shall enter into contracts with the following subcontractors for their portion of the work at prices mentioned:

Pacific Mfg. Co. for mill work, sash, doors and glass.$3,385.00
Burtchael & Crowley, plumbing.................. 1,895.00
P. N. Kuss Co., (or acceptable to owner), painting. 950.00
Century Electric Co., electric work and wiring.... 650.00
Inlaid Floor Co., hardened floors............... 940.00
Schmitt & Co., hot air heating.................. 470.00''

It was further found that the contractor, Magneson, commenced work about June 13, 1910, in the construction of said
residence and garage, and so continued said work until February 11, 1911, when he "abandoned the construction of said
buildings and all work and labor ceased thereon," and no labor
was performed nor any materials furnished to be used, nor
was any used in the construction thereof for a period of thirty
days next immediately thereafter; that on March 22, 1911,
defendants R. A. and Winifred made and filed for record in
the office of the county recorder of Alameda County, and there
was recorded on that day, a notice of abandonment of said
contract by said Magneson on February 11, 1911; that no
notice in writing requiring said Magneson to finish said works
was ever given to said Magneson nor any demand made upon
him as required by said contract, "to wit, the fourth subdivision thereof hereinbefore specifically quoted and set forth."

It is further found that the said defendant, Winifred A.
Perry, never entered into any contract in writing with said
defendants Magneson and R. A. Perry, or either of them, relating to the construction of said buildings; that said Winifred
A. Perry never at any time gave notice pursuant to section
1192 of the Code of Civil Procedure, or otherwise, that she
would not be responsible for the labor performed or materials
furnished in the construction of said buildings, but during
all the time said Magneson was engaged in the construction of
said buildings by the said R. A. Perry he was so engaged with
the knowledge and consent of said Winifred, and all the materials furnished for said buildings were furnished with her
knowledge and consent; that after said Magneson had abandoned said work, to wit, on March 22, 1911, said defendants
R. A. and Winifred commenced to complete said buildings and
completed the same on or about September 6, 1911, and on that
day notice of completion was duly filed by the said Winifred
and defendants R. A. and Winifred that they had expended
the sum of $18,356.59 in the said completion; that said build-
ings were not constructed nor were they completed according

to the plans and specifications and original contract, but "were actually constructed in such a manner that the said buildings greatly exceeded in value the original contract price as agreed upon between the said parties defendant, to wit, the said R. A. and Winifred Perry and said Magneson"; that "no extras were ever agreed upon in writing nor any writing signed with relation to extras by any persons interested or by any of the parties, to wit, the said Perry and Magneson, in pursuance of subdivision 9 of the contract for said building, between the said defendant Magneson and said defendant R. A. Perry hereinbefore specifically set forth; . . . that during the course of the construction of said buildings and prior to the abandonment thereof by the defendant Magneson, said defendant R. A. Perry paid the said Magneson" certain stated sums at different stages of the work amounting in all to ten thousand dollars, "paid on account of the contract price and no more"; that the said defendants Magneson and Perry never at any time, nor did the said defendant Winifred A. Perry ever at any time, fix or attempt to fix, according to the provisions of said contract, or otherwise, by a fair and reasonable valuation or at all, the amount or values of said alterations of, deviations from, additions to or omissions from said contract, in writing, or otherwise"; that the reasonable value of said extra work amounts in the aggregate to $3,866.28, "of which there had been paid, at the time of the abandonment aforesaid by said Magneson, the sum of $1,300.00."

It was also found "that the value of the work and materials done and furnished in the construction of said buildings, including materials then actually delivered on the ground, estimated as near as may be by the standard of the whole contract price (exclusive of the extra labor performed and materials furnished as aforesaid), at the time of the abandonment of the said contract by said Magneson, as aforesaid, was and is the sum of $14,730.00"; that "all of the materials which were furnished by the plaintiffs herein, were furnished to be used, and actually used in the construction of said buildings, and all of the labor performed by these plaintiffs was actually performed upon and in the construction of said buildings . . . all with the full knowledge and consent of the said Winifred A. Perry." The foregoing are the general findings more or less applicable to all the claims involved.

The court then finds the facts as to the specific amounts of labor performed and materials furnished by the several plaintiffs, the filing of their liens, and the amount remaining unpaid in each case, amounting in all to the sum of $7,970.87.

The court found, among other conclusions of law, that the contract between Magneson and R. A. Perry, as recorded, was void, and "that no legal contract was ever made or entered into between the owner of said premises, to wit, Winifred A. Perry and O. M. Magneson, for or with relation to the construction of said buildings"; that the "liens hereinbefore declared in favor of said plaintiffs, and the said several sums hereinbefore stated and declared to be due, owing and unpaid to the said plaintiffs respectively, are prior and superior to the rights, interests and claims of the defendants Winifred A. Perry and R. A. Perry, in and to said premises," and that plaintiffs are entitled to have the "said described land together with the buildings thereon and the premises thereof sold . . . for the satisfaction of said respective liens," etc.

Judgment was accordingly entered.

Defendants appeal from the judgment and from the order denying their motion for a new trial.

The theories upon which respondents urge affirmance of the judgment are as follows:

1. That a valid contract existed which was duly recorded; that it was abandoned, and hence the amount applicable to the liens of plaintiffs should be measured by section 1200 of the Code of Civil Procedure.

2. That no contract existed, because in the construction of the buildings the plans and specifications of the recorded contract were so departed from and so increased the cost of the buildings as actually constructed, as to "constitute a new and independent contract, and render void the recorded contract."

3. That the entire interest of defendant Winifred A. Perry in the premises should be subjected to plaintiffs' liens, because of her failure to give the notice of nonresponsibility required by section 1192 of the Code of Civil Procedure.

The court found that there was a valid contract. If that finding is to stand, the payment of the liens must be determined by section 1200 of the Code of Civil Procedure, and the statutes in force prior to the act of 1911 (Stats. 1911, p. 1313). Section 1183 of the Code of Civil Procedure gives a lien of mechanics and materialmen for labor done or materials furnished, "whether at the instance of the owner, or of any other person acting by his authority or under him," and "in case of a contract for the work between the reputed owner and his contractor, the lien shall extend to the entire contract price, and such contract shall operate as a lien in favor of all persons, except the contractor, to the extent of the whole contract price."

Section 1200 provides that where the contract has been abandoned before completion, "the portion of the contract price applicable to the liens of other persons than the contractor, shall be fixed as follows: From the value of the work and materials already done and furnished at the time of such failure or abandonment, including materials then actually delivered or on the ground, which shall thereupon belong to the owner, estimated as near as may be by the standard of the whole contract price, shall be deducted the payments then due and actually paid, according to the terms of the contract and the provisions of sections 1183 and 1184, and the remainder shall be deemed the portion of the contract price applicable to such liens."

In the recent case of *Roystone Co.* v. *Darling*, 171 Cal. 526, [154 Pac. 15], the history of our mechanic's lien law is very fully shown, and the various decisions of the supreme court are cited which have given construction to the statute as it has been amended from time to time. It was shown in that case that up to the passage of the act of 1911, the supreme court "has followed the rule established by the cases last cited, and has uniformly declared, with respect to such liens, that if there is a valid contract, the contract price measures the limit of the amount of liens which can be acquired against the property by laborers and materialmen; . . . that the contract legally made limits the liability of the owner to lien claimants." See, also, *Ganahl Lumber Co.* v. *Weinsveig*, 168 Cal. 664, [143 Pac. 1025], where the meaning of section 1200, as affecting the liability of the owner in the case of an abandoned valid contract, was very clearly pointed out.

What, then, was the situation when the contract was abandoned and what were the lienors' rights? The court found that the contract price was $23,567. It found that the value of the extra work performed and materials furnished at the time of abandonment was $3,866.28, of which there had been paid the sum of one thousand three hundred dollars; and that the value of the work and materials, including materials then actually delivered at the ground, "estimated as near as may be by the standard of the whole contract price (exclusive of the extra labor performed and materials furnished as aforesaid), at the time of the abandonment of the said contract by said Magneson as aforesaid, was and is the sum of $14,730," of which the sum of ten thousand dollars had been paid.

Respondent states the account thus:

Labor performed and materials furnished	$14,730.00
Value of alterations, etc	3,866.28
Total	$18,596.28
Upon which was paid	11,300.00
Leaving applicable to the liens	$ 7,296.28
The court gave judgment for	7,970.87

—which is $674.59 more than the fund, accepting respondents' method of computation.

But respondent makes no allowance for the cost of completing the buildings which, through no fault of appellants, were left in an unfinished condition. What the *actual* cost of completion was to appellants may be immaterial (*Ganahl Lumber Co.* v. *Weinsveig*, 168 Cal. 664, [143 Pac. 1025]), but as was said in *Hoffman-Marks Co.* v. *Spires*, 154 Cal. 111, 116, [97 Pac. 152]: "When he [owner] is, without any default on his part, burdened with the cost of completing the building, it is but fair and just that he should be relieved of the obligation of paying to the original contractor, or those claiming under him, so much of the contract price as corresponds to the portion of the work left undone. In no other way can he be protected in his constitutional right to have his liability limited to the amount which, by a valid contract, he has agreed to pay."

We have been unable to formulate any equation under the rule of section 1200 as approved by the supreme and appellate courts, which would support the findings of the court for the full amount found subject to the liens, on the theory of a valid contract abandoned by the contractor.

The finding that there was a valid contract and that it was abandoned by the contractor before completion is sustained by the evidence, and unless the judgment can find support upon one or other of plaintiffs' remaining theories, it must be reversed.

Plaintiffs' second theory was that the original contract was rendered void by reason of the alterations in the plans adding so materially to the cost of the buildings. The contract contained the provision quoted above, by which the owner was given the right to make any alterations he might wish to make "from said contract, specifications or plans," which, when made, "shall in no way affect or make void the contract, but will be added to or deducted from the amount of said contract price, as the case may be, by a fair and reasonable valuation." Notice of the provision of the contract was given to all parties concerned by its recordation, and nearly all of them furnished some of the materials or labor constituting these alterations, and no objection was made to any claim, because it was for extras. It would be difficult to express in language more explicit authority to deviate from the plans and specifications than is found in this contract. So far as lien claimants are concerned, alterations are immaterial except where there is an abandonment, and in such case they may be considered in ascertaining the cost of completing the buildings according to the contract, for the contract so expressly provides. (*Johnson v. La Grave,* 102 Cal. 324, [36 Pac. 651].) That the owner may provide in his contract for changes or alterations in the building during its construction without invalidating the contract, we do not doubt.

Witness Quinn, manager of plaintiff Pacific Manufacturing Company, was asked by plaintiffs' attorney whether or not there were changes or alterations made in the construction of the buildings prior to abandonment, and if so, to state what, if any, there were. "A. One of the changes made was in the cornice of the building. The owner took exception to it for some reason or other, and caused the cornice to be torn down and a new cornice was put up in place of it. Another change was made in the pergola after that was in place. The owner . . . objected to the use of beams and had that torn down and a new pergola put in place. And then the owner was dissatisfied with the quality of brick used in the construction of the building and had a special brick manufactured. There were other changes of a minor character. . . . Q. Were there any changes in the interior arrangement of the house, the rooms, to your knowledge? A. No material changes." He testified as to some changes made after abandonment, but we cannot see that they would affect the question of the lienors' rights at the time of abandonment, for they would be taken into account in ascertaining the cost of completion under the contract.

Other witnesses pointed out some changes made in the course of the construction of the building.

The contract called for a "brick veneered and frame residence and garage." The court found that the reasonable value of the changes made, in materials and labor, was $3,866.28; that while said changes did not materially alter the elevations and appearances of said buildings, the same consisted in the use of more expensive material, greater increase in labor, and necessitated the tearing out and replacing of certain work done and performed in the buildings, thereby changing the interior construction as to value and character of materials, and to a certain extent in general appearance.

We do not think that the facts found justified the conclusion of the trial court that the contract was void.

Plaintiffs' third theory calls for the application of section 1192. This claim is that this section of the Code of Civil Procedure makes the title and interest of defendant Winifred absolutely responsible irrespective of the contract, and that the findings and judgment may rest entirely on the fact that she did not give the notice contemplated by section 1192.

Plaintiffs allege in their complaints that "said defendant R. A. Perry, acting for himself and on behalf of the said defendant Winifred A. Perry and with her full knowledge and consent, entered into a contract in writing with the said defendant Magneson," etc. In their answers defendants admit these averments of the complaints.

The finding of the court was, "that defendant R. A. Perry is and was at all times herein mentioned, the reputed owner of the hereinafter described land, buildings and premises, and that Winifred A. Perry is and was at all times herein mentioned, the real owner, to wit, the owner in fee," etc.

The court also found that during all the time that labor was being performed or materials being furnished for said buildings, said defendant Magneson was employed and engaged in the construction of said buildings by the said R. A. Perry with the full knowledge and consent of the said defendant Winifred A. Perry, "and that all the materials furnished or labor performed'' was furnished and performed "with the knowledge and consent of the said Winifred A. Perry."

There was no direct finding that R. A. Perry executed the contract as the agent of his wife, Winifred, nor was there any evidence that she personally contracted with Magneson. The admitted averments of the complaint that defendant R. A. Perry entered into the contract on her behalf, and with her full knowledge and consent, rendered any finding on the fact of his authority to act for her in the matter immaterial. And the finding that "the said Winifred A. Perry never made or entered into any contract in writing with the said defendant R. A. Perry and one Magneson, or either of them, relating to the construction of said buildings," is not inconsistent with the fact that her husband entered into the contract on her behalf and with her full knowledge and consent.

It was said in *Stimson Mill Co.* v. *Braun*, 136 Cal. 122, 125, [89 Am. St. Rep. 116, 57 L. R. A. 726, 68 Pac. 481]: "The materialman and the laborers are protected in their right to a lien by the provision in section 1183 of the Code of Civil Procedure, requiring such contract to be in writing and made a matter of public record. They know that, in accordance with the decisions of this court, the legislature cannot give a right of lien to an extent greater than the contract price. By being placed upon record the contract is open to their inspection and examination, and if they are not content with its provisions, they may decline to furnish any materials for the building or perform any labor thereon. But if they do furnish any, their right to a lien must be limited by the terms of the contract." And as was said in the Roystone case, *supra:* "The contract, legally made, limits the liability of the owner to lien claimants."

In the present case there was a valid contract made on behalf of the owner and with her knowledge and consent, and it seems to us that the owner was not obliged also to give notice under section 1192 of nonresponsibility, in addition to the recorded contract, in order to secure the protection given her by the statute. We have found no case where our supreme court has held that lien claimants may disregard the recorded contract of the owner and proceed against him under section 1192, unless he has also given the notice mentioned in that section. Where the contract is made on his behalf and with his knowledge and consent and is recorded, and the lien claimants so state in their complaints, we can see no reason why the contract should not be the measure of his liability. In short, the owner's liability under section 1192 does not attach when there is a valid recorded contract made in his behalf.

Some other questions are presented in the briefs, but the view we have taken renders their consideration unnecessary.

The learned trial court seems to have found the amount due on the claims upon the theory that the contract was void because of the alterations in the plans and that the owner was liable under section 1192. We think the contract was valid and the owner's liability should be measured by section 1200.

The judgment and order are reversed.

Hart, J., and Ellison J., *pro tem.*, concurred.

A petition to have the cause heard in the supreme court, after judgment in the district court of appeal, was denied by the supreme court on October 23, 1916.

[Civ. No. 1489. Third Appellate District.—August 25, 1916.]

LOUIS BRESLAUER, Respondent, v. McCORMICK-SAELTZER COMPANY (a Corporation), Appellant.

ACTION FOR PERSONAL SERVICES — AMOUNT OF COMPENSATION — PAYMENT OF EXTRA SALARY OUT OF SECRET FUND—EVIDENCE—SUPPORT OF FINDINGS.—In an action to recover an alleged balance due on account of salary as chief clerk and accountant of a general merchandise business, the amount of such salary entered on the books of the company and the receipted card in full for salary is not conclusive evidence of the amount of the plaintiff's compensation, where it is made to appear from the evidence that the plaintiff had for several years been paid an additional amount out of a "secret fund," and that such fund was a recognized part of the machinery of the company kept for paying extra salaries to good employees.

ID.—EVIDENCE—RECEIPT.—A receipt is never conclusive evidence, but is always open to explanation.

APPEAL from a judgment of the Superior Court of Shasta County. James G. Estep, Judge.

The facts are stated in the opinion of the court.

Carr & Kennedy, for Appellant.

W. D. Tillotson, for Respondent.

ELLISON, J., *pro tem.*—This action is brought by the plaintiff to recover of the defendant the sum of $375, balance alleged to be due on account of salary from February 28, 1914, to May 1, 1915.

Plaintiff has judgment for the amount claimed and the defendant appeals therefrom.

The complaint alleges that between the above dates plaintiff rendered services for defendant at its instance and request, each and every month, in the capacity of chief accountant and clerk.

That for said services defendant promised to pay him at the rate of $175 per month, which salary for said time amounted to $2,625.

That defendant had only paid him of said amount the sum of $2,250, leaving a balance due him of $375, which had not been paid and for which judgment is asked.

The answer denied that plaintiff's salary was fixed by agreement at $175 per month, but alleged it was fixed at $150 per month, and alleges that during said period of employment "the plaintiff received and accepted from defendant in payment of said salary the sum of $150.00 for each and every month of said time, amounting for said period to the total sum of $2,250.00, and alleges that said salary has been fully paid and satisfied."

The findings of the court followed closely the allegations and language of the complaint.

The principal contention of the appellant is that the finding of the court "that for plaintiff's services the defendant promised to pay him $175.00 per month," is not sustained by the evidence. That the evidence shows he was only to receive $150 per month, and that this amount has been fully paid to him.

It appears from the record that the defendant is engaged in the general merchandise business in the city of Redding, Shasta County, California, and has in its employ many persons. The plaintiff entered the employ of the defendant in

July, 1901, as chief clerk and accountant, and continued with it until May 1, 1915.

In February, 1910, and for some time prior thereto, the salary of the plaintiff appeared upon the books of the defendant as $125 per month, but for some time he had been receiving, in addition to his "book salary," $25 per month, which was paid to him at the end of the year in a check for three hundred dollars.

The plaintiff testifies that in the latter part of the year 1909, or the early part of 1910, he applied to the defendant for an increase in his compensation or salary. Quoting from his testimony: "I applied to Mr. Saeltzer for an increase of salary. What was said to me: 'You were to receive a book salary of $150 per month.' A salary on a separate fund known as the 'secret fund' of $25 per month. It was said at the time I would get the $25 per month at the end of the year."

He further testified that after this incident his salary was entered on the books of the defendant at $150 per month, which was paid each month, and that three hundred dollars was paid him each year out of the "secret fund," and that this arrangement was carried out from February 28, 1910, to February 28, 1914.

There is no conflict in the testimony as to the fact that the corporation kept a fund or account known as the "secret fund," and no dispute that plaintiff and other employees of the defendant received money from this fund, both before and after February, 1910. And no dispute that from February, 1910, to February, 1914, plaintiff was paid by defendant out of the fund three hundred dollars on four different occasions, making one thousand two hundred dollars in all. This gave him a compensation for his work between those dates of $175 per month. From February, 1914, to May 1, 1915, he only received $150 per month, and received nothing out of the secret fund. The extra $25 per month for the period between the last two dates is the basis of this action.

The defendant denies that it ever agreed to pay the plaintiff at any time any salary in excess of the $150 per month appearing on its books.

The conflict between the parties centers largely around the significance and meaning of this transfer of money from the "secret account" to the plaintiff.

The position of the latter being that the $25 per month was paid to him as a part of his agreed salary out of this fund; the defendant's position is that the three hundred dollars per year paid was a pure gift for good services rendered, and not the result of any contractual liability; that it could give it or not to the plaintiff in any years as it saw fit.

The plaintiff testified that Mr. Saeltzer gave as a reason for not having the books show he was getting $175 per month that he did not want the other employees to know what salary any particular employee was getting. In this he is corroborated by the testimony of Mr. Saeltzer, from which it appears a "secret fund" was kept, and from it other employees besides the plaintiff received extra compensation. His testimony shows that the "secret fund" was a recognized part of the machinery for transacting the business of the corporation.

As to its purpose and use, Mr. Saeltzer testified: "The secret fund was kept to pay extra salaries. To explain salary—for instance, we have a person in our employ who is working for $75 per month and that being a good man. And he says: 'I want to leave; I can make more money.' I don't want to give him more on the books, for the next man would want more salary if I started this. So I would pay him the extra salary out of the secret fund and the board would approve it."

We think this testimony of Mr. Saeltzer clears up the whole situation and corroborates the plaintiff.

It makes manifest that the defendant did not want the books to show, in all cases, the salary that was being paid to an employee, and that they did not. That the "secret fund" was kept for the purpose of paying "the extra salary" (to quote his testimony), extra salary meaning salary agreed upon in excess of that entered on the books, and that plaintiff was paid one thousand two hundred dollars out of this "secret fund" after his salary was raised on the books from $125 per month to $150. That the plaintiff did have an arrangement with the defendant that he was to get $25 per month in addition to his book salary of $150 per month seems clear. And the evidence shows he did receive it for four years. His book salary was raised from $125 per month to $150 per month February, 1910. After this, according to the testimony of Mr. Saeltzer, he secured, in addition to his book salary, the following sums: January 1, 1911, three hundred dollars; May 23, 1912, three hundred dollars; December 22, 1913, three hundred dollars; December 24, 1914, three hundred dollars.

The above testimony of the defendant's manager amply supports the plaintiff's contention that there was a "secret fund." That out of it he was paid three hundred dollars per year extra compensation for several years, not as a gratuity, but as of right under the terms of his contract with the defendant, and that he is entitled to it as of right for the period embraced herein.

Appellant further contends that the plaintiff's testimony is inconsistent with the entries made in the books of the corporation by himself. It is true that for the period here involved the plaintiff's salary was entered upon the books of the corporation as $150 per month. But in view of the plaintiff's testimony that it was a part of his agreement with R. M. Saeltzer that the books should show a salary only of $150 per month, the discrepancy between his actual salary and the book entries stands explained. The entries on the books were in accordance with the contract.

There is other evidence in the record bearing upon the finding under discussion, both in favor of the plaintiff and the defendant. We have examined it all with care, but enough has been referred to to show that the finding of the learned trial judge that plaintiff was working under a contract for an agreed compensation of $175 per month finds substantial support in the evidence.

2. It appears that during the later months of plaintiff's employment the system of paying employees was changed to a time-card system, and employees receipted on the card. The plaintiff signed these receipts. The receipts were worded as follows:

"Received payment in full for period and amount stated, and time recorded on this card."

Counsel for appellant claims that this should be held conclusive on plaintiff that he had been paid his full agreed compensation.

A receipt is never conclusive evidence—is always open to explanation. The explanation contained in the record is sufficient to prevent this receipt from concluding plaintiff.

If the defendant did not want the books of the corporation to show the salary plaintiff was receiving, and the evidence is ample for the drawing of such a conclusion, then it did not want, for same reason, the receipts to show it. It would have been an idle act to have the books show that he was getting only $150 per month, and follow this with a receipt showing he was receiving $175 per month.

3. The stubs of checks and resolutions of the board of directors made months and years after the contract was made with plaintiff were self-serving declarations and properly excluded.

4. It is claimed the court erred in failing to find upon a material issue raised by the answer. In the brief of counsel the allegation of the answer upon which it is claimed no finding was made is quoted as follows:

"That during said time defendant paid to plaintiff and plaintiff received and accepted in payment of said salary, the sum of $150.00 for each and every month of said time, amounting for said period to the total sum of $2250.00."

To properly appreciate the significance of the above language, it must be considered in connection with its context. It is found in paragraph IV of the answer. The first part of the paragraph denies that plaintiff has not been paid all of his salary and, proceeding, says: "Defendant alleges that for said services so rendered by plaintiff to defendant during said time mentioned in the complaint, plaintiff agreed to accept and defendant promised to pay to plaintiff a salary at the rate of $150.00 per month for each and every month during said time and amounting to the total sum of $2250.00" (and alleges that during said time defendant paid to plaintiff and plaintiff received and accepted from defendant in payment of his salary the sum of $150 for each and every month of said time, amounting in said period to the total sum of $2,250, and alleges that said salary has been fully paid and satisfied).

The court has found that the agreed salary was $175 per month, and that of it only $150 per month has been paid, and that the balance is unpaid and due.

The part of the answer above quoted and placed in parentheses, when considered with its context, is no more than a statement that the agreed salary was $150 per month, and that the full amount computed at that rate has been paid and accepted by defendant.

The statement in the answer that his salary was to be $150 per month is the pleader's statement of what the contract of employment was as originally made, and is not and was not intended as a statement that after the services were performed, there was an accord and satisfaction in and by which plaintiff and defendant settled a disputed claim on the agreed basis of $150 per month for the period.

Viewed in this light, the findings of the court fully cover the issue made.

The judgment is affirmed.

Chipman, P. J., and Hart, J., concurred.

A petition to have the cause heard in the supreme court, after judgment in the district court of appeal, was denied by the supreme court on October 23, 1916.

[Civ. No. 1502. Third Appellate District.—August 25, 1916.]

C. J. VATH, Respondent, v. JAMES F. HALLETT et al., Respondents; JAMES J. DAVITT, Appellant.

CONTRACT—LIQUIDATED DAMAGES — PLEADING — INSUFFICIENCY OF COMPLAINT—SUBSTANTIAL BREACH NOT SHOWN.—In an action to recover the sum of money fixed as liquidated damages for the breach of the terms of a contract guaranteeing that in consideration of a loan of a sum of money to a person to permit him to become a member of a retail liquor partnership, the partners would, during the entire period of the leasehold of the premises wherein such business was being conducted, purchase of the lenders "all steam and lager beer and liquors of every kind and character and all incidentals pertaining to the retail liquor business," the complaint fails to state a cause of action, where it is only alleged that on or about a stated date the defendants, contrary to the terms of said agreement and in violation of their obligation thereof, neglected and refused to purchase all lager beer of the plaintiffs as provided in the contract.

APPEAL from a judgment of the Superior Court of Santa Clara County. W. A. Beasley, Judge.

The facts are stated in the opinion of the court.

Hoefler & Morris, and George F. Snyder, for Appellant.

William H. Johnson, for Respondent, C. J. Vath.

ELLISON, J., *pro tem.*—The plaintiff brought this action
to recover of the defendants Davitt and Hallett the sum of
three thousand dollars, alleged to be due under the terms
of a written contract. Two other persons were made defendants under an allegation that they refused to join with the
plaintiff. Davitt and Hallett will be referred to as the
defendants.

The defendant Davitt demurred to the complaint, and his
demurrer having been overruled, he declined to answer and
judgment was entered against him. He appeals from such
judgment.

For a clear understanding of the case it seems necessary
to set out in full the contract sued upon as it appears in the
complaint. It is as follows:

"This agreement made between James J. Davitt and J. F.
Hallett, of the County of Santa Clara, State of California,
parties of the first part, and A. L. Brassy, C. J. Vath and
George Geoffrey, of the same said county and state, parties
of the second part,

"Witnesseth:

"That whereas the said James J. Davitt and J. F. Hallett
are about to enter into partnership in the business of retailing liquor, at number 19 South Second street, in the City of
San Jose, County of Santa Clara, State of California, and
the said J. F. Hallett is desirous of having associated with
him the said James J. Davitt, and the said Davitt, in order
to become associated with the said Hallett, has to raise the
sum of six thousand ($6,000.00) dollars, and whereas the
said parties of the second part are willing to loan to the
said Davitt the said sum of six thousand ($6,000.00) dollars,
in consideration of certain security to be given by to parties
of the second part. One of which is the guaranty of parties
of the first part, on their part, that they will during the entire period of the leasehold, now held by said Hallett, pertaining to said premises, to purchase of said parties of the
second part, all steam and lager beer and liquors of every
kind and character and all incidentals pertaining to the retail
liquor business of and from said parties of the second part.

It being impracticable and extremely difficult to fix the actual damage which may result to parties of the second part from a breach or violation of the terms hereof by parties of the first part. It is agreed that the sum of three thousand ($3,000.00) dollars be and the same is hereby fixed as liquidated damages for which sum judgment may be taken by parties of the second part upon proof of a breach of the terms hereof by parties of the first part.

"JAS. F. HALLETT,
"JAMES J. DAVITT."

Additionally the complaint alleges: "That from the nature of the subject matter of the said contract and the relation of the parties thereto, it would have been, was and still is impracticable and extremely difficult to fix, have fixed, or to now fix the actual damage which plaintiff would sustain by reason of a breach thereof by parties of the first part.

"That on or about the 29th day of May, 1913, the defendants, contrary to the terms of said agreement and in violation of their obligation thereof, neglected and refused to purchase all lager beer of the plaintiffs as provided in said contract."

That at the time of said neglect and refusal defendant Davitt was conducting said retail liquor business.

That plaintiff at all times was ready, able, and willing to comply with all the terms of said contract on his part to be performed, and had done so.

That plaintiff advanced and defendants accepted the six thousand dollar loan provided for in said agreement. That defendants complied with the terms of said contract for a period of about two years after its date.

Judgment is asked for the three thousand dollars and costs.

1. We are of the opinion that the complaint does not state a cause of action and the demurrer thereto should have been sustained. While the contract pleaded is somewhat vague, indefinite, and incomplete, it is manifest that the defendants were to buy of the plaintiff only such beer as they might need from time to time in their business of retailing liquor. There is no allegation in the complaint that they needed any beer on or about May 29, 1913, or that they bought any from any other source. For aught that appears in the complaint, they needed none at about that time.

There is no averment that they ceased to buy of the plaintiff for more than one day.

It is alleged that they failed and refused to buy *all* beer of plaintiff. This allegation would be sustained on a trial by testimony that on the day named the defendants bought ten cases of beer from the plaintiff and only one quart from someone else.

Conceding for the present that the contract is to be construed as one for liquidated damages, yet no recovery can be had unless a substantial breach thereof is alleged and proved.

"This action is brought upon the theory that the sum of two hundred dollars specified in the agreement is liquidated damages for any breach of the requirements thereof, and such is the contention of the plaintiff. For the purposes of the case, the correctness of this proposition will be conceded. In such a case, before any liability to pay the liquidated damages can attach to the party in default, he must have been guilty of a substantial breach of his agreement—a breach that has resulted in something more than mere nominal damages to the other contracting party. This rule is so manifestly just that no discussion of it is necessary." (*Hathaway* v. *Lynn,* 75 Wis. 186, [6 L. R. A. 551, 43 N. W. 956].)

As an application may be made to amend the complaint in the lower court, it becomes necessary to notice some other points raised by appellant.

For several reasons we are of the opinion the contract cannot be the foundation of an action for either liquidated damages or for actual damages.

1. It lacks certainty.

There is no direct promise or agreement on the part of the defendants to buy liquor from the plaintiff. Such promise can only be inferred from the general language of the contract.

The plaintiff agreed to loan defendant six thousand dollars "in consideration of certain security to be given by to parties of the second part. One of which is the guaranty of parties of the first part, on their part, that they will during the entire period of the leasehold, now held by said Hallett, pertaining to said premises, to purchase of said parties of the second part, all steam and lager beer and liquors of every kind and character and all incidentals pertaining to the retail liquor business of and from said parties of the second part." Perhaps a promise on the part of defendants to buy beer, etc., from plaintiff may be inferred from this general language, but it seems unnecessary to definitely pass on the point.

The contract fixes no price at which plaintiff was to furnish beer, etc., to defendant. He did not bind himself to furnish it at any agreed price. The plaintiff did not promise and bind himself to sell beer, etc., to defendant at all. He assumed no obligation to do so, and it was left entirely at his pleasure to sell defendant beer, etc., or not to sell it, and any failure to so furnish and sell would have given plaintiff no cause of action against defendant. An executory contract must have the element of mutuality.

An agreement on part of defendant to buy beer of the plaintiff is not enforceable against the defendant where there is no agreement or promise on the part of the plaintiff to sell such articles to him. Hence the contract cannot be the basis for a suit for damages for not buying of the plaintiff.

The contract is not enforceable as one for liquidated damages.

It will be observed that by the contract the same damage, three thousand dollars, is fixed as the estimated and agreed damages for a complete violation of its terms and for a partial violation.

According to the terms of the contract, if the defendant failed and neglected during the entire five years to buy anything of the plaintiff, the damage would have been three thousand dollars. Whereas, if he bought all beer and other supplies for the saloon during all the five years except the last week of said five years' period, he would also owe plaintiff three thousand dollars.

This shows that no good faith valuation of the damages, which might result from the breach of the contract, was made.

"A good faith valuation of the damages which will result from the breach of a contract is generally upheld and the amount specified recoverable." (Elliott on Contracts, sec. 1559.) And the converse is equally true, viz.: That where the contract on its face shows that no good faith estimate and valuation of the damages that might result from a breach of the contract was ever made or attempted, the amount thus arbitrarily fixed without any reference to the actual damages that may be incurred will not be recoverable as liquidated damages. In 2 Greenleaf on Evidence, section 259, the rule is said to be that it must be "apparent that the damages have already been the subject of actual and fair calculation and adjustment between the parties."

We conclude that the demurrer to the complaint should have been sustained. That the contract is not enforceable as a contract for liquidated damages, and by reason of its lack of mutuality of obligation and uncertainty cannot be the basis of an action for actual damages.

The judgment is reversed, with direction to sustain the demurrer to the complaint.

Chipman, P. J., and Hart, J., concurred.

A petition to have the cause heard in the supreme court, after judgment in the district court of appeal, was denied by the supreme court on October 24, 1916, and the following opinion then rendered thereon:

THE COURT.—The petition for transfer and hearing in this court is denied. We think the judgment was properly reversed upon the first ground stated in the opinion of the district court of appeal, viz.: That the complaint does not state facts showing a substantial breach of the agreement. We are not satisfied of the correctness of the views expressed by the district court of appeal on other points, and withhold the expression of any opinion on such points. Upon a new trial the superior court will not regard as decided or as the law of the case any proposition except the one which is above stated to have our approval.

[Civ. No. 1475.   Third Appellate District.—August 28, 1916.]

GRANT FEE, Respondent, v. McPHEE COMPANY (a Corporation) et al., Appellants.

ACCOUNT STATED—ESSENTIALS OF—NEW CONTRACT.—An account stated is a writing which exhibits the state of account between parties and the balance owing from one to the other; and when assented to, either expressly or impliedly, it becomes a new contract.

ID.—ACTION FOR SERVICES—SUPPORT OF FINDINGS.—In this action to recover an alleged balance due for services in superintending the con struction of certain buildings for a contracting company, it is held that the finding that the document upon which the plaintiff relied as an account stated constituted such an account is supported by the evidence.

ID.—OPENING OF ACCOUNT—FRAUD OR MISTAKE.—In the absence of allegation and proof of fraud or mistake which taints the entire contract, the court will not open and unravel it as if no accounting had been made, but the settlement will be binding except for the errors shown.

ID.—EVIDENCE—PROOF OF OMISSIONS AND ERRORS.—In an action upon an account stated it is proper to allow evidence of omissions and errors therein and find in favor of plaintiff in accordance with the facts.

ID.—INTEREST—ALLOWANCE FROM COMMENCEMENT OF ACTION.—In an action on an account stated, interest is allowable from the date of the commencement of the action.

ID.—SUPERINTENDENCY OF BUILDINGS FOR CORPORATION—PERCENTAGE OF PROFITS—STATUS OF PARTIES.—Contracts between a corporation engaged in the general contracting business and an individual who is to superintend the construction of certain buildings for the former for a percentage of the "net profits" do not make the relationship of the parties that of partners.

ID.—CONSTRUCTION OF TERM "NET PROFITS"—EVIDENCE.—Evidence of similar contracts made between the parties is admissible to assist the court in interpreting the term "net profits."

APPEALS from judgments of the Superior Court of the City and County of San Francisco and orders denying a new trial. E. P. Morgan, Judge.

The facts are stated in the opinion of the court.

William P. Hubbard, for Appellants.

Aitken & Aitken, R. H. Countryman, and Frank W. Aitken, for Respondent.

CHIPMAN, P. J.—Two actions between the same parties are included in the appeal, one having been numbered in the court below 17,022, the other 18,032, both having been tried together. The transcript on appeal covers 1,292 printed pages and the briefs comprise half as many more. The appeals are by defendants from the respective judgments and from orders denying their motions for new trials made in each case, and

354 alleged errors of law are specified in the assignments of errors.

The complaint in the first action, No. 17,022, was filed June 6, 1908. It is therein alleged that defendant McPhee Company was a corporation organized and existing under and by virtue of the laws of California, with its office and principal place of business in the city and county of San Francisco; that defendants Daniel McPhee and Anna McPhee were at all times husband and wife; that defendant Daniel, during all the times mentioned, was doing business under the name and style of McPhee Company; that defendants sued fictitiously as First Doe, Second Doe, and Third Doe were the owners of one share each, and defendants Daniel and Anna McPhee were the owners of 248½ shares each of the capital stock of said corporation, the entire issued capital stock being five hundred shares; "that said defendants other than the defendants sued herein as stockholders of the defendant McPhee Company are indebted to this plaintiff in the sum of $13,649.27 upon and as for and upon an account stated made by and between said defendants except said defendants sued herein as stockholders and this plaintiff." It is then alleged that "said defendants other than those who are sued as stockholders of said defendant corporation within two years last past . . . entered into written agreements with this plaintiff from time to time, by which it was agreed that in the course of the erection and construction of certain buildings, this plaintiff should act as the superintendent thereof and receive forty per cent of the net profits of the erection and construction of said buildings"; that plaintiff performed his part of said contracts and from time to time received various sums of money on account thereof; that on May 28, 1908, plaintiff and defendants "other than said defendants sued as stockholders" entered into an account stated and the amount of the indebtedness to plaintiff was fixed at the sum of $13,649.27, which said defendants promised to pay; that no part thereof has been paid, and that said stockholders are liable for their proportionate amount of said indebtedness.

In a second count of the complaint it was stated "that this plaintiff performed certain work and rendered certain services to defendants other than said defendants sued herein as stockholders of the defendant corporation," and that plaintiff was to receive forty per cent of the net profits received for the

construction of said buildings; that the said profits thereof
were $65,229.56; that forty per cent thereof is $25,991.82;
that plaintiff has been paid $12,342.45, leaving due him the
sum of $13,649.27.   The prayer is for the last-mentioned sum,
judgment being asked against the five stockholders named for
their proportionate amounts.

A demurrer to the complaint was overruled and defendants,
other than those fictitiously named, answered: Denied that
Daniel McPhee ''was doing business under the name and style,
or name or style, of McPhee Company, otherwise or at all except under the name of McPhee Company, a corporation'';
denied that defendant Anna was the owner of any greater
number of shares of the capital stock of said corporation than
ten shares; denied the indebtedness sued for; denied that they
entered into written agreements with plaintiff by which it was
agreed that plaintiff should act as superintendent of the construction of the buildings referred to and should receive forty
per cent of the net profits thereof; denied performance by
plaintiff of the conditions of the contracts alleged; denied
making an account stated and that any amount of indebtedness
was fixed.   The averments of the second cause of action were
specifically denied.

The trial commenced on November 17, 1909, and, before its
conclusion and on December 1, 1909, an amended complaint
was filed, containing two counts.   The allegations were the
same as in the original complaint, with these exceptions:
W. M. Willett, J. F. Campbell, and W. E. Lowe were substituted as defendants for First Doe, Second Doe, and Third
Doe; it was alleged that defendant Daniel McPhee was the
owner of 483 shares and defendant Anna McPhee of ten shares
of the capital stock of said corporation; that the account stated
was for $13,749.27 and that one hundred dollars had been paid
thereon; the amount alleged in the second cause of action to
be due was $15,649.27 and judgment was prayed for that
amount.

A demurrer to the amended complaint was overruled and an
answer was filed with similar denials as those contained in the
answer to the original complaint.

On April 6, 1910, an amendment to the answer was filed, setting up two additional further and separate defenses, in the
first of which it was alleged that in any account stated between

the parties, mistakes, errors, and omissions were made therein by the bookkeeper who prepared "such alleged account stated," and that it showed only gross profits and losses," the items being enumerated and aggregating $14,544.59 "as appearing in favor of the plaintiff herein." It was also alleged, as a further and separate defense, that both counts of the complaint were barred by the provisions of subdivision 1, section 339, of the Code of Civil Procedure.

On April 1, 1912, plaintiff filed an "amendment to amended complaint" to be added to the first count, setting up a mistake by the bookkeeper by which five thousand dollars of the net profits made by the defendant corporation were omitted from the account upon which plaintiff was to receive forty per cent, "and if said account stated had expressed said real intention of plaintiff and the defendant corporation, said account would have shown an additional five thousand dollars of net profits, and said account should and would have been stated for the correct sum due plaintiff, to wit: the sum of $15,749.27." A denial of these allegations was filed by defendants.

The complaint in action No. 18,032, filed July 31, 1908, contained similar averments to those set up in the original complaint in action No. 17,022, alleging an indebtedness of $1,123.78, for which amount judgment was asked. An amended complaint was filed December 1, 1909, containing the same changes as made in the amended complaint filed in the other action on the same date. Answers were filed to both pleadings, denying the material allegations thereof.

Very full findings were filed in each action. A nonsuit was granted as to the defendant Daniel McPhee, doing business under the name of McPhee Company. The judgment in action No. 17,022 was in favor of plaintiff against the corporation for the sum of $14,491.33, with interest from the date of the commencement of the action, the aggregate being $18,529.15; judgment was also entered against defendant Daniel McPhee for $17,899.17, and against defendant Anna McPhee for $370.56. In action No. 18,032, the judgment against the corporation, including interest from the commencement of the action, was $1,427.78; against defendant Daniel for $1,379.20, and against defendant Anna for $28.54.

As is apparent from the pleadings, the corporation defendant McPhee Company was engaged in the general contracting

business in San Francisco and plaintiff was its superintendent
of construction.   Six written agreements were entered into by
the plaintiff and defendant corporation which were received
in evidence and marked, respectively, exhibits 1 to 6.   Exhibit 1 was as follows:

"San Francisco, Cal., April 1/05.

"This is to certify that Grant Fee is entitled to 40% of the
net profits on our contract, Fairmont Hotel dated, Jan. 13/05,
salaries and office expenses to be charged to the contract.

"All money allowed Grant Fee during construction to be
charged against his 40%, on settlement at completion of the
contract.

"McPHEE COMPANY,
"D. McPHEE, Pres't."

Exhibit No. 2 was as follows:

"San Francisco, Cal., Nov. 3/05.

"This is to certify that Grant Fee is entitled to 40% of the
net profits of our contract, Deming Building, located on the
South East corner of Post and Stockton St., S. F.

"Should there be a loss on the building it is agreed that 40%
of the net loss on the Deming Building, is to be deducted
from Grant Fee's share of the profits on our contract, Fairmont Hotel, dated Jan. 13/05."   (Same signatures as to Exhibit No. 1.)

Exhibit No. 3, dated June 25, 1906, certified that plaintiff
was entitled to forty per cent of the net profits on seventeen
specified contracts.

Exhibit No. 4 was dated December 1, 1906, covered three
separate contracts and contained the following clause:
"Should there be a loss on any of the above named contracts it
is agreed that Grant Fee is to assume 40% of such loss the
same to be deducted from his share of the profits."

Exhibit No. 5, dated April 18, 1907, covered four separate
contracts and contained a clause in the same words and figures
as last above quoted.

Exhibit No. 6, dated September 28, 1907, covered two contracts and provided that in case of loss on said contracts,
"Grant Fee is to stand 40% of said loss same to be deducted
from his share of profits on other work."

Appellants, in their opening brief, urge the following general points as demanding reversal of the judgments:

1. There was no account stated.

2. Interest was allowable only from the date of judgment.

3. The judgment rendered was for forty per cent of gross profits and not for forty per cent of net profits.

4. The contracts created the relation of a partnership or joint undertaking between plaintiff and defendant corporation.

5. The court erred in its rulings during the trial.

6. The court erred in other particulars in its findings.

The court found that the defendant corporation entered into written agreements with plaintiff by which it was agreed that in the course of the construction of certain buildings plaintiff should act as superintendent thereof and receive therefor forty per cent of the net profits arising from the construction of said buildings, and that plaintiff performed all the terms and conditions of said agreement on his part to be performed, and there became due plaintiff various sums as his proportion of said net profits; that said proportion at the commencement of the action amounted to the sum of $67,334.46, and that said forty per cent of said net profits amounted to the sum of $26,933,78, of which plaintiff has been paid $12,442.45, leaving due and owing to plaintiff from defendant corporation the sum of $14,491.33, no part of which has been paid; that on May 30, 1908, plaintiff and defendant made and agreed to an account stated of said indebtedness due to plaintiff, and as a result of said accounting the amount of the net profits of defendant on said buildings and the construction thereof was shown to be $65,288.43, and defendants' indebtedness to plaintiff, after charging all debits against him, was fixed and stated to be the sum of $13,749.27, and it was then and there so agreed between plaintiff and defendant, and defendant thereupon promised and agreed to pay plaintiff the said sum of $13,749.27; "that in said account stated and in the making thereof, mistakes, errors, and omissions were made, by which mistakes, errors, and omissions net profits amounting to $2,046.03 made by the defendant corporation McPhee Company in the erection and construction of said buildings upon which plaintiff was to receive forty per cent of the net profits, was omitted from said account," and said account, through said errors, did not represent the real intention of plaintiff and defendant; that said errors were made by the defendants' bookkeeper in erroneously adding up a certain column of figures contained in what defendant called the "Cost Book," showing the sum of money expended by defendant in said work, and through said error there was set down as expenditures the sum of five thousand dollars more than the true sum; that by reason of the mistake as to the said sum of five thousand dollars, or, rather, with certain other mistakes, errors, and omissions of said bookkeeper, the said net profits were in fact $2,046.03 in addition to said $65,288.43, the total net profits being $67,334.46, and the correct amount of net profits due plaintiff should be and is the sum of $14,491.33.

The court found adversely to all the errors, omissions, and mistakes alleged in the answer to have occurred in stating the account, to wit, items in respect of salaries, office expenses, interest, insurance, use of donkey-engine, and as to these the court found that none of said items was "omitted from said account stated in making up said account stated through mistake, error, or omission of said plaintiff and defendant corporation McPhee Company, or through the mistake, error, or omission of the bookkeeper of said defendant corporation," except "the court has allowed $809.00 for insurance and given the defendant corporation credit therefor in ascertaining the net profits as hereinbefore found, and in finding the additional net profits which should have been allowed to the plaintiff in making said stated account." The court also found that defendant's bookkeeper did in fact figure the office expenses to be one thousand eight hundred dollars, which sum is the correct sum and was charged for office expenses in making said account stated. The court also found that neither cause of action was barred by the statute of limitations.

As conclusions of law, the court found the plaintiff was entitled to judgment as we have hereinabove stated.

We shall address ourselves to the principal action (No. 17,022 in the superior court), in which judgment for the larger amount, $18,529.15, was rendered. No question arises as to the ownership of the shares of defendant corporation, ninety-seven per cent of which belonged to defendant D. McPhee—he and his wife owning over ninety-eight per cent of the five hundred shares; nor is there any question as to his authority, as president and manager of the corporation, to represent and act for it during all the time plaintiff was connected with it. There had been no meeting of the stockholders or directors for years, its business being carried on by McPhee. The corporation, in fact, represented his business incorporated. Our reference, when made to the defendant, will mean the corporation.

1. One of the principal questions in the case is whether or not the finding that there was an account stated is supported by the evidence. The account was introduced as exhibit 7, and is as follows:

"San Francisco, May 28/08, 190

M

Statement of McPhee Co. with Grant Fee.
To McPhee Company, Dr.
Contractors

Mill and Yard: Telephone
1308 to 1350 Sixteenth Street   Market 449

1908	Profit	
Borel Bank	$7140.93	
Pacific Union Club	29.75	
	$7170.93	
40%		$2868.27

Nov 17/09
First Page
E P.M.J.

Feb 22/08
Statement of account between McPhee Co.
& Grant Fee.

	Profit	Loss
1906		
To Fairmont Hotel	$23810.80	
Deming		$4326.53
Newhall, Folsom St.	3506.84	
Halleck St.	3095.20	
Pope Estate, Front St.............		$974.63
Pope Estate, Mission St.............	2536.42	
Irwin residence,		
Galvanized iron & sidewalk.........	371.70	
Forward	32320.96	5301.16

Forward	$32320.96	$5301.16
Bush St.	2418.17	
Aronson Bldg. scaffolding	212.87	
Repair work	5291.18	
Lick job	34.30	
Brick work, Call	2835.92	
Call Powerhouse, brick.............	1622.18	
" floors	1932.15	
J. D. Spreckels	78.46	
Borel fence, etc.	9.50	
Sash & frames, Call		1865.95
Halleck St. underpinning...........	138.99	
Dunphy residence	106.87	
Cunningham	19069.42	
Office work		1800.00
	$67070.97	$8967.11
Less loss, ...	8967.11	
Net profit, ...	$58103.86	
Net profit........$58103.86		
40 %.........	$23241.54	
Cash rec'd to & including		
2/21/08	10710.00	
	$12531.54	

Nov 17–09
Second page
E P M. J.

May 23/08		
Transformer house	47.95	
Manhole	11.17	
Call Powerhouse, floor..........		29.35
brick, ...		75.00
	59.12	104.25
		59.12
		45.23

O.K.
A.M.G.

Balance, Feb 21/08...............	$12531.54
Loss,......$45.23	
40%.....	18.09
	$12513.45
Cash rec'd to & including 5/23/08..	1632.45
O. K. McPHEE.......	$10881.00"

The notations, "Nov. 17/09 First page E P M. J" and
"Nov. 17/09 Second page E P M. J.," were made by his
Honor Judge Mogan at the trial.

The notation, "O.K. A. M. G.," on second page was placed
there by defendant's bookkeeper, Mrs. Goodspeed. Otherwise than the notation made by Judge Mogan, the account is
as it was handed to plaintiff by the bookkeeper.

It will be observed that there are two pages comprising this
account, each initialed by the trial judge. The one spoken of
in the testimony as the "second page" is signed: "O.K. McPhee." This account covers transactions concerning the contract made April 1, 1905, in relation to the Fairmont Hotel,
and ending February, 1908, the account having been first
stated February 22, 1908.

The "first page," so called, brings the account down to
May 28, 1908. This page was not signed by McPhee. The
facts as to the preparation of the account and its signing by
McPhee were given in the testimony of plaintiff and of Mrs.
Goodspeed, who was the defendants' bookkeeper. Plaintiff
testified that he asked the bookkeeper to make a statement of
the profits and losses on the different jobs in which he was
associated or had superintended and the moneys drawn by him
and the moneys due him; that she made the statement in
writing and gave it to plaintiff, showing the account down to
February 21, 1908; that he gave the paper to McPhee between
the 1st and 10th of March. He testified: "I told him this
was the statement made up by the bookkeeper, showing the
profits and losses on the different jobs, the amount of money
drawn by me, and the amount of money due me at this date.
. . . He took the paper and said that he would look it over";
that McPhee retained it in his possession until the other account ("first page") was handed him more than two months
later; that at plaintiff's request the bookkeeper continued the
account down to May 23d, 1908, showing the profits and losses

and moneys drawn to that date; that this continuation was a
carbon copy of the prior statement which had been handed to
McPhee; that on May 28, 1908, the bookkeeper prepared a
further statement as to two buildings—the Borel Bank and
Pacific Union Club—just completed; that this statement was
pinned to the prior statement, the two constituting what is
referred to as plaintiff's exhibit 7; the carbon copy of the
February account with its continuations, being the portion
referred to as "second page," and the subsequent account
constituting what is referred to as the "first page." He testified that on May 30, 1908, he gave McPhee "the carbon
copy of that same paper and the extension brought down and
the other business pinned onto it." "Q. Were they attached
together with a pin? A. At that time; yes, sir. Q. And the
papers were in the same condition then as they are now, as
to figures, totals, etc.? A. Yes, sir. Q. Was that written in
lead pencil on that second page 'O.K. McPhee?' A. He
placed that on there that day."

As to what occurred at that time, he testified: "I handed
the paper to Mr. McPhee, and told him that was a statement
of the profits and losses on the jobs, and the moneys that I
had drawn, and what was due me to date, and that Mrs. Goodspeed did not want to put this amount to my credit on the
books without he first O.K.'ed the statement. . . . Mr.
McPhee took the paper and he looked it over for a little while
and O. K.'ed the paper and signed his name to it and handed
it to Mrs. Goodspeed, and told her that was all right, to place
it in the books."

Mrs. Goodspeed testified, "I saw Mr. Fee on that occasion hand this paper to Mr. McPhee; that paper, plaintiff's
exhibit 7, as near as I can remember, was, at that time, in
its present condition and I think both pinned together. As
near as I can remember, Mr. Fee said: 'Mr. McPhee,' he says,
'here is a statement of the profits and losses and the balance
due me as far as I know.' . . . The Court: Q. Did Mr.
McPhee look at the paper? A. Yes, sir. Mr. Aitken:
Q. Then what? A. He looked at it quite a few minutes, and
then he said: 'That is all right, Grant.' Q. Did he sign
it? A. I saw him sign it. . . . Q. Did he say to you, asking about putting it in the books to Mr. Grant Fee's credit?
A. I turned around to Mr. McPhee, and I said: 'Mr. Mc-
Phee, will I put this in the books?' and he said, 'Yes.'"

She testified that McPhee handed the paper to her with this instruction and that later she gave it to plaintiff.

Both before and after this account was stated as plaintiff testified, he had been demanding from McPhee money on account for the purpose of building a house and also to make a contemplated trip east, and these demands amounted to nine thousand dollars; that McPhee made frequent promises to meet his demands, but put him off to await a payment due or soon to become due on the Call Building. "The Court: Q. At that time he had in his possession, and there was due you, you claim, eleven-odd thousand dollars? A. Yes, sir. The Court: Q. But you were only asking a certain sum on account? A. Yes, sir."

After plaintiff commenced the action, plaintiff met McPhee at the latter's request. Plaintiff testified: "Mr. McPhee wanted to know why I had brought suit. I told him I was unable to get the money that was due me; he had promised repeatedly and I could not succeed in getting any of it, and I brought suit to protect myself; that I needed the money and wanted it. . . . He said he owed me the money, but he did not have the money just then. . . . There was no question about his owing me the money. . . . He and I conceded that there was this amount due me of $13,000 and some odd dollars." Later they met me in the office of John R. Aitken, one of plaintiff's attorneys, to talk over the matter. Mr. Aitken testified quite fully to what was said in his office by the parties. Among other things, he testified: "Mr. Fee used words like these: 'You owe me this money; why don't you pay it? Why don't you keep your word?' Mr. McPhee said: 'Well, I owe the money, I know I owe you the money,' or words to that effect, substantially that he owed the amount of money we had sued for. I am trying to give you almost the exact words used by Mr. Fee and Mr. McPhee. . . . Substantially it was this: Mr. Fee said: 'You owe me this money;' and Mr. McPhee said he owed the amount of money that we had sued for. . . . I used the words, stating the amount, $13,649, and Mr. McPhee said that he owed the amount but that he did not have the money and would give his notes at fifteen, thirty, and sixty days for it without security, and I advised Mr. Fee not to accept the offer. . . . The Court: Q. Was the amount mentioned in the

conversation, or was the claim mentioned? A. The amount
was mentioned in the conversation, I know."

It is not necessary to state more of the testimony to show
that McPhee knew the contents of the exhibit 7 and the
amount therein stated as the balance due plaintiff and the
amount plaintiff claimed to be due him.

We think, also, that this exhibit 7 was what the law regards as an account stated. In *Mercantile Trust Co. v. Doe,*
26 Cal. App. 246, 256, [146 Pac. 692], we had occasion to
say: "To turn an account into an account stated, it must
have been rendered with a view of ascertaining the balance
and making a final adjudication of the matter involved in
the account; or, in other words, to bring about a meeting
of the minds of the parties." That this is precisely what was
effected in the case here seems to us plain enough.

In *Gardner v. Watson,* 170 Cal. 570, [150 Pac. 994], the
supreme court very recently said: "Over what in law constitutes an account there was never any question in this state,
and very little uncertainty exists in other states."

Quoting from *Baird v. Crank,* 98 Cal. 293, 297, [33 Pac.
63], the court said: "It must appear that at the time of the
accounting certain claims existed, of and concerning which
an account was stated; that a balance was then struck and
agreed upon, 'and that defendant expressly admitted that
a certain sum was then due from him as a debt' "; and as
was said in *Coffee v. Williams,* 103 Cal. 556, [37 Pac. 504]:
"An account stated is a document—a writing—which exhibits the state of account between parties and the balance
owing from one to the other; and when assented to, either
expressly or impliedly, it becomes a new contract." (See
1 Ruling Case Law, p. 207, tit. "Accounts and Accounting.")

We need to go no further into the books to warrant the
finding of the court that the document here in question was an
account stated.

2. Appellants contend that the account was opened up by
proof of mistakes, errors, and omissions, and hence it ceased
to be an account stated. Defendants' bookkeeper testified
that the account was stated from entries in what were called
"Cost Books," in which were entered all the items of receipts
and disbursements relating to the contracts with plaintiff,
as had been done in agreements not now involved, but similar
previous transactions which had been carried on by the same

parties and had been closed up in the same manner. She
testified that after this account had been stated she discovered that in adding the column showing expenditures on
the Fairmont Hotel, she had made a mistake of five thousand
dollars which affected the profits to that extent on that contract, and made a difference in plaintiff's balance of two
thousand dollars. She also discovered some other minor mistakes, both debits and credits, resulting in $46.03 more to
pass to plaintiff's balance.

"In the absence of allegation and proof of fraud or mistake which taints the entire account, the court will not open
and unravel it as if no accounting had been made, but the
settlement will be binding except for the errors shown." (1
Corpus Juris, p. 721.)

We held in *Adams* v. *Gerig,* 25 Cal. App. 638, 640, [145
Pac. 106], that it was proper for the court, in an action for
an account stated, to allow evidence of omissions and errors
therein and find in favor of plaintiff in accordance with the
facts.

Johnson v. *Gallatin Valley Milling Co.,* 38 Mont. 83, [98
Pac. 883], was a case where an account was stated in relation to an invoice of wheat sold by plaintiff to defendant.
A balance was struck and plaintiff signed at the bottom a
receipt in full payment. He afterward discovered that there
was a shortage in the number of bushels and in the true
balance due, to his disadvantage, and he demanded of defendant to make the correction, which being refused. he
brought the action to surcharge the account stated. Said
the court: "The rules of law applicable to such cases as the
present, wherein one of the parties seeks to avoid the settlement and reopen the account, are simple and of easy application. The balance ascertained from a statement of accounts was formerly held to be the result of so deliberate
an act by the parties as to preclude an examination into
the items for the purpose of correcting errors or mistakes;
but this rule has been so far relaxed that, while the promise
to pay the ascertained balance is in effect a new promise, the
settlement being regarded as the consideration for it, the
settlement does not create an estoppel, but furnishes a strong
prima facie presumption that the result is correct." (Citing cases.)

It was held that the burden of proof is cast upon the party seeking to avoid this new promise and open up to investigation the antecedent dealings between the parties, and he must allege the error, mistake, or fraud on which he relies and establish it by clear and satisfactory evidence. (See, also, note to *Jasper Trust Co.* v. *Lampkin,* 136 Am. St. Rep. 48.)

It was in obedience to this rule that defendant sought to surcharge the account and introduced evidence of what it regarded as errors, omissions, and mistakes.

3. At this point we may dispose of defendant's contention that it was error to find against it in these particulars. The precise point urged is that the judgment rendered was for forty per cent of gross and not forty per cent of net profits, and this because it failed to take into account certain items which defendant contends should have been considered.

Defendant devotes much attention to the cases and text-writers on the question of what constitutes net profits as contradistinguished from gross profits, and the rule by which they are to be ascertained, but he deduces the conclusion that the term "net profits" used in the contracts necessarily implies that the items claimed by defendant should have been included as expenditures, thus reducing proportionately the net profits on the several contracts. Defendants' position might find support were this an accounting of the general business of the corporation between persons mutually interested in such general business, which it is not. There were six separate contracts, each referring to a particular building or buildings, or to particular work at certain places. There was no necessary connection between any two or more of them except as provided in the contracts themselves. Expressly in some and impliedly in others, there was by the terms of the contracts to be a settlement at the completion of each contract. Forty per cent of the net loss in the Deming Building (No. 2) was to be deducted from plaintiff's share of the profits on the Fairmont Hotel contract. No. 3 embraced the Newhall Building and "the net profits on repair work" at certain designated places, and plaintiff was to be allowed his profits "on settlement at completion of the contract and work." No. 4 mentions the second Newhall Building, the Pope Estate Building, and certain work on the Claus Spreckels Building, and the contract provided

that "should there be a loss on any of the above named
contracts, it is agreed that Grant Fee is to assume 40% of
such loss, the same to be deducted from his share of the
profits." No. 5 contained a similar provision as to the work
therein provided for, that is, plaintiff was to share losses
in any of the work therein mentioned. In No. 6, the Borel
Building, and brick work on the Call power-house, the contract reads: "Should there be a loss on the above named
work, it is agreed that Grant Fee is to stand 40% of said
loss, same to be deducted from his share of profits on other
work."

Whether the terms "other work" referred to work mentioned in that contract or in all others is not clear. It is
not very material, since in preparing the stated account
the bookkeeper took up the work from the beginning and
entered the profits and losses on each, and struck a balance,
thus giving defendant the benefit of all losses. But
the contracts show and the evidence was that plaintiff had
nothing to do with the other business of the corporation or
enterprises in which it was engaged, or in the private enterprises or business of McPhee outside of the corporation which
amounted to a large sum and absorbed most of McPhee's
time. The testimony of the bookkeeper and of plaintiff was
that the account was made from entries in defendant's
books showing the receipts and disbursements—the profits
and losses—connected with each contract and building and
piece of work constructed or performed under it. Mrs.
Goodspeed testified that she was then and had been bookkeeper for defendant for about six years. She testified:
"I keep a ledger, journal, cash-book, and the cost books; they
are the books of the McPhee Company." She testified that
she "kept the accounts of the receipts, expenditures, and
disbursements relating to those buildings [referring to the
six different contracts] in the cash-books of the McPhee
Company," and that she made up the document—plaintiff's
exhibit 7—and that it represented "the profits and losses
shown on the books at that time. . . . That is the summary
of the accounts as kept by the McPhee Company in the cost-
book. . . . Q. That is the way you kept the account of these
jobs in the cost book? A. Yes."

Speaking of one of these cost books, and it seems there
were several of them, the witness said: "The book I have

in my hand is the cost book of the McPhee Company, No. 5.
The cost of the various buildings and work done by the Mc-
Phee Company was kept in the journals and ledgers and
the cost books. The items were first entered in the journal
and ledger, and in the cost book right afterward.'' This
cost book No. 5 contained the items as to the Lowe Building, which the witness gave in detail as she did as to the
other buildings of which entries were made in other cost
books commencing with cost book No. 1. For example,
cost book No. 1 contained the items as to the Deming Building—a twenty-one thousand dollar job, in which the loss
was over four thousand dollars, charged against plaintiff.
Cost book No. 2 contained the items as to the Newhall, Folsom, and most jobs on which there was a net profit, and some
other jobs; this book also contained the items as to the Newhall Halleck Street job and the Pope Estate job. Cost book
No. 3 contained the Pope Mission Street job, Irwin residence, Bush Street job, Aronson Building, and other jobs.
No. 4 contained items of repair work. The items of all these
jobs were read into the record ''as shown by the books of the
company.'' The witness testified the date the work mentioned in the contracts ''was completed so far as the McPhee
Company was concerned on the 23d day of May, 1908,'' and
the amount of money drawn by plaintiff on the various jobs,
which, as appeared by the ledger, was $12,385.10 and $157.35
merchandise.

4. We cannot pursue the testimony as to the character
and purpose of these cost books. It showed that they were
kept with the view of recording just what the parties to
the contracts meant should be in them, and what they intended were to be considered in ascertaining the receipts
and expenditures from which were to be computed the net
profits of the work called for. Some time after this action
was begun, Mr. McPhee employed an accountant to examine
the books and make a summary of the net profits after there
had been written into these cost books by McPhee's direction certain items aggregating $36,334.31, the principal item
being McPhee's salary as defendant's president and manager at $1,000 per month, amounting to fifty-five thousand
dollars, of which he directed $29,633.33 to be distributed
upon a proportion fixed by himself among the numerous jobs

embraced in these six contracts. This distribution was entirely arbitrary, as it was in respect of the charges for warehouse and storage, rent, caretaker, interest, and use of a donkey-engine, for it was not possible to say what part of any one of these items was justly chargeable to any particular contract. There was no evidence explaining why, during the period these contracts were running, none of these items had been carried into the cost books, nor was there any evidence that this omission was by mistake. The books had been kept in this way for years, and Mrs. Goodspeed received her education and instruction in bookkeeping from her predecessor, who kept the books under McPhee's directions prior to Mrs. Goodspeed's employment. Some of the items which McPhee directed to be entered in the books, notably his salary, had never before appeared on the books in any form or been considered in any settlement with plaintiff for his services. There never had been, as was shown by the minutes of the corporation, any agreement made by the directors to pay him a salary, or authority given him to charge for his services as president and manager. He knew the system under which his books were being kept and he knew that the items he caused to be entered in the books after the action had been commenced were items never before considered in previous settlements, and had not been entered at any time during the two or three years these contracts were in force. He had in his possession for two months the stated account as first shown him and, presumably, did what he told plaintiff he would do, namely, "look it over." He approved it as presented to him again, with some additions to cover later jobs, and subsequently, and after suit brought, admitted the indebtedness there shown. The burden was on him to show that, through mistake, the account did not include the items he now claims should have been entered on the cost books. He did not meet this burden.

These books were, in fact, so far as they went, duplicates of the journal entries and were placed in the cost books at the same time. Their only office seems to have been to furnish in separate books in convenient form the various items constituting receipts and expenditures relating to the contracts here involved and from which the profits and losses on the contracts could be readily ascertained.

We think the facts and circumstances shown justified the court in rejecting the items written into these books by Mc-Phee's direction after the action was commenced and accepting the cost books as the correct source of the stated account.

5. It is claimed that interest was improperly allowed from the commencement of the action, and should have been, if at all, from the date of the judgment.

Section 1917 of the Civil Code provides: "Unless there is an express contract in writing, fixing a different rate, interest is payable on all moneys at the rate of seven per cent per annum after they become due, on any instrument of writing, except a judgment, and on moneys lent, or due on any settlement of account, from the day on which the balance is ascertained. . . ."

Section 3287 provides: "Every person who is entitled to recover damages certain, or capable of being made certain by calculation, and the right to recover which is vested in him upon a particular day, is entitled also to recover interest thereon from that day, except during such time as the debtor is prevented by law, or by the act of the creditor, from paying the debt."

The general rule is that interest is chargeable on a stated account from its date. (*De la Cuesta* v. *Montgomery*, 144 Cal. 115, [77 Pac. 887]; 22 Cyc. 1511, 1515.)

Where the action is for general damages, or liquidated, or *quantum meruit*, or *quantum valebat*, for the recovery of the reasonable value of goods sold and delivered or services rendered, interest is allowable only from the date of the judgment under the code rule. Here the demands were for "moneys due on settlement of account" and "the balance ascertained" and agreed to as witnessed by the stated account (Civ. Code, sec. 1917); and we think interest was recoverable because the damages were "certain, or capable of being made certain by calculation." (Civ. Code, sec. 3287.) Even under some circumstances, interest may be allowed in an action upon a contract for unliquidated damages. (*Courteney* v. *Standard Box Co.*, 16 Cal. App. 600, 615, [117 Pac. 778].)

The following cases would seem to warrant the charge for interest from the commencement of the action: *McCowen* v. *Pew*, 18 Cal. App. 482, 487, [123 Pac. 354]; *Lane* v. *Turner*,

114 Cal. 396, [46 Pac. 290]; *Cutting Fruit Packing Co. v. Canty*, 141 Cal. 692, 697, [75 Pac. 574]; *Macomber* v. *Bigelow*, 126 Cal. 9, [58 Pac. 312]; *Farnham* v. *California etc. Trust Co.*, 8 Cal. App. 268, 273, [96 Pac. 788].

6. It is further contended that the contracts created the relation of a partnership or joint undertaking between plaintiff and defendant. It is hence claimed that there could be no action other than a suit for an accounting. The pleadings nowhere raise this issue. Ordinarily, in the absence of special authority, a corporation cannot enter into partnership with a private person (10 Cyc. 1142, 1143), and no such authority was shown. A corporation may enter into a contract by which it is agreed that the gains and losses of the venture shall be borne equally (*Bates* v. *Coronado Beach Co.*, 109 Cal. 162, [41 Pac. 855]), but such agreements do not necessarily make the parties partners in legal contemplation.

The question here does not involve the question of partnership as affecting third parties. *Kennedy & Shaw Lumber Co.* v. *Taylor*, 3 Cal. Unrep. 697, [31 Pac. 1122], cited by defendant, only held that the associates were liable as partners to plaintiff. As between themselves, their rights were not involved. In the case here, plaintiff had no interest in the profits as property; he was simply employed under an arrangement by which he was to receive for his services a given sum out of, or a proportion of, the profits. *Berthold* v. *Goldsmith*, 24 How. 536, [16 L. Ed. 762]: "The general rule is," as was stated in *Jernee* v. *Simonson*, 58 N. J. Eq. 282, [43 Atl. 370], "if there is no community of interest in the property of a business, that there is no partnership *inter sese* by mere participation in the profits."

In *Smith* v. *Schultz*, 89 Cal. 526, [26 Pac. 1087], the agreement was to work a farm upon shares. Speaking of the contract, the court said: "It gives no power to one to bind the others; it contemplates no common liability; it does not make one the agent for the others in carrying on any business whatever; it contains no agreement, either express or implied, for the division of any losses, and there is no intimation in it that plaintiff was to be 'liable to third persons for all the obligations of the partnership jointly with his copartners.' (Civ. Code, secs. 2404, 2429, 2442, 2443.) Nor does it contain any agreement among themselves that the party of the one part should be bound to any extent for the obligations of the party of the other part. They were not to be partners, therefore, either as to third persons, or *inter sese.*" This case presents many features similar to the one here. (See, also, *Coward v. Clanton*, 122 Cal. 451, [55 Pac. 147]; 30 Cyc. 376, 377; *Cudahy Packing Co. v. Hibou*, 92 Miss. 234, [46 South. 73, 18 L. R. A. (N. S.) 975, and note, 1032].)

The discussion loses some of its importance in view of the fact that whatever the relation of the parties was, they settled their account with each other and agreed upon the balance due from one to the other.

7. It must not be expected that we can give specific attention to over three hundred and fifty alleged errors. Such an array might give one pause, if each suggested a separate and distinct error. In fact, but few points are involved. For example, after the cost books were identified and the entries explained, as to the different contracts, to each of the hundred or more questions an objection being interposed, plaintiff's counsel would ask the question: "What does the cost book show to be the profits of [naming the job]?" The answer was merely the result of these figures, and was not a conclusion of the witness, and the result was not, as defendant contends, a showing of gross profits; the result clearly was net profits.

8. The motion for nonsuit was directed to this point and was properly overruled. It was discretionary with the court to allow evidence to meet objections made by the motion based on the lack of proof on certain matters. The motion also presented the point that the action should have been in the form of an accounting on the theory that a partnership existed. This point has already been noticed; no partnership was proven.

9. Evidence was admitted that plaintiff and defendant had made similar contracts prior to the ones in the suit. This evidence was objected to. Defendant contended at the trial, and still contends, that these cost books and the profits referred to in the contracts had relation to gross profits and not net profits as claimed by plaintiff. The evidence now urged as inadmissible was introduced to aid the court in viewing the circumstances surrounding the parties, when the contracts were made, and to clear up the situation of the parties at that time

—in short, to put itself in their place. It appeared from the evidence that plaintiff and defendant had been operating from 1901, and up to the time contract No. 1 was made, in a series of jobs not unlike the ones here, and under terms quite similar. In one of them, for example, plaintiff was to receive twenty per cent for his services; in another they were to "divide the profits in half on any work or contracts," and neither of them was to receive a salary, and in all these contracts the McPhee Company was to "finance the jobs." It is true that in the cases where he got fifty per cent, plaintiff was to *procure,* as well as superintend, the jobs, but we cannot see that that affects the question. Plaintiff and defendant had been engaged in doing work for three or four years under substantially the same conditions and circumstances as for the time here involved.

In giving interpretation to their agreement, and to ascertain what they meant by "net profits," it seems to us the court was justified in allowing the evidence. "Previous and contemporaneous transactions may properly be taken into consideration to ascertain the sense in which the parties used particular terms, or to ascertain the subject matter of the contract." (17 Cyc. 671.) The supreme court said, in *First Nat. Bank* v. *Bowers,* 141 Cal. 253, 262, [74 Pac. 856], that "where the meaning of terms is debatable," facts which tend to illustrate or explain the language used in a contract and to place the court or jury as nearly as may be in the situation of the parties, "are always admissible." The courts "may avail themselves of the same light which the parties possessed when the contract was made." (*Merriam* v. *United States,* 107 U. S. 437, [27 L. Ed. 530, 2 Sup. Ct. Rep. 536].)

10. Counsel takes up in his brief each one of these jobs and endeavors to show that the cost books do not correctly exhibit the receipts and disbursements, and hence do not show the net profits. We cannot follow all these intricate details. The bookkeeper testified to the correctness of the accounts in these cost books, and so far as we have been able to analyze the figures and entries upon which her testimony rests, we cannot say she was mistaken.

As we understand the record, the action No. 18,032 involves the same questions *mutatis mutandis* as in No. 17,022, and the decision in the latter covers the decision in the former.

We have endeavored to consider such of defendants' numerous objections as seemed to demand attention, and failing to discover any prejudicial error in the record, the judgments and orders are affirmed.

Ellison, J., *pro tem.*, and Hart, J., concurred.

A petition to have the cause heard in the supreme court. after judgment in the district court of appeal, was denied by the supreme court on October 27, 1916.

[Civ. No. 1509. Third Appellate District.—August 28, 1916.]

HENRY DOERR et al., Appellants, v. FANDANGO LUMBER COMPANY (a Corporation) et al., Respondents.

CORPORATIONS—MORTGAGE BY PRESIDENT — SUBSEQUENT RATIFICATION.— A corporation is estopped from asserting that its president was not authorized by its board of directors to execute a mortgage on the property of the corporation to secure a loan of money to the corporation, where it subsequently made a deed of trust of all its property to a trustee for the purpose of straightening out its affairs, and in such deed made express reference to such mortgage and therein declared that the deed was subject thereto.

ID.—CONVEYANCE OF CORPORATE PROPERTY TO TRUSTEE—RECOGNITION OF MORTGAGE—SCOPE OF RESOLUTION.—The estoppel of the corporation to deny the validity of the mortgage under such circumstances is not affected by the fact that the resolution authorizing the execution of the deed of trust did not expressly vest the board of directors with authority to include in the deed of trust the provision that it should be subject to the mortgage, where the resolution did recite that the object of the deed was to place the properties and business of the corporation in the hands of a trustee for the purpose of operating the business and paying off the indebtedness of the corporation.

ID.—RECEIPT AND USE OF MONEY BY CORPORATION—ESTOPPEL.—A corporation which receives and uses money for the purposes of its business, to secure the repayment of which a mortgage on the property of the corporation is given, is estopped from denying the validity of the obligation.

APPEAL from a judgment of the Superior Court of Modoc County. Clarence A. Raker, Judge.

The facts are stated in the opinion of the court.

Cornish & Robnett, Daly B. Robnett, and N. J. Barry, for Appellants.

Jamison & Wylie, and W. Lair Thompson, for Respondents.

HART, J.—The plaintiffs instituted this suit to foreclose a mortgage upon certain real property of the Fandango Lumber Company, given to secure a loan to the latter of the sum of ten thousand dollars, evidenced by a promissory note executed by the Fandango Lumber Company in favor of the plaintiffs. The property upon which the mortgage was given is located in Modoc County and consists of about two thousand one hundred acres of timber and agricultural lands, upon which a sawmill stands.

The Fandango Lumber Company (to be hereafter referred to variously as the Fandango company and "the company") is a regularly organized corporation, doing business in California, with its principal place of business and offices at Fort Bidwell, Modoc County, this state.

The note to secure which the mortgage in question here was given is set out in full in the complaint. It was executed and delivered to the plaintiffs on the twenty-third day of December, 1911, and is payable on demand.

It is alleged that at the time of the delivery of said note, and for the purpose of securing the payment of the principal sum thereof, and the interest thereupon accruing, the Fandango company duly executed and delivered to the plaintiffs its mortgage, bearing date of December 23, 1911, "conveying the premises described in said mortgage"; that said mortgage was duly acknowledged and certified so as to entitle it to be recorded, and that the same was duly recorded in the office of the county recorder of the county of Modoc. It is alleged that the defendants, W. R. Wilkinson, W. R. Wilkinson, as trustee, and W. R. Wilkinson, as receiver, "have or claim some interest in, or lien on, said mortgaged premises; but all of said claims, if any, have accrued since the lien of said mortgage."

The mortgage is made a part of the complaint, and purports to have been executed by the Fandango company, "by A. G. Duhme, President."

The answer denies all the material averments of the complaint, but, while admitting that Wilkinson, as an individual, claims no interest in, or lien upon, the alleged mortgaged premises, alleges that he, as trustee and as receiver, has and claims some interest in and lien upon said premises.

The answer further alleges that the said A. G. Duhme, as president of the Fandango company, was never at any time authorized by the board of directors of said company, at any meeting thereof, or at all, to borrow any money from the plaintiffs, or to execute and deliver to the latter the said note for ten thousand dollars as evidence of a loan in that amount, or to execute the mortgage, the foreclosure of which is sought by this action; that the transaction involving the execution of said note and mortgage was never ratified by the board of directors of said company.

As an alleged "second and separate" defense, the answer charges collusion between the plaintiffs and the said A. G. Duhme for the purpose of fraudulently bringing about a foreclosure sale of the mortgaged property at which said property would be purchased by the plaintiffs, thereby preventing other creditors of the Fandango company from securing satisfaction of their respective claims against said company, amounting in the aggregate to approximately forty thousand dollars, and which claims are unsecured. No testimony having been offered or received in support of the charge so made, further consideration thereof is obviously unnecessary.

The court found that the Fandango company or its board of directors never at any time or place authorized the said Duhme, as president of said company, or otherwise, to borrow for the company from the plaintiffs the sum of ten thousand dollars or any other sum, or to execute on behalf of said company the note and the mortgage in question; that the said company or its directors never at any time subsequent to the making and delivery of said note and the execution of said mortgage ratified the same or the action of said Duhme in the transaction resulting in the consummation of the loan from the plaintiffs and the giving to them of said note and said mortgage; that, therefore, "the said note and mortgage are not, nor are either of them, the note or mortgage of the said Fandango Lumber Company."

From the findings, of which the foregoing is an epitomized statement, the court concluded as a matter of law "that the said note and mortgage, and each of them, and every part thereof, are void and of no effect as creating any obligation against the said defendants or any of them, or as constituting any lien against the property of said defendants, or any of them, described in said mortgage and complaint, or otherwise.''

Judgment for the defendants followed, from which the plaintiffs appeal, supporting the same by a transcript of the testimony and other proceedings of the trial, prepared in accordance with the provisions of section 953a of the Code of Civil Procedure.

The general question presented is whether the findings vital to the judgment are supported by the evidence.

The salient facts are undisputed, and briefly they are: In the year 1911 the Fandango company found itself in financial difficulties, being heavily in debt and without financial means to carry on its lumber business. It owned extensive properties, including extensive timber land holdings. While the board of directors of said company never at any time expressly authorized Duhme, the president, to borrow on behalf of the company the sum of money for which the note and the mortgage in dispute were given, said board did, nevertheless, at a special meeting thereof, on August 18, 1911, adopt a resolution which, in general language, vested in the directors the authority to borrow money "of whom they see fit" for the company "to run the business." (Trans., p. 47.)

Among those to whom the company was indebted at the time mentioned and whose indebtedness was secured was the Bank of Fort Bidwell. The company had overdrawn its account at said bank by the sum of approximately four thousand dollars, the total indebtedness of the company to said bank being over nine thousand dollars. The bank was pressing the company for a settlement, and Duhme, in the year 1911, went to Minneapolis, Minnesota, for the purpose of making an effort to secure a loan which would be sufficient to liquidate the debt of the company to the said bank. Two of the directors of the company—C. B. and C. D. Eustis—then resided in Minneapolis. After negotiations with the plaintiffs, Duhme and his codirectors, C. B. and C. D. Eustis, succeeded in securing the loan. Before consummating the transaction, however, Duhme telegraphed to the said bank from Minneapolis, asking its consent to mortgage the company's timber lands and plant to secure the proposed loan. The bank, by telegram, replied, under date of December 22, 1911: "Bank consents to your mortgaging timber and plant, providing you have bank in Minneapolis wire us seven thousand dollars for credit Fandango Lumber Company; overdraft now four thousand dollars. Brown advises two thousand in checks outstanding which we will protest if the money is not wired immediately." Thereafter, and on the twenty-third day of December, 1911, the plaintiffs loaned and delivered to Duhme the sum of ten thousand dollars, for which the note set out in the complaint and the mortgage attached to and made a part of that pleading as security for the payment of said note were executed by Duhme in the name and under the corporate seal of the Fandango Lumber Company.

On the twenty-fifth day of June, 1912, in pursuance of a resolution previously adopted by the board of directors of the Fandango company, the said board executed a trust deed, whereby it conveyed to the defendant, W. R. Wilkinson, as trustee, all the property covered by the mortgage in controversy. The object of said deed of trust was to straighten out the affairs of the company, and to this end the trustee was authorized by said instrument to conduct and manage the business of the company, to pay all current operating expenses, and to pay off, as they fell due, the debts of the concern. This deed provides, among other things: "The party of the first part (Fandango Company) covenants and agrees that this deed of trust delivered to the trustee shall be a mortgage upon the premises and property affected thereby, subject only to mortgage . . . to Devereaux, Wallace, Doerr and Bleeker, of Minneapolis," who are the plaintiffs in this action.

The Sunset Lake Lumber Company is a subsidiary corporation, which was organized subsequent to the time at which the mortgage in question was given, for the purpose of taking over the properties and business of the Fandango company and paying all its debts. On the twenty-sixth day of July, 1912, the Fandango company, by deed, conveyed to the said Sunset company all its properties and business for the purposes above mentioned. The defendant, W. R. Wilkinson, was then president of the Fandango company, and as such officer, and for and under the seal of the said company, executed the said deed of conveyance to the Sunset company. That deed expressly recites that it is subject to all the debts of the Fandango company, and subject further: "... to a second mortgage for the sum of ten thousand ($10,000.00) dollars in favor of Thomas F. Wallace, et al., of Minneapolis, Minnesota. . . . "

On September 10, 1912, a complaint reciting, among other facts, the existence of the mortgage in suit and the indebtedness to secure which it was given, and asking for the appointment of a receiver of the Fandango company, was filed in the superior court of Modoc County, by an unsecured creditor of said company. The complaint in said action was verified, and alleged the existence and validity of the mortgage in suit here. Upon the hearing of the application for the appointment of a receiver in said action, the defendant, W. R. Wilkinson, was named for and appointed by the court to that office, and as such took over the control and management of the properties of the Fandango company covered by the mortgage involved herein.

On page 36 of the book containing the record of the proceedings of the meetings of the board of directors of the Fandango company there appears, on a slip of paper pasted on said page, a resolution in typewriting, purporting to have been adopted by the said board on the twenty-fourth day of June, 1912, and purporting to ratify the acts of Duhme in borrowing the money from the plaintiffs and in giving the note and the mortgage in question, evidencing and securing said loan.

It appears from the uncontradicted testimony of Duhme that the money obtained from the plaintiffs on the note and the mortgage in question was applied to the extinguishment of the obligations of the Fandango company, approximately nine thousand five hundred dollars thereof having been paid to the Bank of Fort Bidwell in satisfaction of the debt due it from the company.

Under the evidence, of which the foregoing statement embraces an accurate *résumé*, it cannot justly be held that the findings essential to the support of the judgment are warranted.

Whether the purported resolution of June 28, 1912, pretending to ratify the transaction involving the making and giving of the note and mortgage in controversy here was regularly or legally adopted by the board of directors, is a question. Duhme testified that it was so adopted, while Wilkinson, then a member of the board and president of the corporation, positively declared that he attended all the meetings of the board and that at none was any such resolution even suggested, much less adopted. But, in view of other facts, it is wholly unimportant whether there was or was not a formal ratification of the transaction. For we agree to the following contentions of counsel for the plaintiffs: 1. That the Fandango company ratified the mortgage "when it made a deed of trust of all its property to W. R. Wilkinson, and in that deed expressly referred to plaintiffs' mortgage and made said deed subject to this mortgage, thereby expressly recognizing the obligation." 2. That the Fandango company again ratified said mortgage when its board of directors passed a resolution authorizing a deed of all its property to the Sunset Lake Lumber Company, said conveyance to be subject to the debts of the Fandango company, and which resolution not only expressly recognized the deed of trust theretofore given to Wilkinson, covering all its properties, but recognized by express reference thereto the mortgage of the plaintiffs as a prior and valid lien upon said properties. 3. That, as to the defendant, Fandango company, it is estopped from denying the validity of the mortgage, for the reason that it received, retained, and used, for its legitimate purposes, the consideration for the mortgage, viz., the sum of ten thousand dollars, with full knowledge of the fact that said sum of money had been borrowed for its use in its business and of the fact that said mortgage was given to secure the repayment of said sum of money.

But it is earnestly contended by the defendants that the trust deed to Wilkinson could not have the effect either of ratifying the act of giving the mortgage or of estopping the Fandango company from denying the validity of that instrument, inasmuch as the resolution authorizing the making of said trust deed did not expressly vest the board of directors with authority to include in said deed a provision that it should be subject to the prior lien of the mortgage. The resolution, it is true, did not in express terms refer to the indebtedness to the plaintiffs or the mortgage in question, but it did provide that the object of the trust deed was to place the properties and business of the company in the hands of Wilkinson, as trustee, for the purpose of operating the business of the concern and paying off its indebtedness. The

provision in the trust deed that it was to be subject to the
mortgage and the rights of the mortgagees thereunder may be
assumed to have been the result of the interpretation by the
directors of the language of the resolution providing generally
for the satisfaction of the obligations then existing against
the company; but whether such interpretation was justified
or not—that is to say, whether, in strictness, the board of
directors was authorized or intended by the resolution to be
authorized to insert in the trust deed as a condition thereof
the provision respecting the mortgage—the very fact that said
board did so construe the language of the said resolution in
that particular amounted to a recognition of the mortgage
as imposing a valid obligation upon the Fandango company
as effectually as if express authority to do so had been by
the resolution vested in said board. If, however, this position were unsupportable, then upon either one of two other
considerations, supported by the record, may it justly and
with legal propriety be held that the transaction involving
the execution of the note sued on and the mortgage given to
secure its payment has been ratified, viz.: 1. That the trust
deed has been in existence for a long period of time (executed
June 25, 1912), is still in existence, and has never been repudiated by the corporation, nor is there any repudiation of
it now. It must, therefore, be deemed to have been by the
corporation acquiesced in and all its covenants and conditions,
including any unauthorized conditions or terms, if any, which
it contains, thus ratified. (*Gribble* v. *Columbus Brewing Co.*,
100 Cal. 67, 69, 70, [34 Pac. 527].) 2. Not only does the
resolution authorizing the deed to the Sunset Lake Lumber Company refer to and thus ratify the trust deed and
all its conditions, but the deed itself expressly refers to
and provides that it shall be subject to the mortgage in
question. Here, therefore, we have an express and positive
recognition of the obligation of the mortgage, and this is
the equivalent of the ratification of said mortgage. The conclusion thus declared is in accord with all the cases in which
the facts bear analogy to those of the present case. Indeed,
the proposition that ratification of a contract, the making
of which is unauthorized by one of the principals, may be
effectuated by a recognition, howsoever informally, of the
agreement and the obligations arising by virtue thereof, is
elementary. A familiar and common application of this doc-

trine is to be found in those cases where an agent, in making
a contract for his principal, transcends the scope of his authority as such, and the principal, after the contract has been
made, although not at that time legally bound by its terms,
does some act recognizing the validity of the agreement—
as, for instance, accepting some of the benefits or assuming
some of the burdens thereof. In such case, quite obviously,
the principal will be deemed from his acquiescence in the contract to have ratified the unauthorized act of his agent, and
will be held to its terms and conditions, notwithstanding that
he has not in express language or in a formal manner ratified
the contract. The case here comes within the principle thus
referred to. The giving of the mortgage was not an *ultra
vires* act, and there is no claim that it was. If the act involved the making of an invalid contract, it was, as shown,
merely because of the manner in which it was attempted to
perform the act or make the contract, and, like any other
contract, it is capable of being ratified by conduct or a recognition in some manner of the obligation; and, as stated, the
deed to the Sunset company, which was executed and delivered by the Fandango company when the defendant Wilkinson was president thereof and which, indeed, was executed
by him as president for the company, contains language clearly
and plainly recognizing the mortgage and the obligations
thereof.

We need not refer to all of the many cases holding to the
views above expressed. The case of *Porter v. Lassen County
etc. Co.*, 127 Cal. 261, 270, 271, [59 Pac. 563], is directly in
point here, and it is sufficient for the purposes of this case
to reproduce herein an excerpt or two therefrom. It is held
in that case, quoting from the syllabi thereof: "The subsequent action of a full board [of directors] requiring the mortgagee to make additional advances on the security of his
mortgage, and recognizing its validity in a resolution authorizing a second mortgage upon the property, is a full ratification of the first mortgage." In the text, the late learned
Chief Justice Beatty, who wrote the opinion, said: "The
manner of directing the execution of a corporation mortgage
is by resolution of the board of directors, and here by resolution of the board the mortgage is recognized as valid and
its benefits claimed in behalf of the corporation. It is not
necessary, in order to ratify, to do so in express and formal

terms. Anything is sufficient which clearly and necessarily implies a recognition of the obligation.''

Besides the foregoing considerations, it is very clear that the defendant Fandango company having received, retained, and used for the purposes of its business the money, to secure the repayment of which the mortgage was given, is, and upon a familiar equitable principle should be, estopped from denying the validity of the obligation. As shown, it is not disputed that the corporation received the money and used it in the payment of a part of its debts.

As to the defendant Wilkinson, it is to be observed that both as a trustee under the deed of trust and as a receiver under the appointment of the court he accepted the deed of trust and the office of receiver with full knowledge of the existence of the mortgage, and upon the express condition that his rights and powers in both instances were expressly made subject to the mortgage. Indeed, as seen, as president of the Fandango company, he executed for said company, by authority of the directors duly evidenced and vested, the deed to the Sunset company, and by that act he recognized and admitted not only for the Fandango company but for himself as trustee the validity of the mortgage.

For the reasons herein stated, the judgment is reversed.

Chipman, P. J., and Ellison, J., *pro tem.*, concurred.

A petition to have the cause heard in the supreme court, after judgment in the district court of appeal, was denied by the supreme court on October 27, 1916.

[Civ. No. 1452.   Third Appellate District.—August 30, 1916.]

GEORGE SHELTON, Respondent, v. D. B. MICHAEL et al., Appellants.

CONTRACT—CONSTRUCTION OF WAGON ROAD—JOINT AND SEVERAL LIABILITY OF SIGNERS.—A contract for the construction of a wagon road which recites that "the parties of the first part" (not named but described as "settlers" of a certain school district) agree to pay a named person, described as party of the second part, a certain sum per rod for the building of the road, creates a joint and several liability.

ID.— CONDITIONAL EXECUTION OF CONTRACT — SIGNATURE OF CERTAIN NUMBER OF PERSONS—INSUFFICIENCY OF DEFENSE.—In an action to recover the balance due on such a contract, where it is set up as an affirmative defense that it was agreed that the contract was not to be considered executed until at least a certain number of settlers had signed it, it is not error to refuse to instruct the jury that their verdict should be in favor of the "defendants," if they found that the writing was so executed, in the absence of any such limitation contained in the contract, or of any evidence except that of one of the eight signers that such was the understanding of the parties.

APPEAL from a judgment of the Superior Court of Mendocino County, and from an order denying a new trial.   J. Q White, Judge.

The facts are stated in the opinion of the court.

Charles Kasch, for Appellants.

Robert Duncan, for Respondent.

ELLISON, J., *pro tem.*—The complaint in this action sets forth: That in October, 1914, the defendants (there are nine of them) entered into a written contract with plaintiff in and by which he agreed to construct a wagon road in Mendocino County (describing it), and for his compensation therefor the defendants agreed to pay him two dollars per rod for all that portion thereof that had not been swamped out, and one dollar and fifty cents per rod for all that had been swamped.

That in pursuance of said contract he built 489 rods of road that had been swamped out, and 316¼ rods of road which had not been swamped out, and that the agreed price therefor was $1,367.50. That he had been paid on account thereof three hundred dollars, and there is still due and unpaid to him for constructing said road the sum of $1,067.50, for which amount judgment was asked.

The answer is, first, a general denial of all the allegations of the complaint. It then affirmatively alleges that defendant on October 17, 1914, entered into a contract with plaintiff to build the road for the prices per rod stated in the complaint, and this is followed by:

"That it was expressly understood and agreed by and between the plaintiff and these defendants that before said contract should be made effective and binding on these defendants, or any of them, plaintiff should procure the signatures to said contract of A. E. Arens, Mrs. Ollie Sparks, and Mike Lynch, and it was an express condition and part of the consideration for the signatures of these defendants that plaintiff should secure twelve signatures to said agreement before these defendants, or any of them, should be bound by their said signatures; that it was never intended by plaintiff and these defendants that said contract should be made until at least twelve signatures were appended thereto."

It also alleged that the defendant did not construct the road in a good and workmanlike manner, and did not grade it seven feet wide, as provided in the contract. That large trees were left in the road, making it impossible for travel.

Trial was had with a jury, which found a verdict in favor of the plaintiff for the amount sued for. This was followed by a judgment, from which this appeal is taken, as well as from an order denying a motion for a new trial.

No point is made on this appeal that defendants sustained the defense alleged of improper work being done or that the roadbed was not graded according to contract. The principal point relied upon for a reversal is that defendants, by their evidence, sustained the defense set forth in their answer to the effect that the contract was not to be considered executed until at least twelve settlers had signed it, and that it was delivered to the plaintiff upon condition that it was not to be effective until such number of signatures had been obtained, and that the court erred in not giving certain instructions requested by them applicable to such defense.

For a proper understanding of counsel's position, and the ruling of the court in refusing to instruct as requested, it becomes necessary to consider the legal effect of the contract sued upon and the testimony bearing upon its alleged execution and the instructions requested.

(1) The contract appears in full in the record, and upon a reading of it, it is noticed, first, that the names of the persons who were to sign it as parties of the first part are not stated in the body thereof.

They are only referred to in the first paragraph as "settlers" of a certain named school district in Mendocino County.

It contains no provision that it is not to become a binding contract until signed by at least twelve settlers. Upon this point it is silent.

It creates a joint and several liability: "The parties of the first part agree to pay George Shelton, party of the second part, $2.00 per rod for building the road, etc."

The record shows that there were some twelve or more persons owning land in Mendocino County, upon which was timber suitable for making ties and tan-bark. There was no road leading from any public highway to these lands and no way to get the ties and tan-bark out. All these settlers and land owners were interested in getting a road to these lands. Witness George Shelton testified: "I know all the defendants. They own redwood lands in this county and some tan-bark."

Some of these settlers met at the store of one McFaul to take steps to get the road constructed to these lands.

All of the nine persons who signed the contract were settlers and would be benefited by the construction of the road.

Section 1659 of the Civil Code provides: "Where all the parties who unite in a promise receive some benefit from the consideration, whether past or present, their promise is presumed to be joint and several."

From the facts disclosed by the record, considered in the light of this code provision, it must be held that the contract is joint and several.

(2) The testimony bearing upon the execution of the contract may be summarized as follows: C. A. McFaul, a witness for the defendants, testified that the contract was drawn in his office, and first given to Mr. Michael (one of the defendants) to get signatures. He was to get particular signatures in a particular part of the county. Mrs. Olive Sparks was expected to sign. Mike Lynch was supposed to sign. After

Mr. Michael succeeded in getting some signatures, the contract was turned over to Mr. Shelton. He was to get signers and see Mike Lynch.

"It was supposed there should be twelve at least who would sign."

The defendant D. B. Michael testified: "I had an understanding with Mr. Shelton relative to getting signatures to it. We had a contract drawn up and I signed it first and was to take it and get all the signatures I could in my neighborhood, and he was to take it and get the rest down the coast. I secured the signatures I agreed to get. Mr. Shelton and I had a conversation relative to the number of people who should sign the contract before it would become binding. There were supposed to be twelve signatures. I said to Mr. Shelton that if we could not get over one-half dozen, or something like that, I didn't want it, because I could not afford to pay that much for the road. After I procured the signatures I agreed to procure, I sent the contract to Mr. Shelton."

The defendant Ben Bond testified: "I told him [plaintiff] that I would not put my name to the contract unless it was understood that all of twelve signers should be on the contract. That was agreeable to Mr. Shelton. Mr. Michael had the contract when I signed it, and Mr. Shelton was not present. There are twelve settlers in that country who would be benefited by the road, and I thought they probably all would sign it."

The above is the substance of all the evidence bearing upon this feature of the case.

(3) Several instructions were asked by the defendants as to this phase of the case, but they were all refused; and this refusal is assigned as reversible error.

The instructions were all similar to instruction VIII, and a quotation of it will be sufficient. It is as follows:

"Gentlemen, a delivery on condition is not a complete delivery until the condition is fulfilled. If you find in this case that the writing in evidence was delivered by those who signed it for the purpose of having Mr. Shelton secure twelve signatures thereto, and that it was the intention of the parties that it was not to become binding until twelve signatures were secured, then I charge you, there was no delivery and you must find for the defendants."

It is not reversible error to refuse a requested instruction that is not applicable to the evidence or that presents an erroneous theory of the case.

Referring back to the testimony, it will be observed that the witness McFaul is not one of the defendants. His testimony is not to the effect that there would be no contract unless so many as twelve signed it. His language is indefinite. "It was supposed there would be about twelve who would sign."

The defendant Michael used no language as a witness from which the conclusion can be drawn that he signed it upon the condition that it was to be inoperative unless twelve signatures were obtained to it.

The defendant Bond used language more definite and certain.

No one of the other seven defendants gave any testimony of any understanding or agreement as to the number of signatures it was expected there would be to the contract, or that any of them ever heard of the matter before the trial.

The instruction requested embraced all of the defendants. It is apparent from the evidence above referred to that the instruction was not applicable to it and was too broad. There was no evidence (as the instruction assumed) that any one of eight of the defendants signed the paper for the purpose of having Mr. Shelton secure twelve signatures to it, and no evidence that it was the intention of said eight defendants, or any of them, that the contract was not to become binding until twelve had signed it.

These eight defendants signed a joint and several contract without any limitation or condition, and it would have been error for the court to have instructed the jury as to them and their liability in the language of the refused instruction.

Whether such an instruction directed to the defendant Bond alone should have been given, we need not inquire, as no such instruction was asked.

In the notes to *Benton Co. Savings Bank* v. *Boddicker*, [105 Iowa, 548, 67 Am. St. Rep. 310, 75 N. W. 632], 45 L. R. A. 321, is found quite a full collection of decisions upon the signing of contracts upon an understanding that they were not to be operative until signed by others. We make the following quotation therefrom: "One who signs a joint and several bond, cannot excuse himself from liability upon the ground that it appears on the face of the bond that it was intended to be signed by others who did not sign, unless he declares at the time that he would not be bound unless such signatures were obtained.''

"The requirement that others shall sign must amount to a condition that the bond shall not take effect without its performance as distinguished from a mere expectation that others shall sign." (See, also, *City of Los Angeles* v. *Millus*, 59 Cal. 444.)

(4) There was no error in admitting the contract sued upon in evidence. The alleged error is predicated upon the assumption that the complaint alleges a joint and several contract, and that the contract introduced was not such.

The complaint nowhere attempts to designate the contract as either joint or several or joint and several.

We have already declared that in our opinion the contract was joint and several.

It is claimed that as the figures $25 appear after the signature of the defendant Stevens and the words ''for the swamped road'' after the signatures of defendants Bond and Moller, the contract shows they had only assumed a limited liability, Stevens only for the sum of $25 and the other two named defendants only for money to become due on the part of the road designated as ''swamped.''

In the body of the contract, those defendants, without limitation, promised to pay for the construction of the road, and the words following their signatures are too indefinite to limit their liability. As counsel for respondent suggests, they may have been intended as mere memoranda to be used in some settlement to be made between the defendants.

The case is readily distinguishable from *Moss* v. *Wilson*, 40 Cal. 159, 162, relied upon by appellant. In that case the contract provided: ''The undersigned settlers . . . will pay the sum annexed to their names.'' No such provision is found in this contract. In that case it does not appear that the signers had a joint interest in the act to be accomplished. The record in this case abundantly shows that all the signers were decidedly interested in having the road constructed.

In the brief of appellant it is stated: ''There is a variance in that a different contract was proved than the one alleged. The plaintiff pleaded a contract to build a road and proved a contract to build a road and bridges. The plaintiff testified that he did not build any bridges and that it was understood at the time that he was not to." This is followed by the statement that the plaintiff did not prove performance of the contract he introduced in evidence.

No point is made in counsel's brief that the court erred in admitting proof that it was understood that plaintiff was not to build the bridges. He could not well make such claim in view of the fact that most of the evidence along this line was brought out by him upon cross-examination of witnesses.

Waiving the question whether the contract as to building road and as to building bridges is severable, we think appellant did not raise the point now contended for with sufficient seriousness in the trial court to permit him to ask for a decision upon it here.

The answer set up two separate defenses, but in neither did it allege the contract was different from the one stated in the complaint.

When the contract was offered in evidence, counsel objected on the ground of variance, in that the complaint alleged a joint and several contract, and the contract offered was joint, but said nothing about a variance because of the provision for building bridges. No motion was made for a nonsuit upon the ground of variance.

No instruction was requested to the effect that plaintiff could not recover because he had not built the bridges. Neither court nor counsel were in any way apprised that this point was relied upon or would be. If timely notice had been given thereof in some of the ways suggested, perhaps plaintiff would have asked leave to amend his complaint to show why he had not built the bridges.

An examination of the record fails to disclose that the trial court ruled upon the point or was asked to except by objections to two questions near the end of the trial, and counsel in his brief does not assign these rulings as error, and could not well do so in view of the condition of the record at the time the objections were made. Besides, the evidence that was admitted without objection makes it clear that it was never intended the plaintiff should build the bridges, or if such intent existed at the time the contract was written, it was waived and abandoned by mutual consent.

The plaintiff testified: "I did not build the bridges. I had nothing to do with the bridges. It was the understanding that Michael was to put them in. All the parties said I was not to build the bridges. At the time the contract was signed, it was understood I was not to build the bridges.''

The witness McFaul testified: ''Michael said he would build them [the bridges] on the same day the contract was drawn up.''

The defendant Michael testified: ''At the time the contract was drawn, I said we should have some arrangement made about these bridges, and said at the time I would build the bridges for three hundred dollars if no one else wants to. I heard Mr. Shelton say that he would not have anything to do with the bridges. I have heard these others say they have heard him say so.''

It was not error to admit evidence to prove that money was not deposited in bank as provided in the contract.

The judgment and order are affirmed.

Chipman, P. J., and Hart, J., concurred.

[Civ. No. 1775. First Appellate District.—August 31, 1916.]

SAMUEL JENNINGS, Appellant, v. F. R. JORDAN, Respondent.

REAL ESTATE BROKER—EXCHANGE OF PROPERTIES—FAILURE OF CONSUM-
MATION—COMMISSIONS NOT EARNED.—Under the terms of a contract
for an exchange of properties, wherein each party agreed to convey
title free of encumbrances and to pay the broker who procured the
contract to be executed a commission, the commission is not earned
where the exchange was not consummated by reason of the inability
of one of the parties to convey title to a portion of his property,
and the subsequent mutual abandonment of the contract.

APPEAL from a judgment of the Superior Court of Alameda County, and from an order denying a new trial. Everett J. Brown, Judge.

The facts are stated in the opinion of the court.

Dunn, White & Aiken, for Appellant.

Fitzgerald, Abbott & Beardsley, for Respondent.

KERRIGAN, J.—This action was brought to recover $1,825 alleged to have been earned by Herman Eppinger, Jr., the assignor of the plaintiff, as a commission upon a proposed exchange of certain lands. Judgment went for defendant, and the plaintiff prosecutes this appeal therefrom and from an order denying his motion for a new trial.

On the second day of May, 1914, John Fletcher and the defendant entered into a written contract, under the terms of which Fletcher was to convey to the defendant some 333 acres of land, to be chosen by the defendant from a certain described larger tract of 436 acres in Yuba County, in exchange for a certain apartment house in Alameda County belonging to the defendant, the respective parties agreeing to convey their properties free and clear of all encumbrances. The contract contains various covenants and conditions, and also a provision—the one principally involved in this case—reading as follows: "The parties hereto further mutually covenant and agree that they will each pay to Herman Eppinger, Jr., a commission of Eighteen hundred and Twenty-five dollars." The contract was executed in triplicate, and a copy of it was left with Eppinger. It appears that this contract was entered into as a result of the efforts of Eppinger, but was never consummated by an exchange of the properties; notwithstanding which it is the claim of the plaintiff that he is entitled, as the assignee of Eppinger, to recover from the defendant the sum of $1,825 under the clause of the contract above set out.

The evidence shows that the defendant was ready, able, and willing to carry out his part of the contract, and that he made several ineffectual efforts to that end, and on July 3, 1914, made a formal tender of his deed, and thereupon deposited it in the Oakland Bank of Savings with instructions to deliver it to Fletcher at any time within ten days upon receipt of Fletcher's deed to the land agreed by him to be conveyed. Fletcher was immediately notified of this deposit, and like notice was given to plaintiff's assignor; but Fletcher, within the time limited by the contract or by the aforesaid notice, or at all, made no conveyance to the defendant of the lands agreed by him to be transferred, nor any tender of a deed; and the evidence upon the trial showed that as to part of the land he possessed no title, and that subsequently Fletcher, by his attorney in fact, and the defendant entered into an agreement rescinding the contract of May 2, 1914, and reciting that Fletcher was unable to carry out its terms. The question to be decided is whether under these circumstances the defendant is entitled by virtue of the provision of the contract already set forth to recover from the defendant the sum of $1,825. The trial court held—and we think correctly—that he could not.

There can be no doubt that if A employs B to procure from C a binding agreement to exchange his property for that of A, B has performed his contract and earned his compensation when he has procured such agreement, notwithstanding the fact that C's title proves to be defective, and no exchange of properties takes place. (*Jauman* v. *McCusick*, 166 Cal. 517, [137 Pac. 254]; *Roche* v. *Smith*, 176 Mass. 595, [79 Am. St. Rep. 345, 51 L. R. A. 510, 58 N. E. 152]; 19 Cyc. 270.) But that is not this case. While the theory of the plaintiff, as stated in his brief, is that there was an employment of Eppinger by the defendant and Fletcher, the evidence discloses no such employment, and Eppinger's rights must depend entirely upon the contract actually entered into between the two contracting parties. Eppinger's connection with the matter is testified to by himself as follows: " . . . I brought Dr. Jordan and Mr. Fletcher together and introduced them, and proposed different lines of trade to each one of them, . . . and we finally got down to a basis of trade. Dr. Jordan wanted to go to see the land a second time. I told him I would not go and make a trip the second time until they drew up a contract what they were going to do if the land was satisfactory, and also showing me where I would come in, that I wanted my commission. On the strength of that this contract was drawn up before we went on the second trip." The plaintiff's right to recover, then, must depend entirely upon the terms of the contract entered into between Fletcher and Jordan, to which Eppinger was not a party. Up to that point, so far as the evidence discloses, there was no obligation upon them to pay him anything. The object of the contract actually entered into was to provide for an exchange of the properties of the parties thereto, each agreeing to convey title free of encumbrances, and the provision therein for the payment of a commission to Eppinger must be construed in its relation to the whole contract. Quite apart from the evidence of Jordan, one of the parties to it, that as to him it was not his intention that any commission should be paid unless the exchange of lands was actually effected, such would be the natural and logical construction of the instrument. Unless and until the exchange was consummated the parties would receive no benefit from Eppinger's efforts; and, as we have seen, there was no obligation existing to pay Eppinger anything except that arising from the written agreement under consideration. The provision relating to such payment is not separable from the remainder of the contract; and certainly as to Jordan, when the other party to it found himself unable to comply with its terms and consented to its cancellation (Jordan already having a right to rescind it), the whole contract fell, the provision relating to Eppinger's compensation with the rest. If the broker should suffer any hardship from such construction, it is one inherent in the form of the contract entered into, and which was the only means he chose for his protection. It would certainly be a greater hardship upon the defendant to require him to pay $1,825 for services from which he had received no benefit and which were for the greater part voluntarily rendered.

The case of *Jauman v. McCusick*, 166 Cal. 517, [137 Pac. 254], cited by appellant, though very similar to the case at bar, contains one important difference, which renders the case inapplicable as an authority in plaintiff's favor. There the undertaking to pay the brokers was in terms for the procuring of a certain agreement of exchange which they in fact procured. In that case the court said (page 521): "It is no doubt the general rule that a broker authorized to sell real estate is not entitled to recover the agreed commission unless he shows that he has, in pursuance of his employment and within the time limited therein, found a purchaser ready and willing to purchase the property on the terms specified [citing cases]. Here, however, the defendant's agreement was not simply to pay a commission to the brokers upon their making a sale or exchange of the property. Her agreement was to pay $1,850 for their services in securing the particular agreement which was secured."

There is another material distinction to be noted between the two cases. In the one cited there was merely a mutual abandonment of the contract of exchange because of differences arising between the parties to it; whereas in the case at bar, in addition to the evidence of mutual rescission, it was shown that Fletcher was unable to perform, the title to part of the land, to wit, fifty acres, agreed by him to be conveyed being in another person.

As to this fifty acres, the appellant asserts that there was no showing that Fletcher did not have a conveyance from the parties in whom title was shown to be, and consequently no showing that he was unable to comply with the contract. It is true that a man may take an option on land and agree to sell the land while the title is in another; but that doctrine has no application to the facts of this case, for here the defendant introduced in evidence a deed dated October 28, 1913, showing the title to the fifty acres in question to be in one Josephine Collins, and the *prima facie* presumption is that the title remained in that person at the time when performance was due from Fletcher, less than a year later (Code Civ. Proc., sec. 1963, subd. 32; *Hohenshell* v. *South Riverside L. & W. Co.*, 128 Cal. 627, 631, [61 Pac. 371]). It was incumbent upon the defendant to overcome the presumption. (*Dyar* v. *Stone*, 23 Cal. App. 143, 145, [137 Pac. 269].) It follows that no attempt having been made to do so, the presumption is that Josephine Collins still held the title to that property, and the finding, therefore, of the court that Fletcher was unable to convey the fifty acres must be upheld.

The judgment and order are affirmed.

Lennon, P. J., and Richards, J., concurred.

[Civ. No. 1573.   Third Appellate District.—September 4, 1916.]

WILLIAM EARL, Respondent, v. SAN FRANCISCO BRIDGE COMPANY (a Corporation), Appellant.

NEGLIGENCE — EMPLOYER AND EMPLOYEE — PERSONAL INJURIES FROM ELECTRIC CURRENT—CHANGING SWITCH WITHOUT NOTICE.—An employee of a corporation who receives personal injuries from a powerful electric current while engaged in replacing a fuse in the electrical apparatus of the company, under the orders of its chief engineer, whose duty it was to make the repair, the accident resulting from the failure of a switch, used to protect the employees while

putting in fuses, to perform its functions, the employee having no
knowledge or notice of this change of condition in the switch, and
having every reason to believe that by manipulating the switch the
current would be completely cut off so that the fuse could be inserted without danger, is entitled to recover from his employer
damages for the injury sustained.

ID. — CONTRIBUTORY NEGLIGENCE — FAILURE TO EXAMINE APPARATUS —
WHEN EXCUSED.—Where the proximate cause of the injury was the
failure of the switch to disconnect the current, and this resulted from
a change made by the company unknown to the employee, it was not
negligence for the latter to assume that conditions were as before,
and that the switch would disconnect the current; and he was therefore not chargeable with contributory negligence in not examining
the apparatus.

ID.—KNOWLEDGE OF DANGER—EMPLOYEE ACTING UNDER ORDERS.—If
the employee had full knowledge of the change in such a case he
would not be chargeable with contributory negligence in obeying
orders of the chief engineer under whose direct supervision he was
acting, unless performance thereof was inevitably or imminently
dangerous.

ID. — EMPLOYERS' LIABILITY ACT — ASSUMPTION OF RISK. — Under the
Employers' Liability Act in force at the time of the accident in
question a defense that the employee assumed the risk of the employment was not open to the defendant.

ID.—MEASURE OF DAMAGES—DISCRETION OF JURY.—In actions for damages for personal injuries it must be largely left to the discretion
and sense of justice of the jury, subject to the supervision and correction of the trial court, to determine the amount that will be a
fair compensation for the suffering and misery and financial loss
endured by the injured party.

ID.—INSTRUCTIONS—MEASURE OF DAMAGES.—In an action for damages
for personal injuries, an instruction to the jury that they should
assess the damages, if any, in such sum as they believe under all
the circumstances and evidence plaintiff ought to recover, if standing alone might be misleading, but where it is supplemented by
specific directions as to all the elements of damage that the plaintiff can recover, it cannot be misunderstood.

ID.—STATEMENT OF CLAIM—USING LANGUAGE OF COMPLAINT.—There is
no error in the court stating the claim of plaintiff in the language
of the complaint.

ID.— AFFIRMATION OF THE ISSUE — PREPONDERANCE OF EVIDENCE —
DEFINITIONS OF.—Where the court in the instructions given on behalf
of the defendant sufficiently defined the terms "affirmation of the
issue," and "preponderance of the evidence," if any further elucidation was desired, it should have been requested.

ID.—EVIDENCE—HOSPITAL CHARGES.—A motion to strike out the testimony on cross-examination of a doctor as to the value of the hospital services incurred by the plaintiff in an action for damages for personal injuries, the motion being made upon the ground that he was testifying as to what the usual charges were, and not the actual charges in the case, is made too late, where he had so testified on direct examination without objection.

ID.—EVIDENCE—INADMISSIBILITY OF WRITTEN REPORT.—Where a witness testified from memory with his written report before him that he was at a certain place at a certain time, the report itself was not admissible as corroboration of this testimony.

APPEAL from a judgment of the Superior Court of Solano County, and from an order denying a new trial. A. J. Buckles, Judge.

The facts are stated in the opinion of the court.

H. B. M. Miller, for Appellant.

Walter Shelton, Campbell, Weaver, Shelton & Levy, and Frank R. Devlin, for Respondent.

BURNETT, J.—The interesting argument of appellant is based largely upon the theory that we must discredit and reject the testimony in favor of respondent's contention. It should hardly be necessary to add that we are not permitted to do so, since the statements therein contained are not improbable. Indeed, after a careful reading of the entire record, we can only say that at most a substantial conflict is presented as to the material elements of the alleged cause of action.

The facts, as substantially stated and shown by respondent, are as follows: Appellant at the time of the accident was engaged in dredging a channel near Pinole Flats at Mare Island in Solano County, and for said purpose was using dredgers, pumps, and other machinery and equipment operated by electricity. On the 7th of November, 1913, plaintiff was in the employment of the defendant as an operator in and about one of its pumping stations or substations, and it was his duty, under said employment, "to work with, use, handle and repair the machinery, apparatus and equipment in and about said pumping plant or station." While he was so engaged "he was required by defendant to replace a fuse or connection in the aforesaid apparatus and equipment, and plaintiff, before proceeding to do so, turned or threw the switch provided by defendant to disconnect the electrical current from that portion of said electrical apparatus or equipment where plaintiff was about to insert the aforesaid fuse or connection, but owing to the unsafeness, unsuitableness, unfitness, defectiveness and dangerous and unrepaired condition of said wires, . . . devices and electrical equipment, a powerful and dangerous electrical current of high potential used by defendant on said electrical apparatus and equipment for the purpose of supplying power to be used as aforesaid, was not disconnected from the aforesaid electrical apparatus and equipment, but said electrical apparatus and equipment remained surcharged therewith and defendant carelessly and negligently and knowingly, but without the knowledge of plaintiff, failed to disconnect or cause to be disconnected the aforesaid electrical apparatus and equipment from the aforesaid current, so that when plaintiff undertook to replace the aforesaid fuse or connection as required by defendant, he came in contact with the aforesaid powerful and dangerous current and received the same into and through his body, and suffered great shock and injury.'' Defendant's machinery and apparatus where plaintiff was employed was protected from unusual electric currents by means of fuses which melted or "blew out" and thus automatically disconnected the current when it became too strong. Whenever a fuse blew out, it was the duty of plaintiff to insert another.

Until just prior to the accident, defendant had furnished a switch or cut-off which could be used to disconnect the current, and a fuse could then be put in without any danger; and while this condition prevailed plaintiff had restored many of these fuses.

A few days before the accident, that part of the switch disconnecting the middle phase of the three incoming high-tension wires, burned out, so that it had to be repaired in order to re-establish the connection on the middle wire. The duty to make this repair devolved upon defendant's chief engineer and not upon plaintiff. Instead of restoring the switch to its original condition, the chief engineer connected the middle high-tension wire directly to the middle transformer wire by means of an ordinary wire called a "solid" or "jumper" so that the middle phase could not thereafter be disconnected.

As a consequence, the middle wire was always alive, so that when the two outside high-tension wires were disconnected by throwing the switch, the corresponding wires below the switch, where the fuses had to be inserted, were always charged by a return current from the transformer. Although the fuses in the two outside wires were still kept in use to protect the machinery and had to be replaced when they blew out, the switch to protect the employees while putting in fuses no longer performed its function. While the switch appeared to accomplish its purpose on the wires where the fuses had to be inserted, and apparently disconnected the current in those wires as it had always done, there was a way left open for the current to become a hidden and disguised peril. We must conclude from the record that plaintiff had no knowledge nor notice of this change in the condition of the switch, but, to the contrary, had every reason to believe that by manipulating the switch, the current would be turned off completely so that the fuse could be inserted without danger. Herein lies the negligence of defendant. It consisted manifestly in making such change in the electrical appliances without notifying plaintiff. Of course, if it had not been the duty of respondent to restore the fuses, a different question would be presented. But from the showing made, we must accept it as true that such was the duty of respondent, and, moreover, that the chief engineer specifically ordered him to put in the fuse and in effect assured him that he was not incurring any danger.

Reduced to its simplest form, the case seems clearly to be that a safe place was furnished to plaintiff for his work with certain appliances that he could and did use in a certain manner without danger; that said appliances were changed in a material way without his knowledge; that thereby they could not be safely operated as before; and that, while performing his duty, he was greatly injured in consequence of said change having been made.

The essential features of the situation are covered in the following narrative of plaintiff: "I am thirty-three years old. My occupation has been that of rigger, and for that work I have received from $90 to $125 per month. . . . I was operator on the relay station; my duties were to see that the pump was oiled, well greased and oiled and running; . . . if anything happened, a fuse blown out, we were supposed to put it

back in place, supposed to keep the thing running. I had
been employed there about a month; I had been in the employ
of the San Francisco Bridge Company about two and a half
months; during that time I had worked there on the machine,
on the dredger as a handy man. I was off about four days
before the morning on which I was hurt; I reported for duty
on the dredger, on board the launch, at 7 o'clock, and I was
told to go over aboard the Booster and pack the pump and get
ready to start up, and I did so; two hours later Mr. Purcell,
the chief engineer, came by in the launch and said he was
going to cut in the power from Vallejo and when he did to
start the pump; I started the pump immediately as soon as
the power came into the building. We ran for about ten minutes when the motor burned out; I shut off the power and
stopped the motor and hoisted up the flag to call the launch
up, and they came back, that is, Mr. Purcell and Mr. Squires.
I called them back; it was my duty to accept instructions in
regard to my work from these two men I called back. After
I had thrown the controller so that the power went on and
the motor did not run. Mr. Purcell went out in the back of the
Booster where the transformers are, and he came in directly
afterwards and said, 'Earl, there is a fuse blown; go put one
in.' I took the key to the cut-out and went outside and unlocked the cut-out or switch, that is, the disconnecting switch,
and pulled it out and disconnected the power from the fuse
platform and locked it out. When I pulled the arm of the
connecting switch down and locked it, Mr. Purcell was there;
I asked him if all was ready and he said yes. Then I went
up and caught hold of the thumb-screw and was caught. The
thumb-screw was on the inside wire, that is, the one nearest
the building. I just stayed there burning. I first felt a sen-
sation in the throat here, then the burns down here [indicat-
ing], then I felt the legs burning, both of my legs from here
down here. The key that I had I put in my mouth and had
it there when I was on the wire; I tried to spit it out but
could not; I was tense on the wire and could not do anything
except to hang there. I was in the hospital about five
months; I had to undergo one large operation and three minor
ones; I have not been able to work since that time; some
nights I sleep pretty good and some nights I don't sleep a
single wink; that did not exist before the accident; before my
injury I weighed 168 or 170 pounds, and when I got out of

the hospital I weighed 105; now I weigh about 140 pounds. I was not nervous before the accident. My doctor's bills and expenses at the hospital were between thirteen hundred dollars and fourteen hundred dollars. I had put in fuses lots of times before I was hurt. The correct method of putting in one of these fuses was to take the key and go out and unlock the cut-out and pull down the switch; the cut-off switch is a pole running up the height to the three cut-off leaders, it cuts off the power from the coming-in wires to the fuse wire; I had been in the habit of doing that before this time. *When I went up that day to put that fuse in, I had never been told or advised by anyone and did not know that the cut-out or switch that I had undertaken to disconnect had been changed or modified in any way; I did not notice at any time that morning any change or modification in the cut-off or switch; at the time of the accident when I was up there I saw the wire then at that time, running from the high-tension wire that brings the current in.* It ran to the lower fuse bracket and switch, it was connected with the center wire; I saw that wire from above the switch to the lower fuse bracket, it was joined at one end to the main feed wire and then across the cut-off switch, the middle arm, and extended down below the middle fuse and attach to the lower fuse bracket. It was four days before I was hurt that I had seen that cut-off or switch; it was not then in that condition, it was in good condition."

He further testified that he caught hold of the thumb-screw to put in the fuse when he got to the top of the ladder, and the accident happened immediately, and that he did not know that it was dangerous to come in contact with the wire while "the cut-off was thrown out," nor was he told that "in the condition affairs were in on that platform that the cut-out did not cut the current off."

Applying to the foregoing testimony the familiar legal principles involved in such cases, we reach the conclusion that appellant was rightfully charged with the burden of responding in damages for the injury suffered by plaintiff. Those principles need not be restated, and it is probably sufficient, without quotation, to refer to *Stephens* v. *Pacific Electric Ry. Co.*, 16 Cal. App. 512, [117 Pac. 559]; *Giraudi* v. *Electric Improvement Co.*, 107 Cal. 120, [48 Am. St. Rep. 114, 28 L. R. A. 596, 40 Pac. 108]; *Reeve* v. *Colusa Gas & Electric Company*, 152 Cal. 99, [92 Pac. 89]; *Dow* v. *Sunset Telephone*

Co., 157 Cal. 182, [106 Pac. 587]; *Grimm* v. *Omaha Electric Light and Power Co.,* 79 Neb. 387, [112 N. W. 620].

It is, however, insisted that respondent was guilty of such contributory negligence as to prevent recovery. The real basis for the contention is that respondent is chargeable with knowledge of the dangerous character of the element with which he was dealing. That he was not ignorant of the peril involved in coming into contact with a current of such voltage must be conceded, and that he should be required to exercise care in operating the appliances cannot be disputed; but these considerations are only remotely, if at all, connected with the controversy here. The real danger, the proximate cause of the injury was, as we have already seen, the failure of the switch to disconnect the current, and this by reason of a change made by appellant. It was not negligence on the part of respondent to assume that conditions were as before, and that the switch would disconnect the current. Having the right to assume that the appliance was in the same condition, he was excusable for his failure to make an examination or inspection whereby he might have ascertained what had been done; nor was the difference in the appearance of the equipment so palpable and obtrusive as to compel the conclusion that while hastening to perform his duty, if he had exercised ordinary care he would have discovered the change.

Moreover, plaintiff, as testified to by him, was acting under the direct supervision of the chief engineer and was entitled to rely upon his superior knowledge. In *Price* v. *Northern Electric Ry. Co.,* 168 Cal. 173, [142 Pac. 91], it is said: "He was working under the immediate supervision of a foreman and was not erecting trestle bents or creating them on his own judgment and at his own risk. In the absence of actual knowledge to the contrary, or circumstances under which he would be held to be required to have such knowledge, he had the right to assume, when directed to assist in removing the scaffolding, that the bent had been so braced that it would not fall when the scaffolding was removed. And it cannot be held as matter of law, under the circumstances, that he was guilty of contributory negligence in not observing the absence of bracing, however obvious that fact might have been if he had made an examination to see what the actual condition was." (See, also, *Cumberland Tel. & Tel. Co.* v. *Graves' Admx.* (Ky.), 104 S. W. 356; *Chicago Suburban W. & L. Co.*

v. *Hyslop*, 227 Ill. 308, [81 N. E. 381]; *Green* v. *Varney*, 165 Cal. 347, [132 Pac. 436]; *Lee* v. *Woolsey*, 109 Pa. St. 124.)

Moreover, if plaintiff had full knowledge of the change he would not be chargeable with contributory negligence in obeying orders unless performance thereof was inevitably or imminently dangerous. (*Martin* v. *California Central Ry. Co.*, 94 Cal. 326, [29 Pac. 645]; *Anderson* v. *Seropian*, 147 Cal. 201, [81 Pac. 521]; *Patterson* v. *Pittsburg and C. R. Co.*, 76 Pa. St. 389, [18 Am. Rep. 412]; *Van Duzen Gas etc. Co.* v. *Schelies*, 61 Ohio St. 298, [55 N. E. 998].)

There is room for the application of this principle since there was testimony on the part of appellant that the work done by respondent was not imminently and necessarily dangerous. The chief engineer testified that after the repairs he put in a fuse on the outside wire without injury and that he, an electrical and steam engineer of twenty years' experience, "did not consider it taking a chance" to put in a fuse. Defendant's superintendent, a civil engineer, who was present at the time of the accident, testified that he knew the middle wire was through solid and that he did not warn plaintiff, but that he "did consider that a man had to exercise more care up there after the middle wire was through solid." From this statement it is quite clear that he did not consider putting in the fuse as particularly and obviously dangerous, or else he would have cautioned plaintiff. Upon this theory it is a reasonable conclusion that plaintiff was justified in believing that he could perform the duty intrusted to him without danger if he exercised the care necessarily required in directing and controlling an electric current of such voltage.

In this connection it might be well to state the suggestions of respondent that since plaintiff proceeded carefully and skillfully, there was no more than an assumption of risk if he realized the danger, and that this defense was not open to defendant, the Employers' Liability Act having been in force at the time of the accident. (*Crabbe* v. *Mammoth Channel G. Mining Co.*, 168 Cal. 500, [143 Pac. 714].)

Another point urged upon our attention is that the verdict is excessive and therefore should be set aside. The amount awarded is quite large, but respondent was grievously injured, and we cannot say that it is so disproportionate to the damage done as to compel the conclusion that the jury were controlled by passion or prejudice. We may supplement the testimony of plaintiff on the subject already quoted, by the following statement of Dr. E. A. Peterson, one of the attending physicians: "It was January 15th when I first saw the plaintiff; Dr. Klotz asked me to come over there and help him operate on a man he was going to leave in my charge, as he was going away. I assisted him in the operation, removing the internal condyle of the tibia; he was in my charge from then on; he was in a very critical condition from the inflammation which he had in the bone, which caused a good deal of pain, and we had to remove it, and other bone became infected, and it was necessary to operate on him three times about, to remove pus from under the periosteum, the covering of the bone, and there is nothing more painful, so excruciatingly painful. He was suffering a general condition, as I understand it, he was very much run down, and he had to be put under an anaesthetic three times more. The cause of his condition was the generally weakened vitality, especially as the bone had been burned and rendered very inactive and unhealthy from being burned; this is what we call a complication after a burn. The complications which occurred in this case were unavoidable, and the condition I have described was not due to any neglect that the plaintiff may have received. His pain was so great that opiates would not relieve it. This condition continued from about January 17th to—well, it was a month, anyway, that he was in awful agony. . . . The plaintiff, in my opinion, will never be able to perform labor such as a rigger, or any structural work owing to his present condition."

Dr. Klotz described minutely the patient's condition, and, among other things, said: "The bone was diseased from the electric shock, that is the necrosis, the live bone was destroyed. . . . The nervous condition was due, of course, to the shock and electrical burns that he had. If a person were to receive enough electricity to throw them down and to require artificial respiration and of course burns like the patient had, it would leave him in an awful state afterward. . . . He never will be able to perform such services as a rigger, a person who has formerly worked with his feet, arms and hands."

Of course, in cases like this, there is no certain and absolute measure of damages. It must be largely left to the discretion and sense of justice of the jury, "subject to the supervision and correction of the trial court," to determine the amount that will be a fair compensation for the suffering and misery and financial loss endured by the injured party. The severity of the injury caused by electricity is a matter of general observation, and the courts have been quite liberal in upholding verdicts for large amounts in such cases. As illustrating this tendency of the courts, we may refer to the following cases cited by respondent: *Tedford* v. *Los Angeles Electric Co.*, 134 Cal. 76, [54 L. R. A. 85, 66 Pac. 76]; *Reeve* v. *Colusa Gas and Electric Co.*, 152 Cal. 99, [92 Pac. 89]; *Southwestern Tel. & Tel. Co.* v. *Shirley* (Tex.), 155 S. W. 663; *Hill* v. *Union Light and Power Co.*, 260 Mo. 43, [169 S. W. 345]; *New Omaha Thompson-Houston Electric Light Co.* v. *Rombold*, 68 Neb. 54, [93 N. W. 966, 97 N. W. 1030]; *Goetzke* v. *City of Chicago*, 174 Ill. App. 446.

Some errors in the matter of instructions and rulings of the trial judge are claimed, but they seem to be without substantial merit.

The instruction to the jury that they should assess the damages, if any, in such sum as they believed under all the circumstances in evidence, the plaintiff ought to recover, if standing alone might have been misleading, but it was supplemented by specific directions as to all the elements of damage that the plaintiff could recover and, therefore, could not have been misunderstood as claimed by appellant. (*Zibbell* v. *Southern Pacific Co.*, 160 Cal. 237, [116 Pac. 513]; *Harmon* v. *Donohoe*, 153 Mo. 263, [54 S. W. 453]; *Lamb* v. *City of Cedar Rapids*, 108 Iowa, 629, [79 N. W. 366]; *Denver City Tramway Co.* v. *Martin*, 44 Colo. 324, [98 Pac. 836].)

There was no error in stating the claim of the plaintiff in the language of the complaint. It was certainly proper to inform the jury as to the issues, and it is a mere question of rhetoric whether for this purpose the language of the pleadings or equivalent phraseology should be used.

There is no merit in the contention by appellant of the alleged failure of the court to define "affirmation of the issue" and "preponderance of evidence." As a matter of fact, they were sufficiently defined in the instructions given on behalf of defendant, and if any further elucidation was desired it should have been requested. (*O'Connor* v. *United Railroads*, 168 Cal. 43, [141 Pac. 809].)

The instructions as a whole were very fair and presented every legal phase of the case that was needed for the enlightenment of the jury. Every instruction requested by defendant was given, and in those given on behalf of plaintiff, we find no prejudicial error.

The court properly refused to strike out the testimony on cross-examination of Dr. Klotz as to the value of the hospital services incurred by plaintiff. The motion was upon the ground that he was testifying as to what the usual charges were and not the actual charge in this case, but he had so testified on direct examination without objection, and the motion came too late. Moreover, the testimony of plaintiff as to that point was uncontradicted, and hence the doctor's testimony could not have prejudiced defendant.

Objection is made to the ruling of the court excluding a written report to the company made by William J. Knoll, a witness for defendant. The only purpose of the evidence was to show that the witness was at the station in number 5. The witness had testified from memory with this report before him that he was there at that time, and the report itself was not admissible as corroboration of his testimony. (*People* v. *Eliyea*, 14 Cal. 145; *Baum* v. *Reay*, 96 Cal. 462, [29 Pac. 117, 31 Pac. 561]; Wigmore on Evidence, sec. 763; Elliott on Evidence, sec. 872.)

Two or three other assignments of error are made, but they are so inconsequential as to merit no specific attention.

From an examination of the whole record, we think it can be safely declared that defendant's rights were carefully protected and that the proceedings were free from prejudicial error.

The judgment and order are affirmed.

Chipman, P. J., and Hart, J., concurred.

[Civ. No. 2023. Second Appellate District.—September 5, 1916.]

ALFRED BLANCHARD, Respondent, v. MARK KEPPEL,
Appellant.

SCHOOL LAW—PRELIMINARY ELEMENTARY SCHOOL CERTIFICATE—FEE
FOR.—An applicant for a preliminary elementary school certificate
authorizing him to do practice and cadet teaching in any of the
elementary schools of a county is required to pay the fee of two
dollars provided by section 1565 of the Political Code to be paid
by each applicant for a teacher's certificate, "except for a temporary certificate." The term "temporary certificate," is not used
anywhere in the code as applied to any form of certificate issued
by a county board of education.

APPEAL from a judgment of the Superior Court of Los
Angeles County. Frank G. Finlayson, Judge.

The facts are stated in the opinion of the court.

A. J. Hill, County Counsel, and Hugh Gordon, Deputy
County Counsel, for Appellant.

John W. Luter, for Respondent.

CONREY, P. J.—This is a proceeding in *mandamus*
wherein the defendant has appealed from the judgment. By
the terms of the judgment the defendant, as superintendent
of schools of the county of Los Angeles and *ex-officio* secretary of the county board of education, is required to approve
and present to the county board of education the application
of the petitioner (together with the recommendation of the
president of the State Normal School at Los Angeles) for the
issuance to the petitioner of a preliminary elementary school
certificate authorizing him to do practice and cadet teaching,
without salary, in any of the elementary schools of Los Angeles County, without the payment of a fee of two dollars
demanded by appellant. The superior court held that a
preliminary elementary school certificate as described and referred to in the Political Code in section 1775 (subd. c. of
subd. 1) and in section 1771 (subd. c of subd. 3) is not a
teacher's certificate within the meaning of section 1565 of
that code.

The fee of two dollars demanded by appellant from respondent as an applicant for a preliminary school certificate, is required by section 1565 to be paid by every applicant for a teacher's certificate, "except for a temporary certificate." Section 1543 provides for the issuance of "temporary certificates" good for not exceeding six months, and which are issued, upon certain credentials shown, by the superintendent of schools of the county. Various other forms of certificate mentioned in section 1771 and in other sections of the Political Code are issued by the county board of education. In the list of these last-mentioned certificates we find no reference to a "temporary certificate," but it does include "preliminary elementary certificates" which shall not be valid for a longer period than two years. It does not appear that the code anywhere uses the term "temporary certificate" as applied to any form of certificate issued by a county board of education.

We shall not follow respondent's counsel in his argument based upon alleged unreasonableness of the two dollar fee. The language of the code being in this instance clear and unmistakable, we cannot indulge in a discussion about what the legislature ought to have intended to do.

The judgment is reversed.

James, J., and Shaw, J., concurred.

[Crim. No. 491. Second Appellate District.—September 7, 1916.]

THE PEOPLE, Respondent, v. PHILLIP WINNER, Appellant.

CRIMINAL LAW—PRONOUNCEMENT OF JUDGMENT—DELAY—RIGHT TO NEW TRIAL.—Where judgment is not pronounced upon a person convicted of a crime, within the time prescribed by section 1191 of the Penal Code, he is entitled to a new trial, although the delay in pronouncing judgment was had with his consent.

APPEAL from a judgment of the Superior Court of Kern County, and from an order denying a new trial. Howard A. Peairs, Judge.

The facts are stated in the opinion of the court.

Wesley P. Grijalva, Henry R. Holsinger, and A. B. Campbell, for Appellant.

U. S. Webb, Attorney-General, and Robert M. Clarke, Deputy Attorney-General, for Respondent.

SHAW, J.—Upon an information filed by the district attorney of Kern County the defendant was, on March 16, 1916, convicted of the crime of grand larceny. On March 20th he presented to the court a motion for a new trial, the hearing of which was by the court continued to March 27th, at which time the court, as shown by the minutes thereof, made an entry as follows: "By consent of counsel for respective parties in open court, it is by the court ordered that said motion for a new trial be and the same is hereby submitted upon briefs to be presented within five, five and two days." On April 4th, more than fifteen days after defendant's conviction, the court made an order denying his motion for a new trial. Thereupon defendant, within due time, made a motion for a new trial upon the ground that more than fifteen days had elapsed since the date of the conviction of defendant, and upon the same ground objected to the court pronouncing judgment upon defendant, which motion the court likewise denied. The ruling constitutes error.

Section 1191 of the Penal Code provides that upon a defendant being convicted, "the court must appoint a time for pronouncing judgment which must not be less than two, nor more than five days after the verdict or plea of guilty; provided, however, that the court may extend the time not more than ten days for the purpose of hearing or determining any motion for a new trial, or in arrest of judgment; and provided, further, that the court may extend the time not more than twenty days in any case where the question of probation is considered in accordance with section 1203 of this code, provided, however, that upon the request of the defendant such time may be further extended not more than ninety days additional." And section 1202 of the Penal Code provides that, unless judgment be "rendered or pronounced within the time so fixed or to which it is continued under the provisions of section eleven hundred and ninety-one of this code, then the defendant shall be entitled to a new trial."

As said by the court in *People* v. *Polich,* 25 Cal. App. 464, [143 Pac. 1065], quoting from *Rankin* v. *Superior Court,* 157 Cal. 189, [106 Pac. 718]: "If the judgment was not pronounced within the time limited, a new trial was made imperative if the defendant so desired; he became 'entitled' to it. . . . If the court should refuse a new trial and render judgment against the defendant after the authorized time has passed, its action would be erroneous and the judgment would be reversed on appeal if an appeal should be taken." To the same effect is *People* v. *Okomoto,* 26 Cal. App. 568, [147 Pac. 598]; where it was held that the defendant was entitled to a new trial, but lost his right thereto by reason of not asking for it in the trial court.

Conceding the error, the attorney-general in support of the court's action insists that it was cured by the fact, as shown, that counsel for defendant in open court consented to the postponement of the time for sentence. In support of this contention a number of cases arising under section 1382 of the Penal Code, providing for the dismissal of prosecutions in cases therein specified, are cited. In our opinion such cases are not in point, and throw no light upon the interpretation to be given sections 1191 and 1202, which should be construed in accordance with the plain import of the language used. Thus construed, as held in *People* v. *Polich,* 25 Cal. App. 464, [143 Pac. 1065], and *People* v. *Okomoto,* 26 Cal. App. 568, [147 Pac. 598], the delay beyond the time specified for pronouncing judgment renders it imperative that defendant have a new trial if he asks for it. Prior to the enactment the courts, with consent of parties or otherwise, not infrequently indulged in prolonged delays before pronouncing sentence upon those convicted of crime. Such practice was recognized by the legislature as an evil, to cure which sections 1191 and 1202 were adopted, not as a benefit conferred upon defendant which he might waive, but as a matter of public policy intended to insure a swifter infliction of the penalty which the law requires to be imposed upon those convicted of crime. To uphold the contention of respondent and recognize the consent of the parties as justifying an indefinite postponement of the time for pronouncing judgment beyond that specified for so doing, would not subserve, but on the contrary nullify, the plain purpose and intent of the legislature in adopting the provision.

The judgment and order are reversed and, for the reasons
stated, the court directed to make an order granting defendant's motion for a new trial.

Conrey, P. J., and James, J., concurred.

[Crim. No. 355. Third Appellate District.—September 8, 1916.]

THE PEOPLE, Respondent, v. HENRY CARDER, Appellant.

CRIMINAL LAW—PREJUDICIAL REMARKS OF COURT TO JURY.—It is reversible error in a criminal case, upon the jury returning into
court and reporting their inability to agree, for the court to make
such remarks as, "I don't want to decide any question of fact for
you; *that question though it seems very plain to me*"; and, "You
must try to reconcile the testimony if you can and come to a verdict, gentlemen, if you possibly can. These cases are expensive
to try"; and "*How many contrary ones are there?*" and "Questions
of fact you must decide; *there oughtn't to be any trouble. It's
a case you ought to decide, ought to agree upon and don't make
up your minds that you can't agree, don't get contrary but just
in a good humor, good-natured way work it out.*"

APPEAL from a judgment of the Superior Court of Mendocino County, and from an order denying a new trial.
J. Q. White, Judge.

The facts are stated in the opinion of the court.

Charles Kasch, for Appellant.

U. S. Webb, Attorney-General, and J. Charles Jones, Deputy Attorney-General, for Respondent.

BURNETT, J.—Defendant was convicted of the larceny of
a calf, and he appeals from the judgment and order denying
his motion for a new trial.

Among the alleged errors, the most serious is involved in
certain remarks to the jury made by the trial judge. It
seems that after the case was submitted the jury returned
into court at 3:35 P. M. on Friday, and asked to have certain

evidence read to them. This was done and they again retired. A few hours later they returned to the courtroom and
the foreman informed the presiding judge that in his opinion the jury could not agree. The trial judge then said:
"You must work this out, gentlemen, if there is anything I
can help you in I can do it, and I will be here ten minutes
longer to help you. You oughtn't to make up your mind
you are not going to agree on this kind of a case, simply calls
for the sensible reasoning of men according to the evidence
and talk it over together." Furthermore, in reply to a
juror's question, the court said: "I don't want to decide any
question of fact for you; *that question though it seems very
plain to me.*" A little later he used this language: "You
must try and reconcile the testimony if you can and come to
a verdict, gentlemen, if you possibly can. These cases are
expensive to try."

The jury returned again into court on Saturday morning
at 10:35, and the transcript reveals the following: "Clerk:
Have you reached a verdict, gentlemen? A. We have not.
Court: Well, what can I do for you, gentlemen? Juryman
Yates: Your Honor, please, there isn't a possibility I don't
think in the minds of any of the jury that we can agree. We
have went over the evidence and every particle of that; we
can agree as to what the evidence is but we can't agree on a
verdict. The Court: You can't agree, you think? Juryman:
No, sir, done everything that we could to reach a verdict since
you left here last night. The Court: *How many contrary ones
are there?* Juryman: Two. Court: Well, I tell you, gentlemen, you can work just as good on this, a jury can on holi-
days, Sundays and any other time and the law is all right in
that respect and the court can take the verdict at any time,
too, on Sunday as well as Saturday afternoon; now, if there
is any question of law that you need that you are in doubt
about, why I will give it to you. Questions of fact you must
decide; *there oughtn't to be any trouble. It's a case you
ought to decide, ought to agree upon and don't make up your
minds that you can't agree, don't get contrary but just in a
good humor, good-natured way work it out.* Juryman Cle-
land: Your Honor, we worked all night in there and we have
talked all night. I think we have got it down to where they
say we have made up our minds and no use to argue.
Court: Well, of course men go into the jury-room. They

think their minds are made up and some little question comes
up, they come to the conclusion then they ought to change it.
If they keep working on the theory they are not going to
change their minds, it is made up, of course they will not, but
that's not the way for a jury to do, want to work at it with
the possibility always in view that I may be wrong about this
and I'll change if I am. . . . You think there is no question
of fact the court can help you on by having it read? A. I
don't think so. Court: Well, go back and go to work, gentlemen. The court will be here any time when you agree.''

The jury returned later to have some of the testimony
read. They retired again for deliberation and finally brought
in a verdict of guilty.

We think it quite apparent that from the statements of the
learned trial judge the jury must have concluded that he was
convinced of the defendant's guilt and that as honest men it
was their duty to so find. A portion of the remarks we have
quoted was quite appropriate and calls for no criticism, but
the statements we have italicized constitute, in our opinion,
an infringement of the special prerogative of the jury. It
was proper for the presiding judge to admonish the jury of
their duty to consult together, to listen to argument, and to
endeavor earnestly to reach an agreement, and, although of
somewhat questionable propriety to remind the jury of the
expense of a new trial, such remark could not justly be held
sufficient ground for reversal, nor perhaps even for criticism; but to characterize the two dissentient jurors as *contrary,* and to declare that there should be no trouble about
agreeing upon a case like this, and that it simply called for
the sensible reasoning of men according to the evidence, transcends the proper limits of judicial discretion and authority.
The *contrary* jurors were undoubtedly for acquittal. It is
not likely that if the other ten had been opposed to conviction they would so readily have yielded to the persuasive suggestions of the trial court. Of course, these two jurors had
the same legal and moral right to their opinion of the guilt
of the defendant as had the other ten, and their attitude
should not have been ascribed to obstinacy. That under our
system, in the determination of the guilt or innocence of a
defendant, the jury must be left free from coercion or influence of the trial judge, will not be gainsaid. This right and
privilege accorded by the constitution to one charged with

crime is manifestly fundamental and vital. If serious infractions of it are to be tolerated, then trial by jury becomes a delusive formality.

The case here is controlled by the principle of the decision in *People* v. *Kindleberger*, 100 Cal. 367, [34 Pac. 852], and *People* v. *Conboy*, 15 Cal. App. 97, [113 Pac. 703]. In the former, the trial judge said to the jury: "In view of the testimony in this case the court is utterly at a loss to know why twelve honest men cannot agree." And in the latter, the objectionable remark was: "Now, gentlemen, I think I have read to you about all the instructions you desire upon these points and I suggest to you that *there is no reason why twelve honest, intelligent, reasonable men should not reach a conclusion in this case and I am surprised that you have not done so already.*"

The case at bar for the same reason is equally subject to animadversion and the only reasonable conclusion, as we conceive it, is that the jury were prejudicially influenced against the defendant. It may be said as to this, that the principle is thoroughly considered and the cases reviewed by Mr. Justice Kerrigan in the Conboy decision, *supra,* and therefore we need pursue the subject no further.

The other questions discussed will probably not arise again and we forego specific consideration thereof, but for the reason stated, we think the defendant did not have a fair trial, and the judgment and order are reversed.

Chipman, P. J., and Hart, J., concurred.

[Crim. No. 345. Third Appellate District.—September 9, 1916.]

THE PEOPLE, Respondent, v. W. A. HOWARD, True Name, WALTER H. ALLEN, Appellant.

CRIMINAL LAW—EMBEZZLEMENT—LARCENY.—If one honestly receives goods upon trust, and afterward fraudulently converts them to his own use, he is guilty of embezzlement; but if he obtains possession fraudulently, with intent to convert the same to his own use, and the owner does not part with the title, the offense is larceny.

ID.—WRONGFUL TAKING OF MONEY BY WIFE—HUSBAND AS AIDER AND ABETTOR—EVIDENCE—UNWARRANTED CONVICTION OF GRAND LAR-

CENY.—The conviction of a married man of the crime of grand
larceny on the theory that he aided and abetted his wife in the
wrongful taking of money by her, cannot be sustained, in the
absence of any evidence showing that the taking of the money was
the result of a fraudulent and felonious design of the defendant
and his wife conceived before she obtained employment in the commercial college from which the money was taken, and it is shown
by the evidence presented that the money came into her control
and care while employed in such college as a stenographer, and that
among the duties assigned to her was that of selling small articles
of merchandise, receiving the money therefor, and depositing the
same in the cash register, to which she was given free access to
make change and *permission* to handle the money therein.

ID.—STATEMENT OF DIFFERENT OFFENSES—OMISSION TO CONCLUDE EACH
COUNT WITH PHRASE "CONTRARY TO FORM OF STATUTE"—SUFFI-
CIENCY OF INFORMATION.—An information in three counts, each
stating a different offense, is not prejudicial to the defendant, because of the omission to conclude each count with the statement
that the commission of the offense was "contrary to the form,
force and effect of the statute in such case made and provided,
and against the peace and dignity of the people of the state," etc.,
where the information is ended with such statement.

ID.—DIFFERENT OFFENSES—NUMBER OF PEREMPTORY CHALLENGES.—
Under an information charging more than one offense, the defendant is entitled to but ten peremptory challenges in all, and not
ten as to each offense.

ID.—CHARGE OF DIFFERENT OFFENSES—ELECTION NOT REQUIRED.—
Under an information charging more than one offense, the people
are not required to make an election, before offering proof, upon
which count they intend to rely.

APPEAL from a judgment of the Superior Court of San
Joaquin County, and from an order denying a new trial.
C. W. Norton, Judge.

The facts are stated in the opinion of the court.

Lynch & Cross, for Appellant.

U. S. Webb, Attorney-General, and J. Charles Jones, Deputy Attorney-General, for Respondent.

HART, J.—The defendant was convicted of the crime of
grand larceny, and appeals from the judgment of conviction
and the order denying his motion for a new trial.

The information is in three counts, each stating a different
offense, viz.: The first charging the larceny of $305 in money,

the second the embezzlement of said sum, and the third the receiving of said money knowing it to have been previously stolen.

The attack upon the verdict is upon numerous grounds, which, generally stated, are that the court erred in overruling the demurrer to the information, in disallowing certain *voir dire* questions by the defendant to a certain juror, in denying the challenge by the defendant of a certain venireman upon the ground of actual bias, in refusing to require the people to make an election of the particular count of the several set out in the information upon which they intended to rely, in refusing to allow the defendant thirty peremptory challenges, the theory being that he was entitled to ten such challenges upon each of the offenses stated in the information, in its rulings upon questions involving the legal propriety of the admissibility of certain evidence, and in disallowing certain instructions preferred by the accused. It is further insisted that, if the defendant was guilty of any crime whatsoever, it was not that of grand larceny, of which the jury convicted him, but that of embezzlement. This last point necessarily involves, and its solution depends upon, the question whether the evidence supports the verdict.

Under the several heads above specified, many specific objections to the legal soundness of the result reached at the trial are here interposed and argued in the briefs. Such of these as we deem entitled to special notice and review we shall consider.

The facts, as gleaned from the evidence, may be summarized as follows: In the early part of the month of August, 1915, the defendant and his wife arrived at the city of Stockton and, under the name of Howard, took rooms at a house known as the "Adams Apartments." They were strangers in Stockton, and at said apartments represented themselves as being husband and wife. A few days thereafter they moved to a rooming-house in said city, known as the "McPhee Apartments," where they remained until their departure from Stockton, on the thirtieth day of said month of August. While stopping at the last-named apartments, and about the middle of the month named, "Mrs. Howard" secured employment as a stenographer with a commercial college in said city known as the Western School of Commerce. Said college was incorporated, and at the time of the employment of Mrs. Howard, one John R. Humphreys was president of the corporation and principal of the school, and as such was authorized to employ such assistants as were found necessary to aid in carrying on the business of the institution. When she applied for employment she represented to Humphreys that her name was "Miss Helen Burns," and under that name she accepted the employment. "Mrs. Howard" worked at a desk located in the office of the secretary of the corporation. At about the hour of 12 o'clock, noon, on the thirtieth day of August, 1915, she left the office of the secretary and did not return. A short time after her departure, and after the time at which she should have returned to the office and resume the discharge of her duties, it was discovered upon investigation that the sum of $305 was missing from the cash register which was kept in the office of the secretary.

It transpired that, on the day last mentioned, Howard and his wife met at a point on one of the streets of Stockton and hired a taxi-cab, in which they were driven to Lodi, a distance of a few miles north of Stockton. At Lodi, Mrs. Howard purchased some wearing apparel at one of the stores in said town and Howard, at another store, bought a suit of clothes and a suit case. The clothes worn by him to Lodi he left at the store at which he purchased and donned the new suit. Howard also went to the bank at Lodi and exchanged some gold for paper money. Within a brief time thereafter, Howard and his wife at Lodi boarded a northbound train and went to Sacramento, at which place they bought tickets for the east, and on the said thirtieth day of August together left for the east. They were later arrested in the east and returned to Stockton. While in the east and before their arrest, the defendant, whose true name is Walter Howard Allen, gave his name and registered at hotels variously as "Taylor," "Churchill" and "Howard."

There is, in the record, testimony from which the jury could justly have inferred, as perhaps they did conclude, that the defendant down to the day upon which he with his wife left Stockton, was wholly without financial means, with the exception of five dollars in gold from which he paid for some drinks at a bar for himself and one R. J. Richardson, who, with his wife, also occupied rooms at the McPhee Apart-

ments, and to whom the defendant explained that he had
received the money from his wife.

It further appears that Mrs. Howard, a day or two before
the date of her departure from Stockton, took to her apartments a bank-book which was the property of the institution
by which she was then employed, and that while she and the
defendant were eating their lunch on that occasion, Mrs.
Richardson, wife of the party of that name above referred
to, came into their apartments, whereupon the defendant
picked up the bank-book from the table where it had been
placed by Mrs. Howard, and, addressing Mrs. Richardson,
remarked: "Look what my little girl has banked to-day.
Three hundred and sixteen dollars! Wouldn't that make a
fine trip?" To this Mrs. Howard rejoined: "No, the
straight and narrow path for me."

It was further shown that, on two several occasions, Mrs.
Howard asked the secretary of the corporation, J. W. Rousch,
whether she "should take money received at the school to the
bank," and the secretary replied that she should not.

It was shown, and, in fact, the defendant admitted, that,
within an hour before he and his wife left Stockton for Lodi,
he held a conversation with his wife through the telephone
from a saloon which he had been in the habit of frequenting
while in Stockton, that, within a brief time thereafter his wife
called and talked with him over the same telephone, and that
thereupon the defendant left the saloon, met his wife, and
immediately left with her for Lodi in the manner above
described.

Certain statements made to the sheriff by the defendant
after his arrest were received in evidence at the behest of the
people. Thus it was shown that, among other declarations,
the defendant said that he could not be convicted of any offense which might be charged against him without the testimony of his wife disclosing that he was implicated in the
crime, and that his wife could not testify against him without his consent. He further asseverated his innocence of
any connection with the commission of the crime by his wife,
and declared that he had no knowledge before she took the
money that she intended to do so. He admitted, however,
that, when he met his wife just before leaving Stockton, she
told him that she had taken the money, and that he then
said to her that she had better "beat it," by which he meant

to say that it was better for her to get away from Stockton. He also explained that he registered at hotels in the east under fictitious names only because he desired to protect his wife and so prevent her apprehension, and not because he was himself conscious of having been guilty of committing any wrong in connection with the transaction. These declarations were, as before stated, proved or brought into the record by the people as having been extrajudicially made by the accused.

Thus we have reproduced in substance all the testimony introduced by the people bearing upon the defendant's connection with the crime committed by his wife.

It will not, of course, be disputed that, since the defendant himself did not actually take the money, it must be made to appear, before a conviction of larceny can stand against him, that the taking of the money by his wife constituted larceny. In other words, since the defendant can only be made out a principal in the crime charged by showing that he aided and abetted in the commission thereof (Pen. Code, sec. 971), he obviously cannot be convicted of larceny if the crime in the commission of which he aided and abetted, is that of embezzlement or some other offense than that of larceny.

The distinction between embezzlement, in a general sense, and larceny is thus stated in *People* v. *Tomlinson*, 102 Cal. 19, [36 Pac. 506]: ". . . If one honestly receives goods upon trust, and afterward fraudulently converts them to his own use, he is guilty of embezzlement; . . . if he obtains possession fraudulently, with intent to convert the same to his own use, and the owner does not part with the title, the offense is larceny."

Section 503 of the Penal Code defines embezzlement as "the fraudulent appropriation of property by a person to whom it has been intrusted."

Section 508 of the same code reads: "Every clerk, agent, or servant of any person who fraudulently appropriates to his own use, or secretes with a fraudulent intent to appropriate to his own use, any property of another which has come into his control or care by virtue of his employment as such clerk, agent, or servant, is guilty of embezzlement."

Thus it will be observed that, to constitute the act of taking the money by the wife of the defendant larceny, it must be true and shown that the possession of said money was obtained by her fraudulently or by means of some trick, conspiracy, or artifice, with the felonious intent of converting the same to her own use. If, for illustration, it were clear that Mrs. Howard (or Allen) had designedly and fraudulently and for the purpose and with the felonious intent of taking the money from the possession of the school of commerce, to be converted by her to her own use, sought employment with said school so as to place herself in a position in which she could the more readily execute her evil or felonious design and intent, then, she having under such circumstances taken the money, the crime would be larceny. (*People* v. *Rae,* 66 Cal. 423, 424, [56 Am. Rep. 102, 6 Pac. 1].) On the other hand, if honestly she received possession of the money on trust (*People* v. *Tomlinson,* 102 Cal. 19, [36 Pac. 506]), or if, as a duly employed clerk, agent, or servant of the school, the money came "into her control or care by virtue of her employment as such clerk, agent or servant," and she fraudulently appropriated such money to her own use, or secreted it with the intention of appropriating it to her own use (Pen. Code, sec. 508), then she is guilty of embezzlement and not of larceny of the money. (*People* v. *Tomlinson,* 102 Cal. 19, [36 Pac. 506].)

There are, it will be observed from the testimony presented by the people and thus far and above stated herein, but two circumstances, aside from the fact of flight, which tend in any measure to indicate that the accused aided and abetted his wife in the commission of the felonious taking of the money, viz.: 1. The remark of the defendant that the amount of money shown by the bank-book to be on deposit in a bank in the name of the school would "make a fine trip." 2. The fact of the telephonic communications between the defendant and his wife while he was at the saloon referred to just prior to the time at which he met her and the two together left for Lodi. Whether these circumstances, together with that of flight, were sufficient to warrant a substantial inference that the defendant aided or abetted or advised his wife to take the money, was, of course, a question for the jury. And, conceding that thus the jury might have justly concluded that he did so aid and abet his wife in whatever crime her act constituted, still it will certainly not be contended that those circumstances showed that, prior to her employment by the school of commerce,

there was a conspiracy or understanding between them that
she was to seek and, if possible, secure such employment for
the purpose and with the design and intent of making available to her an opportunity for the felonious asportation of
the money of said school. In other words, it will not be
seriously claimed that those circumstances, whatever may be
their probative value in some other direction, show that the
taking of the money was the result of a fraudulent and felonious design of the defendant and his wife conceived before
she secured employment with the school. The fact of flight,
and the assumption by him of fictitious names after he left
California, are the strongest circumstances which were presented against him. Both these facts, when proved, constitute, it is to be conceded, strong incriminatory circumstances against an accused. But it will not be claimed that
either can have the effect of disclosing, or of serving as the
test for determining, the legal character or nature of the
crime committed. In this case it cannot, of course, be determined from those circumstances when the design to commit
the crime was formed—whether before Mrs. Howard went
to work for the school or after she entered upon the discharge of her duties as an employee of the school. Thus it
is clear that whether the crime committed by the wife was
larceny or embezzlement does not appear from the testimony
thus far considered. We are, therefore, required to examine
and consider the testimony disclosing the circumstances attending her employment and showing the scope and extent
of her duties and authority as an employee of the school to
determine the legal character of the crime committed by her.
Upon this question, the only testimony brought into the case
was that given by the witness Humphreys, principal of the
school and president of the corporation into which the institution had been organized.

It will be recalled that Humphreys testified that he, as
president of the corporation, conducted the negotiations culminating in the employment of Mrs. Allen. He further testified that he employed her as a stenographer; that the desk
at which she performed her duties was located in the office
of the secretary of the corporation; that the corporation kept
a stock of "petty merchandise," such as pencils, paper, etc.;
that among the duties assigned to Mrs. Howard was that of
selling the articles of merchandise mentioned, to receive the

money therefor, and to deposit the same in the cash register, which was kept in the secretary's office; that she, by reason of the authority so conferred on and exercised by her, had "free access to the cash, and made change, sold the merchandise, and had general authority that a stenographer has in an office." "Q. She sold merchandise? A. Yes, sir; had free access to the drawer. Q. Received money from the sale of merchandise? A. Certainly, just as any other employee would. Q. You state that this money that you allege was embezzled from the Western School of Commerce was in the till—the cash register? A. Yes, sir. I do not know that all the money she took was in the cash register because there was other money in the room which was not in the cash register. Q. How much money was in the room at that time? . . . A. Approximately thirteen to fifteen hundred dollars, . . . a large portion of which was in the cash register."

No doubt exists in our minds that the foregoing testimony clearly shows that Mrs. Allen, while in the service of the school, was a clerk or servant of the corporation within the meaning of section 508 of the Penal Code, and, that the money which she is charged to have taken from the corporation came into her "control and care by virtue of her employment as such clerk or servant," there can be no possible room for doubt, in our opinion. She was, by virtue of her employment, authorized to receive money in exchange for goods sold, and to make change from the moneys in the cash register when necessary. In short, as Humphreys testified, she had free access to the cash register, with authority to handle the money deposited therein for any purpose within the scope of her authority as a clerk or employee. The money in the cash register was, to the extent of her authority, and the use to which it was necessary for her to put it as such employee, as clearly and as much intrusted to her control and care as the money in a bank is intrusted to the control and care of the cashier, or the money received into the cash till of a general store is intrusted to the control and care of the sales clerks in such store. If a sales clerk in an establishment dealing in general merchandise, during working hours and while actually performing his duties as such clerk, were to fraudulently take and convert to his own use money from the till, to which he had authorized access, and in which it was his duty to place money received for merchandise and from which it was within the scope of his authority to take money for the purpose of making change, no one would be found to doubt for a moment that his act would constitute embezzlement. The case stated is in no respect different from the present case under the facts as proved at the trial and above stated in substance. Emphasis is, however, placed upon the statement of the witness, Humphreys, in one part of his testimony, that Mrs. Howard was not given *authority* but merely *permission* to handle the money in the cash register. But we cannot perceive that that statement in any way shows a qualification of the authority of Mrs. Howard, under her employment, to receive the money for goods sold and to make change, if required, out of the moneys in the register. "Permission" to do an act is "authority" to do it. Every agent is authorized to do whatever the terms of his agency permit him to do and, stating the proposition conversely, is permitted to perform any act within his authority as agent. Moreover, the contractual relation between the principal and the agent must be determined by the facts upon which the relation is founded, and not by the conclusion of the one or the other of the parties from the facts. Under the testimony of Humphreys and in view of the fact that, as above shown, there is no proof whatever showing that the act of Mrs. Howard in taking the money was the result of a conspiracy between her and the defendant conceived and planned before she entered upon the discharge of her duties under her employment with the corporation, it is clear to us that the crime which the evidence appears to sufficiently show was committed by Mrs. Howard was that of embezzlement, as defined by section 508 of the Penal Code. It therefore follows as a matter of law that there exists a variance between the charge of which the defendant was found guilty and the proof. In other words, the conviction of the defendant of grand larceny under the evidence presented by the record cannot be sustained, since, as we have pointed out, he cannot legally be adjudged guilty of an offense different from that in the commission of which he has aided and abetted.

The conclusion thus arrived at is, of course, decisive of the case, and, therefore, so far as is concerned the result so reached, it is wholly unnecessary to consider other points

made by the defendant. But, in view of a probable retrial
of the case, we deem it proper to review some of those points.

There was no prejudicial error in the order overruling
the demurrer to the information. The particular ground of
objection to the information arises from the absence therefrom at the end of each count the conclusion, "contrary to
the form, force and effect of the statute," etc. At the common law, in cases where several different offenses or different statements of the same offense were set up in different
counts, and where in such cases the rule was disregarded and
the form omitted as so required, the omission was held sufficient to vitiate the accusatory pleading. And there are some
cases which hold that under the code system each count must
be followed by the conclusion mentioned. In this case, after
stating the different offenses, the information ends with
said conclusion, and we think that this was sufficient. The
conclusion referred to, although required by the statute
(Pen. Code, secs. 809, 951), involves a conclusion of law and
is a mere matter of form and not of substance. If an indictment or information states facts disclosing that a public
offense has been committed, the statement that the commission of such offense is "contrary to the form, force and effect
of the statute in such case made and provided, and against
the peace and dignity of the people of the state," etc., adds
nothing to the force of the charge as made, and conveys no
information which does not necessarily inhere in or proceed
from the mere statement of the offense itself. Of course, we
are not thus to be understood as holding that the form in
which the legislature has declared that an indictment or information shall be molded need not be adhered to. To the
contrary, we hold that the form as prescribed must or should
be observed. What we have said relative to the proposition
is only for the purpose of showing that the objection against
the information here goes only to a matter of form, and that,
since that pleading does end with the conclusion required by
the statute, the effect of the omission to end each count with
such conclusion, even if necessary in a strict view of the statute, could not, had he been convicted of the proper crime,
justly be held to have affected or impinged upon the substantial rights of the accused, or in any degree deprived him
of a full and fair trial on the charge of which he was so convicted. While section 4½ of article VI of the constitution

is not applicable to this proposition inasmuch as the cause
must be reversed, still the views above expressed are in harmony with the spirit of that provision of our organic law,
and is, moreover, in perfect harmony not only with the spirit
but with the letter of section 960 of the Penal Code.

2. The contention that the defendant was entitled to exercise ten peremptory challenges on each of the counts, or
thirty in all, is wholly destitute of merit.

The ultimate object of the law in authorizing the statement
of different offenses in the same indictment or information
is to prevent mistrials, and experience has demonstrated that
this can in certain cases the better be accomplished by setting forth several different offenses of the same general class,
thus so framing the accusatory pleading as to authorize,
where the evidence justified it, a conviction of the accused of
the precise crime which the evidence shows he has committed, it often being difficult to determine, until the facts are
all brought out and have been presented in regular and concrete form, what particular crime of several belonging to
the same general class has been committed. And, both in
theory and in fact, it is only that particular offense, if any
at all, which the evidence discloses that the accused has committed upon which he is to be tried or, in the last analysis,
is tried; for, very clearly, he can, in contemplation of law,
neither be tried upon, nor convicted under, all the counts.
It follows that the accused was legally entitled to exercise
the right to interpose but ten peremptory challenges. (Pen.
Code, sec. 1070.)

3. It was not necessary for the district attorney to make
an election, before offering proof, of one particular count, of
the three stated in the information, upon which he intended
to rely for a conviction. As we have already shown, it was
the proper practice for the district attorney to prove the
facts and then ask for a conviction of the accused of that
offense of the several charged legally appropriate to the facts
so proved. Indeed, if, as the attorney for the accused contends is true, it was legally incumbent upon the people to
make an election before any evidence was presented, the very
primary purpose of section 954 of the Penal Code would be
defeated. There would in such case be no efficacy in charging different offenses.

There are no other points to which special attention need be given.

For the reasons herein stated, the judgment and the order are reversed.

Ellison, J., *pro tem.*, and Chipman, J., concurred.

[Civ. No. 2000.   Second Appellate District.—September 11, 1916.]

E. B. YOUTZ et al., Appellants, v. FARMERS & MERCHANTS' NATIONAL BANK OF LOS ANGELES, Respondent.

BANK DEPOSIT—ATTACHMENT OF—SUBSTITUTION OF PARTIES.—Under the provisions of section 386 of the Code of Civil Procedure, in an action brought against a bank by a married woman to recover money on deposit therein in her name, which the bank refused to pay to her because it had been attached for a debt of the husband under the claim that it was his money, the bank has the right, upon payment of the money into court, to have the plaintiff in the attachment suit substituted as party defendant in its place.

ID.—PURPOSE OF SECTION 386, CODE OF CIVIL PROCEDURE—CONSTRUCTION.—The design of section 386 of the Code of Civil Procedure is to enable a party who has been sued upon a contract as to which he admits full liability as to the amount thereof to show that a third party not named in the action claims some right to the proceeds of the contract either by way of complete ownership or that he possesses a lien against the same; and so showing, to deposit the money due in court and have the third party made defendant in his stead, thus placing in positions of adversaries the real parties at interest.

APPEAL from an order of the Superior Court of Los Angeles County substituting a party defendant. Louis W. Myers, Judge.

The facts are stated in the opinion of the court.

Harriman, Ryckman & Tuttle, for Appellants.

J. H. Shankland, for Respondent.

JAMES, J.—Defendant bank in September, 1913, had on deposit in the name of E. B. Youtz, wife of Joshua E. Youtz, the sum of $2,704.83. One Gara Williams commenced an action in the superior court against Joshua E. Youtz in which action judgment was sought in the sum of eleven thousand dollars on promissory notes. A writ of attachment was served upon the defendant bank with notice that all debts or credits owing by the bank to "J. E. Youtz, . . . E. B. Youtz, but belonging to Joshua E. Youtz, or either of them," were attached. The bank made answer to the writ stating the fact as to the name in which the deposit was held. E. B. Youtz thereupon drew her check against the bank for the full amount of the deposit which demand the bank refused to honor. She then brought this action to recover the money. The defendant bank appeared before answering, and by motion asked that the plaintiff in the attachment suit be substituted in its stead, upon the money being deposited in court. In the affidavit of its cashier the bank asserted that the plaintiff in the attachment suit claimed a lien upon the fund upon the ground that the money in fact was the property of Joshua E. Youtz, although deposited by his wife. Other facts showing the pendency of the attachment suit, and the issuance and service of the writ of attachment or garnishment, were set out in the affidavit. No counter-showing of facts appears to have been made, E. B. Youtz resting her opposition to the motion on the claim that the case furnished no sufficient ground to support an order substituting Williams as defendant. The court, upon the full amount of the credit being deposited in its charge, and the further sum of $17.87 interest, made an order substituting Williams in the place of the bank as defendant. It may be here remarked that no point is made that the sheriff should have been made substituted defendant where the attachment suit had not gone to judgment. The court would have the power, nevertheless, to require the sheriff to be brought in, and if it was required to so do we must assume that such action would be taken in the progress of the case. The appeal taken by E. B. Youtz is from the order made as described.

The proceeding taken by respondent was in strict accord with the provisions of section 386 of the Code of Civil Procedure. The design of that statute is to enable a party who has been sued upon a contract as to which he admits full liability as to the amount thereof to show that a third party not named in the action claims some right to the proceeds of the contract either by way of complete ownership or that he possesses a lien against the same; and so showing, to deposit the money due in court and have the third party made defendant in his stead, thus placing in positions of adversaries the real parties at interest. Appellants' counsel insist that the bank could not claim the benefit of section 386 of the Code of Civil Procedure, and secure a discharge from liability toward its depositor, unless a lien in fact was created against the credit in its hands by service of the garnishment process— that Joshua E. Youtz, the defendant in the attachment suit, must have been possessed of the right to maintain an action of *indebitatus assumpsit* against the bank on account of the deposit before any attachment lien could result. *Redondo Beach Co.* v. *California Loan and T. Co.*, 101 Cal. 322, [35 Pac. 896], is cited to this point. The principal conclusion announced in that case was that a mere equitable claim, or a credit not liquidated in the sense that it had become a demand of a fixed and certain amount, could not be reached by attachment process. *Hassie* v. *God Is With Us Congregation*, 35 Cal. 378, is to the same effect. It must be kept in mind that in the cases cited the questions arose between the attachment plaintiff and the garnishee. There is room for distinction, we apprehend, between a case where a person served with garnishment disclaims liability because the debt is unliquidated or is attended by equities held in his favor and a case like this one. Can it be that a debtor, being possessed of money, may place that money to the credit of another in a bank, and that when so placed the credit becomes immune to attachment process issued against all except the nominal depositor? Surely the law will not spend its effort in furnishing to debtors such an easy and reliable means whereby creditors may be defrauded. With notice as to the real ownership of a deposit, and claim made by a third person under attachment process, a banking institution would hardly be justified in honoring the check of the nominal depositor. Section 544 of the Code of Civil Procedure, provides that every person having under his control credits belonging to the defendant, when served with attachment process, becomes liable to the attachment plaintiff for the amount of the credit. In this case Williams claimed that the money to the credit of E. B. Youtz belonged to Joshua E. Youtz, his debtor, and notified the bank of that claim and attached the credit. E. B. Youtz sued the bank for the money. If the money was Joshua E. Youtz' and the bank had full notice of this claim, it would, in our opinion, become liable to Williams in the event that it paid over the money to the wife and the fact was determined to be that Joshua E. Youtz owned the credit. It adopted the most convenient and reasonable course to free itself from liability for costs by asking that the real contending parties be compelled to try out the issue between them.

The final point made in the brief of appellants is that the provisions of section 386 of the Code of Civil Procedure, are in derogation of a party's right not to be deprived of property without due process of law. Using this case as an illustration it is said in argument that the order substituting Williams as defendant in the place of the bank left the plaintiff without recourse in the recovery of damages in the sum of five hundred dollars which she claimed against respondent. If it appeared that this result followed the action of the court, then a case would be presented where the making of the order for substitution would amount to an abuse of discretion. The court is vested with discretion as to the matter of granting such a motion as that here considered. But there is nothing in the statement of plaintiff's cause of action which shows that plaintiff was entitled to recover special damages in any amount, and plaintiff showed no facts in opposition to the motion, which would tend to establish her right to recover on the account last mentioned. The detriment caused by the breach of an obligation to pay money only, is deemed to be the amount due by the terms of the obligation with interest thereon. (Civ. Code, sec. 3302.) The court did require respondent to pay into court the full amount of the deposit with accrued interest to the date of the order.

We are of the opinion that the court was authorized to make the order complained of.

The order is affirmed.

Conrey, P. J., and Shaw, J., concurred.

[Civ. No. 2003. Second Appellate District.—September 11, 1916.]

W. B. MERWIN, Appellant, v. ROSALIA B. SHAFFNER, Respondent.

BROKER'S COMMISSIONS — PROCURING LESSEES FOR REAL PROPERTY — PLEADING—SUFFICIENCY OF COMPLAINT.—In an action to recover commissions alleged to have been earned by procuring a lessee for real property, the complaint states a cause of action, where it is alleged that the defendant made and delivered to the plaintiff an instrument in writing by the terms of which the defendant agreed to pay plaintiff a commission if he procured a lease upon the terms specified in the writing, or other terms acceptable to the defendant, and that plaintiff did procure persons and produced them to defendant who were ready, able, and willing to enter into a lease upon terms which by the written acknowledgment of defendant were acceptable, but that defendant thereafter refused, and continues to refuse, to enter into any lease with such proposed lessees and disclaimed and repudiated any liability to plaintiff for commissions.

ID.—COMMISSIONS—WHEN EARNED.—Where the agreement to pay commissions upon the sale or leasing of real estate is in writing, the agent, as a condition to the earning of his commissions, need only produce to his principal persons who are ready, able, and willing to contract according to the terms proposed or acceptable to such principal.

ID.—OFFER TO LEASE—TIME OF COMMENCEMENT.—An offer in writing to lease real property is not invalid by reason of the failure to specify any time for the commencement of the lease, as it is implied that the term will commence upon the making thereof.

ID.—REPUDIATION OF LIABILITY TO PAY COMMISSION—RIGHT OF AGENT. Where a writing authorizing the procuring of a lessee for real property provides for the time of the payment of the commission "along during the first year," and the liability to pay the commission is repudiated after the rendition of all of the consideration required of the agent, he may sue to recover the amount of such commission.

APPEAL from a judgment of the Superior Court of Los Angeles County. Charles Wellborn, Judge.

The facts are stated in the opinion of the court.

Benjamin E. Page, Arthur C. Hurt, and Arthur F. Coe, for Appellant.

Denis & Loewenthal, and George W. McDill, for Respondent.

JAMES, J.—Plaintiff brought this action to recover commissions alleged to have been earned by procuring a lessee for real property owned by the defendant. A general demurrer to the complaint was sustained without leave to amend. A judgment of dismissal followed, from which this appeal was taken.

In the complaint it was alleged that on or about the twenty-second day of January, 1913, the defendant made and delivered to the plaintiff the following instrument in writing:

"Los Angeles, Cal. Jan. 22nd, 1913.

"W. B. Merwin,

    "424 H. W. Hellman Bldg.,

      "Los Angeles, Cal.

"Dear Sir:

"You are hereby authorized to find a lessee for my property at (611 West 6th street), the east 40 feet of the west 85 feet of lots 1 and 2, block 102, Belleview Terrace Tract, for the term of 99 years, at the annual net rental of $3000.00, payable monthly in advance for the first ten years, and an annual net rental of $4800.00 for the remainder of the 99 years term, payable monthly. Should you secure a lessee acceptable to me on the above terms, or terms acceptable to me, I agree to pay you a commission $2500, payable along during the 1st year. This is exclusively good to you for 60 days from date.

"A building not to cost less than $40,000 to $50,000 on or before 10 years from date of lease, to be built upon the property.

Yours respectfully,
"ROSALIA B. SHAFFNER."

It was then alleged that pursuant to the authority given by this writing the plaintiff procured three individuals to make an offer to lease the property described, the offer being submitted in the following form:

"Los Angeles, Jan. 24, 1913.

"W. B. Merwin & Co.,

    "H. W. Hellman Building,

      "Los Angeles, California.

"Gentlemen:

"On behalf of myself, Mr. Jeff P. Chandler and Mr. Leo S. Chandler, I hereby make you the following proposition: We will lease, for a period of ninety-nine years, the Mrs. R. B.

Shaffner lot, having a frontage of forty (40) feet and a
depth of one hundred twenty (120) feet on the north side of
Sixth street, eighty (80) feet west of Grand avenue, in this
city, at the following rentals, viz.:

"At the rate of $3,000 per year for the first year.

"At the rate of $2400 per year for the next five years.

"At the rate of $3000 per year for the next four years.

"At the rate of $3600 per year for the next five years.

"At the rate of $4200 per year for the next five years.

"At the rate of $5000 per year for the last twenty-nine
years.

"All rentals payable monthly in advance.

"We will agree to build a building upon the property cost-
ing not less than $40,000 within ten years, and we will pay
all taxes and assessments of every kind that may be levied
against or become a lien upon the property during the life of
our lease.   Yours truly,
                                "SHIRLEY C. WARD."

The allegation then follows that the plaintiff communicated
the offer last set out to the defendant, and that the defendant
thereupon made the following indorsement upon the paper
containing the offer:

          "Los Angeles, Calif., January 25, 1913.
"Messrs. W. B. Merwin & Co.,
     "Los Angeles, Calif.
"Dear Sirs:
     "I hereby accept the terms and conditions of the above
agreement.   ROSALIA B. SHAFFNER."

It was then alleged that the persons mentioned in the offer,
of which acceptance was made by defendant, were and continued to be ready, able, and willing to execute a lease upon
the property, and that they did within sixty days from the
22d of January, 1913, communicate to defendant their readiness to execute the lease and offered to so execute it, but that
defendant refused and continues to refuse to enter into any
lease with such proposed lessees, and disclaimed and repudiated any liability to plaintiff for commissions.

We think the demurrer to this complaint was improperly
sustained. The defendant agreed in writing to pay to the
plaintiff a commission if he procured a lease upon the terms
specified by her or other terms acceptable to her. He did

procure persons and produced them to her who were ready, able, and willing, according to the allegations of his complaint, to enter into a lease upon terms which by the written acknowledgment of the defendant were acceptable to her. Considering the allegations of the complaint, no ground appears to excuse the defendant from entering into the lease as proposed and accepted, and the plaintiff having done all that it was conditioned he should do, appears to have fully earned the commission agreed to be paid. The fact that in the offer of Ward and his associates to make a lease no time was specified for the commencement thereof, was not a defect fatal to the validity of the offer. There being no condition specified in the offer as to any different time for the commencement of the lease, it would be implied that the term was to commence upon the making thereof. It has often been held that where the agreement to pay commissions upon the sale or leasing of real estate is in writing, the agent, as a condition to the earning of his commissions, need only produce to his principal persons who are ready, able, and willing to contract according to the terms proposed or acceptable to such principal. In the first instrument signed by the defendant the time for the payment of the commission was stated to be "along during the first year." As it appears in the allegations of the complaint that the defendant refused to enter into any lease at all, but repudiated her liability to pay commission, the well-established rule would apply which permits the other party to the contract in such a case, after having rendered fully all of the consideration to be by him rendered, to sue to recover the amount agreed to be paid. As we view the complaint, it stated a good cause of action and was not subject to the objection raised by the demurrer.

The judgment is reversed.

Conrey, P. J., and Shaw, J., concurred.

A petition for a rehearing of this cause was denied by the district court of appeal on October 10, 1916, and a petition to have the cause heard in the supreme court, after judgment in the district court of appeal, was denied by the supreme court on November 9, 1916.

[Civ. No. 1944. First Appellate District.—September 12, 1916.]

MARIA MACHADO, Respondent, v. FRANK R. MACHADO, Appellant.

MANDATE—EXECUTION ON ALIMONY ORDER—REVOCATION OF.—An order commanding the clerk of the superior court to issue a writ of execution to enforce an order for the payment of alimony *pendente lite* in an action of divorce, will be reversed on appeal, where it is made to appear that the order granting the alimony had been revoked before the making of the order appealed from.

APPEAL from an order of the Superior Court of Santa Clara County made after judgment directing the clerk to issue execution. J. R. Welch, Judge.

The facts are stated in the opinion of the court.

A. M. Free, C. L. Witten, R. V. Burns, and F. H. Bloomingdale, for Appellant.

Joseph Rafael, for Respondent.

THE COURT.—Upon the petition of the plaintiff the court below granted a writ of mandate addressed to the clerk of the court, commanding him to issue a writ of execution to enforce an order for the payment of alimony *pendente lite.* It appears, however, that before the issuance of the writ of mandate the order granting alimony had been revoked, and that the petitioner was not entitled to the amounts for the enforcement of payment of which the execution was issued. Under these circumstances there is nothing for this court to do but to reverse the order appealed from, and that will be the judgment of the court.

[Civ. No. 1995.   Second Appellate District.—September 12, 1916.]

JENNIE EATON et al., Respondents, v. SOUTHERN PACIFIC COMPANY (a Corporation), Appellant.

COSTS—REPORTER'S TRANSCRIPT—APPEAL.—Where a judgment is affirmed on appeal, the respondent is not entitled to recover the amount paid for the reporter's transcript of the testimony taken at the trial, which was obtained solely for the purpose of assisting respondent's counsel in the preparation of amendments to a bill of exceptions proposed by the appellant on its motion for a new trial in the superior court.

ID.—COST OF PRINTING ANSWER TO PETITION FOR REHEARING—WHEN NOT ALLOWABLE.—Where a judgment affirmed on appeal had become final prior to the going into effect of the amendment of 1913 to section 1027 of the Code of Civil Procedure, allowing the costs of printing briefs to a limited amount as part of the costs on appeal, the respondent is not entitled to the cost of printing her brief in answer to the petition of the appellant for a hearing of the appeal in the supreme court after decision by the district court of appeal, notwithstanding the provision of section 1034 of such code that the time for filing a memorandum of costs on appeal is limited to begin after the filing of the *remittitur* in the superior court.

ID.—TIME OF ACCRUAL OF COSTS.—The right of the prevailing party to recover any costs on appeal is obtained by virtue of the judgment as rendered, and this necessarily includes the assumption that he is to have those costs and only those costs to which he is entitled by law at the time of the rendition of such judgment.

APPEAL from an order of the Superior Court of Santa Barbara County taxing costs. Samuel E. Crow, Judge.

The facts are stated in the opinion of the court.

Canfield & Starbuck, for Appellant.

Richards & Carrier, John J. Squier, and John William Heaney, for Respondents.

CONREY, P. J.—Upon a former appeal by the defendant in this case the judgment was affirmed (22 Cal. App. 461, [134 Pac. 801]). The judgment on appeal was rendered July 7, 1913; became final August 6, 1913; an application for a rehearing in the supreme court was denied within thirty

days thereafter; a *remittitur* from this court went down to
the superior court on September 8, 1913. Thereafter respondent filed her memorandum of costs, and appellant applied to the superior court for an order to strike out the
memorandum of costs on the ground that the same had been
illegally filed, and also demanded that certain items in the
cost bill be stricken out upon the ground that they are not
legally allowable as costs of the appeal. The items in dispute
are: (1) One hundred and four dollars paid for a reporter's
transcript of the testimony taken at the trial and which respondent claims as an expense "for transcript of testimony
used by plaintiffs in preparing record on appeal and amendments to defendant's bill of exceptions used upon appeal."
(2) Ten dollars and eighty cents claimed by respondent as
cost of printing answer to defendant's petition for a rehearing in the supreme court. This appeal is by the defendant
from an order denying said motion.

By an amendment to section 1027 of the Code of Civil Procedure relating to costs on appeal, which amendment became
effective on the tenth day of August, 1913, it is provided as
a part of that section that "the party entitled to costs, or
to whom costs are awarded, may recover all amounts actually paid out by him in connection with said appeal and the
preparation of the record for the appeal, including the costs
of printing briefs; provided, however, that no amount shall
be allowed as costs of printing briefs in excess of fifty dollars
to any one party."

The record on this appeal shows that the reporter's transcript was obtained by respondent solely for the purpose of
assisting her counsel in the preparation of amendments to a
bill of exceptions proposed by the defendant on its motion
for a new trial in the superior court. The expense thus incurred was purely an expense in the conduct of the case in
the superior court, and was not a part of the preparation of
the record for the appeal. Therefore the item in question
cannot be allowed even if, as contended by respondent, her
right to costs is governed by the amendment of section 1027.
(*Bank of Woodland* v. *Hiatt*, 59 Cal. 580.)

With respect to the other item, it is necessary to determine
whether respondent's right to costs on appeal accrued prior
to August 10, 1913, or subsequent thereto. The general rule
is that the right to costs accrues at the time when the judg-

ment is rendered, notwithstanding that the judgment has not become final or that entry thereof has been stayed. (Code Civ. Proc., sec. 1033.) Respondent claims, however, that her right to costs on appeal did not accrue until the *remittitur* was sent down to the superior court. This contention is based upon section 1034 of the Code of Civil Procedure, from which it appears that whenever costs are awarded to a party by an appellate court the time within which he may file in the superior court a memorandum of those costs is limited to begin after the filing of the *remittitur*. It seems to us, however, that since the right of the prevailing party to recover any costs on appeal is obtained by virtue of the judgment as rendered, this necessarily includes the assumption that he is to have those costs, and only those costs, to which he is entitled by law at the time of the rendition of such judgment. A judgment on appeal, like a judgment of a trial court, has the force and effect of a judgment from the time of its entry. The fact that within a limited time thereafter a rehearing may be ordered, while it may suspend the operation of the judgment, does not in the meantime deprive the judgment of its inherent attributes as an act of the court, any more than one could say that a judgment of the superior court is no judgment until it has become final. It follows that in the present case respondent is not entitled to recover the cost of printing her brief in answer to the petition for a rehearing in the supreme court.

The order taxing costs and allowing the items above mentioned is reversed, and it is directed that the superior court enter an order disallowing the said items.

James, J., and Shaw, J., concurred.

A petition to have the cause heard in the supreme court, after judgment in the district court of appeal, was denied by the supreme court on November 9, 1916.

[Crim. No. 498. Second Appellate District.—September 12, 1916.]

In the Matter of the Application of JOHN E. SAUL, for a Writ of Habeas Corpus.*

DIVORCE—DENIAL OF RELIEF—AWARD OF CUSTODY OF CHILDREN—POWER OF COURT.—In an action for divorce, the court has power under section 138 of the Civil Code to make an order affecting the custody of the children of the marriage, although the divorce is denied.

ID.—CONSTRUCTION OF SECTION 138, CIVIL CODE.—Section 138 of the Civil Code itself does not state any limitation of its effect to cases in which divorce is denied, and if such limitation be imposed upon the language of the statute it must be a limitation by construction, but such section is designed for the protection of children and should be liberally construed.

APPLICATION for a Writ of Habeas Corpus originally made to the District Court of Appeal for the Second Appellate District.

The facts are stated in the opinion of the court.

Davis & Rush, John S. Cooper, and Wm. A. Gaines, for Petitioner.

Harry A. Chamberlain, for Respondent.

CONREY, P. J.—*Habeas corpus.* The petitioner is held in custody by the sheriff of Los Angeles County under an order made by the superior court of that county, wherein petitioner was adjudged guilty of contempt in that he willfully violated certain orders of that court. The return filed herein by the sheriff sets forth a commitment entered in a certain action wherein John E. Saul was plaintiff and Emma Saul defendant. The commitment is in the form of an order signed by a judge of the superior court which, after reciting that the plaintiff John E. Saul was then before the

---

*On September 28, 1916, a petition of John E. Saul for a writ of *habeas corpus*, similar to the one here considered, was denied by the supreme court. On January 17, 1917, the petitioner was discharged, upon another writ, by the district court of appeal of the second appellate district, upon proof that he had endeavored to bring back the child, Dinah Saul, to California, and was no longer able to comply with the court's order as to that matter.

court in person and with counsel in response to an attachment and arrest for the alleged contempt, continues as follows:

"And it appearing to the satisfaction of the court after a full hearing had, that heretofore, to-wit, on the 25th day of March, 1908, a judgment was duly given and made and thereafter duly entered herein in Book 168, page 184, of Judgments, Records of the County of Los Angeles, State of California, and notice thereof was duly given to the plaintiff herein, John E. Saul, wherein and whereby it, was ordered, adjudged and decreed as follows, to-wit:

" 'That the care and custody of the minor children of plaintiff and defendant be and the same hereby is awarded as follows, to-wit: the care and custody of Eddie Saul and of John Saul to the plaintiff herein; the care and custody of George Saul, Dinah Saul and Walter Saul to the defendant herein.'

"And it further appearing to the court that subsequent to the entry and rendition of said judgment and heretofore, to-wit: on the 18th day of February, 1916, and while the said George Saul and Dinah Saul were in the care and custody of the defendant herein, Emma Saul, pursuant to the terms of said judgment hereinabove referred to, said plaintiff herein, John E. Saul, did by stratagem and fraud and willfully and unlawfully and contrary to the provisions of said judgment, take the said George Saul and Dinah Saul from the custody and care of the defendant herein, Emma Saul, without her knowledge or consent and against her will and took said George Saul and Dinah Saul without the jurisdiction of this court.

"And it further appearing to the satisfaction of the court that said plaintiff, John E. Saul, now has the custody and care of Dinah Saul contrary and in disobedience to the judgment of this court hereinabove referred to.

"And it further appearing to the satisfaction of the court that the said plaintiff, John E. Saul, has refused and still refuses to return and deliver the care and custody of the said Dinah Saul to the defendant herein, Emma Saul, in accordance with and pursuant to the terms of said judgment herein referred to and made a part hereof; and that the said failure to deliver the care and custody of said Dinah Saul consists in the omission to perform an act which is yet in the power of the said plaintiff, John E. Saul, to perform:

"Now, therefore, it is hereby ordered, adjudged and decreed that the plaintiff herein, John E. Saul, is guilty of a contempt of this court and that he be imprisoned in the county jail of the county of Los Angeles, state of California, until he shall have delivered the custody and care of Dinah Saul to the care and custody of Emma Saul, defendant herein.

"You are, therefore, commanded forthwith to convey the said John E. Saul to the jail of the county of Los Angeles, and there commit him until he shall have delivered the custody and care of Dinah Saul to Emma Saul, or be discharged according to law."

In the petition for the writ of *habeas corpus* it is stated that the action of John E. Saul against Emma Saul was tried upon a complaint of the plaintiff and cross-complaint of the defendant and the answers thereto, each of said parties seeking a divorce upon grounds stated in their several pleadings. Copies of those pleadings, and of the findings and judgment, are made part of the petition in this proceeding. It appears therefrom that the court found each party guilty of the misconduct alleged in the complaint and cross-complaint respectively, and for that reason entered its decree denying a divorce. Thereupon, and as a part of the same decree, the court proceeded to award the care and custody of their minor children, some of them to the plaintiff and some of them to the defendant, in the terms quoted in the foregoing order of contempt. That decree was entered in March, 1908, and the minors George and Dinah Saul remained in the custody of their mother, Emma Saul, until they were taken from her by John E. Saul in February, 1916.

The allegations in the petition showing that the action of *Saul* v. *Saul* was for a divorce, and that the petition for divorce was refused, are not denied in the return filed herein; therefore those allegations must be taken as true. (*Ex parte Smith*, 143 Cal. 368, 370, [77 Pac. 180]; *In re Hoffman*, 155 Cal. 114, 119, [132 Am. St. Rep. 75, 99 Pac. 517]; *In re Collins*, 151 Cal. 340, 342, [129 Am. St. Rep. 122, 90 Pac. 827, 91 Pac. 397].) Or if formal proof thereof be necessary, it undoubtedly could readily be supplied in this case. Counsel for respondent in effect admits the facts as stated, but merely relies upon the point that we are limited to an examination of the return. Holding, as we do, that the facts alleged in the petition, showing denial of a divorce in the principal action, are subject to proof herein, we shall, in view of the statements of counsel, consider them as admitted. This will bring us to the petitioner's main proposition, which is, that where in an action for divorce the judgment denies a divorce, the court is without power, then or thereafter in that action, to make an order affecting the custody of children.

Sections 136 and 138 of the Civil Code are found in article IV of the chapter concerning divorce, which article contains sundry general provisions relating to divorce actions. Section 136, under the heading "Maintenance by husband where judgment is denied," reads as follows: "Though judgment of divorce is denied, the court may, in an action for divorce, provide for the maintenance by the husband, of the wife and children of the marriage, or any of them." Section 138, under the heading "Custody and maintenance of minors during actions for divorce," reads as follows: "In actions for divorce the court may, during the pendency of the action, or at the final hearing or at any time thereafter during the minority of any of the children of the marriage, make such order for the custody, care, education, maintenance and support of such minor children as may seem necessary or proper, and may at any time modify or vacate the same." Section 214 of the Civil Code occurs in the title on "Parent and Child" and in the chapter entitled "Children by Birth." Section 214 says: "When a husband and wife live in a state of separation, without being divorced, any court of competent jurisdiction, upon application of either, if an inhabitant of this state, may inquire into the custody of any unmarried minor child of the marriage, and may award the custody of such child to either, for such time and under such regulations as the case may require. The decision of the court must be guided by the rules prescribed in section two hundred and forty-six." Section 246 declares the considerations by which the court is to be guided in awarding the custody of a minor. Where the custody of children is to be awarded, whether in a divorce action or in a separate proceeding under section 214, the superior court is the court having jurisdiction of those matters. It thus appears that there are two classes of actions or proceedings wherein superior courts have jurisdiction to determine the custody of a child at the instance of one or both of its parents. In addition to this, it may be observed that where children are brought before a court in *habeas corpus* proceedings involving adverse claims of right to their custody, the court is not obliged to recognize either parent as entitled to the custody as of right, but may take into consideration such facts as are necessary to enable the court to determine what are the best interests of the children.

The petitioner does not deny the existence of these powers and judicial processes as provided by law. His contention is that the power of the court with respect to the custody of children in a divorce action is wholly derived from the statutes, and that by the terms of the code sections to which we have referred the right to award custody of children in a divorce action is strictly limited as an incidental power to be exercised only when a divorce is granted. On the other side it is contended that the jurisdiction exercised by the superior court in divorce cases is a part of its general chancery jurisdiction which includes the care of children as wards of the court; that since the parents of these children came before the court as a court of equity demanding relief on behalf of their children, and since they might have done that same thing by filing petitions for that purpose without asking for a divorce, no good reason appears why the court, though it denies the divorce, should turn the parties entirely out of court in order that they might come back into the same court to demand separately the same relief as was sought in this action so far as the children are concerned. Such was the opinion of the supreme court of Arkansas, in *Horton* v. *Horton*, 75 Ark. 22, [5 Ann. Cas. 91, 86 S. W. 824]. In that case, as here, no separation of the family was brought about by the court's order. The court merely recognized and found the facts as they existed, and then made an order for the well-being of the children.

The decisions upon this subject are conflicting. In some states it has been held that where the divorce is denied custody of the children may be awarded. (*Horton* v. *Horton*, 75 Ark. 22, [5 Ann. Cas. 91, 86 S. W. 824]; *Hoskins* v. *Hoskins*, 28 Ky. Law Rep. 435, [89 S. W. 478]; *Knoll* v. *Knoll*, 114 La. 703, [38 South. 523].) Decisions cited to the contrary effect are: *Redding* v. *Redding* (N. J.), 85 Atl. 712, 716; *Thomas* v. *Thomas*, 250 Ill. 354, [Ann. Cas. 1912B, 344, 35 L. R. A. (N. S.) 1158, 95 N. E. 345]. See, also, *Davis* v. *Davis*, 75 N. Y. 221, 226, *Robinson* v. *Robinson*, 146 App. Div. 533,

[131 N. Y. Supp. 260], and *Light* v. *Light*, 124 App. Div. 567, [108 N. Y. Supp. 931]. In *Thomas* v. *Thomas*, 250 Ill. 354, [Ann. Cas. 1912B, 344, 35 L. R. A. (N. S.) 1158, 95 N. E. 345], there is a well-reasoned dissenting opinion by Carter, J., closing as follows: "The parties being before a court of equity, what more proper time can there be to adjudicate the rights of the parents to the custody of the children? (2 Nelson on Divorce and Separation, p. 979.) The court having acquired jurisdiction of the subject matter and the parties to the suit at the instance and by the prayer of the plaintiff in error, I cannot reach any other conclusion than that, on the plainest principles of equity, she should be precluded from questioning the jurisdiction of the court which she herself invoked."

Section 138 of the Civil Code, quoted above, recognizes the power of the court in an action for divorce to make orders concerning the custody of the children of the marriage, either during the pendency of the action, or at the final hearing, or at any time thereafter during the minority of the children. If the court at the final hearing in making its decree granting or refusing a divorce is silent with respect to the custody of children, and fails to make any provision for this custody and care, it would seem that this is a complete and final determination of that case. But if the court, in view of the facts found by it, deems that the welfare of the children requires that some order for the custody and maintenance of the children be made and makes that order as a part of its decree, or in specific terms retains the case for the purposes of such custody and maintenance, we find no sufficient reason for holding that such action by the court is beyond its powers as declared in section 138. The section itself does not state any limitation of its effect to cases in which divorce is denied. If such limitation be imposed upon the language of the statute it must be a limitation by construction. But it has been held that the section is designed for the protection of children and should be liberally construed. (*Harlan* v. *Harlan*, 154 Cal. 341, 350, [98 Pac. 32].) It seems to us that this rule of liberal construction may fairly be applied to the question here presented.

The petition herein, and the sheriff's return, show that the petitioner is also detained in custody by virtue of another commitment for a second contempt of the authority of the

superior court, in a matter arising out of the same divorce
action of *Saul* v. *Saul*. In view of our decision upon the
matters herein discussed, it is not necessary to make a further statement, which would involve the same questions and
lead to the same result.

The writ is discharged, and petitioner is remanded to the
custody of the sheriff.

James, J., and Shaw, J., concurred.

[Civ. No. 1948. Second Appellate District.—September 12, 1916.]

HIRAM H. MORE, Appellant, v. BOARD OF SUPERVISORS OF THE COUNTY OF SAN BERNARDINO et al., Respondents.

SAN BERNARDINO COUNTY CHARTER—AMENDMENT CONCERNING COUNTY
OFFICERS — EFFECT OF.—The amendment to the charter of the
county of San Bernardino approved by the electors at the general
election held in November, 1914, and approved by the legislature
by resolution which was filed with the Secretary of State January
30, 1915 (Stats. 1915, p. 1727), which, without naming any of
the seven articles contained in such charter, purported to strike
from such instrument "sections 4, 5 and 6 of said charter" and
insert in lieu thereof the following amendment to be known as
section 4 thereof, to wit: "Section four (4): All county officers
other than supervisors of said county shall be elected at each general election by the qualified electors of said county as is now, or
may be hereafter provided by general law, and all deputies and
assistants to such county officers shall be appointed as is now or
may be hereafter provided by general law; and the powers and
duties of such officers, deputies and assistants shall be such as are
now or may be hereafter provided by general law, and any part of
this charter in conflict herewith is hereby repealed," is fatally
defective as an attempted direct repeal of any sections of the
original charter, because it is impossible to determine what sections
of the charter are intended to be repealed; but such amendment is
effective in that it adds to the charter a new section, and by so doing
impliedly repeals those provisions contained in the original charter
which relate to the same subject matter as the new section and
are in conflict therewith.

ID.—COUNTY OFFICERS—SHERIFF AND CORONER—CHARTER PROVISIONS
NOT REPEALED BY AMENDMENT.—Section 1 of article II of the

charter of the county of San Bernardino which provides for certain
county officers, including a sheriff and a coroner, and section 2 of
the same article which provides that the sheriff shall be *ex-officio*
coroner, were not repealed either expressly or impliedly by the
charter amendment adopted at the general election held in November, 1914.

ID.—CONSOLIDATION OF OFFICES OF SHERIFF AND CORONER — VALID
CHARTER PROVISION.—The office of coroner is a separate office from
that of sheriff, with separate duties and powers as provided by
law, and when the sheriff is performing the duties of coroner he is
in contemplation of law the coroner of the county as distinctly
and completely as any other duly appointed or elected person
would be when lawfully performing those duties, and therefore, the
powers and duties pertaining to the office of coroner are not affected
by the charter provision that the person appointed as sheriff shall
also be the coroner.

ID.—OFFICERS PROVIDED FOR BY CHARTER NOT ABOLISHED BY AMENDMENT.—Such amendment in providing that all county officers other
than the supervisors shall be elected as is now or may be hereafter
provided by general law, and that the powers and duties of such
officers shall be such as are now or may be hereafter provided by
general law, did not intend to refer only to those officers provided
for by general law, and thereby eliminate some county officers provided for by the charter and not by general law, so that such
offices ceased to exist.

ID.—CHARTER PROVISIONS AS TO CONSOLIDATION OF COUNTY OFFICES—
SECTION OF POLITICAL CODE—PROVISIONS NOT SUPERSEDED BY.—The
provisions of the charter of the county of San Bernardino with
respect to the consolidation of county offices, even under such charter
amendment, are not superseded by the terms of section 4017 of the
Political Code upon the same subject, and which does not provide
for the consolidation of the offices of sheriff and coroner, in view
of section 7½ of article XI of the constitution, which provides that
county charters shall provide "for the consolidation and segregation
of county offices."

APPEAL from a judgment of the Superior Court of San
Bernardino County. H. T. Dewhirst, and J. W. Curtis,
Judges.

The facts are stated in the opinion of the court.

Rex B. Goodcell, and Robt. M. McHargue, for Appellant.

T. W. Duckworth, and John L. Campbell, for Respondents.

CONREY, P. J.—In this proceeding the plaintiff applied for a writ of *mandamus* requiring the defendants to appoint some fit and proper person to the office of county coroner of the county of San Bernardino, the plaintiff claiming that there is a vacancy in that office.   From a judgment in favor of the defendants, plaintiff appeals.

Pursuant to the provisions of section 7½ of article XI of the constitution of California, the charter for the county was adopted at the general election of 1912 and thereafter approved by the legislature. (Stats. 1913, p. 1652 et seq.) That charter consists of seven articles; six of those articles contained sections numbered 4, 5, and 6.   Section 4 of article I made it the duty of the board of supervisors, at its first regular meeting after noon of the first Monday after the first day of January, 1915, to appoint each and all of the county officers provided for by the charter or by general law, for a term of four years.   Sections 5 and 6 of that article relate to the appointment and duties of deputies in the several county offices.

At the general election held in November, 1914, the electors of San Bernardino County approved an amendment to the county charter, which amendment was duly approved by the legislature by resolution which was filed with the Secretary of State January 30, 1915. (Stats. 1915, p. 1727.)   That amendment, without naming any article of the charter, purported to strike from the charter "sections 4, 5 and 6 of said charter" and insert in lieu thereof the following amendment to be known as section 4 thereof, to wit: "Section four (4): All county officers other than supervisors of said county shall be elected at each general election by the qualified electors of said county as is now, or may be hereafter provided by general law, and all deputies and assistants to such county officers shall be appointed as is now, or may be hereafter provided by general law; and the powers and duties of such officers, deputies and assistants shall be such as are now or may be hereafter provided by general law, and any part of this charter in conflict herewith is hereby repealed."

Section 1 of article II of the charter provides for certain county officers, including a sheriff and a coroner.   Section 2 of the same article provides that "The following county officers are hereby consolidated: . . . (b) The sheriff shall be *ex officio* coroner." (Stats. 1913, p. 1656.)   Section 4 of article II provides that "Each county officer shall have the powers and perform the duties now or hereafter prescribed by general law as to such officer, except as otherwise provided by this charter; and shall have and perform such other powers and duties as are or shall be prescribed by this charter."

As an attempted direct repeal of any sections of the original charter the amendment is fatally defective, because it is impossible to determine what sections of the charter are intended to be repealed. But the amendment is effective in that it adds to the charter a new section, and by so doing impliedly repeals those provisions contained in the original charter which relate to the same subject matter as the new section and are in conflict therewith. The county officers appointed in January, 1915, will continue to hold their offices until the time regularly appointed by general law for the election of county officers; at which time their successors will be elected the same as if the present officers had been elected under the general law. The charter amendment does not state what county officers shall exist in San Bernardino County. Those officers are designated by sections 1 and 2 of article II, and there is no inconsistency between the amendment and these two sections which would require us to hold that the latter are repealed by implication. The office of coroner is a separate office from that of sheriff, with separate duties and powers as provided by law. The sheriff by virtue of his appointment as sheriff becomes coroner of the county; he is "*ex officio* coroner." When performing the duties of a coroner he is in contemplation of law the coroner of the county as distinctly and completely as any other duly appointed or elected person would be when lawfully performing those duties. Upon the facts of this case we think that there is no sound reason for holding that the office of coroner of San Bernardino County is at this time vacant.

Counsel for plaintiff insist that the amendment, in providing that all county officers other than supervisors shall be elected as is now or may be hereafter provided by general law, and that the powers and duties of such officers shall be such as are now or may be hereafter provided for by general law, intended to refer only to those officers provided for by general law; and that thereby the amendment eliminated some county officers provided for by the charter. Article IV of the charter provides for a county purchasing agent and article VI for a county highway commissioner; defining their powers and duties. It is contended that since the general law does not provide any powers or duties for either of these officers, the offices no longer exist. From this it is argued that the provisions of the charter as to consolidation of certain county officers are no longer effective because such consolidation affects directly and materially the powers and duties of the officer. But we think that the consequences thus contended for do not follow. As we have above suggested, the powers and duties pertaining to the office of coroner are not affected by providing that the person appointed as sheriff shall also be the coroner. Neither do we see any reason for holding here that the offices of county purchasing agent and county highway commissioner are abolished by this amendment. The general law of the state provides for certain county officers, among whom are a sheriff and a coroner, and "such other officers as may be provided by law." (Pol. Code, sec. 4013.) The charter of San Bernardino county is a law. If by general law the legislature shall hereafter prescribe the duties of a county purchasing agent or of a county highway commissioner, such designation of the duties of the office will (under the above quoted amendment of 1915) supersede the description of those duties as now contained in the charter. In the meantime the designation of those duties as contained in the charter is not in conflict with any general law, since the general law has not spoken upon the subject. For these reasons we do not agree with counsel for plaintiff in their contention that the charter is no longer of any effect either as to what county offices exist or as to how they shall be filled or as to what shall be their powers and duties.

Our attention is directed to the fact that in sections 4017 and 4018 of the Political Code it has been enacted that boards of supervisors of counties may by ordinance consolidate the duties of certain officers named in section 4017, and that the consolidation of the duties of sheriff and coroner is not included therein. So it is urged that the effect of the provision of the charter that the sheriff shall be *ex-officio* coroner is to impose upon him duties not imposed upon him by general law; and that under the very terms of the 1915 amendment the powers and duties of sheriff are limited to those provided by general law. Some light may be thrown upon this matter by referring to section 7½ of article XI of the state constitution, which authorizes the framing of charters by counties for their own government. It is therein provided (subd. 4) that county charters shall provide "for the powers and duties of boards of supervisors and all other county officers, for their removal and *for the consolidation and segregation of county offices*, and for the manner of filling all vacancies occurring therein; provided, that the provisions of such charters relating to the powers and duties of boards of supervisors and all other county officers shall be subject to and controlled by general laws." Thus it is seen that when the 1915 amendment of the San Bernardino County charter states that the powers and duties of the county officers shall be such as are or may be provided by general law, it merely repeats in substantially the same words the terms of the constitution on the same subject. Therefore, it is the constitution rather than the charter which constitutes the effective declaration of law upon the subject; a declaration which in the same paragraph above quoted, of the constitution, authorizes county charters to provide for the consolidation of county offices. Having in view these provisions of the constitution, we think that even under the charter amendment there is no valid ground for holding that the charter provisions with respect to the consolidation of county offices are now superseded by the terms of section 4017 of the Political Code upon the same subject.

The judgment is affirmed.

James, J., and Shaw, J., concurred.

[Civ. No. 1929. First Appellate District.—September 13, 1916.]

CENTRAL PACIFIC RAILROAD COMPANY (a Corporation), Appellant, v. EUGENE RILEY (now Deceased, and for Whom has Been Substituted Daniel E. Riley, as Administrator, etc.), Respondent.

DISMISSAL OF ACTION—FAILURE TO PROSECUTE WITH DUE DILIGENCE—STIPULATION DROPPING CASE FROM CALENDAR—ACTION PROPERLY DISMISSED.—An action at issue for over seventeen years and not in the meantime brought to trial, is properly dismissed under the provisions of section 583 of the Code of Civil Procedure for failure to prosecute with due diligence, although the parties sixteen years previous to the service of the notice of the motion to dismiss entered into a stipulation that the action be dropped from the calendar to be reset upon notice.

APPEAL from an order of the Superior Court of Alameda County dismissing an action for lack of prosecution. T. W. Harris, Judge.

The facts are stated in the opinion of the court.

Reddy, Campbell & Metson, Tom M. Bradley, and Harry E. Leach, for Appellant.

Powell & Dow, for Respondent.

THE COURT.—This is an appeal from an order dismissing an action for lack of prosecution.

The action was commenced in January, 1896, and in March, 1897, the answer of the defendant was filed. After the cause had thus been at issue for over seventeen years and not having been in the meantime brought to trial, the same on motion of the defendant was dismissed for failure to prosecute the same with due diligence.

Section 583 of the Code of Civil Procedure provides that: "Any action heretofore or hereafter commenced shall be dismissed . . . on motion of the defendant, after due notice to plaintiff or by the court on its own motion, unless such action is brought to trial within five years after the defendant has filed his answer, except where the parties have stipulated in writing that the time may be extended,"—and the making of an order of dismissal, after the expiration of the five-year period, is mandatory upon the court (*Romero* v. *Snyder*, 167 Cal. 216, [138 Pac. 1002]).

The defendant asserts that a stipulation entered into by the parties sixteen years before the notice of motion to dismiss was served relieved it of the necessity of bringing the action to trial within the five years. The stipulation is as follows:

"It is hereby stipulated that the trial of the above entitled action be, and the same is hereby continued, to be dropped from the calendar, to be reset on notice, subject to the discretion of the court, and a trial by jury is hereby waived." Dated April 13, A. D. 1898.

Under the terms of the stipulation the case was dropped from the calendar, to be reset upon notice, and it was in exactly the same position it occupied prior to the time when it was set, and subject therefore to the provisions of section 583 of the Code of Civil Procedure, above set out. There is nothing in the stipulation which can fairly be construed as taking the case out of the operation of the terms of that section. After the case was dropped from the calendar according to the stipulation, it was still the duty of the plaintiff to see that the case was brought to trial. (*Kubli* v. *Hawkett*, 89 Cal. 638, [27 Pac. 67]; *Mowry* v. *Weisenborn*, 137 Cal. 110, [69 Pac. 971].)

The order is affirmed.

[Civ. Nos. 1937, 1938, 1939. First Appellate District.—September 13, 1916.]

STIMSON CANAL & IRRIGATION CO. (a Corporation), Respondent, v. LEMOORE CANAL & IRRIGATION CO. et al., Appellants.

STIMSON CANAL & IRRIGATION CO. et al., Respondents, v. PEOPLE'S DITCH CO. et al., Appellants.

CUTHBERT BURRELL CO. et al., Respondents, v. PEOPLE'S DITCH CO. (a Corporation), Appellant.

Costs—Action Involving Water Rights—Right of Plaintiff.—An action concerning water rights is an action in the nature of a suit to quiet title to real property, and it falls, so far as regards costs, within the provisions of section 1022 of the Code of Civil Procedure, which declares that costs are allowed, of course, to the plaintiff upon a judgment in his favor in an action which involves the title or possession of real estate.

Id.—Judgment for Part of Demand—Right to Costs.—In an action involving water rights, where the plaintiff recovers a judgment for only a part of its demand, it is nevertheless entitled to its costs.

APPEALS from orders of the Superior Court of Fresno County denying motions to strike out cost bill. Geo. E. Church, Judge.

The facts are stated in the opinion of the court.

E. C. Farnsworth, L. L. Cory, and H. Scott Jacobs, for Appellants.

Frank H. Short, W. A. Sutherland, and M. K. Harris, for Respondents.

THE COURT.—The point involved in the three cases above entitled is identical, and they may be considered together.

The judgment in each case quieted the plaintiff's title to certain water rights subject to the title of the appellant, and the court awarded plaintiff its costs. The appellant moved to strike out the plaintiff's cost bill. From the order in each case denying the motion the appeal is prosecuted.

Jt is conceded that the action concerning as it does the water rights of the parties in a certain river in Fresno County, is an action in the nature of a suit to quiet title to real property. It falls, therefore, so far as regards costs within the provisions of section 1022 of the Code of Civil Procedure, which declares that "Costs are allowed of course to the plaintiff, upon a judgment in his favor, in the following cases: . . . 5. In an action which involves the title or possession of real estate. . . ." While it is true that the plaintiff did not receive all that it asked for in its complaint, nevertheless it recovered a judgment for part of its demand, and is therefore entitled to costs (*Hoyt* v. *Hart*, 149 Cal. 722, 731, [87 Pac. 569]; *F. A. Hihn Co.* v. *City of Santa Cruz*, 24 Cal. App. 365, [141 Pac. 391].) In each case the appellant in its answer also claimed the right to divert certain quantities of water from said river, and also alleged that its rights in that regard were prior to those of the plaintiff. It also recovered judgment for part of what it claimed, and perhaps it was entitled to its costs; but as to this it is sufficient to say that that question is not before us.

The order in each of the cases above entitled denying appellant's motion to strike out plaintiff's cost bill is therefore affirmed.

[Civ. No. 1999. Second Appellate District.—September 13, 1916.]

H. C. COLTON, Respondent, v. EVAN E. ANDERSON et al., Defendants; J. H. RYCKMAN, Appellant.

PROMISSORY NOTE—MATURITY OF PAYMENT OF FIRST INSTALLMENT OF INTEREST—CONSTRUCTION OF INSTRUMENT—ACTION NOT PREMATURELY BROUGHT.—Under the terms of a promissory note dated February 13, 1912, "with interest from November 1, 1911, until paid, at the rate of seven per cent per annum, payable semi-annually," the first installment of interest is due May 1, 1912, and where default is made in the payment of such interest, and the note provides that the whole sum of principal and interest shall become due at the option of the holder in such an event, an action commenced on the twenty-fourth day of June, 1912, to foreclose the mortgage given to secure the payment of such note, is not prematurely brought.

APPEAL from a judgment of the Superior Court of Los
'Angeles County, and from an order denying a new trial.
Paul J. McCormick, Judge.

The facts are stated in the opinion of the court.

Harriman, Ryckman & Tuttle, for Appellant.

H. S. Rollins, for Respondent.

CONREY, P. J.—This is an action for the foreclosure of a
mortgage. The mortgage was given to secure the payment
of two notes which were dated February 13, 1912. The first
note was for seventeen thousand dollars payable on or before
three years after date: "with interest from November 1,
1911, until paid, at the rate of seven per cent per annum,
payable semi-annually; should the interest not be so paid, it
shall become a part of the principal and thereafter bear like
interest as the principal. Should default be made in the
payment of any installment of interest when due, then the
whole sum of principal and interest shall become immediately
due and payable at the option of the holder of this note."
The other note was for five hundred dollars, due in six
months from date, with interest from November 1, 1911,
payable at maturity. No interest having been paid, the
plaintiff on June 24, 1912, declared the whole sum of principal and interest of the first note to be then due and payable, and filed this action for foreclosure of the mortgage.
By supplemental complaint filed August 21, 1912, the action
was made to include the second note. Judgment by default
was entered against the defendants Anderson, makers of the
notes and mortgage, and the only defense presented is that
of defendant Ryckman, who purchased a part of the property subject to the lien of this mortgage. Defendant Ryckman presents this appeal from the judgment and from the
order denying his motion for a new trial.

As stated in the brief of appellant, the only point involved
in this case relates to his contention that the suit was prematurely brought. As to this we are of the opinion that the
plaintiff was entitled to maintain his action by reason of nonpayment of the interest on the larger note on May 1, 1912.
The statement in the note that interest was to be paid from
November 1, 1911, at the specified rate, "payable semi-annu-

ally," clearly made the first installment of interest due May 1, 1912. In view of defendant's claim that the note was uncertain in this respect, the plaintiff introduced evidence which shows beyond any doubt that the intention of the parties was in accord with this interpretation of their note. But we base our decision upon the note itself without reference to such extraneous evidence.

Appellant set up in his answer the further defense that before purchasing the lots which were acquired by him early in May, 1912, he caused inquiry to be made of the plaintiff as to the time when the interest on the seventeen thousand dollar note would fall due, and was assured by the plaintiff that it would not be due until August 13th. In support of this defense we have the testimony of two witnesses. But they are contradicted as to the material parts thereof by the testimony of the plaintiff. Upon this evidence the court found that appellant in buying the lots did not rely upon any statements of the plaintiff regarding said mortgage. At all events, under our construction of the note itself, the defense was not available to appellant.

The judgment and order are affirmed.

James, J., and Shaw, J., concurred.

[Civ. No. 1484. Third Appellate District.—September 13, 1916.]

RICHMOND DREDGING COMPANY (a Corporation), Respondent, v. ATCHISON, TOPEKA & SANTA FE RAILWAY COMPANY (a Corporation), Appellant.

Contract for Filling in Land—Recovery of Balance Due—Pleading—Unwarranted Verdict.—In an action by a dredging company to recover the balance due for material furnished and work performed under a contract for the filling in of a tract of land owned by a railroad company, the jury is not warranted in allowing the plaintiff in addition to the number of cubic yards found to have been deposited multiplied by the contract price per cubic yard, an amount based upon evidence that the hardest part of the work had been done when the plaintiff discontinued the work, in the absence of any averment in the complaint authorizing such additional allowance.

ID.—NATURE OF WORK—MECHANICS' LIEN LAW INAPPLICABLE.—The filling in of a part of a tract of land of fifty or more acres belonging to a railroad company, having for its principal object the location and opening of an avenue across the land and to provide a roadbed to which the line of another railway company might sometime be removed from its present location between the company's tracks and the proposed avenue, is not within the provisions of section 1183 of the Code of Civil Procedure which gives a lien to "all persons . . . performing labor upon, or furnishing materials to be used in the construction, alteration, addition to, or repair, either in whole or in part, of any building . . . , railroad, wagonroad or other structure," etc.

ID.—NUMBER OF CUBIC YARDS DEPOSITED—ACCEPTANCE OF MONTHLY VOUCHERS.—Monthly vouchers made out by the defendant showing the estimated amount due for work done during the previous month and, as provided by the contract, the installment of seventy-five per cent due and twenty-five per cent retained, are not to be regarded as accounts stated, as to the number of cubic yards actually deposited, in the absence of any evidence other than a receipt signed by the plaintiff at the bottom of each voucher for the amount thereof.

ID.—DELAY IN PAYMENT—ACCEPTANCE OF MONEY ON OVERDUE VOUCHERS — LACK OF ESTOPPEL.— The acceptance of money on such vouchers at dates later than provided in the contract, without protest, does not estop the plaintiff from denying that payment for a subsequent month was not tendered in time, where the defendant was notified that prompt payment must be made in the future.

ID.—PLEADING—DAMAGES—FAILURE TO MAINTAIN LEVEES—FAILURE TO CONSTRUCT IN TIME—SEPARATE COUNTS—LACK OF PREJUDICE.—In such an action the setting up as separate causes of action alleged damages for failure to maintain the levees necessary to impound the material deposited, and for the failure to have the levees in readiness at the time promised, is not prejudicial, where there was evidence sufficient to support the verdict on both counts.

ID.—EVIDENCE—LETTERS—LACK OF PRELIMINARY PROOF OF AUTHENTICITY—INSUFFICIENT GROUND OF REVERSAL.—In such action, the admission in evidence of certain letters purporting to have been written by defendant's engineer in charge of the work, which to some extent conceded the defendant's default in failing to construct the levees to impound the material, and which were received by the president of the plaintiff company through the mail, without preliminary proof of their authenticity, is error, but not so prejudicial as to justify a reversal, where the genuineness of the letters was not challenged, and the writer and the recipient were both present in court, and the latter testified that he received the letters from the former through the mail.

APPEAL from a judgment of the Superior Court of Contra Costa County, and from an order denying a new trial. R. H. Latimer, Judge.

The facts are stated in the opinion of the court.

E. W. Camp, H. D. Pillsbury, Platt Kent, and C. E. McLaughlin, for Appellant.

Wm. H. H. Hart, and Frank W. Hooper, for Respondent.

CHIPMAN, P. J.—The action is for damages arising out of a written contract of date January 31, 1910, between defendant as first party, plaintiff as second party, and East Shore & Suburban Railway Company, third party. This latter company is not made a party to the action.

Defendant is the owner of a tract of land situated in the city of Richmond, Contra Costa County, and was desirous of having "said land filled in as herein (by the contract) provided." The area to be filled is particularly described in the contract; the cubic measurement of said area as stated in the contract was "estimated at approximately two hundred and twenty thousand yards," and "the second party agrees to fill, at the rate of fifteen cents per cubic yard, within the area described." A map was attached to the contract as part thereof showing the area to be filled and other facts.

Defendant was to pay plaintiff on "the 15th day of each month, for the work done during the preceding month, seventy-five per cent of the amount estimated by the engineer of the first party to have been earned by the second party during such preceding month and the first party will retain the remaining twenty-five per cent of all monthly estimates of work done until thirty-five days after the completion and acceptance by the first party, of the work herein agreed to be performed. . . . The first party is to construct and maintain any and all levees north of Ohio street necessary or proper to impound the material deposited on the area hereinabove described as lying north of said Ohio street; also such levees as may be necessary to protect its main line between Ohio street and Richmond avenue."

Plaintiff's claim is presented in four causes of action. By the first cause of action it is alleged that plaintiff entered upon the work pursuant to the contract and gave the bond specified therein and continued the work "up to on or about the 17th day of August, 1910"; that the work performed and material furnished "was accepted by the defendant as having been done and supplied in a workmanlike manner and in accordance with the terms of said contract"; that defendant refused to pay plaintiff for its said services and material furnished by plaintiff "during the month of July, 1910, or any part of said money, and in accordance with the terms of said contract, and by so refusing and neglecting to pay such money, defendant rendered, caused, and made it impossible for the plaintiff to further continue performance under the contract; and on or about the 17th day of August, 1910, the plaintiff without fault on its part, did discontinue and suspend work under said contract, although plaintiff was fully equipped and prepared to continue such work and had expended a large amount of money for materials and supplies necessary to complete the same"; whereupon on said last-mentioned day, "plaintiff notified the defendant that plaintiff would perform no further work under said contract because of defendant's neglect and refusal to pay to the plaintiff in accordance with the terms of said contract the amount due, owing and coming to the plaintiff from the defendant for the work and services theretofore performed and labor and material theretofore supplied under said contract"; that plaintiff furnished material and performed work under said contract and in accordance with its terms of the value of $46,575, no part of which has been paid to plaintiff except the sum of $10,575, and there is now due and owing plaintiff from defendant the sum of thirty-six thousand dollars.

The second cause of action is for "work and labor and services heretofore performed and material furnished and supplied by plaintiff for the defendant at the special instance and request of defendant."

In the third cause of action the making of the contract is alleged; furthermore, that the defendant undertook to build the levees called for in said contract, but that it constructed said levees in such a negligent and imperfect manner as that they failed to hold or impound the material deposited on the said area by plaintiff to the great damage of plaintiff; that by reason thereof the defendant so delayed and embarrassed plaintiff as to cause plaintiff to suspend the entire work under said contract, and large amounts of material deposited on said area by plaintiff were not held or impounded thereon; that by reason of defendant's said default, plaintiff was compelled to keep its working forces idle for long periods of time and to pay wages to its employees and rent for a dredger used by plaintiff, all to the loss and damage of said plaintiff in the sum of $6,818.81.

As a fourth cause of action the contract is pleaded and it is alleged that plaintiff on February 12, 1910, notified defendant that plaintiff would be ready to commence operation under said contract as soon as the necessary levees were constructed to impound the material to be dredged and defendant, on or about February 15, 1910, notified plaintiff that proper levees would be constructed on or before February 20, 1910; that on said last-named date plaintiff hired a dredger at large expense and placed it in position to enter upon said work together with a full crew of men to operate the same and was in readiness to commence work on February 25th; that defendant failed and neglected to construct the levees necessary to impound the material to be deposited until March 10, 1910, and thus prevented plaintiff from commencing operations under said contract until March 10, 1910, to its damage in the sum of three thousand dollars.

In the prayer plaintiff asks judgment for thirty-six thousand dollars, the amount claimed in the first and second causes of action, and interest from August 15, 1910; for the further sum of $16,818, the amount claimed in the third cause of action; and for the further sum of three thousand dollars, the amount claimed in the fourth cause of action.

In its answer to the first cause of action defendant denies most of its averments; alleges that it mailed at Los Angeles vouchers for work done by plaintiff, to wit, for March, on April 21, 1910; for April, on May 21; for May, on June 21, and for June on July 20, 1910, amounting in all to $10,596.53, and that plaintiff accepted the said payments and that on or about August 17, 1910, defendant offered to pay plaintiff the amount found to be due for work performed and materials furnished for the month of July, but plaintiff refused and still refuses to accept the same; alleges that at the time of the abandonment of said contract by plaintiff the value of the work done and materials furnished by it was the sum of $21,978.80 and not the sum of $46,575 as set forth in the com-

plaint; denies that there is any sum due and owing plaintiff
save and except the sum of $3,387.57; that there was due
plaintiff for July the sum of $4,080, which sum defendant
tendered plaintiff and was refused, and that there is due
plaintiff for work done and materials furnished from August
1 to August 17, 1910, the sum of $1,837.57; that said contract
was signed, and delivered on March 3, 1910, and not on January 31, 1910, as alleged in the complaint.

Answering the second cause of action, defendant alleges
that there is due plaintiff from defendant the sum of $3,387.57
and no more.

Answering the third cause of action defendant denies that
it has failed to perform the contract and alleges failure of
plaintiff to evenly distribute the material dredged, and that
plaintiff so negligently filled said area that the embankments
constructed by defendant were thereby caused to break and
give way and the progress of the work was thereby delayed.

For answer to the fourth cause of action, denies the averments of the complaint and avers that by the terms of the
contract it was agreed that plaintiff should begin work thereunder not later than April 1, 1910, and alleges the construction of the levees by defendant as called for in the contract.

By way of counterclaim alleges that plaintiff and defendant entered into a written contract on or about March 3,
1910, which provided that the work should be done and completed on or before October 1, 1910; that plaintiff failed to
complete said work and it still remains uncompleted to
defendant's damage in the sum of thirty thousand dollars.

For further and distinct defense alleges the contract attached to plaintiff's complaint; that defendant made payments monthly as therein provided for and plaintiff received
the same except the voucher for the month of July, 1910,
which plaintiff "returned without cashing the same"; that
by accepting said vouchers and payments for the months of
March, April, May, and June, for said work plaintiff "is
estopped from denying that said work was done and performed in accordance with said contract or from denying that
said contract was at all said times and now is in full force
and effect."

For a further defense alleges that "the estimate of the engineer was a condition precedent to the making of such payment," and defendant was unable to obtain the estimates in

time to furnish its voucher "until after the 15th day of the month upon which the payment was to have been made," and that defendant was not in default in respect of March payment; that on September 1, 1910, and before payments could be made under said contract, defendant was served with an attachment in an action wherein plaintiff was defendant and by reason thereof defendant has been prevented from making any further payments.

For further defense alleges that under the terms of said contract the payment to be made thereunder is largely in excess of one thousand dollars and said contract has never been recorded in the office of the county recorder of Contra Costa County, and by reason thereof is wholly void.

The cause was tried with the assistance of a jury and defendant submitted certain interrogatories which, with their answers, follow:

"1. How much do you find from the evidence the defendant has paid to the plaintiff for work done under the contract described in plaintiff's complaint? Answer: $10,575.

"2. How many cubic yards of earth do you find from the evidence was deposited upon the entire area described in the contract that remained there? Answer: 181,500 cu. yards.

"3. How many cubic yards of earth do you find from the evidence was deposited by the plaintiff outside the area described in the contract resulting from overflow through breaks in the levees? Answer: 1,000 cu. yards.

"4. When was the contract described in plaintiff's complaint signed and delivered by the East Shore & Suburban Railway Company? Answer: On or about the 3d of March, 1910.

"6. If you find for the plaintiff, how much do you allow upon the first cause of action, described in plaintiff's complaint? Answer: $19,773.

"7. If you find for the plaintiff, how much do you allow upon the second cause of action in plaintiff's complaint? Answer: Nothing.

"8. If you find for the plaintiff, how much do you allow upon the third cause of action in plaintiff's complaint? Answer: $5,476.50.

"9. If you find for the plaintiff, how much do you allow upon the fourth cause of action in plaintiff's complaint? Answer: $675.

"10. Do you allow the defendant any sum for damages, as set forth in the answer, and counter-claim, and if so, how much? Answer: Nothing."

Judgment was accordingly entered in favor of plaintiff for the sum of $25,925, from which and from the order denying its motion for a new trial, defendant appeals.

1. Appellant contends, first, that the amount found by the special verdict under the first cause of action, to wit, $19,773 (interrogatory 6), was excessive to the extent of $3,123. That conclusion is thus reached:

181,500 cu. yards found by the jury to have been
   deposited on the ground (interrogatory 2) at
   the contract price of 15c per cu. yard, equals.. $27,225.00
Amount paid plaintiff as found by the jury....   10,575.00

               Bal. due $16,650.00

Respondent replies that the interrogatory called for the cubic yards "deposited upon the entire area described in the contract *that remained there,*" and that appellant has overlooked the latter part of the interrogatory; that the jury in reply to it had the right to take into consideration all the materials deposited upon the described area, including that which escaped because of insufficient levees. To meet this reply appellant calls attention to interrogatory 3 which was the finding of the jury that the quantity of earth deposited outside of the area "resulting from overflow through breaks in the levees," was one thousand cubic yards. If this can be held to be the amount of earth which escaped from the designated area and should be considered as earth that did not "remain there," it would add but $150 and the excess would still be $2,973. It is not claimed by plaintiff that it deposited, or had the right to deposit, earth outside the area. Its claim is that where earth deposited in the described area escaped for lack of sufficient levees, it should be compensated therefor. Appellant's answer is that the jury having found the extent of this overflow, the damages are measured by the contract price of fifteen cents per cubic yard.

Respondent, however, makes the further contention as borne out by the evidence, that the work done previous to its suspension, was the hardest and most expensive part of the dredging work, and "the jury had a right to take this fact into consideration in arriving at the amount which respondent had earned under the contract mentioned in the first cause of action."

No special damages are alleged in the first cause of action. The averments are that plaintiff entered upon the work "pursuant to the terms of said contract and continued on the work provided for in and by said contract up to on or about the 17th day of August, 1910." It is further alleged "that all the said work and labor and service done and performed and all material supplied by said plaintiff was done and performed and supplied strictly in accordance with the terms of said contract and was accepted by the defendant as having been done in a workmanlike manner and in accordance with the terms of said contract." The second count was on *quantum meruit* but the jury found that there was nothing due on the second cause of action. (Interrogatory 7.)

Special damages were alleged in the third count for defendant's failure to construct necessary levees and the consequent damages for which the jury allowed $5,476.50, and in the fourth count special damages were alleged for defendant's neglect in not having levees constructed at the time promised, and hence the additional cost to plaintiff by reason of expenses incurred while thus delayed in the work. For this the jury allowed plaintiff $675.50. These three items make up the exact sum found by the general verdict.

It seems to us that there is no allegation in the first cause of action which can be made the basis for damages other than as provided for by the contract, and the agreement there is to pay fifteen cents per cubic yard for earth deposited under the contract. The number of cubic yards was found by the jury and the contract fixed the price to be paid. We can discover no averment in the first cause of action which would authorize the jury to add as further damages an amount based upon evidence "that the hardest part of the work had been done" when plaintiff quit the job. It was expressly alleged that the work was done "strictly in accordance with the terms of said contract," and was "accepted by the defendants as having been done in accordance with the terms of said contract." It was held in *California Wine Assn.* v. *Commercial Union Fire Ins. Co.*, 159 Cal. 49, 52, [112 Pac. 858], that "the special verdicts absolutely control the general verdict"; *Napa Valley Packing Co.* v. *San Francisco Relief and Red Cross Funds,* 16 Cal. App. 461, [118 Pac. 469]. It seems to us

quite clear that the special verdicts were addressed directly to
the issues in the case and responded specifically to each of the
causes of action. These several answers to interrogatories or
special verdicts constituted the basis of the general verdict,
and if any one of these answers or special verdicts was unsupported by the evidence the general verdict cannot stand.

The special verdict upon the first cause of action is not
supported by the evidence. The contract provided that
plaintiff was to be paid fifteen cents per cubic yard for earth
deposited by it, and the jury found the number of cubic yards
deposited both within and without the area. The exact damage, therefore, under the first cause of action, may be ascertained by a simple example in multiplication, and we see no
reason why this may not be resorted to as showing the amount
of plaintiff's damage under the first cause of action. The
contract price for depositing 181,500+1,000 cubic yards of
earth at fifteen cents per cubic yard will give the amount of
plaintiff's damages—$27,375. Deducting payments made of
$10,575 leaves $16,800, the amount due upon the first cause
of action. This amount added to the findings under the
third and fourth causes of action, to wit, $5,476.50 and
$675.50 makes in all the sum of $22,952, instead of $25,925.

2. Appellant claims that the work was of such character
as to bring the contract within the provisions of section 1183
of the mechanics' lien law, and as the contract was not recorded it was void, and plaintiff's only remedy was in an
action on *quantum meruit* for the value of the labor and
material furnished, and the contract price will be taken as
the basis for recovering damages which brings the same result as above shown. (*Laidlaw* v. *Marye*, 133 Cal. 170, [65
Pac. 391]; *Condon* v. *Donohue*, 160 Cal. 749, [118 Pac. 113].)

It is claimed further, however, that plaintiff's recovery
being limited to the contract price as above claimed, the verdict was against law because the jury awarded recovery on
counts under which plaintiff was entitled to nothing (counts
3 and 4), and was denied recovery on count 2, the only one
under which plaintiff had any legal ground for a verdict in
its favor.

We cannot accept appellant's claim that the mechanics'
lien law is applicable. The area to be filled was part of a
tract of fifty or more acres, the property of defendant. As
near as we can determine from the provisions of the contract

and from the map made part thereof, defendant's principal object was to locate and open an avenue, called Ashland Avenue, across defendant's land, and provide a roadbed to which the line of the East Shore & Suburban Railroad Company might sometime be removed from its present location between the defendant's track and the proposed Ashland Avenue. Just why this was deemed necessary or advisable does not appear. The contract reads: "The third party (Suburban Railway) agrees that upon the filling in of said Ashland Avenue to grade, as hereinabove provided, the first party shall have the right to remove the tracks of the third party now situated in part on the area to be filled in under this contract in the following manner: [describing the route or new location of the suburban track]. . . . The cost of the removal and the relocation of said line is to be borne wholly by first party," etc. We do not think that this work can reasonably be held to fall within the provisions of section 1183 of the Code of Civil Procedure which gives a lien to "all persons . . . performing labor upon or furnishing materials to be used in the construction, alteration, addition to, or repair, either in whole or in part, of any building . . . , railroad, wagon-road or other structure," etc. There is no evidence tending to show that defendant intended to make any present use of this filled-in ground for the extension or relocation of its tracks. The moving of the suburban railway company's track to another location cannot be said to be the "construction, alteration, addition to, or repair, . . . of" defendant's railroad, or to be a "structure" connected with said railroad. It did not appear that the fill was necessary to the operation of defendant's road, or for stations, roundhouses, shops, and the like which have been held to be included in the term "railway."

3. We do not think that the monthly vouchers made out by defendant showing the estimated amount due for work done during the previous month, the installment of seventy-five per cent due, and the twenty-five per cent retained as provided in the contract, can be regarded as accounts stated. Appellant claims that "the parties were bound thereby and no recovery can be had except for the unpaid balance." There were four of these for the months of March, April, May, and June, respectively. The first one states the estimated number of cubic "yards dredger filling," but the

others give only the estimated amount of money due, the result of former accounts being carried forward in successive accounts. At the bottom of each is a receipt signed by plaintiff for the amount of the voucher. Beyond this there is nothing to show that they were in effect new agreements or contained the elements constituting an account stated, or that they were intended as a settlement of the number of cubic yards actually deposited.

4. Nor do we think that because plaintiff received money on these vouchers at dates later than the 15th of each month without protest, it is estopped to deny that payment for July was not tendered in time. There might be force in this contention had plaintiff failed to notify defendant that prompt payment must be made in the future. On August 10, 1910, plaintiff wrote defendant as follows: "Because of the fact that our contract with you allows you to retain 25% of the money we have earned and because of the fact that your engineer persists in underestimating the amount of material delivered it is absolutely necessary that we should receive your check for the material delivered during the preceding month on the 15th as our contract specifies. Heretofore your check has arrived anywhere from the 23rd to the 30th of the month instead of on the 15th. Our contract with the power company compels us to pay for the current used on the 15th. Unless we pay our bill the current will be shut off and we will be caused both damage and delay therefore we must demand that we be paid as per contract on the 15th." Notwithstanding this demand, defendant did not offer to pay for the July work as demanded and on August 17, 1910, plaintiff notified defendant in writing that plaintiff considered itself released from "further performance under said agreement," and demanded payment for the work and services performed. The failure to make the payment demanded in compliance with the terms of the contract was a substantial breach thereof, and justified the plaintiff in not proceeding further. (*San Francisco Bridge Co. v. Dumbarton L. & I. Co.*, 119 Cal. 272, [51 Pac. 335]; *Woodruff Co. v. Exchange Realty Co.*, 21 Cal. App. 607, [132 Pac. 598]; *American-Hawaiian Eng. & Con. Co.* v. *Butler*, 165 Cal. 497, [Ann. Cas. 1916C, 44, 133 Pac. 280].)

5. It is urged that the third cause of action included every element of damage which could accrue from the breach of

the contract, and that the damages were duplicated by reason of damages also being awarded under the fourth cause of action; that a party cannot split up a single cause of action and maintain separate actions thereon; that damages arising from a single wrong, though at different times, make but one cause of action. (*Hall* v. *Susskind,* 109 Cal. 209, [41 Pac. 1012].)

This rule of pleading was not invoked by demurrer nor was it raised at the trial. Doubtless the facts constituting the damages could have been set up in a single count and probably should have been, but we cannot see that defendant suffered prejudice by plaintiff's failure to do so. The third cause of action was grounded on defendant's failure to maintain the levees necessary to impound the material deposited, thus causing suspension of work by plaintiff. The fourth cause of action was grounded on defendant's failure to have the levees in readiness at the time defendant promised. There was evidence sufficient to support the verdict on both of these counts.

6. The only remaining error assigned as prejudicial relates to the admission in evidence of certain letters purporting to have been written by Mr. Ball, defendant's engineer in charge of the work. The testimony was conflicting as to the failure of defendant to construct the levees to impound the material. There were two of these letters dated respectively May 2 (exhibit 4), and May 13, 1910 (exhibit 8), each purporting to be signed "R. B. Ball, Division Engineer." The letter of May 2d refers to a conversation previously had with plaintiff, and plaintiff answered this letter on May 3d (exhibit 5); the letter of May 13th (exhibit 8) refers to defendant's letter of May 12th, and all of them dealing with the matter of these levees, and defendant's letters to some extent conceding defendant's default. The letters were produced in court by witness Cutting, president of plaintiff company, who testified that he received these letters in due course through the United States mail. It appeared that on Saturday, Mr. Cutting had a conversation with Mr. Ball and that the letter of May 2d (exhibit 4) was in response to this conversation and to which plaintiff replied on May 3d. Defendant's letter of May 12th was answered by plaintiff by letter the next day. Witness Cutting did not testify to the handwriting of Mr. Ball nor that he knew his signature, nor

that he saw either of the Ball letters written, nor that he was a subscribing witness thereto. On these grounds defendant objected, and it is now urged that the letters were not properly identified. Appellant relies upon the rule as stated in *People* v. *Le Doux,* 155 Cal. 535, 550, [102 Pac. 517], "Where not acknowledged, a private writing must be proved in one of three ways: by anyone who saw the writing executed, or by evidence of the genuineness of the handwriting of the maker, or by a subscribing witness. (Code Civ. Proc., sec. 1940.) Such execution must be shown before it is entitled to admission. (*Sinclaire* v. *Wood,* 3 Cal. 98.)" Mr. Jones states the rule thus: "Before letters are received in evidence there must be, as in the case of other documents, some proof of their genuineness. This is not proved by the mere fact that the letter is received by mail, when the signature is not proved." (Jones on Evidence, 2d ed., sec. 583.)

The evidence shows that Mr. Ball and Mr. Cutting were in frequent, almost daily, communication in connection with the very matters the subject of the letters; sometimes their differences were made known in conversations and sometimes in letters. The evidence showed that the parties acted upon the suggestions in exchanged letters. The genuineness of Mr. Ball's letters was not challenged. He was a witness and in court and could have disclaimed writing them. Cutting no doubt was familiar with Ball's handwriting and his testimony: "That is a letter I received from Mr. Ball on Monday, the 2d day of May, 1910, through the mail" (referring to exhibit 4); again, "that is a letter received by me, received from Mr. Ball, Division Engineer, Santa Fe Railroad" (exhibit 8), we think, under the circumstances, was more than a mere conclusion of the witness. It was stated in *Verzan* v. *McGregor,* 23 Cal. 339, 343: "It is often the case that the main question in controversy is the execution and authenticity of the instrument. And the rule is, that if there be no evidence of authenticity, the instrument cannot be read to the jury; but if there be any fact or circumstances tending to prove the authenticity from which it might be presumed, then the instrument is to be read to the jury, and the question, like other matters of fact, is for their decision."

The rule contended for is sound and is not to be disregarded. It would have been a very simple thing to prove the authenticity of these letters not only by Cutting, but by

their writer who was in court and it should have been done.
We cannot, however, under all the circumstances, say that
the error was so prejudicial as to cause a miscarriage of justice or to justify a reversal.

The judgment is modified by reducing the same from
$25,925 and costs to the sum of $22,952 and costs, with direction to compute interest from the date of the original judgment, and as thus modified the judgment and order are
affirmed, appellant to recover costs on appeal.

Hart, J., and Ellison, J., *pro tem.*, concurred.

[Crim. No. 358.   Third Appellate District.—September 13, 1916.]

THE PEOPLE, Respondents, v. FRANK MARTINEZ, Appellant.

CRIMINAL LAW—BURGLARY—QUALIFICATION OF JURORS—IMPLIED BIAS
—CONTRADICTORY ANSWERS—PROVINCE OF TRIAL COURT—REVIEW
UPON APPEAL.—Where, on the impaneling of a jury for the trial of
a defendant charged with burglary, some of the jurors, in reply to
questions by defendant's counsel, stated that the accused would be
required to produce evidence in his favor to create a reasonable
doubt in their mind as to his guilt, but upon being questioned by
the district attorney each declared that, if accepted as a juror in
the case, he would at all times give the defendant the benefit of the
presumption of innocence until his guilt was satisfactorily proved
and acquit him if, after a full and fair consideration of the evidence by the light of the court's instructions upon the law, he entertained a reasonable doubt of the defendant's guilt, it was the province
of the court, under this state of the record, to determine whether
or not such jurors were disqualified for implied bias; and its discretion will not be disturbed on appeal unless it appears that it has
been abused.

ID.—EVIDENCE — DESCRIPTION OF DEFENDANT AND COMPANION.—In a
prosecution for the crime of burglary, there is no error in permitting the people to prove that the defendant and another man, who
was shown to have been the defendant's companion, applied for and
obtained work together, that the defendant wore a particular kind
of cap, that his companion wore a particular kind and size of shoes,
that footprints in the snow leading to the burglarized premises corresponded in size with the shoes worn by the two men, and that the
remnants of a leather case in which one of the stolen articles was
incased were found a few days after the burg'ary in a town toward

which the defendant and his companion were seen hastily going by foot on the night of the crime.

ID.—STATEMENTS CONCERNING POSSESSION OF STOLEN PROPERTY—ADMISSIBILITY OF.—Statements made by the defendant when placed under arrest, involving conflicting or inconsistent explanations concerning the possession of one of the stolen articles, are properly admitted in evidence, without a preliminary showing that they were voluntarily made, as they do not involve a confession of guilt.

ID.—REASONABLE DOUBT AS TO DEGREE OF CRIME—DUTY OF JURY—INSTRUCTION.—An instruction that "under the information in this case you may, *if the evidence warrant it*, find the defendant guilty of burglary of the first degree or burglary of the second degree. Should you entertain a reasonable doubt as to which of the two degrees he is guilty, *if any*, you will give the defendant the benefit of the doubt and acquit him of the higher offense," contains no intimation that the defendant is guilty of the crime of burglary, but obviously means that, if the jury find by the proper degree of proof that the defendant committed the crime charged, but should entertain a reasonable doubt as to which of the degrees of that crime, *if any*, he was, under the evidence, guilty of, then he would be entitled to the benefit of that doubt and in that case should only be convicted of the lower degree of the crime.

ID.—CIRCUMSTANTIAL EVIDENCE—INSTRUCTION.—An instruction explaining that where circumstantial evidence is solely relied upon for the proof of an accused's connection with the commission of a crime, "any fact essential to sustain the hypothesis of guilt and exclude the hypothesis of innocence," and any single fact from which the inference of guilt is to be drawn, "must be proved by evidence which satisfies the minds and conscience of the jury to the same extent that they are required to be satisfied of the facts in an issue in cases where the evidence is direct," is not argumentative, but if it were, the defendant cannot complain of it, where the record shows that it was given and read to the jury at his request.

ID.—VERDICT OF CONVICTION—CIRCUMSTANTIAL EVIDENCE—SUFFICIENCY OF.—On appeal from a judgment of conviction of burglary in the first degree, it cannot be said that the verdict was not justified, where the proof showed the presence of the defendant and his companion in the town where the crime was committed just before such commission, the correspondence in size of the footprints on the surface of the snow leading to and from the burglarized building with the shoes worn by the defendant and his companion, the finding at a place in which direction the accused were seen traveling, of a part of the leather case in which one of the stolen watches was incased when taken from the building, a short time after the burglary, the possession by one of the parties of one of the stolen watches, and the contradictory statements made by the defendant and his companion in attempting to explain such possession.

APPEAL from a judgment of the Superior Court of Plumas County, and from an order denying a new trial. J. O. Moncur, Judge.

The facts are stated in the opinion of the court.

J. D. McLaughlin, for Appellant.

U. S. Webb, Attorney-General, and J. Charles Jones, Deputy Attorney-General, for Respondents.

HART, J.—The defendant was convicted of burglary of the first degree, and appeals from the judgment and the order denying him a new trial.

He claims that his rights were prejudiced by alleged errors of the court in disallowing challenges of certain veniremen for implied bias, in allowing certain testimony to be received into the record, and in the giving of certain instructions. It is charged that he was prejudiced by alleged misconduct of the district attorney and insisted that the evidence does not support the verdict.

The alleged crime was committed at the town of Portola, in Plumas County, between the hours of 8 and 10 o'clock of the evening of February 13, 1916. The building entered was the property of one Arkin. Therein he carried on the retail drug business and also had living-rooms, where he and his family resided. A portion of the store was occupied by one Johnson as a jewelry-store and repair-shop. On the evening named, Arkin and his family attended a moving-picture show located on the opposite side of the street from the said store. He left the store at about 7:30 o'clock in the evening. Johnson had previously left the store and also attended the picture show mentioned. Arkin returned to the store at about fifteen minutes after 9 o'clock on that evening and discovered that a window to one of his living-rooms in the rear of the building had been broken so as to admit of the easy entrance of a person into the building. An investigation following this discovery disclosed that the jewelry case belonging to Johnson had been broken into and a large quantity of watches, lockets, and other like articles had been abstracted therefrom, aggregating in value the sum of five hundred dollars approximately.

The defendant and another man, known as Ed. Martinez
and also as Ed. Leal, were, within a few days after the burglary was committed, arrested at Gerlach, Nevada, and on the
person of Ed. Martinez was found one of the stolen watches.
Other facts developed at the trial will be stated as we consider some of the points, particularly the contention that the
verdict is not sufficiently supported.

1. Objections by way of challenges for implied bias were
interposed to the legal competency of four of the talesmen to
serve as jurors in the case. These were jurors McKenzie,
Grother, Guidici, and Ohlsen.

In reply to a question upon *voir dire* by the attorney for
the defendant, McKenzie stated that the accused would be
required to "produce evidence in his favor to create a reasonable doubt" in his mind as to the defendant's guilt.
Grother and Ohlsen, also replying to questions by defendant's counsel, made similar replies. Guidici affirmatively
answered the following question propounded by defendant's
attorney: "If there was a reasonable doubt in your mind as
to the guilt of the defendant would you presume, or indulge
in any possibilities that he would be guilty, to overcome that
doubt?" Each of the jurors, however, on being questioned
by the district attorney, declared that, if accepted as a juror
in the case, he would, in determining the question of the guilt
or innocence of the defendant, be governed entirely by the
evidence and the law as the court stated it to them; that he
would, at all times, give the defendant the benefit of the presumption of innocence until his guilt was satisfactorily
proved and acquit him if, after a full and fair consideration
of the evidence by the light of the court's instructions upon
the law, he entertained a reasonable doubt of his guilt.
"Under this state of the record upon the question whether
such jurors possessed such bias as would prevent them from
trying the case fairly and impartially, it was for the court
to determine that preliminary issue, and in all such cases
the court's discretion will not be disturbed on appeal unless
it appears that it has been abused." (*People* v. *Conte,* 17
Cal. App. 771, 777, [122 Pac. 450].) As was well said in
People v. *Ryan,* 152 Cal. 364, 371, [92 Pac. 856], where the
precise proposition under consideration was discussed:
"Many persons, competent as jurors, have not given much
attention to such subjects, are inexperienced as witnesses, and

are unable readily to comprehend the force and effect of the language in which such questions are couched, and they generally answer without reflection as to the effect of their own words. Such contradictions are by no means infrequent, if, indeed, they are not the rule, rather than the exception. The trial court must decide which of the answers most truly shows the juror's mind. . . . Where there are such contradictions its decision is binding upon this court," citing a large number of cases. As is readily to be noted, the challenged veniremen in this case each made conflicting and directly contradictory statements as to the course he would pursue in the discharge of his duty as a juryman—one statement which would disqualify him and another which would make him legally competent to serve—and, under these circumstances, it was, of course, with the trial court to decide, upon his examination as a whole, whether he was in all respects qualified to try the issue fairly and impartially. There is nothing upon the face of the record here indicating that in its decision in any of the instances referred to the trial court abused its discretion and, therefore, the conclusion of that court upon the question is conclusive upon this court.

2. The next assignments involve objections which were made to the reception into the record of certain testimony. The case made against the accused was by evidence of circumstances, no direct proof of his guilt having been presented. The defendant, with Ed. Martinez or Leal, together applied for and secured work as section-hands for the Western Pacific Company at Portola, a few days prior to the date of the burglary. They worked for the company for a few days only. They were subsequently seen together on the streets of Portola. The people, over objection by the defendant, were permitted to prove that the two men applied for and obtained work together; that the defendant wore a particular kind of cap while in Portola; that his companion wore a particular kind and size of shoes; that there was considerable quantity of snow on the ground in Portola at the time of the burglary, this testimony being allowed in connection with testimony that there were observed on the surface of the snow the impressions of human feet and that measurements were made of the footprints so observed which precisely compared in measurement with the shoes of the defendant and his companion; that the remnants of a leather

case in which one of the watches taken from the store was
kept were found a few days after the burglary at a place
called Hawley, a short distance from Portola, and toward
which place the defendant and his companion were seen hastily going by foot in the neighborhood of 10 o'clock of the
night the building was entered, and other like circumstances
tending in a greater or less degree to place upon the accused
and Ed. Martinez or Leal, responsibility for the crime. All
this testimony, it is here claimed, was improperly received.
Not so. The two men were shown to have been companions
and at all times in the company of each other from the time
they procured work with the railroad company until they
were placed under arrest at Gerlach, Nevada. The people,
therefore, were entitled to the benefit of any testimony bearing upon the description of the two men and their wearing
apparel, or which disclosed their joint movements and flight,
or their actions and declarations in the presence of each
other having any tendency to show or point to their guilt of
the crime charged.

3. It was not necessary to make a preliminary showing that
the statements made by the defendant when placed under
arrest, and those made by Ed. Martinez at the same time in
the defendant's presence, were voluntarily made. The statements did not involve a confession of guilt. They merely
involved conflicting or inconsistent explanations of the possession of the stolen watch found in the possession of Ed.
Martinez. In their conversations with the officers, both denied that they were connected in any manner with the crime
or that they had any knowledge of it.

4. The ruling allowing the witness, Johnson, to state a conversation which he testified he overheard between the defendant and Ed. Martinez while they were confined in the county
jail at Quincy, awaiting trial, was not erroneous. The conversation was carried on between the two men in the Spanish
language, and the special ground of the objection to the testimony was that Johnson did not fully understand that language. But the witness testified that he could understand
Spanish when spoken to some extent, and related only that
part of the conversation which he testified that he clearly
understood.

5. It was not error to sustain the objection to the following cross-question to the witness, Johnson: "You had the

same powers of observation as anyone that was with you had,
or didn't you!" The question followed an unsuccessful effort to secure a statement from the witness as to the relative distances between two houses located back of the Arkin
store and between one of those houses and said store. The
question was argumentative in character and, as framed,
called for a conclusion of the witness. But it is probable
that what counsel intended to ask was whether the witness'
opportunity for observation was equal to that of any other
person with him at the time they were inspecting and following the footprints in the rear of the store. But, even so
viewing it and if in that view a proper question, it is very
clear that, inasmuch as the witness, after considerable questioning on that line, showed that he had formed no judgment as to the distances so sought to be shown, he could have
given no more information upon the subject than he did,
whatever his *powers* of observation might be or his *opportunity* for observation on that occasion might have been.

There are some other rulings similar to the last above
considered animadverted upon in the briefs of the defendant,
but even if not strictly correct, they were obviously harmless
in their effect.

6. There was nothing detrimental to the rights of the defendant either in the action of the court in refusing to permit his attorney to explain the object of a certain line of the
cross-examination of the witness, Johnson, and to which the
district attorney objected, or in the language used by the
court in ruling upon the proposition. The witness, Johnson,
had been exhaustively cross-examined upon the question as
to the number of houses situated on a street back of the street
on which Arkin's store is situated. The witness declared that
he was able to remember and say that there was more than
one house on a certain part of the back street, whereupon
counsel asked him: "You are as sure of this as you are of
any other part of your testimony!" to which question an
objection by the district attorney was sustained. Counsel
then attempted to explain that he desired to test the memory of the witness as to the number of houses, and upon objection by the district attorney, the court ruled and said: "I
don't think that particular part is material enough to take
any time with it." The question is of an argumentative
character and one which, though frequently asked of a wit-

ness on cross-examination, is really meaningless. Either an affirmative or negative answer to the question would not have the effect of adding to or detracting from his credibility or the weight of his testimony.

7. It is insisted that the court, in instruction No. 6, as given, told the jury that the defendant was guilty of one or the other of the two degrees of burglary. Said instruction reads: "Under the information in this case you may, *if the evidence warrant it*, find the defendant guilty of burglary of the first degree or burglary of the second degree. Should you entertain a reasonable doubt as to which of the two degrees he is guilty, *if any*, you will give the defendant the benefit of the doubt and acquit him of the higher offense." It seems to us that the language of said instruction is so plain and clear as to put the meaning thereof beyond all doubt or even cavil. It obviously means that, if the jury find by the proper degree of proof that the defendant committed the crime charged, but should entertain a reasonable doubt as to which of the degrees of that crime (Pen. Code, sec. 460), *if any*, he was, under the evidence, guilty of, then he would be entitled to the benefit of such doubt, and in that case should be convicted only of the lower degree of the crime. It would seem to be hardly necessary to say that nowhere in said instruction does the court intimate that the defendant is guilty of the crime of burglary.

8. Instruction No. 16 is challenged upon the ground that it is argumentative. It explained that, where circumstantial evidence is solely relied upon for the proof of an accused's connection with the commission of a crime, "any fact essential to sustain the hypothesis of guilt and exclude the hypothesis of innocence," and any single fact from which the inference of guilt is to be drawn, "must be proved by evidence which satisfies the minds and conscience of the jury to the same extent that they are required to be satisfied of the facts in an issue in cases where the evidence is direct." We see nothing legally objectionable in the instruction; but, if it were amenable to just criticism, the defendant cannot complain of it, since the record shows that it was given and read to the jury at his request.

9. The general instructions preferred by the defendant and disallowed by the court we have carefully examined, and find that they involved the statement of principles fully and

clearly submitted to the jury in the court's charge. It is, therefore, unnecessary to give them special consideration.

10. We cannot say that the verdict was not justified. It at the least appears to be sufficiently supported by the proofs, and this is all that is required to put it beyond the power of a reviewing court to set aside a verdict, so far as the evidence is concerned. We have already stated that the evidence was not direct but consisted wholly of circumstances. Some of the most important of these have been adverted to. It is not necessary to further rehearse them herein. There are, however, several other circumstances of no inconsiderable significance, when considered with the other circumstances, and they are: 1. That, on the evening of the burglary and after Arkin and family and Johnson had left the burglarized building and gone to the picture show, a man answering the description of the defendant as to stature, build, and headgear, was seen standing in a sort of hallway leading into the Arkin drug-store and peering through the window of said store; 2. That, when the defendant and Ed. Martinez were first searched at Gerlach, the watch was not found on the person of either. An Ingersoll watch of the value of one dollar was found on the person of Ed. Martinez, who declared to the officers that that was the only watch they had. In this connection it was shown that after Ed. Martinez was searched he stepped up to and near the defendant, and that the two men were thereafter again searched and a gold watch, positively identified by Johnson as one of the watches stolen from his store, was found on the person of Ed. Martinez; 3. That the defendant was heard to ask Ed. Martinez, while the two were confined in jail, if the latter had "told anything" to the officers, the natural inference from which question was whether Ed. had made any statement to the officers of an incriminatory character concerning the case or their possession of a part of the stolen property.

There is, then, this situation presented here, so far as the proof is concerned: The presence of the defendant and his companion in Portola just before the burglary was committed and thus opportunity to commit the crime available to them; the correspondence in size of the footprints on the surface of the snow leading to and from the building with the shoes worn by the defendant and his companion; the finding at Hawley, in which direction the accused were seen traveling,

of a part of the leather case in which one of the stolen watches
was incased when taken from the store, a short time after
the burglary; the possession by one of the parties of one of
the stolen watches, and the contradictory statements made
by the defendant and his companion in attempting to explain
such possession. These, with the other circumstances mentioned, make out what may well be deemed a strong circumstantial case. At all events, if, as appears to be so, the jury
believed the circumstances and the evidence by which they
were shown, we cannot say, as a matter of law, that they
thus arrived at an erroneous conclusion.

11. The last point calling for consideration involves the
charge of misconduct on the part of the district attorney
during the progress of the trial. The most serious of the
several objections under this head may be shown by the following colloquy: Mr. McLaughlin: "While Mr. Myers [a witness for defendant] is coming, we will ask to strike out all
the testimony in this case in regard to those shoes. The
prosecution had those in their possession at one time, and
could produce them here as an exhibit, if they had used due
diligence; and we object to the shoes being used." Mr. Kerr
(district attorney): "We object to the statement of counsel
that we had the shoes that got away from us before this trial
was started through no fault of the prosecution." Mr. Mc-
Laughlin: "Or defendant." Mr. Kerr: "You tell us where
they are and we will attempt to get them in here." Mr.
McLaughlin: "You probably know as much about their
whereabouts as I do, Mr. Kerr, and we resent the insinuation
in the remark." Mr. Kerr: ". . . I certainly apologize if
he [attorney for defendant] takes it as a personal proposition, for it wasn't meant that way."

It is, of course, always improper for an attorney in the
trial of a case before a jury to make any remark pregnant
with an insinuation that either party to the action, or any
party acting on the suggestion or in the interest of one of the
parties to the action, has suppressed testimony or disposed
of physical objects so that they may not be available for use
as testimony at the trial and which, upon inspection by the
jury, might tend to weaken the case of one of the parties.

In the present case, both the district attorney and the attorney for the defendant, during the course of the discussion, made statements which should not have been made in

the presence and hearing of the jury. While such conduct
on the part of lawyers during the trial of a warmly contested
case is generally the result of their zeal for the interests of
their clients, and not intended as means for bringing some
fact before the jury which it is not legally proper for them
to know, it often results seriously to the rights of the parties
and may lead to gross injustice. In this case, however, it is
reasonably probable that the remarks of the attorneys made
no impression upon the jury. They involved a charge and
counter-charge by two persons, in theory at least hostile to
each other, upon a matter not of overruling importance, since,
as we have shown, there were many other inculpatory circumstances of a convincing character brought out against the
accused than the circumstance of the footprints in the snow
answering to the description of the shoes worn by the defendant and Ed. Martinez at the time of their arrest. The
putting of the shoes themselves in evidence could have accomplished no more than to confirm or confute the testimony
showing that, in size, they corresponded with the footprints;
and if said testimony had been so confirmed or corroborated,
nothing would have been added thereto, and if thus refuted,
then the result would merely have been to destroy only one
circumstance, important, it is true, but which still left many
other circumstances the verity of which did not rest upon
the production of the shoes and which, on their face, were
sufficient to justify a verdict of guilty.

We have not succeeded in discovering the slightest semblance of misconduct by the district attorney in any of the
several other assignments of misconduct on the part of that
official. Those assignments, therefore, do not merit and will
not be given special notice.

We have now considered all the points to which we conceived special attention should be given, and, finding no
prejudicial error in the record, the judgment and the order
appealed from are affirmed.

Chipman, P. J., and Burnett, J., concurred.

GEORGE HAUB, Respondent, v. H. P. COUSTETTE et al., Appellants.

CONTRACT—PLUMBING—ABANDONMENT BY OWNER—REMEDY.—Where a contract to furnish and install the plumbing in a building is abandoned by the owner before completion, the contractor is entitled to recover the reasonable value of the materials furnished and the work performed.

APPEAL from a judgment of the Superior Court of the City and County of San Francisco. Bernard J. Flood, Judge.

The facts are stated in the opinion of the court.

James F. Brennan, for Appellants.

Fabius T. Finch, for Respondent.

KERRIGAN, J.—This is an appeal from a judgment in favor of the plaintiff in an action to recover for certain plumbing materials and for work and labor done and performed by the plaintiff.

Just prior to the opening of the Panama-Pacific International Exposition the defendants, owners of a lot of land near one of its principal entrances, let contracts for the erection of three small stores on their lot. One of those contracts was with the plaintiff, under the terms of which he was to furnish and install the plumbing in said building for a specified sum. Shortly after the opening of the Exposition the defendants, having probably discovered that the improvement of their property no longer promised the profitable investment they had anticipated, discontinued the construction of the stores. The plaintiff had proceeded with the performance of his contract, but certain parts of his work could not be performed until the building had progressed to a certain stage; for example, the toilets could not be installed until the floor had been laid on which they were to rest, and the sinks could not be placed in position until the wainscoting on which they were to hang was ready to receive them. The plaintiff on several occasions indicated to the defendants that he was ready and willing to proceed with and finish his work, and the latter on at least one occasion informed him that they were going to do nothing further with the building. It is plain, according to the testimony accepted by the court, that the defendants had abandoned the construction of the stores. Under these circumstances the court was warranted in finding and deciding, as it did, that plaintiff was entitled to recover the reasonable value of the materials furnished and the work performed. The court found that the reasonable value of the work unperformed called for by the contract was $55, and directed that this amount be deducted from the contract price, and judgment for the balance was accordingly entered in plaintiff's favor.

Such judgment appears to us to be just and legal. The defendants having delayed and prevented the plaintiff from completing his contract, the latter was entitled to recover the reasonable value of the work done. (*McConnell* v. *Corona City Water Co.*, 149 Cal. 60, [8 L. R. A. (N. S.) 1171, 85 Pac. 929].) In *Carlson* v. *Sheehan*, 157 Cal. 692, 696, [109 Pac. 29], the court said: "Where a person agrees to do a thing for another for a specified sum of money to be paid on full performance, he is not entitled to any part of the sum until he has himself done the thing he agreed to do, unless full performance has been delayed, prevented or excused by the act of the other party, or by operation of law, or by the act of God or the public enemy, as specified in section 1511 of the Civil Code. If performance is prevented by the party who is to make such payment, the person doing the things is entitled to payment as for full performance. (Civ. Code, sec. 1512.) And if one party breaks an intermediate covenant of an executory agreement, the other party may treat the entire contract as rescinded and recover in *quantum meruit* for the value of the work he has done under it. (*Cox* v. *McLaughlin*, 76 Cal. 60, [9 Am. St. Rep. 164, 18 Pac. 100].)"

The defendants contend that there is a variance in the findings on the second and third counts, but no pains have been taken to point out the asserted inconsistency, and an examination of the record fails to reveal any merit in such contention.

Judgment affirmed.

Lennon, P. J., and Richards, J., concurred.

[Civ. No. 1992. Second Appellate District.—September 14, 1916.]

ANNA W. RIFFEL, Respondent, v. ARTHUR LETTS et al., Appellants.

ASSAULT AND UNLAWFUL IMPRISONMENT—FORCE USED BY DEFENDANT—QUESTION FOR JURY—APPEAL.—In an action for damages for an assault and battery and for an unlawful imprisonment following an altercation concerning the ownership of a ten-dollar bill, it is for the jury to determine from the evidence whether or not excessive and unnecessary force was used upon the person of the plaintiff, and where there is evidence favorable to the plaintiff upon such issue, the verdict of the jury is conclusive on the appellate court.

ID.—AWARD OF DAMAGES—DISCRETION—EXCESSIVE VERDICT—REVIEW ON APPEAL.—As a general rule, what will be a proper and reasonable compensation for the damages occasioned by injuries to the person is a question committed to the sound discretion of the jury. In considering an attack upon a verdict as excessive the appellate court must treat every conflict of the evidence as resolved in favor of the respondent, and must give him the benefit of every inference that can reasonably be drawn in support of his claim.

ID.—ARREST "WITHOUT LEGAL JUSTIFICATION"—DAMAGES—INSTRUCTION. An instruction defining an arrest, and then stating that "for a private person to take another into custody, without legal justification, and restrain him of his liberty for a time and then turn him loose without taking him before a magistrate, or to a peace officer, is unlawful, and constitutes a trespass upon the liberty of the one so restrained for which he may be compensated in damages," is not prejudicial, for failure to adequately explain the words "without legal justification," where in other instructions, to which no objection is made, the court gives instructions showing the circumstances under which an arrest or imprisonment is legal or justifiable and also the circumstances under which an arrest or imprisonment is not legal or justifiable.

ID.—EVIDENCE—VERDICT NOT EXCESSIVE.—In an action to recover damages for injuries received from an assault and battery and from an unlawful imprisonment, the complaint being in two counts, it cannot be said that a verdict in the sum of two thousand five hundred dollars is excessive, where the jury is instructed that only actual damages are recoverable, and the evidence shows that the plaintiff was an unmarried woman and in good health at the time of the alleged occurrence, that she suffered much humiliation and distress of mind at the time and afterward, caused by being arrested and imprisoned in a caged wagon in a public street and in the presence of her neighbors, and that this caused great nervous excitement and shock, which seriously affected her health for a considerable time after the occurrence.

APPEAL from a judgment of the Superior Court of Los Angeles County, and from an order denying a new trial. Frederick W. Houser, Judge.

The facts are stated in the opinion of the court.

S. F. Macfarlane, and Clair S. Tappan, for Appellants.

T. C. Gould, and Shaw & Stewart, for Respondent.

CONREY, P. J.—The defendant Arthur Letts owns and operates a department store in the city of Los Angeles. The plaintiff purchased certain merchandise in his store and requested that it be delivered to her at her residence, the price to be paid on delivery. The goods were delivered by the defendant Withrow, an employee of Letts, to whom the plaintiff tendered a ten-dollar bill and received the change amounting to $8.65. While this exchange of money was going on the plaintiff suddenly remembered that she had had in her possession two ten-dollar bills; and acting under the belief that she had delivered one of them to Withrow, she attempted to withdraw the bill which she had tendered but which still remained in her hand. According to Withrow's testimony this bill was in his possession and she seized and took it out of his hand. But this is disputed by her, and as the fact is material, it must be deemed that the jury believed her testimony. Thereupon Withrow seized the plaintiff, violently pulled her from place to place in the yard near the door of her house, and finally lifted her up and carried her to the street and placed her in the wagon in a caged inclosure, the door of which he closed and fastened. After some delay and discussion, lasting for about an hour, Withrow and his assistant released the plaintiff from the wagon and went with her into her house, where the missing bill was discovered lying between the pages of a note-book on a table. As a result of the acts of the defendant Withrow, plaintiff received certain bruises upon her shoulder and left leg and suffered serious nervous shock and injury, so that she was confined to her bed for about three weeks. The imprisonment of plaintiff in the wagon took place in the presence of a number of neighbors of Mrs. Riffel, the attention of these persons having been attracted by the noise and violence there occurring.

The complaint in this action is in two counts, whereby she seeks to recover damages on account of the injuries received by her; seeking damages, first, for the assault and battery, and, second, as for a false and unlawful imprisonment. The case was tried to a jury, which returned a general verdict on which judgment has been entered in the sum of two thousand five hundred dollars and costs. The defendants appeal from the judgment and from an order denying their motion for a new trial.

Appellants insist that the evidence was insufficient to justify the verdict of the jury for the reasons: (1) That it was not shown that Withrow acted in an unjustifiable manner in restraining the plaintiff; (2) that in view of the evidence the amount of damages allowed was excessive.

Force may be used by the owner to retake property from a person who has obtained possession of it by force or fraud and is overtaken while carrying it away. As much force as is necessary may be used to retain one's property which a trespasser has taken into possession and is trying to carry away. (*Hodgeden* v. *Hubbard*, 18 Vt. 506; *Gyre* v. *Culver*, 47 Barb. (N. Y.) 592; *Johnson* v. *Perry*, 56 Vt. 703, [48 Am. Rep. 826]; *Hopkins* v. *Dickson*, 59 N. H. 235.) The court gave to the jury instructions correctly stating the law as to these matters. It was for the jury to determine from the evidence whether or not the bill was taken by the plaintiff by force, or taken or withheld with fraudulent intent, and whether or not excessive and unnecessary force was used by Withrow upon the person of plaintiff. As there is evidence favorable to the plaintiff upon these issues, the verdict thereon is conclusive in this court. Therefore, it must be taken as true that the plaintiff had not parted with possession of the bill, that she was acting in good faith, and that the force used by Withrow was excessive even if it had been lawful.

Next, it is claimed that the verdict was excessive in amount. As a general rule, what will be a proper and reasonable compensation for the damages occasioned by injuries to the person is a question committed to the sound discretion of the jury. In considering an attack upon a verdict as excessive

the appellate court must treat every conflict of the evidence
as resolved in favor of the respondent, and must give him
the benefit of every inference that can reasonably be drawn
in support of his claim. (*Kimic* v. *San Jose-Los Gatos etc.
Ry. Co.*, 156 Cal. 273, 277, [104 Pac. 312].) It is admitted
by counsel for respondent that under the first cause of action
as stated in the complaint the damages for injuries from the
assault and battery were limited at the time of the trial to a
period of three months following the date of the transaction.
This being so, it may be that the amount of the verdict under
the evidence in this case would be excessive if applied to the
first cause of action alone. But the plaintiff's recovery also
includes the second cause of action, namely, for an unlawful
imprisonment. The jury was instructed that it must not
allow damages by way of example or penalty, and that as to
the first cause of action the recovery must be limited to facts
or circumstances arising within three months from the date
of the assault. The second cause of action was submitted
under the general instruction authorizing an assessment for
actual damages only. There was evidence showing that the
plaintiff was an unmarried woman about forty-five years of
age and at that time in good health. She suffered much
humiliation and distress of mind at the time and afterward,
caused by being arrested and imprisoned in a caged wagon
in the public street and in the presence of her neighbors.
That this caused great nervous excitement and shock which
seriously affected her health for a considerable time thereafter is indicated by evidence sufficient legally to warrant the
verdict, and we are not justified in setting it aside as excessive, or as having been rendered as the result of passion or
prejudice or anything other than a fair consideration of the
evidence.

Objection is made to the eighth instruction given to the
jury. That instruction defines an arrest and states that "for
a private person to take another into custody, without legal
justification, and restrain him of his liberty for a time and
then turn him loose without taking him before a magistrate,
or to a peace officer, is unlawful and constitutes a trespass
upon the liberty of the one so restrained for which he may
be compensated in damages." Appellants' criticism of this
instruction is that the court failed to adequately explain the
words "without legal justification," and it is contended that

this omission was extremely prejudicial to the defendants as
implying that under the circumstances of the case the plaintiff was entitled to damages. A sufficient answer is that in
other instructions, to which no objection is made, the court
gave instructions showing the circumstances under which an
arrest or imprisonment is legal or justifiable and also the circumstances under which an arrest or imprisonment is not
legal or justifiable.

The judgment and order are affirmed.

James, J., and Shaw, J., concurred.

[Crim. No. 350.   Third Appellate District.—September 1*, 1916.]

THE PEOPLE, Respondent, v. FRANK GOODRUM,
Appellant.

CRIMINAL LAW—ASSAULT TO MURDER—INSANITY FROM USE OF ALCO-
HOLIC LIQUORS—REFUSAL OF INSTRUCTION ON LAW OF SETTLED IN-
SANITY — PREJUDICIAL ERROR.—In a prosecution for the crime of
assault to commit murder, it is prejudicial error to refuse an instruction proposed by the defendant on the law of insanity brought
on by the use of intoxicating liquors that will excuse a criminal act,
where it was expressly admitted by the people that the defendant
was not intoxicated at the time of the assault, and there was evidence introduced which would support the theory that the alleged
insanity of the defendant was the effect of long-continued intoxication prior to the commission of the crime.

ID.—CHARACTER OF MENTAL DERANGEMENT—ERRONEOUS INSTRUCTION—
QUESTIONS OF FACT.—The reading to the jury, as a part of the instructions in the case, of the following language taken from a recent
decision of the appellate court, to wit: "Defendant's normal condition
was that of a sane man. His alleged mental derangement was not
only transient in character, but such condition was the result of his
voluntary acts in the use of alcoholic liquors. Under such circumstances, one prosecuted for the commission of a crime cannot urge
such condition as a defense thereto,"—is prejudicial error, as the
question whether the defendant's mental derangement was only of a
transient character, and his condition the result of his voluntary acts
in the use of alcoholic liquors, was a question solely and exclusively
for the jury.

ID.—TEMPORARY AND SETTLED INSANITY—USE OF INTOXICANTS.—There
is a well-recognized distinction in law between temporary insanity

or mental aberration brought on by voluntary intoxication and "settled insanity" superinduced by long-continued indulgence in alcoholic liquors. A sane person who voluntarily drinks and becomes intoxicated is not excused; but if one, by reason of long-continued indulgence in intoxicants has reached the stage of chronic alcoholism where the brain is permanently diseased and where permanent general insanity has resulted, he is not legally responsible for his acts.

ID.—TEMPORARY DERANGEMENT FROM USE OF INTOXICANTS—EVIDENCE—MOTIVE OR INTENT.—Mere temporary mental derangement resulting from the use of intoxicants, whether it manifests itself in the form of *delirium tremens* or in some milder form, cannot operate to absolve a person from liability for a criminal act, and testimony disclosing that precise mental state at the time the criminal act was committed is admissible only where the existence of a particular purpose, motive, or intent is a necessary element of the crime charged, and then it may be considered by the jury, not as the predicate for the full exoneration of the accused, but solely to enable or assist them in determining the purpose, motive, or intent with which he committed the act.

ID.—SCOPE OF DEFENSE—OPENING ADDRESS OF COUNSEL.—A defendant in a criminal case, in making a defense and proving his case, is not necessarily required to remain strictly within the literal scope of the defense outlined by his counsel in his opening address to the jury.

APPEAL from a judgment of the Superior Court of Tehama County, and from an order denying a new trial. John F. Ellison, Judge.

The facts are stated in the opinion of the court.

J. M. Lee, for Appellant.

U. S. Webb, Attorney-General, and J. Charles Jones, Deputy Attorney-General, for Respondent.

HART, J.—Under an indictment charging him with the crime of assault to commit murder, the defendant was convicted of the crime of assault with a deadly weapon, and was sentenced to imprisonment in the state prison for the term of eighteen months. This appeal is prosecuted by the defendant from the judgment and the order denying him a new trial.

The assault was committed on the wife of the defendant, in the city of Red Bluff, on the twentieth day of December, 1915.

Domestic dissensions had led to the separation of the parties, and for some little time prior to the date of the assault the defendant had not lived with his wife.

The undisputed facts are: That on the said twentieth day of December, between the hours of 5 and 6 o'clock P. M., Mrs. Goodrum and her mother, Mrs. Harriet B. Reyon, who was then stopping at the home of the former, were on their way home from the business part of the city, when they were approached from the rear by the defendant. He placed his hand upon the shoulder of his wife and, addressing her, said: "Belle, I want to speak to you a minute." Both Mrs. Goodrum and Mrs. Reyon turned and faced him, and at the same time the defendant drew a revolver and pointed it in the face of his wife. Mrs. Reyon grabbed the weapon, a tussle ensued, and the weapon was discharged, no one, however, being struck by the bullet. Thereupon the defendant drew a knife and began cutting and slashing his wife about the head and left arm. Several ugly, though not serious, wounds were thus inflicted upon the head, left arm, and hand of Mrs. Goodrum. Mrs. Reyon called loudly for assistance, and finally the defendant desisted from his attack and stepped away a distance of twelve or fifteen feet and threatened and apparently attempted to commit suicide.

Mrs. Goodrum was taken to a drug-store near by, where she received the attention of a physician, and the defendant was placed under arrest, taken to the county jail, and subsequently, on account of a gash across his throat, inflicted by a knife, presumably by himself, and weakness resulting from said wound, was conveyed to the county hospital, where he remained for several weeks.

The defense interposed at the trial was that of insanity, and testimony was introduced to support it, a number of "intimate acquaintances" testifying that in their opinion the defendant was insane on the day upon which the assault was committed. And the defendant himself testified that he had no recollection of the assault or of any incidents connected with himself occurring on that day.

The complaint against the result reached by the jury is based solely upon certain instructions given by the court upon the issue of insanity and also upon the action of the court in rejecting certain instructions proposed by the defendant upon that question.

While it was expressly admitted in court by the district
attorney that the defendant was not under the influence of
intoxicating liquor at the time of the assault, it was the
theory of the people at the trial that if the defendant's mentality was not wholly normal or was, to the extent of rendering him irresponsible, impaired on that occasion, such condition of mind was occasioned wholly by the use by him of
intoxicating liquors for some period of time prior to the assault. And, in harmony with this theory, the court instructed the jury, basing its instructions upon that question
upon section 22 of the Penal Code, which reads as follows:
"No act committed by a person while in a state of voluntary
intoxication is less criminal by reason of his having been in
such condition. But whenever the actual existence of any
particular purpose, motive, or intent is a necessary element
to constitute any particular species or degree of crime, the
jury may take into consideration the fact that the accused
was intoxicated at the time, in determining the purpose,
motive, or intent with which he committed the act."

The court correctly instructed the jury, in accordance with
the provisions of the foregoing section, that temporary insanity produced by the voluntary use of intoxicating liquor is
no excuse for the commission of crime. It is claimed, however, that, since it was admitted that the defendant was not
in an intoxicated condition on the day that the assault was
committed, there was, under the proofs, ample room for the
theory that the alleged insanity of the accused was not of a
temporary character as the result of his voluntary intoxication, but the effect of long-continued intoxication for a period
prior to the time of the commission of the act, and was,
within the meaning of the law, "settled insanity"; that the
court should have instructed upon that theory, and erred to
the prejudice of the defendant by refusing to do so.

In view of the fact that there was some testimony tending
to show that the accused had, previously to the day of the
difficulty, habitually imbibed intoxicating liquors to excess,
and of the further fact that the people admitted that the defendant was not in a state of intoxication on the day of the
assault, we think there is some force to this contention.

There is a well-recognized distinction in law between temporary insanity or mental aberration brought on by voluntary intoxication and "settled insanity" superinduced by

long-continued indulgence in alcoholic liquors. "A sane man
who voluntarily drinks and becomes intoxicated is not excused because the result is to cloud his judgment, unbalance
his reason, impair his perceptions, derange his mental faculties, and lead him to the commission of an act which in his
sober senses he would have avoided. Upon the other hand,
if one, by reason of long-continued indulgence in intoxicants,
has reached the stage of chronic alcoholism where the brain
is permanently diseased, where the victim is rendered incapable of distinguishing right from wrong, and where permanent general insanity has resulted, then, and in such case,
he is no more legally responsible for his acts than would be the
man congenitally insane, or insane from violent injury to the
brain." (*People* v. *Fellows*, 122 Cal. 233, 239, [54 Pac. 830,
832] ; see, also, *People* v. *Travers*, 88 Cal. 233, 239, [26 Pac.
88] ; *People* v. *Rogers*, 18 N. Y. 9, [72 Am. Dec. 484]; *People* v. *Hower*, 151 Cal. 638, 642, 643, [91 Pac. 507].)

While there can be no doubt that the case as made by the
evidence justified the giving of an instruction upon settled
insanity brought about by an incessant and excessive use of
intoxicating liquors for a long period of time prior to the
commission of the assault, we believe that those rejected instructions which purported to contain concrete statements of
the law as applied to the present case were, under the evidence, framed in language entirely too general. The evidence strongly tends to show—indeed, there is no other character of showing upon that subject—that, to whatever extent
the defendant's mentality had been impaired, his condition
in that regard had been caused by the use of intoxicants, but
some of the instructions proposed by the accused but rejected
were so phrased as to have submitted to the jury, if given,
the question, not whether the defendant was afflicted with
settled insanity caused by the use of intoxicating liquors,
but whether from any cause he was the victim of permanent
insanity, as to which latter proposition there was no evidence
presented or received. All the *concrete* instructions on the
question of insanity *in this case* should have been, with
proper qualifications, made applicable solely to insanity
caused by the use of intoxicating liquors, so that the jury
could not have been misled as to the recognized distinction
in law between the mental derangement so caused which
would not excuse a criminal act and the insanity so caused

which would, because of a defect of criminal or any intent necessarily the result of such insanity, excuse such an act. This is not to say, however, that an abstract or a *general* instruction on the question of insanity as applied to crimes should not have been given. To the contrary, we think such an instruction should have been submitted for the purpose of enlightening the jury upon the general proposition that one committing a criminal act while laboring under a state of "settled" insanity resulting from any cause whatsoever cannot be held liable for such act.

But we are of the opinion that the learned trial judge, ordinarily singularly accurate and correct in the statement of pertinent legal principles to juries, permitted himself to be led into error seriously prejudicing the defendant by giving an instruction in which, without qualification, it was declared: "On this subject [that of insanity] the appellate court in a recent decision uses this language, which I will read to you as a part of the instructions in this case: 'Defendant's normal condition was that of a sane man. His alleged mental derangement was not only transient in character, but such condition was the result of his voluntary acts in the use of alcoholic liquors. Under such circumstances, one prosecuted for the commission of a crime cannot urge such condition as a defense thereto.' "

The foregoing language was taken from the opinion in the case of *People* v. *Bremer,* 24 Cal. App. 315, 316, 317, [141 Pac. 222], and the principle stated thereby is unquestionably correct as an abstract proposition. But, as applied to the present case, the instruction plainly invaded the province of the jury. Whether the defendant's mental derangement was only of "a transient character" and his condition the result "of his voluntary acts in the use of alcoholic liquors," was one of the most important questions of fact involved in the case, and one, obviously, whose solution was solely and exclusively a function of the jury. It has been suggested, however, that, since the court declared that it was taken from an appellate court decision, the instruction, so far as it purports to deal with facts, must be viewed as having reference not to the present case but to the case from the opinion in which its language was taken, and that its effect, therefore, so far as this case was concerned, was merely to state the application generally of the rule relating to the effect of voluntary

intoxication upon the commission of a criminal act by one
when suffering from a mental derangement so superinduced.
But we do not feel at liberty to so view the instruction or to
declare that the jury did not understand it as applying particularly to this case.   While the court did explain that the
language was taken from the decision in another case, it also
declared that it would be adopted as part of the instructions
in the case at bar; and from this it is to be assumed, as we
may justly presume the jury assumed, that, according to the
opinion of the court, the facts of this case were precisely the
same as the facts in the case giving rise to the language of
the instruction, and that the principle therein declared was,
therefore, peculiarly applicable and pertinent to the present
case.   In any event, as stated, the instruction, notwithstanding the particular source whence it was derived, was expressly
made a part of the court's charge, and, as declared, it involved a clear instruction upon a vital question of fact in the
case.   And, since the effect of the instruction was to take
from the jury one of the most vital questions of fact in the
case, it cannot, in our opinion, be held that the error in giving it is one of those which may properly be said, after a
review and consideration of the entire record, not to have
resulted in a miscarriage of justice.   It is very true, as well
we may suggest in the present connection, that if the defendant was not wholly irresponsible by reason of insanity when
he attacked his wife, his assault upon her was unprovoked
and of a most atrocious character; but, however vicious and
unjustifiable his attack might have been, he was entitled to
have his only defense, viz, insanity, passed upon and determined solely by the jury.

The judgment and the order are reversed and the cause
remanded.

Chipman, P. J., and Burnett, J., concurred.

A petition for a rehearing of this cause was denied by
the district court of appeal on October 14, 1916, and the following opinion then rendered thereon:

HART, J.—In their petition, counsel for the people say:
"On the outset of this matter we admit that the decision
heretofore rendered in this case is correct in principle, but

we claim that the people tried one case and the court decided another."

The point is that the defendant, at the trial, tried his case solely upon the theory of temporary insanity brought on by "recent indulgence in alcoholism"; that such was the theory upon which the learned trial court instructed the jury, and that this court decided the case upon the erroneous supposition that the defense interposed by the defendant was that he was wholly irresponsible and not accountable in law for his act because of settled insanity superinduced by the excessive use of intoxicating liquors.

In proof of their position, counsel for the people call attention to certain language of the attorney for the defendant in his opening statement to the jury, in which he declared: "In other words, I think, gentlemen, we will show you beyond question in this case that Frank Goodrum, at the time this assault was made, knew nothing about it; that he was simply laboring under a case of *delirium tremens*—simply insane from the effect of alcohol that he had consumed in the week or two before that, and that he was in a state of mind not to be accountable for what he did. We will show you that the acts that he did in the manner in which this offense has been portrayed here were not natural, but unusual —an improbable way of doing that kind of thing; that he had nothing against his wife at any time. Now, I say if we show you that, then that is a defense to this action." Again, in his opening address, the attorney said: "We will show you that he was nervous; that he had all the indications, gentlemen, that make up a case of alcoholic insanity—not drunkenness, gentlemen, but the effects of alcohol after the stimulant has died out—the effect on the nerves. . . . I think I will show you what I have said, and even more on that line."

Thus, it is contended, the counsel for the defendant expressly limited the purpose of proof upon the question of the mental condition of the accused at the time of the commission of the alleged assault to the establishment of the fact that he was suffering only from temporary mental derangement as the result of the use of intoxicating liquors, and this proposition is, it is asserted, emphasized and clearly sustained by the statement of counsel that he would show that the defendant, on the occasion of the assault, was suffering from an

attack of *delirium tremens*, a condition which is a mere temporary effect of alcoholism and not a characteristic of settled
insanity caused by alcoholism.

It is to be conceded that the attorney for the accused, in
his opening statement to the jury, was not altogether happy
in his expressions or the presentation of his case as he proposed to make it. Obviously, mere temporary mental derangement resulting from the use of intoxicants, whether it
manifests itself in the form of *delirium tremens* or in some
milder form, cannot operate to absolve a person from liability for a criminal act, and testimony disclosing that precise
mental state at the time the criminal act was committed is
admissible only where the existence of a particular purpose,
motive, or intent is a necessary element of the crime charged,
and then it may be considered by the jury, not as the predicate for the full exoneration of the accused, but solely to
enable or assist them in determining the purpose, motive, or
intent with which he committed the act. (Pen. Code, sec.
22.)

But we think that the opening statement of counsel is
broader in its scope than the people ascribe to it. Whether
the attorney for the defendant, in his opening statement, did
or did not state to the jury in apt technical language that
he proposed to rely upon the defense of insanity for the complete exoneration of the accused, it is clear to our minds that
said statement clearly enough and so sufficiently shows that
that was what he intended and endeavored therein to say.
On numerous occasions, in the course of his statement, he
declared that he would show, or attempt to show, that the
defendant, when the assault was made, was insane; that he
was suffering from "alcoholic insanity," adding, in one instance, when using the latter language, the statement, "not
drunkenness," thus attempting to emphasize the proposition
that he did not refer to mere temporary mental aberration
or derangement, but to settled insanity; that the accused was
"in a state of mind not to be accountable for what he did,"
and many other like expressions, all indicating with sufficient clearness that what he intended to say to the jury was
that he proposed to prove that the defendant, by the excessive use of intoxicating liquors for a time prior to the assault,
had become afflicted with insanity to a degree that, in a legal

view, he was, at the time of the assault, wholly irresponsible and not accountable for his act.

But a defendant, in a criminal case, in making a defense and proving his case, is not necessarily required to remain strictly within the literal scope of the defense outlined by his counsel in his opening address to the jury. It may happen, as doubtless it has happened, that a lawyer may not succeed in stating his case to the jury in a strictly proper manner or in correct technical nomenclature. This may naturally occur in a criminal case where the attorney for the defendant, generally well learned in the law, has had no experience in the practice of the criminal law, and whose practical familiarity with the rules and doctrines of that branch of jurisprudence is decidedly limited. Hence, that would be a strange, and, indeed, a manifestly unjust rule which would, in a case where his defense had not been properly explained in the opening statement, preclude the defendant from making his case as he intended to prove it, and as he had reason to believe he could only prove it as in complete answer to the charge against him. But, even assuming that the opening statement of counsel for the accused in this case is amenable to the interpretation to which it is subjected by the people, the trial court in this case, so far as the proof was concerned, accorded to the defendant the right to traverse a broader field than the said opening statement, *as so interpreted,* warranted; for it allowed opinion testimony of intimate acquaintances of the defendant that he was insane at the time, or in near proximity to the time, at which the assault occurred. This testimony, even if it may truly be said that the opening statement did not, squarely and broadly brought into the case as a vitally important issue therein the question whether the defendant was insane to the extent that he was so bereft of reason and the power of volition as to have rendered him wholly irresponsible for his act. And the fact that the testimony offered in support of that issue might have been insufficient in probative force to prove it by the requisite degree of proof, or the fact that other witnesses might have given testimony tending to show or even satisfactorily showing that the mental condition of the accused was only temporary and the result of mere drunkenness, could not have the effect of taking insanity from the case as one of the vital issues. The issue was there and some testimony received in its support, and, as declared in our former opinion and as is obviously true, it was wholly for the jury to say whether it was proved to a sufficient degree to entitle the defendant to an acquittal on the ground that thus he was not in a mental condition to be responsible, legally, for the assault. Hence it was, as we have held, error, prejudicial to the accused, for the court to have practically taken that question from the jury, and, moreover, under our view of the record as above pointed out, we may add to what we said in our former opinion that the court further erred to the serious detriment of the defendant by confining the jury to the consideration of the evidence upon the defendant's intoxication to the mere determination by them of the particular "purpose, motive, or intent" with which the accused committed the act. In other words, we think that an instruction on insanity brought on by the use of intoxicating liquors that will, in law, excuse a criminal act, should have been given, and that, such an instruction having been proposed by the defendant and disallowed, the action of the court in that respect constituted prejudicial error.

There can be no possible doubt that the trial court intended to and did, under its conception of the case, give the defendant a fair trial; but we think the scope of the defendant's position in the case was misapprehended by the prosecuting attorney and that the court, erroneously adopting the misconceived theory of the people, made the errors above referred to, and which we think undoubtedly demanded the reversal heretofore ordered.

Rehearing denied.

Chipman, P. J., and Burnett, J., concurred.

A petition to have the cause heard in the supreme court, after judgment in the district court of appeal, was denied by the supreme court on November 9, 1916.

[Civ. No. 1959.   First Appellate District.—September 15, 1916.]

JAMES H. FORMAN et al., Petitioners, v. INDUSTRIAL ACCIDENT COMMISSION et al., Respondents.

WORKMEN'S COMPENSATION ACT—SALESMAN OF REAL ESTATE—INJURIES IN HOTEL FIRE.—Injuries and losses by one employed as a salesman of real estate upon commission do not come within the scope of the Workmen's Compensation Act (Stats. 1913, p. 279), where they resulted from a fire in a hotel in which the employee was spending the night in a town to which he had been sent for the purpose of selling real estate and at which he was to remain indefinitely; and the employee is not entitled to recover compensation under said act from his employer.

APPLICATION originally made to the District Court of Appeal for the Third Appellate District for a Writ of Review to annul the action of the Industrial Accident Commission, awarding an employee compensation for injuries.

The facts are stated in the opinion of the court.

Redman & Alexander, for Petitioners.

Chris. M. Bradley, for Respondents.

THE COURT.—This is an application for a writ of review directed at a proceeding before the Industrial Accident Commission, wherein the respondent, Richard F. James, sought to recover compensation from his employer, James H. Forman, and the insurer of said employer Georgia Casualty Company, for injuries alleged to have been sustained during and in the course of his employment.

The stipulated facts are as follows: Richard F. James was employed by James H. Forman as a salesman for the purpose of selling real estate upon commission. The terms of his employment as such salesman did not call for regular working hours, but it was understood that he should make sales of real estate at any or such times as it was possible for him to secure a customer and complete the sale. Mr. James was directed by his employer to go to the town of Needles for the purpose of selling real estate there and to remain indefinitely. Mr. James went to said town for that purpose, and while there took a room in the White House Hotel, where, on the evening of February 28, 1916, he retired for the night. At or near the hour of 4:15 A. M. of February 29th a fire broke out in the White House Hotel, which destroyed the hotel and in which Mr. James lost his clothing and effects, and was also burned about the hands and arms and face in escaping from the fire. For the injuries thus suffered he made application for compensation from his employer before the Industrial Accident Commission, and upon a hearing was awarded the sum of $365.90. A petition for rehearing was presented and denied by the commission, whereupon the petitioners herein applied to this court for a writ of review.

We are of the opinion that this case is one which does not come within the scope of the Workmen's Compensation Act (Stats. 1913, p. 279). Section 12a of the act provides as follows: "Liability for the compensation provided by this act, in lieu of any other liability whatsoever, shall, without regard to negligence, exist against any employer for any personal injury sustained by his employees by accident arising out of and in the course of the employment. . . . (2) Where, at the time of the accident, the employee is performing services growing out of and incidental to his employment and is acting within the course of his employment as such." It seems clear to us that the injuries and losses which the respondent James suffered cannot be held to have been sustained by an accident arising out of and in the course of his employment, nor to have occurred at a time when the employee was performing service growing out of and incidental to his employment and acting within the course of his employment as such; and that this view is fully sustained by the following authorities: *Gaskell* v. *Van Voorhies Co.*, 2 I. A. C. No. 14, p. 1020; *Green* v. *Shaw*, 5 Butterworth Comp. Cas. 573; *Kitchenam* v. *The Johannisberg*, 4 Butterworth Comp. Cas. 311; *Rodger* v. *Paisley Schoolboard*, 5 Butterworth Comp. Cas. 547; *Milliken* v. *Towle Co.*, 216 Mass. 293, [L. R. A. 1916A, 337, 103 N. E. 898]; *Bryant* v. *Fissell*, 84 N. J. L. 72, [86 Atl. 458]; and particularly the case of *Ocean Accident & Guaranty Co.* v. *Industrial Accident Commission of the State of California*, 173 Cal. 313, [159 Pac. 1041], decided by the supreme court in Bank September 8, 1916, and in which case the foregoing section of the Workmen's Compensation Act is given a very exhaustive review.

The award is therefore annulled.

ALBERT J. CORY, Respondent, v. W. J. HOTCHKISS et al., Appellants.

QUIETING TITLE—ADVERSE POSSESSION—EVIDENCE—BURDEN OF PROOF.—
In an action to quiet title to real property in which the defendants
claim title by adverse possession and also under a purported tax sale,
where the record title to the land is shown to be in the plaintiff, presumptively he was seised of the possession within the time required
by law, and the burden is upon the defendants to show that they or
either of them, having color of title to the land, had held and possessed the same against the plaintiff for the full statutory period
of five years preceding the commencement of the action.

ID.—ABSENCE OF RECORD TITLE—ESSENTIALS OF ADVERSE POSSESSION.—
One who does not connect himself with a record title cannot be said
to have had possession of land under color of title, and therefore,
in order to establish a claim of adverse possession, it is incumbent
upon him to show compliance with the provisions of section 325 of
the Code of Civil Procedure, viz., (1) that the land had been protected by a substantial inclosure; or (2) that it has been cultivated
and improved during his alleged use and occupation of the same, and,
failing in this, his claim falls.

ID.—CLAIM UNDER COLOR OF TITLE—ABSENCE OF POSSESSION.—Where it
does not appear that one claiming land under a tax deed at any time
personally or otherwise occupied and used the land, or that he did
anything with reference to the same after receiving the deed save
to pay the taxes thereon, he cannot sustain a claim of adverse possession.

ID.—LEASING OF LAND—FAILURE TO SHOW EXCLUSIVE USE.—The mere
fact that one of the defendants assumed the ownership of the land
and leased the same to another may be some evidence that it was
his intent to claim the land, but where he fails to show that it was
occupied by his lessee for the statutory period, or that it was not
used by plaintiff or other persons during that time, his mere intent
to claim the land is insufficient to support a claim of title by adverse
possession.

ID.—JOINT CLAIM OF ADVERSE POSSESSION—INSUFFICIENCY OF EVIDENCE.
Where it is alleged in the cross-complaint in an action to quiet title
to land that the title was conveyed by the holder of a tax deed to
one of the defendants (who the evidence does not show ever had possession of the land), for the benefit of himself and the other defendant (who leased the land for grazing purposes), the latter cannot
be said to have connected himself with the purported title of his
codefendant, there being no evidence that he was acting for his
codefendant or for himself and the latter jointly.

APPEAL from a judgment of the Superior Court of Fresno County, and from an order denying a new trial. George E. Church, Judge.

The facts are stated in the opinion of the court.

E. A. Williams, for Appellants.

Drew & Drew, and Frank Kauke, for Respondent.

LENNON, P. J.—The plaintiff in this action sought and recovered judgment against the defendants quieting his title to 160 acres of land situate in the county of Fresno. The defendants' answer denied all of the material allegations of the plaintiff's complaint, and, cross-complaining, claimed title to the lands in dispute by adverse possession, and also under a purported tax sale and deed from the county tax collector to one R. M. Barthold, which was followed by a deed from the latter to the defendant Hotchkiss alleged to have been made and executed for the benefit of Hotchkiss and the defendant Canty. The trial court found that the tax sale which was the basis of the tax collector's deed to Barthold was invalid, for the reason that it was made for an amount in excess of that permitted by law. It is conceded that the evidence sustains this finding, and that, as a consequence, the tax deed did not, as further found by the trial court, convey any title to the land in dispute to Barthold or his purported successor in interest. It is claimed, however, that by reason of the purported deed from the tax collector to Barthold and the deed from him to the defendant Hotchkiss, the defendants had color of title sufficient to support their claim of title to the land by adverse possession under the provisions of section 323 of the Code of Civil Procedure. The record title to the land having been shown to be in the plaintiff, presumptively he was seised of the possession within the time required by law; and therefore the burden was upon the defendants to show that they or either of them, having color of title to the land, had held and possessed the same as against the plaintiff for the full statutory period of five years preceding the commencement of the present action. (Code Civ. Proc., sec. 321.) In support of the burden thus placed upon the defendants they showed that yearly for seven or eight years prior to the commencement of the action the defendant Canty had in writing leased the land in suit to one Pucheu, for the purpose of pasturing sheep thereon, and that during a portion of each of those several years Pucheu did run and pasture as many as three separate herds of sheep upon the land for a period of from two to six months in each year; each band of sheep had a herder, and these herders during the time that the sheep were pasturing were in the habit of traveling back and forth over the land. Bands of sheep belonging to other persons at times traveled across the land to water at a well situated on the southeast corner of the land. Pucheu's sheep were upon the land only during the pasture season, and although during that season he was upon the land once a week, he did not know of his own knowledge whether his herders prevented the sheep of other persons pasturing upon the land leased by him; and because of his lack of knowledge as to where the lines of the land actually ran, he was unable to say whether or not the sheep of other persons had roamed and pastured upon the land at the times his sheep were there. Supplementing the evidence of Pucheu, there was testimony of another witness for the defense to the effect that he knew that Pucheu had pastured sheep upon the land in suit, and that, in so far as he knew, no other sheep were permitted to pasture there.

This is substantially a statement of the evidence introduced at the trial and relied upon by the defendants with reference to the actual use and occupation of the land. It was an admitted fact in the case—and the trial court found—that all taxes levied upon the land in suit subsequent to the date of the tax deed to Barthold were paid by the defendant Hotchkiss, and that the defendant Canty paid nothing for or on account of such taxes. While the evidence shows that the land was neither cultivated, improved nor inclosed, it is conceded that inasmuch as Hotchkiss had color of title to the land, he might have supported his claim of adverse possession by proof of his possession and occupancy of the land for the purpose of pasturage, coupled with proof that he had employed herders to keep his own stock on the land and other stock off. (Code Civ. Proc., sec. 323, subd. 3; *Bullock* v. *Rouse*, 81 Cal. 590, [22 Pac. 919].) However, it does not appear from the record before us that the defendant Hotchkiss at any time personally or otherwise occupied and so used the land, or that he did anything with reference to the same after receiving the deed from Barthold save to pay the taxes thereon. Therefore it cannot be said that he had continuously or at all occupied the land for the purpose of pasturage for the statutory period of five years; and consequently it must be held that his claim of adverse possession was not made out. True, the defendants in their cross-complaint alleged that Barthold conveyed the land to the defendant Hotchkiss for the use and benefit of Hotchkiss and Canty. This allegation, however, was duly denied by the plaintiff's answer to the cross-complaint; and the record is absolutely barren of any evidence showing or tending to show any interest in common between them under the deed or otherwise or that the defendant Canty was in privity or ever claimed any right, title, or interest in the land under or through the defendant Hotchkiss. In so far as the record shows, the source of Canty's right to lease the land to Pucheu does not appear, and certainly there was no showing that in so leasing the lands he was acting for Hotchkiss, or jointly for himself and Hotchkiss. The defendant Canty not having connected himself with the purported title of Hotchkiss, cannot be said to have had possession of the land in dispute under color of title, and, therefore, in order to establish his claim of adverse possession, it was incumbent upon him to show compliance with the provisions of section 325 of the Code of Civil Procedure, viz., (1) that the land had been protected by a substantial inclosure, or (2) that it had been cultivated and improved during his alleged use and occupation of the same. This the defendant Canty did not do, and therefore his defense of adverse possession necessarily failed when measured by the provisions of the code section last cited.

But, aside from this, we are of the opinion that the evidence adduced relative to the use and occupation of the land by Canty's lessee would not have sufficed to support a finding that the defendants, or either of them, had exclusive use and occupation of the land for the statutory period within the intent and meaning of the provisions of section 323 of the Code of Civil Procedure. The mere fact that Canty assumed the ownership of the land and leased the same to Pucheu may have been some evidence that it was the intent of Canty to claim the land; but if, as the evidence shows, he did no more, and that the land was not occupied by Pucheu under the lease in the manner and for the period prescribed by the statute, then of course the mere intent of Canty would not afford any substantial support to the claim of adverse possession; and certain it is that the defendants did not affirmatively show, as they were required to do, that during the time that the land was not used for grazing purposes it was not otherwise used and occupied by the plaintiff or other persons claiming under him or independent of him. The testimony that "this quarter-section is used for nothing after the end of the pasture season" is the only evidence to be found in the record upon this phase of the case; and obviously the scope of that testimony must be confined to the use to which the land was usually put, and clearly cannot be construed as establishing the fact that the land was not occupied during and after the close of the pasturing season. In brief, the proof proffered in the present case in support of the claim of adverse possession, as in the case of *Strauss* v. *Canty*, 169 Cal. 101, [145 Pac. 1012], "was entirely consistent with the view that the possession of this holding under Canty was casual and intermittent," and therefore, as was said in that case, "the court was entirely justified in concluding that the defendant had not proven an exclusive and continued possession sufficient to satisfy the statute."

For the reasons stated, the judgment and order appealed from are affirmed.

Richards, J., and Kerrigan, J., concurred.

[Civ. No. 1841.   First Appellate District.—September 15, 1916.]

N. L. GARDNER, Appellant, v. WILLIS E. STEADMAN, Respondent.

CHANGE OF PLACE OF TRIAL—AFFIDAVIT OF MERITS—AFFIDAVIT OF THIRD PARTY — SECTION 396, CODE OF CIVIL PROCEDURE.—An affidavit of merits, under section 396 of the Code of Civil Procedure, on motion for a change of place of trial, may be made by any person on behalf of the defendant who is sufficiently familiar with the facts of the case to make the same.

ID.—INSUFFICIENT AFFIDAVIT—AMENDMENT.—An affidavit of merits, on motion for a change of place of trial, made by the defendant's wife, which is insufficient by reason of containing affiant's mere conclusion as to defendant's residence, may be amended, and the affidavit of residence and merits of the attorney for the defendant, which is admittedly sufficient in form, may be considered as an amendment to the prior affidavit.

APPEAL from an order of the Superior Court of the City and County of San Francisco changing the place of trial of an action. Marcel E. Cerf, Judge.

The facts are stated in the opinion of the court.

Algernon Crofton, and R. W. Gillogley, for Appellant.

Skinner, Skinner & Henshall, for Respondent.

RICHARDS, J.—This is an appeal from an order changing the place of trial of the action from the city and county of San Francisco to the county of Los Angeles, upon defendant's motion.

The said defendant was sued in the city and county of San Francisco upon a personal obligation and was duly served with process. Within the time required by law he appeared by his attorney of record and demurred, and at the same time filed a demand for a change of the place of trial of the action to Los Angeles County. There was also filed at the same time an affidavit of residence and merits, which affidavit, however, was not sworn to by the defendant but by his wife, who deposed therein that the defendant was temporarily absent from the state of California, and therefore, for that reason, the affidavit was made by her; that the residence of the defendant was some time prior to and at the time of the commencement of the action and thereafter in the county of Los Angeles; that the affiant was familiar with the facts of the case, and had fully and fairly stated the same to Newton J. Skinner, the defendant's attorney, and upon such statement had been advised by him and verily believed that the defendant had a good and substantial defense to the action on the merits. Upon the hearing of the motion plaintiff objected to this affidavit, but upon what grounds does not appear in the record. However, the defendant thereupon asked and obtained leave to file an amended affidavit of residence and merits, and thereafter presented and filed an affidavit of merits and of residence sworn to by Newton J. Skinner, his attorney of record. The plaintiff, in opposition to the motion, presented a counter-affidavit as to the defendant's residence, and upon the hearing the court granted the defendant's motion for a change of the place of trial, whereupon plaintiff prosecutes this appeal.

The first contention of the appellant is that the affidavit of merits made by the defendant's wife and presented on his behalf on said motion was fatally defective and void, for the reason that it was not made by the defendant himself. Section 396 of the Code of Civil Procedure provides that the affidavit of merits upon motion for change of place of trial must be filed by the defendant. The supreme court, construing this section of the code in an early case, decided that this did not mean that the affidavit of merits must be made by the defendant, but upheld the sufficiency of an affidavit of merits made by the attorney. (*Nicholl* v. *Nicholl,* 66 Cal. 36, [4 Pac. 882].) This being so, we see no reason for holding that an affidavit of merits may not be made by any person on behalf of the defendant who is sufficiently familiar with the facts of the case to make the same; and hence that the affidavit of merits in this case made by the defendant's wife was a sufficient compliance with the statute.

The appellant further contends, however, that the affidavit of the defendant's wife, in so far as it purported to be an affidavit of residence of the defendant, was insufficient in point of form, for the reason that it did not contain facts showing that the defendant's residence was in Los Angeles at the time of the commencement of the action, but only contained a mere statement of the affiant's conclusion in that regard, which the appellant insists is insufficient for any purpose, citing the cases of *Bernou* v. *Bernou,* 15 Cal. App. 341, [114 Pac. 1000], and *O'Brien* v. *O'Brien,* 16 Cal. App. 103, [116 Pac. 692]. While it is true that these cases hold that an affidavit of residence when made by another than the defendant himself should contain more than the mere conclusion of the affiant, still we are of the opinion that an affidavit which merely states such conclusion may be made the subject of amendment in the discretion of the court; and in the case at bar the court, upon the application of the defendant, permitted the defendant to file an amended affidavit of residence and merits; whereupon he filed the affidavit of his attorney of record, which it is not contended by the appellant is insufficient in subject matter. But the appellant urges that this affidavit cannot be considered as an amendment to the prior affidavit, and hence should not be received as such. It has been held, however, that the filing of a new affidavit of merits by another affiant is a sufficient compliance with an order of the court permitting an amended affidavit to be filed upon motion for a change of the place of trial. (*Palmer & Rey* v. *Barclay*, 92 Cal. 199, [28 Pac. 226].) This being so, and the affidavit of the defendant's attorney being admittedly sufficient in form and substance to comply with the requirements of section 396 of the Code of Civil Procedure, we think the court committed no error in granting the motion for a change of the place of trial of the action.

The order is affirmed.

Lennon, P. J., and Kerrigan, J., concurred.

[Civ. No. 1942. First Appellate District.—September 15, 1916.]

E. O. REESE, Respondent, v. G. B. AMIGO COMPANY (a Corporation), Appellant.

SALE OF PRODUCE—PLACE OF DELIVERY AND ACCEPTANCE—EVIDENCE.—In an action to recover the price of certain produce alleged to have been sold and delivered to the defendant pursuant to the terms of a written contract, which designated the place of delivery and acceptance as different from the place of shipment, the admission of proof that prior to and at the time of such shipment the authorized agent of the defendant approved and accepted such produce at the point of shipment does not constitute a variance of the terms of the writing by parol, but amounts to evidence of a waiver of such provision of the contract upon the part of the defendant.

ID.—AUTHORITY OF AGENT—CONFLICT OF EVIDENCE—APPEAL.—Where the evidence is conflicting as to whether the person who acted for the defendant was the duly authorized agent for the purpose of accepting the produce at the point of shipment, the finding of the trial court on such issue is conclusive on the appellate court.

APPEAL from a judgment of the Superior Court of Fresno County, and from an order denying a new trial. H. Z. Austin, Judge.

The facts are stated in the opinion of the court.

Chas. A. Lee, and Everts & Ewing, for Appellant.

Short & Sutherland, and Carl E. Lindsay, for Respondent.

THE COURT.—This is an appeal from the judgment and order denying the defendant's motion for a new trial.

The plaintiff, acting for himself and also for two other persons of whom he was the assignee, brought this action against the defendant to recover the contract price of certain Zinfandel grapes alleged to have been sold and delivered to the defendant in September, 1913, pursuant to the terms of three contracts for the purchase of said grapes for that year entered into between the plaintiff and his assignors respectively and the defendant herein, by the terms of which the plaintiff and his assignors agreed to sell and deliver to the defendant first crop Zinfandel grapes, which were to be raised in the county of Fresno and shipped from Kerman, in said county, to said defendant in the city and county of San Francisco, which was designated as the place of delivery and acceptance of said produce. These contracts were made with the plaintiff and his assignors on behalf of the defendant by one Carl A. Heijne, who was the duly authorized agent of the defendant for the purpose of making said contracts. When the first carloads of said grapes arrived in San Francisco they were rejected by the defendant, which refused to receive them as first crop grapes, or to pay for them under said contracts, and refused to receive any more grapes of a like quality; whereupon the plaintiff and his assignors sold the remainder of their crop of grapes to other persons, and then brought this action for the price of the grapes shipped to the defendant as aforesaid.

Upon the trial of the cause the court found that the carloads of grapes so shipped were first crop Zinfandel grapes of the quality required by the terms of said contracts; and also found that the defendant had accepted said grapes as such at Kerman at the time of their shipment from that point, and thereupon rendered judgment in favor of the plaintiff. From an order denying the defendant's motion for a new trial, it has prosecuted this appeal.

The first contention of the appellant is that the court erred in the admission of evidence tending to show that Carl A.

Heijne continued to act as the authorized agent of the defendant up to and including the time of the shipment of said grapes, and tending to show that prior to and at the time of said shipment said Heijne, purporting to act as the duly authorized agent of the defendant, had approved the quality of said grapes and accepted them as sufficient under the contract at the point of their shipment. It is the appellant's contention that this proof tended to vary the terms of the written contracts between the parties, which provided that the place of delivery and acceptance of said grapes should be the city and county of San Francisco. We are of the opinion, however, that such would not be the effect of the introduction of such evidence, but that the proofs thus adduced would simply amount to evidence of a waiver on the part of the defendant of the provisions of its contracts with regard to the place of delivery and acceptance of the grapes. We are of the opinion that the defendant might, through its duly authorized officers or agents, have accepted and received said produce at Kerman instead of requiring that they be delivered at San Francisco, and that the place of acceptance should be there. The only question, therefore, presented on the record is as to whether said Carl A. Heijne was the duly authorized agent of the defendant for the purpose of acceptance of said produce at Kerman. Upon this subject the evidence is clearly conflicting, with the preponderance rather in favor of the view that Heijne acted as the agent of the defendant throughout the cropping season, and that his ostensible authority was such as would have entitled him to have bound the defendant by his approval and acceptance of the grapes at the place of their shipment. This being so, the finding of the court to the effect that the goods were delivered and accepted at Kerman will not be disturbed.

The appellant further contends that the evidence in the case is insufficient to show that the grapes were first crop and of the quality required by the contracts in question; but as to that matter also the evidence is in conflict, and for that reason this further finding of the court will not be disturbed.

The final contention of the defendant is that there was a conspiracy between Heijne and the plaintiff and his associates, by which unmarketable grapes were to be shipped to the defendant and the contract thus violated, so as to enable the plaintiff and his associates to evade it and sell the remainder of their crop at a higher price upon a rising market. This defense does not appear to have been pleaded nor in fact presented upon the trial of the cause in the lower court; but aside from this, we do not think the evidence is sufficient to sustain the appellant's contention.

The judgment and order are affirmed.

A petition to have the cause heard in the supreme court, after judgment in the district court of appeal, was denied by the supreme court on November 14, 1916.

[Civ. No. 1579. Third Appellate District.—September 15, 1916.]

WILLIAM GRANT, Respondent, v. CHARLES A. WARREN, Appellant.

SALE OF BONDS—PAYMENT OUT OF PROCEEDS OF MARBLE QUARRY—FAILURE TO WORK QUARRY—MEASURE OF DAMAGES.—Where a sale of mortgage bonds of a corporation owning a marble quarry is made upon condition that the purchase price of such bonds, other than the amount paid upon their delivery, should be made by the vendee causing a corporation to be organized for the working of the quarry and having such corporation enter into an agreement with the vendor to pay to the latter such balance out of the proceeds of the quarry, and the vendee thereafter repudiates his agreement to work the mine, the measure of the plaintiff's damage is the full balance due in cash, and not the amount of the royalty that the quarry might have yielded had it been worked.

APPEAL from a judgment of the Superior Court of Tuolumne County, and from an order denying a new trial. G. W. Nicol, Judge.

The facts are stated in the opinion of the court.

Thomas B. Dozier, and Reid & Dozier, for Appellant.

Harding & Monroe, Grant & Zimdars, Beverly L. Hodghead, and W. H. Bryan, for Respondent.

BURNETT, J.—The appeal is from the judgment and also the order denying a motion for a new trial. It is virtually

conceded, however, by appellant that by reason of irregularities as to the statement on motion for a new trial we are, in
effect, limited to the consideration of the appeal from the
judgment and to the determination of whether the findings
support said judgment.

The findings necessary for an understanding of the situation are as follows: "That heretofore and on the 26th day of
March, 1912, the plaintiff was the owner of five hundred and
ninety-five per cent first mortgage bonds of the par value of
five hundred dollars each, issued by the Columbia Marble
Quarries, Inc., a corporation. That the payment of said
bonds was secured by a first lien, mortgage or deed of trust
made by said Columbia Marble Quarries, Inc., on that certain
property situated in the county of Tuolumne, state of California, which property is more particularly described in the
complaint on file herein. That said property included a certain marble quarry hereinafter referred to as the marble
quarry property. That at the time of the issuance of said
bonds and continuously up to and until the time of the sale
thereof, as hereinafter found, the said Columbia Marble Quarries, Inc., was the owner of said marble quarry property
subject to said bonded indebtedness.

"That on or about the 26th day of March, 1912, this plaintiff sold and delivered to the defendant, Charles A. Warren,
the said five hundred and ninety bonds upon the following
express terms and conditions, that is to say: First: That the
said defendant should immediately pay to plaintiff the sum
of fifteen thousand dollars as a part of the purchase price
of said bonds.

"Second: That said defendant, upon receiving delivery and
possession of said bonds should immediately proceed to sell,
or cause to be sold, the property described in the deed of
trust made to secure the payment of said bonds, in accordance with the powers conferred upon the holder or holders
of said bonds by such deed of trust, and at the sale thereof
should purchase said property and hold the same upon certain trusts for the use and benefit of this plaintiff; that is to
say: the said defendant agreed to cause a corporation to be
organized for the acquiring, owning and operating of said
marble quarry property and that he would cause and procure
said corporation to enter into a proper written agreement
with this plaintiff whereby it should pay plaintiff beginning

eighteen months from the 26th day of March, 1912, the sum
of fifty cents for each and every ton of marble taken out and
shipped from said quarries until there should be paid to
plaintiff the further sum of twenty-eight thousand dollars
as the balance of the purchase price of said five hundred and
ninety bonds.

"That it was further agreed that such royalties should be
paid on the 15th day of each and every month for all marble
shipped during the previous month, and that all such royalty
or royalties should be a first lien charge against said marble
quarry property."

Then follows a finding to the effect that Warren, on the
delivery to him of said bonds, paid therefor the said sum of
fifteen thousand dollars, and proceeded to sell said property
under the terms of said trust and thereupon purchased the
same; that he organized a corporation known as the Warren
Marble Company; that he acquired control of its corporate
stock and of said corporation and dominated its policy and
business affairs; that said corporation, "at the behest and
instigation of said Charles A. Warren and with full knowledge of the claims of this plaintiff against said property and
in violation of such claims and without the knowledge or consent of this plaintiff, the said Warren Marble Company on
or about the first day of July, 1912, made a certain mortgage
or deed of trust, mortgaging and conveying said marble
quarry property to the defendant, the Savings Union Bank
and Trust Company, for the purpose of securing the payment of one hundred bonds of the denomination of one thousand dollars each." That said mortgage was duly acknowledged and was recorded on July 29, 1912; that after said
mortgage was recorded, the said corporation made and delivered to plaintiff the agreement attached to the complaint and
marked Exhibit "B," providing "that this contract and all
moneys payable thereunder shall be a first lien and charge
against the said marble quarry property and against the real
property herein described"; that at the time of the delivery
of said Exhibit "B" plaintiff believed it constituted a first
lien and charge against said property; that he had no knowledge or notice of the creation of said bonded indebtedness
of one hundred thousand dollars nor of the making or recording of said deed of trust, and that defendants Warren
and the Warren Marble Company repeated to him that said

agreement constituted a first lien and charge upon said property.

It is also found that plaintiff performed all the conditions of his agreement; that immediately after he discovered that "said bonded indebtedness had been created and had been made a lien and charge upon the said marble quarry property prior to the lien or charge of said agreement Exhibit 'B,' this plaintiff demanded of said defendants Charles A. Warren and the Warren Marble Company that they cancel and annul said bonded indebtedness and said mortgage or deed of trust, and make said agreement Exhibit 'B' a first lien or charge against said property, but that said defendants and each of them refused and have failed so to do," and that said defendants notified plaintiff that they did not intend engaging in the business of operating and carrying on said marble quarry enterprise and of quarrying and shipping marble from said quarry, and that they did not intend to perform the terms and provisions of said agreement Exhibit "B."

The findings disclose, as stated by respondent, that Warren broke his contract: "First, by conveying the property to the corporation without reserving a first lien to plaintiff; and without which lien no one would have a right to extract marble from the quarry. Second, by impressing the property so conveyed, with the first lien of one hundred thousand dollars in priority to plaintiff's security, thus putting it out of his power to perform his contract with plaintiff. Third, by repudiation of plaintiff's right to have the first lien. Fourth, by notice to plaintiff that neither Warren nor the company intended to operate the quarry or pay the royalty."

The groundwork is thus laid for a judgment in favor of plaintiff unless there be merit in the contention of appellant that, the action being for damages, there should be a specific finding as to the actual pecuniary detriment suffered by plaintiff in consequence of the violation of the contract on the part of appellant. It is argued that for aught that appears to the contrary, there may have been no actual loss to plaintiff as a result of said dereliction. For instance, among other considerations, it is suggested that the quarry, if worked, might not have yielded sufficient to pay any portion of said royalty, and reference is made to section 3358 of the Civil Code, providing that "Notwithstanding the provisions of this chapter, no person can recover a greater amount in

damages for the breach of an obligation than he could have
gained by the full performance thereof on both sides, except
in the cases specified in the articles on exemplary damages
and penal damages, and in sections 3319, 3339, and 3340," it
being claimed that the present case does not fall within any
of said exceptions.

But we do not regard this action as technically one for
damages. It is rather a suit to recover the balance due on
the purchase price of property that has been completely transferred to the vendee. There would, of course, be no question
if the promise to pay the said twenty-eight thousand dollars
had been absolute. In other words, if Warren had promised
to pay the said amount on delivery of said property by the
vendor and had failed or refused to do so, plaintiff could
maintain his action immediately. Here the promise was to
pay the balance out of the proceeds of the mine, it is true,
and, therefore, was conditional, but in consequence of Warren's failure to give the promised security and his repudiation of his agreement to work the mine, the law treats his
promise as an absolute and unconditional one, and holds him
to an obligation to pay said balance in cash. The authorities
seem to take this view of the situation, and we may follow
respondent in his quotations from some of the cases.

In *Wolf* v. *Marsh,* 54 Cal. 228, the action was upon a note
for a certain amount containing this provision: "This note is
made with the express understanding that if the coal mines
in the Marsh Ranch yield no profits to me, then this note is
not to be paid and the obligation herein expressed shall be
null and void." Defendant thereupon conveyed the property, making it impossible for him to operate the mine or derive any profit. In holding him liable on the note, the supreme court said: "When he did that he violated his contract
and the note at once became due and payable."

In *Love* v. *Mabury,* 59 Cal. 484, the contract for the payment for work done on a mine contained this clause: "And
the balance of nine hundred dollars to be paid out of the first
proceeds of the mine after deducting expenses." The court
declared: "That the contract contemplated that the defendants were to work the mine 'out of the first proceeds of which,
after deducting expenses,' the balance was to be paid, does
not admit of doubt. And we are of the opinion that the
failure and refusal to commence to work it within a reason-

able time after the completion and acceptance of the labor and materials bestowed upon the property, rendered them liable for the balance due therefor."

In *Poirier* v. *Gravel*, 88 Cal. 79, [25 Pac. 962], the suit was upon a written promise to pay a stated sum containing this provision: "The said sum to be so paid in installments in such amounts and at such times as I shall realize each month from such products after payment of all costs and expenses of the gathering or obtaining and selling such products. The said sum of money to be paid only and exclusively from such products of said land as I may be entitled to, and no other property of mine shall be subject to said debt or obligation." The defendant conveyed the property and thereafter derived no profit. It was said by the court: "This being so, the balance unpaid became immediately due and payable and the plaintiff could maintain an action for the recovery thereof."

In *Bagley* v. *Cohen*, 121 Cal. 604, [53 Pac. 1117], the balance due was to be paid "out of the profits realized by me from my business of packing raisins at Malaga, during the present season." Defendant conveyed the property and it was held that "his liability became thereupon fixed and absolute."

In *Carter* v. *Rhodes*, 135 Cal. 46, [60 Pac. 985], the agreement provided: "And one thousand dollars balance to be paid only out of the net proceeds of the working of the one-half interest in said mineral claim conveyed, and in no event shall the one thousand dollars, or any part thereof, become a personal claim against the party of the second part—that is, the appellant." The court said: "By the sale of his interest in the mine, the appellant put it out of the power of the respondent to receive the thousand dollars from the net proceeds of that interest and appellant became at once personally responsible to pay the thousand dollars."

The cases where the defaulting party failed to give security as promised for the balance of the consideration are of the same tenor. Among the citations, we may refer to *Carnahan* v. *Hughes*, 108 Ind. 227, [9 N. E. 80], *Wheeler* v. *Harrah*, 14 Or. 325, [12 Pac. 500], and *Cook* v. *Stevenson*, 30 Mich. 243.

In the first of these, it is said: "It is abundantly settled that where goods are sold upon credit, the purchaser agreeing as part of the contract to execute notes payable at a future day for the purchase price, the refusal of the purchaser to execute the notes according to the contract entitles the seller to maintain an action for such refusal, and the measure of damages is the full price of the goods sold.''

In the Wheeler case, *supra,* the court says: ''The naked obligation of the defendant was not sufficient to obtain the credit; nor would it have been received, and the property delivered, without the promise of security as agreed. When credit is given for the price of goods sold on the condition that the purchaser's note, with surety, be given therefor, and this condition is not complied with, but the property is taken by the purchaser, he is liable for the price at once, and before the expiration of the proposed term of credit.''

In the Michigan case, *supra,* it was declared as to the defendant: ''By refusing or failing to keep that term in the agreement which was introduced to assure him delay, he entitled the other party to insist upon the resulting alternative of immediate payment.''

Some of the cases refer to the amount recovered as ''damages,'' and declare that the vendor will be entitled to recover as damages the whole value of the goods, it being suggested, though, that there may be ''a rebate of interest during the stipulated credit.'' Such rebate, it may be stated, was allowed in the case at bar.

If we regard the amount recovered as damages, it is apparent that no other just rule could be applied in determining the amount. It is impossible, in other words, to say just how much would have been taken from the quarry and what the payments to plaintiff would, therefore, have been, but this difficulty was created by the refusal of appellant to perform his contract. He therefore is in no position to say that respondent must prove his actual damages, but the law holds him to the measure that he himself prescribed.

We think the foregoing consideration is decisive of the case, and the judgment and order are affirmed.

Chipman, P. J., and Hart, J., concurred.

A petition to have the cause heard in the supreme court, after judgment in the district court of appeal, was denied by the supreme court on November 14, 1916.

[Crim. No. 631. First Appellate District.—September 18, 1916.]

THE PEOPLE, Respondent, v. FRANK AMBROSE, Appellant.

CRIMINAL LAW — RELEASE FROM CUSTODY PENDING TRIAL — FALSE AND WORTHLESS BAIL BOND—SUFFICIENCY OF INDICTMENT.—An indictment alleging that the defendant, acting in concert with his three codefendants, "did unlawfully, willfully, and fraudulently conspire, combine, confederate, and agree to obtain the release and discharge from custody" of a prisoner (who was confined in the county jail pending trial upon an indictment which charged him with the commission of a felony), "by presenting to the superior court of the state of California in and for the city and county of San Francisco a fraudulent, worthless, and void bail bond," states facts sufficient to constitute the offense denounced by the terms of subdivision 5 of section 182 of the Penal Code.

ID.—COUNSELING OF CODEFENDANT TO BECOME SURETY—EVIDENCE—UN-WARRANTED CONVICTION.—In such a prosecution, where the only evidence adduced which tended in any way to connect the defendant with the alleged conspiracy was that he advised and counseled one of his codefendants to become a surety on the bond, and to swear that he was owner of property which stood of record in his name, but in fact belonged to the defendant, his conviction is unwarranted.

APPEAL from a judgment of the Superior Court of the City and County of San Francisco, and from an order denying a new trial. Frank H. Dunne, Judge.

The facts are stated in the opinion of the court.

John D. Harloe, for Appellant.

U. S. Webb, Attorney-General, and John H. Riordan, Deputy Attorney-General, for Respondent.

THE COURT.—In an indictment returned to the superior court of the city and county of San Francisco the defendant herein, jointly with three other persons, was charged with the crime of criminal conspiracy. The appeal is from the judgment of final conviction and from an order denying a new trial.

Subdivision 5 of section 182 of the Penal Code, under which the indictment evidently was drawn, denounces as a criminal conspiracy the conduct of two or more persons who conspire "to commit any act . . . for the perversion or obstruction of justice, or due administration of the laws." The charging part of the indictment alleges that the defendant, acting in concert with the three codefendants, "did unlawfully, willfully, and fraudulently conspire, combine, confederate, and agree to obtain the release and discharge from custody" of one Joseph Monahan (who was confined in the county jail pending trial upon an indictment which charged him with the commission of a felony), "by presenting to the superior court of the state of California in and for the city and county of San Francisco a fraudulent, worthless, and void bail bond." The indictment further alleged that two of the co-defendants had agreed to falsely swear, and did so swear, when qualifying as sureties upon the bail bond of Monahan, that they were each worth the sum of two thousand five hundred dollars, the amount fixed as bail, over and above their just debts and liabilities, and that they were respectively the owners of certain real estate situated in the county of Yolo and the city and county of San Francisco.

Apparently the only connection which the defendant Ambrose had with the conspiracy charged, in so far as the allegations of the indictment are concerned, is to be found in the concluding paragraph of the indictment, which alleged that he advised and counseled Shaney, one of the codefendants who became a surety on the bond, "to execute said bond and to swear that he was the owner of said property." It will be noted that the indictment does not charge that it was the intent and purpose of the defendant and his alleged co-conspirators to do anything more by the preparation and presentation of the bail bond in question than to procure the release of Monahan upon bail pending his trial upon the felony charged against him. Neither expressly nor by necessary implication does the indictment allege that the release of Monahan upon worthless bail was procured primarily for the purpose of permitting him to abscond and thereby evade the possible penalties of a trial and conviction. Nevertheless, we are of the opinion that the indictment states facts sufficient to constitute the offense charged against the defendant, and that therefore his demurrer was properly overruled by the trial court. True it is that release from custody upon bail pending trial is ordinarily the constitutional and statutory

right of every person charged with crime; but it is equally
true that it is neither the constitutional nor statutory right
of a person to be so released by means of a false and worthless bail bond; and it seems certain to us that the procurement of the release in that manner is a perversion of the due
administration of the law, and therefore comes within the
denunciation of subdivision 5 of section 182 of the Penal
Code.

We are satisfied, however, upon a review of the evidence
adduced upon the entire case that the judgment against
this defendant cannot be sustained. The only evidence adduced upon behalf of the people tending in any way to connect the defendant with the alleged conspiracy may be stated
in substance to be that the codefendant Shaughnessy qualified
as a surety upon the bail bond in question under the name
of Shaney; that the property which at the time of qualifying
he swore he owned stood of record in the name of Shaney;
that the property originally belonged to Ambrose; that the
latter had placed it of record in the name of Shaney at a
time when he was having trouble with his wife; that Shaughnessy, with the knowledge and consent of the defendant
Ambrose, pretended to be the owner of the property, and
on one or two occasions exercised acts of ownership over the
property by borrowing money secured by mortgages upon it
executed and acknowledged in the name of Shaney; that one
Barkley, attorney for Monahan, called upon Ambrose for
the purpose of having him procure Shaughnessy as a bonds-
man, giving as security the property in question; that the
defendant Ambrose stated to Barkley that he had no objection to Shaughnessy going upon the bond, and that when
Shaughnessy mentioned the subject of going upon the bond
Ambrose replied, "If you desire it, go on the bond; it is all
right; I think Monahan is all right." Incidentally it was
shown in evidence that Shaughnessy was sometimes known as
Shaney.

In the face of this evidence we do not think it can be said
that the bond, as regards Shaughnessy's qualifications to
serve thereon, was valueless. Even though the defendant
Ambrose claimed to have been the real owner of the property, nevertheless inasmuch as the record title was in the
name of Shaney, and that Shaughnessy, under the name of
Shaney (by which he was sometimes known), duly executed

and acknowledged the bond, there can be no doubt that the property standing in the name of Shaney could have been resorted to in satisfaction of a breach of the bond had one occurred. This being so, it cannot be held that the evidence sustains the allegation of the indictment to the effect that Ambrose counseled and advised his codefendant Shaughnessy to execute and qualify upon a false and worthless bond. It may be conceded that the evidence shows that the codefendant Gilfeather, who qualified as surety upon the bond, perjured himself when he swore upon qualifying that he was the owner of certain property situate in the city and county of San Francisco, and that therefore, in so far as Gilfeather was concerned, the bond was false and valueless; but aside from the fact that the indictment does not charge Ambrose with having counseled and advised Gilfeather to execute the bond and qualify as a surety thereon, we have been unable to find in the record any evidence showing, or tending to show, any connection of the defendant Ambrose with his codefendant Gilfeather in the preparation and presentation of the bond. In short, in so far as the evidence shows, whatever Ambrose may have done in the transaction was independent of anything done by Gilfeather. This being so, it cannot be said that the conspiracy charged in the indictment was sustained by the evidence adduced at the trial.

This conclusion makes it unnecessary to refer to and decide the other points presented upon the appeal.

For the reasons stated the judgment and order appealed from are reversed.

[Civ. No. 2007. Second Appellate District.—September 18, 1916.]

EDNA R. BELLINGER, Respondent, v. JAMES B. HUGHES et al., Appellants.

NEGLIGENCE—COLLISION OF PEDESTRIAN WITH AUTOMOBILE—ERRONEOUS INSTRUCTION—CONTRIBUTORY NEGLIGENCE.—In an action to recover damages for personal injuries received by a pedestrian as the result of a collision with an automobile while crossing a city street over which a street-car was then passing, it is prejudicial error to instruct the jury, without any qualifications whatever, that "If an automobile driver, not being able to see a street crossing which he is approaching because of a passing street-car, instead of stopping his machine, merely changes its direction so as to go around the car and in doing so comes suddenly upon and runs into and injures a person, he is guilty of gross negligence, and is liable for all damage proximately caused thereby," where the answer alleges contributory negligence, and there is evidence supporting the claim that plaintiff had her eyes turned away from the automobile, the approach of which she had noticed, and that she stepped back to escape collision with a passing motorcycle.

ID.—NEGLIGENCE—WHEN QUESTION OF LAW.—It is only where the undisputed facts are such as to leave but one reasonable inference, and that of negligence, that the court is justified in taking the question from the jury.

APPEAL from a judgment of the Superior Court of Los Angeles County, and from an order denying a new trial. Grant Jackson, Judge.

The facts are stated in the opinion of the court.

C. J. Willett, for Appellants.

G. A. Gibbs, and Elliot Gibbs, for Respondent.

SHAW, J.—Action to recover damages for personal injuries. Judgment was rendered for plaintiff, from which, and an order denying defendant's motion for a new trial, he prosecutes this appeal.

The injury, damages for which are sought, was the result of a collision between an automobile operated by defendant Hughes and plaintiff while she was crossing from the north side of Colorado Street, in Pasadena, to the south side thereof, at a point along the east line of Los Robles Avenue which at right angles intersects Colorado Street. The record here presented is not only meager, but to a large extent unintelligible, by reason of the fact that a map or plat, not brought up in the record, was used by witnesses, who pointed out thereon positions and places knowledge of which is necessary to a proper understanding of the relation of the parties to the location where the injury occurred. But to the court this evidence, without the map, is meaningless.

Numerous errors are assigned, only one of which, however, we deem necessary to consider, as upon this we are of the opinion that the judgment and order must be reversed. This error consists in giving to the jury, without qualification thereof, an instruction numbered 17, as follows: "If an automobile driver not being able to see a street crossing which he is approaching because of a passing street-car, instead of stopping his machine merely changes its direction so as to go around the car and in doing so comes suddenly upon and runs into and injures a person, he is guilty of gross negligence and is liable for all damage proximately caused thereby." It appears that a street-car track was maintained along Colorado Street west of Los Robles Avenue, which at the intersection was extended in a southerly direction along the latter street. Immediately before the time of the injury a street-car operated upon said line was on the track at a point just west of the line of Los Robles Avenue and about to turn southerly into said avenue, when plaintiff, who was crossing Colorado Street, and had reached a point therein about half or two-thirds of the way between the street-car tracks and the curb, saw the automobile on the south side of Colorado Street and near the west line of Los Robles Avenue. She testifies that this automobile appeared to be held up by the street-car, which was about to turn in front of it into Los Robles Avenue, or for other reasons had slowed down. At all events, she says she was sure, since the street in front of her over which she was crossing was clear, that she had time to reach the south curb line thereof before the automobile would reach the line of her travel in effecting the crossing. When eight or ten feet from the south curb line of Colorado Street she was struck by the motor car and knocked down. There is evidence, though contradicted, tending to show that plain-

tiff at the time she was struck by the automobile was facing
east—that is, in the direction in which the automobile was
going—and when "she got just beyond the tracks that are in
the center of the street she got out of the way of a passing
motorcycle." Plaintiff testified that she "saw the automobile plain enough" when it was approaching just back of the
street-car. As to whether any signal was given by the operator of the automobile by horn or bell, and as to the speed at
which it was operated—whether rather fast, as testified to by
one witness, moderate speed, or slowly, as testified by others—
the evidence is likewise conflicting.

The answer alleged contributory negligence on the part of
the plaintiff, and since there was evidence which, if believed
by the jury, would establish such fact, the question as to
whether or not plaintiff was guilty of contributory negligence which constituted the proximate cause of her injury,
should have been submitted to the jury for determination;
and had it so found, this court could not have disturbed such
verdict. The claim, as to which there was a conflict of evidence, that plaintiff had her eyes turned away from the automobile the approach of which she had noticed, and that she
stepped back to escape a collision with a passing motorcycle,
if believed, might justify a conclusion of negligence on the
part of plaintiff. And her own testimony to the effect that
the distance between the line upon which she was crossing
the street and the approaching automobile was little more
than the intervening space of Los Robles Avenue (width,
however, not shown), might be deemed well calculated, if
believed by the jury, to constitute a sufficient warning to her
of danger from which, by the exercise of ordinary care, she
could escape. Reasonable minds might have differed as to
whether or not, under the circumstances, she was justified in
concluding that the motor would not continue its progress,
and as to whether she should not at least have looked in the
direction of the approaching automobile, and this even though
no sound of the horn or other signal was given. "The fact
of negligence is generally an inference from many facts and
circumstances, all of which it is the province of the jury to
find." (*Schierhold* v. *North Beach & M. R. R. Co.*, 40 Cal.
453.) In *Davis* v. *Pacific Power Co.*, 107 Cal. 563, 575, [48
Am. St. Rep. 156, 40 Pac. 952], it is said: "It is only where
the undisputed facts are such as to leave but one reasonable

inference, and that of negligence, that the court is justified
in taking the question from the jury." Where either negligence is set up as a cause of action or contributory negligence
pleaded as a defense, it seldom happens that the question is
so clear from doubt that the court can undertake to say as a
matter of law how the jury should find upon such issues. It
is apparent, we think, that plaintiff relied upon the course of
the automobile being obstructed by the street-car which she
had reason to think was about to turn into Los Robles Avenue
ahead of the automobile. Whether an inference of negligence on the part of the plaintiff in not further watching
the approach of the automobile was justified depended upon
whether she was justified in this reasoning. As said in *Johnson* v. *Thomas*, 5 Cal. Unrep. 256, [43 Pac. 578]: "It
was certainly an inference upon which minds might well differ, and hence proper to be submitted to a jury, under proper
instructions." The evidence shows that the position of the
street-car was such as to partially at least obstruct the automobile driver's view of the street crossing, and that he did
not see the plaintiff until after his automobile had passed the
street-car, when he came suddenly upon plaintiff, which facts
bring the case directly within the instruction given. Nevertheless, if the jury were satisfied that plaintiff was guilty
of contributory negligence which was the proximate cause of
her injury, she was not entitled to recover. In effect, the
jury was told to disregard all evidence tending to prove contributory negligence on the part of plaintiff, and in effect
took from it the consideration of all evidence tending to show
negligence and carelessness on her part. Such we do not
conceive to be the law. Whether such act on the part of the
automobile driver would constitute negligence and render him
liable for damages caused by a collision, would depend upon
the degree of care required in the operation of his machine,
and this in turn would depend upon the dangerous character
of the machine, its size, weight, the speed at which it was
operated, the noise it made, condition of the streets, and other
conditions which might be mentioned. (*Simeone* v. *Lindsay*,
6 Penne. (Del.) 224, [65 Atl. 778].) Whether plaintiff was
warranted, after she saw the approaching automobile a short
distance away, knowing that it would cross the line of her
travel, in not further watching the approach thereof, was a
question upon which minds might well differ, and hence it

should have been submitted to the jury. Respondent attempts to justify the giving of this instruction upon the authority of *Gregory* v. *Slaughter*, 124 Ky. 345, [124 Am. St. Rep. 402, 8 L. R. A. (N. S.) 1228, 99 S. W. 247], the syllabus of which reads as follows: "The driver of an automobile is guilty of gross negligence in driving his car at high speed across the intersection of two much used streets and around the end of a street-car which obstructs his view of the crossing, so that upon finding a pedestrian directly in the path of the car he cannot avoid a collision with him." There is no evidence here, however, that the intersection of Colorado Street and Los Robles Avenue was a *much used* street. On the contrary, it might be that it was seldom traveled or crossed. Nor does the evidence show that the defendant ran his automobile around the end of the street-car, and the evidence cannot as a matter of law be said to justify the conclusion that the car was being driven at a *high rate* of speed, or at other than a moderate rate of speed.

It is true that the court elsewhere in the instructions told the jury that even though it found defendant guilty of negligence in managing the automobile, its verdict must be in his favor if they found that plaintiff was guilty of negligence constituting the proximate cause of the injuries received; and also told them that if plaintiff in the exercise of ordinary care, by looking or listening, might have observed the automobile approaching, and did not exercise such care, she was guilty of negligence which would prevent her recovery. Instruction No. 17, however, was given without any qualifications whatever, and it is impossible to reconcile it with other instructions. The evidence tended clearly to show the facts upon which the jury were therein told that defendant was guilty of gross negligence and liable for damages, and was well calculated to mislead the jury in arriving at its verdict. Under these circumstances, our conclusion is that it constitutes prejudicial error.

The judgment and order appealed from are, therefore, reversed.

Conrey, P. J., and James, J., concurred.

[Civ. No. 1547.   Third Appellate District.—September 19, 1916.]

BEN E. TORMEY, Appellant, v. FRANK N. MILLER, Respondent.

ATTACHMENT—RELEASE—SUBSEQUENT BANKRUPTCY OF DEFENDANT—ENTRY OF QUALIFIED JUDGMENT—LIABILITY OF SURETIES—RIGHT OF PLAINTIFF.—Where in an action for goods sold and delivered the property of the defendant is attached and afterward released upon the giving of an undertaking conditioned that if the plaintiff should recover judgment the sureties upon demand would pay the amount thereof, the plaintiff is entitled, where the defendant by way of supplemental answer sets up his adjudication and discharge in bankruptcy since the commencement of the action, to have a special or qualified judgment entered against the defendant with a perpetual stay of execution, for the purpose of enforcing the liability of the sureties on the undertaking.

ID.—PROCEDURE—MOTION FOR ENTRY OF QUALIFIED JUDGMENT AT CLOSE OF TRIAL.—Under such circumstances, it is proper procedure to enter such a judgment upon motion made at the conclusion of the trial of the issues raised by the original pleadings and supplemental answer.

ID.—PLEADING — ATTACHMENT AND RELEASE — EVIDENTIARY MATTERS.—Under such circumstances it is not necessary to the entry of the judgment against the defendant, for the special purpose of fixing and enforcing the liability of the sureties on the undertaking, that the plaintiff should plead the issuance of the writ of attachment, its levy, the giving of the undertaking for the release, or the release of the property, as the same are purely evidentiary matters.

ID.—APPEAL FROM JUDGMENT—REVIEW OF ERRORS OCCURRING DURING TRIAL.—In such an action alleged errors in excluding proof of the issuance of the writ of attachment and the execution of the undertaking are reviewable upon appeal taken from the judgment, where the appeal was taken after the abrogation by the legislature of 1915 of the right to appeal from an order denying a new trial (Stats. 1915, p. 209).

APPEAL from a judgment of the Superior Court of Butte County.   H. D. Gregory, Judge.

The facts are stated in the opinion of the court.

Milton Newmark, and Clarence A. Shuey, for Appellant.

Lon Bond, for Respondent.

HART, J.—The defendant in this action was awarded judgment, from which this appeal, supported by a bill of exceptions and a stipulation admitting as true certain facts, is prosecuted by the plaintiff.

The facts as agreed upon by the stipulation of the parties are with accuracy synoptically stated in the opening brief of counsel for the plaintiff, and we, therefore, adopt said statement thereof, together with the statement of the legal propositions submitted here for decision by the appellant.

"Appellant brought an action in the superior court of this state for Butte County, against respondent, for goods sold and delivered. A writ of attachment was issued in said action directed to the sheriff of Butte County and placed in his hands for execution. A bond was thereafter made, executed and delivered, and thereupon the attachment was released and discharged. By the obligation of said bond, the sureties undertook 'that if the said plaintiff shall recover judgment in said action we will pay to the said plaintiff upon demand the amount of said judgment together with the costs not exceeding in all the sum of $1200, gold coin of the United States.'

"Thereafter, and within four months of the commencement of the attachment suit, respondent filed a petition in the District Court of the United States for adjudication as a voluntary bankrupt, and thereafter was duly adjudged a bankrupt and discharged of his debts by order of said District Court. Respondent filed a supplemental answer in the attachment suit, setting up his discharge in bankruptcy as a defense. Upon these issues the case was tried, and at the trial counsel for plaintiff, in his opening statement, told the court that he proposed to ask for judgment against the defendant with a perpetual stay of execution against the property of said defendant for the purpose of maintaining his rights against the bondsmen.

"The allegations of the complaint in regard to the incurring of the indebtedness sued upon and non-payment were admitted by stipulation of counsel for respondent. The bankruptcy proceedings culminating in the order of discharge were also admitted by stipulation, and this constituted the sole defense interposed to the action. Plaintiff offered evidence establishing the facts in regard to the issuance of the writ of attachment, the execution and delivery of the under-

taking, which evidence was excluded by the trial court upon
defendant's objection that it was incompetent, irrelevant and
immaterial. The bond was also offered and similarly excluded. At the conclusion of the trial plaintiff again asked
for judgment against defendant with a perpetual stay of execution against the property of said defendant. Judgment
went for defendant. The question of law thus presented and
raised by the exclusion of the testimony in regard to the issuance of the attachment and the execution of the bond and
also by the absolute judgment in favor of the defendant, relates to the right of a plaintiff under such circumstances to
a qualified judgment against the defendant sufficient to preserve his rights against the sureties arising out of the bond
given to release the attachment. By the terms of the bond,
recovery of a judgment is made a prerequisite to an action
against the sureties.''

It is not questioned but, indeed, is admitted by the stipulation of counsel for the defendant, that but for the special
plea setting up by way of supplemental answer the fact of
the defendant's discharge from his debts under the federal
bankruptcy law, the plaintiff would have been entitled to
judgment against the defendant for the amount of the debt
sued for. By reason of the adjudication in bankruptcy,
however, the defendant's property could not, obviously, be
resorted to in execution or satisfaction of any judgment obtained against him by the plaintiff or, for that matter, by
any other person suing upon an obligation created prior to
and consequently affected by the adjudication. But, as seen,
the plaintiff contends that the effect of the defendant's discharge in bankruptcy was not to destroy his rights originally
created by the lien of the attachment, or, speaking with respect to the case as it appears, his rights against the sureties
on the undertaking given to discharge the attachment levied
upon the property of the defendant to secure his judgment.

The contention so urged is clearly in harmony with the
construction placed by the courts upon certain provisions of
the bankruptcy law. Indeed, counsel for the defendant does
not combat or dispute the soundness of the proposition, but,
as we shall presently see, bases his resistance to this appeal
solely upon grounds involving procedure.

Section 67d of the federal bankruptcy law provides:
''Liens given or accepted in good faith and not in contempla-

tion of or in fraud upon this act, . . . shall not be affected
by this act.''

Section 16 of said act reads: ''The liability of a person
who is a codebtor, or guarantor or in any manner surety
for, a bankrupt shall not be altered by the discharge of such
bankrupt.''

The courts have uniformly held, in cases like the present,
that, under the foregoing sections, while the adjudication,
when pleaded, will, of course, have the effect of granting immunity to the defendant from the execution of any judgment
obtained against him from his property, such adjudication
cannot operate to destroy the rights of the plaintiff under
the undertaking given to release the attachment, or, in other
words, will not itself relieve the sureties on the undertaking
of their obligations thereunder. (See *Bank of Commerce* v.
Elliott, 109 Wis. 648, [85 N. W. 417]; *Hill* v. *Harding*, 130
U. S. 699, [32 L. Ed. 1083, 9 Sup. Ct. Rep. 725], and cases
therein cited; *Smith* v. *Lacey*, 86 Miss. 295, [109 Am. St.
Rep. 707, 38 South. 311]; *United States Wind Engine &
Pump Co.* v. *North Penn. Iron Co.*, 227 Pa. St. 262, [75 Atl.
1094]; *Rosenthal* v. *Nove*, 175 Mass. 599, [78 Am. St. Rep.
512, 56 N. E. 884].) The principle is discussed and approved in *Harding* v. *Minear*, 54 Cal. 502, and *Holloday* v.
Hare, 69 Cal. 515, [11 Pac. 28]. As was said by the supreme
court of Wisconsin, in *Bank of Commerce* v. *Elliott*, 109 Wis.
648, [85 N. W. 417]: ''The language of the bankrupt act,
preserving a lien incident to a debt, by implication preserved
the debt, notwithstanding its discharge, so far as is necessary to make the lien effective.''

The above cases further hold that where, under such circumstances as are present in the case at bar, the defendant
has pleaded and proved his discharge after the attachment
had been levied upon his property and said attachment released upon the giving of the undertaking, the remedy of the
plaintiff against the sureties on the undertaking must be
made effectual, if at all, by the entry of a qualified judgment
against the defendant for the amount found to be due on
the account declared upon; that is to say, that, in order to
enable the plaintiff to reap the benefit of his attachment,
which can be obtained in this case only by proceeding against
the sureties on the undertaking upon the giving of which said
attachment was dissolved, he is entitled to have a judgment

entered against the defendant with a perpetual stay of execution, so as to prevent the plaintiff from enforcing the judgment against him, and leave him at liberty to proceed against the sureties. (*Smith* v. *Lacey*, 86 Miss. 295, [109 Am. St. Rep. 707, 30 South. 311], and the other cases above cited.)

As has been shown, in the present case, the undertaking given for the release of the attachment provided, as a condition precedent to the right of the plaintiff to a recovery against the sureties thereon or to maintain an action against them on the undertaking, that a judgment shall have first been rendered and entered against the defendant. Indeed, it is obviously true that, if no judgment in the attachment suit were entered against the defendant, there would be no predicate for the support of an action against the sureties, the obligation of the latter being to pay the debt only when it should be established by a judgment.

Excerpts from the opinions in a few of the cases above referred to will be sufficient to disclose the reasons for or the theory of the rules above considered.

In *Danforth Mfg. Co.* v. *Barrett & Co.*, 138 Ill. App. 244, which was concerned with an action commenced in a justice's court, judgment was rendered against the defendant, who appealed, giving an appeal bond with surety conditioned for the payment of any judgment obtained against the defendant, if the latter defaulted in the satisfaction of the same, it is said: "It is admitted in argument by appellant that it is proper for a trial court to enter a judgment against a defendant with a perpetual stay of execution in order that the plaintiff in said judgment may enforce the same against the sureties on a bond given upon an attachment levied more than four months prior to the bankruptcy of the defendant, as held in *Hill* v. *Harding*, 116 Ill. 92, [4 N. E. 361], and *Hill* v. *Harding*, 130 U. S. 699, [32 L. Ed. 1083, 9 Sup. Ct. Rep. 725]. But it is contended . . . that this rule should not be applied where the plaintiff or claimant has acquired no lien under his judgment; and that there should be no judgment against the appellant in this case because the sureties on the appeal bond are not liable.

"On this record the sureties on the appeal bond are not before the court, and we cannot determine their rights and liabilities. It will be time enough to determine the question of their liability when a proper case is presented for our consideration involving that question.

"In view of this question of the liability of the sureties on the appeal bond—a question not necessary for us to decide and which we do not decide—the proper judgment in this case is a special judgment against appellant for the amount due to appellee with a perpetual stay of execution. Such a judgment against appellant can work no harm to it, and will not interfere with any rights or privileges acquired by its discharge in bankruptcy."

In *United States Wind Engine & Pump Co. v. North Penn. Iron Co.*, 227 Pa. St. 262, [75 Atl. 1094], the supreme court reversed the judgment, with directions to enter a special judgment against the defendant, with a perpetual stay of execution, for the purpose of enabling the plaintiff to proceed against the surety upon a bond given to secure the release of an attachment levied upon the property of the defendant. The court there said: "The appellee has secured its discharge in bankruptcy, and its personal liability is gone; but that does not constitute any reason why a judgment against it should not be entered for the special purpose of fixing and enforcing the liability of the surety. The surety took the risk of the appellee's insolvency—a risk that the appellant was supposedly protected against by the very bond in question. So it would be most unfair to allow the substitution of the bond for the goods attached, and then to deny the formal relief necessary in order to enforce its terms against the surety. There is nothing in our law, or practice, or in the announced public policy of the state, to require such a ruling."

Further quotation is not necessary, it being sufficient to say, as we have before declared, that all the other cases above cited are to the same effect.

It is true that section 67c of the Bankruptcy Act provides that a lien arising from the attachment of a debtor's property and so created within four months before the filing of a bankruptcy petition by the litigant debtor shall be dissolved by the adjudication of such debtor to be a bankrupt, if: "1. It appears that said lien was obtained and permitted while the defendant was insolvent and that its existence and enforcement will work a preference; or 2. The party or parties to be benefited thereby had reasonable cause to believe the defendant was insolvent and in contemplation of bankruptcy; or 3. That such lien was sought and permitted in fraud of the provisions of this act." It is asserted in the brief of appellant that the bankruptcy proceedings in the case at bar were instituted within four months after the levy of the attachment. We find nothing in the record justifying this statement, hence we do not know when, with respect to the time at which the attachment lien was created, the proceedings in bankruptcy were commenced by the defendant. But it is altogether immaterial whether the attachment lien in this case was created within four months prior to or within four months after the commencement of the bankruptcy proceedings, since the attachment had, by virtue of the undertaking, been dissolved before the proceedings in bankruptcy were begun. As seen, the bond or undertaking was given for the express purpose of effecting a release of the attachment, the attachment was accordingly released, and such release operated as a sufficient consideration to support the obligation of the bondsmen. It has repeatedly been held that the bondsmen are, under such circumstances, liable. (*Rosenthal* v. *Perkins*, 123 Cal. 240, [55 Pac. 804]; *San Francisco Sulphur Co.* v. *Aetna Indemnity Co.*, 11 Cal. App. 695, [106 Pac. 111]; *In re Maaget*, 173 Fed. 232, [23 Am. Bankr. Rep. 14]; *McCombs* v. *Allen*, 82 N. Y. 114; *King* v. *Will J. Block Amusement Co.*, 126 App. Div. 48, [111 N. Y. Supp. 102].)

The Rosenthal case involved an action against the sureties on an undertaking given to release an attachment. The defendant in the attachment suit, one Brusie, had the attachment released upon giving an undertaking for that purpose. Within a month after the levy of the writ of attachment, Brusie filed his voluntary petition in insolvency under the State Insolvency Act of 1880. That act contained a provision that the effect of the commencement of insolvency proceedings was to dissolve any attachment levied within one month next preceding the commencement thereof. The defendants (sureties on the bond) contended that "the effect of this provision was to dissolve the attachment in *Rosenthal* v. *Brusie*, and render impossible the return of the released property to the attaching officer, and hence to destroy the obligation of their undertaking." After showing that the contract involving the undertaking embodied two alternative promises, viz., that the released property would be redelivered and applied toward the satisfaction of the judgment, or the sureties would pay the value thereof, not exceeding the amount of the judgment, and that if an agreement is in the alternative, and one branch of the alternative cannot by law be performed, the party is bound to perform the other," the court said: "It is clear, for reasons which need not be enlarged upon, that if at the time the proceedings in bankruptcy is instituted there is no attachment in force on which the proceeding can operate, if the attachment lien has already been discharged by a bond for that purpose, then the liability of sureties on the bond is not affected by the subsequent bankruptcy of their principal. (*McCombs* v. *Allen*, 82 N. Y. 114, and cases cited; *Easton* v. *Ormsby*, 18 R. I. 309, [27 Atl. 216]; Insolvent Act, sec. 45, last proviso.) The mistake of defendants lies in supposing that the lien of the attachment in *Rosenthal* v. *Brusie* continued on the attached goods after they had been released to Brusie in consequence of the delivery bond. Our statute and the inferences which follow from the decisions of this court seem to put the question at rest. Upon the execution of the bond, such as was given by defendants, 'an order may be made, releasing from the operation of the attachment any or all of the property attached.' (Code Civ. Proc., sec. 554.) It is impossible that property can be 'released from the operation of the attachment' if it yet remains subject to the attachment lien. . . . We are satisfied that no lien of the attachment persisted on the goods in this case after the release to the owner.''

Our conclusion from all the authorities which we have examined and to many of which special attention has been directed in this opinion is that there is no provision in the Federal Bankruptcy Act with which the judgment asked for by the plaintiff in this action would be in conflict. In other words, there is no language in said act which prevents the rendering or entering of such a judgment, and our opinion is that the court below should have entertained the motion of the plaintiff for a special or qualified judgment against the defendant, and that, in refusing to do so, and in disallowing the above-indicated proof offered by the plaintiff in support of said motion, the court erred to the prejudice of the latter.

As stated above, the defendant has not in his brief or otherwise assailed or challenged the legal propositions above considered, but, as we understand him, he denies the propriety of their application to the case in hand, and further maintains that, even if this case in the abstract presented an appropriate instance for their application, the plaintiff did not properly proceed in the court to make them or to justify a review of the ruling of the court denying him the remedy sought.

In support of this position it is declared: "1. There is absolutely no mention made in any of the pleadings of a writ of attachment having been issued or a bond to prevent its levy having been given. There was, therefore, no issue presented as to those matters. 2. The findings fully covered all the issues raised. 3. The specifications of particulars wherein plaintiff claims the evidence insufficient to support the decision is in fact addressed to the conclusions of law and not to findings of fact. 4. The notice of intention to move for a new trial fails to specify as one of the grounds, 'errors in law, occurring at the trial, and excepted to,' etc., the only grounds of the motion being: Insufficiency of the evidence to justify the decision and that the decision is against law."

The reply to the first of the above-stated propositions is, in our opinion, that, since the ultimate question at issue was whether the plaintiff was entitled to any sort of judgment against the defendant under the issues as finally framed, the fact of the issuance of the writ of attachment, the fact of its levy upon the property of the defendant, the fact of the giving of the undertaking for the purpose of effecting a release of the attachment, and the fact of such release, were purely evidentiary, or constituted mere evidence upon which the court might predicate its conclusion upon said question. It was, therefore, even if proper, unnecessary to plead those facts.

Nor can we conceive of a more appropriate procedure to which the plaintiff might have resorted for the protection and preservation of his rights against the sureties than that adopted. The trial of the case was, of course, necessary, notwithstanding the special plea set up by the supplemental answer and its availability as a perfect defense to the action, if proved. If it transpired, as it did transpire, that the special plea could be established, then the plaintiff, still concerned with the ultimate decision, was entitled to a judgment in form which could do the defendant himself no possible harm, but which would preserve to him (the plaintiff) certain rights arising out of the controversy to which he was justly and legally entitled.

As to the fourth proposition above stated, it is sufficient to say that whether the grounds upon which the plaintiff founded his motion for a new trial were or were not such as to warrant the trial court in legally considering and passing upon the alleged errors involved in the rulings of the court excluding proof of the attachment and the bond given to secure the release thereof is, so far as this appeal is concerned, wholly immaterial. Indeed, under the existing system for taking appeals in this state, it was not necessary for the plaintiff to move for a new trial to authorize this court to review the errors mentioned, and, so far as is concerned our right and authority to do so, it may be assumed that no motion for a new trial was in fact made. The appeal here was taken after the abrogation by the legislature of 1915 of the right to appeal from an order denying a new trial (Stats. 1915, p. 209, amending sec. 963, Code Civ. Proc.), and the said errors may, therefore, be reviewed by this court on the appeal from the judgment, notwithstanding that the court below might have been justified in denying the motion for a new trial because of the insufficiency of the grounds upon which the motion was based, as designated in the notice of intention, to point the errors relied upon. (Code Civ. Proc., sec. 956.) The last named section provides: "Upon an appeal from a judgment the court may review the verdict or decision, and any intermediate *ruling,* proceeding, order or decision which involves the merits or necessarily affects the judgment, *or which substantially affects the rights of a party. . . .*" (Italics ours.) The motion for a new trial was made upon the minutes of the court, and the errors occurring at the trial were preserved by a bill of exceptions, duly settled, for use on the appeal from the judgment. (Code Civ. Proc., sec. 950.) The errors are, therefore, legally before this court for review, and quite manifestly they "involve the merits," "necessarily affect the judgment," and most unquestionably "substantially affect the rights of" the plaintiff.

The judgment is therefore reversed and the cause remanded for further proceedings in accordance with the views herein expressed.

Chipman, P. J., and Burnett, J., concurred.

———————

[Crim. No. 347.   Third Appellate District.—September 19, 1916.]

THE PEOPLE, Respondent, v. AMEDIO FINALI, Appellant.

CRIMINAL LAW—MURDER—SELF-DEFENSE—DOCTRINE OF APPARENT DANGER—INCONSISTENT INSTRUCTION.—In a prosecution for the crime of murder, where the plea made by the defendant is that of self-defense, an instruction that there must have been a present ability on the part of the assailant to accomplish his criminal design in order to justify the person assailed in taking his life is inconsistent with the doctrine of apparent danger to one who is assailed, but is not so misleading as to have caused a miscarriage of justice, where the evidence shows whatever real or apparent necessity defendant believed to exist for the killing was created by his own fault.

ID.—PLEA OF SELF-DEFENSE—WHEN NOT AVAILABLE—SEEKING OF QUARREL.—An instruction that self-defense is not available as a plea to a defendant who has sought a quarrel with a design to force a deadly issue and thus, through his fraud, connivance, or fault, create a real or apparent necessity for the killing, is proper, where the evidence shows that whatever real or apparent necessity the defendant believed to exist for the killing was created by his own fault.

ID.—DOCTRINE OF SELF-DEFENSE.—The doctrine of self-defense presupposes that one who would avail himself of it has, without his fault, found himself in threatened danger of serious bodily injury, to avert which the law gives him the right to resort to extreme measures. But the plea is not available to him where he willfully and without any necessity for his own protection creates the danger with which he is threatened.

ID.—RETURN OF JURY FOR FURTHER INSTRUCTIONS—RIGHT OF DEFENDANT. Upon the return of the jury for further instructions while deliberating on the verdict, the defendant is not entitled as a matter of right to have read to them instructions not called for, or to have all of the instructions upon a given subject read, when such as are read are stated to be satisfactory to them.

ID.—Argument of District Attorney—Comment upon Failure of Defendant to Deny Self-incriminatory Statement—Lack of Prejudice.—In such a prosecution, while it is wrong for the district
attorney in his argument to the jury to make reference to the fact
that the defendant, while on the witness-stand, had failed to make
denial of a somewhat self-incriminatory statement which he made at
the time of his arrest and which was introduced in evidence, such
misconduct is not prejudicially erroneous, under section 4½ of article
VI of the constitution, where the jury was fully advised as to the
subject matter of such statement through other testimony.

ID.—Misconduct of District Attorney—When Ground for Reversal.
Where misconduct of the district attorney is claimed as prejudicial,
if attention is called to it and the court instructs the jury to disregard it and not allow themselves to be influenced by it, the misconduct must be flagrant and obviously prejudicial to justify a
reversal.

APPEAL from a judgment of the Superior Court of
Shasta County, and from an order denying a new trial. J. E.
Barber, Judge.

The facts are stated in the opinion of the court.

Braynard & Kimball, for Appellant.

U. S. Webb, Attorney-General, and J. Chas. Jones, Deputy Attorney-General, for Respondent.

CHIPMAN, P. J.—Defendant was informed against by the
district attorney of Shasta County for the crime of murder,
and at his trial was convicted of manslaughter and sentenced
to imprisonment for the term of seven years in the state
prison. He appeals from the judgment of conviction and
from the order denying his motion for a new trial.

Defendant shot and killed Vincenzo Coudera on Sunday at
about half-past 4 o'clock in the afternoon of November 28,
1915, at the warehouse (sometimes called stable by witnesses)
of Giacossa & Bellone, near the Mammoth mine, in Shasta
County. Defendant justifies the killing on the plea of self-
defense. Defendant and deceased met near this warehouse
shortly before the homicide; they were but casually acquainted with each other; defendant had been told that deceased had said that defendant was watching for one Tony
Claro every evening with intent to assault him; at the meet-

ing of defendant and deceased above referred to, deceased
was pointed out by one Peselli as the person who had made
the statement, whereupon defendant asked deceased why he
had made such statement to Claro; deceased denied that he
had made it and defendant replied that he, deceased, did
make the statement because Tony so told defendant.   Thereupon defendant extended his hand toward deceased, whether
in a threatening manner or by way of assault or as an invi-
tation for an encounter, does not clearly appear.   However,
the two men grappled and a scuffle ensued, in the course of
which they fell to the ground, defendant on top of deceased.
Bystanders interfered and the two separated, defendant walk-
ing away a few steps.   When deceased arose he picked up a
stone and threw it at defendant, hitting him on the left
shoulder, and immediately ran into the warehouse and closed
the door.

The eye-witnesses were Italians, whose testimony was taken
through interpreters.   Several exhibits were introduced to
assist the jury in understanding the facts and circumstances
surrounding the homicide, among which was the bullet causing the death of deceased, taken from the body of the deceased, the latter's clothing worn at the time, defendant's
revolver, the door through which, as was claimed by the
prosecution, the fatal shot was fired and in which two bullet
holes appeared, the door casing or four by four scantling to
which the door was latched when closed, and which showed
an indentation claimed by the prosecution to have been made
by one of the bullets when the first shot was fired, sundry
photographs, diagram of the warehouse premises, and two
or three other exhibits, none of which was sent up with the
record.   Obviously, we are deprived to some extent of the aid
which these exhibits afforded the jury.   For example, defendant claims that the bullet found in the body of deceased
was a fragment only, and that the first shot fired by defendant struck a beer bottle which the deceased threw at defendant, and that the bullet was split and a fragment of it caused
the death of deceased, and not one of the bullets that went
through the door of the warehouse.   The scantling or door
case was introduced and the indentation found on it was
shown to the jury in support of the theory of the prosecution that the bullet from the first shot struck the edge of this
door casing and passed on into the building.   The second

shot was shown to have gone through the door and the bullet hole was in line with a bullet hole through the opposite side of the building. The third shot concededly went through the door, and the position of the hole tended to show that it was where deceased was pushing at the door.

We think, however, that the evidence found in the record is quite sufficient to justify the verdict without having these exhibits before us to explain the testimony.

It appeared that when the first altercation occurred the parties were within two or three feet of the warehouse door; when defendant released the deceased and the latter got up, defendant moved away two or three steps and was standing sidewise to deceased when the latter threw the rock, hitting defendant on the left shoulder as above mentioned. Deceased immediately ran into the warehouse, the keeper, Fracchia, with him, and closed the door and both braced themselves against it on the inside, deceased next to the latch and Fracchia next to the hinges. When defendant was hit with the stone he ran after deceased and reached the door about the same time the two other men had closed it. He immediately endeavored to force it open, kicking and pushing it and calling to deceased to "come out." It was testified by witnesses who were outside of the warehouse that defendant had his revolver in one hand while he was trying to force the door open. It was in evidence that during this struggle on the part of defendant to open the door and deceased and Fracchia to hold it fast, it was opened and closed a few inches at intervals, during one of which deceased threw or struck with a quart beer bottle which he had picked up with one hand while pushing with the other and at about the same instant defendant fired the first shot. The bottle was broken into pieces, some of them falling within and some without the door. The evidence does not show how the bottle was broken. Defendant was not hit with it. He testified that he shot Coudera because he thought he was about to hit him with the bottle. Fracchia testified that he heard the bottle strike and break against the door casing just before the shot was fired. After the first shot the door was shut and Fracchia and deceased remained pushing against it. The second and third shots followed in quick succession, the last one, it is claimed by the prosecution, being the one that hit and killed the deceased. When deceased was hit he exclaimed, "I am shot in the stomach," and Fracchia cried out to stop shooting, that one of them was wounded. Deceased staggered back from the door to another part of the warehouse and shortly afterward expired. The door was opened and among others defendant went in, looked at deceased, and immediately left, and was the next day arrested at the town of Tehama.

Fracchia testified: "Q. Now, when Coudera came inside the warehouse, what did he do? A. He shut the door right away. Q. Was the door open or closed when Coudera came inside? A. Open. Q. When Coudera closed the door what did he do? A. He put himself right away against the door. Q. And how did he hold the door? A. With both hands. (Witness illustrates.) Q. What did you do? A. I put myself also against the door. (He explained the relative position of the two men, deceased on his right, next to the door latch.) Q. When you and Coudera placed yourselves against the door as you have illustrated, what next occurred? A. Finali was pushing at the door and we was pushing back. Q. Did Finali say anything as he was against the door on the outside? A. He was saying to open the door—'Open, open.' Q. While Finali was pushing against the door from the outside and you and Coudera were against the door on the inside, what happened to the door, if anything? A. It happened that after he pushed the door several times, Coudera got ahold of a bottle. Q. When you say, 'He pushed the door several times,' whom do you refer to? A. I think it was Finali; I couldn't see outside. (It elsewhere appeared that defendant was the only person pushing the door from the outside.) Q. Where did Coudera get the bottle? A. From the floor. Q. And what part of the floor? A. To the right side—north side. Q. And how far was the bottle from the door on the north? A. More or less, a foot and a half. (A photograph was shown witness on which he located the place where the bottle was. He also illustrated how Coudera reached out and got the bottle with his right hand while pushing against the door with his left hand.) And when Finali pushed the door he (Coudera) done like that (illustrating as if throwing an object with the right hand). Q. Which hand, right or left, did Coudera reach for the bottle? A. With the right one. Q. At the time that Coudera reached with his right hand for the bottle, where was his left hand? A. At the door. Q. What did Coudera do with the bottle after he got it in his right hand? A. He held it there for a little while and while the other was pushing at the door, he threw it at him—he threw it. He threw it. Q. And was the door open or closed at that time? A. When he threw the bottle, the door was open a little bit. Q. What happened when Coudera threw the bottle? A. When Coudera threw the bottle, I heard the report of the bottle, and the shot, 'Pom! Pom!' Q. What happened to the bottle? A. The bottle broke. Q. When did the bottle break with reference to the time that you heard the shot? A. First I heard the sound of the bottle and then the shot of the pistol. Q. What do you mean by the sound of the bottle? A. The sound of the explosion of the bottle. Q. How did the bottle break, if you know? A. That I don't know. Q. Did the bottle break inside the door or outside the door? A. Inside the stable. Q. When the bottle broke what did Coudera do? A. He put himself against the door." He was asked to illustrate: "A. Like that. (Witness illustrates by arising and facing the wall, bending forward slightly and placing both hands flat against the wall.) Q. What occurred after Coudera placed himself in a leaning position with both hands against the door as you have illustrated? A. It occurred that the shots were fired. Q. How many shots were fired? A. Three shots. Q. How many shots were fired after Coudera placed both hands against the door in a leaning position immediately after the bottle was broken? A. Two shots. Q. After the two shots were fired, what happened? A. I heard Coudera say, 'Oh, I am wounded in the stomach.' Q. And what did Coudera do after he said that? A. He turned around and walked to the little room. Q. When you heard the bottle break did you hear another noise? A. When the bottle broke I heard the fire of the pistol—the shot of the pistol. Q. When Coudera said: 'I am wounded,' what did you do? A. Then I began to holler, 'Stop! Stop! He is wounded.' . . . Q. From the time that Coudera came inside the warehouse, closed the door and leaned against the door, did he at any time let go of the door with both his hands? A. I never saw him move from the door." He testified that the door opened two or three times, as he estimated it, before the first shot was fired, once he thought eight or ten inches.

Witness Benedetti went into the warehouse about the same time deceased entered it and from a point fifteen or twenty feet from the door saw and heard what took place in there. He testified: "Q. At the time the bottle broke, was the door open or closed? A. There was about that much open (showing). Q. State how many inches? A About a foot or foot and a half. Q. Was Fracchia against the door or leaning against the door when the last two shots were fired? A. He was at the door pushing. Q. What happened after the last shot was fired? A. Mr. Coudera went backward and he was wounded here (indicating in the breast). . . . Q. Did anyone say anything after the last shot was fired? A. Mr. Fracchia told him not to fire any more—told Mr. Finali not to fire any more." He testified that Coudera had the bottle in his right hand and was "pushing against the door this way (showing)."

The autopsy showed that the bullet entered the body of deceased "between the first and second cartilages on the right side—in front, . . . the bullet entered near the apex of the lungs, passed down through the base, through the diaphragm, through the liver, and passed out between the eleventh and twelfth ribs and entered and lodged in the back about three inches from the spine on the right side of the body, about one inch from the skin—general course was down and back." Dr. Sanholdt, who made the autopsy, testified that the cause of death was "bleeding from the vena cava, which was torn by the bullet"; that a man with such a wound would live but a short time—"it is only the matter of a moment. Q. As much as a minute? A. I don't think so. . . . He might utter a few words but I doubt if he could make any coherent sentences." He testified that the point where the bullet lodged was about twelve inches lower than the point of entrance, and that the bullet encountered no bone in its passage.

We think the jury were warranted in finding that the fatal shot was fired through the door while deceased and Fracchia were holding it shut and endeavoring to keep defendant from entering. The position of deceased at the door—a position one would naturally assume in pushing with his hands against a door to hold it fast—would account for the entrance of the bullet as described and its course backward and downward. It is true this might possibly have happened had the bullet struck the bottle and had a fragment of it been deflected toward deceased. Bullets take eccentric courses sometimes after entering the body. But the evidence was that deceased did not exclaim that he was shot until the third shot was fired and while he and Fracchia were pushing at the door, and the evidence was also that had he received this wound from the first shot, it would have immediately disabled him from making any further physical effort toward keeping defendaît out of the building. But if it be conceded that the first shot was the fatal one, we cannot see that it was justified upon any view of the doctrine of self-defense. Defendant was clearly the aggressor. With revolver in hand he was trying to force his way through the door, which was being held to prevent his entrance. Having succeeded in pressing it partially open, the deceased was the one then in danger, and had he given defendant a fatal blow with the bottle, the doctrine of self-defense and the right to act upon appearances might have been available to deceased.

Defendant could not by his own willful act create a situation giving rise to appearances which he could interpret as endangering his life and thereupon kill the person he was assailing. As was said in *People* v. *Hecker*, 109 Cal. 451, 462, [30 L. R. A. 403, 42 Pac. 307, 311] : "A man may not wickedly or willfully invite or create the appearances of necessity, or the actual necessity which, if present to one without blame, would justify the homicide."

Defendant lays much stress upon the fact that deceased hit him with a rock after they had separated from the first encounter. Had defendant overtaken deceased in the heat of the moment and suitably punished him for this assault, he might not have been blameworthy. But he lost this opportunity by deceased having reached a harbor of safety where he was in no position to do defendant further harm. Thenceforth defendant was clearly the aggressor. Under the circumstances disclosed, the plea of self-defense in killing deceased was not open to him. It seems to us that the jury exercised much charity in finding that the homicide was "upon a sudden quarrel or heat of passion," and but manslaughter.

2. The court instructed the jury quite fully on the law of self-defense and the right of one being assailed to act upon appearances. It is not objected that these instructions were incorrect, but it is objected that the court in the same connection instructed the jury as follows: "There must have

been a present ability on the part of the assailant to accomplish his criminal design in order to justify the person assailed in taking his life." It is contended that there was conflict in the evidence as to whether deceased struck at defendant through the open space when the door was open, or whether deceased threw the bottle at defendant through the opening and whether the bottle was broken by the bullet at the first shot or struck the door casing and was broken, and that there was a conflict in the evidence as to whether the shot was fired before, at the time, or after the bottle was thrown. In this state of the evidence it is claimed "that the jury may have believed, under this instruction of the court, that the bottle was broken before the first shot was fired, and that the door was closed when the last two shots were fired, and that therefore, as a matter of law, deceased at neither time had the present ability to inflict injury upon defendant and defendant was in no real danger."

We think the instruction was inconsistent with the doctrine of apparent danger to one who is assailed and was out of harmony with other instructions given upon the subject, and, taken alone, was an incorrect statement of the law. It must not be forgotten, however, that in no view of the evidence could it be reasonably said that deceased was the assailant. And when the door was pushed open by defendant, who was at that moment the real assailant, armed with a deadly weapon, which the sequel showed he intended to use, deceased had a right to defend himself against the threatened danger. By doing so, his relation toward defendant was not changed. Throughout their argument the learned counsel of defendant seem to hold that deceased became the assailant in having struck defendant with a rock after the latter had withdrawn from the first encounter, and that notwithstanding deceased had taken refuge in the warehouse, defendant had a right to pursue and punish him and still be within the protecting aegis of the doctrine of self-defense should deceased resist. This doctrine must not be confused with the *lex talionis.* The doctrine of self-defense presupposes that one who would avail himself of it has, without his fault, found himself in threatened danger of serious bodily injury to avert which the law gives him the right to resort to extreme measures. But, as we have already pointed out, the plea of self-defense is not available to him where he willfully and with-

out any necessity for his own protection creates the danger
with which he is threatened.   The law of self-defense is a law
of necessity, and ceases with the disappearance of the necessity.   Whatever may be said of the instruction, however, we
are quite convinced that, error though it be, we cannot for
a moment believe that the jury were so far misled by it as
to have caused a miscarriage of justice, and unless we can
so say we are forbidden to reverse the judgment.   (Sec. 4½,
art. VI, Const.; *People* v. *O'Bryan*, 165 Cal. 55, [130 Pac.
1042] ; *People* v. *Bartol*, 24 Cal. App. 659, [142 Pac. 510] ;
Vallejo & N. R. R. Co. v. *Reed Orchard Co.*, 169 Cal. 545,
[147 Pac. 238].)

3. The court instructed the jury as follows: ''Self-defense
is not available as a plea to a defendant who has sought a
quarrel with a design to force a deadly issue and thus,
through his fraud, connivance, or fault, create a real or apparent necessity for the killing.''   It is claimed that the instruction was not applicable to the facts because there was no
evidence that either a real or apparent necessity for the killing was created by the fraud, connivance, or fault of defendant.   The instruction was based upon the principle announced
in *People* v. *Hecker*, 109 Cal. 451, [30 L. R. A. 403, 42 Pac.
307].   We think the evidence showed that whatever of real
or apparent necessity defendant believed to exist for the killing was created by his fault.   He had no right to break into
the warehouse by force to assault deceased or to punish him
for an assault previously made on defendant by deceased, and
if, in doing so, danger to defendant appeared, it was of his
own creation.

4. After the jury had been considering the case some time,
they came into court and asked for the instructions on justifiable homicide to be again read to them.   The court read its
instructions on the subject, including the reading of section
195 of the Penal Code.   On the suggestion of defendant's attorney, the court read still other instructions on the subject
given at defendant's request.   Defendant then asked to have
a particular instruction read—''that the defendant need not
wait until the blow is struck before acting in his own protection.''   ''The Court: No, I will only act on the request of
the jury.   The Court: Is that all you wish, gentlemen?   A
Juror: Are we entitled to know what the penalties are in each
degree?   The Court: No, that is entirely in the discretion of

the court. The Juror: That is what I thought. The Court:
The court has told you about that heretofore. I will read
you this, gentlemen." The court then read one of its instructions in connection with the rule of reasonable doubt and
stating the law as to the right of the jury to fix the punishment should the defendant be found guilty of murder in the
first degree. The jury were then asked if they desired any
further instructions and all answered satisfied.

The jury being still unable to agree came into court again
and requested "a little information on one little point, and
that is, what creates a reasonable doubt." The court read its
instructions on that subject and asked the jury if they desired anything further. "The Foreman: That seems to be
the only thing, your Honor. The Court: Is that plain enough
to you, gentlemen? (An affirmation is given to the court.)"
The jury retired and later brought in their verdict. Defendant was not entitled as matter of right to have instructions read which the jury had not called for or to have all
the instructions on a given subject read when such as were
read were satisfactory to the jury.

5. The court refused certain instructions requested by defendant on the ground that they were presented too late for
consideration by the court: (a) As to the right of self-defense
having been revived, after defendant withdrew from the first
conflict, by deceased having hit him with a rock; (b) defendant not bound to retreat in the face of danger; (c) reasonable
doubt as to who opened the door and for what purpose it was
opened, and that such doubt should have been resolved in
favor of defendant. Whether or not the reason given by the
court was sufficient need not be considered, for we do not
think the defendant was prejudiced by the court's ruling.
The hitting of defendant with a stone by deceased after defendant had withdrawn from the first conflict did not so far
revive defendant's right to self-defense as to justify him in
forcing a second conflict, as appeared by the evidence, and
killing deceased because in doing so he believed himself to
be in danger of great bodily injury. The doctrine of retreat
in the face of apparent danger had no application, since defendant was the assailant. There was no evidence warranting the assumption that deceased opended the door for any
purpose or raising any doubt on that question.

6. Two instructions were refused, for one of which rulings the court assigned no reason and as to the other that it was covered elsewhere. The latter related to the doctrine of defendant's right to act upon appearances which was, as the court said, fully covered elsewhere in the instructions.

The other instruction proceeded on the assumption that deceased was the assailant at the time he was killed, and that defendant acted upon the reasonable belief that he was in danger of receiving great bodily harm from deceased at that moment.

7. In the course of his argument to the jury, the district attorney referred to an instance within his knowledge, of a bullet in passing through the front end of a wagon split in its course into two parts, hitting each horse and another part performing an equally freakish thing. Defendant objected and the district attorney asked the court to instruct the jury to disregard the illustration and confine themselves to the evidence, which the court did.

The defendant at the time of his arrest made a somewhat self-incriminatory statement which was introduced in evidence. The district attorney referred to the fact that defendant, when on the witness-stand, did not deny the truth of the statement. Upon defendant's objection as misconduct prejudicial to defendant's rights and motion that the court instruct the jury to disregard the same, the district attorney said: "While we do not feel that there is anything prejudicial, at the same time we have no objection to the court's giving the instruction," and the court thereupon gave the requested instruction.

In his closing argument to the jury the district attorney stated that he did not believe Coudera (deceased) had ever made the statement to Tony Claro attributed to Coudera, for the reason that defendant did not call Claro as a witness to prove it, though subpoenaed by defendant and excused.

Where misconduct of the district attorney is claimed as prejudicial, the more recent decisions of the supreme court hold that, if attention is called to it and the court instructs the jury to disregard it and not allow themselves to be influenced by it, the misconduct must be flagrant and obviously prejudicial to justify a reversal. Such was the misconduct of the district attorney in *People* v. *Tufts*, 167 Cal. 266, [139

Pac. 78] , *People* v. *Derwae*, 155 Cal. 593, [102 Pac. 266] , and other cases cited by defendant.

In the present case the record shows that the district attorney exhibited commendable carefulness in the conduct of the trial, not to trench upon the rights of the defendant. No evidence was offered or admitted as to which defendant has assigned error. There was no attempt by the district attorney to repeat the objectionable statements. The reference to the eccentricities of a bullet was of no particular significance and, in fact, had as much application to defendant's theory as to the people's.

As to the nonappearance of Claro as a witness, the reference could not have injured defendant, for whether it was true or not that he told defendant what deceased said had very little if any significance. Reference by the district attorney to defendant's failure to deny his extrajudicial statement, while violative of the defendant's right to remain silent without prejudice for so doing, the statements of defendant were as to circumstances connected with the homicide about which the jury had full knowledge through testimony of witnesses. We may safely adopt what was said in *People* v. *Kromphold*, 172 Cal. 512, [157 Pac. 599]: "While it was wrong for the district attorney to comment at all on the failure of defendant to testify upon this subject, it would be most unreasonable to assume, in the light of the attitude of the trial judge in the matter and the nature of the remarks, that the jury could have been influenced to the prejudice of the defendant by the statement complained of. (See *People* v. *Sansome*, 98 Cal. 235, [33 Pac. 202].) Certainly one cannot hold that this statement 'has resulted in a miscarriage of justice.' (Sec. 4½, art. VI, Const.)"

The defendant was ably defended, and every opportunity given him to meet the evidence in support of the charge. We think the verdict was justified by the evidence and that no prejudicial error occurred at the trial which would warrant a reversal.

The judgment and order are affirmed.

Burnett, J., and Hart, J., concurred.

[Civ. No. 1546.   Third Appellate District.—September 20, 1916.]

E. S. BAXTER, Respondent, v. CHICO CONSTRUCTION COMPANY (a Corporation), Appellant.

NOVATION—STATUTE OF FRAUDS—PAYMENT FOR SUPPLIES FURNISHED THIRD PERSON—VERBAL PROMISE OF CORPORATION.—A verbal promise made by the foreman of a corporation engaged in the construction of a dam that the corporation would pay for certain supplies which had been furnished to the person who had the contract for the hauling of the necessary gravel for the work, is binding on the corporation, and without the statute of frauds, where it is shown that such foreman had authority to hire and discharge men and to procure needed supplies, and that the promisee accepted the new promise and canceled the antecedent obligation.

APPEAL from a judgment of the Superior Court of Yuba County.   Eugene P. McDaniel, Judge.

The facts are stated in the opinion of the court.

Guy R. Kennedy, for Appellant.

W. H. Carlin, for Respondent.

BURNETT, J.—We think a rational conclusion from evidence disclosed by the record is found in the following statement of facts as claimed by respondent: Defendant had a contract for constructing within a given time a concrete dam for the impounding of water for irrigation.   It sublet to one James Kirby the work of hauling the necessary gravel to the dam site.   Defendant's headquarters were at Chico, Butte County, and the dam was being constructed some forty or fifty miles away, in the foothills of Yuba County.   Plaintiff was conducting a general merchandise store a few miles from this site.   The work was begun, and while hauling the gravel, Kirby incurred a bill at the store for the sum of $298.20 for supplies of various kinds, including groceries and a considerable quantity of beer and whisky.   Up to about October 17, 1913, defendant had been represented at this place by its superintendent or foreman, a Mr. Cuddeback, and he was succeeded by a Mr. Jack McGeehan, each of them having authority to hire and discharge men, buy necessary supplies, incur bills in connection therewith, and represent defendant in the prosecution of the work. At said date, Mr. Kirby had a large amount of gravel on the way near plaintiff's store and plaintiff demanded the payment of his bill, refused to extend any further credit to the subcontractor, and was about to commence suit and attach the gravel. This was communicated to foreman Cuddeback, and his successor, Mr. McGeehan, took up the matter and informed plaintiff that he would communicate with the president of defendant by telephone. To plaintiff's knowledge, he did have such communication with the president, who was then at Chico, went direct to plaintiff's store, assisted plaintiff and his clerk in figuring up the amount due and unpaid, ascertained it to be $298.20, told plaintiff that in his talk with the president of defendant over the phone, the president stated that defendant would pay the bill, and McGeehan further declared that he, the foreman, would O. K. the bill, had a statement of the bill made out which he, in fact, initialed and sent to defendant at Chico, stated to plaintiff that defendant desired him to continue giving credit to Kirby, and that it would pay for all necessary articles furnished to him thereafter. Plaintiff thereupon accepted defendant's promise thus made to pay the then existing bill of $298.20, released Kirby from all claim in connection therewith, stopped the proceedings to attach, or at least abstained from any action, and looked solely thereafter to defendant for payment, and further carrying out his promise, furnished additional merchandise to Kirby in the sum of $81.20, looking to defendant alone for payment therefor.

The foregoing are the most favorable inferences in favor of the judgment that can be drawn from the evidence, but that, of course, is no objection here, if they are substantially supported at all.

The following quotation from plaintiff's testimony would seem to disclose said support: "My store is a little less than a mile from the dam. James Kirby had a subcontract from the defendant for the hauling of gravel for the construction of the dam. In doing that work, he ran a bill with me for general merchandise. Ed. Fleming was on the ground representing Mr. Kirby, and at first Pete Cuddeback was the foreman and representative of defendant, and he was succeeded by Jack McGeehan. On October 20, 1913, James Kirby owed

me $298.20, and I told his foreman, Mr. Fleming, that I
wouldn't furnish any more supplies unless it was fixed up.
Mr. Fleming went to Oroville, came back in a couple of days,
and said Pete Cuddeback, who went to the phone and talked
with Mr. Polk, the engineer for defendant in charge of the
work, and after talking with him, told me to fix up the
amount owed me by Kirby and send it to the defendant, and
that it would be paid and defendant would be responsible for
it. Then Mr. Fleming and Jack McGeehan, who was then
foreman and representative of the defendant, took my books,
added up the account, which came to $298.20, and made out
the statement introduced in evidence themselves, and Jack
McGeehan took it, saying that he would O. K. it and send it
to the defendant. I then and there accepted this promise on
behalf of defendant and I released James Kirby, canceled
his indebtedness, and from this time on looked to the defendant alone for the payment of this bill. As a further inducement and consideration to defendant for assuming this bill,
I promised Jack McGeehan that I would go ahead and let
Kirby have thereafter anything that was necessary to complete the contract, which Mr. McGeehan, for defendant, asked
me to do and stated the defendant would pay the same. Had
not defendant assumed the prior account, I would not have
done this, as I was going to attach, but having obtained this
promise from the company, I released Mr. Kirby and then
furnished additional supplies to Mr. Kirby thereafter in accordance with the direction obtained from Mr. McGeehan,
amounting to $81.20.''

There is thus shown a novation, and it is excepted from
the operation of the statute of frauds by virtue of subdivision
3 of section 2794 of the Civil Code, excluding the case ''where
the promise, being for an antecedent obligation of another,
is made upon the consideration that the party receiving it
cancels the antecedent obligation, accepting the new promise
as a substitute therefor,'' etc.

We can see no valid objection to the course permitting
plaintiff to testify that he did cancel the antecedent obligation and accepted the new promise. These were facts, and
no one was better qualified than plaintiff to testify concerning
them. The court would not be bound by his declaration to
that effect, but they constituted evidence which we cannot
say was insufficient to support the court's finding.

We think, also, that there was sufficient showing that the foreman or superintendent had authority to bind the company in the promise to pay for the supplies.

There is no dispute that Cuddeback and McGeehan had the same authority, and the former testified that: "My authority was to go ahead with the construction of the dam, hire men, discharge them, buy what supplies were needed for the work." Mr. Fleming also testified that Mr. McGeehan was general foreman for the Chico Construction Company, that "he hired and discharged laborers and supervised the work and ordered supplies."

There is also strong circumstantial evidence in the fact that McGeehan, immediately after telephoning to the president of said company, made said agreement with plaintiff. He would quite naturally repeat to plaintiff what was said to him by his superior. It is altogether improbable that he would immediately make a contract entirely different from his instructions. It is true that there is a difference between the testimony of plaintiff and McGeehan as to this, but we must accept the version of the former.

The proposition involved in the case seems simple, and, as we cannot say that the conclusion drawn from the evidence by the trial judge is unreasonable or unsupported, we think the judgment should be affirmed, and it is so ordered.

Chipman, P. J., and Hart, J., concurred.

[Civ. No. 1542. Third Appellate District.—September 20, 1916.]

RECLAMATION DISTRICT No. 730, Respondent, v. M. INGLIN, Appellant.

CONDEMNATION OF LAND FOR LEVEE—EVIDENCE—OPINION OF VALUE—OTHER SALES—IMPROPER REDIRECT EXAMINATION.—In an action in eminent domain brought by a reclamation district, to condemn a strip of land as a part of a right of way for a levee, it is error to permit the plaintiff upon redirect examination of one of its trustees, who had on direct examination given his opinion as to the market value of the strip, to state that he based his opinion upon what other lands in the district of a similar character as to quality had been sold for to the district, although the defendant

on cross-examination brought out the fact of other sales and the
prices at which they were made, but such error is without prejudice, where it is obvious from the verdict that the jury did not
accept the testimony of the witness as to value.

ID.—OTHER SALES AND PRICES OBTAINED—PROPER CROSS-EXAMINATION
—LIMITED PURPOSE.—In such an action it is proper to bring out
on the cross-examination of a witness as to value the fact of other
sales in the district and the prices at which they were made, for
the purpose of testing the witness' knowledge and impeaching his
opinion, but not for the purpose of fixing the value of the strip
in suit.

ID.—VALUE OF LAND—RIGHT OF OWNER.—The owner of land sought to
be condemned is entitled to its actual market value for the most
valuable use or uses to which it is adapted or may be put, and the
prices at which other lands of like quality and adaptation and similarly situated may have been sold cannot reasonably be accepted as
a just criterion for measuring, and finally ascertaining. the actual
value of the land sought to be taken.

APPEAL from a judgment of the Superior Court of Yolo
County.   N. A. Hawkins, Judge.

The facts are stated in the opinion of the court.

Hudson Grant, and George Clark, for Appellant.

Arthur C. Huston, and Harry L. Huston, for Respondent.

HART, J.—This action is in eminent domain, and the appeal is by the defendant from the judgment in condemnation
entered upon the jury's verdict.

The plaintiff is a reclamation district, entirely situated in
Yolo County, organized as such under the laws of this state,
the object for which it was organized being, as its name naturally implies, "to reclaim from overflow, flood, and seepage
waters all the lands lying within the boundaries of said district."

The defendant is the owner of a tract of land situated
within the boundaries of said district, and it is alleged in the
complaint that a certain specifically described strip of said
land, consisting of 9.8 acres, is necessary as a "right of way
. . . to excavate, build, construct, repair and maintain canals,
drains, levees, embankments, and other works necessary for
the reclamation of the lands in said district, and also to ob-

tain material for the construction, maintenance, and repair thereof, and for the purpose of reclaiming the lands within said district from overflow and seepage waters.'' The strip of land sought to be taken by this action and which was by the verdict and the judgment condemned for the purposes above indicated constitutes a portion of the entire tract of land, situated in said district, owned by the defendant.

The answer alleges that upon the strip of land sought to be condemned are located the defendant's house, barn, and fences, and also a large, carefully constructed levee, and that all of said improvements ''are to be taken or damaged by said plaintiff''; that the value of the house, barn, and fences is the sum of $9,655.65, the value of the land itself is in excess of the sum of $3,430.00, and that the value of the said levee is the sum of $2,725.65. It is further alleged that the said house, barn, and fences cannot be used by defendant, if left upon said right of way, and that to make any convenient use of the same, upon the taking of said right of way and the construction of said proposed improvements, it will be necessary to move said buildings and fences from said land, and that the placing and setting of the buildings on new foundations and the rebuilding of said fences will be at an expense and to the damage of the defendant in the sum of one thousand dollars; that the total damages suffered by the defendant by reason of the taking of said right of way and the construction of said proposed improvements, exclusive of the damage that will be suffered by the land not taken, ''of which the part taken is a part, is the sum of $8,680.65''; that the damage which will accrue to the portion of the land not sought to be condemned will, by reason of the severance therefrom of the portion condemned and the construction of the improvements in the manner proposed by the plaintiff, amount to the sum of one thousand dollars.

The jury assessed and fixed the aggregate damages suffered by the defendant by reason of the taking of the strip of land at the sum of $2,862.95, the several items of said damages being found as follows:

Value of the land taken....................$2422.95
Cost of removal and relocation of structures
    upon said land........................... 400.00
Cost of removal of hay from barn.............   40.00

The jury found that no damage whatever will accrue to the land not condemned by reason of the severance therefrom of the strip taken.

The points urged by the defendant against the legal integrity of the judgment involve alleged errors of the trial court in permitting certain testimony to be given and in disallowing a certain instruction proposed by him and bearing upon the testimony referred to.

The witnesses for the defendant estimated the value of the land sought to be condemned, variously, at $400, $375, $350, $325, and $300 per acre. The plaintiff's witnesses expressed the opinion that it was worth no more than $50 per acre. One of the witnesses for the plaintiff testified that the particular strip involved here could be used, if it remained the property of the defendant, for the purposes of a levee only—that "it is useless for anything else."

The testimony to which objection was made by the defendant at the trial was that of W. S. Kendall, one of the trustees of the plaintiff.

On direct examination, he stated it to be his opinion that the market value of the strip of land involved in this action was $50 per acre. On cross-examination, he was asked whether he knew that several other tracts of land situated in said district belonging to other parties and which was adapted and had been devoted to the raising of alfalfa had been sold at prices ranging from $130 to $150 per acre in near proximity to the time at which the summons in this action was issued. His replies to the questions so propounded were that he had heard of such sales. On redirect, counsel for the plaintiff thus questioned the witness: "Mr. Huston: Explain to the jury why you placed the valuation of $50 an acre on this tract of land. Witness: Because it is what everybody in the district got." This answer was, on motion of the defendant, stricken out. Thereupon counsel for the plaintiff, naming six different owners of land in said district, asked the witness if he knew of the sales by said owners of their said lands, to which an affirmative reply was returned. "Mr. Huston: What did you hear was the sale price of these several tracts of land? Witness: Fifty dollars an acre." The witness then proceeded to say, on redirect, that the lands sold by the other parties named were in all respects similar in quality and in productive capacity to the land of the defendant and from which the strip in question was proposed to be taken. All this testimony was duly and regularly objected to by the defendant, and the objections overruled.

On cross-examination, the witness was questioned: "Are you judging of the value of the Inglin lands by what these lands will produce? A. No, sir. Q. Are you endeavoring to fix the value on these lands simply by the standard of valuation which prevailed in the transfers to the district which were mentioned and enumerated by Mr. H. L. Huston in his questions to you? A. Yes."

Upon the conclusion of the witness' testimony, and before he left the witness-stand, counsel for the defendant moved to strike out all of said testimony on the ground that the basis of the witness' estimate of the value of the land in dispute was the prices at which other lands in the district had been sold, and that such prices do not constitute the legal criterion for estimating or determining value in a case of this character. The motion was denied.

Although the witness, we think, sufficiently qualified himself to give testimony upon the question of value by declaring that he had for many years been engaged in buying and selling real estate for himself and others, and that he had seen and was acquainted with the land in controversy, it is very clear that his testimony plainly and, indeed, conclusively showed that his opinion upon the value of the land in question was based entirely upon what other lands in said district of a similar character as to quality had been sold for to said district. The law provides that the owner is entitled to the actual value of the land sought to be condemned at the date of the issuance of summons in the action to condemn (Code Civ. Proc., sec. 1249), and the standard adopted by the witness is not the proper one for the estimation and (finally) the ascertainment of such value. The owner of the land is entitled to the actual market value of the land for the most valuable use or uses to which it is adapted or may be put, and the prices at which other lands of like quality and adaptation and similarly situated may have been sold cannot reasonably be accepted as a just criterion for measuring and, finally, ascertaining the actual value of the land sought to be taken. The reasons for this are obvious, and hardly need be stated, although, it may be suggested that, in looking for such reasons, it may readily be conceived how a person might, through force of circumstances beyond his control, sell his land at a price far below its actual value, or how he might make such a sale through improvidence or for want of good judgment.

It is true that counsel for the defendant, in the cross-examination of Kendall, first brought out the fact of other sales of lands in the district and the prices at which they were made. As cross-examination, the questions and answers were proper, not, however, for the purpose of fixing the value of the land in dispute, but only "for the purpose of testing the witness' knowledge and impeaching his opinion." (*Estate of Ross*, 171 Cal. 64, 66, [151 Pac. 1138]; see, also, *Central Pac. R. R. Co.* v. *Pearson*, 35 Cal. 247, 262; *Clark* v. *Willett*, 35 Cal. 534, 544; *Santa Ana* v. *Harlin*, 99 Cal. 538, 544, [34 Pac. 224]; *Spring Valley W. W.* v. *Drinkhouse*, 92 Cal. 528, 532, [28 Pac. 681]; *De Freitas* v. *Suisun City*, 170 Cal. 263, [149 Pac. 553].) But such cross-examination does not justify the plaintiff on redirect examination, which often amounts in practical effect to an examination in chief, to take up the question of sales of other lands and thus show by the witness the prices paid by purchasers of such other lands; for the reason of the rule permitting the fact of the sales of other lands to be gone into on cross-examination ceases with the cross-examination. While in all cases witnesses may, upon their examination in chief, give the reasons upon which they base their opinions, they should never be allowed to go into details of particular sales or transactions. (2 Lewis on Eminent Domain, 3d ed., sec. 654.) It follows, of course, that the court not only erred in allowing the question of sales of other lands and the prices paid for such lands to be gone into on the redirect examination of the witness, Kendall, but erred in refusing to grant the motion to strike out the testimony of said witness, it having been made clearly to appear from said testimony that the witness had based his opinion upon the question of value wholly upon incompetent matters. (*San Diego Land etc. Co.* v. *Neale*, 88 Cal. 50, 63, [11 L. R. A. 604, 25 Pac. 977]; *Pierson* v. *Boston Elevated Ry.*, 191 Mass. 223, 233, 234, [77 N. E. 769].)

But we think the errors thus considered were not prejudicial, for it is obvious from the verdict that the jury did not accept the testimony or opinion of the witness, Kendall, upon the question of the value of the property proposed to be taken. As seen, the strip to condemn which this action was brought consisted of a fraction of over nine acres of the defendant's land, the total value of which, together with the improvements, the jury assessed at $2,422.95, or, approximately, if not precisely, at $265.52 per acre.

But it seems to be the theory of counsel for the defendant that but for the testimony of Kendall the jury might have found that the defendant suffered some damage from deterioration in the value of his land by reason of the severance therefrom of the strip in question. No such assumption is justified on the record as it is presented here. We have already stated that other witnesses testified that the land of the defendant was not damaged by reason of the severance of the strip in dispute therefrom. These same witnesses further testified that the land in question was of no greater value than $50 per acre. There is a mere brief recital in the transcript of the testimony of these witnesses, and the record before us does not disclose the basis of their estimate of the value of the land in controversy or the reasons, if any they gave, for the opinion that the actual value of said land does not exceed the sum of $50 per acre. We must therefore assume that the testimony of the witnesses referred to was in all respects competent, and that they adopted a proper criterion for estimating the value of the land. There is therefore a pronounced conflict in the evidence both upon the question of value and the question whether the remainder of the defendant's land would be damaged by reason of the severance therefrom of the strip in dispute.

Thus viewing the record as it appears before us, in so far as it concerns the evidence, it is plainly manifest that the jury were afforded a very wide latitude within which to exercise their judgment as to the actual value of the land sought to be taken, viz., from the sum of $50 to the sum of four hundred dollars per acre, and there is nothing appearing upon the face of the record which would warrant us in declaring that the actual value of the land was in excess of the amount at which it was fixed by the jury.

For the same reason for which we hold the errors in admitting the above-considered testimony to be without prejudice to the rights of the defendant, the action of the court in refusing to give a certain one of the instructions proffered by the defendant, while erroneous, was without prejudice. The substance of the said instruction was: "During the progress

of this case some reference has been made in the testimony
and in the argument to prices paid to others than defendant
for the land constituting a part of the right of way for the
river-front levee of Reclamation District No. 730. You are
instructed that the prices which may have been paid for rights
of way to other persons for the levee along the river-front
constitute no test for the fixing of the value of the defendant's lands in this cause. . . . And you will, accordingly, disregard, in determining the value of the defendant's land, any
reference, either in the testimony or in the argument, to payments made to others for rights of way.''

As before declared, it is obvious that the jury were not
governed, in the determination of the question of value, by
the testimony of those witnesses who expressed the opinion
that the value of the land in dispute did not exceed the sum
of $50 per acre, although, as suggested, so far as the record
here shows, they would have been justified in predicating
their verdict upon the testimony so given other than that by
the witness, Kendall. The total value fixed by the jury, however, as is obvious, was over five times the sum of $50 per
acre, or, approximately, $34.40 less than three hundred dol-
lars, the minimum amount at which the value of the land
was estimated by the defendant's witnesses.

There was neither prejudice to the defendant nor a miscarriage of justice by reason of the errors complained of
(Const., art. VI, sec. 4½; *Vallejo & N. R. Co. v. Reed
Orchard Co.*, 169 Cal. 545, [147 Pac. 238]), and the judgment is accordingly affirmed.

Chipman, P. J., and Burnett, J., concurred.

[Civ. No. 1804.   First Appellate District.—September 21, 1916.]

TIDEWATER SOUTHERN RAILWAY COMPANY (a Corporation), Appellant, v. CAREY M. VANCE, Respondent.

CORPORATION—SUBSCRIPTION FOR STOCK—PAYMENT BY NOTE—RIGHT TO RECALL IN EVENT OF DISSATISFACTION WITH PURCHASE—VALIDITY OF AGREEMENT.—An agreement made by a fully organized corporation with a subscriber for a certain number of shares of its stock that the subscriber should have the right at any time within ten months after the date of the subscription agreement to cancel his subscription by recalling his note, if dissatisfied with his purchase, is enforceable against the corporation, where it is not shown that any later subscriber was defrauded by reliance upon such subscription, or that any subsequent creditor relied thereon in dealing with the corporation, or that there was any secrecy contemplated or connived at by the subscriber in the making of such agreement.

APPEAL from a judgment of the Superior Court of Fresno County.   H. Z. Austin, Judge.

The facts are stated in the opinion of the court.

Meredith, Landis & Chester, for Appellant.

Johnston & Jones, and W. B. Good, for Respondent.

RICHARDS, J.—This is an appeal from a judgment in favor of the defendant in an action brought to recover the sum of $625, alleged to be due upon a promissory note executed and delivered by the defendant to the Tidewater Southern Railroad Company and by it assigned and transferred to the plaintiff herein.

The facts of the case are undisputed.   On December 14, 1911, the defendant executed a subscription for five hundred shares of the capital stock of the Tidewater Southern Railroad Co., for which he agreed to pay $625 on or before ten months after date, giving his promissory note for that amount.   The authorized agent of the corporation who solicited and received the subscription had two copies thereof, one marked "Original" and the other "Duplicate," both of which were signed by the defendant and the agent on behalf of the corporation, the original being retained by him for the company and the duplicate being delivered to the defendant. On the back of the duplicate the following memorandum was written: "Dec. 4, '11· Ten months after date if holder of this contract is for any reason dissatisfied we agree to return note or cash equivalent.—H. C. Coffin, Tidewater Southern Railroad Co." This writing was not indorsed on the back of the original subscription retained by the agent for the company. Within ten months of the date of his subscription the defendant requested the return of his note, which request the corporation refused to comply with, but, on the contrary, transferred the note to the plaintiff herein, who brought this suit.

The defendant pleaded the foregoing facts by way of defense to the action, and upon proof of the same judgment went in his favor. Wherefore the plaintiff prosecutes this appeal.

The only material point involved in this appeal relates to the validity of the agreement indorsed upon the defendant's duplicate copy of his subscription which purported to entitle him to recall his note. The appellant contends that this collateral agreement not having been indorsed upon the original stock agreement and filed with the company, and thus brought to the knowledge of other stockholders and subscribers for stock and to the creditors of the corporation, is void. In support of this contention the appellant relies chiefly upon the case of *Quartz Glass Mfg. Co. v. Joyce*, 27 Cal. App. 523, [150 Pac. 648]. In that case, however, the question involved was the validity of a stock subscription agreement by the terms of which the promissory note given for the purchase price of the stock was to be paid out of dividends to be thereafter declared by the corporation. The court held that this practically amounted to a gift of the stock in violation of the provision of section 359 of the Civil Code, and that the said agreement of the parties having that effect was therefore void. It is true that the court in that case also adverted to the quite well-recognized rule that secret collateral agreements as to stock subscriptions, by which the subscriber gains an advantage over other subscribers, are void, for the reason that such secret advantages are in the nature of a fraud upon subsequent subscribers and upon persons who afterward become creditors of the corporation. The

authorities cited in that case and amplified by the appellant
herein refer in the main to subscriptions for the stock of
corporations prior to the incorporation of the company or
during the initial stages of its life when sales of its stock
are being promoted, and when subsequent subscribers have
relied upon the integrity upon their face of prior subscriptions. This, however, is not the situation presented in the
instant case. The Tidewater Southern Railroad Company had
been fully organized before the respondent's subscription to
its stock was made, and it does not appear that there was
any later subscriber who could have been defrauded by his
reliance upon the respondent's subscription; nor does it appear that there was any subsequent creditor of said corporation who could or did rely thereon in dealing with said
corporation; nor is it shown that there was any secrecy contemplated or connived at by the respondent in the making
of the collateral agreement by which he was permitted within
ten months thereafter to cancel his subscription by recalling
his note; nor that he had any knowledge of the fact that the
authorized agent of the corporation failed to also indorse
such agreement upon the original subscription which said
agent retained on behalf of the corporation. Whatever
secrecy there was in respect to this agreement was imparted
entirely by the corporation itself through the act or neglect
of its authorized agent; and this being so, and no rights of
subsequent subscribers or creditors being involved in the case,
it would be a manifest fraud upon the defendant to permit
the corporation to take advantage of its own wrong by repudiating its agreement while enforcing the defendant's note,
which was evidently given only because of the reservation in
said agreement permitting its recall.

This case is in many respects similar to the case of *Schulte
v. Boulevard Gardens Land Co.,* 164 Cal. 464, [Ann. Cas.
1914B, 1013, 44 L. R. A. (N. S.) 156, 129 Pac. 582], wherein
the court made use of the following apt language applicable
to the instant case: "The right to return the stock and recover the sum agreed to be paid upon such return was a
material and indivisible part of the consideration upon which
the plaintiff agreed to become a stockholder. As between the
parties, it would be manifestly unjust to permit the corporation to retain the money paid by plaintiff and at the same
time repudiate the promise which it gave in exchange for the

money.   The obligation to pay upon the return of the shares
the sum agreed to be paid is not to be viewed as a new undertaking arising after the plaintiff has assumed the relation of
stockholder.   The sale to plaintiff was conditional.   He never
became a stockholder except subject to the qualification that
he might return his shares upon the stipulated terms.''
(*Schulte* v. *Boulevard Gardens Land Co.*, 164 Cal. 464, [Ann.
Cas. 1914B, 1013, 44 L. R. A. (N. S.) 156, 129 Pac. 582].)

The case at bar presents an even stronger instance for the
application of the rule above laid down, for the respondent
herein never in fact became a stockholder of the corporation,
since no stock was to be issued to him until his note was paid.

The judgment is affirmed.

Lennon, P. J., and Kerrigan, J., concurred.

A petition to have the cause heard in the supreme court,
after judgment in the district court of appeal, was denied by
the supreme court on November 21, 1916.

[Civ. No. 2002.   Second Appellate District.—September 21, 1916.]

A. F. MACK, Respondent, v. HENRY EUMMELEN,
Defendant; CITIZENS' SAVINGS BANK, Appellant.

ACTION TO ESTABLISH TRUST — PLEDGEE OF STOCK — INTERVENTION
AFTER JUDGMENT—KNOWLEDGE OF ACTION—LEAVE PROPERLY RE-
FUSED.—In an action to establish a trust in corporate stock, a bank
to whom the stock had been pledged as security for a loan is properly denied leave to intervene where such application is not made
until after judgment, and it is shown that the president of the
bank had knowledge of the pendency of the action long prior to
the time of trial and had discussed the case with the defendant.

ID.—INTERVENTION—WHEN NOT ALLOWED.—Any person who has an interest in the matter in litigation, or in the success of either of the
parties, or an interest against both, may intervene in the action
or proceeding at any time before trial, but the law does not contemplate that a person thus interested may willfully omit to intervene, and then compel a retrial of the case because it has gone
against his interests.

APPEAL from a judgment of the Superior Court of San Diego County. W. R. Guy, Judge.

The facts are stated in the opinion of the court.

Andrews & Lee, and Albert J. Lee, for Appellant.

Doolittle & Morrison, for Respondent.

CONREY, P. J.—In this action it appears that the plaintiff and the defendant Eummelen purchased from one W. H. Bentley 840 shares of stock of a corporation known as the Bentley Ostrich Farm. Eummelen acted for himself and Mack in the negotiations and represented to Mack that the price was fifty thousand dollars, of which each of the two purchasers was to pay one-half. Mack paid twenty-five thousand dollars; Eummelen paid only five thousand dollars, and each of them received from Bentley 420 shares. The court found facts establishing fraud in the transaction, as charged by the plaintiff, and held the defendant as trustee for the plaintiff of 280 shares of the stock which had been transferred by Bentley to the defendant. The defendant was ordered to indorse and transfer those 280 shares to the plaintiff, and it was further ordered that in default of his so doing before the fifteenth day of August, 1913, the judgment should operate as a transfer to plaintiff of all of the defendant's right, title, and interest therein. The facts constituting the fraud were not discovered by the plaintiff until March, 1912. The action was commenced on August 12, 1912, and the judgment was entered on August 4, 1913.

On August 14, 1913, the appellant, Citizens' Savings Bank, filed a petition asking the superior court to set aside and vacate the judgment and admit petitioner as a defendant, with leave to answer, and in that application and accompanying affidavits it was set forth that on June 20, 1912, Eummelen pledged to the plaintiff, as security for a loan of twenty-four thousand dollars, the said 420 shares of stock of the Bentley Ostrich Farm standing in his name; that at the time of filing the petition the bank was still the pledgee of those shares of stock for that indebtedness; that the bank had no notice or knowledge of the pendency or termination of the action until August 11, 1913. Counter-affidavits were filed showing that the president of the bank was acquainted with the fact of the pendency of this action and understood the nature thereof long prior to the time when it came on for trial, and during that period of time discussed the case with the plaintiff; that in that conversation in November, 1912, Mr. Irwin, president of the bank, told the plaintiff that he had the entire matters of Eummelen in his hands and suggested that the case be settled out of court. It was further stated in plaintiff's affidavit that in January, 1913, he had another conversation with Mr. Irwin, in which that gentleman stated that he had discussed the case with defendant Eummelen and had advised the latter that he had nothing to fear therein. It is shown in the affidavit of Bentley that on April 21, 1913. which was the day before the trial of this action, Mr. Irwin stated to Bentley that plaintiff had no chance of winning this case. The motion or petition of the bank was presented upon these affidavits and by order of court was denied. From that order the Citizens' Savings Bank presents this appeal.

Counsel for appellant in their argument have urged sundry errors which they claim were committed by the court in the trial of the case and on account of which they think the judgment should be reversed. If the court was justified in overruling the motion to vacate and set aside the judgment for the reasons stated in the petition, it follows that appellant has no rights as a party to the action, and on this appeal it is not necessary to consider any alleged errors committed at the trial. The order denying the application is based upon implied findings in favor of the plaintiff with respect to the issues raised by the petition and covered by the affidavits. We must therefore assume that with full knowledge of the pendency of this action and of its purposes the bank silently stood by until the case had been tried and until judgment had been rendered against the defendant. This being so, the court was justified in denying the petition and in refusing to recognize petitioner's belated assertion of a right to intervene in the action. "At any time before trial, any person, who has an interest in the matter in litigation, or in the success of either of the parties, or an interest against both, may intervene in the action or proceeding. . . ." (Code Civ. Proc., sec. 387.) The law does not contemplate that a person thus interested may willfully omit to intervene, and then compel a retrial of the case because it has gone against his interests.

(*Hibernia etc. Soc.* v. *Churchill*, 128 Cal. 633, [79 Am. St. Rep. 73, 61 Pac. 278].)

The order is affirmed.

James, J., and Shaw, J., concurred.

A petition to have the cause heard in the supreme court, after judgment in the district court of appeal, was denied by the supreme court on November 20, 1916.

[Civ. No. 1922. First Appellate District.—September 22, 1916.]

A. G. AINSWORTH et al., Appellants, v. ENOCH MORRILL, Respondent.

EXCHANGE OF REAL PROPERTY—HOMESTEAD—REFORMATION AND SPECIFIC ENFORCEMENT.—A husband and wife are not entitled to have a written contract for an exchange of real property reformed and then specifically enforced where the writing consisted of a written offer made and signed only by the husband and accepted in writing by the defendant, and the property of the plaintiffs was encumbered with a homestead declared by the wife.

ID.—HOMESTEAD—ENCUMBRANCE—STRICT COMPLIANCE WITH STATUTE. The policy and purpose of section 1242 of the Civil Code is to prevent the destruction or encumbrance of a homestead by either spouse acting alone, and a purported conveyance or encumbrance of the homestead by either spouse not made in strict compliance with the requirements of such section is invalid and inoperative for any purpose.

APPEAL from a judgment of the Superior Court of Alameda County. T. W. Harris, Judge.

The facts are stated in the opinion of the court.

Lindley & Eickhoff, and Russell T. Ainsworth, for Appellants.

Redmond C. Staats, and James M. Koford, for Respondent.

THE COURT.—In this action the plaintiff sought to have reformed and then specifically enforced a written contract executed by and between the plaintiff A. G. Ainsworth and the defendant Morrill, for an exchange of certain real property. The defendant's general and special demurrer to the plaintiff's fourth amended complaint was sustained, and the plaintiffs declining to further amend, judgment was entered for the defendant, from which the plaintiffs have appealed.

The facts pleaded and relied upon for a cause of action are substantially these: The plaintiffs are, and at all times mentioned in the complaint were, husband and wife and living together as such in the county of Napa. The plaintiff Minerva L. Ainsworth was the owner of certain real property situate in the county of Napa, and the defendant Morrill was the owner of certain real property situate in the county of Alameda. Both properties were at the time of the making of the contract encumbered with mortgages, and the property of the plaintiff Minerva L. Ainsworth was further encumbered with a right of way and a homestead declared by her. The contract in controversy consisted of a written offer made and signed only by the plaintiff A. G. Ainsworth, which was accepted in writing by the defendant Morrill.

In our opinion the plaintiffs' complaint does not and cannot be made to state a cause of action, and therefore the defendant's demurrer was rightfully sustained upon that ground alone. It affirmatively appears from the allegations of the complaint that the contract in suit was not signed and acknowledged by the plaintiff Minerva L. Ainsworth; and we have no doubt that its effect, if valid and enforceable, would be an encumbrance upon the homestead previously declared by her within the meaning of section 1242 of the Civil Code, which provides that "The homestead of a married woman cannot be conveyed or encumbered unless the instrument by which it is conveyed or encumbered is executed and acknowledged by the husband and wife." Although the contract was signed only by the plaintiff A. G. Ainsworth and was executory in its nature, nevertheless its tendency was to cast a cloud upon the property involved, and to that extent at least constituted an encumbrance upon the existing homestead. The policy and purpose of section 1242 of the Civil Code is to prevent the destruction or encumbrance of a homestead by either spouse acting alone; and it is well settled that a purported conveyance or encumbrance of the homestead by either spouse not made in strict compliance with the requirements of that section is invalid and inoperative for any purpose. (*Freiermuth* v. *Steigleman*, 130 Cal. 392, [80 Am. St. Rep. 138, 62 Pac. 615].) Clearly, under the pleaded and admitted facts of the present case the defendant would not be entitled to have the contract in controversy reformed and enforced as against either or both of the plaintiffs; and conversely it must be true that the plaintiffs can have no rights under the contract superior to those accorded by the law to the defendant. It is elementary that a void agreement has no standing in the law, and consequently it can neither be reformed nor enforced.

The judgment appealed from is affirmed.

A petition to have the cause heard in the supreme court, after judgment in the district court of appeal, was denied by the supreme court on November 20, 1916.

[Civ. No. 1790. First Appellate District.—September 25, 1916.]

MARY L. WATERS, Administratrix, etc., Appellant, v. J. C. NEVIS, Respondent.

BANK DEPOSIT — JOINT OWNERSHIP — RIGHT OF SURVIVORSHIP — CONSTRUCTION OF DEPOSIT AGREEMENT.—The deposit by two persons of a sum of money in a bank in a joint account and under a written agreement that the same and any additional money deposited, and all accumulations thereof, shall be payable to and collectible by them, or either of them, during their joint lives, and then belong absolutely to and become the absolute property of the survivor, without reference to or consideration of the original or previous ownership of such moneys, creates a joint ownership in the moneys with the right of ownership in the survivor upon the death of the other depositor.

ID.—COMPETENCY TO EXECUTE AGREEMENT—FINDINGS ON CONFLICTING EVIDENCE—APPEAL.—In an action brought after the death of one of the parties to such a deposit agreement to recover the amount of the deposit, based upon the ground that the deceased was incompetent to execute such an agreement, where the evidence is conflicting, the findings of the trial court as to competency are conclusive on the appellate court.

APPEAL from a judgment of the Superior Court of Sacramento County. Peter J. Shields, Judge.

The facts are stated in the opinion of the court.

Shinn & Hart, L. A. Kottinger, and Milton Shepardson, for Appellant.

Elliott & Atkinson, for Respondent.

RICHARDS, J.—This is an action brought by the plaintiff, as administratrix of the estate of Antone H. Waters, deceased, to recover the sum of $1,240, alleged to be money had and received by the defendant Nevis from Antone H. Waters, under the circumstances detailed in the complaint, and when, it is alleged, that said Waters was incompetent to conduct any transaction. The complaint was unverified. The answer was a general denial. The evidence was quite voluminous. The court found the facts in the defendant's favor and rendered judgment accordingly. The plaintiff prosecutes this appeal.

The facts of the case, concerning which there is little if any dispute, show that Antone H. Waters was a man of Portuguese extraction, who had accumulated some considerable property, but who during the closing years of his life had become afflicted with various physical ailments, and having also become estranged to some extent from his family, had, in about the year 1913, gone to live at the home of the defendant Nevis, whom he had known for a number of years. While living there, and in the month of February, 1914, said Waters and Nevis went together to the National Bank of D. O. Mills & Co., in Sacramento, and there deposited the sum of $1,240 in a joint account and under a written agreement, which contained the following words: "The money now deposited and also money which shall at any time be deposited by us or either of us with the National Bank of D. O. Mills & Co. in this account No. 8340, will be so deposited by us and is to and will be received and held by it with the understanding and upon the condition that the same and all dividends and interest thereon and all accumulations thereof are payable to and shall be collectible by us or either of us during our joint lives, and then belong absolutely to and be the sole and absolute property of the survivor of us, or the heirs, administrators or assigns of such survivor, without refrence to or consideration of the original or previous ownership of such moneys or any part of the same.'' The money remained on deposit at said bank until May 22, 1914, when it was withdrawn by Nevis. Waters died on December 21, 1914. It is the contention of the appellant that for a considerable period prior to the transaction at the bank, and for all the rest of his life thereafter, Waters was mentally incompetent to conduct a business transaction, and particularly to comprehend the nature and effect of the particular transaction by which the defendant Nevis became a party to the deposit of the money in question and the alleged owner thereof after the death of Waters.

It is not seriously insisted by the appellant that the defendant Nevis would not have become the joint owner of the money deposited in the bank under the foregoing agreement, with the right of survivorship thereto upon the death of Waters, had the latter been capable of making and had made the deposit of his money in that form. The construction of deposit agreements of the kind shown here has been practically settled since the decision of the case of *Booth* v. *Oakland Bank of Savings*, 122 Cal. 19, [54 Pac. 370], which has been upheld in the following cases: *Carr* v. *Carr*, 15 Cal. App. 480, [115 Pac. 261]; *Drinkhouse* v. *German Sav. & L. Soc.*, 17 Cal. App. 162, [118 Pac. 953]; *Denigan* v. *Hibernia Sav. & L. Soc.*, 127 Cal. 137, [59 Pac. 389]; *Estate of Hall*, 154 Cal. 527, [98 Pac. 269]. The appellant's contention that Nevis' withdrawal of the money in question in May, 1914, was an act of bad faith toward Waters, which operated to terminate his rights to any portion thereof and destroy the trust relation created by the bank deposit, cannot avail against the finding of the court upon sufficient evidence that the withdrawal of said money was accomplished with Waters' consent; and even were it otherwise, the *status* of the parties would not be changed by such withdrawal. (*Sprague* v. *Walton*, 145 Cal. 228, [78 Pac. 645].)

This brings us to the main and, in fact, only contention upon which the appellant relied in the trial court, viz., that of Waters' mental incompetency during the period including the date of the deposit agreement and continuing up to the time of his death. The testimony upon this subject was, as we have seen, quite voluminous and very conflicting. The trial court having heard all of said testimony, and having observed both parties and the witnesses in the case, made its findings in the defendant's favor upon the question of the mental competency of the decedent during the period in question. This being so, and a careful examination of the record showing that a real and substantial conflict exists, it follows that under the well-settled rule of this court the findings of the trial court will not be disturbed.

The judgment is affirmed.

Lennon, P. J., and Kerrigan, J., concurred.

A petition for a rehearing of this cause was denied by the district court of appeal on October 25, 1916, and a petition to have the cause heard in the supreme court, after judgment in the district court of appeal, was denied by the supreme court on November 23, 1916.

[Civ. No. 1711. First Appellate District.—September 26, 1916.]

W. C. DANIEL, Respondent, v. SADIE B. CALKINS et al., Appellants.

BROKER'S COMMISSIONS — FINDING OF PURCHASER — CONFLICT OF EVIDENCE—APPEAL.—In an action brought to recover a sum of money alleged to be due as the commission of a real estate agent in securing a purchaser for the property of the defendant pursuant to a written contract of authorization and also an alleged oral agreement as to the amount of the commission to be received in the event of a sale, where it is found on conflicting evidence that the plaintiff procured a purchaser, the finding will not be disturbed on appeal.

ID.—AMOUNT OF COMPENSATION—EVIDENCE—PAROL AGREEMENT.—In an action to recover a broker's commission in securing a purchaser of real property pursuant to the terms of a written authorization of sale which designated the "net" amount which the owner was to receive upon the sale and which provided that "no percentage as a commission" was to be paid to the broker, it is not error to permit the plaintiff to introduce evidence of an oral agreement that he was to receive as compensation for his services all over the net sum stated in the writing as the purchase price of the property.

ID.—COMMISSIONS—WHEN EARNED.—Under the terms of such a written
authorization, the broker is entitled to his compensation when he
produces a purchaser who is ready, able, and willing to buy the
property for any sum up to or in excess of the net amount specified in the writing.

APPEAL from a judgment of the Superior Court of Santa
Clara County, and from an order denying a new trial. W. A.
Beasly, Judge.

The facts are stated in the opinion of the court.

Owen D. Richardson, for Appellants.

Earl Lamb, and R. J. Glendenning, for Respondent.

RICHARDS, J.—This is an appeal from a judgment and
order denying the defendants' motion for a new trial.

The action was brought to recover the sum of $550 alleged
to be due as the commission of a real estate agent in securing a purchaser for the property of the defendant, Sadie B.
Calkins, pursuant to a written contract of authorization and
also an alleged oral agreement as to the amount of commission to be received in the event of a sale. The evidence in
the case discloses that the plaintiff was a real estate agent
residing and doing business as such at Sunnyvale, in the
county of Santa Clara, in the year 1912; that during the
month of July of that year the defendant, Sadie B. Calkins,
was in possession of a piece of real estate of which she was
shortly to become the owner, and that in that month and at
her request the plaintiff took a Mr. Deckman (who subsequently became the purchaser of the property) out to see it
with a view to buying it; that the price of twelve thousand
five hundred dollars was quoted to him at that time by plaintiff, and he said he would take the property at that figure;
but when the plaintiff reported these facts to Mrs. Calkins
she said that she had decided not to sell, but later, in the
meantime having received title to the property, she requested
the plaintiff to reopen negotiations with Mr. Deckman. It
was at or about this time that the following writing was executed between the parties:

"Sunnyvale, Cal. August 23, 1912.

"W. C. Daniel: I hereby authorize you solely to sell for
me and my account the following described real estate . . .

for the sum or price of $11,700.00 net; and I agree to pay
you no per cent as a commission on said sale when made.   I
further agree to furnish a complete abstract of title to date
of transfer.   This authorization to remain in full force and
effect for thirty days, after which notice must be given in
writing to terminate this contract.

"(Signed)   Sadie B. Calkins.

"Witness: (Signed)   W. C. Daniel."

At the time of the execution of the foregoing writing the
plaintiff testifies, and the court finds, that an oral agreement
was made between the parties to the effect that in the event
of his success in securing a purchaser for the premises, the
plaintiff was to receive as his compensation a sum equal to
the difference between the net price specified in said writing
and such price as the property should be sold for.   In the
meantime the plaintiff corresponded by telegrams and letters
with Mr. Deckman, who was at the time in the east, but who
later and during the life of the plaintiff's written contract
came to California, re-examined the property, and finally
purchased it directly from the owner for the sum of twelve
thousand dollars.   After the consummation of such sale the
plaintiff demanded as his commission a sum equal to the difference between the amount named in the written authorization as the net sum to be received by the owner and the sum
actually paid by the purchaser of the property, to wit, the
sum of three hundred dollars.

The trial court rendered judgment in plaintiff's favor for
said sum, and from said judgment and from the order denying a new trial, the defendants prosecute this appeal.

The first contention of the defendants is that the evidence
is insufficient to sustain the finding that the plaintiff procured Deckman as a purchaser of the property.   In respect
to this issue there is a substantial conflict in the evidence,
and this being so, the finding of the trial court will not be
disturbed.

The next and chief contention of the appellants is that the
court erred in permitting the plaintiff to introduce evidence
of the oral agreement between the parties to the effect that
the plaintiff was to receive all over the net sum stated in the
writing as the purchase price of the property.   In making
this contention it is apparently conceded by the appellants
that when an agent's authorization is written, the amount of

his compensation in the event of a sale may be agreed upon orally. This concession is doubtless made in the light of the authorities sustaining this view. (*Toomy* v. *Dunphy*, 86 Cal. 639, [25 Pac. 130]; *Kennedy* v. *Merickel*, 8 Cal. App. 381, [97 Pac. 81]; *Baird* v. *Loescher*, 9 Cal. App. 65, [98 Pac. 49]; *Naylor* v. *Adams*, 15 Cal. App. 354, [114 Pac. 997].) The appellants, however, insist that the oral agreement between the parties as to the sum to be received or retained as the agent's compensation is void, for the reason that it undertakes to vary the terms of a written instrument by parol, and that the ruling of the trial court in admitting evidence of such oral agreement was error. The clause in the writing which it is argued is varied and in fact abrogated by the oral agreement, according to the appellants' contention, reads as follows: "I agree to pay you no per cent as a commission on the amount of said sale when made." This clause standing alone might support the appellants' contention; but it is to be interpreted in connection with the entire writing, with the nature and object of the contract, and with the circumstances attending its creation. Contracts between real estate agents and owners of real estate by which the former are given authority to engage in activities having for their object the sale of the latter's property are entered into for the mutual material benefit of the parties to such contracts, and are to be so construed as not to defeat these objects when such construction is reasonably deducible from their terms. The foregoing clause in the written authorization of the plaintiff is to be read in the light of the preceding clause in such writing with which it is connected in the conjunctive, and which designates the net amount which the owner is to receive upon the sale of the property; and it is upon said "amount of said sale" that "no percentage as a commission" is to be paid. The use of the term "net" and specifying the amount which the owner is to receive carries the plain implication that the selling price of the property is to be some larger sum, the excess of which is undisposed of by the terms of the written agreement. This being so, the oral agreement of the parties to the effect that the agent should retain such extra sum as the compensation for his services in the premises does not vary the terms of the writing, but only amplifies it so as to effectuate the mutual material interests of the parties in entering into it. The court, therefore, did not err in admitting the evidence of such oral agreement, nor in its finding predicated upon such evidence.

The final contention of the appellants is that the plaintiff never in fact produced a purchaser ready and able and willing to purchase the property in question for the price at which the agent offered it to such purchaser. This argument is predicated upon the evidence in the case showing that the lowest price quoted to the prospective purchaser by the plaintiff was the sum of $12,250, which sum the purchaser was never shown to be willing to pay. The views above expressed as to the construction to be placed upon the plaintiff's written authorization to the effect that he was to endeavor to make a sale of the property for such sum in excess of the net amount which the owner was to receive, necessarily implies that in his offers of the property to prospective purchasers he was to fix a larger sum than said net amount as the lowest purchase price of the property, and if he found a purchaser who was ready and willing and able to buy the property for any sum up to or in excess of the net amount specified in his written authorization he would be fulfilling its terms and also the terms of the oral understanding of the parties supplementing their written agreement; and if such purchaser when found saw fit to deal directly with the owner, and the owner with him, within the life of the plaintiff's agency, and to consummate a sale of the property for a sum equal to or in excess of the owner's net figure, the agent would be none the less the procuring cause of such sale, and would under the authorities be entitled to his reward. (*Briggs* v. *Hall*, 24 Cal. App. 586, [141 Pac. 1067].)

This disposes of every material contention of the appellants in the case.

Judgment and order affirmed.

Lennon, P. J., and Kerrigan, J., concurred.

[Crim. No. 351. Third Appellate District.—September 26, 1916.]

THE PEOPLE, Respondent, v. CHARLES F. PRECIADO, Appellant.

CRIMINAL LAW—APPEAL—STATEMENT OF "GROUNDS" AND "POINTS"—CONSTRUCTION OF SECTION 1247, PENAL CODE.—In an application for an appeal, made under section 1247 of the Penal Code, it is sufficient if the application states the *grounds* of the appeal, without specifying the *points* upon which the appellant relies, as there is no substantial distinction intended in the use of the two words.

ID.—EMBEZZLEMENT—ESTABLISHMENT OF DEFENSE OF INSANITY—DEGREE OF PROOF—ERRONEOUS INSTRUCTIONS.—In a prosecution for the crime of embezzlement, wherein the principal defense made was that the defendant at the time of the commission of the alleged offense was not responsible, because he was incapable of understanding the nature and quality of the act on account of his then insanity, it is erroneous for the court to instruct the jury in three or four different instructions that the defense of insanity must be "clearly proved," "clearly established," or "satisfactorily established," although the jury was also instructed that the defense of insanity may be established by a preponderance of the evidence.

ID.—INSANITY—PROOF OF DEFENSE—PREPONDERANCE OF EVIDENCE.—The defense of insanity may be established by a preponderance of the evidence, and trial courts are not allowed to qualify the rule by requiring a higher degree of proof.

ID.—EMBEZZLEMENT OF TAX MONEYS—PLEA OF ONCE IN JEOPARDY—EVIDENCE—TAKING OF MONEYS AT SAME TIME.—In the prosecution of a tax collector for the alleged embezzlement of certain moneys paid to him as such officer by certain persons, wherein he interposed the plea of once in jeopardy based upon his acquittal of the alleged embezzlement of moneys paid to him by other parties, it is error to refuse him permission to show in support of his plea that both sums were taken at the same time.

ID.—ACQUITTAL—WHEN A BAR.—Where the offense on trial is a necessary element in, and constitutes an essential part of, another offense, and both are in fact but one transaction, a conviction or acquittal of one is a bar to the prosecution of the other.

APPEAL from a judgment of the Superior Court of Madera County, and from an order denying a new trial. Charles O. Busick, Judge presiding.

The facts are stated in the opinion of the court.

Lee D. Windrem, R. R. Fowler, Joseph Barcroft, and H. I. Maxim, for Appellant.

U. S. Webb, Attorney-General, and J. Charles Jones, Deputy Attorney-General, for Respondent.

CHIPMAN, P. J.—Defendant was informed against by the district attorney of the county of Madera for the crime of embezzlement. He was tried and convicted, and thereafter moved for a new trial, which was denied. He thereupon appealed from the judgment and the order denying his motion for a new trial.

1. The attorney-general has made a motion to dismiss the appeal principally upon the ground that defendant, in his application for an appeal under section 1247 of the Penal Code, failed to file or present to the trial judge an application containing a statement of the grounds and points on which he relies. The contention is that defendant should have stated in his application not only the *grounds* of his appeal, but should also have specified the *points* on which he relied; that the statute is mandatory in its requirement that the application contain a statement of "grounds" and "points." Section 1247 provides that upon an appeal taken from any judgment or order of the superior court, in any criminal action, where such appeal is allowed, "the defendant . . . must, within five days, file with the clerk and present an application to the trial court, stating in general terms the grounds of the appeal and the points upon which the appellant relies, and designate what portions of the phonographic reporter's notes it will be necessary to have transcribed to fairly present the points relied upon. If such application is not filed within said time, the appeal is wholly ineffectual and shall be deemed dismissed and the judgment or order may be enforced as if no appeal had been taken." The section also provides that the court shall, within two days after such application is made, direct the phonographic reporter who reported the case to transcribe such portion of his notes as in the opinion of the court "may be necessary to fairly and fully present the points relied upon by the appellant." It will be observed that while the terms "grounds" and "points" are conjunctively stated in the earlier part of the section, the direction as to the portion of the reporter's notes

necessary to have transcribed is that the transcription shall
be such as "to fairly present the points relied upon," and
further along in the section it is made the duty of the court,
"after such application is made," to direct the reporter to
transcribe such portion of his notes as may be necessary to
present "the points relied upon by the appellant." The
term "points" as above shown, it seems to us, was used as
embracing "grounds" as well as "points," and, as there used,
indicates that the legislature did not intend that an appellant should lose his appeal as "wholly ineffectual" unless in
his application he specifically and separately states therein
that his reasons for the appeal are to be deemed both the
"grounds" and "points" upon which "appellant relies."

The application was entitled: "Settlement of Grounds on
Appeal under Sec. 1247 P. C." Then follows title and cause.

The application recites the proceedings, the trial, verdict,
motion for new trial, order denying motion, judgment, and
notice of appeal from the judgment and order. It then
states: "That said appeal is taken upon the following general grounds," and the grounds (briefly stated) were as
follows:

1. Once in jeopardy; 2. Errors in rulings with reference
to the allowance of challenges for cause; 3. Misconduct of
district attorney; 4. Errors of the court in its rulings upon
evidence; 5. Errors of the court in the interrogation of witnesses; 6. The verdict is contrary to law; 7. The verdict is
contrary to evidence.

The application specifically mentioned portions of the record called for and also for "the entire transcript of the testimony taken in said action."

With this application before the court, it made an order
directing the phonographic reporter "to transcribe the following portions of the testimony and proceedings given and
had in the above-entitled cause." Then follow in the order
the portions of the testimony and proceedings specifically
called for in the application, including "all the testimony
given at the trial, and all objections, rulings, and exceptions
made and taken at the trial." This order was complied
with, and the entire record is now here for review and
appears to be in authentic form.

The statute only requires that the application state "in
general terms the grounds of the appeal and the points upon

which the appellant relies." The grounds stated in the present case were specific enough to indicate upon what errors defendant would rely, and he designated the portions of the reporter's notes which were deemed "necessary to have transcribed to fairly present the points relied upon." Section 1248 of the Penal Code provides that: "If the appeal is irregular in any substantial particular, but not otherwise, the appellate court may, . . . order it to be dismissed."

It was said in *Estate of Nelson*, 128 Cal. 242, [60 Pac. 772]: "The right of appeal is conferred by the constitution, and statutes and rules of procedure for its exercise are to be liberally construed; and no appeal will be dismissed upon technical grounds, where there has been no violation or disregard of any express rule of procedure." Unless we can say that the failure of defendant to state in his application that the "grounds" therein set forth were also the "points" on which he relied is a fatal "violation or disregard" of the provisions of section 1247, the motion, in our opinion, must be denied. We cannot so hold. We fail to appreciate respondent's argument that there is, in contemplation of the statute, a substantial distinction intended in the use of the terms "grounds" and "points." By stating "in general terms the grounds," we think the defendant complied with the statute sufficiently to entitle his appeal to be heard.

2. The principal defense made in the case was that defendant, at the time of the taking of the money, was not responsible, because he was incapable of understanding the nature and quality of the act on account of his then insanity. The court gave the following instructions:

"You are instructed that in prosecution for crimes the defense of insanity is often interposed, and thereby becomes a subject of paramount importance in criminal jurisprudence. A due regard for the ends of justice and the welfare of society no less than mercy to the accused requires that it should be thoroughly and carefully weighed. It is a plea sometimes resorted to in cases where aggravated crimes have been committed under circumstances which afford full proof of the overt acts and render hopeless all other means of evading punishment. While, therefore, it ought to be viewed as a not less full and complete than it is a humane defense when satisfactorily established, yet it should be examined into

with great care lest an ingenious counterfeit of the malady
furnish protection to guilt.

"Insanity as used in this sense means such a diseased and
deranged condition of the mental faculties as to render a
person incapable of distinguishing between right and wrong
in relation to the act with which he is charged, and to establish a defense on the ground of insanity it must be clearly
proved that at the time of committing the act the party accused was laboring under such a defect of reasoning from
disease of the mind as to not know the nature and quality
of the act he was doing, or if he did know it, that he did not
know he was doing wrong.

"Hence you are instructed that in order for insanity to be
available as a defense in this case, the defendant herein must
establish by a preponderance of evidence that he was so diseased and deranged in mind as to render him incapable of
distinguishing between right and wrong, and it must appear
from such preponderance of evidence that he was so incapable
of distinguishing between right and wrong in relation to the
particular offense charged in the information, and it must appear, further, by such preponderance of evidence that he was
in such a mental condition as to be incapable of distinguishing between right and wrong in relation to the act with
which he is charged in the information upon the particular
date so charged and designated in the information.

"You are instructed that the law of this state does not
recognize the defense of insanity based upon claims that a
defendant committed the crime while laboring under an un-
controllable or irresistible influence, nor does it recognize
that form of insanity commonly known as emotional insanity
beginning on the eve of the criminal act and ending with its
consummation. Such forms of insanity have no legal standing in this state as a defense to crime. It is necessary that
insanity, in order to be a defense, it must be clearly proved
that at the time of committing the act the party accused was
laboring under such a defect of reason and from disease of
the mind as not to know the nature and quality of the act he
was doing, or if he did know it, that he did not know he was
doing what was wrong."

In *People* v. *Wreden*, 59 Cal. 392, the defense was insanity, and among the instructions was the following: "I charge

you that when insanity is relied upon as a defense, the burden of proof is with the defendant, and the proof must be such in amount that if the single issue of sanity or insanity of the defendant should be submitted to the jury in a civil case, they would find that he was insane, or, in other words, that *insanity must be clearly established* by satisfactory proof; it is not sufficient that you should entertain a reasonable doubt as to his sanity, but the proof must be satisfactory and the fact of insanity *clearly established.*" (Italics the court's.) The court referred to the rule as previously well settled that "insanity, in order to constitute a defense in a criminal action, need not be proved beyond a reasonable doubt, but that it might be established, 'by mere preponderating evidence.' " Referring to the instruction, the court said: "Is not the expression *clearly* 'established by satisfactory proof' the full equivalent of 'established by satisfactory proof beyond a reasonable doubt?' How can a fact be said to be clearly established so long as there is a reasonable doubt whether it has been established at all? There can be no 'reasonable doubt' of a fact after it has been clearly established by satisfactory proof." After giving the definition of "clearly" according to Webster, and after stating the definition of reasonable doubt as defined by Chief Justice Shaw, the court said: "A juror would have no excuse for saying that he did not 'feel an abiding conviction to a moral certainty' of the truth of a fact which had been '*clearly* established by satisfactory proof.' Such proof, if any could, would convince and direct the understanding, and satisfy the reason and judgment of a conscientious juror. Under the instruction given it was the duty of the jury to require that the defense of insanity should at least be proved beyond a reasonable doubt. This was error."

In *People* v. *Wells*, 145 Cal. 138, [78 Pac. 470], the instruction was, as the court stated, "almost in the exact language of the one condemned in *People* v. *Wreden*." Said the court, after quoting what is above taken from the opinion in that case: "We have not been referred to a case, nor do we know of one in this court, overruling or modifying the decision in *People* v. *Wreden*, 59 Cal. 393. On the contrary, in *People* v. *Allender*, 117 Cal. 81, [48 Pac. 1014], the court instructed the jury that the burden rested upon the defendant of proving his insanity by a preponderance of evidence

merely," and the court referred to the fact that such had
been the rule in this state for a period of thirty years.

The latest discussion of the question by the supreme court
is found in *People* v. *Miller*, 171 Cal. 649, [154 Pac. 468].
In that case the trial court instructed the jury correctly as
to the rule that a preponderance of the evidence is sufficient
where insanity is pleaded, but it gave a further instruction
as to what was meant by the term "preponderance of the
evidence," as follows: "Preponderance of the evidence
means that degree of evidence which proves to a moral certainty, or, in other words, that degree of proof that produces
conviction in an unprejudiced mind, regardless of the number of witnesses from whom it proceeds."

Chief Justice Angellotti, speaking for the court, shows
quite clearly that the definition thus given was substantially
the same as that of proof beyond a reasonable doubt, and
therefore violated the rule that insanity may be established
by a preponderance of the evidence merely. The court said:
"That such is the effect of the instruction given is shown by
what is said in *People* v. *Wreden*, 59 Cal. 393, and *People* v.
Wells, 145 Cal. 142, [78 Pac. 470], where it is held that an
instruction declaring that insanity 'must be clearly established by satisfactory proof' is the full equivalent of one
making it incumbent on a defendant to establish insanity
beyond a reasonable doubt."

As we understand this reference to the case of *People* v.
Wreden, the court intended to give its approval of what was
there said, and because of such approval it followed that the
instruction in the Miller case was error; that is, that in the
Wreden case the instruction called for proof equivalent to
the proof called for in the Miller case, or, in other words,
both instructions meant the same thing and both were
erroneous.

In the present case the only instruction given defining
what is meant by preponderance of the evidence was as follows: "By a preponderance of the evidence is meant the
greater weight of the evidence—that which is the more convincing of its truth. It is not necessarily determined by the
number of witnesses for or against a proposition." Notwithstanding this definition, the jury were told that the defense
of insanity is to be received as "a humane defense when *satisfactorily established*"; again, in another instruction, "to
establish the defense of insanity it must be *clearly proved*";

again, in another instruction, "It is necessary that insanity, in order to be a defense, it must be *clearly proved*," etc. How else could the jury have understood the instruction that insanity may be established by a preponderance of the evidence than that this preponderance must be "satisfactorily established" and "clearly proved?"

In the case of *Beach* v. *Clark*, 51 Conn. 200, the action was on a promissory note on which defendant was indorser as an accommodation to plaintiff, and as security therefor he held certain personal property conveyed to him by plaintiff. The trial court instructed the jury that "if the defendant held the property in question as collateral security, the burden of proof is on him to clearly prove his authority to sell." This was held error, the supreme court of errors saying: "The use of that word [clearly] required the defendant to assume a heavier burden than the law imposed upon him. The law only required him to prove by a preponderance of proof the material fact on which he relied. The charge required him to do more than that: to prove it clearly, without uncertainty, free from doubt or question. It required him to prove it with substantially the same amount of proof that is required to substantiate a criminal charge; and that is not the law. . . . For this reason there must be a new trial."

In *Hall* v. *Wolf*, 61 Iowa, 559, [16 N. W. 710], the action related to the sale of certain personal property. The instruction given was that the sale "should be clearly and fairly proven." Said the court: " 'Clearly and fairly proven' imports more than a mere preponderance of evidence. In the case of *West* v. *Druff*, 55 Iowa, 335, [7 N. W. 636], an instruction was held to be erroneous which required 'clear and satisfactory evidence' to satisfy the jury of an issuable fact. That instrument [instruction?] cannot be distinguished from the one now under consideration."

In *French* v. *Day*, 89 Me. 441, [36 Atl. 909], the action was trespass and the court instructed the jury: " . . . It is incumbent on the defendants to show, by a clear preponderance of the evidence and by convincing proof, their right to do it in order to prevent a verdict against them." In discussing the instruction, the court said: " 'Preponderance' means to outweigh; to weigh more. A 'clear preponderance' may mean that which may be seen, is discernible, and may be appreciated and understood. In this sense, the expression might be unobjectionable; but it may convey the idea, under emphasis, of certainty, beyond doubt, and very likely would do so to the common mind. At any rate, the expression is equivocal and mischievous. 'Convincing proof' may be said to mean that degree of certainty required to sustain a given postulate. But that view assumes that the hearer knows the rule that governs such case, which jurors are not supposed to know, but of which they should be informed. The two expressions, coupled, must have conveyed to the jury an erroneous basis for their verdict. Exceptions sustained.''

In *McEvony* v. *Rowland,* 43 Neb. 97, [61 N. W. 124], the instruction required that the transaction "must be clearly established.'' The court said that the party "is not required to satisfy the jury in such a case, beyond question, that the sale is an honest one. A preponderance of the evidence is all that is required (citing *Stevens* v. *Carson,* 30 Neb. 544, [9 L. R. A. 523, 46 N. W. 655]). The word 'clearly' means without uncertainty.''

Some of the qualifying terms which have been held to import a higher degree of proof than is meant by a preponderance of evidence are stated in 17 Cyc., pages 763, 764, namely: "an abiding conviction," a "clear conviction," "convinces," "clearly," "fully," "clearly and satisfactorily," etc.

The rule in some other jurisdictions is not the same as our supreme court in an early day declared it. But where the rule has been followed that the defense of insanity may be established by a preponderance of the evidence, the appellate courts have held that no higher degree of proof should be required, and that it is error to charge the jury by language importing any higher degree of evidence to be necessary to establish such defense.

The attorney-general cites *People* v. *Hoin,* 62 Cal. 120, [45 Am. Rep. 651], as an instance where the supreme court inferentially approved of the rule that this defense must be clearly proved. In that case the quotation from the opinion of Chief Justice Tindall was used to illustrate what constituted insanity such as would be accepted as a defense and not the character of proof necessary to establish it. This will at once be seen by reading the instruction which was under discussion. The court was composed of the same members when the case cited was before the court as when the case of *People* v. *Wreden* was decided, and it is not to be supposed that if the court had changed its opinion upon so important a rule, it would have failed to mention its decision in the Wreden case. Whatever may be found in decisions, the rule is firmly established that the defense of insanity may be established by a preponderance of the evidence merely, and that being the rule, trial courts are not allowed to qualify it by requiring a higher degree of proof.

In the instant case nothing appears in the record to lead to a suspicion that the plea of insanity was a subterfuge, and put forward as a means of escaping punishment. Expert and nonexpert testimony was introduced for and against this defense, sufficient in quantity and forcefulness to have prevented the reviewing court, under the settled rule, from interfering with the verdict whichever way the jury may have decided the issue.

It is contended by the attorney-general that the trial court having so clearly instructed the jury that the defense of insanity may be established by a preponderance of the evidence, the jury could not have been misled by the instruction to which complaint is made. The same contention was urged in *People* v. *Miller*, 171 Cal. 649, [154 Pac. 468], where "the jury," as the supreme court points out, "were explicitly and correctly instructed that it was not necessary for defendant to show his insanity beyond all reasonable doubt, but only by a preponderance of evidence, as in civil cases . . . that, in other words, insanity may be established by a preponderance of evidence merely." In the Miller case the error arose in the definition which the trial court gave to what constitutes preponderance of evidence. In the present case, the error arose from the fact that the learned trial court in three or four different instructions on the subject instructed the jury that the defense must be "clearly proved," "clearly established," "satisfactorily established," and these expressions were so closely related to the instructions as to the preponderance of evidence being sufficient that we do not feel at liberty to say the jury were not influenced by them.

Whether the judgment should be affirmed notwithstanding such error, under the provision of section 4½, article VI, of the constitution, as was said in the Miller case: "We are satisfied that the evidence was of such a nature that such a conclusion may not fairly be reached." We do not wish to be

understood as holding that there was not sufficient evidence
to warrant the verdict or that the insanity of the defendant
was not shown by a preponderance of the evidence. What
we mean to say is that upon this issue the record discloses a
condition of facts presented by the defendant from which,
under the rule of preponderance of the evidence, the jury
might reasonably have found in favor of the theory of
insanity.

3. A plea of once in jeopardy was interposed and defendant claims that upon the evidence he was entitled to a verdict of acquittal. It appeared that defendant was put upon
his trial for having embezzled certain funds from the county
paid to defendant as tax collector by Carrie M. Hammel,
such embezzlement having been committed on the first day of
December, 1913. Upon this charge defendant was acquitted.
Thereafter a complaint was filed in the justice's court charging him with the embezzlement of certain funds on the first
day of December, 1913, paid in to him as tax collector by
Seth Mann and Myrtle Mann. On his arraignment, after
having been held to answer, he pleaded former acquittal.
Later and when he was brought to trial, by leave of court,
the district attorney amended the information by changing
the date of the alleged embezzlement to November 1, 1913.
The trial resulted in a disagreement of the jury, and upon
his retrial defendant was convicted and from that conviction
the present appeal is taken. It appeared that defendant
received a check for the amount alleged to have been embezzled on October 29, 1913, and that the check was cashed
on November 3, 1913. It also appeared that defendant made
his verified return in due form of all *moneys* received by him
as such tax collector from October 1 to November 1, 1913.
The claim of defendant is that the money received from this
check, on November 3, 1913, was not due to the county until
after his settlement with the treasurer on the first day of
December, 1913, and hence falls within the same time as the
charge upon which he was tried and acquitted, that is, of
having on December 1, 1913, embezzled certain moneys paid
in to him as tax collector by Carrie M. Hammel. Section
3753 of the Political Code requires the tax collector, on the
first Monday in each month to ''settle with the auditor for
all moneys collected for the state or county, and pay the
same to the county treasurer, and on the same day must de-

liver to and file in the office of the auditor a statement, under
oath, showing: 1. An account of all his transactions and
receipts since his last settlement; 2. That all money collected
by him as tax collector has been paid.''

The charge is that defendant embezzled certain money on
November 1st, whereas the evidence was that the money
alleged to have been embezzled was the proceeds of a check
which, while it was received October 29th, was not cashed
until November 3d, and the proceeds became part of the
funds for which defendant was to account at the end of the
latter month. It is contended that having been embraced
in his return for November, this money was included in the
return of the money paid in by Seth Mann and Myrtle Mann
for the alleged embezzlement of which he was tried and acquitted; that, hence, the only question is, "Are the two offenses a part of the same criminal act?"

It was held in *People* v. *Meseros*, 16 Cal. App. 277, [116
Pac. 679], that "proof of the embezzlement or larceny of
checks, in the county of the venue, will not support a charge
of embezzlement or larceny of the money therein. The
contention that checks are money is without support."
(Syllabus.)

Once in jeopardy and former acquittal are favored pleas
(12 Cyc. 364), and "the right not to be put in jeopardy the
second time is as sacred as the right of trial by jury, and is
guarded with as much care by the common law and by the
constitution." (Black, C. J., in *Dinkey* v. *Commonwealth*,
17 Pa. St. 126, [55 Am. Dec. 542].) It seems to be a well-
settled rule that where the offense on trial is a necessary
element in, and constitutes an essential part of, another
offense, and both are in fact but one transaction, a conviction
or acquittal of one is a bar to a prosecution of the other.
In *People* v. *Stephens*, 79 Cal. 428, [4 L. R. A. 845, 21 Pac.
856], the prosecution was for libel, and the question was
whether there may be as many prosecutions for libel maintained upon a single article published in a single issue of a
newspaper as there are false and defamatory statements concerning a single individual in such article. "The second
prosecution," said the court, "is for a libel contained in the
same article and published in the same issue of the same
newspaper as the first. The words alleged to be defamatory
are not the same in both informations. If they were, the

case would be a plain one. But the publication in both cases was one and the same act. . . . In *Regina* v. *Erlington*, 9 Cox C. C. 86, Cokburn, C. J., said: 'It is a fundamental rule of law that out of the same facts a series of charges shall not be preferred.' '' Cases are cited to the rule that "the state cannot split up one crime and prosecute it in parts." (See the rule discussed in *People* v. *McDaniels*, 137 Cal. 192, [92 Am. St. Rep. 81, 59 L. R. A. 578, 69 Pac. 1006].) An elaborate and illuminating note is found in 92 American State Reports, upon the identity of offenses in a plea of former jeopardy. The note is very full upon the "carving" or "splitting" of offenses. The general rule is there stated: "The instance above given, of the larceny of several articles at one time and place by one act of theft, is one of frequent occurrence. In such a case, by the great weight of authority, there is but one offense. The state may, if it sees fit, prosecute the theft of all the articles at once, or it may select what it wishes and prosecute for the larceny of that part, but it cannot split the single larceny into as many charges as there are articles stolen and make of such charges the basis of successive prosecutions. The second and subsequent prosecutions are, then, for the same offense." It is unnecessary to cite further authority.

At the trial the defendant, in proof of his plea, offered in evidence the transcript and proceedings at the trial when he was acquitted. The court sustained the objection offered by the district attorney that the evidence was irrelevant and immaterial, remarking: "I think the proper evidence is the indictment or information on file." And as to this—the only evidence allowed by the court except the verdict of acquittal—the court said: "It appears on the face of the indictment there are two separate and distinct offenses charged, and the acquittal on the former trial on information No. 323 is not the same offense charged in the information No. 341, and the motion to dismiss the information No. 341 and dismiss the case against the defendant is denied."

Of course, the two informations show two different offenses committed at two different times. The second one was amended purposely to so show. But this would not preclude the defendant from showing as matter of fact that both sums of money alleged to have been embezzled were taken at the same time, or rather, it was the duty of the prosecution to show that the embezzlement was committed as alleged in the information.

We think it was error to confine defendant in the proof in support of his plea to the face of the information on which he was acquitted. We do not mean to hold that the defendant could not be convicted of embezzling the money received November 3d in payment by Seth and Myrtle Mann of their taxes, if, as a fact, he did appropriate it on that day to his own use. That question does not arise. It is claimed that the money embezzled was shown by a shortage in his accounts at the end of November and that this shortage arose from his having at that time—December 1st—failed to account for both the Hammel and Mann money, and that in both instances the taking was at the same time out of the combined funds received during that month. Whatever the fact was, defendant had a right to show that the taking of the money in both instances was one and the same transaction. In other words, if the money embezzled on December 1st included in part both the Hammel and Mann moneys, the offense could not be split into two charges and he be convicted of both.

As there must be a new trial, we have thought it proper to consider the point raised on the plea of once in jeopardy. Other errors are claimed, but we do not find it necessary to consider them.

The judgment and order are reversed.

Hart, J., and Burnett, J., concurred.

A petition to have the cause heard in the supreme court, after judgment in the district court of appeal, was denied by the supreme court on November 25. 1916.

[Civ. No. 2001. Second Appellate District.—September 27, 1916.]

ALVINA VALENCIA, Respondent, v. PHILIPP MILLIKEN, Appellant.

ACTION FOR RAPE—WEIGHT OF UNCORROBORATED TESTIMONY—QUESTION FOR JURY—APPEAL.—In an action to recover damages for a criminal assault upon a single woman, the weight to be given uncorroborated testimony is a matter solely for the consideration of the jury, unless it is inherently improbable, and its conclusion is conclusive upon the appellate court.

ID. — ARGUMENT TO JURY — COMPARISON OF CHILD WITH DEFENDANT — LACK OF PREJUDICIAL ERROR.—In such an action a remark made by plaintiff's counsel in his argument to the jury, requesting them to compare the child to which the plaintiff gave birth with the defendant, is not prejudicial, in the absence of anything in the record showing whether or not it bore any resemblance to the defendant, or that the defendant was prejudiced by the remark.

ID. — PREVIOUS CHASTITY OF PLAINTIFF — EVIDENCE OF DAMAGES—INSTRUCTION LIMITING EVIDENCE—LACK OF PREJUDICE.—The defendant is not prejudiced by the giving of an instruction limiting the purpose of evidence of previous chastity of the plaintiff to the question of damages suffered, where his defense is an alibi, and not that the plaintiff consented to the act.

ID.—COMPENSATORY DAMAGES FOR "ACT COMPLAINED OF"—PROPER INSTRUCTION.—An instruction that compensatory damages should be given in such amount as will fairly compensate the plaintiff for the injury she has received by reason of the "act complained of," "taking into consideration her physical suffering and disability during pregnancy and in childbirth, if the jury should find the pregnancy was the result of defendant's act, also her mental suffering, shame, and disgrace, and her loss of social standing, and all other harm they find she suffered as the natural result of the wrong," is not an invasion of the right of the jury by telling them that damages should be awarded regardless of whether she gave her consent or not.

APPEAL from a judgment of the Superior Court of Riverside County, and from an order denying a new trial. F. E. Densmore, Judge.

The facts are stated in the opinion of the court.

Miguel Estudillo, for Appellant.

Richard L. North, A. Orfila, and V. Rapp, for Respondent.

SHAW, J.—As appears from the complaint, defendant, on or about December 19, 1911, with force and violence, made an indecent assault upon plaintiff, who at the time was a chaste and virtuous single woman over the age of twenty-one years, and then and there, without her consent, debauched and carnally knew her, as a result of which she became pregnant, and on September 17, 1912, gave birth to a child, to her damage in the sum of twenty-five thousand dollars; all of which allegations were by defendant denied.

The case was tried before a jury, which brought in a verdict in favor of plaintiff in the sum of four thousand dollars. Defendant moved for a new trial upon the ground of insufficiency of the evidence, errors in law occurring at the trial, and irregularities in the proceedings of plaintiff and the attorneys for plaintiff, which motion was overruled. The appeal is from the judgment and an order of court denying defendant's motion for a new trial.

Appellant devotes a large part of his brief in support of his contention that the evidence is insufficient to justify the verdict of the jury. No purpose could be subserved in quoting at length the detailed acts of defendant in accomplishing his purpose, as related by plaintiff. Her statement, if true, clearly shows that she was, on December 19, 1911, against her will, ravished and debauched by defendant, as a result of which she gave birth to a child on September 17, 1912. As declared in criminal cases, the weight to be given testimony in prosecutions for rape, even if uncorroborated, is a matter solely for the consideration of the jury, *unless it is inherently improbable* (*People* v. *Ah Lung*, 2 Cal. App. 278, [83 Pac. 296]; *People* v. *Benson*, 6 Cal. 221, [65 Am. Dec. 506]; *People* v. *Hamilton*, 46 Cal. 540); and a less stringent rule is applicable here, since it is a civil action, wherein a preponderance of the evidence is all that is required to establish a fact. Not only do we find nothing improbable in plaintiff's story when all the circumstances are considered, but her testimony is strongly corroborated by that of her father and mother, to the effect that defendant did, on the afternoon of the day named, accompanied by plaintiff, leave their house in a buggy for a ride, from which trip he returned with her that evening, when plaintiff immediately, in the presence of defendant, informed her parents of the fact that the defendant had so abused her; that he then admitted the fact, as

stated by plaintiff, and promised the father that he would
marry his daughter within two weeks; that the clothing of
plaintiff was torn and blood-stained; that the father accompanied by plaintiff visited the isolated place where the latter
stated defendant had pulled her from the buggy, and found
evidence of the struggle which plaintiff testified she had with
defendant in an effort to protect her virtue. Defendant denied *in toto* the testimony of plaintiff; denied that he made
any admissions or had any conversation with the father and
mother; denied that he had gone riding with plaintiff or had
seen her or her parents at all on the day referred to; and
asserted that at the time when the offense is alleged to have
been committed he was elsewhere, and a part of the time at
the house of his brother, where he remained during the night,
in which claim he was corroborated by his brother and one
other person. The weight to be given this conflicting evidence was clearly a matter for the determination of the jury,
and its conclusion thereon in favor of plaintiff and against
the alibi which defendant sought to establish must, so far as
this court is concerned, be deemed conclusive. Appellant
cites the case of *Lind* v. *Closs*, 88 Cal. 6, [25 Pac. 972], to
the effect that where in prosecutions for rape the circumstances tend to throw discredit upon the uncorroborated testimony of the prosecuting witness, the court in reviewing
such testimony should be liberal in granting a new trial, to
the end that justice may be done. For the reasons stated,
however, the rule announced in that case is not applicable to
the facts in the case at bar.

It appears that the child, nearly a year old at the time, was
produced in court, and in addressing the jury plaintiff's attorney said: "I call your attention, gentlemen, to the child
in question and ask you to compare it with the defendant."
Defendant objected to the use of this language in argument
to the jury, on the ground there was no evidence that the
child was that of the defendant, and asked the court to instruct the jury to disregard the remarks of counsel. The
testimony of plaintiff was that the child to which she gave
birth nine months after the alleged act of intercourse with
her by defendant was that of the defendant. The record is
silent as to whether or not it bore any resemblance to defendant. For aught that appears to the contrary, its lack of resemblance might have constituted strong evidence in his

favor. If, on the other hand, it resembled the alleged father, it would be convincing evidence, not of the alleged violence, but of the act of intercourse with him which it was necessary for plaintiff to establish. There existed no controversy as to the birth of the child, and it was competent for plaintiff to testify that defendant was the father thereof. (*State* v. *Miller*, 71 Kan. 200, [6 Ann. Cas. 58, 80 Pac. 51].) And it has also been held that a child may be exhibited to the jury in order that they may consider and determine whether or not there may be any resemblance to the defendant. (*State* v. *Danforth*, 73 N. H. 215, [111 Am. St. Rep. 600, 6 Ann. Cas. 557, 60 Atl. 839].) In *State* v. *Danforth*, *supra*, it is said: "All of the cases concede, in effect, that there may be cases in which the maturity of the child or the character of the peculiarities relied upon as a ground of resemblance or dissimilarity render the child competent evidence on the issue of paternity. The objections urged to the competency of the evidence go rather to its weight than to its relevancy." In 1 Wigmore on Evidence, section 166, it is said: "The sound rule is to admit the fact of similarity of specific traits, however presented, provided the child is in the opinion of the trial court old enough to possess settled features or other corporal indications." In our opinion, since the child is not before us, the matter complained of was a question peculiarly within the province of the trial court to determine. At all events, it devolves upon appellant to affirmatively show prejudicial error, and there is nothing in the record here presented upon which we can assume, even if the court erred, that defendant was prejudiced by the ruling.

Complaint is made that the court erroneously instructed the jury as follows: "Whether or not plaintiff was chaste and virtuous prior to the alleged assault is not material to the maintenance of this action, and should you find from the evidence that she was not, that alone would not justify you in finding for the defendant. Whether or not she was chaste prior to the alleged assault is only material for the purpose of showing the damages which she may have suffered by reason of the alleged assault." The chastity of plaintiff prior to the assault was made an issue in the trial, and there was conflicting evidence touching the question. In our opinion, evidence as to the chastity of plaintiff was not only material touching the question as to the measure of damages, as stated by the court, but likewise material as tending to show the probability or nonprobability of resistance on the part of the prosecutrix; "for it is certainly more probable that a woman who has done these things voluntarily in the past would be much more likely to consent than one whose past reputation was without blemish, and whose personal conduct could not truthfully be assailed." (*People* v. *Johnson*, 106 Cal. 289, [39 Pac. 622].) Conceding, however, that the court erred in thus limiting the purpose for which such evidence was to be considered by the jury, it is nevertheless impossible to perceive how defendant could have been prejudiced thereby, since his defense, being an alibi, was not based upon the fact that plaintiff had consented to the act. Hence, conceding the error, defendant's substantial rights could not have been prejudiced by reason thereof.

The court instructed the jury that "Compensatory damages should be given in such amount as in your judgment will fairly compensate her for the injury she has received by reason of the act complained of, taking into consideration her physical suffering and disability during pregnancy and in childbirth, if you find the pregnancy was the result of the defendant's act, also her mental suffering, shame, and disgrace, and her loss of social standing, and all other harm you find she suffered as the natural result of the wrong." Objection is made to this instruction upon the ground that it invades the right of the jury, telling it that damages should be awarded to plaintiff regardless of whether she gave her consent or not. We do not so construe it. Read in connection with other instructions, and also as stated therein, they are to compensate her for the wrong by reason of the *act* complained of. "The act complained of" was the rape alleged to have been committed upon plaintiff by defendant.

Numerous assignments of error are predicated upon rulings of the court in admitting and rejecting evidence. Conceding some of the questions calculated to elicit immaterial testimony, we are unable to perceive that any prejudice could have resulted therefrom. The questions: "Did you become unconscious at any time while you were struggling with him?" "Did he say anything while he was doing this?" "Were you or were you not unconscious at the time he set you up?" "Before this assault were you as large physically as you are now?" were all proper, not only as tending to show damage, but for the further reason that they bore upon the question of her power to resist the defendant. In response to the last question plaintiff replied that she weighed 140 to 145 pounds at the time the act was committed, whereas at the time of the trial she weighed 215 pounds. This testimony was certainly proper, since defendant claims that, as he weighed only 155 pounds, it was improbable that he could forcibly rape a woman weighing 215 pounds. It was made to appear that after the commission of the act plaintiff remained on friendly terms with defendant, and she was asked the reason for such continued relations. Her answer to the effect that he always "promised Papa that he would come and get married, and we expected that he would keep his word," shows the materiality of the question. It is also claimed that the court erred in admitting the testimony of a physician as to the period of gestation. The ground of this objection is that such period is a matter of common knowledge, and not one requiring expert testimony. Conceding this to be true, how could defendant have been prejudiced by the answer? It is also claimed that the court erred in striking out the following testimony given by witness Mendez for the defense: "Last summer I saw Frank Truhillo and Alvina Valencia at Urbita Springs. It was last year I saw them." It is impossible to perceive how such fact could be material to any issue involved in the case. There were numerous other objections, in character as trivial and unimportant as those to which we have adverted. No purpose could be subserved by a more extended reference thereto. Suffice it to say, we find no error which in any event could have resulted in a miscarriage of justice. (Const., art. VI, sec. 4½.)

The judgment and order are affirmed.

Conrey, P. J., and James, J., concurred.

[Civ. No. 1915.   First Appellate District.—September 28, 1916.]

EDWARD L. KNORP, Appellant, v. BOARD OF POLICE COMMISSIONERS, etc., et al., Respondents.

POLICE OFFICER — REINSTATEMENT — MANDAMUS — STATUTE OF LIMI-
TATIONS.—The right of a member of the police department of the
city and county of San Francisco, whose resignation was accepted
on account of collapse due to mental strain, to be reinstated, is barred
by laches and the provisions of sections 338 and 343 of the Code of
Civil Procedure, where the *mandamus* proceeding to compel such
reinstatement was not instituted until some seven years and eight
months after the date of his certificate of discharge from the state
hospital to which he was committed, although the proceeding was
instituted within the statutory period after his restoration to capacity pursuant to the provisions of section 1766 of the Code of
Civil Procedure, where the petition for such restoration failed to
show that there had been any previous guardianship proceedings.

INSANE PERSONS—RESTORATION TO CAPACITY—ABSENCE OF GUARDIAN-
SHIP PROCEEDINGS — JURISDICTION OF OFFICERS OF ASYLUM. — The
superior court is without jurisdiction, under the provisions of section 1766 of the Code of Civil Procedure, to restore to capacity a
person adjudged to be insane and committed to an insane asylum,
without having been put under guardianship, as such jurisdiction,
in the absence of guardianship proceedings, is vested exclusively in
the officers of the hospital.

APPEAL from a judgment of the Superior Court of the
City and County of San Francisco, and from an order
denying a new trial.   James M. Troutt, Judge.

The facts are stated in the opinion of the court.

Von Schrader & Cadwalader, for Appellant.

Percy V. Long, City Attorney, and D. S. O'Brien,
Assistant City Attorney, for Respondents.

LENNON, P. J.—In this proceeding the plaintiff sought a
writ of mandate against the defendants, sitting as the board
of police commissioners of the city and county of San Francisco, commanding them to reinstate the plaintiff as a member of the police department of said city and county.   The

appeal is from a judgment entered in favor of the defendants, and from an order denying the plaintiff a new trial.

The facts of the case are practically undisputed and, in so far as they are pertinent to a discussion of the paramount point in the case, are, substantially stated, these: On the sixth day of November, 1899, the plaintiff became a member of the police department of said city and county, and was thereafter an active member of the department until June, 1901, when he "collapsed on account of mental strain." The records of the police commission show that on July 2, 1901, the plaintiff's application for leave of absence for three months without pay was granted by the board, and that on September 24, 1901, he tendered his resignation as a member of the police department, which was accepted "to take effect from ——." On November 22, 1901, the plaintiff was adjudged to be insane by the superior court of said city and county, and committed to the care of the Napa State Hospital, where he remained as a patient and an inmate until November 16, 1902, when he was released on leave of absence in care of his brother, George H. Knorp. Thereupon plaintiff returned to San Francisco, where he resided with his brother until May 24, 1904, when he in person applied for and procured from the medical superintendent of the Napa State Hospital a certificate discharging him from the custody and control of said institution upon the ground of his mental recovery. Thereafter, on October 24, 1911, he petitioned the superior court of the city and county of San Francisco for an order restoring him to capacity pursuant to the provisions of section 1766 of the Code of Civil Procedure, and the court made the order. The trial court in its findings of fact, among other things, found that plaintiff's resignation as a member of the police department was tendered by him and accepted by the board of police commissioners on September 24, 1901, and that his cause of action for reinstatement was, as pleaded in the answer of the defendants, barred by the provisions of sections 338 and 343 of the Code of Civil Procedure and the laches of the plaintiff.

The latter, we think, is fully sustained by the evidence. The action was not instituted until March 26, 1912, some seven years and eight months after the date of the medical superintendent's certificate finally discharging the plaintiff from the custody and control of the state as recovered. That

date, in our opinion, must be taken as the time when the
plaintiff was restored to capacity, rather than October 24,
1911, the date of the decree of the superior court which purported to judicially determine his restoration to capacity.
The plaintiff's petition to be restored to capacity, which was
the basis of the decree of the superior court, did not aver
that he had been under guardianship by virtue of the provisions of sections 1763 and 1764 of the Code of Civil Procedure, at the time of his commitment for insanity to the state
hospital; and consequently the superior court had no jurisdiction to hear and determine the question of the plaintiff's
mental capacity.   Such jurisdiction, in the absence of guardianship proceedings, was vested exclusively in the officers
of the state hospital (*Kellogg* v. *Cochran*, 87 Cal. 192, [12
L. R. A. 104, 25 Pac. 677]), and therefore the plaintiff's discharge from the hospital upon the ground of his recovery
was an adjudication by competent authority that he was sane
on the day and date of his discharge.   (*Kellogg* v. *Cochran*,
87 Cal. 192, [12 L. R. A. 104, 25 Pac. 677].)   The case of
Aldrich v. *Barton*, 153 Cal. 488, [95 Pac. 900] has no application to the facts of the present case.   There the patient
had been away from the state hospital for many years, claiming all the while, without opposition from the officers of the
hospital, to have been discharged and at liberty under a purported order of discharge; and the supreme court held that
under those circumstances the officers of the state hospital
lost the custody and control of the patient, and were therefore ousted of jurisdiction to make a second certificate of
discharge.   That case recognizes the right of the medical superintendent of a state hospital to release a patient on parole;
and that is precisely what was done in the present case.
During his leave of absence the plaintiff was constructively
in the custody and under the control of the state; and it was
not essential to the exercise of jurisdiction to discharge the
plaintiff that he should have been actually confined in the
state hospital at the time the certificate of discharge was applied for and granted.   (*People* v. *Geiger*, 116 Cal. 440, [48
Pac. 389].)   The certificate of discharge dated May 24, 1904,
was at least *prima facie* proof of the plaintiff's restoration
to capacity upon that date (*Aldrich* v. *Barton*, 153 Cal. 488,
[95 Pac. 900]), and nothing appearing to the contrary, the

presumption must prevail that he was then and ever since has been sane.

It is not disputed that the plaintiff's purported resignation as a member of the police department was accepted and dealt with by the board of police commissioners upon the theory that it took effect immediately, notwithstanding the fact that the records of the commission show that it was to take effect at a time not specified. In short, it is not disputed that the plaintiff was ousted from his position as a police officer by the board on September 24, 1901, the date of his purported resignation; that being so, his cause of action for reinstatement accrued upon that date; and giving him credit for the time during which he was under the disability of insanity, the statute, in our opinion, commenced to run against his cause of action upon May 24, 1904, the date of his restoration to capacity, as shown *prima facie* by the medical superintendent's certificate of discharge, and consequently his cause of action was barred by the statute of limitations. (Code Civ. Proc., secs. 352, 338, 343; *Farrell* v. *Board of Police Commrs.*, 1 Cal. App. 5, [81 Pac. 674]; *Jones* v. *Board of Police Commrs.*, 141 Cal. 96, [74 Pac. 696]; *Dodge* v. *Board of Police Commrs.*, 1 Cal. App. 608, [82 Pac. 699].)

It was not contended upon behalf of the plaintiff in the court below, nor is it contended here, that he did not have knowledge of the fact that his purported resignation was accepted and treated as having gone into effect as of the date of its tender; and his only excuse for not sooner instituting his action is that he could not do so until he had been restored to capacity by the decree of the superior court. But such decree, as has been pointed out, was, under the facts of the present case, neither a necessary nor a valid adjudication of his competency, and consequently will not avail to toll the statute of limitations, nor relieve him from the penalty of his undoubted laches in instituting the action.

We need not concern ourselves with the question as to whether or not the evidence sustains the finding that the plaintiff did in fact tender his resignation, and that the same was accepted and took effect immediately, for the fact still remains that the plaintiff, under and by virtue of his purported resignation and its acceptance, ceased to be a member of the department from the date thereof; and even if it be conceded that he was thereby wrongfully deprived of his office, the finding upon the statute of limitations and the laches of the plaintiff being supported by the evidence, it alone will suffice to support the judgment.

This disposes of all of the points presented in the appeal which we deem worthy of discussion.

The judgment and order are affirmed.

Kerrigan, J., and Richards, J., concurred.

A petition to have the cause heard in the supreme court, after judgment in the district court of appeal, was denied by the supreme court on November 27, 1916.

[Civ. No. 2006.   Second Appellate District.—September 28, 1916.]

F. F. COPP, Respondent, v. GUARANTY OIL COMPANY (a Corporation), Appellant.

PROMISSORY NOTE—DEFAULT IN INTEREST—EXERCISE OF OPTION—TENDER—CONFLICTING EVIDENCE—APPEAL.—In an action to recover on a promissory note, which contained a provision that if interest payments were not made when due, the whole sum of principal and interest should become immediately due and payable at the option of the holder, the finding of the trial court, on conflicting evidence, that the option to mature the note had been exercised prior to the alleged tender of the overdue interest is conclusive upon the appellate court.

ID.—AGREEMENT NOT TO SELL NOTE—KEEPING OF PLEDGED STOCK AVAILABLE FOR VOTING PURPOSES—RIGHT OF PAYEE AFTER DEFAULT.—An agreement made at the time of the execution of a note and as a part of the consideration therefor that the payee would not negotiate or sell or allow the note to go out of his possession other than to deposit it in a bank until the same became due, and that he would keep certain stock delivered to the payee as collateral security at all times available, so that the maker of the note could use or vote the stock in any stockholder's meeting of the corporation, is not to be construed as an agreement which would hinder the payee from transferring the note after default had been made in the payment of interest, or for the purpose of collecting the debt.

APPEAL from a judgment of the Superior Court of Los Angeles County, and from an order denying a new trial. Fred H. Taft, Judge.

The facts are stated in the opinion of the court.

Weaver, McCracken & McKee, for Appellant.

Clair S. Tappan, for Respondent.

JAMES, J.—This action was brought upon a promissory note executed by the defendant. Plaintiff had judgment, and a motion made by the defendant for a new trial was denied. The appeal is taken from the judgment and also from the order denying the motion.

The promissory note, which evidenced an indebtedness of fourteen thousand one hundred dollars, was dated at Los Angeles, June 14, 1911, and made payable "on or before two years after date." It contained a provision that if interest payments were not made when due, "then the whole sum of principal and interest shall become immediately due and payable at the option of the holder." In December, 1911, an installment of interest became due, and it was because of default in the payment of this interest that the plaintiff declared an option to mature the full amount of the note. On the 29th of January, 1912, written notice was given to the defendant company of this election on the part of the plaintiff and this action was shortly thereafter brought. The payee of the note was W. H. Fuller, who, after the December interest payment became due, indorsed the note to this plaintiff. As collateral security there was delivered to the payee with the note and afterward transferred to his indorsee thirty thousand shares of the Lucky Boy Oil Company stock. In the answer of the defendant issue was raised as to the matter of the note being indorsed to this plaintiff, and it was denied that any default had been committed in the matter of the payment of interest at the time of the alleged election of the plaintiff to declare the whole amount of principal and interest due. In the separate defense, more particular reference to which will be hereinafter made, one of the allegations was that before the original payee had indorsed the note to plaintiff, tender had been made to such

payee of the amount of interest due on the note, together
with compound interest, all of which the payee refused to accept. It appeared in evidence that prior to the time this
action was brought, the representative of defendant called
upon the attorney for this plaintiff and made request to be
allowed to pay the interest, both simple and compound, which
had then accrued; that the attorney for plaintiff informed
such representative of defendant that he had no authority
to accept anything except the full amount of principal and
interest. There was a conflict in the testimony as to when
this conversation was had. Two witnesses for the defendant
testified that it occurred on the twelfth day of January, 1912
(this action having been commenced early in March of the
same year). There was no dispute in the evidence showing
that on the twenty-ninth day of January, 1912, a letter was
written by the attorney for this plaintiff to the defendant,
notifying defendant of the election of the plaintiff to declare
the whole amount of the note, both principal and interest,
due on account of the default in the payment of the installment of interest which had become due in December, 1911.
The attorney for the plaintiff testified that the conversation
had with the representatives of defendant, wherein an offer
was made to pay overdue interest, occurred after the dispatch
and receipt by them of the letter wherein the option was exercised to mature the note. In the presence of this conflict
in the testimony, the findings of the trial court wherein they
are adverse to the appellant's contention as to that matter
must be sustained. We find in the transcript the record of
statements made by the learned trial judge, wherein it was
suggested as the view of the court that it was immaterial as
to whether any tender of interest was made before or after
the receipt of the written notice of election to mature the
note, because, as stated by the judge, when the parties appeared at the office of plaintiff's attorney they were told that
the attorney had no authority except to collect the full
amount of the note. The trial judge declared that such a
statement made under such circumstances was sufficient to
mature the note and to show an election on the part of the
plaintiff so to do, and that any offer then made by the defendant to pay the interest then owing was ineffectual. We
are hardly prepared to agree with the trial judge in this
view, but we cannot disturb the judgment because of such

erroneous conclusion, for the reason that the findings as made cover the issues presented and declare that no tender as alleged was ever made. The trial court received all of the evidence touching the matter of this tender; so there was no ruling adverse to appellant by which it was prevented from showing the facts according to its contention. It may have been that, with all of the evidence before him, the trial judge in making up the findings reconsidered the passing conclusion made by him in the course of the trial and determined that the tender, if made, was made as the testimony introduced on the part of plaintiff showed, to wit, after the receipt by the appellant of the letter of January 29th notifying it of the election of plaintiff to collect the entire amount of principal and interest.

There are other matters alleged in the special defense set up in the answer as to all of which the trial judge refused to hear any testimony. Appellant very earnestly contends that such special matters constituted good defenses and that it should have been allowed to make proof of them. We quote the material portion of the answer setting up the matters adverted to:

"That at the time of the making and delivering of said promissory note by the defendant, the said W. H. Fuller agreed as a part of the consideration thereof that he would not negotiate or sell or allow said note to go out of his possession other than to deposit it in the First National Bank of Los Angeles until the same became due and that he would keep the said certificates of stock for the 30,000 shares of stock in the Lucky Boy Oil Company at all times available so that the defendant could use or vote them in any stockholders' meeting of the Lucky Boy Oil Company; that at the time of the making and executing of said note, the said defendant was the owner of a certain large portion of the capital stock of said Lucky Boy Oil Company; that the stock owned by the defendant and the said 30,000 shares owned by the said W. H. Fuller constituted more than a majority of the issued stock of said Lucky Boy Oil Company, and that the defendant purchased said 30,000 shares of stock from said W. H. Fuller for the purpose of giving to it, the defendant, the stock control of said Lucky Boy Oil Company; that at the time of said contract, the said W. H. Fuller well knew such fact and then and there well knew that the said Guar-

anty Oil Company was purchasing said 30,000 shares of stock
for the sole purpose of acquiring a majority of the stock of
said Lucky Boy Oil Company; that said Lucky Boy Oil Company is a corporation organized and existing under and by
virtue of the laws of the territory (now state) of Arizona,
and that said W. H. Fuller had been for many years the attorney of said company; that at the time of the making and
executing of the note mentioned in the complaint of the
plaintiff, the said W. H. Fuller was a member of the board
of directors of the defendant company; that at the time the
defendant executed and delivered said note and acquired
said 30,000 shares of stock, the said W. H. Fuller represented and stated to the defendant that no more stock could
be issued from the treasury of the Lucky Boy Oil Company;
that said Guaranty Oil Company believed said statement of
said W. H. Fuller and relied upon the same, and would not
have purchased said stock if it had not believed that said
statement was true and correct, and the said representation
of the said W. H. Fuller was the inducement which caused
said Guaranty Oil Company to purchase said stock and to
give said note; that after the said W. H. Fuller had made
said representations, this defendant discovered that the same
were false and untrue, and that said Lucky Boy Oil Company did have the right and authority to issue and sell other
stock out of its treasury other than the issued and outstanding stock at the time of the execution and delivery of said
note; that said Guaranty Oil Company did not know that it
did not have such right until long after the execution and
delivery of said note; that after said transaction, said Lucky
Boy Oil Company did issue and sell other stock out of its
treasury, whereby the defendant was deprived of the control,
or the right to control, the corporate affairs of said Lucky
Boy Oil Company; that said defendant attempted by a legal
proceeding to have the issue of stock by said Lucky Boy Oil
Company cancelled and set aside but was unable to procure
the same; that thereafter the said W. H. Fuller, in violation
of his agreement not to negotiate or sell or allow said note
or said stock of said Lucky Boy Oil Company to go out of
his hands, as the defendant is informed and believes, and on
such information and belief alleges, to make it appear that
the said F. F. Copp was a *bona fide* holder of said note for
value, caused said pretended endorsement to be made

thereon, assigning and negotiating said note to the said plaintiff, whereas in truth and in fact, as the defendant is informed and believes, and on such information and belief alleges, to make it appear that the said F. F. Copp was a *bona fide* holder of said note for value, caused said pretended indorsement to be made thereon, assigning and negotiating said note to the said plaintiff, whereas in truth and in fact, as the defendant is informed and believes, and on such information and belief alleges, said endorsement was made without any consideration whatever; that it appears on the face of said note that the same is non-negotiable, and that thereupon the said plaintiff, if she ever acquired any interest or any right to sue upon said note took it subject to the aforesaid defenses existing between the defendant and said W. H. Fuller."

It may be conceded in discussing the propositions to follow that any defenses which the maker of the note might have urged against its payee were equally available as against this plaintiff. The note was non-negotiable in form. (*Smiley v. Watson*, 23 Cal. App. 409, [138 Pac. 367].) We think, however, that none of the special matters set up in the answer, as we have quoted them, would constitute a defense in this action. As to the alleged agreement on Fuller's part not to negotiate or sell the note or allow it to go out of his possession, and that he would keep the certificates of stock available for use, this should not be construed as an agreement which would hinder him from transferring it after default had been made in the payment of interest. There is no allegation that the thirty thousand shares of stock of the Lucky Boy Oil Company were not at all times available for the defendant's use in the stockholders' meetings. As to the alleged representation by Fuller that no more stock could be issued from the treasury of the Lucky Boy Oil Company, it does not appear from the allegations that such statement was more than an opinion of the said Fuller, or that he made the statement with intent to deceive or with the knowledge that it was untrue. It appears in the same allegations of the answer that the defendant itself was the holder of a large number of shares in the Lucky Boy Oil Company, and presumptively as such stockholder it would have knowledge or the means of readily ascertaining the fact as to the condition of any stock that remained in the treasury of the corporation. All of the alleged errors predicated upon the refusal of the court to hear testimony offered by the defendant related to the special matters set up in this answer, and, in the view we take of the case, were without prejudice to the appellant. The findings in their general form cover the issues presented, and there is some evidence to be found in the record to sustain the determination of the trial judge as to the facts.

The judgment and order are affirmed.

Conrey, P. J., and Shaw, J., concurred.

A petition for a rehearing of this cause was denied by the district court of appeal on October 26, 1916, and a petition to have the cause heard in the supreme court, after judgment in the district court of appeal, was denied by the supreme court on November 27, 1916.

[Civ. No. 1990.   Second Appellate District.—September 28, 1916.]

NEWHALL LAND AND FARMING COMPANY (a Corporation), Respondent, v. JULIETTE A. BURNS et al., Appellants.

VENDOR AND PURCHASER—EXTENSION OF TIME OF PAYMENT OF INSTALLMENT OF PURCHASE MONEY—CONSTRUCTION OF AGREEMENT—TIME AS OF THE ESSENCE OF THE CONTRACT INCLUDED.—Where an agreement extending the time for making payment of an installment of the purchase price of real property expressly provided that the agreement was "subject to all of the terms, covenants, and conditions" of the original contract of sale, such provision had the effect of carrying into such agreement all of the terms and conditions of the original contract, including the provision that time was of the essence of the contract, and no express declaration in such agreement to that effect was essential.

ID.—DEFAULT—TERMINATION OF RIGHTS OF VENDEES.—Under the terms of such an extension agreement, the default in making the payment at the time therein provided, unexcused and not waived, ipso facto terminated the rights of the vendees under the original contract.

ID.—ACTS OF VENDEES AFTER DEFAULT—RIGHT TO DECLARE TIME OF ESSENCE NOT WAIVED.—The right to declare time of the essence of

such contract after default in making payment is not waived by the
vendor in thereafter making no protest against the efforts of the
vendees to sell the property and in the making of surveys, where
the contract contained no requirements that the vendees should perform such acts.

ID.—TENDER OF DEED—WHEN UNNECESSARY.—Where under the terms
of such a contract the deed to the property had been delivered to a
third party with instructions to deliver to the grantees upon payment of the price, no further tender of the deed was necessary to
declare a forfeiture upon default of the vendees.

APPEAL from a judgment of the Superior Court of Los
Angeles County, and from an order denying a new trial.
Charles Wellborn, Judge.

The facts are stated in the opinion of the court.

John C. Miles, for Appellants.

Campbell & Moore, for Respondent.

SHAW, J.—Defendants prosecute this appeal from a judgment entered in favor of plaintiff quieting its title to certain
lands described in the complaint, and likewise appeal from
an order of court denying their motion for a new trial of
said action.

Defendants base their claim to an interest in the lands
upon two contracts alleged to have been executed by plaintiff, the first of which was dated January 31, 1912, whereby
plaintiff, for a consideration of seven hundred and fifty
thousand dollars, to be paid as therein stipulated, agreed to
sell and defendant Burns and one R. E. Muncy agreed to
purchase the property in question. At the time of the making of this contract there was paid to the plaintiff the sum
of five thousand dollars, and the agreement was placed in
escrow with the Citizens' National Bank of Los Angeles, "to
be delivered only in the event of the payment of the sum
of forty-five thousand dollars ($45,000) on or before May
1st, 1912." Burns and Muncy failed to pay this forty-five
thousand dollars, and on April 29, 1912, they, with plaintiff,
executed an agreement reciting the fact that the contract
was not to be delivered except upon the payment of forty-
five thousand dollars on or before May 1, 1912, which payment they were unable to make, and agreed in writing that

such contract should be canceled and annulled, and that Burns and Muncy waived all claims to or interest in said agreement, and consented to the forfeiture of said sum of five thousand dollars paid by them to plaintiff.

As found by the court upon ample evidence, no fraud or duress entered into the execution of this latter agreement for the cancellation of the contract and forfeiture of the five thousand dollars paid thereon; and hence this contract may be eliminated from further consideration.

Thereafter, on May 2, 1912, a contract similar in terms and conditions between plaintiff and defendant Burns alone was prepared, wherein plaintiff agreed to sell and Burns agreed to purchase the property in question for the sum of seven hundred and forty-five thousand dollars, payable as follows: "Forty-five Thousand Dollars ($45,000) on or before June 1st, 1912, at the Citizens' National Bank of Los Angeles, with which this agreement is deposited in escrow, to be by said bank delivered to the party of the second part upon receipt of said payment"; the contract further specifying the time for the payment of other stipulated installments of the purchase price covering the whole thereof. This contract provided: "That time is hereby made the essence of this agreement, and of each and every one of the covenants, terms and conditions hereof. . . . That any neglect, failure, or default in making any one or more of the payments of principal or interest hereinbefore provided for, or in complying with any of the other covenants, terms, or conditions of this agreement, at the time or times and in the manner hereinbefore specified, or at the expiration of any extension thereof in writing made by the party of the first part, or any violation of any of such covenants, terms, or conditions, upon the part of the said party of the second part, shall, at the option of the party of the first part, cause a forfeiture of all of the rights, privileges and interests of the said party of the second part under this agreement." Burns made default in the payment of the forty-five thousand dollars so stipulated to be paid on or before June 1, 1912, and upon payment of which the escrow holder was to deliver said contract to her. Whereupon, on June 1, 1912, in consideration of the payment of $750, plaintiff in writing agreed "to extend the time for the payment of the sum of forty-five thousand dollars ($45,000) due and payable on this day to July 1st, 1912, subject to all of the terms, covenants and conditions of the agreement between the parties hereto bearing date of 2nd day of May, 1912, a copy of which is deposited with the Citizens' National Bank of Los Angeles in escrow to be delivered to the party of the second part upon the payment of said sum of forty-five thousand dollars ($45,000)." Defendant again made default in the payment of the forty-five thousand dollars, time for the making of which was so extended to July 1, 1912. It appears that after July 1, 1912, there were some negotiations between plaintiff and defendant Burns, as a result of which defendants claim a verbal extension of time to July 15, 1912, was given within which to pay the forty-five thousand dollars. As to this claim, however, upon sufficient evidence, the court found adversely to defendants. Not only does the claim rest upon an oral alteration of the terms of a written contract (if there was one), but there was no consideration for such alleged extension.

The chief contention of appellants is that the written instrument whereby defendants were given until July 1st within which to pay the forty-five thousand dollars so stipulated in the contract to be paid June 1st, and upon the making of which the contract was to be delivered to defendant Burns, did not in express terms provide that time should be made the essence of said agreement for the extension of time of payment. The original contract, dated May 2, 1912, did in the strongest terms provide that time should be the essence thereof, and the agreement providing for the extension expressly provided that such agreement was "subject to all of the terms, covenants and conditions of the agreement between the parties hereto bearing date of 2nd day of May, 1912." The sole purpose of the latter agreement was to extend the time as stated for the payment of the sum of forty-five thousand dollars, and to this extent only was the contract modified. Clearly, the effect of the language last quoted was to carry into the agreement for the extension all of the terms and provisions of the contract to which it related. When defendants failed to make the payment within the time so extended, the position of the parties was identically the same as though such contract providing for the extension had never been executed. This being true, and conceding that instead of the contract being placed in escrow to be delivered to Burns only upon payment of forty-five thousand dollars by July 1st it had been actually delivered to her, a case is presented as to which the language used by the supreme court in *Glock* v. *Howard etc. Co.*, 123 Cal. 1, [69 Am. St. Rep. 17, 73 L. R. A. 199, 55 Pac. 713], is applicable. Defendants' right to an interest in the land was only such as the contract gave, and it gave no right save and except upon compliance with the conditions contained therein. No notice was required to terminate defendants' rights under the contract (see *Commercial Bank* v. *Welden*, 148 Cal. 601, [84 Pac. 171]), but their default on July 1, 1912, in making the payment of forty-five thousand dollars, unexcused and not waived, *ipso facto* terminated all rights they might have acquired by compliance with such provision. (*Champion Gold Min. Co.* v. *Champion Mines*, 164 Cal. 205, [128 Pac. 315].)

Appellants, however, claim that plaintiff in allowing the defendants to proceed under the contract after the fifteenth day of July, 1912, made the conditions of the original contract mutual and dependent, by reason of which fact plaintiff waived its right to declare time of the essence of the contract. In support of this contention appellants cite authorities to the effect that where the contract requires a party to do certain acts in the performance of which he has made default but afterward performs the acts, which performance is accepted by the other party, such acceptance constitutes a waiver as to time. (*Howard* v. *Thompson Lumber Co.*, 106 Ky. 566, [50 S. W. 1092]; *Smith* v. *Sanitary District*, 108 Ill. App. 69.) The acts done by defendants and as to which plaintiff entered no protest were efforts to sell the land and the alleged making of surveys, acts not called for by the contract, and in the doing of which plaintiff had no interest, since there was no provision in the contract requiring them to sell the land or make surveys. The only acts pursuant to the terms of the contract the performance of which, if accepted by plaintiff, would have constituted a waiver as to time would have been the performance of the covenants contained in the contract, none of which, as shown by the evidence, was performed by defendants. If after making default defendants had tendered the forty-five thousand dollars and plaintiff had accepted the same, clearly it would have constituted a waiver under which, notwithstanding the fact said sum had not been paid as stipulated, defendants would have been entitled to delivery of the contract, and the performance of other covenants therein as stipulated would have entitled them to performance on the part of the plaintiff.

It is further claimed that plaintiff, in order to have placed the defendants in default, should have tendered a deed before declaring a forfeiture, in support of which *Cleary* v. *Folger*, 84 Cal. 316, [18 Am. St. Rep. 187, 24 Pac. 280], is cited. It appears from the contract that as payments were made to the Citizens' National Bank deeds to specified parts of the property were to be delivered to defendants, one of which deeds, as provided in the contract, to a piece of land designated as Tract A, was to be delivered, together with the contract, upon the payment of the forty-five thousand dollars. This deed was deposited with the Citizens' National Bank in escrow, to be delivered by said bank to defendant Burns with the contract upon payment of said sum. Since the deed was signed and left with the bank to be delivered to defendants upon payment of the amount, no further tender was necessary. Hence, assuming a fact not true, that the contract was at the time of its date delivered to defendant Burns, and assuming further that there was a consideration for its execution, nevertheless, since any rights thereunder depended upon her paying the sum of forty-five thousand dollars on or before July 1st, she, by making default in said payment, lost all right to enforce the contract against plaintiff. (*Glock* v. *Howard etc. Co.*, 123 Cal. 1, [69 Am. St. Rep. 17, 43 L. R. A. 199, 55 Pac. 713], and *Champion Gold Min. Co.* v. *Champion Mines*, 164 Cal. 205, [128 Pac. 315].)

Moreover, the fact that the contract was never delivered is fatal to the assertion not only of any claim of interest in the land on the part of defendants, but as well to any right to recover the five thousand dollars so paid at the time of the making of the first contract, January 31, 1912, or the recovery of the $750 paid for an extension of time within which, as provided in the second contract, to pay the forty-five thousand dollars. Defendants allege in their answer that the contract was executed, and this is true in the sense only that it was signed by the plaintiff; but according to its express terms, *it was not to be delivered*, but *deposited in escrow* until July 1st, when, if Burns paid the forty-five thousand dollars, the escrow holder was instructed to deliver it to defendant. In other words, the effect of the transaction was, at most, for a consideration of five thousand dollars, to give defendants an option to acquire a contract for the purchase of the land upon the terms and conditions contained therein, upon payment of forty-five thousand dollars by July 1, 1912. They neglected and failed to exercise such option by paying the forty-five thousand dollars by July 1, 1912, and hence the contract was never delivered.

The appeal is without merit, and the judgment and order are affirmed.

Conrey, P. J., and James, J., concurred.

<hr />

[Civ. No. 1574. Third Appellate District.—September 28, 1916.]

SLAMA TIRE PROTECTOR CO. (a Corporation), Appellant, v. G. A. RITCHIE et al., Copartners, Respondents.

CONTRACT FOR PURCHASE AND SALE OF TIRE PROTECTORS—RELATIONSHIP CREATED — UNCERTAINTY OF CONTRACT — FINDINGS CONCLUSIVE.— Upon an appeal taken from the judgment in favor of the defendants in an action to recover an alleged balance due on account of a certain quantity of tire protectors shipped to them by the plaintiff, where the single question presented by the appeal is whether the contract upon which the action was founded was one whereby the plaintiff agreed to sell and the defendants agreed to buy the protectors at the prices and upon the conditions specified in the contract, or was one whereby the plaintiff agreed to ship or make consignments of the protectors to the defendants upon the understanding or condition that the protectors to be so shipped or consigned should be paid for only when they were sold by the defendants, and the contract upon its face is ambiguous and uncertain as to the nature of the relation which the parties intended thereby to establish between themselves, the finding of the trial court will not be disturbed.

ID.—RELATIONSHIP CREATED BY CONTRACT—UNCERTAINTY—CONSTRUCTION OF TRIAL COURT—APPEAL.—Where a writing is so characterized by ambiguity and uncertainty as to the nature of the relation which the parties intended thereby to create between themselves that either of the two constructions of the contract urged by the respective parties might upon reasons equally cogent be sustained, it is not within the proper or legal functions of a court of review to declare that the construction given the writing by the trial court should be rejected and supplanted by the other construction of which the instrument is susceptible.

ID.—NATURE OF TRANSACTION—UNCERTAINTY OF CONTRACT—QUESTION OF FACT.—Where the contract is uncertain or not clear as to its purpose and effect, the question whether the transaction of which it purports to be the evidence is a sale or a bailment is to be determined from all the circumstances giving rise to it, and on conflicting evidence a question of fact is presented for the jury's determination.

APPEAL from a judgment of the Superior Court of Kings County, and from an order denying a new trial. M. L. Short, Judge.

The facts are stated in the opinion of the court.

Miller & Miller, for Appellant.

H. Scott Jacobs, and H. P. Brown, for Respondents.

HART, J.—This appeal is by the plaintiff from the judgment and the order denying it a new trial.

The controversy arises out of a contract entered into between the plaintiff and the defendants, as copartners, at Kansas City, Missouri, on the eighth day of October, 1910. Said contract is made a part of the complaint.

The plaintiff is a corporation organized under the laws of the state of Nebraska.

The defendants, at the time of the making of the contract mentioned, were copartners, doing business in the city of Sacramento, under the firm name of Ritchie & Heriot.

The single question presented by this appeal is whether the contract upon which the action is founded was one whereby the plaintiff agreed to sell and the defendants agreed to purchase certain tire protectors at the prices and upon the conditions therein specified, or was one whereby the plaintiff agreed to ship or make consignments of the tire protectors to the defendants upon the understanding or condition that the protectors to be so shipped or consigned should be paid for only when they were sold by the defendants; or, to put the proposition in another form, it is, whether the parties to the con-

tract intended it to operate only to create between them the
relation of principal and agent or that of creditor and
debtor, or, in other words, whether the delivery of the goods
to the defendants was intended by the agreement to constitute an absolute sale thereof. The proposition thus stated
calls for a construction of said contract, or, what practically
amounts to the same thing, involves the question whether the
court's findings, which necessarily involve and exemplify its
construction of the contract, derive sufficient support from
the evidence.

The contract in full reads as follows:

"AGREEMENTS.

"Made this eighth day of October, 1910, by and between
Slama Tire Protector Company, Kansas City, Missouri,
known as the party of the first part and Ritchie and Heriot
of Sacramento, California, known as party of the second
part, witnesseth:

"That whereas, Party of the first part is engaged in selling
Tire Protectors, known as Slama Tire Protector, which pro-
duct is protected by various letters patent of the United
States of America, and

"Whereas, the party of the second part is desirous of purchasing and selling said Protectors in the States of Washington, Oregon, California, Arizona and Nevada.

"Whereas, the party of the first part is willing to permit
party of the second part to sell said protectors in accordance
with terms mentioned herein.

"Now, therefore, In consideration of the premises and of
One Dollar by each of the parties hereto, the other in hand
paid, receipt whereof is hereby acknowleged, said parties do
covenant and agree to and with each other as follows:

"1. The parties of the second part agree to purchase from
said first party a total of five hundred pair of above referred
protectors for each year of this contract to be taken either on
or before expiration of each year of contract and such quantity that is purchased over the stipulated amount can be
applied toward total purchases of next succeeding year's
purchases.

"2. Said second party agrees that they will not sell any of
said protectors at less than the established list prices attached herewith, marked Exhibit A, when selling to the con-

sumer nor allow any of their sub-agents to violate this agreement.

"3· The second party agrees to spend the sum of Two Thousand Dollars ($2,000.00) annually during the life of contract towards advertising said protectors in manner they see fit for the benefit of the sale of such protectors and all expenditures for such advertising to be reported by verified statements to said first party. It is also understood that any amount spent over and above this sum, can be applied toward making total of the amount to be spent during the life of this contract.

"4· The party of the first part agrees to furnish party of the second part such quantities of circular matter with the said second party's name printed thereon at any time they are requested to do so and in such quantities as will be necessary for the second party to properly circularize the territory covered and allotted to said second party.

"5· The said party of the first part agrees to turn over all inquiries, orders and business coming from the territory or states specified herein.

"6. Said first party agrees to supply a sufficient stock of said protectors to meet all reasonable demand to said second party and a report of stock on hand is to be made the first day of each month to said first party by said second party. All goods taken from such stock to be paid for as provided hereinafter. New and unused protectors are only to be considered as stock on hand. All stock on hand to be kept fully insured, and all freight and storage charges to be paid by second party and in the event of any of said goods being returned for any reason, freight is to be prepaid back to the factory.

"7· The price to be paid to first party for such protectors as they shall purchase will be list price as per Exhibit A. attached herewith, less discount of 30 per cent therefrom with an additional discount of 5 per cent for cash, payable the tenth of each month of net cash, if paid at the end of each month. If the said second party shall comply with all the terms and conditions of this contract and as soon as the total purchases paid for, amount to two hundred fifty pair (250) then the said first party will allow an additional discount of 5 per cent from all protectors purchased. Should these same conditions be complied with and the total paid for purchases amount to five hundred pair (500) then another 5 per cent will be allowed, thus making a total discount from the list price in that event amount to 30-5-5 per cent and the extra 5 per cent for cash. In the event of the maximum discount being reached, permission is given as a matter of convenience to figure a total net discount of 40 per cent.

"8· Privilege is given to said second party to call and advertise our product under the name of 'The Armor Plate Tire Protector.'

"9· The life of this contract shall be for a term of five (5) years, but shall not be assignable by the party of the second part."

Annexed to the contract is a schedule containing a list of the prices which the defendants were to pay for the goods consigned to them by the plaintiff under the terms of the agreement and for not less than which they were to sell them to the public.

The complaint avers: "That under and pursuant to said contract plaintiff shipped to defendants at Sacramento, California, at defendants' instance and request, between the eighth day of October, 1910, and the first day of May, 1911, tire protectors of the value $18,700.45, estimated at the price provided for in said contract; that, as plaintiff is informed and believes, and on such information and belief alleges, all of said tire protectors so delivered to defendants as aforesaid have been sold by defendants."

It is alleged that of the sum above mentioned there has been paid by the defendants to the plaintiff the sum of $2,741.75, only, and that there is consequently due the latter from the former the sum of $15,958.70.

A general demurrer to the complaint having been overruled, the defendant Ritchie answered.

The answer admits the making of the contract mentioned in the complaint; admits the shipment to the defendants by the plaintiff of a certain quantity of the protectors, but denies that they were of the value of $18,700.45, averring, however, that they were of the value of $28,333.45; denies that said tire protectors so delivered to the defendants have been sold by said defendants, but admits that of the protectors so delivered to the defendants the latter have sold "about $6.275 worth, only," which amount it is alleged has been paid to the plaintiff.

The answer sets up a number of special defenses and counterclaims growing out of alleged breaches of the agreement by the plaintiff, said counterclaims amounting in the aggregate to the sum of forty-two thousand dollars. As to these, however, it may here be remarked that the court found, and appears to have been justified in so finding, that the defendant was entitled to nothing on the counterclaims pleaded by him. They, therefore, need not be further noticed.

It is further alleged in the answer that, after the contract in question was made, the partnership existing between Ritchie & Heriot at the time of the execution of said instrument, was, by the mutual consent of said partners, dissolved, and that the said contract was thereupon assumed by the said Ritchie, "who continued to transact the business theretofore conducted by the said copartnership."

The court found that the pleaded contract was entered into between the parties as alleged in the complaint; that the plaintiff shipped to the defendants at Sacramento tire protectors of the value of $18,700.45; that the defendants did not sell all the protectors so shipped, but did sell a portion thereof, amounting in value to the sum of $2,741.75; that all of said goods were shipped to and received by the defendants to be paid for when sold, and not otherwise; that no part of the said sum of $18,700.75, the value of the protectors shipped to the defendants, has been paid by the said defendants, except the sum of $2,741.75, "but the court finds that it is not true that there is a balance due from the said defendants to plaintiff in the sum of $15,958.70, or any other sum."

It must be conceded that the contract, upon its face, is rather ambiguous and uncertain as to the nature of the relation which the parties thereto intended thereby to establish between themselves. That the construction placed upon it by the trial court, as evidenced by its findings, is reasonable and sustainable by certain language of the instrument, no one reading the writing will for an instant doubt. On the other hand, language is used from which the conclusion might justly be justified that the intention was that, while the defendants were to enjoy the exclusive right and privilege of selling the tire protectors within the territory designated in the contract, they were, nevertheless, to be required to purchase the goods outright from the plaintiff on the terms and conditions of the agreement, and that each order or shipment was to constitute an absolute sale.

The preamble to the contract contains the declaration that "the party of the first part is willing to *permit* party of second part to *sell* said protectors in accordance with the terms mentioned herein." Among the terms of the contract is a provision that the prices at which the defendants are to sell the article must not be less than the established prices indicated in the schedule attached to the contract exhibiting a list of prices, "nor allow any of their *subagents* to violate this agreement." This language, viewed by the light of that of the preamble above referred to, appears to make it very clear that the intention was that the defendants were by the contract to act as mere selling agents of the plaintiff. As counsel for the defendant well suggest: "The idea of subagents must presuppose an agent. . . . There could be no reason for the expression, 'subagent,' unless the parties had in mind that the second parties were the agent of the first party in the matter of the distribution of these protectors."

Again, the third paragraph of the contract binds the defendants to the obligation of expending the sum of two thousand dollars each year during the life of the contract for the purpose of advertising the protectors and to render to the plaintiff a verified statement of expenditures for such purpose. Such a provision is a most unusual one in a contract providing for the absolute or unconditional sale of a commodity. If the contract was intended as one for the absolute sale of the article at the prices specified therein, is it reasonable to suppose that the defendants would have bound themselves for a period of five years to the expenditure of such a large sum each year of the five for such a purpose? Indeed, if it had been intended as such a contract, is it reasonably to be supposed that the plaintiff, having received its price for its goods, would have exacted such an agreement from the purchaser? The burden imposed by said provision as a condition upon which a party might acquire the rights and authority of a selling agent for another would not be, *per se,* an unreasonable one; for, as counsel for the defendant suggest, the clause may the more reasonably be construed as involving an agreement on the part of the defendants to expend the amount required for advertising as a *bonus* for the right and privilege of acting as the selling or distributing agents of the plaintiff within the designated territory. Then there is the clause whereby it is covenanted that the plaintiff will supply the defendants with a sufficient "stock of said protectors to meet all reasonable demands," the defendants to report to the plaintiff on the first day of each month the amount of stock on hand. Said clause further provides that the defendants were to keep the stock on hand fully insured. Such conditions as these are rarely to be found in a contract of sale, but are peculiarly appropriate to a bailment or some other transaction by which it is not intended that the consignee of the goods shall acquire title thereto.

Thus we could proceed and point out other language of the contract which, taken alone or viewed in connection with the provisions of the instrument above referred to, clearly implies that the contract was intended to establish the relation of principal and agents between the parties and not intended as a contract for the sale of the goods; but it is unnecessary further to examine the contract for this purpose. The instrument is presented herein in full, and there can be no difficulty in observing from its language that the conclusion arrived at by the court below as to its legal nature, scope, and effect involves a reasonable view of the language of the writing.

We do not say that the provisions of the contract above specifically adverted to are wholly inconsistent with the theory that the transaction was intended as a contract of sale. What we do say is that the provisions are perfectly consistent with a contract creating an agency. Indeed, as declared, some of them are very rarely to be found incorporated into a contract for the absolute or unconditional sale of goods. And it should further be noted that the plaintiff appears to have proceeded in this action upon the theory that the transaction involved only a conditional sale of the protectors to the defendants. The complaint alleges, upon the information and belief of the plaintiff, that all of the protectors shipped to the defendants had been sold by the latter. If the transaction was in fact an absolute sale of the goods, why such an allegation in the complaint? What material difference could it make to the plaintiff whether the goods were or were not sold by the defendants if, in truth, the sale was absolute and title to the goods passed to the defendants? The averment is obviously wholly inconsistent with the theory of an absolute or unconditional sale.

As suggested, however, it must be admitted that the contract contains some language which, if considered by itself or without reference to or consideration of other language of the instrument, might warrant the construction to which the writing is subjected by the plaintiff, viz., that it involves an agreement for the absolute sale of the tire protectors to the defendants. Indeed, it may justly be assumed to be true that the instrument is so characterized by ambiguity and uncertainty as to the nature of the relation which the parties intended thereby to create between themselves that either of the two constructions of the contract urged by the respective parties might, upon reasons equally cogent, be sustained. The question, therefore, then arises, assuming, of course, that no competent testimony extrinsic to the writing itself reflecting light upon the real intention of the parties has been received: Is it, in such a situation, within the proper or legal functions of a court of review to declare that the construction given the writing by the trial court should be rejected and supplanted by the other construction of which the instrument is susceptible? Manifestly, no reason can be conceived which would support an affirmative reply to that question. The appeal court could not adopt such a course in such a case without resorting to the exercise of arbitrary power. So, if there were no other evidence in this record but the instrument itself which throws or tends to throw any light on the relation which the parties by the contract intended to establish between themselves, we would feel constrained —indeed, it would be our duty—to uphold the construction given the contract by the trial court, as evidenced by its findings.

But there was introduced and received in the case some evidence extrinsic to the instrument itself which we think tends to support the trial court's construction. After the contract was made and a large stock of protectors had been shipped to the defendants, considerable correspondence by mail was carried on between the parties. Some of these letters were introduced in evidence. Excerpts from a few will be sufficient to indicate that the plaintiff understood the contract to call for a payment for the goods shipped to the defendants only when the latter sold the same.

In one of the plaintiff's letters to the defendants the following language was used: "It is also much to be regretted to note the exceptional dry weather California is experiencing, especially this being your first year with the Protectors and as you say, so much depends upon the weather in your section of the country. No doubt, however, when the rains do start, you will make up for lost time, which is surely hoped for, as you know by my previous letters that this amount of stock we have with you, has put us in a rather tight financial circumstances and caused us to borrow money from the banks in order to meet our own obligations which were necessarily increased on account of the anticipated business from you. We really realize your condition on account of the weather and have enough faith in you to know that if the business is to be had, you will get it. All we want is that you play the game square and you will find us easy people to get along with."

In the same letter reference is made to a proposition by the defendants to sell a portion of their territory to a Mr. Kaar for the sum of one thousand dollars, and the plaintiff wrote: "We were very much interested, however, in noting your proposition to Mr. Kaar and would like to know just what territory you intended turning over to him for this amount and also your reason for making a proposition of this kind. We were wondering if you are getting dissatisfied with the proposition or thought that Salt Lake City was a little out of your territory."

Again, the following letter, under date of February 24, 1911, was addressed by the plaintiff to the defendants: "We hardly know how to express ourselves in replying to your telegram in which you inform us that you have not sold any protectors for two months, and in this telegram you say there is none to make this month. We, of course, realize the dry weather had something to do with the sales falling off, but when they are reduced from what they were to absolutely nothing, we cannot help but think something is wrong, and you in our position would, of course, think likewise.

"We have treated you absolutely square in all of our dealings with you and expect the same from you. *If it is your intention to discontinue handling our protectors we wish you would say so at once and return what new unused stock you*

*have on hand by prepaid freight and remit for the balance
due us as per our agreement.*

"Stock that has been put to use is not returnable."

It is not necessary to enter herein upon an analytical examination of the above letters to show that their language clearly implies the relation of principal and agent between the parties. The letters sufficiently speak for themselves in that respect.

Other letters passing between the parties were introduced in evidence. In the place of presenting herein extracts therefrom, it is sufficient to say that said letters contained language clearly indicating that both parties to the contract understood the agreement to have been intended, not as a contract for the absolute sale of the goods, but merely to vest in the defendants the authority of agents in the sale of said goods within the several states named.

Many other significant considerations revealed by the correspondence between the parties might be mentioned, all tending to support the theory that the contract was intended as, and in fact was, a contract of agency, or, at the most, a conditional sale, the protectors consigned to the defendants to be paid for only when the goods consigned to the defendants were sold by them.

In addition to the foregoing considerations, the statements rendered to the defendants by the plaintiff of protectors shipped to the former may be referred to as indicating the view the plaintiff had of the character or nature of the contract. These statements were uniformly marked "consignment," and from this fact it is reasonably inferable that the plaintiff regarded the shipments under the contract as mere consignments and not as a delivery on the sale of the goods.

Our conclusion is, from all the facts and circumstances of the transaction involved here, as disclosed by the contract itself and other documentary proofs, that the court's findings are sufficiently supported; that, under the terms of the contract, as it is warrantably construed by the court, there could not be a completed sale until the defendants sold the goods to third parties. Until that occurred, the consignee was under no obligation to pay the listed prices therefor, and could have been compelled to surrender the goods to the consignor upon demand. (*Vermont Marble Co.* v. *Brow,* 109 Cal. 236, [50 Am. St. Rep. 37, 41 Pac. 1031].)

It is true, as the authorities declare, "the distinction between agency contracts creating bailments and contracts of sale is not always clear, . . . and in some cases a contract may be construed as creating merely an agency as between the parties where, as between the parties and a third person, it might be given the effect of a sale." (6 Corpus Juris, p. 1091.) There is no question of the rights of third persons involved in the transaction with which we are presently concerned.

After all, however, where the contract is uncertain or not clear as to its purpose and effect, the question whether the transaction of which it purports to be the evidence is a sale or a bailment is to be determined from all the circumstances giving rise to it, and, on conflicting evidence, a question of fact is presented for the jury's determination. (6 Corpus Juris, p. 1087.)

But counsel for the plaintiff contend that the "terms of selling these goods were to be determined by the defendant, and that he agreed to pay a fixed price for the goods," and declare that therefore the case here comes within the rule that where the consignee or factor is to sell upon terms fixed by himself, and is bound to pay to the consignor a fixed price, the contract is one of sale. (21 Am. & Eng. Ency. of Law, p. 520.) The contract here, however, expressly provides, as will be observed from a perusal of it, that the "second party agrees that they will not sell any of said protectors at less than the established list prices attached herewith, marked Exhibit A, when selling to the consumer, nor allow any of their sub-agents to violate this agreement." Thus it is plainly manifest that the defendants were not at liberty under the contract to fix their own minimum prices in selling the goods, but were to be governed in that respect entirely by the prices fixed by the consignor—the plaintiff itself.

We have neither been shown nor found a substantial reason for declaring that the trial court's construction of the contract is erroneous, and the judgment and the order are accordingly affirmed.

Chipman, P. J., and Burnett, J., concurred.

[Civ. No. 1570.   Third Appellate District.—September 28, 1916.]

J. H. THOMPSON, Respondent, v. SOUTHERN PACIFIC COMPANY et al., Defendants; SOUTHERN PACIFIC COMPANY, Appellant.

NEGLIGENCE—COLLISION AT RAILROAD CROSSING—OBSTRUCTIONS—FAILURE TO STOP AND LISTEN—CONTRIBUTORY NEGLIGENCE.—In an action for damages for personal injuries received from a collision between an automobile driven by the plaintiff and a freight train of the defendant at a grade crossing on a public highway, the plaintiff is guilty of such contributory negligence as to preclude recovery, where it is shown by his own testimony that the view of approaching trains at the place of the accident was obstructed by a dense growth of sunflowers and weeds, which was well known to the plaintiff, and that he did not, upon approaching the crossing and while within the lines of the right of way of the railroad company, stop his machine, or look or listen for an approaching train.

ID.—OBSTRUCTED VIEW AT CROSSINGS—DUTY OF TRAVELERS.—While it is true that the rule requiring the traveler to *stop* at railroad crossings and look and listen for approaching trains is not an absolute one, yet if the view is obstructed he must place himself in a position where he can use his faculties of observation to advantage.

ID.—LACK OF NEGLIGENCE OF TRAIN OPERATIVES—RIGHT TO ASSUME—ERRONEOUS INSTRUCTION.—An instruction advising the jury that the plaintiff had the right to assume that the defendant's employees would observe the law requiring them to ring the bell and sound the whistle when approaching the crossing is erroneous.

ID.—ACTION AGAINST RAILROAD COMPANY AND TRAIN OPERATIVES—JUDGMENT EXONERATING AGENTS—ACQUITTAL OF COMPANY.—In such an action, where recovery is sought against the railroad company and its servants, based upon the acts of the latter in running the train at a high rate of speed without sounding any warning of its approach, an acquittal of the latter of negligence is an acquittal of the company.

APPEAL from a judgment of the Superior Court of Tulare County, and from an order denying a new trial. W. B. Wallace, Judge.

The facts are stated in the opinion of the court.

Power & McFadzean, for Appellant.

Alfred Daggett, Lamberson, Burke & Lamberson, and J. A. Chase, for Respondent.

BURNETT, J.—It is conceded by respondent that appellant has made a fair statement of the facts and we may, therefore, substantially adopt the same. The action is for personal injuries to plaintiff, resulting from a collision between an automobile driven by him and a freight train of appellant. The collision occurred July 18, 1912, about 4 o'clock P. M., at a grade crossing of a public highway. The crossing is located about one mile south of Dinuba, in the county of Tulare, and the train was, at the time of the accident, in charge of defendant Keith, as engineer, and defendant Rhone, as conductor. Defendant Waller was the fireman. Appellant and its trainmen were jointly charged with negligence.

The amended complaint in substance alleges that bordering the public highway on which the accident occurred on the south, and adjoining the railroad right of way on the west, there was at the time of the accident, and for a long time prior thereto had been, an orchard belonging to one Weddle; that the defendants had negligently permitted to grow up and mature on said right of way where the same crosses the public highway a dense growth of sunflowers and weeds; that the vegetation had grown to such height that a person traveling in a vehicle in an easterly direction along the highway across the railroad right of way could not see the railroad track or a locomotive engine or a train of cars upon it for any distance when looking in a southeasterly direction, until he reached a point near and almost immediately upon the railroad track; that the train of cars which collided with plaintiff's automobile was traveling upon its track from the southeast to the northwest; that at the time of the accident, the plaintiff, who was traveling along said highway in an easterly direction, brought his machine down to a slow gait at a point about one hundred and twenty yards west of the crossing, moved slowly toward the crossing, and looked for an approaching train; that because of the presence of the fruit trees in the Weddle orchard, and the sunflowers and weeds on appellant's right of way, he did not see any engine or cars on the track until he was practically upon the track; that before he got near the track he listened, but could not hear any train approaching the crossing; that when he reached the crossing, defendant and appellant, which was operating the train by and through its codefendants,

Keith, Waller, and Rhone, at a high rate of speed and in a careless, reckless, and negligent manner, ran into said automobile and seriously injured plaintiff.

It is alleged that the defendants Keith, Waller, and Rhone did not have control over the train; that they omitted to ring any bell. sound any whistle, or give any warning whatever as the train approached the crossing; that if defendants had sounded the whistle at a distance of eighty rods from the crossing. and had continued to ring the bell or sound the whistle from that point until they reached the crossing, the plaintiff would have known of the approach of the train, and would not have gone upon the track and been injured.

The answer denied all the allegations of the complaint except those in reference to the corporate capacity of appellant and the existence of said orchard, and affirmatively alleged that the train was carefully and properly run; that plaintiff was driving his automobile at a speed of about thirty miles per hour; that the whistle was blown and the bell sounded; that plaintiff, as he approached the crossing, did not look or listen for an approaching train; that if he had done so, he would have known that the train was approaching the crossing, and that he was guilty of contributory negligence which directly and proximately caused the injuries. The jury rendered a verdict in favor of plaintiff against the Southern Pacific Company for $17,946.55, but against plaintiff as to said trainmen, Keith, Waller, and Rhone.

It appears that plaintiff, in company with one West Lee, left Dinuba about 4 o'clock in the afternoon of the day of the accident. In leaving the town they crossed the railroad approximately one-half or three-fourths of a mile northwest of the crossing where the accident happened, and proceeded in a southerly direction until they came to a county road leading in an easterly direction toward the railway. They traveled along this roadway and in an easterly direction until the automobile collided with the train. As they crossed the railway in leaving the town of Dinuba the witness Lee looked down along the railroad track in a southeasterly direction toward the town of Monson and saw the smoke of a train beyond the crossing at which the accident occurred. Lee and the plaintiff say that there was a rough place in the county road upon which they were traveling, about one hun-

dred and fifty yards west of the crossing, near a stone cul-
vert, and that plaintiff brought his automobile down to a
slow gait and thereafter moved slowly toward the railroad
crossing. They and their witnesses testified that there was
one row of tall sunflowers extending along the south side of
the county road and into the railroad right of way, to within
a few feet of the railroad track, and that there was another
row of tall sunflowers extending southeasterly from the south
side of the county road along the fence which separates the
railroad right of way from the Weddle orchard. Lee's estimate of the height of these sunflowers was six or seven feet.

The westerly or southwesterly boundary of the railroad
right of way from the center line of the railroad track, measured along the center line of the highway, is about seventy
feet. Plaintiff testified that as he approached the crossing he
looked in a southeasterly direction, and that he listened for
the purpose of ascertaining whether or not there was a train
approaching the crossing, but that he did not see or hear one.

As to his knowledge of conditions at the crossing, he testified as follows: "I knew that trains were passing up and
down the road frequently and I was somewhat familiar with
the road. I do not know how often I have been over that
road, but I believe I had been over it once that day, and I
had had occasion to be over it many times previous to that
time, but I went usually another way and didn't go over this
crossing. I noticed the sunflowers, or other weeds or wild
oats there about ten days before the accident. At that time
I particularly noticed the sunflowers and wild oats, and this
other vegetation, and that is the reason I approached as cau-
tiously as I could, and I knew they were there on the occasion
of making this approach to the railroad track on the eighteenth
day of July."

As to his automobile, he testified: "My automobile was in
good condition and repair, both as to brakes and otherwise,
and I could stop it within a distance of three or four feet by
applying the brakes. I could have stopped it by the emer-
gency brake, or the foot brake, or by shifting my gearing
across to the other side of the disc. I could have set it back
so that it would not have moved a foot after that."

As to his conduct while within the railroad's right of way,
he was asked this question: "Now, when you were approaching the crossing, and while you were within the lines of the

right of way of the railroad company—still on the county
road, of course—did you stop your machine, or look or listen
for an approaching train?'' And he answered: "I did not.
I could not have seen it if I did, unless I got out of the
machine and walked up to the track." By this answer he
showed very clearly, under the decisions, that he was chargeable with such contributory negligence as to preclude recovery. In other words, he did not exercise that due care for
his own safety which the law demanded of him. It was his
duty to stop and look and listen, at some point where such
conduct would be effective. According to his own testimony,
he knew of the obstructions to his view. But if he had not
known of them before, he certainly observed them that day
when he attempted to see if any train was approaching.
Common prudence under such circumstances would dictate
that he bring his machine to a full stop before attempting to
cross the track. If he had done so, he would undoubtedly
have heard the train approaching. But to exercise due care,
under the situation as revealed by him, the consensus of the
opinion of prudent men would require him, if necessary to
ascertain whether his life was in danger, to get out of his
machine and go forward a few feet on foot in order that the
matter might be placed beyond peradventure. We may say,
in passing, that the testimony of plaintiff as to the obstruction of the view seems almost incredible in the light of the
whole record, but accepting his statement as true, his mis-
fortune is attributable to his own carelessness.

In *Herbert* v. *Southern Pacific Co.,* 121 Cal. 227, [53 Pac.
651], it was said: "But the cases arising from injuries suffered at railroad crossings have been so numerous, and upon
certain points there has been such absolute accord, that what
will constitute ordinary care in such a case has been precisely
defined, and if any element is wanting, the courts will hold
as matter of law that the plaintiff has been guilty of negligence." The rule of conduct at railroad crossings is therein
stated, and it has been recognized and enforced in all the
subsequent decisions of the supreme court.

In *Green* v. *Southern Cal. Ry. Co.,* 138 Cal. 1, [70 Pac.
926], it was held that "as a general rule, one approaching a
railroad track must stop and listen, and the only exception
to such rule is that there may be particular instances where
the circumstances would not call for such precaution." And

in the consideration of the facts of that case, it was said:
"The fact that they looked to the east as they passed the
gate, or opening, farther up the street as above noted, which
was of little benefit to them, is no excuse for not looking or
listening at points near the track, where such looking or listening would have been effective."

In *Chrissinger* v. *Southern Pacific Co.*, 169 Cal. 619, [149
Pac. 175], the rule is stated as follows: "A person approaching a railroad track, which is itself a warning of danger, must
take advantage of every reasonable opportunity to look and
listen. Undoubtedly, the question of contributory negligence
or freedom from it is ordinarily one for the jury, but where,
as here, the standard of conduct is so obvious as to be applicable to all persons, and the plaintiff has failed to measure
up to that standard under the circumstances shown, he is not
entitled to have his case go to the jury."

In *Griffin* v. *San Pedro etc. R. R. Co.*, 170 Cal. 772,
[L. R. A. 1916A, 842, 151 Pac. 282], after reciting the facts,
the supreme court said: "From these facts it is clear that
Mr. Griffin neglected the simplest and plainest precautions
for the safety of himself and the others in the automobile.
It is the duty of a traveler on a highway approaching a railroad crossing to use ordinary care in selecting a time and
place to look and listen for coming trains. He should stop
for the purpose of making such observations when necessary.
It is his duty to use all his faculties, and it is not enough if
he merely listens, believing that the people in charge of any
approaching engine will ring a bell or sound a whistle. . . .
He [Mr. Griffin] had his car under perfect control. The
brakes had been tightened that day. He was running at a
very low rate of speed, and it would have been easy for him
to stop a short distance beyond the fence corner at a place
of complete safety and one well suited to observation. Failing to do this amounts to contributory negligence on his
part." It may be said that Mr. Griffin's negligence in that
case was no more manifest than that of plaintiff in the case
at bar.

It is true, as declared in the opinions, that the rule requiring the traveler to *stop* is not an absolute one. If the view
is entirely unobstructed, the traveler, while going toward a
crossing, may see whether a train is approaching in dangerous proximity. Of course, in a case like that it would be idle

to require the traveler to stop to find out something that he
can ascertain just as well without stopping. He must, however, avail himself of the vision, and if he is exercising ordinary care, he need not stop except to allow an approaching
train to pass so as to avoid a collision. But where the view
is obstructed, he must place himself in a position where he
can use his faculties of observation to advantage. In such
case he stops—not primarily to avoid a collision—·but to
ascertain whether a collision is threatened. Whereas, if the
view is unobstructed, if he stops, it is to allow the approaching train to pass.

It appears entirely clear to us that the foregoing is decisive
of the controversy, and that it is really unnecessary to notice
other points. However, we may briefly call attention to two
other grounds of criticism that would demand a reversal of
the judgment.

Among the instructions given by the court was the following: "The plaintiff, in approaching the railroad crossing on
the public highway, referred to in the pleadings in this case,
had a right to rely upon the performance by those on the
locomotive of every act imposed by the law upon them when
approaching a crossing. In the legal sense, he was innocent
of negligence, unless there was a want of ordinary care and
prudence on his part. . . . The degree of caution required is
relative to the risk; but no person is bound to assume that
another will abandon any reasonable precaution, or violate
the obligation imposed upon him by the laws of the land.
Plaintiff was authorized to assume that all other persons
using the public highway would do so with due care, and it
cannot be imputed as negligence that he did not anticipate
that the servants or agents in charge of a railroad train on
said highway would not perform their duty of ringing a bell
or sounding a whistle as the law required. He had the right
to assume, until he reached a point where he would look up
and down the track, that no train was approaching the crossing, because there was no sound of an engine, bell, or of a
whistle."

If the traveler had the right to assume that defendant's
employees would observe the law requiring them to ring the
bell and sound the whistle when approaching the crossing,
he would, of course, have a right to rely upon receiving such
information of approaching danger and would be entirely

excusable for neglecting to avail himself of any other source of knowledge. Again, if he had a right to so assume, if no bell, as a matter of fact, was rung or whistle sounded, he would have a right to assume that no train was in fact approaching, and he would not be chargeable with negligence if he acted upon that assumption and proceeded to cross the track.

In *Huston v. Southern California Ry. Co.*, 150 Cal. 703, [89 Pac. 1093], it is said: "It is not the law of this state that a person approaching a railroad crossing is authorized to assume that the person operating a train will not in any way be negligent in that operation. This doctrine has been asserted in some of the states, but is opposed to the law as laid down in the decisions of this state and of the supreme court of the United States. Such a rule would abrogate the doctrine of contributory negligence in all such cases."

There is manifestly another fatal error lurking in the last clause of the instruction. Therein, the court plainly invaded the province of the jury in a matter of vital importance. It was probably an inadvertence to declare that "there was no sound of an engine, bell, or of a whistle," but the effect was the same, whether the statement was intentionally made or not. If the evidence had all been in favor of respondent's contention, it might be said that such declaration was without prejudice, but on this point there was a sharp conflict in the testimony. The engineer, the two brakemen, and the firemen testified that the whistle was sounded and that the bell was rung up to the crossing, and had been ringing constantly for about two miles, back from the crossing. It is plain, therefore, that the question should have been left to the jury without any suggestion or statement as to the fact by the court.

Again, it is plain that the negligence of appellant, if any, which was the proximate cause of the injury, consisted in running the train at a high rate of speed without sounding any warning of its approach. But these acts of commission and omission were the acts of appellant's agents whom we have already mentioned. Appellant did not, of course, actually participate in running the train, but it is liable, if at all, upon the theory that it is responsible for the want of care on the part of its servants. The jury found, however, that said servants were not guilty of any negligence. It

would follow that appellant was acquitted of any dereliction in running the train.   In *Bradley* v. *Rosenthal,* 154 Cal.
420, 425, [129 Am. St. Rep. 171, 97 Pac. 875], it is held that
where recovery is sought, based upon the act or omission of
an agent, which the principal did not direct, and in which
he did not participate, an acquittal of the agent of negligence
is an acquittal of the principal, because the principal's
responsibility is cast upon him by law because of his relationship to his agent.

There is some contention that appellant did actually participate in the accident by reason of permitting the growth
of weeds so as to obstruct the view of the track.   But from
respondent's standpoint upon the assumption that he was
exercising ordinary care, it is quite clear from the record that
he would have been apprised of the danger if the bell had
been properly rung and the whistle sounded.   He can justify
his cause of action only upon the theory that these precautions were omitted.   If he had conceded that these usual
warnings were sounded, he would have had no cause with
which to go to the jury, as he showed no reason why he would
or could not have heard them in time to avoid the collision.
Indeed, he alleges in his complaint that he would have heard
the warning if it had been given.   The presence of the weeds
simply emphasized the importance and duty of great care on
the part of those in charge of the train, and we repeat that
since they were acquitted of negligence, the jury, to be consistent, should have gone a step further and exonerated the
appellant.

The judgment and order are reversed.

Chipman, P. J., and Hart, J., concurred.

[Civ. No. 1764. First Appellate District.—September 29, 1916.]

ROSENBAUM ESTATE COMPANY (a Corporation), Respondent, v. ROBERT DOLLAR COMPANY (a Corporation), Appellant.

LANDLORD AND TENANT—CONTINUANCE OF TENANCY UPON EXPIRATION OF LEASE—CONSTRUCTION OF ORAL AGREEMENT—TIME OF PAYMENT OF RENT.—An oral agreement made between the parties to a written lease just prior to its expiration providing that the lessee might remain a tenant of the premises "from month to month at the same rental" as stipulated in the lease, contemplates that the rental shall be continued to be paid in the same manner as provided in the lease.

ID.—REMOVAL FROM DEMISED PREMISES—UNFITNESS FOR HABITATION—NOTICE TO REPAIR.—A tenant is not warranted in removing from demised premises under the provisions of sections 1941 and 1942 of the Civil Code, where no definite notice to repair is given.

APPEAL from a judgment of the Superior Court of the City and County of San Francisco, and from an order denying a new trial. Marcel E. Cerf, and E. P. Shortall, Judges.

The facts are stated in the opinion of the court.

Nathan H. Frank, and Irving H. Frank, for Appellant.

Heller, Powers & Ehrman, for Respondent.

KERRIGAN, J.—This is an appeal from a judgment in favor of the plaintiff and from an order denying the defendant's motion for a new trial in an action to recover rent.

The defendant had been in possession of certain premises belonging to the plaintiff for five years, under a written lease which, among other things, provided that the rent should be three hundred dollars a month, to be paid in advance on the first day of every month. Just prior to the expiration of the written lease the parties orally agreed that the defendant might remain a tenant of the premises "from month to month at the same rental" provided for in the written lease. The defendant accordingly remained in possession of the premises for six months under this new arrangement, paying the rent in advance on the first day of each month up to December

31, 1913, and on January 5, 1914, upon two days' notice to the plaintiff that it would vacate the premises, it removed therefrom.

The first contention of the appellant is that the rent during the period that it occupied the premises from month to month was not payable in advance but at the end of the month; and that this action having been begun on the 19th of January, 1914, for the rent of the premises for that month, was prematurely brought, and that the finding of the court that the rent was payable in advance is without support in the evidence.

We are unable to agree with this view. From the record it appears that the defendant was to remain in possession of the premises from month to month and to pay the same monthly rental as was provided for in the written lease. We think the arrangement contemplated the payment of the rent in advance. An important incident of the rent is the time of its payment; and the phrase, "at the same rental," as employed by the parties in this instance, was undoubtedly, in view of their subsequent conduct, intended to cover both the amount of the rent and the time of its payment. Under section 1945 of the Civil Code, if the tenant had simply remained in possession of the premises after the expiration of the written lease, and nothing had been said between the parties, and the landlord had accepted rent, the law would have conclusively presumed that the hiring was on the same terms as the expired lease; and we think it can hardly be said that where there is an express agreement that the tenant shall remain in possession from month to month at the same rental, the parties contemplated any change in the time of payment of the rent from that which had previously prevailed. Had there been no previous hiring, the appellant's position would be very strong, that the time of payment would be as provided for in section 1947 of the Civil Code, viz., at the end of the period of the hiring; but the circumstances of the verbal renting in this case, and the course thereafter pursued, sufficiently attest the understanding of the parties that the tenant was to continue to pay the rent in advance. Where the meaning of a contract is doubtful, the acts of the parties done under it afford one of the most reliable means of arriving at the intention of the parties. (*Mayberry* v. *Alhambra etc. Water Co.*, 125 Cal. 446, [54 Pac. 530,

58 Pac. 68]; *Keith* v. *Electrical Engineering Co.*, 136 Cal. 178, 181, [68 Pac. 598].) In our opinion, therefore, having remained in possession of the premises after the thirty-first day of December, 1913, the tenant was liable for rent for the month of January, 1914, unless it was warranted in removing therefrom under the terms of sections 1941 and 1942 of the Civil Code, which provides that the lessor of a building intended for occupation by human beings must, in the absence of an agreement to the contrary, put and keep it in a condition for such occupation; and that if repairs to the premises are necessary, and are not made after reasonable notice, the lessee may vacate the premises and shall be discharged from further payment of rent—which brings us to the second contention of the appellant, viz., that the neglect of the landlord to make repairs of the character indicated justified the appellant in summarily vacating the premises, and relieved it from the obligation to pay any further rent.

The evidence shows that the basement of the premises (in which was conducted the bookkeeping department of the defendant's business, giving employment to ten persons) was very damp during the greater part of the last two years of the tenancy. It does not appear, however, that the defendant gave to the plaintiff any definite notice to repair. True, according to the evidence introduced by the defendant, the attention of the plaintiff was called to the condition of the basement, and on one occasion repairs were made; but apparently the defendant, realizing that the building stood on filled land over which the waters of San Francisco Bay formerly flowed, and which was subject to seepage, and expecting in the near future to move into a new building, concluded to tolerate the condition of the basement. This view is borne out by an examination of all the evidence in the case, and especially by the circumstance that the defendant, at the termination of the written lease, entered into the present oral lease after it had known for eighteen months the condition of the premises about which it now complains. It is true that one of the witnesses for the defendant testified that three days before the vacation of the premises the condition of the basement on account of accumulated seepage had become acute, and could no longer be tolerated; but there was no attempt to show that the condition could not be remedied, or that any notice was given to the plaintiff to repair the defect and make the premises habitable. The only notice then given by the defendant was a letter written on January 3d to the effect that on the fifth day of that month the defendant would vacate, which letter the plaintiff received on the day the defendant moved out.

Complaint is made that the defendant was not permitted to introduce evidence as to the effect upon the health of the defendant's employees of the condition of the basement; but the court permitted proof of such condition, and stated that it would itself draw its conclusion as to its effect upon the health of the occupants. We see no error in this ruling.

Judgment and order affirmed.

Lennon, P. J., and Richards, J., concurred.

[Civ. No. 1490. Third Appellate District.—September 30, 1916.]

DAVID E. COVEY, Respondent, v. NATIONAL UNION FIRE INSURANCE COMPANY OF PITTSBURGH (a Corporation), Appellant.

FIRE INSURANCE LAW—OCCUPANCY OF BUILDING—EVIDENCE.—A private dwelling is not vacant or unoccupied within the meaning of a clause in a policy of insurance providing that the company will not be liable for loss or damage from fire occurring while the building is vacant or unoccupied beyond the period of ten days, where, at the time of the fire, the occupant of the premises for the period of one year next preceding the fire was in the act of removing from the premises, but had not completed such removal nor surrendered possession to the landlord, although he had actually removed himself and his family from the premises.

ID.—DISAGREEMENT WITH AMOUNT OF LOSS CLAIMED—INSUFFICIENCY OF NOTICE.—Where a policy of fire insurance provides that the company shall be deemed to have assented to the amount of the loss claimed by the insured in his preliminary proof of loss, unless within twenty days after the receipt thereof the company shall notify the insured in writing of its disagreement with the amount claimed, a notice of disagreement given by letter mailed on the twentieth day after the receipt of such proof of loss to the insured residing in a different place, and received two days after the mailing, is not given in time.

ID.—DEMAND FOR APPRAISEMENT—INSUFFICIENCY OF NOTICE.—Where a policy of fire insurance provides that if for any reason not attributable to the insured or to the appraiser appointed by him, an appraisement is not had and completed within ninety days after the preliminary proof of loss is received by the company, the insured is not to be prejudiced by the failure to make an appraisement, and may prove the amount of his loss in an action brought without such appraisement, a demand for an appraisement given by letter mailed before the expiration of said ninety-day period but not received until after its expiration is not within time.

APPEAL from a judgment of the Superior Court of Shasta County.   James G. Estep, Judge.

The facts are stated in the opinion of the court.

Sterling Carr, for Appellant.

Braynard & Kimball, for Respondent.

CHIPMAN, P. J.—The cause was tried by the court without a jury and plaintiff had judgment for eight hundred dollars, as damages for loss by fire against which defendant had issued its policy of insurance. Defendant appeals from the judgment under the alternative method.

The following were stipulated as facts in the case: The policy took effect July 13, 1913, and was for one year; the insured building was destroyed by fire October 1, 1913, about the hour of 2 A. M.; notice of the fire was received by defendant October 21, 1913, and on November 19, 1913, proof of loss was filed with defendant; by letter dated December 8, 1913, defendant wrote plaintiff notifying him of its "total disagreement of the amount claimed" by plaintiff, and that defendant "admits a loss of $290.91 on the property described in above-mentioned policy"; this letter was mailed at San Francisco on December 9, 1913, and was received by plaintiff on December 12, 1913; on December 31, 1913, plaintiff brought an action on said policy for eight hundred dollars, in all respects the same as the present action; the first action was dismissed April 4, 1914, and the present action was commenced on April 8, 1914; on February 16, 1914, defendant mailed to plaintiff "a demand for arbitration" by letter dated at San Francisco on that day, and directed to plaintiff at "Millville,

Shasta County, California," notifying him that defendant "failed to agree as to the amount of loss caused by fire of October 1st, 1913, to the building described in . . . Policy No. 5116 . . . as admitted in our notice to you dated December 8, 1913"; and stated that "this company demands an appraisement of the loss . . . and names L. N. Bursen a competent and disinterested appraiser," and calls upon plaintiff to appoint an appraiser and so notify defendant; "this notice was received at Millville by Mr. Covey February 20, 1914. No appraiser was ever appointed by Mr. Covey and no notice was ever taken of this demand."

The policy in question was what is known as the standard California form. Certain of its provisions are more or less applicable to the case in hand and will be given in the order found in the policy, omitting intermediate provisions, as follows:

"$800.   On the two story frame dwelling and its adjoining and connecting additions . . . and all permanent fixtures therein and attached thereto, property of assured, while occupied only as a private dwelling, situate (as per diagram) on the north side of Main street in Whitmore, Shasta County, California. . . .

"This policy is made and accepted subject to the foregoing stipulations and conditions and those hereinafter stated, which are hereby specifically referred to, and made part of this policy, together with such provisions, agreements or conditions as may be endorsed thereon or added thereto, etc. . . .

"Unless otherwise provided by agreement endorsed hereon or added hereto, this company shall not be liable for loss or damage occurring . . . (f) while a building herein described whether intended for occupation by owner or tenant, is vacant or unoccupied beyond the period of ten consecutive days.

"This company shall be deemed to have assented to the amount of the loss claimed by the insured in his preliminary proof of loss, unless within twenty days after the receipt thereof . . . the company shall notify the insured in writing of its partial or total disagreement with the amount of loss claimed by him and shall notify him in writing of the amount of the loss, if any, the company admits on each of the different articles or properties set forth in the preliminary proof or amendments thereto.

"If the insured and this company fail to agree, in whole or in part, as to the amount of loss within ten days after such notification, this company shall forthwith demand in writing an appraisement of the loss or part of loss as to which there is a disagreement and shall name a competent and disinterested appraiser, and the insured within five days after the receipt of such demand and name, shall appoint a disinterested appraiser and notify the company thereof in writing, and the two so chosen shall, before commencing the appraisement, select a competent and disinterested umpire. . . .

"A loss hereunder shall be payable in thirty days after the amount thereof has been ascertained either by agreement or by appraisement, but if such ascertainment is not had or made within sixty days after the receipt by the company of the preliminary proof of loss, then the loss shall be payable in ninety days after such receipt."

1. It is contended by appellant that the findings to the effect that the insured building was totally destroyed by fire "while occupied as a private dwelling" is not supported by the evidence. The premises were under lease by plaintiff to one Moses C. Tribble, who testified that he had been living in the house with his family for "something over a year" as a "dwelling-house"; that on September 28, 1913, he commenced to move his family and household effects; that he did not "move all his household effects or personal property from the house before it was destroyed by fire"; that he did not sleep in the house after the night of September 27th. He was asked what remained at the place after he removed his wife and was there on the night of the 30th of September. "A. I know there was stuff there left in my care. The stuff didn't belong to me, left in my care. Had some household things, junk there that would naturally accumulate with farming, and so it was there, and what there was I could not say. I would not confine myself down. Q. Was there any furniture there? A. No, sir. . . . Q. And then all there was left there was some chickens running around the yard and this accumulation of things? A. Yes, sir." He testified that he was at the premises about 4 o'clock in the afternoon of September 30th. "I had some chickens there and I was trying to catch these chickens and get them and take them and move them up to the place where I was moving to. Q. Did you at any time notify Mr. Covey that you were about to move from the

premises? A. Well, I think, yes. I think I told Mr. Covey that I intended to move but as to the exact day that I told Mr. Covey, I could not say. Q. As to the time when you would move? A. Yes, because it was on account of the health of my wife. She was down with rheumatism and I didn't know really when I could move. Q. Yes. Who had the key to the dwelling at the time of the fire? A. The key was in my possession."

Plaintiff testified that he was at the premises on September 30th, the day before the fire. "Q. Was there anybody upon the premises at that time? A. Yes, sir; Mr. Tribble was there. . . . Q. Was he a tenant of the property? A. Yes, sir. Q. Your tenant? A. Yes, sir. Q. And what were the conditions there with reference to whether or not the property was occupied at the time that you were there? A. It was occupied, yes; the man had his stuff there, was hauling some of his stuff off, and catching his chickens and one thing and another. His poultry was there. . . . Q. Do you know whether any of his household goods were still upon the property? A. Yes, we went through the house and seen some boxes and household things there. Don't know what he had boxed up, something another. . . . Q. Had Mr. Tribble at that time turned over the key to the premises? A. No, sir." On cross-examination he testified that Tribble told him he was moving off. "Q. But Mr. Tribble told you, did he not, that he was going to move out that day? A. No, sir; didn't say he was going to move that day. Q. Never said so? A. He said he was moving out. Q. As a matter of fact, he did move out that day? A. I don't know. No, sir, I don't think so." He testified that Tribble had been in possession of the premises for "something over a year"; that he was paying $75 per year and had paid his rent in full; that he learned that Tribble was going to move away "somewhere near the 30th, about that day I think is the first I can remember." It was admitted that the "building was totally destroyed."

We think the situation at the time the fire occurred, to wit, 2 A. M., October 1st, briefly stated, was as follows: Plaintiff's tenant was not in actual physical possession of the premises, but had the right of possession and was still in the act of moving his effects therefrom; that he was the recognized tenant and retained possession of the keys to the building, and that he had not surrendered possession to his landlord; that his intention was to reside elsewhere, and to that end had removed his family and most of his household goods, but his intention was to return to get what remained of his personal property.

The court found: "It is not true that at the time of the destruction by fire of said premises, to wit, on the first day of October, 1913, said premises described therein and so insured by said policy of fire insurance were not occupied only as a private dwelling, and it is not true that said premises" at said time were "wholly or at all vacant and unoccupied, or vacant or unoccupied." The contention of appellant is that this finding is unsupported by the evidence. The cases are numerous in which the terms "occupied," "vacant," "occupied and vacant," "occupied or vacant," are defined, and are by no means harmonious. All agree that existing conditions when the policy is issued have much to do with arriving at the intention of the parties. A different construction is given to these terms in case of loss by fire where the premises were by the insurer known to have been occupied by a tenant when insured, as was the case here, from that given where the insured was the owner and the occupant. Also consideration is given to the character of the premises and the use to which they are being put. In the case of *Omaha Fire Ins. Co.* v. *Sinnott,* 54 Neb. 522, [74 N. W. 955], the policy provided that the insured house was and should continue to be occupied, and it was claimed that this warranty was broken by reason of the house becoming unoccupied and continuing to be vacant before the fire. Said the court: "The evidence most favorable to this contention was, in effect, that while the policy was in force, to wit, about July 11, 1894, the owner of the insured property notified her tenant to vacate it; that immediately thereafter the tenant began to remove his furniture to another house, to which he went with his family. When the fire took place, however, he had not yet removed his cook-stove and some other personal property. Under these conditions, we cannot say that the jury improperly concluded, from a consideration of the evidence, that the house was not occupied at the time of the fire." In cases of tenancy, it is reasonable to assume that the parties contemplated that some space of time might necessarily elapse after the tenant's family had moved from the premises before the tenant could remove all his household goods or possession could be given

to the landlord or to another tenant. In the case of *Norman*
v. *Missouri etc. Ins. Co.*, 74 Mo. App. 456, a distinction is
drawn between the terms "vacant" and "unoccupied." In
that case the tenant had, on the evening of October 5th, taken
his family to a neighborhood house and had removed a part
of his furniture, leaving a part in the building, but retaining
the keys and possession until he should have time the next
day to remove the remainder of his household effects. During the night of the 5th and 6th, at about 1 o'clock in the
morning, the building and contents were destroyed by fire.
The court held the company liable notwithstanding the provision of the policy that "as soon as buildings become vacant
the insurance shall be void," and that the building was not
vacant.

Weidert v. *State Ins. Co.*, 19 Or. 261, [20 Am. St. Rep.
809, 24 Pac. 242], was a case where one McNett, a tenant,
moved into the premises in April and lived there until June
15th or 20th, when he moved away, but a hired man or some
member of the family "was there at the house every day to
see if things were all right . . . , that they went down there
to see that nothing was destroyed." The fire occurred on
the night of July 9th. The court held that conceding to the
fullest extent all the facts that this evidence tends to prove,
no occupancy of the premises was shown after McNett moved
out. The provision of the policy involved was as follows:
". . . or if any change shall take place in the title, possession,
or occupancy" without immediate notice to the company and
its consent obtained, "this policy shall . . . be null and void."
Several cases are cited in the opinion supporting the view
there taken, but, as in the principal case, the occupant seems
to have moved away from the premises and was using the
former dwelling as a sort of place of storage for some portion
of his household effects.

In *Norman* v. *Missouri etc. Ins. Co.*, 74 Mo. App. 456, the
court said: "Removal was *in fieri*, not complete. If the tenant had, on the evening of October 5th, taken his family to a
neighbor's house, leaving his household goods packed and
ready for moving the next day, could it with any show of
reason be said that the building was vacant? Surely not.
Neither could it be said to be vacant if the tenant had taken
away a portion and left a portion for removal the following
day. The house would not in either event be vacant, though

unoccupied.'' The court seems to have held to the strict meaning of "vacant," a distinction which we do not think is unbending or may be arbitrarily applied.

The circumstances existing at the time must necessarily be factors in determining whether or not the building is unoccupied or vacant. These terms may, therefore, be treated as synonymous in their meaning. This was shown in *Herrman* v. *Adriatic Ins. Co.*, 85 N. Y. 162, [39 Am. Rep. 644], a case in which it was held as a general proposition that "for a dwelling-house to be in a state of occupation, there must be in it the presence of human beings as at their customary place of abode, not absolutely and uninterruptedly continuous, but that must be the place of usual return and habitual stoppage."

Cummins v. *Agricultural Ins. Co.*, 5 Hun (N. Y.), 554, was a case where the policy provided that if the dwelling-house became vacated by the removal of the owner or occupant, "the policy shall be null and void until the written consent of the company at the home office is obtained." It was held that the provision, "vacated by the removal of the owner or occupant," means an abandonment of the house as an actual place of residence, permanently or temporarily. A mere temporary absence of the family from the house for a night or a day would not be such a removal."

In *Bennett* v. *Agricultural Ins. Co.*, 50 Conn. 426, the insured building was occupied by a tenant, and the policy provided that if the dwelling should "cease to be occupied as such . . . the policy shall cease and be of no effect." The proof showed that the house was occupied about a month and a half in the spring of 1880, that it was thereafter again occupied, and that the tenant moved out about 6 o'clock in the evening on the day preceding the fire, and the house remained unoccupied until it was destroyed by fire, about 2 o'clock the next morning. "This," said the court, "was clearly a violation of this condition of the policy." That case is easily distinguishable from the present case. There was a complete abandonment of the dwelling, the tenant leaving nothing in the house and having surrendered possession completely and having no occasion to return for any purpose. It was not a temporary absence, but an actual giving up of the premises. The length of time the building was unoccupied was, therefore, an immaterial factor.

A tenant moved out of an insured dwelling on Tuesday and on Wednesday morning the owner took possession, and with his servants, began cleaning it and moving in goods, and were continuously so engaged during the working hours of each day until Friday evening; intending that the family should be fully domiciled there Saturday, but meanwhile lodging and taking their meals elsewhere. On Friday night the house was burned, and it was held that the policy had not become void on the ground of vacancy or nonoccupancy. (*Eddy* v. *Hawkeye Ins. Co.*, 70 Iowa, 472, [59 Am. Rep. 444, 30 N. W. 808].) "There is no case to which our attention has been called," said the court, "which holds that a house is vacant or unoccupied by the mere fact of the physical absence of the occupants for a day or night." The case of *Shackleton* v. *Sun Fire Office*, 55 Mich. 288, [54 Am. Rep. 379, 21 N. W. 343], is cited in the opinion. In that case the tenant vacated the house June 19th, and the owner took possession, put her furniture in the building, but, for what seemed to be good reasons, she did not take her meals nor lodge in the house, and it was destroyed by fire on July 4th. It was held that the house was not vacant or unoccupied within the meaning of the contract. Said the court: "Nothing apparently was wanting to complete personal possession, except that she lodged and took her meals at her father's, a few rods off. Those facts were not conclusive against her occupancy."

We can see no reason why the rule should be different where a tenant is moving into a house than where he is moving out. In both cases he is in possession of the house and has some or all of his goods there, but for sufficient reasons he finds it necessary temporarily to lodge elsewhere while moving in or moving out, as the case may be. No fixed and unbending rule seems to be deducible from the adjudicated cases. The courts take into consideration all the circumstances and attribute such intention to the parties in entering into the contract as would appear consonant with reason. As was said in the Michigan case last above referred to, the facts in this case "are not conclusive against the tenant's occupancy."

2. The court found that defendant did not serve its notice of disagreement or demand for appraisement within the time required by the policy, and that plaintiff complied with and

performed all of its terms on his part. This finding is challenged. The policy provided that the company "shall be deemed to have waived assent to the amount of the loss claimed by the insured in his preliminary proof of loss, unless within twenty days after the receipt thereof . . . the company shall notify the insured in writing," etc. (see provision *supra*). Defendant, at San Francisco, mailed a letter to plaintiff, residing at Whitmore, Shasta County, on the twentieth day after the receipt of proof of loss, which letter was received by plaintiff two days later. Defendant contends that "the mailing of the notice of disagreement within the twenty days is sufficient under the terms of the policy even though it is not received until after the expiration of the twenty days." Respondent contends that where, as here, the loss was total and so conceded, there was no occasion for arbitration, and appellant was not prejudiced by the ruling of the court. However this may be, we think defendant failed to give the notice contemplated by the policy. In *Winchester v. North British etc. Co.*, 160 Cal. 1, [35 L. R. A. (N. S.) 404, 116 Pac. 63], the defendant made demand for the appointment of appraisers, but the notice did not reach plaintiff's attorney in fact until after the expiration of sixty days. It was held that "the failure to serve such notice upon the insured within sixty days after service of proof of loss amounted to a waiver." The policy read: "The sum for which the company is liable pursuant to the policy shall be payable sixty days *after due notice*," etc. The question there was as to the time when the action could be brought. The language of the present policy is, "unless within twenty days after the receipt" of proofs of loss, the company *"shall notify* the insured," etc.

It appears from the transcript in the Winchester case that due proof of loss was made on May 14, 1908, and on July 8th, within sixty days after proof of loss, defendant duly posted a letter addressed to plaintiff's attorney in fact, giving notice of its disagreement, etc. The court found that said demand "was received by plaintiff's attorney in fact on the eighteenth day of July, 1908, and more than sixty days after the service of said proof of loss." In the present case the notice was received two days too late; in the Winchester case four days too late. We think the Winchester case decisive of the point.

3. Defendant was equally in default in sending its demand for an appraisement. Proof of loss was filed with defendant on November 19, 1913. On February 16, 1914, defendant mailed a letter at San Francisco, directed to plaintiff at Millville, Shasta County, notifying plaintiff that it demanded an appraisement of the loss. This notice was received by plaintiff on February 20, 1914, which the court found "was more than ninety days after the said preliminary proof of loss was received by said defendant." The policy provided: "If for any reason not attributable to the insured or to the appraiser appointed by him, an appraisement is not had and completed within ninety days after said preliminary proof of loss is received by this company, the insured is not to be prejudiced by the failure to make an appraisement and may prove the amount of his loss in an action brought without such appraisement." Not having received notice in time, plaintiff was not compelled to submit to an appraisement of the loss, and the case stands as though no appraisement was had. Defendant recognized the policy as still in force after the action was first commenced by demanding an appraisement, and we do not think plaintiff is now estopped from claiming that the demand for arbitration was not made in time.

Defendant admitted a liability of $290.91 in its letter of December 8, 1913, and also in its answer. The principal question of fact was as to the actual loss, defendant claiming that it did not exceed the above amount. Other questions are matters largely of technical law. The loss was total, and there was evidence sufficient to support the finding that "the actual cash of plaintiff's interest in said dwelling-house was at the time of said loss on the first day of October, 1913, more than the said sum of eight hundred dollars."

The judgment is affirmed.

Hart, J., and Burnett, J., concurred.

A petition to have the cause heard in the supreme court, after judgment in the district court of appeal, was denied by the supreme court on November 27, 1916.

[Civ. No. 1935. First Appellate District.—October 2, 1916.]

MAUDE E. HANDY, Respondent, v. ROZELVIN B. HANDY, Appellant.

PRACTICE—TIME OF TRIAL—INSUFFICIENT NOTICE—PRESENCE IN COURT —REFUSAL OF CONTINUANCE—DISCRETION NOT ABUSED.—It is not an abuse of discretion to refuse a motion made by the defendant for a continuance of the trial of an action, based upon the fact that he had not received a full five days' notice of the time fixed for the trial, where he had filed his answer, was present in court when the case was called for trial, and filed no affidavit setting forth the reasons why he was unable to proceed, or why his witnesses were not present, or who they were, or what they would testify to if present.

ID.—NOTICE OF TRIAL—CONSTRUCTION OF SECTION 594, CODE OF CIVIL PROCEDURE.—The provision of section 594 of the Code of Civil Procedure, requiring as a condition to proceeding with a trial proof that the adverse party has had five days' notice of such trial, has reference only to proceedings taken against a party in his absence, and has no application to cases in which both parties are represented and present when the case is called for trial.

APPEAL from a judgment of the Superior Court of the City and County of San Francisco. Frank H. Dunne, Judge.

The facts are stated in the opinion of the court.

W. C. Cavitt, for Appellant.

F. A. Berlin, for Respondent.

KERRIGAN, J.—This is an appeal from a judgment in an action to foreclose a mortgage on real property given to secure a promissory note for four hundred dollars, the attack upon the judgment being based upon the fact that the trial court denied a motion of the appealing defendant to postpone the trial of the action.

At the time set for the trial of the action the appellant, by his counsel, appeared in court, and moved for a continuance of the trial, stating that he had not received the five days' notice prescribed by law; that he had not had time to find the appellant nor subpoena a witness who lived out of the city and county of San Francisco, where the action was pending. No showing for a continuance was made under the provisions of section 595 of the Code of Civil Procedure; and it is clear that the motion was based entirely upon the fact that the appellant had not received a full five days' notice of the time fixed for the trial.

Section 594 of the Code of Civil Procedure provides: "Either party may bring an issue to trial or to a hearing, and, in the absence of the adverse party . . . may proceed with his case, and take a dismissal of the action, or a verdict or judgment, as the case may require; provided, however, if the issue to be tried is an issue of fact, proof must first be made to the satisfaction of the court that the adverse party has had five days' notice of such trial."

The supreme court, in the case of *Sheldon* v. *Landwehr*, 159 Cal. 778, [116 Pac. 44], construing that section, held that it had reference only to proceedings taken against a party in his absence, and that it had no application to a case like the one here, in which both parties were represented and present when the case was called for trial. "When," says the court, "the party has actually known that the case was set for a certain time, and appears at that time, he is not entitled to a continuance in the absence of a claim showing that he has not had such knowledge long enough to enable him to properly appear. It is in each case a question for the discretion of the trial court."

In the present case the appellant had filed his answer; he was present in court when the case was called for trial, and he made no legal showing to the effect that the notice which he had received was insufficient to enable him to prepare for trial; in other words, he filed no affidavit setting forth the reasons why he was unable to proceed to trial, or why his witnesses were not present in court, or who they were, or what they would testify to if present. Moreover, with one possible exception the answer of the defendant raised no substantial issue and was frivolous. All the circumstances of the case cast a suspicion on the good faith of the application and induce the belief that it was intended only for delay. We think, therefore, that the defendant was not entitled to the postponement demanded.

The judgment is affirmed.

Lennon, P. J., and Richards, J., concurred.

A petition to have the cause heard in the supreme court, after judgment in the district court of appeal, was denied by the supreme court on December 1, 1916.

[Civ. No. 2008. Second Appellate District.—October 2, 1916.]

FRANK MARTZ et al., Respondents, v. PACIFIC ELECTRIC RAILWAY COMPANY (a Corporation), Appellant.

NEGLIGENCE—ELECTRIC RAILWAY CROSSING—CAUTION IN APPROACHING. The rule requiring a person upon approaching a railroad track with intent to cross it to exercise his faculties in order to ascertain whether a train is approaching, is applicable to electric railroads operated under conditions similar to the operation of steam railroads.

ID.—DEATH OF AUTOMOBILE DRIVER—COLLISION WITH ELECTRIC RAILWAY-CAR AT CROSSING—ABILITY TO SEE APPROACHING CAR—FINDING.—In an action for damages for the death of an automobile driver from a collision with a rapidly moving electric railway-car at a crossing, where the question presented to the jury was whether or not a person traveling, as was the deceased, and using reasonable care in observing, would have seen the approaching car, notwithstanding the obstruction of trees and brush along the highway, and notwithstanding the further obstruction made by poles erected at intervals between the railway tracks and carrying the power wires, the conclusion of the jury must be accepted on appeal.

ID.—APPROACHING RAILROAD CROSSING—FAILURE TO USE FACULTIES—INFERENCE FROM PHYSICAL FACTS—CONTRIBUTORY NEGLIGENCE.—Where the physical facts shown by undisputed evidence raise the inevitable inference that the person approaching a railroad crossing did not look or listen, or that having looked and listened, he endeavored to cross immediately in front of a rapidly approaching train, which was plainly open to view, he was, as matter of law, guilty of contributory negligence.

APPEAL from a judgment of the Superior Court of Los Angeles County, and from an order denying a new trial. Wm. D. Dehy, Judge presiding.

The facts are stated in the opinion of the court.

Joseph Scott, A. G. Ritter, and J. B. Joujon-Roche, for Respondents.

CONREY, P. J.—This action was brought by the widow and three minor children of Frank Martz to recover damages on account of the death of Martz, alleged to have been caused by the negligence of the defendant company. The defendant denied the charges of negligence, and set up the defense of contributory negligence on the part of the deceased. The defendant appeals from the judgment and from the order denying its motion for a new trial.

At about 2 o'clock in the afternoon of the first day of February, 1912, Frank Martz was traveling in his automobile in a southerly direction on Santa Anita Avenue in the county of Los Angeles, and was approaching a point where that highway is crossed by the tracks of defendant company. At the crossing a collision took place between the automobile and a car of the defendant. Immediately east and west of Santa Anita Avenue the railroad occupies a private right of way. It is a double-track railroad which runs east and west across the avenue, but curves toward the south at a point beginning about one hundred yards west of the avenue. The curve is such as that at a distance of one thousand feet west of Santa Anita Avenue cars beyond that point are not visible from the avenue. Appellant claims that the evidence is such as to compel the conclusion that no negligence was established on the part of the defendant, and also very earnestly contends that contributory negligence on the part of the deceased was conclusively established. For these reasons it is claimed that the court erred in refusing to instruct the jury to render a verdict for the defendant.

At the same time when Mr. Martz coming from the north was approaching the railroad, an express car of the defendant was traveling in an easterly direction on defendant's southerly track. Santa Anita Avenue is constructed in two roadways separated by a row of eucalyptus trees down the center. On the westerly side of the west roadway of Santa Anita Avenue, and north of the defendant's right of way, there was at the time of the collision a small white building about thirty-two and one-half feet long, located about forty-seven feet west of the westerly line of the highway, and about forty-three feet north of the south track. Along the westerly side of the west roadway was a row of tall eucalyptus trees, about ten feet apart. A sign-board, marked "Railroad Crossing—Look Out for the Cars," had been placed at the intersection of the right of way with the westerly roadway, and the railroad tracks were raised slightly above the level of the roadway upon which Martz was traveling, thereby rendering the tracks plainly visible to one occupying his position. No persons but the motorman and conductor of defendant's car (so far as the evidence shows) saw the deceased at the time of the accident, and they saw him only for an instant immediately preceding the collision. There is no testimony from any observer as to whether the deceased looked or listened for the approach of the car. The motorman testified that his car was traveling eighteen or twenty miles an hour, and that the deceased was traveling "as fast as I was going, maybe a little faster." In addition to the foregoing undisputed facts, appellant claims that the evidence shows that the branches of the eucalyptus trees were high above the traveler's head, and did not materially obstruct the traveler's view in looking to the west; and that the tracks with poles and wires were plainly visible to the traveler; and that it is also certain that Martz "made no effort to avoid the approaching train, for the marks of his automobile on the ground showed that he was headed due south and had not swerved in either direction." Appellant admits that there was conflict in the evidence as to whether warning was given by blowing of the whistle on defendant's car, but claims that the negative testimony of plaintiff's witnesses that they heard no whistle blown is not entitled to credit as against the positive testimony of other witnesses who said that they heard the whistle. Appellant further admits that the evidence as to the rate of speed at which defendant's car was traveling varies from eighteen to thirty miles an hour. There is evidence tending to show that the branches of the eucalyptus trees were above the traveler's head, but there is also testimony that there was an undergrowth extending upward from the ground, and that the limbs of the trees came down and met this undergrowth; that there were sprouts growing up from the trees which were as much as five feet long; that these were suckers from the roots of the trees and grew out like a bush. Under these conditions it is likely that there would be spaces through which one traveling along the road, as the deceased was traveling before he came to the small building, possibly could have seen an approaching car, and that a large part of the space so occupied by the trees was so obstructed that through the space thus occupied it was impossible to have seen the cars. The question presented to the jury was whether or not a person so traveling and using reasonable care in observing would have seen the approaching car, notwithstanding the obstructions of trees and brush along the highway, and notwithstanding the further obstruction made by poles erected at intervals between the railroad tracks and carrying the power wires. We are not warranted in saying that as a matter of law, under these conditions, the deceased would have seen the car if he had made a reasonable effort to use his powers of observation before he reached the point where the building entirely obstructed his view in that direction. Therefore, as to this fact, we must accept the conclusion of the jury. And we are likewise bound by their implied finding that no warning whistle was sounded by the motorman.

Assuming, then, that Martz was not negligent in failing to observe the approaching car while he was farther north than the above-mentioned building, or while he was traveling along the road opposite that building, we must now consider the situation as it existed between the point in the avenue where the building no longer obstructed his view to the west and the south track of the railroad where the collision occurred. The testimony of the witnesses is aided by certain photographs shown in the record. As above stated, the building was forty-three feet north of the south railroad track, and about forty-seven feet west of the westerly line of the highway, which would be probably about sixty feet west of that part of the highway in which the automobile was traveling. Under these conditions the railroad tracks west of Santa Anita Avenue along which the electric car would approach the crossing would be plainly visible from the automobile during at least the last sixty feet of its approach to the south track. And, as shown by the photographs, the curve of the railroad is such that the approaching

railroad car would have been plainly visible if it was anywhere within one thousand feet of the crossing.

The evidence shows that Mr. Martz was fifty-two years
old, in good health, and had been using this automobile
nearly a year. On the day of the accident he was driving
alone. It appears that he had never driven over this railroad crossing until that day. But as above shown, the railroad track at the point of crossing, and a sign-board of
warning, were in plain view in front of the deceased as he
came down the road. This being so, even if (as we must
assume to be the fact) he had not seen any approaching car
before coming opposite the white building, it was his duty to
approach the crossing with reasonable care to have his automobile under control. If we assume that he did this, then
when he came within sixty feet of the southerly railroad
track he was in a safe situation at all events. If there was
no approaching car within a distance of one thousand feet,
he would have ample time to cross. For at the rate of thirty
miles per hour the railroad car would require at least twenty-
three seconds to reach the point of intersection; whereas the
automobile, even at a five-mile rate, would be across in eight
seconds. On the other hand, if the approaching railway car
was anywhere within the distance of one thousand feet, Mr.
Martz must have seen it if he made the most ordinary use
of his faculties, and this at least he was bound to do.
(*Griffin* v. *San Pedro etc. R. R. Co.*, 170 Cal. 772, [L. R. A.
1916A, 842, 151 Pac. 282].) The rule is applicable to electric railroads operated under conditions similar to the operation of steam railroads. (*Loftus* v. *Pacific Elec. Ry. Co.*, 166
Cal. 464, [137 Pac. 34].) And if the car thus observed by
the deceased was approaching at such speed, and was then
within such distance as to cause reasonable apprehension of
danger, it was negligence on the part of the automobile driver
to attempt such a crossing. Such attempt would be the
voluntary assumption of a risk, and for injuries resulting
therefrom, and which the defendant then had no further
opportunity to avoid, the law does not intend to provide
compensation.

The only other alternative state of facts which seems possible under the evidence is that Mr. Martz came down the
avenue and into the zone of danger at a rate of speed which
was reckless under the circumstances, and thus heedlessly

placed himself where the concurrent negligence of the defendant caused his death. In this case also there is no right of recovery. Where the physical facts shown by undisputed evidence raise the inevitable inference that the person approaching a railroad crossing did not look or listen, or that having looked and listened, he endeavored to cross immediately in front of a rapidly approaching train that is plainly open to his view, he is as matter of law guilty of contributory negligence.

It seems clear that there is no situation shown upon any possible state of facts consistent with the evidence which can authorize a verdict such as was rendered in this case. The defendant was clearly entitled to a verdict in its favor. Having reached this conclusion, we deem it unnecessary to discuss alleged errors in the instructions given to the jury. With respect to the objections urged against those instructions, we express no opinion.

The judgment and order are reversed.

James, J., and Shaw, J., concurred.

A petition to have the cause heard in the supreme court, after judgment in the district court of appeal, was denied by the supreme court on December 1, 1916.

[Civ. Nos. 1993 and 2017. Second Appellate District.—October 2, 1916.]

MAY CATLIN, Administratrix of the Estate of John Catlin, Deceased, Respondent, v. UNION OIL COMPANY OF CALIFORNIA (a Corporation), Appellant; WILLIAM M. RILEY et al., Respondents.

NEGLIGENCE—EXPLOSION OF GASOLINE—SALE FOR KEROSENE—PROXIMATE CAUSE.—In an action for damages against an oil company and a grocer for the death of a patron of the latter from an explosion of gasoline sold to the deceased by the grocer for kerosene, where it is shown that the oil company in filling an order of the grocer for kerosene had mistakenly made a delivery of kerosene and gasoline mixed, and that the grocer upon discovering such mistake, notified the company thereof and the latter agreed to

take the oil back, but before the oil was taken back the grocer
relying upon his experience in dealing in such oils, and upon a
personal test made by him, sold the oil which caused the explosion,
the direct and proximate cause of the damage was the intervening
act of the grocer, and not the negligence of the oil company.

ID.—PROXIMATE CAUSE—WHAT CONSTITUTES.—Proximate cause is that
cause arising out of a breach of duty which in a natural and continuous sequence produces the damage complained of.

ID.—INTERVENING ACT OF NEGLIGENCE—LIABILITY OF ORIGINAL WRONG-
DOER.—If the negligent acts of two or more persons, all being
culpable and responsible in law for their acts, do not concur in
point of time, and the negligence of one only exposes the injured
person to risk of injury in case the other should also be negligent,
the liability of the person first in fault will depend upon the question whether the negligent act of the other was one which a man
of ordinary experience and sagacity, acquainted with all the circumstances, could reasonably anticipate or not. If such a person
could have anticipated that the intervening act of negligence
might, in natural and ordinary sequence, follow the original act
of negligence, the person first in fault is not released from liability
by reason of the intervening negligence of the other. If it could
not have been thus anticipated, then the intervening negligent person alone is responsible.

ID.—NEGLIGENCE—WHEN QUESTION OF LAW.—While it is true that
questions involving alleged negligent action which turn upon the
proposition as to what should be expected of an ordinarily reasonable man under the circumstances, present mixed questions of law
and fact which generally should go to the jury under proper instructions as to the law, leaving the deductions of fact to be made
by the verdict, yet, on the other hand, where the facts are undisputed and clearly settled, and the dictates of common prudence
point to only one reasonable conclusion, the question is then one of
law for the court, and a verdict may be either directed or a nonsuit granted.

ID.—EVIDENCE—CHARACTER OF FLUID—STATEMENTS OF DECEASED—IN-
COMPETENT TESTIMONY.—Statements made by the deceased immediately after the explosion to the effect that the fluid used was
gasoline are inadmissible, being self-serving and expressive of the
opinion and conclusion of the witness.

ID.—MANNER OF FILLING LAMP—CONTRIBUTORY NEGLIGENCE—QUESTION
FOR JURY.—The question whether the deceased was guilty of contributory negligence at the time of the explosion by reason of the
fact that he was engaged in filling an oil-lamp with the fluid,
while he had a lighted miner's lamp on his cap, is one for the jury,
where there was expert testimony that a lamp could be thus filled
with reasonable safety, and without great danger, provided the
fluid was coal-oil of ordinary quality.

APPEAL from a judgment of the Superior Court of Los Angeles County, and from an order denying a new trial. Willis I. Morrison, Judge.

The facts are stated in the opinion of the court.

Lewis W. Andrews, A. V. Andrews, Thos. O. Toland, Andrews, Toland and Andrews, W. H. Bowers and Cedric E. Johnson, for Appellant.

R. T. Lightfoot, Walter Whitworth, J. W. Whitworth, and E. B. Drake, for Plaintiff and Respondent.

A. G. Alm, for Respondents, William M. Riley et al.

JAMES, J.—This action was brought to recover damages for the death of John Catlin, alleged to have been caused by the negligent acts of the defendant Union Oil Company and William M. Riley. Mary E. Riley, the wife of William M. Riley, was also sued, but the action was dismissed as to her in the course of the trial. The jury returned a verdict in favor of the plaintiff and against the defendant Union Oil Company for the sum of seventeen thousand dollars, on which judgment was entered. By the verdict it was found that William M. Riley was not liable for damages in any sum. The defendant Union Oil Company appealed from the judgment, and from an order denying its motion for a new trial.

In November, 1912, William M. Riley was conducting a grocery store at the town of Sawtelle in Los Angeles County. Among other classes of merchandise he dealt regularly in fuel oils, including gasoline and kerosene. The oils he stored in a little outbuilding some thirty feet or more away from the store proper. In this outbuilding he had a tank for gasoline and one for coal-oil or kerosene. On about the 15th of November, that being Friday of the week, he gave an order to the Union Oil Company to deliver to him sixty gallons of kerosene. The tank-wagon belonging to the oil company made delivery. The kerosene tank had a capacity of sixty gallons. The tank was not empty, but contained twenty gallons of the fluid before the quantity delivered that day was added to it. Hence, the driver of the oil-wagon was only able to put into the tank forty gallons of the sixty gallons ordered. There were four or five empty five-gallon cans inside of the oil-room, and into these cans was poured the remaining twenty gallons, which completely filled both the tank and the other receptacles mentioned. Almost immediately after the tank-wagon had left his place, Riley, according to his testimony, took one of the five-gallon cans which had been filled as described, and delivered it to a customer; for another customer, either that evening or the following morning, he drew a gallon from the tank which had been filled; and for a third customer he made delivery of another gallon, evidently from the same supply. Complaint was very soon made by the patron who had received the five-gallon can that there was something the matter with the oil, and complaint also came from one of the persons who had received a single gallon. On Saturday morning, being the next day after the delivery of the oil, Riley got back all of the oil about which complaint had been made that he was able to secure, including the five-gallon can which he had delivered to the first customer. He testified that one of the single gallons of oil returned he poured back into the large tank; that he then had the four five-gallon cans of oil which had been filled by the tank-wagon, and of the contents of these he proceeded to make tests. Riley had for a number of years, both in the east and in California, had experience in the handling of both kerosene and gasoline as a dealer. He testified that in making his tests he dipped splinters of wood into the cans, noted the smell of the fluid, and also the rapidity with which it evaporated from the sticks; that by this means, and also by noting the odor of the fluid, he made up his mind that two of the five-gallon cans contained gasoline and two contained coal-oil; that he made a further test of the fluid in the two cans which he had concluded was gasoline by taking a small quantity thereof and placing it upon a stove where, when it was subjected to heat, it flashed up quickly. He made no further tests of the contents of the other two cans, being satisfied that these cans contained coal-oil. On cross-examination he testified that had the oil been mixed he did not know whether he would have been able to determine from the tests he made if it was gasoline or kerosene. He testified further that he took the two cans which he had determined contained gasoline, labeled them with a label showing their true contents, and placed

them up on the large gasoline tank. Then, as he testified,
he delivered one of the five-gallon cans believed to be coal-oil
to the patron by whom the five gallons of gasoline had been
returned; that there then remained on the floor of the oil-
room one five-gallon can of coal-oil which had been a part
of the delivery received on the preceding day; that the same
evening (Saturday) at about dark or dusk, one of the children of Catlin came and wanted kerosene oil; that he (Riley)
informed the child that because of insurance regulations he
could not handle illuminating oil after dark, and that as
the child insisted that the family had no oil, he told her
if she would bring a small can the following morning (Sunday), as he made no deliveries on that day, he would give
her sufficient to last until Monday, when he would deliver
the remainder of the five gallons; that on Sunday morning
one of the Catlin children returned with a gallon can which
he (Riley) filled from the five-gallon can sitting on the floor
of the oil-room, and that the next morning he delivered the
four gallons remaining in the can at the Catlin home, where
he poured the oil into an empty can customarily used for
that purpose. John Catlin, the deceased, at the time of his
death was forty-four years of age, in good health, weighing
about one hundred and eighty-five pounds. As his wife testified, he was a "strong" man, and had had no illness or
needed the attention of a physician. He had been married to
the plaintiff, his wife, for twenty-three years, and there sur-
vived him besides the widow, four children aged respectively:
Bessie, nineteen; Pauline, seventeen; Howard, thirteen;
Fred, eleven. He had been a miner, but at the date of the
accident his regular employment was that of a carpenter's
helper, at which work he earned $2.75 per day. His life
expectancy was 25 years. On Tuesday evening following
the receipt of the oil delivered by Riley, being at work laying
some cement in his cellar, Catlin had occasion to make use of an
oil-lamp. He was already carrying in a miner's cap on his
head a small lamp such as miners customarily use. This
small lamp was lighted and remained so until after the explosion which produced the injuries from which Catlin later
died. Catlin went to the rear of the house in or about a
screen porch in order to fill the larger oil-lamp which he
intended to use, and apparently started to pour what he
assumed was coal-oil or kerosene from the large can into the

lamp, when the explosion occurred. Mrs. Catlin, as she testified, heard the noise of an explosion, and almost immediately her husband ran to the front of the house, covered with fire, and rolled in the grass, calling for help. She tried to smother the flames with bedclothing and, with the help of a neighbor, the fire was finally extinguished. One witness, a Mr. Tucker, who assisted in extinguishing the fire burning on the person of Catlin, testified that when he reached Catlin the latter said: "Oh, Mr. Tucker, put this fire out on me; I am burning up. Do something for me quick—I was filling the lamp and it exploded, and before I could throw the can it exploded also—put the fire out; I am burning up—I have handled gasoline and coal-oil all my life; I am an old miner. Why should anything of this kind happen to me? I am sure that it was gasoline." On cross-examination this witness added that while on the way to the hospital the injured man had said that he had filled lamps before "when they were lit," and had never had one act that way. Catlin in his injured condition was removed immediately to a hospital, where he died two days later. It appeared without dispute that the driver of the appellant company, instead of delivering sixty gallons of coal-oil as directed, delivered in part coal-oil and in part gasoline, and that the mistake came about in this way: The tank-wagon from which deliveries were made, was divided into three compartments, one in front, one in the middle, and one at the rear. These compartments were entirely separated one from the other, and connected with each at the rear of the wagon was a stopcock or faucet; that customarily gasoline was carried in the forward tank and kerosene in the two rear ones; that on the day when the delivery to Riley was made the driver started to load his wagon and had commenced to fill the forward tank with gasoline; that desiring to attend to his team, he asked one of the other employees, an agent of appellant, to complete the filling of the forward tank, and to put kerosene into the two rear ones. These latter he knew to be empty at the time; that this employee after completing the filling of the forward tank with gasoline, filled the middle one with kerosene as directed, but through some error of understanding or judgment, put gasoline into the rear compartment. The driver testified that in delivering oil in quantities as large as that ordered by Riley, he customarily used two five-gallon measures having handles on them, and drew from two faucets at the same time; that he followed this custom in making the delivery to Riley, and drew from the faucets connecting with the two rear compartments, filling his two measures thus at the same time, emptying them and refilling them until the desired quantity had been secured. Riley, the grocer, testified that he was familiar with this practice, and noted that the driver followed it on the Friday when he made delivery of the oil. The driver explained that in consequence of this practice of drawing two measures at a time, and as each measure when filled would completely fill a five-gallon can, the four cans filled with the last twenty gallons of oil desired by Riley, should have contained unmixed fluid; that is, two should have contained gasoline and two kerosene. This conclusion would be in accordance with the tests made by Riley. There is some discrepancy between the testimony of Riley and the testimony of the driver of the wagon, wherein the driver stated that when he returned on Monday, to take away the oil, he found one five-gallon can full of coal-oil still standing near the door of the oil-house. Riley had testified that he had placed two of the five-gallon cans on top of the gasoline tank and marked them with the word "gasoline," and that of the two remaining which he had determined to be kerosene, he had delivered one to the first patron who had returned the gasoline, and had taken the other to fill the Catlin order. Riley testified that there was in another portion of the oil-room at that time, perhaps five gallons of coal-oil which he had received at a prior date, and which was not included in the Friday delivery of mixed oil. Fred Catlin, the eleven-year old son of the deceased, who had obtained the gallon of oil from Riley on Sunday morning, testified that when he called for the oil Riley first went to the fifty-gallon tank and said: "I think this is mixed"; that Riley then went to a five-gallon can and drew therefrom the gallon of oil and handed it to him, saying: "I guess this is coal-oil." The lamps used by the Catlins were ordinary glass lamps with no aperture separate from the wick-holder through which oil might be introduced into the bowl. To complete the narrative of facts it is necessary to refer to an occurrence which took place on Saturday, before any of the oil tested by Riley was resold. When the first oil put out by Riley on Friday and

Saturday morning had come back to him with the report that
something was wrong with it, he made his tests of the oil in
the five-gallon cans as has been hereinbefore described. He
then phoned to the branch office of the Union Oil Company
through which he did business, and after getting the ear of
the driver who had delivered to him the oil, told this driver
that a mistake had been made, that his oil had been mixed
on him. Riley testified that he told the driver to come and
take back the oil Sunday morning. He testified: "They told
me they would come on Sunday, but did not come until Monday." The driver of the wagon admitted receiving notification from Riley that the oil was mixed; that at the time of the
conversation over the telephone he had stated to Riley that
it was impossible that a mistake had been made, but that
if such was the case the wagon had been loaded up "wrong"
on him. He testified that he believed he said he would
take the oil back; further, that he was not convinced that
a mistake had been made until he went for the oil on Monday
morning. He denied having promised to return on Sunday
morning, and said that he could not have done so because
Riley did not keep his store open on Sunday. There was testimony from which the jury was authorized to draw the
conclusion that had the oil delivered to Catlin been kerosene,
and not gasoline, the ignition of the oil and vapor and consequent explosion would not have occurred. In short, there
was sufficient proof, in a circumstantial way at least, upon
which the jury was authorized to make the deduction which
is implied from the verdict, to wit, that the oil delivered to
Catlin was much more inflammable and explosive in its
character than kerosene, and that it was in fact gasoline.

Appellant first urges that there is a defect in the foundation of plaintiff's case which requires that the judgment be
reversed. This contention is referred to the evidence which,
it is urged, fails to show that the negligence of appellant
was the proximate cause which produced the death of plaintiff's intestate. No contention is made but that the mistake
of appellant's agents in delivering both gasoline and kerosene in the place of kerosene to Riley, the grocer, was negligence for which the corporation might, in some circumstances, be held responsible in damages. It is, however,
insisted that whatever negligence was first committed by
appellant in delivering mixed oil, this negligence ceased to

be of active effect in the line of causation when Riley, the
grocer, discovered that he had received gasoline and kerosene mixed. It is argued that when Riley notified the driver
that the oil was mixed, and it was understood that the driver
would return and take it back, all responsibility of appellant ended; that the subsequent acts of Riley in selling the
oil were the acts of an independent, responsible person which
interrupted the chain of causation and furnished in law the
last efficient cause of the damage. Proximate cause has
been defined many times in the decisions, and by text-writers,
to be that cause arising out of a breach of duty which, in
a natural and continuous sequence, produces the damage
complained of. The original negligent act may be separated
from the untoward event by great periods of time and many
other connecting acts, negligent or non-negligent. The latter may be acts of third persons not in any representative
sense the agents of the first wrongdoer. There is a qualification, however, to the last-named condition, and that is this:
When there is no privity of contract between the first
wrongdoer and the person suffering damage, and the negligent act falls within the class concerning things which carry
no menace or threat of probable damage to third persons,
the liability of the first party will extend no further than
to his immediate co-contractor. This rule applies generally
to cases where breach of contract has been committed in the
furnishing of merchandise, or building of tools, machines,
etc., which in their very nature are not calculated to produce damage when of imperfect construction or composition.
The mislabeling of poisons, inflammable oils, explosives, and
like dangerous substances is so fraught with possibilities of
danger to purchasers as to charge the first vender with a
responsibility for damages, even though the mismarked substance has passed through the hands of a number of intermediate venders. (*Elkins Bly & Co.* v. *McKean*, 79 Pa. St.
493; *Riggs* v. *Standard Oil Co.*, 130 Fed. 199; *Wellington*
v. *Downer Kerosene Oil Co.*, 104 Mass. 64; *Thomas* v. *Winchester*, 6 N. Y. 397, [57 Am. Dec. 455].) The interrupting
event which will disturb the train of causation may be the
negligent act of a responsible person. "If the negligent
acts of two or more persons, all being culpable and responsible in law for their acts, do not occur in point of time,
and the negligence of one only exposes the injured person

to risk of injury in case the other should also be negligent, the liability of the person first in fault will depend upon the question whether the negligent act of the other was one which a man of ordinary experience and sagacity, acquainted with all of the circumstances, could reasonably anticipate or not. If such a person could have anticipated that the intervening act of negligence might, in a natural and ordinary sequence, follow the original act of negligence, the person first in fault is not released from liability by reason of the intervening negligence of another. If it could not have been thus anticipated, then the intervening negligent person alone is responsible." (1 Shearman and Redfield on Negligence, 6th ed., sec. 34.) Thus it has been held that where a defendant had negligently constructed a fence and some panels having fallen out, these panels were picked up by a third party and placed against the fence in an insecure position from which they again fell, injuring a child, the defendant was held to have furnished the proximate cause of the injury, notwithstanding that had the panels been allowed to remain where they had first fallen no injury would likely have resulted; the court saying: "When there is danger of a particular injury which actually occurs, we must surely say that it is the usual, ordinary, natural and probable result of the act of exposing the person or thing injured to the danger." (*Fishburn* v. *Burlington & N. W. Ry. Co.*, 127 Iowa, 483, [103 N. W. 481].) The case last cited contains a collection of authorities treating of proximate cause and its relation to other acts intervening before the injury and contributing to the cause. No difficulty is encountered in giving a definition to the phrase "proximate cause." The difficulty in many cases is to determine which, among several concurring causes, is the active, efficient, and producing agency in working the damage. In following the train of causation to the end of a prolonged chain of acts involving perhaps negligence on the part of third persons, the test as to the original wrongdoer's liability depends upon whether, as a reasonable man, in all the circumstances of the case, he could or should have anticipated that the damage complained of might probably occur. As said by Justice Strong in *Milwaukee & St. Paul Ry. Co.* v. *Kellogg*, 94 U. S. 469, [24 L. Ed. 256]: "The primary cause may be the proximate cause of a disaster, though it may operate through suc-

cessive instruments, as an article at the end of a chain may
be moved by a force applied to the other end, that force being
the proximate cause of the movement, or as in the oft cited
case of the squib thrown in the market place. The question
always is: Was there an unbroken connection between the
wrongful act and the injury, a continuous operation? Did
the facts constitute a continuous succession of events, so
linked together as to make a natural whole, or was there some
new and independent cause intervening between the wrong
and the injury? . . . The inquiry must, therefore, always
be whether there was any intermediate cause disconnected
from the primary fault, and self-operating, which produced
the injury.'' In some of the cases first cited in this opinion,
where oils and medicines had been sold in a manner not indicating their true character, or bearing some mistake in label,
it seems to be intimated that the original vender who caused
the mistake to be first made will be held liable, unless some
of the intermediate sellers have been guilty on their part of
negligence in dispensing the oil or drug. Such is the court's
intimation in *Wellington* v. *Downer Kerosene Oil Co.*, 104
Mass. 64; *Elkins, Bly & Co.* v. *McKean*, 79 Pa. St. 493, and
Thomas v. *Winchester*, 6 N. Y. 397, [57 Am. Dec. 455]. The
facts in this case show that Riley, the grocer, had had long
experience in the handling of kerosene and gasoline and that
he was a dealer in such merchandise. Appellant suggests
and insists that the legal situation illustrated by the evidence
here is no different than had appellant's driver, immediately
after delivering the oil to Riley, notified him that a mistake
had been made, and that gasoline and kerosene had been
mixed and that the company would take back the oil. In the
latter case it is argued, and the conclusion suggested seems
logical, that had Riley determined then to dispose of some
of the mixed oil, relying upon his own judgment or knowledge in the matter of determining its true character, the responsibility for any damage which might result would not
attach to the appellant corporation, but that for any mistake made by the groceryman which might result in damage
to his patrons, Riley alone could be held accountable. There
is no doubt at all but that Riley would have had the right
to depend upon the implied representation made by the company that the oil was of the particular kind ordered by him,
where he was not put upon notice of the fact that kerosene

had been mixed with the more inflammable liquid. On Saturday, after the several lots of oil had been returned to Riley, and had been found to contain gasoline, and Riley had proceeded to make his own tests, he then had the conversation with the agent of appellant and the agreement clearly implied from what is admitted to have been then stated was that the company would take the oil back. Riley, as an experienced handler of oils, knew of the highly inflammable quality of gasoline, and it could hardly be said that the appellant, in order to absolve itself from liability, should have specifically advised him not to sell any of the liquid. Riley himself admitted that he would not have been sure in his own mind from the tests made of the two five-gallon cans which he supposed contained coal-oil, of the exact character of that oil, providing it had been mixed with gasoline and had not been entirely one or the other. He testified that he made fire tests of the liquid from the two cans which he concluded contained gasoline, but that he contented himself with noticing the odor and the rapidity with which the liquid from the other two cans evaporated. We cannot on the admitted facts distinguish this case from a case where the oil had been sold as claimed, and upon notification from Riley to the company of the state of affairs the company had immediately dispatched their wagon to take the oil back, and that while the wagon was waiting outside for that purpose Riley tested up some of the oil and sold it with the same disastrous consequences which did ensue. It was not incumbent upon appellant to have taken more steps than it did to prevent the independent action of Riley. Its responsible duty to third persons had ended. We have already pointed out that Riley was a dealer in both gasoline and coal-oil, and he had had many years' experience in handling those commodities. He himself testified that he had received and sold gasoline and kerosene for about ten years. In the view we take of the case, the intervening act of Riley was that of a culpable, responsible person, and that it interrupted the chain of causation and furnished the direct and proximate cause of the damage. In the case where poison was mislabeled as a harmless drug (*Thomas* v. *Winchester*, 6 N. Y. 397, [57 Am. Dec. 455]), it seems quite clear that had the retail druggist who received from the defendant, and later dispensed the poison, had notice of the fact that the drug had been mislabeled and

notice of its true character, his act in dispensing it, even
though after the making of some tests, would be an act for
which the original vender would not be liable. As the court
there said: ''The wrong done by the defendant was in putting the poison, mislabeled, into the hands of Aspinwall, as
an article of merchandise, to be sold and afterward used, as
the extract of dandelion, by some person then unknown.''

But it is said by respondent that, under the facts and circumstances shown in evidence, it became a question solely for
the jury to resolve as to whether there had been any negligence on the part of the plaintiff. It is true that questions
involving alleged negligent action which turn upon the
proposition as to what should be expected of an ordinarily
reasonable man under the circumstances, present mixed questions of law and fact which generally should go to the jury
under proper instructions as to the law, leaving the deductions of fact to be made by the verdict. This is always the
case where the evidence is conflicting. However, it has been
uniformly held that where the facts are undisputed and
clearly settled, and the dictates of common prudence point
to only one reasonable conclusion, the question is then one of
law for the court and a verdict may be either directed or a
nonsuit granted. (1 Shearman and Redfield on Negligence,
6th ed., sec. 56.) Our supreme court has repeatedly applied
this rule. (*Glascock* v. *Central Pac. R. R. Co.*, 73 Cal. 137,
[14 Pac. 518]; *Baddeley* v. *Shea*, 114 Cal. 1, [155 Am. St.
Rep. 56, 33 L. R. A. 747, 45 Pac. 990]; and a number of other
cases which it is unnecessary to cite.) We think in this case
that it must be said that there should be no difference of
opinion in the mind of any reasonable man, but that the
appellant was shown to have exercised reasonable caution,
when its driver informed Riley, the dealer, that he would
take the oil back upon being informed by Riley that the fluid
was mixed. No assurances were made to Riley designed to
dissuade him from his conviction that the oil had been mixed,
but the transaction or sale to him was agreed in effect to be
rescinded. Riley himself had had abundant proof that the
fluid delivered was not unmixed kerosene.

It is contended that prejudicial error was committed by the
trial court in refusing to strike out portions of statements
made by the deceased Catlin. As has been narrated, Catlin
immediately after the explosion, and while he was upon the

grass in front of his house covered with fire, made a statement to the witness Tucker as to how the accident occurred, and then said: "I am sure that it was gasoline." He made another statement to which attention has not heretofore been called, to witness Siemsen, who arrived on the ground a few moments after Tucker came. In that statement, after some words had passed between the two men, the deceased said to Siemsen that "there must have been something in that coaloil." Both of these statements appellant moved the court to strike out on the ground that they were not a part of the *res gestae,* that they were self-serving and expressive of the opinion and conclusion of the witness. It may be assumed that the statements made by the deceased were sufficiently contemporaneous with the occurrence as to admit them in proof as part of the *res gestae* (*Elkins, Bly & Co.* v. *McKean,* 79 Pa. St. 493), but it does seem quite clear that the particular sentences objected to could not have been competent in any case; they were not statements expressive of how the accident occurred, for the witness had already described what had happened, but presented purely the opinion and conclusion of the deceased as to the fluid which he was using being gasoline. The matter of the establishment of the fact as to the character of the fluid involved was one of the crucial issues in the case, and one as to which there was a conflict in the evidence. This statement coming from the deceased may have had deciding weight in settling the important question, and that consideration therefore clearly illustrates the prejudice suffered by appellant. For a discussion of what constitutes proper testimony where statements of the actors are claimed to be a part of the *res gestae,* we refer to *Heckle* v. *Southern Pacific Co.,* 123 Cal. 441, [56 Pac. 56]; *Williams* v. *Southern Pacific Co.,* 133 Cal. 550, [65 Pac. 1100].

As to the claim made that Catlin, as a matter of law under the facts shown in evidence, was guilty of contributory negligence, we think that contention should not be sustained. While it may appear to the ordinary mind as a heedless act for a man to fill a lamp with an open flame on his cap, at the same time, it must be borne in mind that there was evidence given by a witness, who was shown to have some expert knowledge on the subject, that such a thing might be done with reasonable safety and without great danger of the oil or vapor being ignited, if the fluid used was coal-oil of ordinary lamp quality. Under this state of the evidence, it was for the jury to settle the question as to whether the deceased acted with reasonable caution in the circumstances. The case of *Riggs* v. *Standard Oil Co.*, 130 Fed. 199, cited by appellant, presented different facts. In the decision the district judge held that the pouring of oil by the person injured into a fire-box of a stove in which were live coals was contributory negligence which would prevent a recovery, even though the oil furnished was not of the high flash test required. The injured person in that case actually brought the oil in contact with fire. Hence it was clear that of whatever higher test the oil might have been, nothing could have prevented its ignition; the conclusion of negligence was irresistible. It is contended that the court erred in refusing to give certain instructions offered on the part of appellant. It was error not to instruct the jury in accordance with the conclusions expressed in the foregoing as to the conditions under which the first negligence of the appellant ceased to be of contributing influence in the chain of causation. Appellant was entitled to an instruction, as we view the case, that as a matter of law under the facts shown, responsibility, if any, was that of Riley, the immediate vender of Catlin. In other respects the charge as given by the trial judge appears to have contained in the main a correct exposition of the law. Those instructions furnishing more explicit advice on the subject of contributory negligence might well have been given, but we think it was not error to have refused them. As to the alleged excessive amount of the verdict, we would not feel justified in reversing the cause for that reason. (*Morgan* v. *Southern Pac. Co.*, 95 Cal. 501, 508, [30 Pac. 601]; *McGrory* v. *Pacific Electric Ry. Co.*, 22 Cal. App. 671, [136 Pac. 303].)

The judgment and order are reversed.

Conrey, P. J., and Shaw, J., concurred.

ANNUNZIATA BARSI, by SERAFINE BARSI, the Guardian of Her Person and Estate, Appellant, v. J. A. SIMPSON, Respondent.

NEGLIGENCE—MALPRACTICE IN SETTING OF FRACTURED ARM—EVIDENCE —PROPER SETTING—EXPERT TESTIMONY.—In an action against a physician and surgeon for damages for alleged malpractice in the setting of a fractured arm, the plaintiff is not prejudiced by the sustaining of an objection to a question asked an expert witness, who caused to be made certain X-ray plates of the bones some two months after the fracture, as to whether a fracture set in the manner shown by the plates was a proper setting, where the witness later in his testimony made the statement that if the fracture had been properly set in the first place, there would have been no angulation at that time, and also testified fully as to how the operation should have been performed.

1a.—EVIDENCE—ADMISSION SUBJECT TO MOTION TO STRIKE OUT—AB-SENCE OF MOTION—APPEAL.—Where evidence is admitted subject to a motion to be thereafter made to strike it out if certain proof is not supplied, and no such motion is made, the adverse party cannot be heard on appeal to say that the ruling of the court was erroneous.

1b.—PROPER TREATMENT OF ARM—TRAINED NURSE.—A trained nurse, who was superintendent of the operating-room of a large hospital, and who witnessed the performance of the operation on the plaintiff by the defendant, is properly permitted to testify, that from her experience, the treatment was proper.

APPEAL from a judgment of the Superior Court of the City and County of San Francisco, and from an order denying a new trial. John Hunt, Judge.

The facts are stated in the opinion of the court.

Louis Ferrari, for Appellant.

Chickering & Gregory, and Evan Williams, for Respondent.

THE COURT.—The appeal is by plaintiff from an order denying his motion for a new trial.

The plaintiff suffered a fracture of the left arm between the wrist and elbow on the fifteenth day of March, 1913, and on the same day employed the defendant, a physician and surgeon, to set the fracture. Thereafter the defendant set the fracture, and it is claimed on behalf of the plaintiff that the defendant failed to use due care in this respect, by reason of which certain permanent injuries to the plaintiff resulted. The sole claim of negligence, as appears from an examination of the complaint, is that the defendant, at the time the arm was set, did not bring the ends of the fractured bones into position. There is no claim that any subsequent treatment given by the defendant was improper in any way, nor is any contention made on behalf of the plaintiff that the verdict, which was in favor of the defendant, is not sustained by the evidence.

The points relied upon for reversal fall under two heads: First, the action of the court in admitting or rejecting offered testimony; second, the instructions given by the court, and the refusal of the court to give certain instructions offered by the plaintiff.

Dr. Guido Caglieri, who was the first witness for the plaintiff, testified that he had caused to be made certain X-ray plates of the bones some two months after the arm had been fractured. The witness was asked whether a fracture set in the manner shown by the plates was a proper setting. The question was objected to on the ground that it assumed something not in evidence, viz., that the fracture was set in that manner. The objection was sustained. Assuming that the ruling of the court was erroneous, still it was a harmless error, for the witness later in his testimony said that if the fracture of the arm had been properly set in the first place there would have been no angulation at that time; and the witness further testified fully as to how the operation upon the arm should have been performed. Considering the testimony of this witness as a whole, he in effect answered the question to which the objection just noted was sustained.

The next contention of this plaintiff is that the trial court committed prejudicial error in permitting defendant to ask Dr. Isaac W. Thorne on cross-examination a question which assumed facts not in evidence; but the question was permitted with the understanding that the defendant would later supply the omitted facts; and, as there is no claim now made that the facts assumed were not thereafter proven, it follows that the plaintiff is without any substantial ground of complaint on this score. Moreover, it is clear that the court permitted the question to be asked with the idea that such evidence was admitted subject to a motion to be thereafter made to strike it out if the defective proof was not supplied. No such motion was made. Consequently plaintiff cannot now be heard to complain of this ruling. (*Tarpey* v. *Veith*, 22 Cal. App. 289, [134 Pac. 367].)

Maud Compton, a trained nurse, who was at the time the superintendent of the operating-room of a large hospital, witnessed the performance of the operation on the plaintiff by the defendant, and testified that from her experience as a trained nurse she would say that Dr. Simpson's treatment of the injured arm was proper, and not subject in any respect to adverse criticism. Passing the point made by the defendant that the question was answered before the objection was made, and that therefore it cannot now be considered, we think the question of whether or not the witness was qualified to testify as an expert was a matter within the sound discretion of the court; and there being no showing of a clear abuse of that discretion the ruling of the trial court will not be disturbed. (*Vallejo etc. R. R. Co.* v. *Reed Orchard Co.*, 169 Cal. 545, 575, [147 Pac. 238].) Instances of cases where others than medical practitioners have been allowed to give their opinion on medical matters are found in the following cases: *Lund* v. *Masonic Assn.*, 81 Hun, 287, [30 N. Y. Supp. 775]; *Robinson* v. *Exempt Fire Co.*, 103 Cal. 1, [42 Am. St. Rep. 93, 24 L. R. A. 715, 36 Pac. 955]; *Kimic* v. *San Jose & Los Gatos Ry. Co.*, 156 Cal. 379, 391, [104 Pac. 986, 991]. In the last-mentioned case a professional nurse was allowed to so testify, and the court said: "There can be no doubt that one who is shown to be a graduate nurse and to have been constantly engaged in the calling of a professional nurse for five years, may properly be called upon to give evidence of the character elicited by the question asked."

There are two other points made as to the admission of evidence, but they are without any substantial merit; as is also the objection to certain of the instructions of the court, and we see no necessity for a detailed discussion of them.

The order appealed from is affirmed.

[Civ. No. 1291.   Third Appellate District.—October 4, 1916.]

WESTERN NATIONAL BANK (a Corporation), Respondent, v. GEORGE W. WITTMAN, Appellant; J. G. LEIBOLD et al., Defendants and Respondents.

CORPORATION—PROMISSORY NOTE SIGNED BY PRESIDENT AND SECRETARY —SUFFICIENCY OF AUTHORIZATION.—A promissory note of a corporation signed by its president and secretary requires no ratification by the directors or stockholders, where the same was so executed in strict conformity to a resolution of the board of directors authorizing the corporation to borrow from a bank an amount of money not to exceed at any one time a certain sum, and empowering the president or vice-president, together with the secretary or treasurer, to execute its promissory note or notes therefor to such bank for all such sums so borrowed upon such terms in respect to amount or rate of interest or otherwise as might be agreed upon.

ID.—INDORSER AND GUARANTOR — SUFFICIENCY OF CONSIDERATION— —ULTRA VIRES ACT—DEFENSES NOT AVAILABLE.—An indorser and guarantor of the payment of such note cannot be heard to say that it was executed without consideration, or that it was *ultra vires*, where its genuineness was admitted by the corporation and its validity recognized by numerous payments made thereon and an acquiescence of several years.

ID.—AGREEMENT BETWEEN CORPORATION AND CREDITORS—CONDITION— GUARANTOR NOT RELEASED.—An indorser and guarantor of the payment of such a note is not released by a subsequent agreement made between the corporation and its creditors relating to a settlement of the debts of the corporation, where the agreement expressly provided that it should be void, unless signed by all creditors, and it in fact was not so signed.

APPEAL from a judgment of the Superior Court of the City and County of San Francisco, and from an order denying a new trial. K. S. Mahon, Judge presiding.

The facts are stated in the opinion of the court.

J. J. Dunne, for Appellant.

Gavin McNab, B. M. Aikins, A. H. Jarman, and W. F. Williamson, for Respondent.

J. J. Lermen, for Defendants and Respondents.

CHIPMAN, P. J.—Plaintiff commenced the action by verified complaint to recover the balance due on a certain promissory note.   Judgment went against defendants Geo. W. Wittman and J. G. Leibold for the sum of $7,076.82, with interest
from date of the judgment and costs.   Defendant vehicle
company, maker of the note, did not answer.

The appeal is from the judgment and order denying his
motion for a new trial by defendant Wittman alone.   The
promissory note in suit reads as follows:

"9000.00.   San Francisco, Cal., March 30, 1907.

"One day after date, for value received, California Vehicle
& Harness Co., a corporation, organized and existing under
the laws of the State of California, promises to pay to the
Western National Bank of San Francisco, likewise a corporation, or order, at its banking house in this city, the sum of
nine thousand 00/100 dollars in United States gold coin of
the present standard, with interest thereon in like coin from
date until paid, at the rate of six per cent per annum, said
interest to be paid monthly, and if not so paid to be added
to the principal and thereafter bear interest at the same rate.
Should default be made in the payment of interest as herein
provided, then the whole sum of principal and interest shall
immediately become due and payable.

"(Signed)   J. G. LEIBOLD, Pres.
"(Signed)   L. HOLT, Secy."

On the back of the note is indorsed: "J. G. Leibold and
Geo. W. Wittman," and then:

"San Francisco, for value received, we, or either of us,
guarantee the payment of the within note and interest according to its terms, and we, or either of us, hereby waive presentation thereof to the maker, demand of payment, protest
and notice of non-payment.

"(Signed)   J. G. LEIBOLD,
"(Signed)   GEO. W. WITTMAN."

Stamped on the back of the note are various sums of interest and principal.

Defendant Leibold in his answer admitted, by not denying,
the due execution of the note, the indorsements and guarantee and that the vehicle company received consideration for
its note, but alleged want of consideration passing to him
for his indorsement; denied that the whole or any part of

said note or interest is now or ever was due from this defendant.

Defendant Wittman's answer is of considerable length, a summary of which he states in his brief as follows:

"The answer denies that the corporation defendant executed the note sued on, or that it ever authorized anyone to execute that note; and alleges that the note is not and never was the note of the corporation defendant. It also denies that either Wittman or Leibold ever indorsed or guaranteed the payment of any note of the corporation defendant. It denies that no part of the principal has been paid, that the whole or any part of the principal or interest is due, owing or unpaid, and that the plaintiff is the owner or holder of the note in question. The answer then sets up as a separate defense that the note is *ultra vires* and void, because issued by Leibold and his secretary, Laura Holt, to take up a private and personal indebtedness of Leibold to the plaintiff corporation, without authority from or ratification by the board of directors of the defendant corporation, all to the knowledge of the bank. It further sets up, as an additional separate defense, that no consideration for this note ever passed to the corporation defendant. It further sets up, as an additional separate defense, the fraud of the plaintiff and of Leibold in inducing the defendant Wittman to go upon the note, and it further sets up as an additional separate defense, under section 2819 of the Civil Code, the execution of a contract without the consent of the defendant Wittman, he being unindemnified, which contract suspended the plaintiff's rights and remedies against the defendant corporation."

It appeared that prior to March 23, 1907, defendant Leibold was engaged in business in San Francisco under the name of Leibold Harness Company, and was indebted to plaintiff in the sum of nine thousand dollars, evidenced by Leibold's promissory note. On that day defendant, the vehicle company, was incorporated by three persons, one of whom was in Leibold's employment. Neither Wittman nor Leibold was then a corporator. After this date and prior to the execution of the note sued upon, Leibold transferred his business to the vehicle company and the latter assumed all the liabilities of the Leibold Harness Company, including the bank indebtedness of nine thousand dollars, and agreed to and did issue a block of the stock of the vehicle company to Leibold as consideration for his business. Leibold was then made a director and president of the corporation and defendant Wittman, having invested some money therein, became a stockholder in and was made vice-president of the corporation. Thereafter Leibold, on behalf of the corporation, applied to plaintiff for a loan of nine thousand dollars, and was told by an officer of the bank that the corporation would have to execute its note for the loan, which must be indorsed by the principal stockholders. On March 30, 1907, at a meeting of the board of directors of the corporation defendant, held at its office, all directors and the secretary, L. Holt, being present, defendant Wittman offered and defendant Leibold seconded a resolution which was adopted, authorizing the corporation to borrow from the Western National Bank an amount of money not to exceed at any one time the sum of nine thousand dollars, "and that either the president or vice-president, together with the secretary or treasurer of this corporation are hereby empowered to execute its promissory note or notes therefor to said Western National Bank of San Francisco, for all such sums so borrowed, upon such terms in respect to amount or rate of interest or otherwise as may be agreed upon." The resolution directed the secretary to deliver to said bank "a copy of these resolutions properly certified by her in evidence of the authority of the persons hereinbefore named to make said loans and execute the notes as above specified." A duly certified copy of this resolution was delivered to plaintiff, the promissory note above set out was also delivered to and accepted by the bank and the amount, nine thousand dollars, placed to the credit of the vehicle corporation, in its regular checking account. Later, on April 3, 1907, the corporation drew its check for nine thousand dollars and paid the note of said Leibold, which had been assumed by the corporation. This note of the corporation is the obligation which appellant Wittman now contends was not authorized or executed by the vehicle corporation, and is the note on which it subsequently paid various sums of both principal and interest, and is the note for the unpaid balance of which this action was brought.

Section 2792 of the Civil Code provides that no other consideration need exist "where a guaranty is entered into at the same time with the original obligation, or with the acceptance of the latter by the guarantee, and forms with that obligation a part of the consideration to him." Section 2806 of the same code provides that: "A guaranty is to be deemed unconditional unless its terms import some condition precedent to the liability of the guarantor." Section 3116 provides that: "Every indorser of a negotiable instrument, unless his indorsement is qualified, warrants to every subsequent holder thereof, who is not liable thereon to him: First. That it is in all respects what it purports to be. Second. That he has a good title to it. Third. That the signatures of all prior parties are binding upon them." Fourth: That if dishonored, the indorser will pay the same unless exonerated under certain provisions of the code not here applicable.

Appellant contends that the note sued on is invalid and void for many reasons: (a) Because, though signed by the president and secretary, their acts were never authorized or ratified by the directors or stockholders; (b) because contrary to public policy declared in section 2228 et seq., of the Civil Code; (c) the note is not evidentiary of any consideration flowing from the bank to the vehicle company.

The note in question was authorized by the unanimous vote of the directors. No ratification was necessary. It was executed in strict conformity to the resolution passed by the directors, and the money derived from the loan was placed to the checking account of defendant corporation and was used in the payment of an obligation assumed by the corporation as part consideration for the business and property conveyed to it by Leibold. As the governing body of the corporation, the directors were the persons and only persons who, in their official capacity, could execute the note. Sued as he was in his individual capacity, and being both an indorser and guarantor of the note in such capacity, appellant will not be heard to do the very things which the code sections, *supra*, say he may not do. We can discover no principle of public policy violated in the transaction, nor can we see that there was a failure to show consideration flowing to the vehicle corporation. Aside from the presumption of consideration arising where the obligation is in writing, and aside from the provisions of the code, *supra*, there was a consideration in that the money received for the note was subsequently used to pay an obligation of the corporation. The genuineness of the corporation note was never questioned by the corporation and is here admitted. The corporation recognized its validity by

numerous payments made on the note and by an acquiescence
of several years. Neither can we see that appellant has established his claim that the note was *ultra vires* in the sense that
it was beyond the power of the directors to bind dissenting
stockholders or of the legal rights of creditors. The articles
of incorporation empowered the corporation, among other
things:

"1st. To manufacture, buy, sell, import, export and generally deal in all kinds of harness, saddlery . . . and all goods,
wares and merchandise, etc. . . .

"4th. To borrow and lend money, etc. . . .

"6th. To receive, hold, store, buy and sell and generally
deal in goods, wares and merchandise of any kind, etc."

The corporation was formed to conduct the same kind of
business which, with the property forming part of it, Leibold
conveyed to the corporation. There was express authority
given by the articles to transact this business, and part of its
business was to pay its obligations assumed in consideration
for the property it received from Leibold. There were no
dissenting stockholders or directors at the time the note was
executed nor for some months thereafter, and there is none
now so far as we know except defendant Wittman, and he it
was who moved the resolution authorizing the note to be executed, and who guaranteed its genuineness and that he would
pay it if the corporation did not. Furthermore, Wittman
testified that he knew, or supposed, that the note was delivered to the bank; that the corporation received credit for
it and "understood that they took up that old note with this
new one."

It was legal for the parties, in forming the corporation, to
exchange its stock for the property conveyed to it by Leibold.
(*Turner* v. *Markham*, 155 Cal. 562, [102 Pac. 272].) Having taken over the harness business of Leibold for the purpose
of conducting it, and having assumed his liabilities connected
with that business, it was as much within its power to pay
its debts as to conduct the business for which it was formed.

It is further contended that Wittman was discharged by
reason of a certain agreement which it is claimed was entered into in February, 1908, between the vehicle corporation,
its creditors and Leibold. This agreement purports to be
"between the California Vehicle & Harness Company, a California corporation, party of the first part, and the under-

signed creditors of the said corporation, parties of the second part, and J. G. Leibold, of the City and County of San Francisco, California, party of the third part." By its terms, the first party conveyed to the third party the property of the first party in trust to collect the accounts of the corporation, to sell and dispose of the stock of goods on hand, to purchase such additional goods as were necessary for carrying on the said business, to render an account monthly of receipts and disbursements. "As soon as said party of the third part has in his hands sufficient funds wherewith to do so, a dividend of ten (10) per cent shall be made to each one of the parties of the second part, upon the amount of their respective claims; providing, however, the interest on said claims shall be kept paid according to the terms of the respective existing contracts. . . .

"This agreement shall be void and of no effect unless the same be executed by all of the creditors of said corporation as the parties of the second part hereto."

The court found among other facts, in respect of the agreement: "That it is not true that during the operation of said agreement the plaintiff's rights in respect of its original obligation sued on in this action, should cease and become suspended; that it is not true that said agreement was entered into against the will of said defendant Wittman; and in respect to the agreement, mentioned and referred to in paragraph IX of the answer of said defendant Wittman, the court finds that a certain agreement was drawn and was attempted to be executed by said California Vehicle & Harness Co. and all its creditors, and that said agreement was signed by plaintiff; that said agreement specifically provided as follows, to wit: [Then follows the clause above quoted requiring all the creditors to sign.] That said agreement was not signed by all of the creditors of said California Vehicle & Harness Co. and said agreement was never executed and did not become operative."

The evidence supported this finding. But it is contended that because plaintiff signed the agreement and received payments claimed by appellant to have been made under this agreement, plaintiff is bound by it. There was evidence that a payment of nine hundred dollars was made in June, 1908, shown by the indorsement on the note as on account of the principal, and this was exactly ten per cent of the face of the note. Whether or not it was received under the agreement did not appear, except by the fact that Leibold paid it to the bank while acting under the agreement, and by the circumstance that it was ten per cent of the principal of the note. The only officer of the bank called as a witness by defendant, testified: "Q. I will ask you if it is not a fact that the bank did accept payments from Mr. Leibold on the note under that agreement? A. I could only say now after seeing the note that payments were made to the bank. By whom they were made and under what circumstances, I could not say."

Cases such as *Daneri* v. *Gazzola*, 139 Cal. 416, [73 Pac. 179], cited by appellant, do not support his contention. In the case cited, the defendants were sureties on the note; the payee agreed in consideration of part payment and that the interest would be kept paid as it matured, to dismiss the action and extend payment one year. This agreement was carried out without the consent or knowledge of the defendants. The court held that this operated a release of the sureties. No such facts exist here. Assuming that the agreement took effect, it was merely an arrangement by which Leibold was to manage the business and pay the obligation when he could out of the earnings. No time was fixed for payments, and no extension of time given by the creditors, and there was no consideration passing to plaintiff as a creditor for the agreement. It was said in *Stroud* v. *Thomas*, 139 Cal. 274, [96 Am. St. Rep. 111, 72 Pac. 1008]: "A surety is not discharged by an extension of time to the principal debtors without consideration. Part payment of the interest or principal of a note after maturity is not a consideration for an extension of time; and the surety is not discharged by an agreement to forbear suit against the principals, founded upon such part payment, though carried out by the creditor."

Under sections 2822 and 2823 of the Civil Code, mere delay on the part of the creditors to proceed against the principal does not exonerate the guarantor, and a partial satisfaction of the obligation of the guarantor will reduce it, but will not otherwise affect the obligation.

We think, however, that as by the express terms of the agreement it was to be null and void unless all creditors signed it, the court rightly held that it never became operative.

We discover no alleged errors in rulings of the court during the trial which were prejudicial or call for consideration. The judgment and order are affirmed.

Burnett, J., and Hart, J., concurred.

[Civ. No. 1778.   First Appellate District.—October 6, 1916.]

JOSEPH RAFAEL, Respondent, v. THOMAS F. BOYLE, as Auditor of the City and County of San Francisco, Appellant.

CIVIL SERVICE COMMISSION—POWER TO EMPLOY PRIVATE COUNSEL—SAN FRANCISCO CHARTER.—The civil service commission of the city and county of San Francisco has no power, express or implied, to employ private legal counsel at the expense of the city and county to defend the commission in legal proceedings, when the city attorney is ready and willing to perform such services, as such officer, by virtue of article V, chapter 2, section 2 of the charter of said city and county, is alone authorized to conduct the legal business of the municipality.

APPEAL from a judgment of the Superior Court of the City and County of San Francisco.   John J. Van Nostrand, Judge.

The facts are stated in the opinion of the court.

Percy V. Long, City Attorney, and Robert M. Searls, Assistant City Attorney, for Appellant.

Joseph T. Curley, for Respondent.

KERRIGAN, J.—This is an appeal from a judgment granting a peremptory writ of mandamus directed against the defendant herein, commanding him to audit a certain demand against the treasury of the city and county of San Francisco.

In brief the facts are as follows: William A. Kelly, an attorney at law, was employed by the members of the civil service commission of said city and county to defend them in certain legal proceedings.   At the time of such employment the commission had received from the city attorney certain written opinions contrary in tenor to its views as to the legality of certain matters then before it. In each of these matters the commission, disregarding the city attorney's opinion, acted in accordance with its own judgment; and thereafter legal proceedings were commenced in the superior court against said commission to determine the legality of its action. Notwithstanding that the commission had acted contrary to his views in these matters, the city attorney was ready and willing to appear in court and defend said suits. The members of the commission, however, ignored the offer, and by resolution engaged William A. Kelly to defend them in the proceedings. A total compensation of five hundred dollars was agreed upon. The city attorney was not consulted further in the matter nor requested to appear. In accordance with his agreement Kelly appeared for the commission in said actions, and thereafter he presented his demand drawn on the city treasurer for payment of the agreed compensation, which demand was approved by the civil service commission and by the board of supervisors, and passed to the auditor, defendant herein, for audit. That officer declined to audit the demand on the ground of illegality; Kelly assigned his claim to the petitioner herein, who brought the proceeding here under review. Judgment was rendered in favor of the petitioner as prayed, and defendant takes this appeal.

The sole question presented for determination is whether or not under these facts the civil service commission had the power to retain an attorney at the expense of the city when the city attorney was ready and willing to perform the necessary legal services. It is contended by the respondent that under the broad provisions of article XIII of the charter of the city and county of San Francisco, the right to retain, counsel other than the city attorney is incidental to the very nature and life of the civil service system as therein created.

Nowhere in the charter is express power conferred upon the civil service commission to engage private counsel, but it is insisted by petitioner that this power is implied in section 20, article XIII of that instrument, providing that the commission shall have power "to institute and prosecute legal proceedings for violation of any of the provisions of this

article.'' We are of the opinion that such contention cannot
be maintained.

Whether attorneys may be employed in behalf of a municipal corporation depends upon the proper construction of
the law under which such employment is sought to be sustained, the nature of the service to be performed, or, in the
absence of legal provisions pertaining thereto, the character
of the litigation or legal controversy involved. There is
much variety in the charters and statutes of different jurisdictions relating to law officers of municipal corporations.
In general, unless forbidden by law, when necessity arises
therefor and the interests of the municipal corporation require it, the employment of attorneys has usually been sanctioned. (2 McQuillin on Municipal Corporations, sec. 501.)
It is usual, however, to find in municipal charters or laws
applicable to the government of local public corporations,
provisions dealing with the conduct of the municipality's
legal business. Such is the case in the charter of San Francisco, which provides for a legal department, the head of
which is known as the city attorney, and whose duties are set
forth in article V, chapter 2, section 2, as follows: ''He must
prosecute and defend for the city and county all actions at
law or in equity, and all special proceedings for or against
the city and county; and whenever any cause of action at law
or in equity or by special proceedings exists in favor of the
city and county he shall commence the same when within his
knowledge, and, if not within his knowledge, when directed
to do so by resolution of the board of supervisors. He shall
give legal advice in writing to all officers, boards, and commissions named in this charter, when requested so to do by
them, or either of them, in writing, upon questions arising
in their separate departments involving the rights or liabilities of the city and county. He shall not settle or dismiss
any litigation for or against the city and county under his
control unless upon his written recommendation he is ordered
to do so by the mayor and supervisors.''

This express provision clearly indicates an intention that
the city attorney should handle all the legal work of the various departments of the city government, except where special
provision is made for additional counsel. The manifest intention of the framers of the charter in the adoption of this
provision was to systematize the conduct of the city's legal

business, and to limit the power of the authorities to incur
expenditures for this character of service; and the mere power
given the commission to institute and prosecute legal proceedings does not imply that this above-quoted provision of
the charter should be inoperative with regard to the civil service commission so as to empower it to employ another
attorney to perform the duties belonging to the law officer
of the municipality. The charter having provided a city
attorney upon whom the board can call when a defense to
any suit is necessary, it by implication makes it incumbent
upon the board to avail itself of his services, and it cannot
ignore this provision and employ some other attorney to render those services which it is the duty of the city attorney
to perform. (*Denman* v. *Webster*, 139 Cal. 452, [73 Pac.
139]; *Merriam* v. *Barnum*, 116 Cal. 619, [48 Pac. 727].)

The judgment is reversed.

Lennon, P. J., and Richards, J., concurred.

[Civ. No. 1571. Third Appellate District.—October 6, 1916.]

R. A. CORSON, Respondent, v. CHARLES CROCKER
et al., Appellants.

Irrigation District—Levying of Assessment—Manner and Form.—
Under the provisions of the act of 1897 (Stats. 1897, p. 254), authorizing the organization and government of irrigation districts,
it is not necessary that the levying of an assessment by the board
of directors for the purposes of the district shall be by or in the
form of a resolution.

Id.—Assessment-roll and Delinquent List—Certification not Essential.—Under the provisions of such act, it is not necessary
that the assessment-roll and delinquent list be certified by any
person or officer of the irrigation district.

Id.—Description of Property Assessed — Sufficiency of.—Under
such act, assessed property described as "Modesto Bl'k 123, lots
1 to 5 inclusive," in the assessment-book under the heading "Description of Property," is sufficient.

Id.—Sufficiency of Designation of Land.—Where the designation
of the land in the assessment-book is such as to afford the owner

the means whereby the land may readily be identified, or does not mislead or is not calculated to mislead him, it is sufficient.

ID.—PUBLICATION OF DELINQUENT NOTICE—EVIDENCE—SUFFICIENCY OF. The *prima facie* showing made through proof of the collector's deed that notice of delinquency was duly published is not overcome by testimony that the numbers of a certain newspaper had been examined and that the notice was found in but one issue, where it is not shown that the notice was published in such newspaper.

ID.—DATE OF CERTIFICATE OF SALE.—Under the provision of such act requiring that the collector must make out in duplicate a certificate of sale of property sold for delinquent assessment "dated on the day of sale," a certificate is not void because dated on a day subsequent to the sale, where it is recited therein that the property may be redeemed within twelve months from the date of sale, which date of sale is stated in the recital.

APPEAL from a judgment of the Superior Court of Stanislaus County. L. W. Fulkerth, Judge.

The facts are stated in the opinion of the court.

F. W. Reeder, and Charles S. Conner, for Appellants.

E. H. Zion, and L. L. Dennett, for Respondent.

HART, J.—This is an action to quiet title to certain real estate. The plaintiff had judgment, from which this appeal is prosecuted by the defendant, Josephine Arata, upon a transcript of the record prepared in pursuance of the provisions of section 953a of the Code of Civil Procedure.

The plaintiff claims title under a deed executed by the Modesto Irrigation District, a corporation, the property in dispute lying within the boundaries of said district, and having been sold on default of the owner in the payment of an assessment levied thereon by the district in the year 1905.

The appealing defendant challenges the validity of the sale and deed, and the objection so made presents the only questions involved in the controversy.

The lands in question consist of lots 1, 2, 3, 4, and 5, in block 123, of the city of Modesto, and, as stated, are embraced within the limits of the said irrigation district, and were assessed to the appealing defendant.

The appellant was the daughter of one Giovanni Arata, who died testate on the twenty-second day of March, 1897.

With the mother, and other surviving children of the deceased, she was made a devisee in trust of a certain designated portion of the residue of his estate, of which the lots in dispute constituted a part. The record discloses that the lots in question were, together with lots 6, 7, 8, 9, and 10, in the same block, by the trustee conveyed by deed to one Susan Springsteen, on the second day of February, 1903, and that said deed was duly recorded in the office of the county recorder of Stanislaus County on the fifteenth day of December, 1903. This conveyance appears to have been executed prior to the partition of the residue of the said estate and the assignment to the devisees in trust of their respective interests therein in severalty. But it is further made to appear that a partition suit was subsequently filed in the superior court of Stanislaus County, wherein and whereby the several interests of the parties in the residue of the estate were set off to them in severalty, and that by the decree in said action the appellant was awarded title in fee to the particular lots involved in this controversy.

The above recital is important only because thus it is made to appear that the record shows that legal title to the lots in dispute was, notwithstanding the conveyance to Springsteen, still in the appellant, and that the assessment involved herein was properly made against the lots in the latter's name.

By finding No. 4 the court in effect found that the plaintiff's title was deraigned from the sale of the property for the satisfaction of the assessment above referred to, and further found that for more than five years prior to the commencement of this action he and his predecessors in interest have been in actual, exclusive, and continuous possession of said lots, which possession was founded on the ''certificate of sale and deed for delinquent irrigation assessment, issued by the Modesto Irrigation District, . . . and has himself and his said predecessors in interest paid all taxes and assessments of any kind and description and character levied on or against said property for the said period of five years preceding and immediately prior to the date of the filing of the complaint herein.''

By finding No. 5, the court further found: ''Fifth: That the said assessment of the Modesto Irrigation District, for the nonpayment of which said premises were sold, was duly and regularly levied according to law, and that the said irrigation district and its officers complied with all the provisions of law prior to and leading up to the sale and the issuance of the certificate hereinbefore referred to, and that thereafter a deed was duly and regularly issued by the Modesto Irrigation District conveying to the predecessors in interest of the said plaintiff the said premises, and that all proceedings leading up to said deed were duly and regularly taken and that the said deed conveyed to and vested in the grantee therein named a good and perfect title to the said premises, free from all claims and demands of every character of the defendants, Josephine Arata, Assunta Arata, as trustee, and all persons holding by, through or under them."

The appellant claims that said findings are not supported by the evidence, and thus the objections urged against the legality of the assessment and sale of the property in question are raised. These objections, specifically stated, are: 1. That it does not appear that the board of directors of the said irrigation district had, in proper form, and previously to the levying of the assessment, passed a resolution authorizing the assessment; 2. That the assessment-roll and the delinquent list "are not certified"; 3. That "the assessment-book and delinquent roll show that this property was not properly listed, being under the head of 'fractional or metes and bounds' rather than under 'city' or 'town' or 'city' or 'town lots' "; 4. That notice of delinquency is shown to have been published for one week only, whereas the statute requires that publication of such notice shall be for two weeks; 5. That the certificate of sale is void because it was dated on a date subsequent to the day upon which the sale was made.

The Modesto Irrigation District was organized under the provisions of an act of the legislature of 1897, entitled, "An act to provide for the organization and government of irrigation districts, and to provide for the acquisition or construction thereby of works for the irrigation of the lands embraced within such districts, and, also, to provide for the distribution of water for irrigation purposes." (Stats. 1897, p. 254 et seq.)

Section 43 provides for the sale by the tax collector of the district of all lands within the district upon which assessments duly levied under the act have not been paid. Section 45 provides that, upon a sale of real property for delinquent assessments being made, the collector, after receiving the amount of the assessments and costs, "must make out in duplicate a certificate, dated on the day of sale, stating (when known) the name of the person assessed, a description of the land sold, the amount paid therefor, that it was sold for assessments, giving the amount and year of the assessment, and specifying the time when the purchaser will be entitled to a deed. The certificate must be signed by the collector, and one copy delivered to the purchaser, and the other filed in the office of the county recorder of the county in which the land is situated."

Section 48 of said act provides:

"The matter recited in the certificate of sale must be recited in the deed, and such deed duly acknowledged or proved is *prima facie* evidence that,

"(a) The property was assessed as required by law.

"(b) The property was equalized as required by law.

"(c) That the assessments were levied in accordance with law.

"(d) The assessments were not paid.

"(e) At a proper time and place the property was sold as prescribed by law and by the proper officer.

"(f) The property was not redeemed.

"(g) The person who executed the deed was the proper officer."

The action is, as seen, one to quiet title, in which the plaintiff alleges that he is the owner in fee of the property in dispute. The plaintiff having supported his claim of ownership by proof of a tax deed to the property, said deed containing all the matters recited in the certificate of sale, as required by the statute, and having been duly acknowledged, a *prima facie* case was thus made by the plaintiff, and the burden was thereupon devolved upon the appellant to establish her title to the property by a preponderance of the evidence. To do this it was requisite that she should show some defect or defects in the assessment or other proceedings leading to the sale and, finally, to the execution of the tax deed to the purchaser at the tax sale, fatal to the legality of the sale or said deed. As before stated, she made an attempt at such showing but we think without success. The points made against the validity of the assessment we shall consider in the order in which they are above stated.

1. The act of 1897 authorizing the organization and government of irrigation districts nowhere expressly requires that the levying of an assessment by the board of directors for the purposes of the district shall be by or in the form of a resolution. The law, of course, requires the board of directors to levy an assessment, when necessary, but whether this act be done by a mere motion, or in the form of a resolution, is immaterial so long as it constitutes the action of the board and the proceeding is otherwise properly carried out and duly preserved in the records of the board or the books required to be kept for that purpose. (Act of 1897, secs. 34 and 39, pp. 265, 267.)

The reply to the proposition that the "assessment-roll and delinquent list are not certified" is the same as the answer given above to the proposition that the board did not proceed to levy the assessment in the form of a resolution. Counsel have not pointed to any provision of the act in question requiring the assessment-roll and delinquent list to be certified by any person or officer of the district, and, after a careful examination of the statute, we have found no such requirement. It ought not to be necessary to suggest that the governing body of the district was required to take no step in the tax proceedings not expressly or by necessary implication required by the statute.

3. The next objection is that the assessment-book and delinquent list disclose that the property was not properly listed. The specific objection is as above stated.

Section 35 of the Irrigation Act provides, *inter alia:* That the assessor must prepare an assessment-book, with appropriate headings, in which must be listed all real property within the district, in which must be specified, in separate columns, under the appropriate head: (a) the name of the person to whom the property is assessed . . . ; (b) land by township, range, section, or fractional section, and when such land is not a congressional division or subdivision, by metes and bounds, or other description sufficient to identify it, giving an estimate of the number of acres, locality, and the improvements thereon; (c) city and town lots, naming the city or town, and the number and block, according to the system of numbering in such city or town, and the improvements thereon.

By stipulation of counsel on both sides, the memoranda of the map of the city of Modesto were received in evidence and considered in lieu of the map itself, and from the memoranda so received it appears that the lots in question were delineated on said map and described as lots 1, 2, 3, 4, and 5, in block 123, in said city. It is admitted that that portion of the city of Modesto embracing said lots is included within the boundaries of the Modesto Irrigation District. In the assessment-book of said district for the year 1905, as well as in the delinquent assessment-book of said district for said year, the property in dispute is listed and described as follows, under the heading: "Description of Property": "Modesto, Bl'k 123, lots 1 to 5, inclusive." In the assessment-book, the assessed value of the property is stated and in the delinquent assessment-book the value of said property is given under substantially the same heading.

The description of the property as above shown was in substantial compliance with the requirements of the statute, and it was sufficiently clear and definite to facilitate the ready identification and location of the land by means of the deed itself, and, therefore, sufficient to apprise the owner that an assessment-lien subsisted upon the lots, and so enable her to discharge such lien. If the designation of the land in the assessment-book is such as to afford the owner the means whereby the land may readily be identified, or does not mislead or is not calculated to mislead him, it is sufficient. (Cooley on Taxation, p. 745; *San Gabriel Co.* v. *Wittmer Co.*, 96 Cal. 635, [18 L. R. A. 465, 31 Pac. 588]; *Best* v. *Wohlford*, 144 Cal. 733, 736, [78 Pac. 293]; *Baird* v. *Monroe*, 150 Cal. 560, 569, [89 Pac. 352].) As before suggested in another form of expression, the description of the lots here fully measured up to the test thus stated.

4. We cannot say that the trial court was not justified in finding, as impliedly it did so find, that the statutory requirement as to the publication of notice of delinquency was complied with. Section 41 of the statute provides that such notice must be published by the collector of the district in a newspaper published in each county in which any portion of the district may lie for the period of two weeks. The record here does not show in what particular newspaper said notice was ordered to be published. One of the attorneys for the appellant, however, was sworn as a witness, and tes-

tified that he had examined several numbers of the "Weekly News" (presumably a newspaper), and that he had found the notice referred to published in one issue only of said newspaper. This constituted all the showing that was made which tended in any degree to disclose that the notice had not been published as prescribed by the statute; and it was wholly with the trial court to decide whether the showing so made was sufficient to overcome the *prima facie* showing through proof of the deed that the notice referred to was published as required. If the appellant had shown by clear and direct proof that the "Weekly News" was a newspaper published in Stanislaus County, in which the district is situated, that the notice had been by the collector, within twenty days after the delivery of the assessment-book to him by the secretary of the board, given to said newspaper and no other published in said county for publication therein, and that said notice had not been published in said paper for and during the full time prescribed by the statute, there would then have been a sufficient showing of noncompliance with the requirement of the statute in that regard to have overcome the effect of the deed as *prima facie* proof of the due regularity of all the proceedings leading to the sale and the execution of the deed. It is very clear that no such showing was made by the appellant. Indeed, so far as we are given direct information to the contrary upon the subject by the record, the collector might have ordered the publication of the notice in some newspaper published in Stanislaus County other than the "Weekly News," and that the notice was published in accordance with the mandate of the statute upon that subject.

5. The point that the certificate of sale is void because it was not dated on the day of the sale is without substantial merit. The point has its inspiration in the language of section 45 of the act. It will be recalled that that section reads, in part: "After receiving the amount of assessments and costs, the collector must make out in duplicate a certificate, *dated on the day of the sale*, stating," etc. The sale in this case was made on the twentieth day of February, 1906, and the certificate of sale dated the third day of March, 1906.

The certificate, it is to be observed, recites that the property may be redeemed from said sale "within twelve months from the date of said purchase, viz.: this 20th day of Feb-

ruary, 1906, by the person and in the manner as provided
by law," etc. Thus (the certificate being in duplicate, one
of which is to be recorded in the office of the county recorder)
the most important object thereof was fully effectuated, viz.,
the giving of notice to the owner of the date of the sale and
of the time when the purchaser will be entitled to a deed
upon his (the owner's) default in redeeming the property
within the time prescribed by the law and stated in the certificate. It thus must become clearly manifest that the mere
dating of the certificate on some day subsequent to the day
of the sale is not of material importance. It has so been
held. The state of Idaho has a statute which contains a
provision as to the dating of the certificate of a tax sale in
the precise language of section 45 of the statute here in
question. In *McCowan* v. *Elder*, 19 Idaho, 153, [113 Pac.
103], the tax sale was had on the 8th of July, 1904, and the
certificate of sale was dated July 9, 1904. The supreme
court of Idaho, replying to an objection to the certificate
similar to that urged here, held that the language of its
statute regarding the dating of the certificate was merely
directory, and held the certificate in that case to be good.
And, in the recent case of *Bruschi* v. *Cooper*, 30 Cal. App. 682,
[159 Pac. 728], this court, having a similar proposition
before it, cited and approved *McCowan* v. *Elder*, in so far as
it held the language of the statute as to the dating of the
certificate to be directory.

Besides the objections to the assessment proceedings above
considered, the point is made that the property was sold for
less than the total amount actually due on the assessment.
There is no real ground for the support of the point, it being
made to appear that certain items which counsel for the appellant have added to the assessment and penalties as computed by the assessor were figured in lead pencil on the face
of the assessment-book and constituted no part of said book.
The explanation, as shown by the record, is as follows:
That the delinquent assessment involved herein showed the
amount of the assessment to be $20.40, to which were to be
added five per cent, amounting to $1.02, and costs amount-
ing to fifty cents, making the assessment and penalties total
the sum of $21.92; that the assessment-book for the year
1905 contained three columns, entitled as follows: the first,
"Amount of tax for semi-annual interest bonds"; second,

"Amount of tax for redemption of bonds," and third, "Amount of tax for general purposes"; that none of said three columns was used in the assessment of the property in question, and the same were blank and vacant, and that, in compiling and preparing said delinquent assessment, the assessor used the assessment-book of the irrigation district and, for convenience, "used the said three blank columns for the purpose of computing and determining the amount of costs and five per cent additional and the total assessment and the penalties," the same, as stated, being figured in lead pencil on the face of the assessment-book in said three columns. The figures so made appeared as follows: "$.50 in the column entitled, 'Amount of tax for semi-annual interest on bonds'; $1.02 in column entitled, 'Amount of tax for redemption of bonds,' and $21.92 in column entitled, 'Amount of tax for general purposes.'" Quite clearly, the addition of the three amounts would make the total assessment $23.44, whereas, as the record unquestionably shows, the actual amount due on the assessment, including the amount of the assessment and the sums of fifty cents and $1.02, penalties, etc., was $21.92, for which sum the property was sold.

It is further pointed out that the court found (finding 4) that the plaintiff had acquired title to the lots in controversy by adverse possession, and that there is no evidence to support said finding. Assuming this to be true, it is also true that the court by its fifth finding found that the plaintiff obtained title to the property by the tax sale and deed, and this finding is sufficient to support the decree quieting plaintiff's title to said property. Finding 4 is further and otherwise criticised, but the judgment could stand secure on the fifth finding with finding 4 entirely eliminated, and it is, therefore, immaterial whether the last-mentioned finding is or is not justly amenable to the criticism referred to.

We have found nothing in the record which would warrant us in holding that the decree assailed by the appellant is not justified by the facts and the law.

The judgment is accordingly affirmed.

Chipman, P. J., and Burnett, J., concurred.

[Civ. No. 1415. Third Appellate District.—October 7, 1916.]

JOE MATH, Respondent, v. CRESCENT HILL GOLD MINES CO. OF CALIFORNIA (a Corporation), Appellant.

ACTION FOR SERVICES—CROSS-COMPLAINT FOR MONEY LOANED AND GOODS SOLD—FAILURE TO FIND ON ISSUE—REVERSAL OF JUDGMENT. Where in an action to recover for services performed in working a mine, the defendant filed a cross-complaint alleging an indebtedness to him for money loaned and goods sold, and the plaintiff in his answer to such pleading denied the indebtedness, and evidence was admitted on such issue, a finding thereon was essential, and where omitted, the judgment must be reversed on appeal.

ID.—FINDINGS—MATERIAL ISSUE—APPEAL.—A judgment will be reversed on appeal where there is a failure to make a finding on a material issue.

APPEAL from a judgment of the Superior Court of Plumas County, and from an order denying a new trial. J. O. Moncur, Judge.

The facts are stated in the opinion of the court.

J. D. McLoughlin, and L. N. Peter, for Appellant.

L. H. Hughes, for Respondent.

HART, J.—An opinion affirming the judgment and the order appealed from in this action was filed by this court on June 19, 1916. A rehearing was within due time granted on the petition of the appellant for the reason, as stated in the order granting the rehearing, that the petition called "attention to some evidence that seems to have been overlooked when the case was decided." The former opinion contained the following statement of the facts and the issues as the same are presented in the pleadings of the respective parties:

"Plaintiff worked as a miner for defendant, at its mine in Plumas county, from February 15, 1912, to October 28, 1913, a total of six hundred days. In the first cause of action set up in the complaint it is alleged that plaintiff entered into an agreement with defendant whereby the former was to

work as a miner at the rate of $3.50 per day, 'and as a part
of said agreement it was understood and agreed between
plaintiff and defendant that if plaintiff refrained from demanding any pay for his said services until a sufficient
amount of money had been realized from the proceeds of
said mine for that purpose, the defendant would pay plaintiff double the amount of his said wages, to wit, the sum of
seven dollars per day.'   It is then alleged that said mine 'did
on or before the said twenty-eighth day of October, 1913,
produce and yield to defendant a sufficient sum of money
as the proceeds thereof to pay the said plaintiff for his said
labor at the rate of seven dollars per day for the period of
his employment as aforesaid.'   It is also alleged that a demand was made by plaintiff on defendant for a statement
of the earnings and proceeds of the mine and for payment
of the amount due, but that defendant refused to comply
with said demands.   The receipt of $75 on account is admitted
and judgment is asked for $4,125.

"The second cause of action sets up the employment of
plaintiff and his rendition of labor for six hundred days
and 'that said services were and are reasonably worth $3.50
per day'; that no part thereof has been paid except the sum
of $75.00, and judgment is demanded in the sum of $2,025.

"A demurrer to the complaint, generally and for ambiguity, uncertainty and unintelligibility, was overruled and
defendant answered: Admitted an agreement with plaintiff
whereby he was to work for defendant, but denies that it
was as set out in the complaint; admitted that plaintiff performed six hundred days' labor 'but denies that defendant
was to pay for such work or labor, or that the plaintiff was
working for defendant'; denied that the mine yielded to
defendant 'a sufficient sum of money as the proceeds thereof
to pay plaintiff for his said labor at the rate of seven dollars per day, or any other sum, or at all for his said labor';
admitted plaintiff's demand for a statement but avers that
defendant 'could not understand what kind of statement was
expected to be furnished to plaintiff; defendant demanded of
plaintiff that he make his demand in writing so that defendant would be enabled to comply with plaintiff's demand, but
defendant denies that a statement of the moneys paid and
yielded to defendant by and from the operation of the said
mine . . , was refused plaintiff, or that defendant does now

continue to refuse to furnish such statement to plaintiff; admitted that no payment was made plaintiff and alleged that none is due.

"As 'a further defense and answer,' defendant 'alleges that plaintiff was not in the employ of the defendant at any time or at all between the nineteenth day of February, 1912, and the twenty-eighth day of October, 1913, and alleges further that plaintiff with others was working in the said . . . mine, and was to receive as compensation for his said labor and work, his *pro rata* of the net profits derived from the mining and milling of the ores mined by them . . . up to the sum of seven dollars per day.'

"Answering the second cause of action, defendant denied the employment of plaintiff or that he rendered work to defendant, and repeated the allegation that plaintiff and others were to receive a *pro rata* of the net profits; admitted that plaintiff was paid nothing by defendant.

"A cross-complaint sets up an indebtedness by plaintiff to defendant for money loaned and goods and merchandise furnished, of the value of $98.20, and judgment is prayed against plaintiff for that amount. In an 'Answer to Amendment,' defendant denied that $75 was paid plaintiff as wages, but alleged that said sum was a loan.

"Findings were filed: That plaintiff performed six hundred days' labor for defendant under an agreement that 'plaintiff should receive for his said services the sum of $3.50 per day and to pay for his board the sum of $1 per day and if plaintiff refrained from demanding pay for his said services until an amount of money sufficient to meet the sum had been realized from the proceeds of the operation of said mine, that plaintiff should receive the sum of $7 per day, less the said amount for board; that there was not received from the operation of said mine a sufficient amount of money to pay plaintiff for his said work; that plaintiff is entitled to receive $3.50 per day for six hundred days; that defendant is entitled to credit for $75 advanced to plaintiff; that defendant is entitled to credit for board for 616 days at $1 per day,' and judgment was rendered for plaintiff in the sum of $1,409.

"The appeal is from the judgment and from an order denying defendant's motion for a new trial."

Counsel for the appellant vigorously contend in their petition for a rehearing, as likewise they argue in their briefs originally filed herein, that the only permissible conclusion from the testimony of the plaintiff himself was that the agreement upon which he relies here for a recovery does not require the defendant to pay him any compensation whatever until the money was taken from the mine "and in case of failure to take it from the mine he would get $3.50 per day, and that before he could claim the latter amount he would have to allege and prove some misconduct on the part of the defendant or that the mine had failed to produce the money within a reasonable time." And it is further asserted that upon the question of what is "reasonable time," no issue was tendered by the complaint nor evidence offered or received.

The agreement not having been reduced to writing, its terms must necessarily be learned and the intention of the parties as to its nature, scope, and effect necessarily ascertained from the evidence. We have, upon further consideration of the record, concluded that, for a reason to be hereafter explained, the judgment must be reversed. While it may technically be true that there is evidence in the record which supports the trial court's conception of the agreement, as evidenced by its findings, still, on the whole, the evidence as to the nature of the agreement or upon the question of what the parties actually intended should be the precise occasion on which the plaintiff would be entitled to demand and receive pay for his services at the rate of $3.50 per day is, as the learned trial judge in his written opinion, giving his reasons for the conclusion reached, in effect declared, unsatisfactory, and it appears to us to be so much so that, since the judgment must be reversed, a retrial of the issues of fact should be had, in which event the facts bearing upon the transaction may, it is to be hoped, the more clearly and satisfactorily be disclosed. It will, therefore, be unnecessary for us to consider in detail the evidence in this opinion.

As to the criticism of the plaintiff's complaint, however, it is proper that we should say that, it being alleged in the first count or cause of action therein stated that the mine "did, on or before the twenty-eighth day of October, 1913, produce and yield to defendant a sufficient sum of money as the proceeds thereof to pay the said plaintiff for his said labor at the rate of $7 per day for the period of his employment," it was obviously unnecessary to plead therein that the mine had failed, within a reasonable time, to produce the money with which to pay the plaintiff, assuming that it is true that the understanding between the parties was that the plaintiff was entitled to the payment of no compensation whatever until the mine did produce the money required to make such payment. Nor was it necessary to plead the matter as to "reasonable time" in the second cause of action, which was cast in the form of a common count, upon a *quantum meruit*. To have done so would have necessitated the pleading of the express agreement almost in its entirety—that is to say, it would have been necessary to plead not only the agreement to employ the plaintiff (which necessarily is pleaded in said count), but also the condition upon which he would be entitled to demand and receive his compensation. This, it seems to us, would have been inconsistent with the essential theory upon which an action on an implied contract proceeds.

The plaintiff, in his second cause of action, proceeded precisely as is required where the action is in the *quantum meruit* form of a common count, and in such case the defendant is entitled to interpose any defense, which, if proved, will countervail the claim of the plaintiff that any sum is due and owing to him from the defendant as the "reasonable value" of services alleged to have been performed. In this case, either with or without pleading it, the question of "reasonable time" could have been introduced by the defendant as a defense to the second cause of action. In other words, the actual agreement between the parties, as the defendant understood it, could have been shown by the latter, without pleading such agreement, as a defense to the plaintiff's claim, as set forth in said cause of action, that the defendant was indebted to him in a sum representing the reasonable value of the alleged services rendered by him to and for the defendant.

As above stated, however, it will be necessary to order a reversal of the judgment, and this for the reason that the court failed to make a finding upon a material issue.

As seen, the defendant filed a cross-complaint in which it is alleged that the plaintiff is indebted to the defendant for money loaned and for goods and merchandise furnished and delivered to the plaintiff, at the latter's special instance and request, in the sum of $98.20.   In his answer to the cross-complaint, the plaintiff denied the indebtedness so alleged.

There was some testimony supporting the above-mentioned allegation of the cross-complaint, and it was this evidence that this court said in the order granting the rehearing had been overlooked in the preparation of the former opinion.

The plaintiff himself testified that the defendant, through Mr. Oddie, its president and manager, had furnished him a bill of groceries, etc., amounting in value to the sum of $80, for which he had not paid.   The court made no finding upon this issue.

It is, of course, well settled that if any material issue is left unfound, it is ground for reversal of the judgment. (Hayne on New Trial and Appeal, Rev. ed., p. 1317.)

For the reasons herein stated, both the judgment and the order are reversed and the cause remanded.

Chipman, P. J., and Burnett, J., concurred.

A petition to have the cause heard in the supreme court, after judgment in the district court of appeal, was denied by the supreme court on December 14, 1916.

[Civ. No. 1568.   Third Appellate District.—October 7, 1916.]

NANCY SHELLMAN et al., Respondents, v. ELLA L. HERSHEY et al., Appellants.

NEGLIGENCE—FALL IN MAKING EXIT FROM OPERA HOUSE—DANGEROUS AND UNSAFE PASSAGEWAY—LIABILITY OF LESSEES.—In an action against the owners of an opera house and the lessees thereof to recover damages for personal injuries sustained by a spectator at an entertainment held therein, in passing out through a side door, which had been opened during the performance by the manager and agent of the lessees, at the request of spectators, for ventilating purposes, the lessees are liable in damages for such injuries, where it is shown that the door was not used or intended to be used as an exit or entrance, and that it was left open, unguarded, and unlighted at the close of the entertainment and with no step to aid a person in reaching the sidewalk three feet below.

ID.—NONLIABILITY OF OWNERS.—The owners of the opera house are not
liable in damages for such injuries, where it is shown that such door
was not intended to be used and never was used for the convenience
of patrons, but was intended for the use of and to be used only by
lessees to take in and out stage properties and for the purpose of
occasionally sweeping dirt through, or to air the house.

ID.—NUISANCE CREATED BY LESSEES—LESSOR NOT LIABLE.—Where property is demised, and at the time of the demise is not a nuisance, and
becomes so only by the act of the tenant while in his possession,
and injury happens during such possession, the owner is not liable.

APPEAL from an order of the Superior Court of Yolo
County denying a new trial. N. A. Hawkins, Judge.

The facts are stated in the opinion of the court.

George Clark, and Black & Clark, for Appellants.

A. C. Huston, and H. L. Huston, for Respondents.

CHIPMAN, P. J.—This is an action commenced by plaintiffs to recover damages for an injury suffered by plaintiff
Nancy Shellman in passing out through a doorway of the
Woodland Opera House owned by defendants, the Hersheys,
and under lease to defendants Henry and Giesea. The cause
was tried by the court without the aid of a jury, and plaintiff
had judgment for two thousand dollars and costs of suit.

Defendants, the Hersheys, moved for a new trial which was
denied. They appeal from the order. Defendants Henry
and Giesea appeal from the judgment on a separate transcript
No. 1569, but do not appeal from the order.

The Woodland Opera House is situated on Second Street of
the city of Woodland. The main entrance and exit of the
auditorium is on Second Street at the southeast corner of the
building. Along the east wall opening into the auditorium,
about midway of the building, is a door opening from the
dress-circle. It was in stepping out of this door that plaintiff,
Mrs. Shellman, fell and received the injury of which she complains. The interior of the opera house is similar to most
playhouses. In the center next to the stage is the parquet ·
surrounding the parquet by a half-circle are the dress-circle
seats extending back to the rear wall; at the center of the
rear wall is an exit door eight and a half feet wide leading
from the dress-circle into the main entrance area; the center

aisle passes from this door down through the dress-circle and parquet; aisles also lead from this door along the south, east and west walls down to the stage. The defendants, the Hersheys, are and have been for many years the owners of this opera house and at the time of the accident, on the evening of May 29, 1912, it was under lease to defendants Henry and Giesea. It had been let by the lessees to the graduating class of the high school of Woodland for an entertainment that evening, for which a rental of $25 was paid to the lessees. Admission to the entertainment was free and the house was crowded with spectators, many standing in the aisles for lack of seating capacity. It is alleged in the complaint: "that the entrance to said opera house is on Second Street in the city of Woodland; that said opera house is so constructed that a door bearing the same relative position to the entrance leads onto Second Street from the main auditorium of the theater; that said door is built three feet above the sidewalk on Second Street; that during all times herein mentioned, there was no light over said door, and said door was not protected or guarded in any way, or at all; that said door as built and situated in said theater is unsafe, insecure, and dangerous to the patrons of said theater. That on the twenty-ninth day of May, 1912, said theater or opera house was leased to L. Henry and F. A. Giesea, but said door was in said building and was so built and located, and was not connected with the sidewalk by any steps or otherwise, or at all, and was not protected or guarded as above described, and was an unsafe and insecure and a dangerous passageway as above described, prior to the leasing of said opera house to said L. Henry and F. A. Giesea; that said owners had during all of the times herein mentioned full knowledge of the unsafe, insecure, and dangerous character of said door, and negligently permitted it to remain in such condition, and failed to properly or at all to safeguard it. That on the evening of the twenty-ninth day of May, 1912, plaintiff, Nancy Shellman, above named, attended a public entertainment at said opera house; that during said performance the above described door was left open; that at the close of said performance, as the spectators were leaving the building, plaintiff, Nancy Shellman, believing that said door was an exit from said theater, walked through said door and was violently precipitated upon the sidewalk; that at the time said plaintiff walked through said door it was unguarded and unprotected, and there was nothing about said door to warn plaintiff of its dangerous or unsafe character. That by reason of said fall, the left arm of plaintiff, Nancy Shellman, was broken at the elbow; that the bones in said elbow were broken in such a way that they could not and did not properly mend; that said elbow is now stiff''; that she was otherwise injured as set forth in much detail.

In their answer, "defendants deny that said door was constructed for use as an entrance or exit or that it was in any manner necessary" for such use, or that defendants or either of them directed or sanctioned the use of said door as an entrance or exit in the use of said opera house; "admit that said door was not connected with the sidewalk by any steps or otherwise . . . because said door was not an entrance to, or exit from, the said opera house in the use thereof by persons going into, or coming out of said opera house at the time the same was used for public entertainment." Deny that said door as built is or was unsafe or dangerous or that any act of defendants caused the same to be unsafe or dangerous; deny that on May 29, 1912, or at any other time, defendants had full or any knowledge that said door was unsafe or that they permitted it to remain unsafe; allege that when said opera house was leased to said Henry and Giesea, it was never understood that in the management thereof "said doorway should at any time be or remain open as a means of entrance or exit . . . for the use of persons going into or leaving the same; . . . that on the occasion of giving said entertainment and after the audience was assembled, some person, whose name cannot be ascertained, requested one Robert Eastham, who at said time was employed by said L. H. Henry and F. A. Giesea, lessees of said opera house, to unlock said door; that said Eastham did thereupon, and pursuant to said request, unlock and open said door and allowed the same to remain open but all without authority, consent, or knowledge of defendants hereby answering, or either of them''; that said plaintiff, Mrs. Shellman, entered said opera house without any charge therefor and voluntarily; that the injury suffered by her in leaving said entertainment was caused by her own negligence "in an effort to leave said opera house speedily and by an unusual means and by stepping out of the doorway mentioned in the complaint, which said doorway could be plainly observed . . . and, if the said Nancy Shellman suffered the injuries mentioned in the complaint, they were the direct result of her negligent and careless conduct in so endeavoring to leave said opera house."

The findings of the court are substantially in accord with the averments of the complaint, and are challenged by defendants as not supported by the evidence. A diagram was introduced showing the sidewalk elevation along Second Street. "It shows the sill elevation and floor elevation of the door; in front of that door there is a concrete sidewalk; it is two feet five inches from the sidewalk to the sill of the door; it is nine inches from the sill of the door to the floor of the opera house. There is no step between the sill and the sidewalk. The door is seven feet four inches by three feet four inches. The door opens outward into the street."

Plaintiff, Mrs. Shellman, testified as follows: "I went to the opera house that evening by going up the front steps, the wide steps, on Second Street, and I went down into the lower floor of the opera house, walked around the wall, down to the door. I walked around there, there were no seats so I stood up there until the entertainment was over. There were a great many that did stand up. There wasn't seats. I was standing near the door, not a great ways from the stage, a yard or so from the door. The door was open all the time. I think people were going out there, that is why I stepped out. I thought they were going out there. There was several in between the door and myself where I stood and that is why I stepped out there. I thought I could step out there. The floor in the opera house inclines toward the rear. It seemed to me it was much lower there as I went down the side of it, it seemed so much lower that I could step right out on the sidewalk, that is why I stepped out. I thought I could step on to the sidewalk. The Court: Did you see the sidewalk when you stepped down? A. No, sir. Q. It was dark? A. Yes. Q. You looked out from a light room into the dark street? A. Yes, there was no light there as far as I could see, but I supposed I could step right on to the sidewalk. Mr. Huston: State whether or not there was anything there to prevent you from going out? A. No, sir; nothing there and nobody to tell me, nobody guarded the door. Q. The door was not guarded in any way? A. No, sir. Q. State whether or not the door was standing open or closed? A. Yes, it was standing open. The Court: Was that a warm night? A. Yes, sir; it was warm, the 29th of May; it was very pleasant and warm. Mr. Huston: When was the first time you noticed the door was open? A. It was open all the time, I think, during the entertainment. Q. Just state to the Court how that door or opening looked to you that night. A. Well, it looked to me like a door right down near the sidewalk that I could step right out and without any harm, of course, or I wouldn't have stepped out. Mr. Huston: That is all."

On cross-examination, she testified that she had been at the theater twice before, and both times had entered and left by the main entrance and did not see the other door on those occasions. "There was no light in front of the door through which I stepped. There was no light only on the inside, the lights were inside the house. Q. Had there been a light at that exit or doorway through which you went the night you hurt your arm would you have been able to see whether there was or was not a step there or would you have been able to see how far the sidewalk was from the doorsill? A. Yes, I think I could have seen if there had been a light there. Mr. Clark: But you are rather emphatically of the opinion that there was no light there? A. Yes, sir. Q. You are a lady sixty-seven years of age, you stated? A. Yes, sir. Q. And in stepping through an exit that you never went through before you paid some attention to where you were stepping, you looked before you as you walked, didn't you, to that exit? A. Why, I walked to the door and just stepped, I just stepped through, I thought it was right on to the sidewalk of course, or I wouldn't have stepped through. Q. You were looking out of that doorway as you came to the doorway? A. Yes, I was looking out; I just started and went to that door and just stepped right through thinking I could step right on to the sidewalk. Q. Did you pay attention to where you were stepping? A. Yes, sir. Q. Did you endeavor as you went through the door to look to see whether you were stepping safely toward the sidewalk? A. I had no thought that it wasn't safe."

Witness Eastham was the lessee's manager in charge of the theater at the time of the accident. He testified that he had the key to the door referred to and opened it and left it open during the entertainment. He testified: "It was very warm that night, and it was very warm in there and oppressive, and someone came and asked me to open the door, some one requested me, that there was a lot of ladies there about to faint but who it was I don't remember, so I unlocked the door but not for an exit. Q. You had been manager of the opera house for some time? A. Yes." He testified that it was not any one of defendants who made the request; that he had charge of the theater for Henry and Giesea and let the theater to the board of education and collected the rental for the lessees who had the theater for 1911 and 1912. The lease bears date August 26, 1910, and was executed by "Ella L. Hershey and Cornelia A. Hershey, executrices of the last will and testament of D. N. Hershey, deceased, the parties of the first part." It was admitted that when the lease was made, the defendants Hersheys owned the opera house, and that witness Eastham had been in charge of the opera house three seasons under other tenants before the lease to Henry and Giesea was executed, and had the key in his possession all the time. He testified that this particular door was used occasionally "to sweep some of the dirt out that way or take something in that way, but was never used as an exit or entrance"; that while he had charge "there was no box or step leading to that door whereby a person could step into that from the outside"; that he had no instructions from the lessees with reference to that door; that the Hersheys never gave him any instructions about that door; that it was locked that night before the witness opened it, and was always kept locked during entertainments; that he had been acquainted with the building since its construction and there never had been any step placed at that door, and that to make use of it as an exit or entrance a step would have been necessary.

Witness Clary was asked whether, during the time he was city marshal, the city trustees ever gave him any instructions in reference to the opera house. Over objection, the court allowed the answer if "connected with the defendants in some way." Answering yes, the witness was asked what the directions were. "A. Well, the board ordered me to notify them that they had to repair the sidewalk, and fix the step for a kind of fire-escape there." Defendants' counsel moved to strike out the answer as immaterial, irrelevant, and incompetent. Motion denied. "Mr. Huston: The step you mention was in reference to this door at the opera house? A. Yes, sir. Q. In obedience to these instructions, did you notify the de-

fendants Hershey concerning this condition?" Over defendants' objection, the court allowed the answer. "A. I know
that I told Mr. Webber and I don't know but I think I wrote
them a notice. Mr. Huston: To whom did you address your
notice? A. To Mrs. Hershey." An objection was allowed to
precede the answer on the same grounds and that it is not
the best evidence. "The Court: The objection will be sustained unless it is connected, but for the present it will be
overruled. Mr. Huston: You mailed this notice in the regular
course of business? A. Yes, sir. Q. You also notified Mr.
Webber? A. Yes, sir. Q. What connection, if any, did Mr.
Webber have with this opera house? A. He was manager.
Q. He had charge of it? A. Yes, sir. Q. What, if anything,
did they do in reference to this notice that you gave them?
Mr. Clark: Our objection is going to this. The Court: Same
ruling. A. Put a box there for a step. Mr. Huston: At this
same door? A. Yes; put a box on the sidewalk at that door.
Q. When was that? A. That was after I told Mr. Webber,
they put it there for a step." He testified that this was in
1909 while he was marshal and that his term expired in 1910.
Defendants' attorneys moved to strike out all the testimony
of Clary on various grounds: that no foundation was laid for
it, nothing to connect the Hersheys with the transaction, and
other grounds. "Mr. Huston: Mr. Clary, you put that letter
in the postoffice at Woodland? A. Sure. Q. Mrs. Hershey
lives in the city of Woodland? A. Lives in Woodland. Mr.
Huston: This proof is offered in furtherance of our allegation
in the complaint to the effect that the defendants Hershey
had prior knowledge and actual knowledge of this door and
its dangerous condition prior to the time of the accident. The
Court: It doesn't appear who this man Webber is. Mr. Huston: Mr. Clary says he was the manager of the opera house.
The Court: You say you told Mr. Webber this? A. Yes, I
told him. The Court: The motion to strike out is denied."

Recalled as a witness for defendants, he testified: "I know
the side door of the opera house was never used as an exit or
as an entrance. I have been there in the opera house at per-
formances. I have been there when people were going in
and out."

Witness Curson, a city trustee from 1907 to 1911, testified
that Clary was night watchman up to the time he was appointed marshal, and that during that time "the board gave

him directions to enforce some matters that the building committee of the board was asked to look into regarding fire-escapes, etc., and the protection of the building, and I think Mr. Clary was authorized to notify the owners of the building that such steps were necessary for the protection of the public at large in regard to fire-escapes, etc.''

Witness Eastham was recalled as a witness for defendants. He testified that he received the keys to the theater from Mr. Farrell, president of the Great Western Theatrical Circuit, and was employed by him and was the only manager of the opera house from that time; that the Farrell lease was made on August 1, 1908, and continued until Henry and Giesea took the theater; that ''Mr. Webber had nothing to do during that time with the booking of the shows or attending to that opera house''; that Webber was employed at one time as manager, previous to Mr. Farrell's time. He testified that he had known the opera house ever since it was built, and that in using it ''the entrance and exit to that lower auditorium for performance purposes has been through the main entrance over at the south wall.''

Defendant Cornelia Hershey testified that she and her mother acted for the others of the family in leasing the theater; that they got some notice about fixing the sidewalk in 1912, which was attended to, and the work done, but that she had been unable to find among their papers any notice sent them by Mr. Clary relative to that side door; that she knew there was no step there and that it was in that condition when they took the premises and when they leased them to tenants; that no step was ever maintained there, and the door had never ''been used as an exit or entrance to the opera house down to the time of this accident.'' She testified that she and her mother, as executrices, leased the opera house to the Great Western Theatrical Circuit, August 1, 1908, and that Mr. Eastham acted as manager. She testified that she never got any notice from Mr. Clary telling them to put steps at that central side door; that she ''got a notice from Mr. Scott regarding the fixing of the sidewalk in 1912,'' and it was done; that she had made it a practice to keep all papers served upon them, and had searched the files but could find no notice from Mr. Clary relative to that side door.

We do not think there can be any doubt of the lessee's liability. They, through their agent and manager, opened the door in question and left it open under circumstances such as would and did lead the plaintiff, Mrs. Shellman, to believe that she could safely pass out at that door. Although this door was not used or intended to be used as an exit or entrance, the tenants are chargeable with knowledge that in opening and leaving it open, unguarded, and unlighted, with no step to aid a person in reaching the pavement, the passage out by that door was dangerous and unsafe. This situation was one of their own creation for which upon well-settled principles they were liable.

A much more serious question arises as to the owners' liability. They knew that this door had no step leading from it to the sidewalk; they knew this when they leased the premises to their codefendants, for it was in the same condition it had been in ever since they inherited the property in 1903 at the death of the original owner. But the uncontradicted testimony was that this particular door was not intended for use as an exit or entrance for patrons of the theater, and had never been used for that purpose in all the years of defendants' ownership. The only use to which it had ever been put was "only occasionally to sweep some of the dirt out that way or to take something in that way, but it was never used as an exit," and it was "always kept locked." Defendants, the Hersheys, had never given any directions concerning this door and personally had nothing to do with the management of the theater. Their liability must spring, if at all, from the single fact that they knew the location of this door, and also knew that no step or steps had been placed there.

Witness Clary's testimony that he "mailed notice to Mrs. Hershey," that he "deposited it in the postoffice at Woodland," does not meet the statutory requirements of such form of service, and at most would be but *prima facie* evidence which was rebutted by the testimony of Cornelia Hershey that no such notice was received. His testimony that he served the notice when city marshal was disproved by the record showing that in 1909 when he said he served the notice, he was not the city marshal. He was night watchman, however, and he was no doubt honestly mistaken as to when he became city marshal. If he served the notice in either capacity, it would be equally effective, but the proof of service is insufficient.

As to his having notified Webber, this may be taken
as established. But Webber was not then the manager.
Eastham was manager under the then lessee, Farrell's company. But, assuming that such notice was given to the
Hersheys while the theater was under lease to the Farrell
company, it would have conveyed no new fact to the Hersheys, for they admit that there never had been a step placed
at this door. Their defense is that this door was not intended
to be used, and never was used for the convenience of patrons
to the theater, and was intended for the use of and used
only by the lessees to take in and out stage properties, and
was used occasionally to sweep dirt through or to air the house,
but never as an exit or entrance for patrons or during per-
formances.

Respondent relies upon the rule stated in note E to the case
of *Griffin* v. *Jackson Light & Power Co.*, 92 Am. St. Rep. 526;
"No person can create or maintain a nuisance upon his premises and escape liability for the injury occasioned by it to
third persons. Nor can a lessor so create a nuisance and then
escape liability for the consequences by leasing the premises
to a tenant. Prior to and at the time of the lease, it was the
duty of the lessor to put an end to the nuisance. If he fails
to do this, and leases the premises with the nuisance on them,
he may be deemed, and is deemed, to authorize the continuance
of the nuisance, and is therefore liable for the consequences
of such continuance. Whether, therefore, the defect be one
of original construction, or arises from a failure to repair, or
from the maintenance on the premises of any condition endangering the health or safety of strangers, whatever its nature, *if it constitute a nuisance,* the lessor will be responsible
for its consequences if he leases the premises with the nuisance
upon them, and thus authorizes its continuance." Among
the cases cited in support of the text is *Kalis* v. *Shattuck,* 69
Cal. 593, [58 Am. Rep. 568, 11 Pac. 346] in which injury
arose from an awning falling upon a person while passing
under it. The tenant of the premises allowed the awning
to be used by sight-seers going upon it, thus causing it to fall.
It was not built or intended for such use, but only as a cover
for the sidewalk from sunshine and rain, and was properly
constructed for that purpose. The lessor was held free from
liability for the injury. Said the court: "It is well settled
that a landlord is not liable for such consequences, unless;

1. The nuisance occasioning the injury existed at the time
the premises were demised; or, 2. The structure was in such
condition that it would be likely to become a nuisance, in
the ordinary and reasonable use of the same *for the purpose
for which it was constructed and let* and the landlord failed
to repair it (citing cases); or, 3. The landlord authorized or
permitted the act which caused it to become a nuisance occasioning the injury." Quoting from *Gandy* v. *Jubber*, 5
Best & S. 485, "To bring liability home to the owner the
premises being let, the nuisance must be one which was in
its very essence and nature a nuisance at the time of letting,
*and not something which was capable of being thereafter ren-
dered a nuisance by the tenant. . . .*"

In notes B and C (p. 524) to the case from which respondents extract note E, *supra*, in 92 Am. St. Rep., the liability
of the lessor of real property to third persons is considered.
Note B points out the nonliability of the lessor to third persons for injuries arising from a nuisance not on the premises
at the time of the lease, but which was erected or created by
the tenant alone without the license or consent of the lessor.
Note C is as follows: "The same considerations control where
the nuisance is occasioned by a *misuse* by the lessee of the
premises, or of appliances which were thereon at the time of
the lease. It is not sufficient to render a lessor liable that the
premises leased by him are capable of a use which will prove
a nuisance to strangers. 'If a landlord demise premises which
are not in themselves a nuisance, but may or may not become such, according to the manner in which they are used
by the tenant, the landlord will not be liable for a nuisance
created on the premises by the tenant. He is not responsible
for enabling the tenant to commit a nuisance if the latter
should think proper to do so. (Citing cases.) In such a
case it may be said, in one sense, that the landlord permitted
the tenant to create the nuisance, but not in such a sense as
to render him liable. (Citing cases.) The landlord will not
be liable for the use of the premises in such a way as to do
harm, *merely because there was a manifest possibility of
their being used in such a way.*' (Citing cases.) . . . Where,
therefore, the premises, while capable of improper use, may
be used in an ordinary manner without the creation of a
nuisance, the lessor is not chargeable with the improper uses

of them by the tenant which results in a nuisance." (Citing cases.)

In *Owings* v. *Jones*, 9 Md. 108, the court, referring to *Rich* v. *Basterfield*, 4 Manning, Granger & Scott, 56 Eng. Com. Law, 784, said: "After a full review of all the cases, and that too after a second argument, we understand the court to deduce, at least the two following principles from the numerous adjudications to which reference is had: First: That where property is demised, and at the time of the demise is not a nuisance and becomes so only by the act of the tenant while in his possession, and injury happens during such possession, the owner is not liable; but second: that where the owner leases premises which are a nuisance, or must in the nature of things become so by their user, and receives rent, then, whether in or out of possession, he is liable."

Further reference to authorities seems unnecessary. We think it results from the principles above stated that the only question here is: Was this side door to the theater a nuisance when the premises were leased to defendants Henry and Giesea, or did it become such for the time being when the tenants used it for a purpose other than that for which it was designed and had, from the day the house was built, been used to the moment the present tenant misused it? We think the premises were not a nuisance when demised, and became so because of the manner in which the tenants used them on the night of the accident. It follows that the defendants, the Hersheys, are not liable for the injury complained of.

It is not necessary to consider any of the other alleged errors.

The order is reversed and a new trial granted as to defendants, the Hersheys.

Burnett, J., and Hart, J., concurred.

A petition to have the cause heard in the supreme court, after judgment in the district court of appeal, was denied by the supreme court on December 4, 1916.

[Civ. No. 1569. Third Appellate District.—October 7, 1916.]

NANCY SHELLMAN et al., Respondents, v. ELLA L. HERSHEY et al., Appellants.

NEGLIGENCE—INJURIES IN MAKING EXIT FROM OPERA HOUSE—PLEADING —SUFFICIENCY OF COMPLAINT AGAINST LESSEES.—In an action against the owners and the lessees of an opera house to recover damages for personal injuries received by a patron in making her exit therefrom, the complaint sufficiently states a cause of action against the lessees, where it is alleged that they were the lessees of the premises on the day of the accident, and the nuisance and the accident are fully described.

APPEAL from a judgment of the Superior Court of Yolo County. N. A. Hawkins, Judge.

The facts are stated in the opinion of the court.

E. M. Rosenthal, for Appellants.

A. C. Huston, and H. L. Huston, for Respondents.

CHIPMAN, P. J.—This is an appeal by defendants Henry and Giesea from the judgment in the case of like title, No. 1568, *ante*, p. 641, [161 Pac. 132], this day decided, and is here on the judgment-roll alone. The only question presented arises on a general demurrer.

The complaint alleged ownership of the premises in defendants, the Hersheys; that defendants Henry and Giesea on the day of the accident were lessees of the premises; that the premises are a public place of amusement let for hire; describes what was claimed to constitute the nuisance complained of; that the theater on the day mentioned was leased to defendants Henry and Giesea; that said nuisance existed in the theater prior to the letting to Henry and Giesea and at the time of the accident and describes fully the accident and alleges amount of damages.

We think a cause of action was sufficiently stated against these appellants. There was no special demurrer. The case was fully tried on all issues. It must be assumed, in the absence of a bill of exceptions, "that the evidence presented in support of the findings was competent to establish the facts alleged, and was received at the trial without any objection, and was sufficient to sustain each of the facts found." (*Cutting Fruit Co.* v. *Canty,* 141 Cal. 692 [syllabus], [75 Pac. 564].)

The judgment as to defendants Henry and Giesea is affirmed.

Burnett, J., and Hart, J., concurred.

[Civ. No. 1527.   Third Appellate District.—October 10, 1916.]

TUOLUMNE COUNTY ELECTRIC POWER AND LIGHT COMPANY (a Corporation), Appellant, v. CITY OF SONORA (a Municipal Corporation), Respondent.

MUNICIPAL CORPORATION—LIABILITY FOR ELECTRICITY FOR STREET LIGHTING—FAILURE OF PROOF.—An electric light and power company engaged in furnishing electricity for lighting dwellings, business places, and streets of a municipal corporation, cannot recover in an action against the city for current consumed in the street lights between the hours of 7 o'clock A. M. and 4:30 o'clock P. M., where the complaint alleges that such current was furnished at the instance and request of the municipality, but the evidence shows that the city expressly notified the power company that it would only pay for electricity furnished between the hours of 4:30 oclock P. M. and 7 o'clock A. M.

APPEAL from a judgment of the Superior Court of Tuolumne County.   G. W. Nicol, Judge.

The facts are stated in the opinion of the court.

J. B. Curtin, and W. H. Mahoney, for Appellant.

J. C. Webster, for Respondent.

BURNETT, J.—The action was for the recovery of the sum of $2,425.37 for electrical energy claimed to have been furnished by plaintiff and consumed by defendant in the street lights of said city. For years plaintiff, which is a public service corporation purchasing its electricity from the

Sierra and San Francisco Power Company and then selling it to consumers, has been engaged in furnishing electrical energy for lighting dwellings, business places, and the streets in said city of Sonora. From its substation along the side of Washington Street, the main street of said city, for more than ten years prior to October 1, 1913, the plaintiff had two main power lines, and to these, other lines extending along the sides of the other streets were attached, thus forming the system by which electric lights were furnished for houses and streets. During these years, one of these main lines from the substation carried what is called the day circuit current of twenty-four hours, the other, what is called the night circuit current, both of which currents were turned on and off at said substation. The night circuit was loaded one-half hour after sunset and turned off one-half hour before sunrise—this period being recognized generally as the standard hours for street lighting, and the day circuit was left continuously turned on so as to have twenty-four hours always of continuous service on that line. More than ten years prior to October 1, 1913, the trustees of said city, for the purpose of lighting the streets, caused wires from the center of the street to be connected with plaintiff's night service main line, an incandescent light being attached to the end of each of these wires. The light was anchored on the opposite side of the street so that each light would be suspended over the middle of the street at a given height. By this method, most of the streets were lighted during this period of time, and all street lights were connected with and received current from plaintiff's night circuit line. During this period the city of Sonora owned all of the wires extending from plaintiff's main night service line into the streets, and also owned all bracket street lamps. When the street lighting system was constructed, no automatic switches or devises of any kind were connected therewith or constructed thereon, so as to turn on or off independent of other consumers' hours, any of the street lights, the entire street lighting system being regulated as to that by a switch at said substation, controlled and operated by the Sierra and San Francisco Power Company. As the electric current flowed through the said main night circuit line, it ran out into the street lamps and bracket lamps, and thus the streets were lighted.

With knowledge of these facts and without any previous notice to plaintiff, the trustees of Sonora on September 15, 1913, adopted and passed to print, to take effect on October 1, 1913, the ordinance in controversy here, which appears in full in the transcript. The title of said ordinance is: "An ordinance fixing the rate which may be charged and collected by any person, firm, or corporation furnishing, distributing, or delivering electric current for lighting, heating, power and other purposes to the inhabitants of the city of Sonora, California; providing for the installation of meters and regulating the installation of electric current and prices to be charged for labor and supplies therefor, and fixing a penalty for the violation of any of the provisions of the ordinance." Section 11 provided: "Electric current furnished or distributed to consumers in the city of Sonora, except for street lights, shall be an all day and all night service and shall be furnished every day for twenty-four hours each day, and electric current furnished for street lighting shall be from 4:30 P. M. of each and every day to 7 o'clock A. M. of the following morning." This section, it may be said, was amended on the 18th of June, 1914, so as to read: "Electric current furnished or distributed to consumers in the City of Sonora, except for street lights, shall be an all day and all night service and shall be furnished every day for twenty-four hours each day, and electric current furnished for street lighting shall be from one-half hour after sunset to one hour before sunrise each night."

When plaintiff saw the publication of this ordinance of September 15th, it addressed the following letter to said trustees:

"Sonora, Cal., Sept. 25, 1913.

"To the Trustees of the City of Sonora,

"Sonora, California.

"Gentlemen:

"The Tuolumne County Electric Power and Light Company on and after October 1, 1913, will furnish twenty-four hour service to all it's customers as required by Ordinance No. 63 of the City of Sonora and in order to so do it will be necessary to leave for said twenty-four hours, power on what is now our night circuit. As all the street lighting apparatus for lighting the city streets is the property of the City, it will be necessary for the Trustees of said City to turn off

the street lights between seven A. M. and four thirty P. M.
each day otherwise the power thus used between said hours
will be charged for as provided in said ordinance.

"The obligation of this Company ceases when it furnishes
power to the city's connection. . . ."

The street lights were not turned off, and the city of Sonora
enjoyed the unique and illuminating experience of street
lamps burning day and night. In passing, it may not be
amiss to venture the conjecture that strangers must have regarded with some degree of astonishment, if not of admira-
tion, the spectacle of prodigality thereby exhibited.

Plaintiff presented its bill for the whole amount of electric
energy consumed by said lights, and it was allowed for the
said hours so contemplated by said section 11. Plaintiff declined to accept such payment in full and hence the suit.

Appellant contends in the first place that "the duty of such
a corporation is fully performed when it has brought its commodity safely and conveniently to the door of the consumer.
Within that door the company is not by law obliged and may
not by law be compelled to go for any purpose foreign to the
public service it is called upon to render, and that the purpose here contemplated is foreign is abundantly established."
(*Ex parte Goodrich,* 160 Cal. 418, [Ann. Cas. 1913A, 56, 117
Pac. 451, 456].)

It is argued that if the light company desired to raise or
lower the lights from their present height across the street,
it would have no right or power to do so because the lights
and wiring connected with the same belong to the city. So if
the company desired to put a longer wire from its main wire
to the street lamps, it would have no right to do so for the
same reason. It would also have no right to put new lamps
on the streets in place of the old ones, or in any manner to
interfere with the city's street lamps. These circumstances
are mentioned to illustrate appellant's contention that it has
done its full duty when it turns on its electrical energy in
the main lines to which the city street lamps are connected,
and that then it "has brought its commodity safely and conveniently to the door of the consumer and beyond that the
company is not by law obliged and may not be by law compelled to go."

Again it is claimed that since the city of Sonora is a consumer of electrical energy, the same rule of law will control

it as would control a private individual, and herein is cited
Davoust v. *City of Alameda*, 149 Cal. 70, [9 Ann. Cas. 847,
5 L. R. A. (N. S.) 536, 84 Pac. 761], wherein is quoted the
following from *Touchard* v. *Touchard*, 5 Cal. 307: "A corporation by the civil and common law, is a person, an artificial
person; and although a municipal corporation has delegated
to it certain powers of government it is only in reference to
those delegated powers that it will be regarded as a government. In reference to all other of its transactions, such as
affects its ownership of property in buying, selling, or granting, and in reference to all matters of contract, it must be
looked upon and treated as a private person, and its contract
construed in the same manner and with like effect as those
of natural persons."

Lastly, it is claimed that when the "company loaded its
electrical energy in its main night service line for the twenty-
four hours required and to which line the city more than ten
years ago, attached its streets lamp wires," it had done all
that could be required of it and then it "became the duty
of the city to take care that it used only so much of that
commodity as it required for street lighting purposes and
not permit any that had entered its doors to go to waste
and to prevent any waste, if it was necessary, to attach or
furnish any appliance to turn on or off the 'commodity'
when not required." It is insisted that the duty to so attach and furnish said appliance devolved upon the city and
not upon the company. As authority for this proposition,
attention is directed to *Hunt* v. *Marianna Electric Co.*, 114
Ark. 498, [L. R. A. 1915B, 897, 170 S. W. 96], wherein it
appears that said company for several years had been operating a system or plant in which the generator of electricity
produced what is known as "133-cycle current of electricity,"
and plaintiffs had installed motors and machines for conducting their business adapted to this cycle system; that the said
company was proceeding to change the kind and character
of machinery operated by them into what is termed a "60-
cycle system," so that it would not operate the motors used
by plaintiffs and the citizens generally, and that the company
was demanding of the users of its electricity that they bear
the expense of the readjustment and repairs to their various
motors so that they could be operated. It appears further

that plaintiffs had demanded of the company to readjust said motors for said purpose, to the end that the company might carry out its contract and agreement with them and the public to properly serve electricity, but that the company refused to do so and was proceeding to change its system to the great injury of plaintiffs. It was held that the company was not bound at its own expense to alter the consumers' fixtures so that they would be adapted to the use of the new current, even though many of the fixtures had been bought from the company and were suitable only for the current formerly furnished, it appearing that the change was not made capriciously. The court said: "In our judgment, it not having been alleged that the change was needlessly or capriciously made, we think this expense should be borne by the plaintiffs. Otherwise, having become a part of the operating expense of the company, this would be an item to be considered in fixing the rates to be charged all consumers of electricity, and would be an expense to be borne at least by the public generally, rather than by those owners who were required to supply themselves with new appliances.''

It is contended that the rule applies with stronger force here for the reason that plaintiff did not change its system "of its own volition from night service to day service of twenty-four hours. The light company here was compelled to turn in twenty-four hours of load on what it theretofore had only loaded from one-half hour after sunsent to one-half hour before sunrise, and if it failed to do so it was guilty of misdemeanor and subject to a fine,'' and the claim is that the trustees knew that if they did not put in some device to turn off the current, the lights would burn for twenty-four hours, and hence arises the responsibility of the city for the whole amount consumed.

It is also claimed that from the showing made the inference must be drawn that the whole amount was furnished upon the demand and at the instance and request of defendant city. In this connection, some authorities are cited, among them *Babbitt* v. *Chicago & A. Ry. Co.*, 149 Mo. App. 449, [130 S. W. 367]; Abbott's Trial Evidence, 358, and *San Francisco Gas Co.* v. *San Francisco*, 9 Cal. 453. In the first, it is said: "It has been held that the specific word 'demand' need not be used in making such a request, but it is sufficient if any words are used which are understood by both parties to be a demand. Furthermore, it has been held that the existence of a demand may be shown by circumstantial evidence, or may be inferred from the acts and declarations of the parties as proven by direct evidence.''

In the second, it is declared: "In general, there must be evidence that the defendant requested plaintiff to render the service, or assented to receiving their benefit, under circumstances negativing any presumption that they would be gratuitous. The evidence usually consists in: First, an express request precedent to the service; or second, circumstances justifying the inference that plaintiff in rendering the services expected to be paid, and defendants supposed or had reason to suppose and ought to have supposed that he was expecting pay, and still allowed him to go on in the service without doing anything to disabuse him of this expectation; or, third, proof of benefit received, not on an agreement that it was gratuitous and followed by an express promise to pay.''

In the San Francisco Gas Co. case, it is held that "under some circumstances a municipal corporation may become liable by implication. The obligation to do justice rests equally upon it as upon an individual. It cannot avail itself of the property or labor of a party and screen itself from responsibility under the plea that it never passed an ordinance on the subject. As against individuals, the law implies a promise to pay in such cases, and the implication extends equally against corporations.''

Thus far it would seem that the case for appellant is very persuasive, as it appears that it furnished the electric energy, and that it was used by respondent, and the implication would arise that it was furnished at the instance and request of said respondent although attention is called to no direct evidence to that effect.

Another feature, however, is injected into the situation through the action taken by the council when it received the said written notification from appellant that it would furnish electricity for the entire twenty-four hours and hold respondent liable for it. To that communication the city replied as follows:

"Sonora, Cal., Sept. 27, 1913.

"Tuolumne Co. Elec. Power & Lt. Co.,
  "Sonora, California.

"Gentlemen:

"In reply to your communication of the 25th inst. the Board of Trustees of the City of Sonora desire to inform you that the ordinance of the City of Sonora, being Ordinance No. 63, requires any person, firm or corporation supplying electric current for consumption in the City of Sonora for street lighting only from 4:30 o'clock P. M. to 7 o'clock A. M. the following morning, and it requires any person, firm or corporation engaged in that business in the City of Sonora to so furnish electric current for the purpose of lighting the streets, and it prohibits any charge to be made for any electricity furnished in excess of the amount required. See Section 4 of said ordinance. The obligation of such company is to furnish and supply electricity in the manner required by the ordinance and at the times required and its obligation does not cease merely when it furnishes power to the City's connection. *The City will pay for electricity furnished at the time and in the manner provided for in said ordinance and not otherwise, as long as said ordinance remains in effect. Any electric current furnished other than that required by ordinance, unless specifically requested by proper authorities, will not be paid for by the City of Sonora, but must be furnished, if at all, without charge to the City of Sonora.*

"The lighting company is required to equip its system to comply with the requirements of the ordinance. The City does not want street lights at other times than required by the ordinance and is not required to turn off the lights."

The foundation of appellant's cause of action is thus swept away. The theory to which appellant's claim is anchored embodied in the allegations of the complaint is that the electricity was furnished at the *instance and request* of respondent, and to prove this, there must be some evidence either direct or circumstantial that defendant "requested plaintiff to perform the services or assented to receiving their benefit under circumstances negativing any presumption that they were to be gratuitous." In other words, the party to be charged must either directly authorize the services, or by his declarations or silence he must acquiesce in the action of the one performing and avail himself of the services performed.

Here there was neither express promise nor acquiescence, nor was there conduct by silence or otherwise on the part of the city that would justify any expectation that the city would pay for the additional service that was not demanded in said ordinance. To the contrary, the city, by the terms of said ordinance, requested and demanded that the energy be furnished for street lighting during certain hours only, but it went still further and notified appellant by letter that it did not want any longer service, that it had no use for it, and that if it was furnished, it would not pay for it, but it must be furnished gratuitously. If, in the face of this repudiation of any contractual relation as to the extra electricity, the company persisted in allowing the current to flow into the city's lines during the entire twenty-four hours, it certainly cannot claim that it was done "at the instance and request" of respondent.

No case cited by appellant is parallel to this in this essential feature. As we have already intimated, if the city had used said electric energy and remained silent as to remuneration, an altogether different situation would be presented. In such case, the law as well as principles of equitable dealings would create the implication that the service was performed at the instance and request of the city. Assuredly it is not true, as alleged in the complaint, that "plaintiff herein at the special instance and request of defendant has furnished and delivered electrical energy" during the entire period.

Again, it cannot be said in any proper sense that said electrical energy was used by the city during the additional hours already referred to. It answered no municipal purpose. It was well known that the city desired the electricity for lighting the streets, and there was, of course, no such need during the daytime. Instead of being used during said hours, it was simply allowed to go to waste. It was of no benefit whatever to the city and it is true, as found by the court, "that the defendant has never at any time mentioned in plaintiff's complaint had any use whatever for electricity for lighting its streets in the daytime and never at any of said times purchased or procured and accepted electricity from plaintiff for such use, and plaintiff has never at any of said times, at defendant's request, furnished or delivered any electric energy for street lights in the daytime."

It is true that until the said ordinance was amended, the city demanded electricity for a portion of the day, but there is no controversy as to that.

It seems clear that the plaintiff utterly failed to make out its case as presented by its complaint. As far as this action is concerned, it seems immaterial as to whose duty it was to furnish appliances to prevent the waste of electrical energy. If appellant is right in its contention that such burden should be borne by the city, then probably an action for damages would lie for its failure to prevent the waste, but in view of the undisputed showing we do not see how it can be held that an action on contract can be maintained by plaintiff.

The judgment is affirmed.

Chipman, P. J., and Hart, J., concurred.

A petition to have the cause heard in the supreme court, after judgment in the district court of appeal, was denied by the supreme court on December 7, 1916.

[Civ. No. 2180. Second Appellate District.—October 12, 1916.]

LOUISE B. DAHNE, Petitioner, v. SUPERIOR COURT OF THE COUNTY OF SAN DIEGO, Respondent.

DIVORCE—APPLICATION FOR COUNSEL FEES AND COSTS—ALLEGED NON-RESIDENCE OF WIFE—RIGHT TO PRIOR HEARING OF APPLICATION.— A wife who is without means to prosecute an action for divorce is entitled to have an application made by her for attorney's fees, court costs, and alimony *pendente lite* heard and determined in advance of the question raised by the defendant as to her alleged nonresidence, and consequent lack of jurisdiction of the court.

ID.—RESIDENCE IN DIVORCE ACTIONS—CONSTRUCTION OF SECTION 128, CIVIL CODE.—Section 128 of the Civil Code relative to residence of the plaintiff in actions for divorce does not impose any limitation on the jurisdiction of the superior court in such actions, but simply prescribes certain facts essential to the making out of a case warranting a divorce, and allegations in regard to residence stand upon the same footing as any other allegation of facts showing the right to a divorce.

APPLICATION for a Writ of Mandate originally made to
the District Court of Appeal for the Second Appellate District to compel the Superior Court to hear and determine an
application for counsel fees, court costs, and alimony *pendente
lite* in an action for divorce.

The facts are stated in the opinion of the court.

C. C. Kempley, and Holcomb & Kempley, for Petitioner.

W. Jefferson Davis, for Respondent.

JAMES, J.—Petition for mandate to compel the superior
court of the county of San Diego to hear and determine the
application of Louise B. Dahne made for the purpose of
securing to her in a divorce action against Eugenio Dahne
an allowance to cover attorney's fees, court costs, and alimony
pendente lite. This petitioner filed her complaint in due form
in the superior court, alleging, among other things, that she
had resided in the state for one year and in the county of San
Diego for ninety days next preceding the commencement of
her action; and further set forth that she was without means
or money with which to prosecute the action. The complaint
was duly verified. The matter of her application for the allowance referred to first coming on to be heard, the defendant
filed a demurrer, alleging among other grounds that the court
had no jurisdiction over his person. He also made a motion
to quash the service of summons and dismiss the action on the
ground that he was not a resident of the state of California,
but was a resident of Brazil, and that he was in the state of
California for a temporary purpose as representative of the
department of agriculture, industry, and commerce of the
government of Brazil. The argument is made that the
domicile of the husband is in law the domicile of the wife,
and that as the defendant was a Brazilian subject and had
no intention of remaining permanently in the state, the wife
could claim no residence here sufficient to entitle her to bring
an action for divorce. We do not understand the law to be
that a citizen of a foreign country may not, even under the
alleged facts asserted by petitioner's husband, be deemed in
a divorce action to have acquired such residence as the code
(Civ. Code, sec. 128) requires. But that is a matter which

need not here be considered. Counsel for the defendant insisted upon the right to have the question of the plaintiff's residence determined in advance of the hearing on the application for an allowance of attorney's fees and costs, and in this contention he was sustained by the trial judge who, as appears from the petition and return herein, has refused to consider the motion for such allowances. On the other hand, the court proposes to proceed in advance of the trial of the case to a hearing of the motion to dismiss the suit and to determine the truth of the allegation of plaintiff's complaint that she has been a resident of the state of California for a period of one year and of the county of San Diego for a period of ninety days next preceding the commencement of her action. The question presented is as to whether the plaintiff, this petitioner, in view of her verified assertion that she is without means to live or prosecute the action, is entitled to have her application heard in advance of the trial of the main issues. As appears from the petition, the trial judge is of the opinion that the question of the plaintiff's residence, where challenged, must be first established before any jurisdiction rests in the court to make to her any allowance provided to be made under the provisions of the Civil Code. We cannot agree with the view taken by the learned trial judge on that proposition. In the case of *Estate of McNeil*, 155 Cal. 333, [100 Pac. 1086], it is said: "Section 128 of the Civil Code, relative to residence of the plaintiff, does not impose any limitation on the *jurisdiction* of the superior court in the matter of divorces, but simply prescribes certain facts essential to the making out of a case warranting a divorce, and allegations in regard to residence stand upon the same footing as any other allegation of facts showing the right to a divorce." Admitting, as we must for the purpose of this motion, that the petitioner is without means to prosecute her divorce action, is to admit that she is without means of meeting the objection raised by the defendant as to one of the material issues in the case. That issue is to be treated as any other issue of fact, and the wife should in a proper case be furnished with funds by her husband in order that she may employ counsel and produce such evidence as may be available to her. To say that she is entitled to have her motion for a preliminary allowance heard by the court before being required to meet the defendant on issues regularly proposed by the complaint is not to say that the court must make such allowance, for that is a matter which the discretion of the trial judge will regulate altogether upon the hearing of the motion. But it appears clear to us that the petitioner is entitled to have her application considered in advance of the determination of any question of residence which the defendant has sought to interpose in advance of the trial.

Peremptory writ of mandate is ordered to be issued, requiring respondent superior court to proceed in accordance with the conclusions expressed in this opinion; petitioner to have her costs.

Conrey, P. J., and Shaw, J., concurred.

A petition to have the cause heard in the supreme court, after judgment in the district court of appeal, was denied by the supreme court on December 11, 1916.

———————

[Civ. No. 1389. Second Appellate District.—October 12, 1916.]

LUVISA DELLARINGA, Appellant, v. E. T. HOOKER et al., Respondents.

DISMISSAL OF ACTION—ORDER SETTING ASIDE—APPEAL—AFFIRMANCE OF ORDER.—Upon an appeal taken from an order setting aside an order dismissing an action entered upon the written request of the attorneys for the plaintiff, the order appealed from must be affirmed, where the record shows that the defendant prior to the order of dismissal had filed an answer asking for affirmative relief, and no stipulation authorizing the dismissal is furnished.

APPEAL from an order of the Superior Court of Kern County setting aside an order dismissing an action. Paul W. Bennett, Judge.

The facts are stated in the opinion of the court.

W. W. Kaye, Rowen Irwin, and Emmons & Hudson, for Appellant.

John F. Poole, for Respondents.

JAMES, J.—This appeal was taken from an order of the superior court made on the motion of defendant E. T. Hooker. This order directed that an order of dismissal of the action theretofore entered upon the written request of the attorneys for the plaintiff, be set aside. The action was to quiet title and defendant Hooker had answered prior to the request made for the dismissal of the action, in which answer he set up ownership in the property in controversy and asked for an adjudication to be made in his favor. A clerk's transcript was prepared under the alternative method of appeal, and that is the only document which has been filed in this court. At the time set for oral argument, no counsel for appellant appeared, and counsel for respondent being present stated that the controversy had been settled and that only moot questions were therefore now involved. However, the appellant, upon being advised of the suggestion made, has failed to furnish any stipulation upon which to authorize the court to enter an order of dismissal. We are left without any argument offered by the appellant to sustain the appeal taken. An examination of the record discloses to our minds no reason why the order of the court should be disturbed.

The order is affirmed.

Conrey, P. J., and Shaw, J., concurred.

[Civ. No. 2044. Second Appellate District.—October 12, 1916.]

ROY KIRKPATRICK et al., Petitioners, v. INDUSTRIAL ACCIDENT COMMISSION et al., Respondents; JAMES McLEOD, Applicant.

WORKMEN'S COMPENSATION ACT—DEATH OF EMPLOYEE OF TEAMING COMPANY—HIRING OUT OF TEAM AND EMPLOYEE TO THIRD PARTY—LIABILITY OF EMPLOYER.—Under the terms of the Workmen's Compensation, Insurance and Safety Act, a person engaged in the business of contract teaming and hauling is liable to the dependent parents of an employee for his accidental death while engaged in hauling lumber for a lumber company, where he, in pursuance of a request made to his employer by the lumber company for a team and driver, was directed by his employer to perform such work.

ID.—MEANING OF TERMS "EMPLOYER" AND "EMPLOYEE."—The Workmen's Compensation, Insurance and Safety Act, in sections 13 and 14 thereof, furnishes its own definition of the terms "employer" and "employee." The former term includes every person who has any person in service under any contract of hire, express or implied, and the latter term includes every person thus in the service of such employer.

ID.—COMPENSATION TO DEPENDENTS OF KILLED EMPLOYEES—CONSTITUTIONALITY OF ACT.—The provisions of the Workmen's Compensation Act authorizing the payment of compensation to dependents of employees whose death has resulted from injuries received in the course of their employment, are constitutional.

APPLICATION for a Writ of Review, originally made to the District Court of Appeal for the Second Appellate District, to review an order made by the Industrial Accident Commission awarding compensation for death.

The facts are stated in the opinion of the court.

Hickcox & Crenshaw, for Petitioners.

Christopher M. Bradley, for Respondents.

CONREY, P. J.—A writ was issued in this proceeding to review an order of the Industrial Accident Commission whereby it awarded to the dependent parents of one Jay McLeod compensation for his accidental death while in the employ of Roy Kirkpatrick, defendant in that case and one of the petitioners herein. Jay McLeod was regularly employed by Kirkpatrick as a driver and teamster in connection with Kirkpatrick's business, which was that of contract teaming and hauling. On that day the Blinn Lumber Company requested the Pasadena Transfer Company to furnish a team and driver for the delivery of some lumber. The Pasadena Transfer Company called upon Kirkpatrick to furnish a team and driver to fill this order. Thereupon Kirkpatrick directed McLeod to take his team and do the hauling required. As Kirkpatrick did not have a wagon suitable for hauling lumber, a wagon of the Pasadena Transfer Company was used. While using said wagon and the horses of Kirkpatrick in hauling lumber for the Blinn Lumber Company the accident occurred which resulted in the death of McLeod. The Southwestern Surety Insurance Company is the insurance carrier for Kirkpatrick, and had insured him against liability for compensation for injuries sustained by his employees in connection with his business.

Petitioners' first contention is that at the time of the accident McLeod was not the employee of Kirkpatrick, but was the employee of the Blinn Lumber Company, and that therefore Kirkpatrick was not liable for compensation to McLeod or to his dependents. The argument is based upon rules which often have been enforced in cases arising out of injuries to third persons through negligence of employees, and cases arising out of negligence resulting in injuries to employees, wherein it became necessary to determine who was the employer or master responsible for the acts of the servant or liable for injuries to the servant. It has sometimes been held that where the direct or immediate employer furnishes his servant to a third person to do work of the latter, and places the employee under the exclusive control of such third person in the performance of the work, the employee becomes for that particular purpose the servant of him to whom the employee is furnished; with resultant responsibility on the part of the employer whose work is being done. An instance of this kind is shown in *Cotter* v. *Lindgren*, 106 Cal. 602, [46 Am. St. Rep. 255, 39 Pac. 950]. It was there held that the defendant, who was the first or general employer of the servants whose negligence caused plaintiff's injuries, was not responsible for their negligence, because the work in which the servants were employed was not work of the defendant, and the defendant had not at that time the control or right to control or supervise the conduct of the servants in doing that work. But even in negligence cases it does not always follow that the general employer is freed from responsibility by the mere act of hiring out his employees to third persons to be used by them in the performance of their work. Thus in *Stewart* v. *California Improvement Co.*, 131 Cal. 125, [52 L. R. A. 205, 63 Pac. 177, 724], the defendant company had employed one Conger as engineer to manage a steam-roller owned by it. The steam-roller, with the engineer in charge, was hired out by the company to the city of Oakland for use in rolling and leveling a street, such use being under the direction of the superintendent of streets. The plaintiff suffered injuries caused by negligence of the engineer, who carelessly let off steam from the engine without giving warning thereof, thereby frightening the plaintiff's horse. It was held that under the given circumstances the relation of master and servant existed between the defendant company and its engineer, and not between the city of Oakland and said engineer. "Here the city simply hired the use of the street-roller outfit from the defendant company—to wit, the roller, engine, and the engineer to manage the same—for so much a day. The city's agent—foreman of the street superintendent—only directed or supervised how and where the street should be rolled; he did not have the control or management of the engine; this was subject entirely to the judgment of the engineer, the servant of the owner, the defendant company, who had selected and employed him for that special purpose, paid him his wages and had the sole right to discharge him." So here, the Industrial Accident Commission may well have concluded from the evidence that the Blinn Lumber Company simply hired the use of the team and driver to deliver its lumber, without in any way interfering with the control or management of the team by McLeod as servant of Kirkpatrick, who had selected and employed him for that special purpose, who paid him his wages, and had the sole right to discharge him. The evidence thus tending to support the commission's finding of fact to the effect that McLeod at the time of receiving his injuries was in the employ of Kirkpatrick, such findings are final and will not be reviewed in this proceeding, since they present only questions of fact and not of law.

The Workmen's Compensation, Insurance and Safety Act, in sections 13 and 14 thereof, furnishes its own definition of the terms "employer" and "employee." The term "employer" includes every person who has any person in service under any contract of hire, express or implied. The term "employee" includes every person thus in the service of such employer. The decisions in negligence cases such as those above mentioned are not necessarily controlling in cases like the present; for the liability of the employer in this case arises, not from any wrong done by him, but from the statute which imposes such liability upon persons bearing toward each other the relation of employer and employee as defined in the statute. While this appears to be the first case in this state in which the courts have been called upon to review an award of the commission for injuries received by an

employee hired out by one employer to another, the same
questions have been presented under the workmen's compensation acts in other states.   In *Re State Workmen's Compensation Comm. (Dale v. Saunders Bros.)*, 218 N. Y. 59, [112
N. E. 571], the award was made to a widow and children for
the death of one Frank Dale.   The general employer in that
case, like Kirkpatrick in this case, was engaged in the teaming business and in hiring out teams with drivers for truck-
ing purposes.   Dale was sent with a team to work for one
Walsh, by taking sand from Walsh's sand-pit and delivering
it to his customers.   The court of appeals, after referring to
the rules which we also have mentioned as applied in negligence cases, declared that the question in this case was not
one of responsibility for negligent injuries inflicted upon
strangers, nor upon an employee; that the doctrine of *respond-
eat superior* had no application there, nor were the rules of
employers' liability for negligence controlling; and it was
held that Dale was working for Saunders Bros. as a teamster;
that he was engaged in teaming, not in the operation of a
sand-pit.   In like manner it might be said in the present case
that McLeod was engaged in teaming, which was the business
of Kirkpatrick, and not in the lumber business, which was
the business of the Blinn Lumber Company.

In *Rongo* v. *R. Waddington & Sons*, 87 N. J. L. 395 (94
Atl. 408), a similar case arose.   There the supreme court of
New Jersey determined that the petitioner, who had been
injured in the course of his employment, was the employee
of Waddington & Sons, the contracting teamsters who employed him by the day, and who had let him out for the day
to haul sand and other building materials for a third person.
In this, as in the New York case, the terms of the statute
were not identical with those of the California statute.   They
are sufficiently alike, however, to indicate the trend of opinion.
In the New Jersey case it was determined that the person
to whom the team and driver had been furnished by Waddington & Sons could not be held liable as the employer.   He
"had no direct dealings with the petitioner; he had nothing
to say on the question how much wages petitioner should
be paid; the only contract that he made was a contract with
Waddington for the supply of a team consisting of a wagon,
horses and driver, for which he paid as a team.   There was
of course ample evidence to justify an award as against

Waddington, and this is what we think the court ought to have done.''

Petitioners further contend that "Kirkpatrick not being the immediate employer, would be considered as a principal and intermediate contractor, and would be excluded from liability under subdivision 1 of subdivision d, section 30, of the Workmen's Compensation, Insurance and Safety Act.'' Even without taking into consideration the effect of section 30 under the construction given to it in *Carstens* v. *Pillsbury*, 172 Cal. 572, [158 Pac. 218], and *Sturdivant* v. *Pillsbury*, 172 Cal. 581, [158 Pac. 222], we are of opinion that Kirkpatrick does not occupy any different relation than that of an "immediate employer," as those words are used in said section 30.

Finally, petitioners contend that the act under consideration, so far as it provides or attempts to provide for compensation to others than employees, is unconstitutional. This question has been determined adversely to petitioners' contention, by a recent decision of the supreme court. (*Western Metal Supply Co.* v. *Pillsbury*, 172 Cal. 407, [156 Pac. 491].)

The award is affirmed.

James, J., and Shaw, J., concurred.

[Civ. No. 2088. Second Appellate District.—October 12, 1916.]

HENRY J. KRAMER, Petitioner, v. INDUSTRIAL ACCIDENT COMMISSION OF THE STATE OF CALIFORNIA et al., Respondents.

WORKMEN'S COMPENSATION ACT—REVIEW OF AWARD—REFERENCE TO EVIDENCE—WHEN PERMISSIBLE.—In a proceeding to review an award made by the Industrial Accident Commission, where the findings are meager in detailing the facts upon which the commission based its conclusion, the evidence may be referred to, not to vary or contradict the findings of fact, but for the purpose of explaining or supplementing the same.

ID.—INJURY TO PERSON EMPLOYED AS JANITOR AND GARDENER—PRUNING OF FIG TREE—GARDEN LABOR—COMPENSATION NOT AWARDABLE. A person employed as janitor for a dancing academy in a building which was also used by his employer for the purpose of a residence, the duties of which position were to take charge of the rooms, sweep and dust the same, and in general keep them in order, and also employed as a gardener to look after and care for the grass, flowers, shrubbery, and trees growing upon the lot and upon the adjoining lot, which latter lot the employer used for garage purposes, is not entitled to compensation for injuries received in pruning a fig tree upon the latter lot, as such injury arose in the course of his employment as gardener, and not as janitor, which first-named employment is excluded from the operation of the Workmen's Compensation, Insurance and Safety Act by section 14 thereof, which excepts employees engaged in farm, agricultural, or horticultural labor, or in household domestic service.

APPLICATION for a Writ of Certiorari originally made to the District Court of Appeal for the Second Appellate District to review an award made by the Industrial Accident Commission.

The facts are stated in the opinion of the court.

Jones & Evans, Gibson, Dunn & Crutcher, and Norman S. Sterry, for Petitioner.

F. M. Shepard, and Christopher M. Bradley, for Respondents.

SHAW, J.—*Certiorari* to review the action of the Industrial Accident Commission in awarding benefits to Oscar Ohlsson, an employee of petitioner Henry J. Kramer.

The findings are, unfortunately, meager in detailing the facts upon which the commission based its conclusion. Such being the case, we may refer to the evidence, not to vary or contradict the findings of fact, but for the purpose of explaining or supplementing the same. (*Matter of Rheinwald*, 168 App. Div. 425, [153 N. Y. Supp. 598].) It appears that Ohlsson was an employee of Kramer, who conducted a dancing academy in a building which was also used by him for the purpose of a residence. Adjoining the lot upon which this building stood was a lot, upon the rear of which there was a garage, reached by a driveway from the street, along which there grew some peach and palm trees, the branches of which overhung the driveway, thus interfering with the free use thereof, and some twenty-five feet from which was a growing fig tree. Kramer did not own this adjoining lot, but was permitted by the owner thereof to use the garage, and Ohlsson had been directed by Kramer to trim the branches of the palm and peach trees which overhung the driveway. On both lots were plots of grass, flowers, trees, and shrubbery. The evidence, without conflict, shows that Ohlsson was employed by Kramer in the capacity of a janitor, the duties of which position were to take charge of the rooms, sweep and dust the same, and in general keep them in order; and also employed as a gardener to look after and care for the grass, flowers, shrubbery, and trees growing upon both lots, and that he performed services in both capacities.

The commission found that Ohlsson was injured by accident "while in the employment of . . . Henry J. Kramer as a janitor of a dancing-hall and house and garden laborer." (2) "That said accident and injury arose out of and happened in the course of said employment, and occurred while the said employee was performing service growing out of, incidental to, and in the course of his employment, and was as follows: While pruning a fig tree upon a lot adjacent to that occupied by his employer, and in part used by such employer, a garage used by such employer being located thereon and the driveway thereto on such property having along its border palm and peach trees which applicant had been instructed to trim, applicant stepped upon and was pierced in the ankle by a palm thorn, which occasioned serious disability. That the pruning of such fig tree without specific instructions so to do, did not constitute misconduct on the part of the applicant or take him outside the scope of his employment, but was such an act as any employee might reasonably perform incidental to the course of his employment."

It thus appears that Ohlsson was employed in a dual capacity; that is, in the capacity of a janitor for a dancing hall and a house and garden laborer. A janitor is defined to be "one who is employed to take care of a public building." As generally understood, the term refers to a person employed to take charge of a building and rooms therein and keep the same clean and in order. (*Fagan* v. *Mayor,* 84 N. Y. 348.) For the purpose of this case we may assume that the employment of a person in such capacity brings him within the operation of the statute. Section 14 of the act excludes from its operation employees engaged in farm, agricultural, or horticultural labor, or in household domestic service. In the light of the evidence we construed the finding that Ohlsson was employed as a house and garden laborer, as referring to household domestic service mentioned in section 14, and the caring for the flowers, grass, trees, and shrubbery growing upon the two lots. In other words, the service performed by Ohlsson as a house laborer consisted of household domestic service, while that performed by him in the capacity of a garden laborer consisted in horticultural labor. Clearly, the labor of caring for grass lawns, trees, shrubbery, and flowers is horticultural in character. (See definitions of horticulture in Standard Dictionary and American Encyclopedia.) Ohlsson was thus employed for the performance of services in two capacities; one that of janitor, falling within the terms of the act; the other as a house and garden laborer, employees engaged therein being excluded from its operation. Hence, if the injury sustained by Ohlsson was due to an accident while he was engaged in labor as and under his employment as a gardener, he would not be entitled to the benefits of the act, unless the service was incidental to the work of janitor. The pruning of this fig tree without specific instructions so to do might well be regarded as within the scope of his employment as gardener, since the proper care thereof required such work to be done. It did not, however, interfere with the use of the driveway, and the pruning thereof had no connection with the work of janitor which by any stretch of the imagination could render it incidental thereto. Therefore, the conclusion of law as found by the commission, that at the time of the injury "the applicant employee was not engaged in any of the occupations or employments excepted by section 14 of the Workmen's Compensation, Insurance and Safety Act from the provisions of said act," is without support in the facts found. (*Southern Pacific Co.* v. *Pillsbury et al.*, 170 Cal. 782, [151 Pac. 277].) The New York compensation act does not apply to all employees, but to those only engaged in certain occupations there designated as extrahazardous, while the California act applies to all except those designated as being excluded when engaged in certain work. This being true, the decisions of the New York courts in like cases furnish a rule which we think should be followed in the case at bar. In the case of *Gleisner* v. *Gross,* 170 App. Div. 37, [155 N. Y. Supp. 946], a part of the duties of an employee was to operate boilers and elevators, designated as extrahazardous. He had other duties to perform, however, which were not within those so classed by the legislature, and was injured while performing some of the latter duties. In holding that he was not entitled to recover, the court said: "Regardless of the contractual or colloquial designation of the duties or position of an injured employee, the question remains in every instance as to the work which he was in fact doing and the extent to which his work came within the category of the enumerated employments. The actuality, rather than the appellation, is the sound basis for the commission's action in determining whether an employee met with mishap in the course of an enumerated employment." In the case of *In re Sickles*, 156 N. Y. Supp. 864, the defendant was engaged as warehouseman in storing fruit, and also engaged in buying and selling fruits. An employee of the defendant was engaged part of the time in connection with defendant's business as a warehouseman, designated as extrahazardous, and part of the time as a salesman in buying and selling fruit, which latter calling was not within the operation of the statute. He was injured while engaged in the latter business, and it was held that he was not entitled to recover compensation therefor. The court there said: "The difficulty is that the employer was engaged in two entirely distinct kinds of business, one of which was not within the protection of the statute, and that the claimant was injured in performance of his duties, which at the time of the injury solely had reference to that kind of business not thus protected." So, too, where an employee of a common carrier engaged in both intra and inter state transportation is injured, his right to recover under the federal statute will depend upon the character of his service at the time of his injury; that is, if at the time of the injury he was engaged in interstate work, he may recover under federal statute; otherwise, his rights are measured by the state law. (*Illinois C. R. Co.* v. *Behrens*, 233 U. S. 473, [Ann. Cas. 1914C, 163, 10 N. C. C. A. 153, 58 L. Ed. 1051, 34 Sup. Ct. Rep. 646]; *Colasurdo* v. *Central R. R. Co. of N. J.*, 180 Fed. 832; *Erie R. Co.* v. *Jacobus*, 221 Fed. 335, [137 C. C. A. 151].) Our conclusion is that the injury sustained by Ohlsson arose out of and was in the course of his employment, not as a janitor, but while engaged in garden labor, which is in the nature of and included within the term "horticultural labor," for which he is not entitled to the benefit of the act.

The award is, therefore, set aside and annulled.

Conrey, P. J., and James, J., concurred.

[Civ. No. 2005. Second Appellate District.—October 12, 1916.]

PATRICK J. HARTNETT, Respondent, v. JOHN C. WILSON et al., Copartners, etc., Appellants.

CONTRACT FOR PURCHASE OF STOCKS ON MARGIN—PLEDGE TO SECURE BROKERS — ACTION TO RECOVER PLEDGED PROPERTY — PLEADING—SUFFICIENCY OF COMPLAINT.—In an action in replevin to recover certain certificates of stock and a certain bond deposited with a firm of stockbrokers engaged in the business of buying and selling stocks and bonds on margin, and otherwise, as collateral security for any debt that might accrue from the plaintiff to the defendants on account of any loss caused by reason of any contract that plaintiff might make with defendants whereby defendants might purchase of or for, or sell to or for, plaintiff, on margin, shares of the capital stock of various corporations, the complaint states a cause of action where it is alleged that in none of the various contracts entered into was there any intention on the part of either party that there should be delivery of the shares of stock bought or sold, but that only the difference between the contract price and the market price of said shares should be paid, and only such difference was ever paid.

ID.—EVIDENCE — UNLAWFUL CHARACTER OF TRANSACTIONS — GENERAL QUESTIONS—LACK OF PREJUDICE.—In an action to recover the possession of such certificates and bond, the defendants are not prejudiced by the rulings of the court in permitting the plaintiff to show the character of many of the transactions in a general way, where previous thereto a great deal of evidence had been received covering particular details of many of the transactions, showing their unlawful character.

ID.—RULES OF NEW YORK STOCK EXCHANGE—PROOF PROPERLY EXCLUDED.—The rules of the New York Stock Exchange in regard to buying and selling stock are properly excluded in such an action, where there was no evidence that the defendants were members of such exchange, or transacted any of the plaintiff's business through it.

ID.—VALUE OF PROPERTY—TIME OF DEMAND FOR DELIVERY.—The value
of the property involved in such an action is to be computed according to its value at the time when demand for delivery was made,
and not as of the date of the original deposit.

ID.—TRIAL—REFUSAL OF CONTINUANCE—DISCRETION NOT ABUSED.—It
is not an abuse of discretion to refuse a continuance of the trial
at the close of the plaintiff's evidence in order to permit the defendants to obtain evidence to meet the amendment made to the plaintiff's complaint on the day of trial, which showed that the dealings
were to include cotton, as well as corporate stock, in the absence of
any showing that the witness whose attendance was required would
or could testify as to the lawful character of the cotton transactions.

ID.—APPEAL—BANKRUPTCY OF APPELLANTS PENDING DETERMINATION—
RIGHTS OF RESPONDENT.—Upon an appeal taken from the judgment
and order denying a new trial in such action, the right of the
respondent to have the appeal determined is not affected by the
bankruptcy of the defendants pending the appeal, and if the appeal
be affirmed, the plaintiff is entitled to recover the property or to
assert his rights under the appeal bond.

APPEAL from a judgment of the Superior Court of Los
Angeles County, and from an order denying a new trial.
Charles Wellborn, Judge.

The facts are stated in the opinion of the court.

Hartley Shaw, for Appellants.

Arthur Wright, for Respondent.

CONREY, P. J.—This is an action of replevin brought by
the plaintiff to recover certain certificates of stock and a certain bond, alleged to be his property, in possession of the
defendants and unlawfully detained by them. The defendants were partners doing business under a firm name as stockbrokers engaged in the business of buying and selling stocks
and bonds on margin and otherwise. The complaint shows
that on July 30, 1912, a series of transactions began between
the plaintiff and the defendants wherein, as it is alleged, contracts were made between the parties, whereby the plaintiff
employed the defendants to purchase for him shares of the
capital stock of corporations on margin, without any intention
on the part of either of the parties for delivery of the shares
sold or bought, and without any actual delivery of such shares

or any agreement for such delivery. It is alleged that each of said contracts provided that only the difference between the contract price and the market price of said shares on divers days should be paid, and only such difference was ever paid. On the day of trial of this action the complaint was amended so as to show that the transactions included purchases and sales by the defendants as principals, and included bales of cotton as well as corporation stock.

On several dates, beginning on August 8th, the plaintiff deposited with defendants the certificates and the bond, one at a time, until all of them had passed to the possession of defendants. It was alleged that the property was deposited as collateral security for any debt that might accrue from the plaintiff to defendants on account of any loss caused by reason of any contract that plaintiff might make with defendants whereby defendants might purchase of or for, or sell to or for, plaintiff, on margin without intention to deliver, shares of the capital stock of divers corporations, or bales of cotton; that since said delivery of the certificates and bond plaintiff has entered into divers verbal contracts with defendants whereby the plaintiff sold to or for defendants, and divers other verbal contracts whereby the plaintiff purchased of defendants shares of the capital stock of corporations or bales of cotton on margin; that in each instance and in every case and as agreed to in each of said contracts, there was no intention either on the part of the plaintiff or on the part of the defendants to deliver by the party selling or to receive by the party purchasing any of said shares or bales of cotton, and no shares of capital stock or bales of cotton were ever delivered by plaintiff to defendants or by defendants to plaintiff, as the case might be, and no agreement was ever made for such delivery or receipt; that each of said contracts provided that only the difference between the contract price and the market price of said shares or bales of cotton on divers days should be paid and only such difference was ever paid; that said certificates and bond were deposited with the defendants for no other purpose than as so stated. By their answer the defendants raised issues upon the material allegations of the complaint, both as to the ultimate facts and the evidentiary facts thus pleaded, other than as to plaintiff's ownership and deposit of the certificates and bond. The case was tried upon those issues with resulting findings and judgment in favor of

plaintiff, awarding to plaintiff possession of each of said
certificates and said bond; it being further provided in each
instance that if delivery or return of the property cannot be
had, plaintiff should recover the value thereof as stated in the
judgment. These values were severally stated and in the
aggregate amounted to $5,017.50. The defendants appealed
from the judgment and from an order denying their motion
for a new trial.

It is not disputed that the complaint states facts sufficient
to entitle the plaintiff to recover. (*Willcox* v. *Edwards*, 162
Cal. 455, [Ann. Cas. 1913C, 1392, 123 Pac. 276] ; Cal. Const.,
art. IV, sec. 26.) Appellants also admit that the evidence is
sufficient to justify the court in finding that all of the transactions involved were of the character alleged, except those
involved in the account of one M. T. Zorn. We are satisfied,
however, that the Zorn transaction was like the others. The
defendants maintained an office in the city of Los Angeles in
which they kept a blackboard for market quotations and maintained a telegraph operator, a manager, a bookkeeper, and
agents for soliciting business. One of these agents, Mr. C. H.
Marshall, introduced the plaintiff to that place of business,
and suggested that there was a chance for plaintiff to make
some easy money there by buying stock on margin. Upon
being informed that plaintiff had never done business of that
kind, Marshall compared it to horse-racing. He said: "It is
just about the same as making a book. You bet that the stock
will either go up or down. If you bet it goes up and it goes
up, you win the equivalent of what you bet or what you buy."
The transactions which followed, and which are set forth at
great length in the record as occurring between the plaintiff
and the defendants, were of the nature thus described and
nothing else. After the plaintiff had invested a few hundred
dollars there came a time when he was called upon for more
cash to protect his margins, but did not have the money. In
lieu of cash the defendants accepted from plaintiff the certificate for ten shares of Northern Pacific Railroad stock as collateral for plaintiff's account. The other deposits were made
from time to time under like circumstances.

At the office of defendants the plaintiff was made acquainted with Mr. Zorn. Plaintiff's testimony concerning
Zorn is not disputed and in substance is as follows: "He had
some deals on there in corn, and they were calling him for

two hundred dollars. He asked me if I would give him a
loan, or he would lose a whole lot of money, he claimed. I
brought this certificate up the next morning and I told Mr.
Marshall to protect this corn.'' It is unnecessary to follow
this matter through its devious course wherein the Zorn account was manipulated and shifted into plaintiff's name and
the deposited shares of stock used for purposes not intended
or authorized by the plaintiff. In further discussion of the
case we will make no further separate mention of the Zorn
transaction.

Appellants next contend that since the burden was on plaintiff to show the unlawful character of the transactions, and
since there were many of those transactions, the court erred
in allowing the plaintiff to make this proof in a wholesale
manner and by general questions, for if any of these were
lawful transactions and indebtedness arose out of them, defendants were entitled to hold plaintiff's collateral therefor.
A great deal of evidence was received covering particular
details of the several transactions, including numerous statements in writing made by the defendants. The character of
the business of the defendants was thus thoroughly exposed
to view. The facts as to the manner in which the business
was done were almost wholly within the knowledge of the
defendants and were not known to the plaintiff. This is
peculiarly true of that portion of these transactions well along
toward the end of them, when (the plaintiff then being
''ahead of the house'') the defendants got the plaintiff drunk
for three days, during which time numerous transactions
occurred, and then or soon thereafter nearly all of the
''losses'' occurred whereby they claimed that his collateral
had been absorbed. The principal objection made by appellants under this head is to the following question put to the
plaintiff by the court: ''Subsequent to the time that you put
up these collaterals was there ever any stock you owned sold
by them for you in Los Angeles or anywhere else, after you
put up these collaterals?'' to which the plaintiff answered,
''No, sir.'' Objection was made that the question was too
general and called for the conclusion of the witness. This
matter must be considered in the light of occurrences immediately preceding the asking of this question, as shown in several pages of the transcript. Plaintiff's showing of facts had
progressed to a point where it was appropriate for the court

to intervene for the purpose of shortening the record and saving a large waste of time which would be consumed in proving the details of many transactions of apparently the same character. If any of those transactions were of different character and involved actual and legitimate sales, it would have been an easy matter for the defendants to point out the transactions upon which they relied to protect their claim to these collaterals. But this they did not do, and we are unable to see that the defendants were prejudiced by the ruling of the court.

The defendants called as their witness at the trial one Ellis M. Harris, who on and after November 1, 1912, was the manager of their Los Angeles office, and propounded to him the following question: "Do you know what the rules of the New York Stock Exchange are in regard to buying and selling stock?" Objection to this question was sustained, and was properly sustained, unless the rules of that exchange were in some way material and of benefit to the defendants. Some of the statements of account furnished by the defendants to the plaintiff contained a statement in the following form: "It is agreed between broker and customer: 1. That all transactions are subject to the rules and customs of the New York Stock Exchange and its clearing-house." There is no evidence that the defendants were members of the New York Stock Exchange, or transacted any of the plaintiff's business through that exchange, and if we may suppose that the rules of the New York Stock Exchange prohibit mere gambling and fictitious transactions, that fact would be of no value to the defendants if, in truth, the transactions between them and the plaintiff were not conducted in accordance with those rules. Neither at the time when the foregoing question was asked of the witness Harris, nor at any other time, was evidence offered tending to show that in any instance there was a genuine purchase by the plaintiff or a genuine sale by him. It is true that, referring to two or three orders received from the plaintiff, Mr. Harris testified that the orders were transmitted to New York, that the orders were executed and that the cotton mentioned was bought; but there is nothing to show that the word "bought" was used in any other sense than in the multitude of other transactions in which that word was current in the business of defendants. Harris admitted that never in his experience as an employee of the defendants did he know of cotton being actually delivered. As a specific instance: In referring to the last five hundred bales of cotton "bought" for the plaintiff (and which previously had been "sold" for him), the amount involved would be about sixty thousand dollars, and he said: "We did not get sixty thousand dollars from anybody, nor deliver any cotton at all." "Q. Isn't it true that those losses were merely differences between different days of the price of cotton? A. Different prices at which he bought and sold cotton." He said that the contracts were held by their correspondent in New York; and that he did not know whether plaintiff knew or not that there was any such transaction. Under the circumstances shown by this and by all of the evidence in the case, it is manifest that any rules of the New York Stock Exchange, whatever they might be, could not affect the plaintiff's rights in this case.

Appellants contend that the court erred in its findings as to the value of the property involved. At the trial an attempt was made by the attorneys for the respective parties to agree upon these values. Plaintiff's attorney claimed that he was entitled to the value of the property as of the dates when the certificates and bond were deposited. Defendants' attorney claimed that the value should be taken as of December 17, 1912, the day when plaintiff made his demand for their return to him. As to the latter date, defendants' answer admitted values amounting to only $4,848.75. The answer of defendants had admitted values at the date when the properties were deposited by the plaintiff with the defendants, which admitted values in the aggregate amounted to $5,017.50, or $168.75 more than the values at the time of the demand. The court in its decision adopted the larger figures, proceeding evidently upon the theory that the value should be fixed as of the earlier dates. Appellants now contend that the court's findings as to values are wholly without support in the evidence, because there is no evidence of the value of the property at the time of the trial, which they now for the first time contend is the time for which the values should have been fixed. It is provided by the Code of Civil Procedure, section 667, that "In an action to recover the possession of personal property, judgment for the plaintiff may be for the possession or the value thereof, in case a delivery cannot be had, and damages for the detention." As no damages for the detention of the property

were allowed, that element need not be considered. It is said
that there is only one decision upon this precise point. In
Phillips v. *Sutherland*, 2 Cal. Unrep. 241, [2 Pac. 32], it was
held that in an action of this kind, where the judgment is in
the alternative, the value of the property should be fixed as
of the day of the trial as being nearest to the time when the
property would be delivered. Under the stipulations made as
above stated, we do not think that the losing party should be
allowed on appeal to object for the first time that the findings
are wholly unsupported by the evidence. In substance he
conceded that on any theory of the case the values to be found
by the court would amount to at least $4,848.75. So far as
this matter is concerned, the only relief to which he should be
entitled would consist in reducing the amount of the judgment by deducting therefrom the sum of $168.75. This may
the more readily be done because, unless controlled by the decision above cited, it is our opinion that the value of the property at the time when demand for its delivery was made is
the value which should prevail.

It is contended by appellants that the court erred in refusing to allow a continuance at the close of the evidence presented on behalf of the plaintiff. When the plaintiff presented his amendment to the complaint at the beginning of
the trial, the defendants made no objection thereto, but stated
that they would desire to have a continuance. The court responded that the plaintiff might introduce his evidence, and
that whenever it became necessary in the interest of fair play
to get the defendants' evidence on the transactions in cotton,
the court would adjourn the trial of the case for such time as
was necessary. After the plaintiff had rested his case, the
attorney for appellants stated that on account of the cotton
transaction having been received as part of the evidence, he
would want further time before he could finish putting in his
defense; that it would be necessary for the defendants to show
that the deals in cotton were actually made, and he was not
prepared to produce such evidence at that time. He said
that the man Marshall was not then in the employment of the
defendants, and they had no means of communicating with
him, and did not know whether they could find him or not.
He said he wanted to prove that the cotton deals were actually
carried out on the New York exchange; that there was a telegraph line from their office to New York, and messages were

received in New York about this cotton, and the cotton was bought and sold according to the order and report got back to Los Angeles and given to the plaintiff. Upon suggestion of defendants' attorney that he could put the evidence in the form of an affidavit, the court stated: "It is not necessary. I am assuming every word you say to be true, and no affidavit is necessary; but I say, assuming all that you have said to be correct, I do not see any reason for a continuance." The following also occurred: The Court: "But you don't claim that this man ever owned any cotton in his life, or put up one cent of money as the purchase price of the cotton?" Defendants' attorney: "It does not make any difference whether he ever owned any cotton in his life or not. The court has stated that it is perfectly legal to make a contract to sell something he hasn't got." Thereupon, the continuance having been denied, the defendants introduced the testimony of several witnesses. One of them, the witness Harris, manager of the office of defendants, referred to the cotton deals as follows: "Two or three days after I came to Los Angeles [which would be two or three days after November 1, 1912], I asked Mr. Hartnett for some more money to protect us on some cotton that we were carrying for him; he told me he wouldn't be able to take care of it at that time, and we bought in five hundred bales, I think, November 6th, and I told him we would put a stop loss order on the remaining five hundred bales at 1215. I told him it would be bought in when it reached 1215. He said if it would go up there, it would have to be closed out, if it reached that point before he heard from the east. He made no objections to my closing it out. That is one of the two cotton transactions I spoke of before. The other one is the one we bought in the day I first spoke to him about margin, because he said he didn't have any money, and he would lighten up his load by buying in half his commitments, which was five hundred bales. These two days were about five days apart, I think. The day he told me we had better lighten up his load by buying five hundred, I entered an order to buy five hundred bales January cotton at the market. It was bought. The other time there was an order entered with our New York correspondent to buy if it reached a certain point. That was bought too at 1215." Defendants made no further attempt than as above shown to prove the good faith and reality of their transactions with plaintiff.

Let the statements made by defendants' attorney be treated
as a substitute for an affidavit; they nevertheless were not
sufficient to require that the court grant a continuance. It
was not stated that Mr. Marshall could or would testify to the
facts referred to by the attorney; nor that other witnesses
upon whom the defendants must rely were not within call on
the day of the trial. For aught that appears, the defendants
themselves were then in court or at their office in Los Angeles.
It may be that books, contracts, and other documents were in
the hands of the defendants which, together with testimony
of defendants or of their bookkeepers and other agents in
the city where the case was on trial, would have proved all of
the facts covered by the statement made in connection with
the application for a continuance. Moreover, the allegations
of fact introduced into the case by the amendment of the complaint at the day of the trial were all of evidentiary matter
which would have been provable in the case without such allegations. This was an action for the recovery of personal
property wherein the plaintiff had alleged all the facts necessary to a complaint in that kind of an action, including the
facts of ownership by the plaintiff and his right to immediate
possession and the wrongful possession by the defendants, the
demand for a return of the property and refusal thereof.
The defendants were fully acquainted with the facts upon
which the determination of the case must depend and adequately warned of the nature of the plaintiff's claims. Our
conclusion is that the refusal of a continuance under the circumstances shown did not constitute an abuse of the discretion
vested in the court as to that matter.

In addition to the foregoing matters directly involved in the
appeals herein, we are required to consider a motion presented
by counsel for appellants whereby they ask for an order staying all proceedings in the action on the ground that since the
rendition of the judgment appealed from, and since the time
of the appeal, the defendants have been duly discharged in
bankruptcy. The motion is accompanied by a certified copy
of an order duly made in the district court of the United
States for the Northern District of California, discharging the
defendants from all debts and claims provable under the acts
of Congress relating to bankruptcy, and which existed on the
seventh day of November, 1914, when the petition for adjudication of bankruptcy against them was filed; with the usual

exceptions, none of which require attention at this time. Respondent in reply to the motion shows that the appeal from the judgment herein was taken and a stay bond filed by appellants on the sixteenth day of July, 1913, which was about sixteen months prior to the commencement of the bankruptcy proceedings. That an undertaking was given as required for a stay of proceedings under section 943 of the Code of Civil Procedure, and was conditioned that the defendants will obey the orders of the appellate court upon the said appeal. Respondent concedes that this court may appropriately make an order perpetually staying execution as against the appellants themselves; but insists that he is entitled to an affirmance of the judgment in order that he may prosecute his rights under the bond. That he is so entitled, and that an action may be maintained upon such bond, we do not doubt.

Regardless of the suggestion thus made with respect to the existence of a stay bond, we also think that appellants are not on this motion entitled to anything more than is thus conceded to them by counsel for respondent. The principal object of the judgment was to enforce the plaintiff's right to have certain personal property restored to his possession. If that property remains in the possession or under the control of the defendants, it may be redelivered to the plaintiff, in which event the alternative money judgment would be of no consequence. We are not aware of anything in the bankruptcy proceedings which would prevent such return of his property by the defendants to the plaintiff. The respondent is entitled to a determination of this appeal, so that if the judgment be affirmed he may recover that property; and since the condition of the bond was that the defendants would obey the order of this court upon the appeal (which upon an affirmance of the judgment would in substance be an order for the return of the property), we see no reason why the respondent is not equally entitled to a determination of the appeal so that if the judgment be affirmed he may assert his rights with respect to that bond. All the protection to which the appellants are entitled by reason of a discharge in bankruptcy will be obtained by them under an order perpetually staying proceedings by execution or otherwise, against them, to realize upon the alternative money judgment which was rendered against them.

The order denying defendants' motion for a new trial is affirmed. The judgment is modified in that portion thereof providing for the amount to be recovered in case a delivery or return of the property cannot be had, by substituting for the sum of $1,287.50 the sum of $1,200; and for the sum of $1,270 the sum of $1,250; and for the sum of $1,460 the sum of $1,398.75; and for the aggregate sum of $5,017.50 the sum of $4,848.75. As thus amended, the judgment is affirmed; without prejudice to the right of appellants to apply to the superior court for an order perpetually staying execution as against them, upon those parts of the judgment which provide for recovery by the plaintiff against the defendants of any sum or sums of money in case a delivery or return of the described personal property or any thereof cannot be had.

James, J., and Shaw, J., concurred.

[Civ. No. 1595. Third Appellate District.—October 14, 1916.]

E. F. RICH et al., Petitioners, v. SUPERIOR COURT OF MENDOCINO COUNTY et al., Respondents.

JUSTICE'S COURT—APPEAL—SUFFICIENCY OF UNDERTAKING.—An undertaking on appeal from the justice's court from a judgment for the payment of money in a sum equal to twice the amount of the judgment and costs (an amount in excess of one hundred dollars), and conditioned that if proceedings be stayed the appellant will pay the amount of the judgment appealed from, and all costs if the appeal be withdrawn or dismissed, or the amount of any judgment and all costs that may be recovered against him in the action in the superior court, is sufficient, under section 978 of the Code of Civil Procedure, as an undertaking for the payment of costs on the appeal and to give the superior court jurisdiction of the appeal, regardless of its sufficiency as an undertaking to stay execution.

ID.—DISMISSAL OF APPEAL—INSUFFICIENCY OF UNDERTAKING—JURISDICTION OF SUPERIOR COURT.—The superior court has jurisdiction to hear and determine a motion to dismiss an appeal taken thereto from the justice's court on the ground that a sufficient undertaking had not been filed.

31 Cal. App.—44

ID.—JURISDICTION—MEANING OF RULE.—The rule that when a court
once obtains jurisdiction of the subject matter of an action, it then
has jurisdiction to decide a question arising therein erroneously as
well as correctly, has no application to a case where the very question to be determined is whether the court has the legal authority
to hear and determine the matter before it. The rule simply means
that when the court has jurisdiction of the subject matter of the
action, and makes error during the course of the trial or in its final
decision, such error is correctible, not through a jurisdictional writ,
but solely by appeal.

APPLICATION for a Writ of Review originally made to
the District Court of Appeal for the Third Appellate District
to secure an annulment of an order dismissing a justice's
court appeal.

The facts are stated in the opinion of the court.

Charles Kasch, for Petitioners.

Frank W. Taft, for Respondents.

HART, J.—One Harvey Carlton, on the twenty-first day
of June, 1916, recovered judgment against the petitioners in
the justice's court of Little Lake Township, in the county of
Mendocino, for the sum of $115.35, together with costs of
suit, taxed at $8.75. Thereafter, and within the time allowed
by law, the petitioners appealed from said judgment to the
superior court, in and for the county of Mendocino, said appeal being upon questions of both law and fact. The petitioners, in due time, filed the following undertaking:

"Whereas, on the 21st day of June, A. D. 1916, a judgment
was entered in said justice's court against defendant in favor
of plaintiff, for one hundred and fifteen and 35/100 dollars
and costs.

"Defendant has appealed from said judgment to the Superior Court of the County of Mendocino; and he wants proceedings stayed pending appeal. Now the undersigned jointly
and severally undertake in the sum of two hundred and
forty-eight and 70/100 dollars, that if proceedings be stayed
appellant will pay the amount of the judgment appealed
from, and will pay all costs if the appeal be withdrawn or
dismissed, or the amount of any judgment and all costs that

may be recovered against him in action in the Superior Court, and will obey any order made by the Court therein.

"Dated this 26th day of June, A. D. 1916.

"E. F. RICH.

"GERTRUDE RICH.

"J. D. BARNWELL.

"LOUIS BILODEAU."

Thereafter the respondent noticed a motion to dismiss the said appeal on the ground that no appeal bond, or deposit in lieu thereof, had been filed for the purposes of the appeal and that the superior court, therefore, had failed to acquire jurisdiction of said appeal. Said motion came on for hearing and was heard on the twenty-first day of August, 1916, and on the twenty-eighth day of August, 1916, the respondents herein made and entered an order dismissing said appeal on the ground set forth in the notice of motion and above stated.

The petitioners claim that the undertaking filed by them and above quoted herein was and is legally sufficient to support the appeal, and that therefore the respondents, in ordering the appeal dismissed, exceeded their jurisdiction.

The proceeding here is for a writ of review to secure an annulment of the order dismissing said appeal.

Section 978 of the Code of Civil Procedure provides that "an appeal from a justice's or police court is not effectual for any purpose, unless an undertaking be filed with two or more sureties in the sum of one hundred dollars for the payment of the costs on the appeal." The same section provides that, if a stay of proceedings be claimed, there shall be filed a like undertaking, "in a sum equal to twice the amount of the judgment, including costs, when the judgment is for the payment of money," etc.

The undertaking in the case involved herein, it will be observed, is for a sum equal to twice the amount of the judgment and the costs, and while it is possible that its sole purpose might have been to effect a stay of proceedings, it obligates the sureties to pay all costs which may accrue by reason of the appeal, if the same be withdrawn or dismissed, or to pay "the amount of any judgment and all costs that may be recovered against him in the action in the superior court," and to "obey any order made by the court therein."

It is clear that the sureties, by their undertaking, bound themselves to pay the costs on appeal, and the bond, being in

an amount in excess of one hundred dollars, is in all respects
sufficient for that purpose.   Whether it was also sufficient to
stay proceedings, is wholly immaterial, so far as the appeal is
concerned.   To perfect his appeal, the statute makes it in-
dispensably necessary for the appealing party to file an undertaking in the sum of one hundred dollars for the payment
of the costs on appeal, and when this is done, the court to
which the appeal is taken acquires jurisdiction thereof, and
obviously cannot be divested of such jurisdiction by the mere
failure of the appellant to file a stay bond.   Nor is its validity
as an appeal bond destroyed by the fact that it also purports
to be given to stay execution.   (*Edwards* v. *Superior Court*,
159 Cal. 710, 714, [115 Pac. 649]; *Ward* v. *Superior Court*,
58 Cal. 519; *Jones* v. *Superior Court*, 151 Cal. 589, [91 Pac.
505].)

The undertaking in the case of *Edwards* v. *Superior Court*,
159 Cal. 710, [115 Pac. 649], contained the following condition, between which and the condition of the undertaking
herein involved it will readily be perceived no substantial
difference exists:

"The condition of the above undertaking is such that the
said Edwards et als. obtained judgment, before James G.
Quinn, Justice of the Peace of Oakland Township, in and for
the County of Alameda, State of California, on the 25th day
of October, 1909, for $73.20, principal sum, and for $9.50
costs; and whereas the above bounden F. E. Miller (defendant
and appellant) is desirous of appealing from the decision of
said justice to the Superior Court in and for the County of
Alameda, and a stay of proceedings is claimed.   Now, if the
above-bounden shall well and truly pay or cause to be paid
the amount of the said judgment and all costs, and obey any
order the said Superior Court may make therein, if the said
appeal be withdrawn or dismissed, or pay the amount of any
judgment and all the costs that may be recovered against
the said appellant in the said superior court, and obey any order
the said court may make therein, then this obligation to be
null and void; otherwise to remain in full force and virtue."

Chief Justice Beatty, who prepared the main opinion in
that case, among other things, said: "The latest decision of
this court upon that point (*Jones* v. *Superior Court*, 151 Cal.
589, [91 Pac. 505]), is a conclusive affirmance of the sufficiency of the undertaking under section 978 of the Code of

Civil Procedure. It may be doubted whether the decision in that case successfully distinguishes the case of *McConky* v. *Superior Court*, 56 Cal. 83, in which section 978 appears to have been differently construed, but if that case was not distinguishable it was certainly overruled—and I have no doubt properly overruled—for the construction there given to section 978 was only reached by disregarding the express terms of the statute, i. e., by the substitution of the word 'or' for 'and' with the effect of requiring two undertakings, each containing the same condition, where one was amply sufficient for every conceivable purpose—and that in a class of actions where simplicity of procedure and economy are a most important *desideratum.*"

In a concurring opinion, the other members of the court said:

"We concur in the order denying a writ on the ground that the bond is sufficient to confer jurisdiction on the superior court. The undertaking is in more than the sum of one hundred dollars, and is conditioned for the payment of the costs on the appeal. It thus contains all that is required by section 978 of the Code of Civil Procedure, to make the appeal effectual. . . . Whether or not it is effectual to operate as a stay bond is not here involved. We express no opinion on this point, nor do we think it necessary for the decision of this case to question the correctness of *McConky* v. *Superior Court*, 56 Cal. 83.''

The Edwards' case ''is a conclusive affirmance of the sufficiency of the undertaking'' in ''the present case,'' under section 978 of the Code of Civil Procedure, as a bond for the payment of costs on appeal.

The learned counsel for the respondents argue, however: "It is elementary that, if a court has jurisdiction to decide a question correctly, it also has jurisdiction to decide it incorrectly, and to hold that a court exceeds its jurisdiction in granting a motion to dismiss would compel us to hold that it exceeds its jurisdiction in denying such motion. Therefore, a rule which holds that the superior court exceeds its jurisdiction in either granting or denying a motion must, perforce, hold that the superior court cannot pass upon a motion at all. A litigant could, under such a rule, appeal to the superior court without filing any bond whatever and the superior court would be without jurisdiction to dismiss it.''

The reasoning is clearly and wholly fallacious. The superior court has the right and the power to pass upon and decide a motion to dismiss an appeal taken thereto, and where the motion is based upon the ground that the undertaking required by section 978 of the Code of Civil Procedure for the indemnification of the costs accruing by reason of the appeal has not been filed, it is not only within the power, but it is the duty, of the court to dismiss the appeal or, speaking more accurately, the attempted appeal, since, as stated, the section named makes the filing of such an undertaking one of the essential and, indeed, indispensable requisites for conferring upon such court jurisdiction to hear and determine an appeal thereto from a justice's or police court. The rule that when a court once obtains jurisdiction of the subject matter of an action, it then has jurisdiction to decide a question arising therein erroneously as well as correctly, has no application to a case where the very question to be determined is whether the court has the legal authority to hear and determine the matter before it. The rule simply means that when the court has jurisdiction of the subject matter of the action, and makes error during the course of the trial or in its final decision, such error is correctible, not through a jurisdictional writ, but solely by appeal. Obviously, if the trial court is called upon to decide whether it has jurisdiction of the subject matter of the action and determines the question erroneously, or, having no jurisdiction, nevertheless claims it, it can be prevented from proceeding to exercise the usurped authority or, having exercised it, its action may be annulled and vacated by means of the remedy appropriate thereto.

For the reasons herein given, the order made by the respondents in this proceeding dismissing the appeal by the petitioners herein from the judgment of the justice's court of Little Lake Township, Mendocino County, in the action wherein said Harvey Carlton was plaintiff and the said petitioners were defendants, is hereby annulled, set aside, and vacated.

Chipman, P. J., and Burnett, J., concurred.

[Civ. No. 1806. Second Appellate District.—October 17, 1916.]

A. H. REHKOPF, Appellant, v. JOE WIRZ et al., Respondents.

LANDLORD AND TENANT—ABANDONMENT OF PREMISES—UNQUALIFIED TAKING OF POSSESSION BY LESSOR—ACTION FOR DAMAGES NOT MAINTAINABLE.—Where the possession of demised premises is vacated by the lessees prior to the expiration of the term, the lessor cannot maintain an action for damages in a sum equal to the difference between the rent which should have been paid under the lease and the amount for which he was able to rent the property for the period of the unexpired term, where he, upon being informed by the lessees of their intention to vacate the premises, took possession of the property and made a new lease thereof, without making any further demand upon the lessees, or in any manner informing them of the course which he would pursue.

ID.—REPUDIATION OF LEASE BY TENANTS—ACCEPTANCE OF POSSESSION FOR BENEFIT OF LESSEE—DUTY OF LESSOR.—Where a tenant abandons the leased property and repudiates the lease, the landlord may accept possession of the property for the benefit of the tenant and relet the same, and thereupon may maintain an action for damages for the difference between what he was able in good faith to let the property for and the amount provided to be paid under the lease agreement. But a lessor who chooses to follow that course must in some manner give the lessee information that he is accepting such possession for the benefit of the tenant, and not in his own right and for his own benefit.

ID.—UNQUALIFIED ACCEPTANCE BY LESSOR—RELEASE OF LESSEE.—An unqualified taking of possession by the lessor, and reletting of the premises by him as owner to new tenants, is inconsistent with the continuing force of the original lease. If done without the consent of the tenant to such interference, it is an eviction, and the tenant will be released. If done pursuant to the tenant's attempted abandonment, it is an acceptance of the surrender and likewise releases the tenant.

APPEAL from a judgment of the Superior Court of Imperial County. Franklin J. Cole, Judge.

The facts are stated in the opinion of the court.

Dan V. Noland, and Walter B. Kibbey, for Appellant.

McPherrin & Nichols, for Respondents.

CONREY, P. J.—This is an action whereby the plaintiff seeks to recover damages for breach of the covenants of a written lease of real property. The court having granted defendants' motion for a nonsuit, judgment was entered, from which plaintiff appeals.

The lease was for three years, beginning April 1, 1913. Defendants paid the rent monthly in advance for the period of one year and vacated the premises a few days prior to April 1, 1914. Thereupon the lessor took possession of the premises and advertised for another tenant. During the month of April, 1914, he obtained another tenant to whom he leased the premises for a term of three years, beginning May 1, 1914, and at a rate of rental less than that provided for in the lease which had been made to defendants. Plaintiff claims damages in a sum equal to the difference between the rent which would have been paid under the lease of the defendants and the amount for which he was able to rent the property for the period of the unexpired term of the defendants.

Where a tenant abandons the leased property and repudiates the lease, the landlord may accept possession of the property for the benefit of the tenant and relet the same, and thereupon may maintain an action for damages for the difference between what he was able in good faith to let the property for and the amount provided to be paid under the lease agreement. (*Bradbury* v. *Higginson*, 162 Cal. 602, [123 Pac. 797].) But a lessor who chooses to follow that course must in some manner give the lessee information that he is accepting such possession for the benefit of the tenant and not in his own right and for his own benefit. If the lessor takes possession of property delivered to him by his tenant and does so unqualifiedly, he thereby releases the tenant. (*Baker* v. *Eilers Music Co.*, 26 Cal. App. 371, [146 Pac. 1056]; *Welcome* v. *Hess*, 90 Cal. 507, [25 Am. St. Rep. 145, 27 Pac. 369].) An unqualified taking of possession by the lessor and reletting of the premises by him as owner to new tenants is inconsistent with the continuing force of the original lease. If done without the consent of the tenant to such interference, it is an eviction, and the tenant will be released. If done pursuant to the tenant's attempted abandonment, it is an acceptance of the surrender and likewise releases the tenant.

In this case the plaintiff's testimony presents the facts clearly and without conflict. The defendants informed the plaintiff that they were going to leave the ranch. They did leave, and omitted payment of the installment of rent which, according to the terms of the lease, fell due April 1, 1914. Without making any further demand upon the defendants, or in any manner informing them as to the course which he would pursue, the plaintiff took possession and made a new lease of the land as above stated. Upon these facts the plaintiff failed to establish any right of action for the damages claimed by him. In *Auer* v. *Penn*, 99 Pa. St. 370, [44 Am. Rep. 114], it was stated that if the tenant gives up the demised premises, the landlord may re-enter and relet, and that such action on his part raises no presumption of acceptance of a surrender, since it is for the advantage of the tenant that he should do so. Referring to that case and that proposition, the supreme court of California in *Welcome* v. *Hess*, 90 Cal. 507, [25 Am. St. Rep. 145, 27 Pac. 369), declared that while there are many cases which hold to this view, "the weight of authority and the better reason is the other way." It follows that the evidence in this case, although construed as favorably as possible to the plaintiff, was insufficient to establish his case and the court was right in granting the nonsuit.

In examining the evidence we have not overlooked the proposed alteration of the lease, which alteration was signed by the lessor and delivered by the lessor to the defendants for their approval, nor the evidence of the circumstances connected with that proposed change in the terms of the lease. The defendants did not sign the proposed supplemental agreement, and it does not appear that any of the things which they did after it was delivered to them amounted to an acceptance or part performance. Throughout the transaction they appear to have acted consistently with the terms of the original lease until the time when they abandoned the premises and thereby offered to surrender the same, which surrender must be deemed to have been accepted by reason of the acts of the plaintiff as above stated.

The judgment is affirmed.

James, J., and Shaw, J., concurred.

A petition to have the cause heard in the supreme court, after judgment in the district court of appeal, was denied by the supreme court on December 14, 1916.

[Crim. No. 513. Second Appellate District.—October 17, 1916.]

In the Matter of the Application of EUGENIA N. DUPES, for a Writ of Habeas Corpus.

DIVORCE—CUSTODY OF CHILDREN—APPEAL—STAY OF PROCEEDINGS.—In an action for divorce an order included in the interlocutory decree awarding the father the custody of the minor children of the parties is stayed by the taking of an appeal from such decree by the wife, and the trial court has no jurisdiction pending the appeal to order that such children be taken from the possession of their mother and given to their father.

ID.—EFFECT OF APPEAL—REMOVAL OF JURISDICTION.—The effect of the perfecting of an appeal is to stay all further proceedings upon the judgment or order appealed from or matters embraced therein in the court below, and to remove the subject matter of the adjudication from the jurisdiction of such court.

APPLICATION for a Writ of Habeas Corpus originally made to the District Court of Appeal for the Second Appellate District to secure the custody of minor children.

The facts are stated in the opinion of the court.

MacKnight & Fitzgerrell, and P. N. Myers, for Petitioner.

Chas. N. Sears, and E. J. Emmons, for Respondent.

SHAW, J.—The facts are as follows: On February 25, 1916, T. W. Dupes filed a complaint in the superior court of Kern County, wherein he prayed for a decree of divorce from Eugenia N. Dupes and the award to him of the care, custody, and control of Janice and Bernard Dupes, minor children of the parties, who it appears were at the time living with their mother. By answer and cross-complaint, Eugenia N. Dupes asked that she be awarded the decree of divorce and likewise awarded the care and custody of the children; each of said parents alleging the other's unfitness to have control of them. Pending the trial an order was issued to Eugenia N. Dupes requiring her to show cause why an order should not be made awarding the custody of the children to their father, and this matter coming on for hearing, the court, pursuant to stipulation of the parties, on March 6, 1916, made an order, subject to such further order as might be made, awarding the custody of the children to the mother. The case was tried and, on July 22, 1916, the court made findings in said action upon which, as a conclusion of law, it found that T. W. Dupes was entitled to a decree of divorce, and that Eugenia N. Dupes was unfit to have the custody and care of the minor children, and awarding their custody to the father. Three days thereafter, to wit, on July 25, 1916, the defendant in said action, Eugenia N. Dupes, perfected an appeal from said interlocutory judgment. After the appeal had been perfected, and on July 26, 1916, the court made an order reciting that, whereas, before the hearing of said action upon its merits, to wit, on March 6, 1916, an order had been made awarding the care, custody, and control of said minor children to the defendant Eugenia N. Dupes, and the court having at the conclusion of the trial of the action found that defendant was not a fit and proper person to have the care of said children, and it having appeared by the evidence introduced that T. W. Dupes was a proper person to whom their care and custody should be awarded, ordered that said temporary order made on the sixth day of March, 1916, be vacated, and the care, custody, and control of said children awarded to their father, T. W. Dupes. Thereafter, on July 31, 1916, the court by an order directed the sheriff of Kern County to take into his custody and deliver to the court said Janice and Bernard Dupes, to be disposed of according to the order of court; and further ordered that a copy of the order so made be delivered to the mother then having possession of the children. The sheriff complied with this order and took from the mother the possession of the children and produced them in court; whereupon, on the same day, to wit, July 31, 1916, the court ordered the sheriff to immediately deliver the children to their father.

By the return made in response to the writ, T. W. Dupes bases his right to the custody, care, and control of the minors upon the findings of fact showing petitioner's unfitness to have charge of the children, and upon the interlocutory decree made July 22, 1916, awarding the custody of the children to the plaintiff in said action; and also upon the order of the superior court made after the perfecting of the appeal from said interlocutory decree (and which said order purported to vacate and set aside the order awarding the custody of the children to Eugenia N. Dupes on March 6, 1916), pursuant to which the sheriff was on July 31, 1916, directed to take possession of the children and deliver them to the father.

The effect of the perfecting of an appeal is to stay all further proceedings upon the judgment or order appealed from or matters embraced therein in the court below. (Code Civ. Proc., secs. 946, 949.) It operates to remove the subject matter of the adjudication from the jurisdiction of the court below pending the appeal, and suspends the power of that court to enforce its order until the appeal is determined. (*Ex parte Queirolo*, 119 Cal. 635, [51 Pac. 956].) "The effect of the appeal is to remove the subject matter of the order from the jurisdiction of the lower court, and that court is without power to proceed further as to any matter embraced therein until the appeal is determined." (*Vosburg v. Vosburg*, 137 Cal. 493, [70 Pac. 473].) The fitness of the respective parties as custodians of the children was one of the issues involved in the action and tried by the court, and as to which it found the mother, Eugenia N. Dupes, was not a proper person to have control of the children; that the father was a fit person to whom the control should be awarded, and so ordered. The mother, however, under and by virtue of the order of March 6th awarding her the custody of the children, had possession of them and, since the stay of proceedings pending appeal has the legitimate effect of keeping the subject thereof in the condition in which it was when the stay of proceedings was granted (*Schwarz v. Superior Court*, 111 Cal. 113, [43 Pac. 580]), it would seem clear that the decree from which the appeal was perfected should constitute no ground upon which respondent could found his right to the custody of the children. This being true, the order awarding their custody to T. W. Dupes, as embodied in the decree from which the appeal was perfected, left in full force and effect the order of March 6th, under which petitioner was awarded control of the children. Since by perfecting the appeal the subject of the litigation was removed from the lower court, it would seem equally clear that the court was without jurisdiction to make the order of July 31st purporting to vacate and annul the order of March 6th, and directing the sheriff to take the children from the mother and deliver them to the father. Our conclusion is that the appeal stayed all proceedings upon the decree and order embraced therein, and removed the case from the trial court, thus depriving it of jurisdiction to make any order as to the subject matter thereof pending the appeal. Hence neither the findings, decree based thereon, nor the order made after the appeal was taken purporting to vacate the order of March 6th, constitute any ground for respondent's asserted right to the control and custody of said minors. (See *Vosburg* v. *Vosburg*, 137 Cal. 493, [70 Pac. 473], and *Ex parte Queirolo*, 119 Cal. 635, [51 Pac. 956].)

It is also claimed that petitioner is not a fit and proper person to have the care and control of said minors. Specific acts of neglect of the children occurring prior to the trial, and a course of misconduct pursued by petitioner prior thereto, are set forth in the return, to prove which numerous affidavits are presented. These affidavits, however, relate to acts of omission and commission on the part of petitioner, as stated, occurring before the trial of the issues involved in the litigation and therein relied upon to show her unfitness. Pending the appeal, a new proceeding involving the same question cannot be based thereon.

It is ordered that the custody of said Bernard Dupes and Janice Dupes be by T. W. Dupes, the respondent herein, surrendered and restored to petitioner, Eugenia N. Dupes.

Conrey, P. J., and James, J., concurred.

[Civ. No. 1958. First Appellate District.—October 18, 1916.]

PACIFIC COAST CASUALTY COMPANY (a Corporation), Petitioner, v. A. J. PILLSBURY et al., as Commissioners, etc., Respondents; MRS. J. CASSELL, Applicant.

Workmen's Compensation Act—Death of Errand Boy in Elevator Accident—Disregard of Instructions—Annulment of Award.—An award of compensation made by the Industrial Accident Commission for the death of an errand boy, who met his death while endeavoring to ascend to the floor of the building upon which his employer had its place of business, by means of a freight elevator operated by himself, is beyond the jurisdiction of the commission, where the undisputed evidence shows that the deceased had been

expressly warned not to ride in, or attempt to operate, the freight
elevators in the building under penalty of discharge, and that
notices were posted at, or near, the entrance of such elevators of
similar import, and there is no evidence that the alleged disregard
of such instructions and warnings on the part of employees was
ever brought to the notice of their employer, or of any negligence
from which such knowledge would be chargeable.

APPLICATION for a Writ of Review originally made to
the District Court of Appeal for the First Appellate District
to review an award of compensation made by the Industrial
Accident Commission.

The facts are stated in the opinion of the court.

T. T. C. Gregory, for Petitioner.

Christopher M. Bradley, for Respondents.

THE COURT.—This is an application for a writ of review
directed against the Industrial Accident Commission by the
petitioner, who is the insurer of the Simon Millinery Company
of San Francisco, which company was the employer of one
Simon Cassell, an errand boy, who was killed in an elevator
accident during the time of his employment by said company.

The facts of the case as disclosed by the record are briefly
these: The deceased, Simon Cassell, entered the employment
of the Simon Millinery Company as an errand boy about one
month prior to the accident in which he met his death. The
place of business of the Simon Millinery Company was in the
Lincoln Building, situate near the corner of Fifth and Market
Streets in said city. There were several passenger and freight
elevators in said building. The tenants in the portion of the
building fronting on Market Street used chiefly the freight
and passenger elevators near the entrance to said building on
said street. There was also a freight and passenger elevator
chiefly used by tenants in that portion of the building fronting upon Fifth Street, and it was in the freight elevator near
the Fifth Street entrance that the deceased met with the accident which caused his immediate death. On the third day of
September, 1915, the deceased was directed by his employer,
the Simon Millinery Company, to go to a certain place on
Mission Street and obtain some piping. He went upon said

errand, and, returning with the piping, attempted to enter the
building and ascend to the floor upon which his employer had
its place of business by way of the freight elevator near the
Fifth Street entrance, and in so doing to operate the elevator
himself. In some manner not made very clear by the evidence he was crushed and killed in the attempt to thus operate
this elevator.

There was evidence introduced before the commission that
upon entering the employment of the Simon Millinery Company the deceased had been expressly warned not to ride in or
attempt to operate the freight elevators under penalty of
immediate discharge. There was also some evidence before
the commission tending to show that notices were posted at, or
near, the entrances to both freight elevators in the building
warning persons against attempting to operate or ride in them
without the presence of the regular operator of said elevators.
There was also some evidence before the commission that these
warnings or notices had been occasionally disregarded by certain of the employees of the Simon Millinery Company, and
that upon several occasions the errand boys had ridden up and
down in the freight elevators of the building in violation of
the express warning and instruction not to do so. We have
examined the record carefully for the purpose of determining
whether there is any evidence therein that these instances of
the disregard of the instructions and warnings on the part
of its employees were ever brought to its notice, and as to
whether or not there is any evidence showing that the employer was derelict in not taking notice of the fact that its
orders were being disobeyed by its employees; but upon such
examination we have failed to find any evidence whatever of
any such knowledge on the part of the employer, or of any
such negligence on its part from the fact of which such knowledge would be chargeable. This being so, we are of the opinion that the finding of the Industrial Accident Commission
"that the deceased and other employees of the defendant frequently operated said Fifth Street elevator by themselves
without reproof or discipline by said defendant," and also the
finding "that the signs placed by the owners of said building
upon the doors of the elevators were habitually disregarded
without protest," and also the finding "that the protection of
its employees from serious bodily injury or death in connection with the operation of such elevators was not made plain

to them nor to Cassell in a manner suited to the intelligence of a person of his age,'' are without evidence to support them, and are contrary to the evidence in the case; and that since these findings of fact were essential to the recovery of the applicant before the Industrial Accident Commission, the action of that body in awarding such compensation without any evidence sufficient to sustain said findings was beyond the jurisdiction of the commission, and hence that a writ of review would properly lie, and that such writ should issue, and that the action of the commission in awarding such compensation should be annulled.

It is so ordered.

A petition for a rehearing of this cause was denied by the district court of appeal on November 16, 1916, and the following opinion then rendered thereon:

THE COURT.—The petition for rehearing is denied. We are of the opinion that the undisputed evidence in the case showed that the deceased had been expressly warned not to ride in, or attempt to operate, the freight elevators in the building in which he met his death, under penalty of discharge, and that notices were posted at, or near, the entrance of such elevators of similar import, and that the disregard of such warning by the employee must, in the absence of evidence mitigating such disobedience, be held to constitute such willful misconduct as would prevent a recovery before the commission, where, as in the instant case, there is no evidence tending to show that the disregard of its warnings, orders, and notices was condoned by the employer.

[Civ. No. 2042.   Second Appellate District.—October 19, 1916.]

NATIONAL BANK OF BAKERSFIELD (a Corporation), Appellant, v. W. R. WILLIAMS, as Superintendent of Banks, etc., Respondent.

BANKING ACT—SALE OF PROPERTY—LIABILITY FOR TAXES—CONSTRUCTION OF ORDER AUTHORIZING SALE.—An action cannot be maintained against the superintendent of banks to recover of him, as the grantor of certain real property belonging to an insolvent banking corporation, the amount of the taxes which the grantee was required to pay to protect the property from sale on account of delinquency, notwithstanding such taxes were a lien on the property but not due at the time of the conveyance, where such conveyance was made pursuant to an order of court directing such official to make a conveyance of only such right, title, and interest as the insolvent had in the property, and neither the order, nor the deed, made any reference to taxes.

ID.—DEED—USE OF TERM "GRANT"—COVENANT AGAINST TAXES—WHEN NOT IMPLIED.—While the use of the word "grant" in a conveyance implies a covenant against encumbrances made or suffered by the grantor, and while taxes which were at the date of the grant a lien upon the property conveyed are embraced therein, nevertheless the covenant implied from the use of the term "grant" must be deemed limited by the subject matter of the conveyance.

ID.—SALE UNDER ORDER OF COURT—JUDICIAL SALE—APPLICABILITY OF DOCTRINE OF CAVEAT EMPTOR.—A sale made by the superintendent of banks under an order of court in accordance with the provisions of the Banking Act is a judicial sale, to which the doctrine of caveat emptor applies.

ID.—CONFIRMATION OF SALE—NONESSENTIAL ELEMENT.—A confirmation of such a sale is not required, as the order authorizing the sale is sufficient confirmation.

APPEAL from a judgment of the Superior Court of Kern County.   Howard A. Peairs, Judge.

The facts are stated in the opinion of the court.

C. L. Claflin, for Appellant.

Hiram W. Johnson, Jr., and A. A. DeLigne, for Respondent.

SHAW, J.—This is an appeal by plaintiff from a judgment entered in favor of defendant upon the court sustaining a general demurrer to the former's amended complaint, without leave to amend.

Briefly stated, the facts so far as pertinent are as follows: At the times in question the business and assets of the Kern Valley Bank, a corporation organized for the purpose of conducting a banking business, were in charge of defendant as superintendent of banks, and in process of liquidation.

In accordance with section 136 of the Banking Act of 1909 (Stats. 1909, p. 115), which provides that "the superintendent of banks shall collect all debts due and claims belonging to it, and upon the order of the superior court may sell or compound all bad or doubtful debts, and on like order may sell all real and personal property of such bank on such terms as the court shall direct," defendant filed a petition in the superior court praying for an order of court empowering and directing him to sell certain real estate therein described to plaintiff for the sum of thirty-one thousand dollars. After due notice, the petition was heard, at which time the court called for other bids and, none being received, the court "ordered, adjudged, and decreed that the said W. R. Williams, Superintendent of Banks of the State of California, and Trustee of the Kern Valley Bank, a corporation in liquidation, be and he is hereby authorized, empowered, and directed to accept the offer of said The National Bank of Bakersfield to sell the property hereinafter described for the sum of Thirty-one Thousand Dollars ($31,000) and he is hereby authorized, empowered and directed to execute unto said The National Bank of Bakersfield a deed conveying to said The National Bank of Bakersfield all the right, title, and interest in said Kern Valley Bank, a corporation in liquidation, to all that certain real property commonly known as the banking premises of said Kern Valley Bank [followed by description of property], upon the payment to said W. R. Williams for and in behalf of said Kern Valley Bank, a corporation in liquidation, the sum of Thirty-one Thousand Dollars ($31,000)." Pursuant to this order directing him so to do, defendant sold and conveyed to the plaintiff all the right, title, and interest of the Kern Valley Bank to said real estate, which property at the time was subject to state, county, and municipal taxes (not then due) for the then current year, the lien for which had attached in March preceding. No reference to taxes was made in the deed or in the order pursuant to which it was made, and defendant refusing to pay them, plaintiff, in order to protect the property from sale on account of delinquency, paid the same and brought this action to recover upon implied covenants contained in the deed.

It is conceded the superintendent of banks, in the absence of such order, had no power to make the sale and conveyance. Hence, since he was acting as an instrument of the court, the duty of which was to direct the sale upon such terms as it might specify, the power of such agent must be measured by the terms of the order under which he acted. Looking to the order, it appears that he was directed to accept the offer of plaintiff and authorized "to execute unto said The National Bank of Bakersfield a deed conveying . . . all the right, title, and interest in said Kern Valley Bank . . . to all that certain real property," etc. The deed followed the language of the order; the words of transfer used, however, being *"grant, bargain, and sell all the right, title, and interest"* of the Kern Valley Bank. While the use of the word "grant" in a conveyance implies a covenant against encumbrances made or suffered by the grantor (Civ. Code, sec. 1113), and while taxes for the fiscal year, which were at the date of the grant a lien upon the property, are embraced therein (*McPike* v. *Heaton,* 131 Cal. 109, [82 Am. St. Rep. 335, 63 Pac. 179]), nevertheless the covenant implied from the use of the term "grant" must be deemed limited by the subject matter of the conveyance. The order of court, which is the measure of defendant's power, directed a conveyance only of such right, title, and interest as the grantor had in the property, and the deed transferring such interest must be construed as a conveyance of such interest subject to defects in title, liens, or encumbrances of whatsoever nature. (*Sweet* v. *Brown,* 12 Met. (Mass.) 175, [45 Am. Dec. 243].) "Where a deed purports to convey only the right, title, and interest of the grantor, the scope of the covenant of warranty may be limited by the subject matter of the conveyance." (2 Devlin on Deeds, sec. 931.)

Moreover, we are of the opinion that the transaction possesses every element of a judicial sale, to which, if true, the doctrine of *caveat emptor* applies. (*Webster* v. *Haworth,* 8 Cal. 21, [68 Am. Dec. 287]; 3 Freeman on Executions, sec. 335; 17 Am. & Eng. Ency. of Law, p. 1010.)

Appellant claims that, conceding the sale and conveyance were required to be made upon an order of the superior court, no provision is made in the law for an order confirming the same, and hence it is lacking in one of the essential elements of a judicial sale. In our opinion, there is no merit in this contention. It is conceded that the sale could not have been made in the absence of an order of court. As appears from the record, respondent presented a petition showing that he had received an offer for the property; whereupon notice was given of the hearing of the petition, and at the hearing thereof the court itself called for bids thereon and, none being received, directed that the sale be made to plaintiff, and directed defendant, upon the payment of the purchase price, to execute a deed conveying the grantor's right, title, and interest therein to plaintiff. The order itself constituted a confirmation of the sale thus directed to be made, and there remained nothing to confirm. In Freeman on Void Judicial Sales, section 1, it is said: "The true test is, that it (the sale) must be one which is, in contemplation of law, made by the court, and there may be circumstances when such is the case, though there is no pre-existing order directing or authorizing the sale, as where the property is in the hands of a receiver appointed by the court and given power by law to make sales thereof, or of an executor upon whom a power of sale is conferred by the will, if the sale must be reported to, and confirmed by the court." A judicial sale is defined in the American and English Encyclopedia of Law, volume 17, page 953, as follows: "A judicial sale is a sale made under the process of a court having competent authority to order it, by an officer duly appointed and commissioned to sell, which sale, as a general rule, becomes absolute only upon confirmation by the court." Here the sale was made by the court through an officer by law designated in such cases to make the conveyance of the property when so ordered by the court and upon the terms specified therein. It was made under a procedure authorized by law, and in substance is the same as that adopted in effecting sales of property by receivers of national banks as provided by section 5234 of the Revised Statutes of the United States, [5 Fed. Stats. Ann., p. 170; U. S. Comp. Stats., sec. 9821], which transactions are held to constitute judicial sales. Thus, in *Schaberg's Estate* v. *McDonald*, 60 Neb. 493, [83 N. W. 737], it is said: "A sale made by a receiver of a national bank under an order of a court of competent jurisdiction is a judicial sale." And in *In re Third National Bank*, 4 Fed. 775, it is said: "A sale by a receiver of the property of a national bank, under an order of court, in accordance with the provisions of section 5234 of the Revised Statutes, constitutes a judicial sale."

The judgment is affirmed.

Conrey, P. J., and James, J., concurred.

———

[Civ. No. 1924. First Appellate District.—October 19, 1916.]

AUGUSTA VRAGNIZAN, Respondent, v. SAVINGS UNION BANK AND TRUST COMPANY (a Corporation), as Executor, etc., Appellant.

ACTIONS—ABATEMENT AND SURVIVAL OF CAUSES OF ACTIONS—TORTS.— An action arising out of a tort, unconnected with contract and which affects the person only and not the estate, is purely personal, and abates with the death of the wrongdoer, while an action virtually founded upon contract, though nominally in tort, survives against the tort-feasor's legal representatives.

ID.—HUSBAND AND WIFE—SETTLEMENT OF PROPERTY RIGHTS—RECOVERY OF CONCEALED PROPERTY—ACTION NOT ABATED UPON DEATH.—An action to recover one-half of the value of certain property concealed by a husband from his wife upon the settlement of their property rights during the pendency of an action for divorce, is in the nature of an action for the recovery of an interest in property, and does not abate with the death of the husband.

ID.—MAINTENANCE OF ACTION—DECREE OF DIVORCE NOT A BAR.—The maintenance of such an action is not barred by the decree in the suit for divorce, where such decree dealt only with the status of the parties.

ID.—PLEADING—OFFICIAL CAPACITY OF EXECUTOR.—An allegation in the complaint that on a stated day letters testamentary were duly and regularly issued to the defendant executor, and that such defendant ever since has been and now is the duly qualified and acting executor of the will of the deceased husband, is a sufficient allegation of official capacity, in the absence of a special demurrer. Where such allegation is admitted in the answer, such admission has the effect of a stipulation of the fact, which renders the allegation of more specific facts unnecessary.

ID.—FALSE REPRESENTATIONS—STATEMENT IN DIVORCE PROCEEDINGS—
RIGHT OF ACTION NOT AFFECTED BY.—The fact that most of the
false representations made by the deceased upon which the plaintiff
relied were not made to her personally, but by the testimony of the
deceased and in affidavits filed by him in the action for divorce,
does not affect the right of the plaintiff to maintain the action.

APPEAL from a judgment of the Superior Court of the
City and County of San Francisco. Marcel E. Cerf, Judge.

The facts are stated in the opinion of the court.

Pillsbury, Madison & Sutro, and Felix T. Smith, for
Appellant.

Arthur H. Barendt, for Respondent.

KERRIGAN, J.—This is an action based on a claim presented against the estate of the decedent for approximately
six thousand dollars, of which sum the plaintiff alleges she was
defrauded in a settlement of property rights had between herself and the decedent during the pendency of a suit for divorce
in which they were the parties. Plaintiff obtained judgment,
and the defendant appeals.

After the plaintiff and the decedent had been married and
living together as husband and wife for a period of about
thirty years, the decedent on September 11, 1908, culminated
a long course of cruel treatment of the plaintiff by threatening to kill her and by driving her and their children from
home. The next day, in anticipation of a divorce proceeding
being brought against him by his wife, he withdrew from two
savings banks, where he had on deposit community funds to
the amount of ten thousand one hundred dollars, the sum of
six thousand dollars, and placed the same in a safe deposit
box which he rented that day. A few days thereafter the
plaintiff commenced an action against decedent for divorce
on the ground of extreme cruelty. In a counter-affidavit upon
a motion for counsel fees, costs, and alimony, as well as in his
verified answer to the plaintiff's complaint and by testimony
in open court, the decedent represented that the only money
he had was the four thousand one hundred dollars remaining
on deposit in the said savings banks. He also represented in
his affidavit, answer, and oral testimony that a partnership,

in which he had been theretofore interested, had been dissolved and that he was no longer interested in that business, whereas it was admitted at the trial of the present action that such representations were untrue, and that in fact his partnership in such business continued to the time of his death, and it was also stipulated by the parties to this action that during all the time between the commencement of said proceeding in divorce, and his decease, he was in receipt from the partnership of a net income of forty dollars per month. On the twelfth day of April, 1909, the plaintiff, believing the representations of the decedent, entered into an agreement of settlement of their property rights with him, under the terms of which they divided equally all the money which he had on deposit at the time in the savings banks above mentioned, viz., four thousand one hundred dollars. At about three months after the making of this contract the decedent redeposited the six thousand dollars with an additional nine hundred dollars in the banks from which the six thousand dollars had been withdrawn. The decedent by the terms of his will left five dollars to each of his two children. He was of a secretive nature, and consequently the plaintiff knew little concerning his business affairs. Plaintiff herself is unable to read or write the English language, and for years has suffered from an incurable deafness. In her complaint, among other things, she alleges that she was induced to enter into the agreement of settlement by the fraudulent misrepresentations of the decedent; that she did not learn the falsity of his representations until shortly after his death; that if she had known the facts with reference to the property owned by the decedent at the time of the agreement she would not have accepted the property delivered to her in settlement of her property rights. In her prayer she asks judgment for one-half of the value of the property concealed from her by decedent.

In support of the appeal the defendant claims that this is an action based on fraud and deceit, and that therefore it abated with the death of the decedent. It is sometimes said that at common law all causes of action *ex contractu* survive, whereas all those based on tort die with the person. But neither of these statements is strictly accurate. As to the former, for example, a breach of promise of marriage is an action arising *ex contractu*, yet it does not survive. Nor do all actions in tort die with the person. The true test is not so much the form of the action as the nature of the cause of action. When the action arises out of a tort, unconnected with contract, and which affects the person only and not the estate—such as assault and battery, false imprisonment, malicious prosecution, personal injuries—the action is purely personal and abates with the death of the wrongdoer. But when the action is virtually founded upon contract, though nominally in tort, it survives against the tort-feasor's legal representatives. (1 Cyc. 60; 1 C. J. 340, 362; 1 R. C. L. 22; *Lee v. Hill,* 87 Va. 497, [24 Am. St. Rep. 666, 12 S. E. 1052]; *Payne's Appeal,* 65 Conn. 397, [48 Am. St. Rep. 215, 33 L. R. A. 418, 32 Atl. 948].) And in the case of a tort resulting in the wrongful acquisition of personal property, the law imposing on the wrongdoer the duty of returning that property to the owner, the obligation at common law might be treated as *quasi* contractual, and the neglect to perform it a breach of such contract; in which case the damage resulting from the tort is substantially the value of the property, and the damage resulting from the breach of contract is measured substantially in the same way. Similarly, in determining the question of survival, at common law the substantial cause of action might properly be treated as founded in contract (1 R. C. L. 24.)

In the present case it appearing from the allegations of the complaint that the plaintiff was entitled to a divorce from the decedent on the ground of extreme cruelty, she was entitled at the very least to one-half the community property (Civ. Code, sec. 146; *Gorman v. Gorman,* 134 Cal. 378, [66 Pac. 313]); and she settled with her husband apparently on the theory that she was receiving one-half of the community personal property, and that the agreement of settlement recognized this right. Later, and after his death, on discovering that she had been deceived as to the amount of money decedent had on hand at the time of the settlement, she promptly commenced this action to recover one-half of the property which decedent had thus concealed from her. Such an action is not purely a personal action for tort. It may be treated under the authorities as founded upon contract; and certainly it is in the nature of an action for the recovery of an interest in property. If one believes a false statement of another, and such false statement is the direct means of obtaining the property of such person, there is a legal injury to the rights

of property, and the owner has an action for the property or
its value based on the fraud, and also in some jurisdictions
on the implied contract to return the property or the proceeds
thereof, which legally or equitably belong to the original
owner.   In the case at bar the plaintiff at the time of settlement was entitled to at least one-half of the community property, and if the divorce proceeding had included an adjudication of property rights the court could not have awarded her
less (*Gorman* v. *Gorman, supra*), but believing a false statement of the decedent as to how much community property
there was, and receiving by agreement with her husband one-
half thereof, she took less than she would have been entitled to
receive under an adjudication by the court.   Accordingly it
would appear that she has been injured in a right of property,
and has an action to recover the amount of which she was defrauded.

In *Henderson* v. *Henshall*, 54 Fed. 320, [4 C. C. A. 357], the
facts constituted an action for damages for false representations concerning real property, and to the contention that the
cause of action did not survive the death of the plaintiff the
court said: "There may be some question as to the survival
of a thing in action arising out of a personal injury, but the
thing in action in this case arises out of the violation of a
right of property, which, by the express language of section
954 of the Civil Code of California, passes to the personal
representatives of the deceased," for that section provides that
"a thing in action arising out of the violation of a right of
property, or out of an obligation, may be transferred by the
owner.   Upon the death of the owner it passes to his personal
representatives."   And it necessarily follows that if the thing
in action would pass to the legal representatives of plaintiff on
her death, it would survive the death of the defendant.   The
court further said: "The wrong which was the subject of the
action was not merely a personal injury inflicted upon the
decedent, and the damages claimed the measure of her bodily
or mental suffering; but the wrong was to the estate of the
original plaintiff whereby it became diminished in value."
Here the court quotes from Pomeroy's Remedies and Reme-
dial Rights, section 147, as follows: "It is now the general
American doctrine that all causes of action arising from torts
to property, real or personal—injuries to the estate by which
its value is diminished,—do survive and go to the adminis-

trator or executor as assets in his hands." In the case of
Fox v. *Hale & Norcross S. M. Co.*, 108 Cal. 478, [41 Pac. 328],
the defendants were charged with a conspiracy to defraud a
mining company in which the plaintiff was a stockholder, and
one of the defendants died after judgment against him but
before the entry thereof; and on the subject of the abatement
of the action with the death of that defendant the court said:
"The right of the plaintiff to maintain the action against the
executors of Hobart is fully recognized by section 1584 of the
Code of Civil Procedure. (See, also, *Coleman* v. *Woodworth*,
28 Cal. 567.) It falls within the rule given by Lord Mansfield in *Hambly* v. *Troutt*, Cowp. 371: 'Where the property is
acquired which benefits the testator, there an action for the
value of the property shall survive against the executor.' "
See, also, *Shiels* v. *Nathan*, 12 Cal. App. 604, [108 Pac. 34],
which is a case very similar in its facts to this case, except
that there the contract of settlement itself expressly provided
that the plaintiff should receive one-half of the community
property, which provision of the contract having been broken
it was held that an action for damages for the breach would
lie.

Passing to the next question, it must be held, we think, that
the decree in the suit for divorce of *Vragnizan* v. *Vragnizan*
is not a bar to this action. The pleadings in that case placed
in issue the question of the property rights of the parties, but
thereafter the plaintiff and defendant, as the code permitted
them, withdrew that question from the consideration of the
court, and prior to the entry of the decree made the agreement upon which this action is founded. The plaintiff, therefore, is not estopped by the decree in the divorce proceeding
from maintaining this action. That decree is final, it is true,
as to every point which either expressly or by implication
was in issue and the decision of which is essential to support
the judgment; but the decree in this instance dealt only with
the status of the parties; and certainly no decision with respect to their property rights was essential to sustain such a
decree. (1 Freeman on Judgments, 465, 468; *Senter* v.
Senter, 70 Cal. 619, 625, [11 Pac. 782]; *Coats* v. *Coats*, 160
Cal. 671, 679, [36 L. R. A. (N. S.) 844, 118 Pac. 441]; *Tabler*
v. *Peverill*, 4 Cal. App. 671, 679, [88 Pac. 994]; *In re Bur-
dick*, 112 Cal. 387, 397, [44 Pac. 734].)

Defendant complains that the allegation in the complaint that on the fifth day of June, 1913, letters testamentary were duly and regularly issued to the defendant executor, who has ever since and now is the duly qualified and acting executor of the will in the estate of said Vragnizan, deceased, is a mere conclusion of law, and that the complaint therefore must be held insufficient. We think this allegation of the official capacity of the defendant sufficient in the absence of a special demurrer. Moreover, the allegation is admitted in the answer, which is in effect a stipulation of the fact; and this rendered the allegation of more specific facts unnecessary. (*Collins* v. *O'Laverty*, 136 Cal. 31, [68 Pac. 327]. See, also, *San Francisco etc. Land Co.* v. *Hartung*, 138 Cal. 223, [71 Pac. 337].)

Defendant also contends that the complaint fails to show that the representations upon which the plaintiff relies were addressed to her, and therefore it is argued that they cannot be the basis of an action for deceit. In the main, the complaint depends upon statements made by the decedent, as before stated, in his oral testimony and in his affidavit and verified answer, and therefore were not made directly to her; but it is reasonable to assume that they were made with the intention of deceiving her, and she believing these representations, was induced thereby to make a settlement with the decedent for less than she otherwise would have accepted, and certainly for less than she was entitled to—the property being community property, and the decedent having treated her with extreme cruelty. Under these circumstances, how can it be successfully asserted that the representations upon which she acted were not addressed to her? However this may be, it is alleged in the complaint in so many words "that said decedent repeatedly communicated with plaintiff through their son, and urged her to make a settlement of their property rights, and stated that he had no other money save and except the sum of four thousand one hundred dollars in the two savings banks, and that if plaintiff would agree to make a settlement of their property rights he would give her one-half of said money, etc."

It is further argued that so far as the plaintiff depends upon affidavits and statements made by the decedent in court, they are privileged, and cannot be made the foundation of an action of deceit, and that it is not alleged in the complaint

that decedent, by his representations in the former action.
intended to induce any action on the part of the plaintiff.　It
is further contended that nowhere is it alleged in the complaint that the testator had any reason to believe that the
representations made by him were false.　We think these and
other points made by the defendant cannot be seriously urged.
and it is not necessary to specifically discuss them.

For the reasons heretofore stated the judgment is affirmed.

Lennon, P. J., and Richards, J., concurred.

A petition to have the cause heard in the supreme court,
after judgment in the district court of appeal, was denied by
the supreme court on December 18, 1916.

[Civ. No. 1904. Second Appellate District.—October 19, 1916.]

MARVIN G. TRACY, Respondent, v. K. SUMIDA, Appellant.

JUSTICE'S COURT APPEAL—AMENDMENT OF COMPLAINT—LACK OF JURIS-
DICTION.—The superior court is without jurisdiction upon an appeal
taken to it from a judgment rendered in an action in a justice's
court upon a contract to recover a sum of money less than three
hundred dollars, to permit the complaint to be amended so as to
state a cause of action for a sum in excess of three hundred dollars.

ID.—EXTENT OF JURISDICTION OF SUPERIOR COURT.—Where jurisdiction
is derived through an appeal from a judgment rendered in the justice's court, the superior court cannot, by permitting an amendment
of the complaint, acquire jurisdiction in excess of that of the justice's court from which the appeal was taken.

ID.—APPEAL FROM JUDGMENT OF SUPERIOR COURT—LACK OF JURISDIC-
TION OF DISTRICT COURT OF APPEAL—DISMISSAL.—A judgment
rendered on a justice's court appeal is not within the appellate
jurisdiction of the district court of appeal, and an appeal taken
therefrom must be dismissed.

APPEAL from a judgment of the Superior Court of
Tulare County.　J. A. Allen, Judge.

The facts are stated in the opinion of the court.

Earl A. Bagby, and Farnsworth & McClure, for Appellant.

Bradley & Bradley, for Respondent.

SHAW, J.—This action was commenced in the justice's court to recover a balance of $171.80, alleged to be due plaintiff from defendant for wood furnished by plaintiff to defendant under a contract so to do. Defendant answered, denying all the allegations of the complaint, and also filed a cross-complaint wherein he asked judgment against plaintiff. The case was tried by the justice, who gave defendant a judgment for $6.85 and costs, from which the plaintiff appealed to the superior court. After perfecting the appeal plaintiff, by leave of court, filed an amended complaint in said action wherein the cause of action based upon the contract was stated in the sum of $990.40, for which he asked judgment. Defendant demurred to this amended complaint upon the ground, among others, that the court had no jurisdiction of the action set out in said amended complaint. The demurrer was overruled; whereupon defendant filed his answer, consisting of a general denial, and a cross-complaint upon which he asked for judgment against plaintiff in the sum of $842.45. Trial was had by a jury which rendered a verdict in favor of plaintiff for $150, and from the judgment entered thereon defendant prosecutes this appeal.

Clearly, the action as brought, since it was upon a contract to recover a sum of money less than three hundred dollars (Code Civ. Proc., sec. 112), was one over which the superior court had no jurisdiction, except upon appeal. The effect of the amendment made in the superior court was to convert the action into one over which the justice's court had no jurisdiction; hence the case was one over which the superior court could not, by virtue of its appellate powers, derive jurisdiction by the procedure of an appeal. In *Heath* v. *Robinson*, 75 Vt. 133, [53 Atl. 995], it is said: "An amendment which, had it been made before the justice, would have ousted that court of its jurisdiction, . . . must consequently oust the county court of its appellate jurisdiction upon the same condition." To the effect that where jurisdiction of an action is derived from a justice's court on appeal from a judgment rendered therein the superior court may not, by permitting an amendment of the complaint, acquire jurisdiction in excess

of that of the justice's court from which the appeal is taken.
see *Pecos etc. Ry. Co. v. Canyon Coal Co.*, 102 Tex. 478, [119
S. W. 294]; *Missouri etc. Ry. Co. v. Hughes*, 44 Tex. Civ.
App. 436, [98 S. W. 415]; *Rose v. Christinct*, 77 Ark. 582,
[92 S. W. 866]; *Flanagan v. Reitemier*, 26 Ind. App. 243,
[59 N. E. 389]. In our opinion, since the jurisdiction of a
justice of the peace in an action to recover money upon contract is limited to an amount not in excess of three hundred
dollars, the jurisdiction of the superior court on appeal from
a judgment rendered therein is likewise limited to such an
amount. In other words, the superior court by virtue of the
appeal acquires only such jurisdiction as the justice of the
peace had.

Conceding, however, as claimed by appellant, that the superior court erred in its rulings and erroneously assumed
jurisdiction to try and render judgment upon the cause of
action over which it had no jurisdiction, nevertheless such rulings cannot be reviewed by this court on appeal from the judgment rendered. Cases of this character originating in justice's courts cannot be brought by appeal to this court.
(*Williams v. Mecartney*, 69 Cal. 556, [11 Pac. 186]; *Pool v.
Superior Court*, 2 Cal. App. 533, [84 Pac. 53]; *Cox v. Southern Pacific Co.*, 2 Cal. App. 248, [83 Pac. 290].) We agree
with respondent's contention that the appeal should be dismissed, and it is so ordered.

Conrey, P. J., and James, J., concurred.

[Civ. No. 1463.   Third Appellate District.—October 19, 1916.]

PACIFIC POWER COMPANY (a Corporation), Respondent, v. STATE OF CALIFORNIA et al., Appellants.

[Civ. Nos. 1460, 1461, 1462.   Third Appellate District.—October 19, 1916.]

MONO COUNTY IRRIGATION COMPANY (a Corporation), Respondent, v. STATE OF CALIFORNIA et al., Appellants.

APPEAL—JUDGMENT IN FAVOR OF STATE—PARTY AGGRIEVED.—The state of California is a party aggrieved and has the right of appeal from a judgment in its favor in an action brought against it to condemn land, notwithstanding the state in its answer denied any ownership in the land, and declared that the United States was the owner thereof.

ID.—DEFAULT IN FILING OF BRIEF—SUFFICIENCY OF EXCUSE.—An appeal taken by the state from a judgment will not be dismissed for the failure of the appellant to file its points and authorities within the prescribed time, where it is made to appear that the time to file its briefs was inadvertently allowed to expire by reason of misunderstandings between representatives of the attorney-general's office and the deputy attorney-general, who had charge of the litigation, as to the obtaining of an extension of time from the court.

APPEALS from judgments of the Superior Court of Mono County.   W. S. Wells, Judge presiding.

The facts are stated in the opinion of the court.

U. S. Webb, Attorney-General, and John T. Nourse, Deputy Attorney-General, for Appellants.

Wm. O. Parker, and J. D. Murphy, for Respondent.

BURNETT, J.—A motion has been made to dismiss the appeal in each of the above-entitled causes. The facts are identical and the cases may be considered together. The motion is made upon the grounds: "(1) That the said defendant and appellant is not a 'party aggrieved' by the judgment in this case within the provisions of section 938 of the Code of Civil Procedure of the state of California.   (2) That the said defendant and appellant has failed to comply with the provisions of rule II, subdivision 4 of the rules of this court in that it has failed to file its printed points and authorities within the period prescribed.''

As to the first point, it may be said that the state of California was the only party against whom the action was brought, except certain fictitious parties, and it is the only party against whom a judgment was obtained, said judgment being ''that the plaintiff is entitled to judgment in its favor herein as prayed for in its complaint herein, and that it be adjudged and decreed in and by said judgment that the corporation plaintiff pay as compensation and damages to the said defendant, the state of California, for the land herein sought to be condemned, the sum of twelve hundred dollars,'' etc.

It is true that defendant in its answer had denied ''that the defendant state of California claims to be or is the owner of the property sought to be condemned in said action and particularly described in paragraph IV of said complaint,'' and alleged ''that by reason of the facts hereinbefore set forth, the state of California is improperly joined as a party in said action and that the whole fee estate and interest in the land described in paragraph IV of said complaint is in the United States of America and not in the state of California,'' but the court was more generous toward the defendant than was demanded by its claims, and it was found that ''it is not true that by reason of the facts, or any of the facts set forth in said answer, or by reason of any facts, the state of California is improperly joined as a party to this action; and it is not true that the whole fee or any part of the fee or any interest in the lands herein sought to be condemned is in the United States of America and not in the state of California.'' This was followed by a finding that the value of the land was one thousand two hundred dollars, and this, by the judgment, as we have before set out. The court, therefore, having found that defendant was the owner of the land and having decreed its condemnation, it would necessarily follow that appellant is an aggrieved party. It is said in *Estate of Colton,* 164 Cal. 5, [127 Pac. 643], ''Under our decisions, any person having an interest recognized by law in the subject matter of the judgment, which interest is injuriously affected by the judgment, is a party aggrieved and entitled to be heard upon appeal."

As to the second point, the rule requires that "thirty days after the filing of the transcript, the appellant shall file with the clerk his printed points and authorities with proof of the service of one copy thereof upon the attorney or attorneys of each respondent who shall have appealed separately in the superior court." It is further provided, however, that the time may be extended for good cause shown. In this case, the time was extended but the period thus enlarged had expired a few days before the motion to dismiss the appeal was given. Appellant, though, was ready and was granted permission to file its opening brief at the time said motion came on for hearing.

To excuse its failure to file the brief in time, appellant filed the affidavit of John T. Nourse, deputy attorney-general of the state, in which, among other things, he declared: "That he had charge of the litigation involved in the above entitled actions on behalf of the State of California, appellant therein; that on or about the 21st day of December, 1915, affiant filed in this Court his affidavit in support of appellant's application for an extension of time to file its opening briefs in each of said cases, setting forth that the appeals in each of said cases involved the question presented in the case entitled *Deseret Water, Oil, and Irrigation Company* vs. *State of California,* then pending before the Supreme Court of the United States, and that there was no attorney of record in the said actions on appeal in this Court; that affiant believed that if any attorney should appear of record in said action, a stipulation would be entered into continuing the hearing of said appeals until the determination of said Deseret case; that the complaints in each of the above entitled actions were endorsed by Parker & Parker, as attorneys for each of the plaintiffs; that all of the proceedings therein were conducted by Pat R. Parker who on the 2nd day of January, 1915, became Judge of the Superior Court in and for the County of Mono . . . ; that on numerous occasions the said Pat R. Parker informed affiant that his father, William O. Parker, had long discontinued the practice of the law, that he was no longer associated with him, and that he (William O. Parker) was not associated with him in any of said actions; . . . that said William O. Parker is not the successor to Parker & Parker and never

has been, but said firm has long since been dissolved; . . .
that said William O. Parker never has been at any time an
attorney or counsel for any of the respondents in any of the
above entitled actions . . . : that all the extensions of time
to file appellant's briefs in said actions were obtained from
this Court by the representatives of the Attorney General's
office, located in the City of Sacramento and affiant had assumed that the time of appellant to file its said briefs was
being protected in that manner and the representatives of
said office assumed that affiant, intending to prepare the briefs
in said actions, was protecting the time of appellant to file
its briefs, and that by reason of these misunderstandings, and
by reason of the press of official business of said office, including matters involving the recent primary election and
preparation for the coming general election, the time to file
said briefs was inadvertently allowed to expire.''

It is further stated ''that affiant was led to believe that
another attorney would be substituted for said Parker &
Parker and that he would be notified of the same so that he
might obtain a stipulation continuing these cases, and that he
received no such notice.''

It has been often stated that courts in the determination of
such motions as far as possible should lean toward a hearing
of the case upon its merits. It may be said also that, manifestly, a large discretion is committed to the court in the exercise of its judgment as to whether a party should be relieved
from such default. The rule itself is, of course, somewhat
flexible and may be set aside when justice requires it.

We have no reason to doubt the good faith of appellant, and
as we are impressed with the showing made to excuse the
delay and believing that it is the better policy to consider
the merits of the cause, the motion to dismiss the appeal in
each of said cases is denied.

Chipman, P. J., and Hart, J., concurred.

[Civ. No. 1829. Second Appellate District.—October 20, 1916.]

MARY WILLS, Respondent, v. SOUTHERN PACIFIC COMPANY, Appellant.

RAILROAD CORPORATION—FAILURE TO FENCE TRACK—KILLING OF DO-
MESTIC ANIMAL—RIGHT OF ACTION—CONSTRUCTION OF CODE.—The
provisions of section 485 of the Civil Code, as that section existed
prior to the amendment of 1915, giving a right of action against a
railroad company for the killing or maiming of a domestic animal
upon its line of road which passes through or along the property of
the owner thereof, in case of the company's failure to fence the
track, are not intended to be for the benefit of the owners of stock
running at large, but the right of action there given exists only in
favor of one having some interest in land adjoining the right of way
of the railroad.

ID.—ACTION BY LESSEE—INTEREST IN LAND—FAILURE OF PROOF.—In
an action against a railroad corporation for damages on account of
the loss of certain horses of the plaintiff which were killed by a
collision with one of the defendant's trains by reason of the negligence of the defendant in permitting the gate in its fence inclosing
its right of way to be left open and the animals to stray thereon
from adjacent land, the right of the plaintiff in or to the land is
not established by proof that she leased the land from a third party,
without any further proof that such party owned the land, or any
interest therein, or that he was in possession of it, or that the plaintiff obtained possession through him.

ID.—CLOSING OF GATES—DUTY OF RAILROAD CORPORATIONS—ERRONEOUS
INSTRUCTION.—An instruction declaring it to be the duty of a railroad corporation to keep gates in fences along its tracks closed on
all proper occasions to prevent stock from adjoining lands from
passing upon its right of way, is erroneous, in that it imposes upon
such a corporation the absolute duty of keeping the gates closed,
whereas in fact its only duty is to use reasonable care to keep them
closed.

APPEAL from a judgment of the Superior Court of Tulare
County, and from an order denying a new trial. W. B. Wallace, Judge.

The facts are stated in the opinion of the court.

Power & McFadzean, for Appellant.

J. C. Thomas, for Respondent.

CONREY, P. J.—Pursuant to the verdict of a jury, judgment was entered in favor of the plaintiff for the sum of six hundred dollars damages on account of the loss of certain horses of the plaintiff which were killed on the defendant's railroad track. The defendant appeals from the judgment and from an order denying its motion for a new trial

There is in the complaint an allegation of negligence by the defendant in running and managing its train whereby the horses were killed. The evidence shows that they were killed by a collision with one of defendant's trains. But there is no evidence of carelessness or negligence in the running of the train, and the judgment cannot be sustained unless a cause of action has been established upon another theory of the case arising from the provisions of section 485 of the Civil Code. We refer to that section as it existed prior to the amendment of 1915. It is therein enacted that "Railroad corporations must make and maintain a good and sufficient fence on either or both sides of their track and property. In case they do not make and maintain such fence, if their engine or cars shall kill or maim any cattle or other domestic animals upon their line of road which passes through or along the property of the owner thereof, they must pay to the owner of such cattle or other domestic animals a fair market price for the same, unless it occurred through the neglect or fault of the owner of the animal so killed or maimed. . . . "

The provisions of the foregoing section are not intended to be for the benefit of the owners of stock running at large, but the right of action there given exists only in favor of one having some interest in land adjoining the right of way of a railroad. It has been held that the interest of a lessee in the land constitutes a sufficient ownership under the statute. (*Walther* v. *Sierra Ry. Co.*, 141 Cal. 288, [74 Pac. 840].) And there are intimations that a licensee in possession of land under a license from the owner is included in the benefit of the statute. *McCoy* v. *Southern Pacific Co.*, 94 Cal. 568, [29 Pac. 1110], where it was said that such license (in that case derived from lessees) did not confer upon the licensee any rights as against the railroad company which the licensors themselves did not possess; that he stood in the place of the lessees and possessed only such rights as they could have enforced.

In the present action it is alleged in the complaint that on the twenty-sixth day of January, 1914, the plaintiff was the owner and possessed of certain horses, and that said horses were lawfully upon certain described land, from which land the horses strayed in and upon the track and ground occupied by the railroad. It is alleged that the defendant so carelessly and negligently permitted its gates in its fences to remain open that it permitted said horses to go from the pasture of the plaintiff upon the said railroad track. These are the only facts alleged which in any way connect the plaintiff with any ownership or right of occupancy of land adjacent to the railroad. Unless such allegations can be construed as declaring that the plaintiff owned the land or was in occupancy thereof as tenant or licensee, it must follow that the complaint does not state a cause of action. Without deciding that the complaint is sufficient in this respect, we will assume its sufficiency for the purpose of considering the evidence bearing upon the supposed issue. And we will here note that the complaint was unverified, and that all of its allegations are denied.

It was shown that there was a fence separating the railroad right of way from the land described in the complaint; that there was a gate in the fence; and that on and before the date of the killing of the horses they were kept by the plaintiff in the field upon which that gate opened. The plaintiff testified that she leased the premises described in the complaint from one P. T. Clark, and the court received in evidence a document identified by the plaintiff, which was in terms a lease of those premises by Clark to her. All of the foregoing evidence was received over objections duly made by defendant's counsel. No effort was made by the plaintiff to show that Clark owned the land or owned any interest therein, or that he was in possession of it, or that plaintiff obtained possession through him. So far as the record shows, Clark may have been in every respect an absolute stranger to said premises both as to title and possession.

There is evidence sufficient to establish the facts that the defendant negligently permitted the gate to remain open, and that the horses strayed from the field to the railroad tracks and were killed without any fault of the plaintiff. We have stated the evidence merely for the purpose of considering whether it is sufficient to establish any right of the plaintiff in or to the land on which she was keeping her horses. We are of the opinion that it is wholly insufficient for that purpose. As the record does not show who was the owner of the land, or where he was at any time, it may be that the plaintiff's occupancy there was entirely without his knowledge or consent, and that she was a mere trespasser. If so, the statute upon which she must rely in this case gives her no cause of action against the defendant.

With regard to the errors claimed in the refusal of instructions, and in the giving of instructions by the court to the jury, it seems necessary to refer here to instruction No. 1 given by the court as follows: "You are instructed that the laws of this state require railroads to maintain fences beside their tracks, and if they make a gate in the fence, it is a part of the fence, and when there is a road across their track with a gate in the fence across it, they are under the same duty to keep it in repair when erected as it is regarding any other part of the fence, and also it is their duty to keep such gate closed at all proper occasions to prevent stock from adjoining lands from passing upon the right of way of said roadbed." The objection urged is that the instruction imposes upon the defendant the absolute duty to keep the gate closed, whereas in fact its only duty was to use reasonable care to keep it closed. In *Johnson v. Southern Pacific Co.*, 11 Cal. App. 278, 285, [104 Pac. 713], the court said: "Had the defendant erected and maintained a good and sufficient gate, it would have been required only to exercise reasonable diligence in keeping the gate closed;" citing and quoting from Thompson on Negligence, section 2059. In the case at bar no claim has been made that the gate was insufficient or out of repair. On the contrary, the testimony of the plaintiff's own witnesses proves that the fence was sufficient to turn stock and that the gate was better than the fence. It seems that the horses strayed out of the field because some person whose identity was not ascertained left the gate open on the afternoon preceding the night when these horses were killed. Therefore, clearly the question for the jury to determine was as to whether the defendant had used reasonable diligence in the matter of keeping its gate closed. Therefore, the instruction as given was not only erroneous, but also it was seriously prejudicial to the defense. The judgment and order are reversed.

James, J., concurred.

Shaw, J., concurred in the judgment.

[Civ. No. 1921. First Appellate District.—October 25, 1916.]

CHARLES J. PEASE, Respondent, v. J. F. FITZGERALD, Appellant; CALIFORNIA MAIL ORDER HOUSE, T. W. WITHOFT, Trustee, etc., Respondent.

ASSIGNMENT OF PLEDGED COMMERCIAL PAPER—RIGHTS OF ASSIGNEE.—A pledgee of commercial paper may assign and deliver the same, and, in the event of such transfer, the assignee holds it in the same capacity as the original pledgee, and may bring suit to collect the collateral note when due.

ID.—ACTION BY ASSIGNEE—FRAUD IN PROCUREMENT OF NOTE—DEFENSE WHEN NOT AVAILABLE.—In an action brought by the assignee of a pledged promissory note to recover the amount alleged to be due thereon, the maker cannot set up as a defense to the action that the note, which was given as the purchase price of certain corporate stock for which he subscribed, was procured through the false and fraudulent representations of the agent who acted for the corporation, where such defendant at the time of making his subscription, signed a memorandum attached thereto to the effect that his subscription was based upon the printed literature and printed statements of the corporation, and that no representations made by its agents not in accordance therewith should be binding upon the corporation.

APPEAL from a judgment of the Superior Court of the City and County of San Francisco, and from an order denying a new trial. Franklin A. Griffin, Judge.

The facts are stated in the opinion of the court.

Brittan & Raish, and W. E. Davies, for Appellant.

Robert R. Moody, and Edwin L. Forster, for Respondent Pease.

Franklin T. Poore, for Respondent Withoft.

RICHARDS, J.—This is an appeal from a judgment in favor of plaintiff in an action brought to recover the sum of one thousand dollars and interest alleged to be due upon the promissory note of the defendant, J. F. Fitzgerald, and from an order denying said defendant's motion for a new trial.

The facts out of which the action arose were these: On the eighth day of February, 1912, the defendant, J. F. Fitzgerald, executed and delivered to the California Mail Order House, a corporation, a promissory note for the sum of one thousand dollars as the purchase price of one thousand shares of its capital stock for which he subscribed on that day. The transaction was conducted on behalf of the corporation by one Hugh Wyncoop, as its agent, who is alleged by the said defendant Fitzgerald to have made to him certain false and fraudulent representations as to the assets and solvency of the corporation. The said defendant, however, at the time of making his said subscription, signed a memorandum attached thereto to the effect that his subscription was based upon the printed literature and printed statements of the corporation, and that no representations made by its agents not in accordance therewith should be binding upon the corporation. On April 20, 1912, the California Mail Order House executed and delivered to the American National Bank of San Francisco its promissory note for the sum of two thousand five hundred dollars, and at the same time assigned and delivered to the said bank as security for the same the promissory note of the defendant Fitzgerald. On April 30, 1912, the California Mail Order House paid to the bank $1,435.82 on account of its note but no further sum, and on May 11, 1912, the bank indorsed and delivered to the plaintiff and respondent in this action the Fitzgerald note. On May 24, 1912, the California Mail Order House was adjudged a bankrupt, and one T. W. Withoft was appointed trustee. On October 30, 1912, the present suit was brought.

In his answer the defendant Fitzgerald set forth several defenses, chiefly relying, however, both in his pleading and at the trial, upon the defense that the note had been procured through the false and fraudulent representations made by said Wyncoop at the time of his stock subscription, upon the discovery of which he had taken steps to rescind the transaction. Upon the trial he was permitted to testify fully as to these matters. The court gave judgment in plaintiff's favor, and from such judgment and the order denying a new trial the defendant Fitzgerald prosecutes this appeal.

The first point urged by the appellant is that the assignment and transfer of his promissory note by its pledgee, American National Bank, to the plaintiff, was illegal and void for the alleged reason that a pledgee of commercial paper has no right to sell the same, but must collect the amount due thereon at maturity, and apply the proceeds to the payment of the principal debt.

Whatever may be the rule in other jurisdictions from which the appellant draws for authority supporting his contention, the rule is well settled in this state that a pledgee of commercial paper may assign and deliver the same, and in the event of such transfer the assignee holds the same in the same capacity as the original pledgee, and may bring suit to collect the collateral note when due. (*Cushing* v. *Building Assn.*, 165 Cal. 731, [134 Pac. 324]; *Brittain* v. *Oakland Bank of Savings*, 124 Cal. 282, [71 Am. St. Rep. 58, 57 Pac. 84]; *Williams* v. *Ashe*, 111 Cal. 180, [43 Pac. 595]; *Dewey* v. *Bowman*, 8 Cal. 145.)

The appellant in his closing brief herein practically admits that this is the settled rule in this state, but urges that in the event of such transfer the assignee takes the note subject to all of the defenses which the maker might have urged against the original payee. It is not necessary, however, to discuss or decide this point, for the record discloses that the appellant was permitted upon the trial of the cause to fully present his defenses to the note, and that the court found that neither of the two chief defenses to the payment of the obligation was sufficiently made out. We think the evidence sufficiently sustains the finding of the court in that regard. The defendant was not entitled to rely on the oral statements of the agent Wyncoop in the face of his own express written agreement that only the printed statements of the corporation were to be regarded in making subscriptions to its stock.

The effort of the appellant to rescind his agreement after his discovery that Wyncoop's statements were false was clearly not sufficiently carried into effect to work a rescission of his agreement or furnish a defense to the payment of his note.

We discover no error in the record before us.

Judgment and order affirmed.

Lennon, P. J., and Kerrigan, J., concurred.

A petition to have the cause heard in the supreme court, after judgment in the district court of appeal, was denied by the supreme court on December 21, 1916.

––––––––––

[Crim. No. 494. Second Appellate District.—October 25, 1916.]

THE PEOPLE, Respondent, v. JOSE ANDRADE, Appellant.

CRIMINAL LAW—APPEAL—FAILURE TO APPEAR—AFFIRMANCE OF JUDGMENT.—Where on an appeal taken in a criminal case the appellant's counsel fails to appear at the time set for oral argument, it is proper to move for an affirmance of the judgment under the provisions of section 1253 of the Penal Code.

APPEAL from a judgment of the Superior Court of Tulare County, and from an order denying a new trial. W. B. Wallace, Judge.

The facts are stated in the opinion of the court.

Ralph H. Walker, and Edwards & Smith, for Appellant.

U. S. Webb, Attorney-General, and Robert M. Clarke, Deputy Attorney-General, for Respondent.

JAMES, J.—The defendant was convicted of the crime of murder and by the verdict of the jury his punishment was fixed at imprisonment for life. Judgment in accordance with that decision was regularly made. A motion for a new trial being presented was denied by the court, and an appeal was taken from the judgment and order. The transcript on appeal was filed on May 13, 1916. No brief was offered to be filed on the part of appellant until October 17th. At the last-mentioned date a brief was deposited in the office of the clerk of this court. At the time set for oral argument on the calling of the calendar on October 24, 1916, appellant's counsel did not appear, and the attorney-general moved for an affirmance under the provisions of section 1253 of the Penal Code. The motion was properly made under

the sanction of the statute, and it would have been altogether
appropriate that the judgment asked for be entered. However, as the charge is that of murder, and the defendant was
convicted of the first degree of that crime, we have felt it
fitting that some examination be made of the record in order
to determine as to whether the defendant was properly convicted. There was a former trial in this case and upon an
appeal being taken, a new trial was ordered to be had because of certain errors committed by the trial court. It was
from the judgment pronounced and order made after the
second trial that this appeal was taken. We have carefully
examined the record and are convinced that the evidence
heard by the jury fully sustains the verdict, and that no material errors were committed by the trial judge which would
entitle defendant to have the judgment set aside. The facts
of the case, as disclosed by the evidence, were in brief as follows: Defendant in January, 1915, was one of a party of
woodchoppers engaged on a ranch in the county of Tulare;
on about the ninth day of January, their work at the ranch
being finished, they prepared to go to Visalia. The deceased
happened by their camp, riding in a country wagon and driving a mule. He stopped and talked with the men, all of
whom were Mexicans, and offered them wine which he had in
a jug, of which all partook. Deceased assisted them in repairing a wagon, and then requested the defendant to accompany
him while he went to secure more wine. The defendant at
first demurred, but was finally persuaded to go, and the two
men rode away together. They visited an Italian, who sold
them more wine, and later left his place. Cook, the deceased,
was not seen again alive, but on the following morning his
dead body was found in a road. The *post mortem* examination disclosed that Cook had been struck on the back of the
head, where the blow had cut the scalp and slightly fractured
the skull; there were two bruises upon his face, a bruise upon
a shoulder, and a bullet wound near one of his ears. The bullet
which produced this wound was found lodged in the brain
of the deceased near the side of the head opposite from the
point of its entrance. The defendant was arrested in another county. After being brought back to Tulare he made
a statement to the sheriff in which he admitted having killed
Cook, but said that Cook had gotten out on the ground and
after abusing him (the defendant), had pulled him roughly

out of the wagon and kicked him in the side; that he (the
defendant) had thereupon shot Cook and had immediately
gone away. This statement was shown to have been repeated
in the presence of other persons, and it was shown to have
been voluntarily made. Taking all of the circumstances disclosed by the evidence, including the condition of the body
of the deceased and the statements made by the defendant,
the jury was fully authorized to conclude that the use of the
deadly weapon by defendant was unjustified and that his act
in shooting Cook was malicious.

The judgment and order are affirmed.

Conrey, P. J., and Shaw, J., concurred.

[Civ. No. 1621. Second Appellate District.—October 27, 1916.]

DEVELOPMENT BUILDING COMPANY (a Corporation),
Appellant, v. F. B. WOODRUFF, Respondent.

ATTACHMENT—ORDER RELEASING LEVY—EXEMPT PROPERTY—CONFLICT OF
EVIDENCE—APPEAL.—Upon an appeal from an order vacating and
setting aside the levy of an attachment, the appellate court is not
authorized to review the evidence and make a different finding,
where the trial court upon evidence definitely tending to support
the defendant's claim determined that the property attached was
exempt from attachment under subdivision 4 of section 690 of the
Code of Civil Procedure.

APPEAL from an order of the Superior Court of Los
Angeles County quashing the levy of an attachment. John
M. York, Judge.

The facts are stated in the opinion of the court.

Williams, Goudge & Chandler, for Appellant.

F. B. Woodruff, for Respondent.

CONREY, P. J.—Under a writ of attachment duly issued
in this action the sheriff levied upon certain personal property of the defendant. Thereafter, upon motion of the de-

fendant, the court made an order vacating and setting aside
the levy made against said property, from which order the
plaintiff appeals.

The defendant is an attorney at law, and the motion was
made upon the ground that the personal property seized was
his professional and necessary law office furniture and, as
such, exempt from execution or attachment. (Code Civ.
Proc., sec. 690, subd. 4.) In support of this motion respondent presented to the court an affidavit in which he stated
that on the day of the levy, and for several years prior thereto, he was in the actual possession and enjoyment of said
property, and was using the same in the actual practice of
his profession, the same being his necessary office furniture
as described. A counter-affidavit was filed wherein an agent
of the plaintiff stated that on the date of the levy, and for
some time prior thereto, the described property was used by
persons other than the defendant, and during that period
of time was not being used by the defendant and was not
necessary to him in his business as an attorney at law. Omitting further facts detailed in the affidavits, it is sufficient to
observe that they present a conflict of evidence upon the issues
as to whether or not the property in question was necessary
office furniture then in use by the defendant in the practice
of his profession. The superior court having determined that
issue of fact in favor of respondent upon evidence definitely
tending to support respondent's claim, we are not authorized
to review the evidence and make a different finding. From
the facts found the conclusion necessarily followed that the
property was exempt from attachment.

The order is affirmed.

James, J., and Shaw, J., concurred.

[Civ. No. 1990. First Appellate District.—October 28, 1916.]

ALBERT E. GOLDEN, Petitioner, v. SUPERIOR COURT
OF THE CITY AND COUNTY OF SAN FRANCISCO,
Respondent.

JUDGMENT—SALE OF STOCK BY PLEDGEE—STRIKING OUT OF INJUNCTIVE
ORDER—LACK OF JURISDICTION.—Where in an action involving the
ownership of certain shares of stock in the possession of the defendant, it is apparent from the pleadings and the findings that the
purpose of the action was to have it declared that the defendant
held the stock as pledgee, and to prevent him in the meantime from
making an absolute sale of it, the court has no jurisdiction to entirely strike from the judgment rendered the provision enjoining
the defendant from making any sale of the stock to any person
save the plaintiff, but it has the right to modify the phraseology
of the injunctive part of the judgment to the extent of making it
clear that the defendant might sell the stock as pledgee, and in no
other way.

APPLICATION originally made in the District Court of
Appeal for the First District for a Writ of Review to set aside
an order striking from a final judgment an order for an
injunction.

The facts are stated in the opinion of the court.

James H. Boyer, for Petitioner.

T. C. West, for Respondent.

THE COURT.—This is an application for a writ of review
directed against the superior court of the city and county of
San Francisco, for the purpose of having set aside and annulled a certain order of that court, by which a final judgment,
after its affirmance by the district court of appeal, was modified in a material respect, by striking therefrom an order for
an injunction, restraining the defendant in that action from
making a sale of certain stock. The action had been brought
for the purpose of having declared that the defendant held
certain shares of stock as pledgee, the stock having been given
as security for a loan of $1,125. The defendant, appearing
by answer, set up the claim that he was the owner of the
stock absolutely. The court, however, decided against him

on that issue, made its findings accordingly, and entered a judgment that the plaintiff should have the stock surrendered to him upon payment to the defendant of the sum of $1,125, the amount of the loan; and as a part of the judgment the court enjoined the defendant from making any sale of the stock to any person save the plaintiff. The judgment was appealed from, and was affirmed by the district court of appeal of the second district, and a petition to the supreme court for a rehearing was denied. Subsequently, when the *remittitur* went down, the defendant went into the court below and moved that the judgment be modified by striking therefrom the order for injunction, which motion the court granted upon the theory that the judgment originally was a conditional one, that is to say, that the note representing the loan and the stock involved in the suit should be surrendered to the plaintiff and the note canceled upon condition that he pay the sum of $1,125, and that the plaintiff not having made said payment within a reasonable time the court was justified in striking out from the judgment that part of it relating to the injunction.

The court, we think, was in error in believing that it was a conditional judgment. As stated before, the action was simply one to have declared a lien upon the stock that had been pledged to the defendant, and to prevent the defendant in the meantime from making an absolute sale of it. That purpose was plainly indicated by the complaint, the answer, and the findings of the court. While the judgment is too broad in the sense that it prevents a sale of any kind, the very evident intent of the action was to prevent a sale by the defendant save and except as a pledgee, and the court below would have had a right to modify the phraseology of the injunctive part of the judgment to the extent of making it clear that the defendant might sell the stock as a pledgee and in no other way; but in striking out the injunctive part of the judgment entirely it made a material modification of the judgment itself, and thereby deprived the defendant in that action of a very substantial right which he had secured by the litigation. This the court had no jurisdiction to do, and for that reason we are of the opinion that the order complained of should be annulled, vacated and set aside.

It is so ordered.

[Crim. No. 506. Second Appellate District.—October 28, 1916.]

THE PEOPLE, Respondent, v. MILTON A. SMITH, Appellant.

CRIMINAL LAW—REFUSAL TO PROVIDE FOR WIFE—IGNORANCE OF PRESENCE WITHIN STATE—UNWARRANTED CONVICTION.—The conviction of a husband of willfully neglecting to provide his wife with the necessaries of life, as provided in section 270a of the Penal Code, is not warranted where it is shown that he left her in another state, and had no information of her presence in this state until he was arrested.

ID.—LACK OF MEANS OF SUPPORT—PROOF BY WIFE.—In such a prosecution it is necessary that the wife should show that she was without other sufficient means of support at the time of the alleged offense.

APPEAL from a judgment of the Superior Court of Kern County, and from an order denying a new trial. Howard A. Peairs, Judge.

The facts are stated in the opinion of the court.

Homer E. Johnstone, for Appellant.

U. S. Webb, Attorney-General, and Robert M. Clarke, Deputy Attorney-General, for Respondent.

CONREY, P. J.—In this action the defendant has been convicted of the offense described in section 270a of the Penal Code, in that on or about March 24, 1916, in the county of Kern, he did willfully, etc., neglect, refuse, and omit to provide his wife with necessary food, clothing, shelter, and medical attendance, he having the ability to so provide and not being justified in so refusing or failing to provide for her "by any misconduct on the part of the said wife." The defendant appeals from the judgment and from an order denying his motion for a new trial.

The defendant and the prosecuting witness, Florence E. Smith, were married in the state of Washington in August, 1907, and lived together in that state until September, 1911, when the defendant moved to Portland, Oregon. Some time later he came to California, and for a year or two prior to March 24, 1916, and on that date, was living at Bakersfield in

Kern County. There was some correspondence between the husband and wife while he was in Portland. Afterward it appears that for some time she did not know where he was living; but in the latter part of the year 1915 she learned that he was living in Bakersfield. She did not then communicate with the defendant, but after waiting some five or six months she came to California and arrived at Bakersfield on March 24, 1916. Without any delay she made the complaint upon which this prosecution is founded, and the defendant did not know of her presence in California until he was arrested on this charge. The only evidence that Mrs. Smith at any time prior to the commencement of this action was without means of support is found in her testimony wherein she states that during the time of their separation she never received any money from the defendant; and in her affirmative answer to a question inquiring whether during the time of their separation she had "at any time been in want."

The defendant is not prosecuted for having abandoned and left his wife in a destitute condition; for if such offense was committed by him at all it was not in the state of California. Also it may well be doubted whether any refusal or neglect of the defendant to provide his wife with the necessaries of life while she was absent from California, can be construed into an offense committed at the place of the husband's residence and against the laws of California. If the defendant had received information of her presence in this state and then if, without legal justification, he had refused or neglected to provide his wife with food, clothing, etc., she having need of such support from him, such facts no doubt would constitute an offense against the provisions of the Penal Code. But it seems clear to us that the provisions of the code under which the defendant is prosecuted in this action are not intended to authorize a punishment of the husband for neglecting to provide for his wife before he knows of her presence within the state. Neither do we think the judgment can be sustained without evidence that the wife was without other sufficient means of support at the time of the alleged offense. (*People* v. *Selby*, 26 Cal. App. 796, [148 Pac. 807].)

Having reached the conclusion above stated, we deem it unnecessary to discuss the numerous propositions urged in

31 Cal. App.—47

the brief of defendant's counsel wherein he claims errors in the rulings of the court and in the instructions given, and in the refusal to give instructions requested by the defendant.

The judgment and order are reversed.

James, J., and Shaw, J., concurred.

[Civ. No. 1544.   Third Appellate District.—October 30, 1916.]

CITY STREET IMPROVEMENT COMPANY (a Corporation), Appellant, v. CHARLES E. LEE, as Mayor, etc., Respondent; NELLIE FURGERSON et al., Interveners and Respondents.

STREET LAW—SECOND IMPROVEMENT—EFFECT OF FILING OF OBJECTIONS—SANTA ROSA CHARTER.—Under the provisions of the charter of the city of Santa Rosa relating to the public streets thereof and their improvement (Stats. 1905, pp. 891 to 898, inclusive), where a street of that municipality, or any part thereof, has once been improved, and after such improvement has been made, proceedings are taken by the governing body of the municipality to again improve the street, timely written objections filed by the owners of the prescribed amount of the frontage of the property fronting on the line of the proposed improvement has the effect of barring further proceedings in relation to the proposed improvement for the period of six months.

APPEAL from a judgment of the Superior Court of Sonoma County.   Emmet Seawell, Judge.

The facts are stated in the opinion of the court.

L. M. Hoefler, and George F. Snyder, for Appellant.

John T. Campbell, for Respondent Lee.

R. M. F. Soto, for Interveners and Respondents.

HART, J.—The petitioner, a corporation, filed a petition in the court below for a writ of mandate to force the mayor of the city of Santa Rosa, a municipal corporation, to enter into a contract with the said petitioner for doing certain street work on Santa Rosa Avenue, in said city.

The respondent, mayor, answered the petition, and certain property owners, whose property abuts upon said street and which would, as a consequence, be assessed for the improvement which had been proposed to be made on said avenue, providing the proceedings were legal and valid, filed a complaint in intervention. The court, upon the trial of the issues made by the answer and the complaint in intervention, rendered and entered a judgment dismissing the writ.

The petitioner brings the case to this court on an appeal from said judgment.

On the twenty-first day of September, 1915, the council of the city of Santa Rosa, proceeding in accordance with the provisions of the charter of said city relating to the public streets thereof and their improvement (Stats. 1905, pp. 891 to 898, inclusive), passed a resolution of intention to order the improvement of Santa Rosa Avenue, a public street in the said city, from the south side of the bridge over Santa Rosa Creek, southerly to the south city limits, where not already paved and improved, by grading the roadway thereof and constructing thereon an asphaltic pavement of a character fully and clearly described in said resolution. The said resolution of intention and notices of the passage of the same were duly and regularly posted, as required by section 72 of the charter.

On the ninth day of October, 1915, and within twenty days from the first day of the posting of said notices, the owners of more than two-thirds of the frontage of the property fronting on said proposed work, which embraced portions only of said avenue not already improved, filed written objections to the said proposed work. The complaint, in this connection, alleges: "That not more than two blocks of the said Santa Rosa Avenue, including street crossings, remained ungraded to the official grade and unimproved; that a block or more on both sides of the unimproved portions of said Santa Rosa Avenue was, at all times herein mentioned, and now is, improved with the same character of improvements specified in the said Resolution of Intention."

Thereafter, and within due time, and after the posting of notice as required calling for the same, sealed proposals or bids for doing the work according to the plans, specifications, and estimates previously made and filed by the city engineer and which were approved and adopted by the council, were received and the council on the twenty-seventh day of October, 1915, opened and examined and publicly declared said proposals, and rejected all said proposals or bids except that of the petitioner herein, who was then by said council declared to be the lowest responsible bidder for the doing of said proposed work and awarded to it the contract.

Thereafter, and within three days after the expiration of the five days within which the owners of a majority of the frontage of the property upon the line of the proposed work might themselves have taken the work at the same price or bid at which the contract was awarded to the petitioner, the latter signed and presented to the respondent, mayor, for his signature, a form of written contract for the performance of said work and improvements at the prices specified in its said bid, said form of contract providing in detail that the petitioner would do all the work according to the specifications adopted for that purpose. With the said form of contract, the petitioner presented to the mayor a bond duly executed by it, and sufficient in all respects, conditioned for the faithful performance of the said contract. The said mayor, without specifying or suggesting any objections to the form of the contract presented to him by the petitioner, or to the bond offered at the same time, refused to execute said contract or any contract for the doing of said work.

The respondent, mayor, answered the complaint, admitting all the allegations thereof, but alleged, in the nature of a special plea in bar, that in the year 1888, by due proceedings had by the city council of said city of Santa Rosa in pursuance of the provisions of the then existing charter of said city, Santa Rosa Avenue was regularly ordered to be improved in accordance with certain plans and specifications adopted by said council for that purpose; that said avenue was, in said year, improved as so ordered after proceedings regularly had for the letting of the contract to do said work; that, in due course, the street commissioner reported to the council that the work and improvement had been completed, and that the council thereupon accepted the street as so improved; that, on the sixth day of July, 1893, the city council of said city, acting in pursuance of the provisions of section 20 of the general street law of 1885, known as the "Vrooman Street Law" (Stats. 1885, p. 160), passed an ordinance, numbered 150, accepting, as improved in the year 1888, as above indicated, Santa Rosa Avenue, from the south bank of the Santa Rosa Creek southerly to the city line.

The complaint in intervention also pleads said ordinance No. 150, and further points out a number of objections to the proceedings leading to the ordering of the work to be done on the portions of Santa Rosa Avenue described in the resolution of intention adopted by the council on the twenty-first day of September, 1915, and, finally, to the awarding of the contract to do the work described in said resolution to the petitioner.

We do not conceive it to be necessary to consider all the points urged by the respondents against the validity of the proceedings leading to the awarding of the contract by the council to the petitioner. We think the judgment should be sustained for the reason that, in our opinion, the council never acquired jurisdiction to order the work proposed to be done, and this proposition will now be considered.

According to the complaint, the resolution of intention described the work or improvement proposed to be done or made substantially as follows: "To improve Santa Rosa Avenue, a public street in the City of Santa Rosa, Sonoma County, California, from the south side of the bridge over Santa Rosa Creek, southerly to the south City limits, where not already paved and improved, by grading the roadway thereof and constructing thereon an asphaltic pavement consisting of three (3) inches of asphaltic concrete foundation covered with an asphaltic concrete wearing surface two (2) inches in thickness, the finished surface of which shall be to official grade."

The court made the following finding: "That on the eleventh day of May, 1888, the Council of said City of Santa Rosa, by an order in due form, did order that Santa Rosa Avenue should be graded and graveled, with common gravel, to the established grade, under plans and specifications therefor to be adopted and furnished by the City Engineer of said City, and further ordered the sidewalks to be graveled, with common gravel, to the official grade and curbing for sidewalks to be placed; that thereafter a contract was duly let for the doing of said work and the said Santa Rosa Avenue, from the south side of the bridge to the southerly City limit, was graveled with common gravel, curbs for sidewalks were laid and the sidewalks were graveled, with common gravel, all to the official grade, as required by ordinance, and said street work was thereafter accepted by said City of Santa Rosa as herein set out; that thereafter an assessment was made in due form of law against the owners of property fronting on the line of said work for the costs, and expenses of said work, and the contractor collected from the owners of the property the several amounts against them, as shown in said assessment.''

The appeal here is upon the judgment-roll alone. Therefore, notwithstanding that there is neither by the defendant nor the interveners a denial of the allegations of the complaint "that not more than two blocks of the said Santa Rosa Avenue, including street crossings, remained ungraded and unimproved,'' from which allegation it is to be implied that there were two blocks on said street ungraded and unimproved, it must be presumed that there was evidence which justified the above finding, and that Santa Rosa Avenue was in the said year 1888 improved under due proceedings by the city council in the manner described by said finding from the south side of the bridge southerly to the south limits, which embraced the two blocks designated or specified in the resolution of intention of September 21, 1915.

Section 72 of the charter of the city of Santa Rosa provides (among other things) that the filing of written objections to the proposed improvement of one block or more of a street by the owners of two-thirds of the frontage of the property fronting on the proposed work within twenty days from the first day of the posting of notice of the resolution of intention to order such improvement will operate, *ipso facto*, to bar further proceedings in relation to the doing of said work for a period of six months. The said section then proceeds: "When not more than two blocks, including street crossings or intersections, remain ungraded to the official grade, or otherwise unimproved, in whole or in part, and a block or more on one or both sides upon said street has been so graded or otherwise improved, said Council may order such work or improvement mentioned to be done upon said ungraded or unimproved part of said street notwithstanding such objections, and said work shall not be stayed or prevented by any written objections, unless the Council shall deem the same proper.''

Counsel for the petitioner contend that the case here comes within the exception thus made by said section 72 with reference to the effect of written objections by the property owners upon the power of the council to order the work to be done. This position is doubtless founded on the allegation of the complaint, and expressly admitted by the answer of the mayor and not denied in the complaint of the interveners, that "a block or more on both sides of the unimproved portions of said Santa Rosa Avenue was at all times herein mentioned, and now is, improved with the same character of improvements specified in said Resolution of Intention," etc.

We cannot agree to the contention. As we have shown, it must be accepted as an established fact in this case that at least that portion of Santa Rosa Avenue embraced within the resolution of intention had once been improved after proceedings regularly had by the city council under the then existing law empowering the municipality of Santa Rosa to coerce the improvement of its streets at the expense of the property owners; and our judgment is that where a street or any part thereof has once been improved under a law containing provisions similar to those of section 72 of the charter in question, and after such improvement has been made, proceedings are taken by the governing body of a municipality again to improve said street, timely written objections filed by the owners of the prescribed amount of the frontage of the property fronting on the line of the proposed improvement will have the effect of barring further proceedings in relation to the proposed improvement for the period of six months. In other words, we think that in such a case the provision of section 72 of the charter first above referred to applies. That provision is fashioned after or the same as the provision upon that subject in the Vrooman Act. We think it is not reasonable to suppose that, a street having been once improved at the expense of the property owners and to their satisfaction, the legislature, or, in this case, the framers of the charter or the people who ratified and so made it the organic law of the municipality, intended that the governing body of the latter should be vested with an unhampered or a discretionary power of again ordering such street to be improved at the expense of the property owners in the face of a protest regularly filed by the latter against the proposed improvement. The provision that further proceedings shall be barred for six months upon the due filing of written objections by the property owners was doubtless inspired to some extent by the consideration that owners of property subject to taxation for street improvements might not be prepared at the particular time at which streets were called up for improvement to meet or discharge the burden thus to be imposed upon them, and that a postponement of the work for the period designated might be sufficient to enable them to do so; or, it may be, that the framers of the act, in incorporating that provision into the law, conceived that the judgment of the property owners as to the necessity of the improvement at the particular time should be deferred to; but whatever might be the underlying motive for the provision, whether one or the other of the two above suggested or both combined, there can be no less reason or propriety for applying the provision to the case where, as here, the street has once been improved under the direction of the municipal authorities and it is proposed to again improve it, than to the case where a street has been called up for the first time for improvement. Indeed, we think there is a much stronger reason for applying the provision to the situation presented here, since the proceedings involved here, if consummated, will result in taxing the property owners the second time for the improvement of said street.

We have found no direct authority which supports the above views and the conclusion declared. But there is in the case of *City Street Imp. Co.* v. *Babcock,* 139 Cal. 690, 693, [73 Pac. 666], an expression, which involves, however, a mere dictum, the question not being directly before the court, that would seem to indicate that the supreme court leaned to the conclusion to which we have been led. Speaking of that part of section 3 of the Vrooman Act which, like the latter part of section 72 of the charter involved here, makes an exception, where similar conditions exist, to the rule that written objections duly filed by property owners will bar further proceedings in relation to the proposed improvement of a street, the supreme court in that case said, although expressly disclaiming any intention to decide the question therein: "It is certainly doubtful if this exception applies at all to a block which has been previously improved."

The position above taken cannot be affected by a consideration of the fact, which is alleged in the complaint and nowhere denied, thus imparting to it the dignity of a finding, that at some time since the year 1888, not definitely stated or disclosed, a block or more on both sides of the blocks proposed to be improved had been improved by the construction thereon of asphaltic pavement, etc., and that the blocks proposed to be improved are to be in like manner and character improved. To repeat, what we believe to be the true meaning or intent of section 72 of the charter, so far as it relates to the effect of the due filing of written objections to work proposed to be done, is that where a street or any part thereof has once been improved under the law authorizing such improvement, and thereafter it is sought again to improve it under the same authority, the proceedings looking to the second improvement must be regarded and treated as the same in all essential particulars as those necessary for the improvement of a street in the first instance or where a street or no part thereof has ever theretofore been improved, notwithstanding that at some time subsequent to the first or original improvement other parts of said street had been again improved.

Our conclusion, as stated in the outset, is that, since the property owners on the parts of Santa Rosa Avenue proposed to be improved by the resolution of intention of September 21, 1915, in due time filed sufficient objections to the proposed improvements, the council was wholly without authority or jurisdiction to order the work to be done, and, consequently, its action in awarding the contract to the petitioner to do the work was absolutely void.

The judgment appealed from is, accordingly, affirmed.

Chipman, P. J., and Burnett, J., concurred.

[Civ. No. 1414.   Third Appellate District.—October 31, 1916.]

COLUSA AND HAMILTON RAILROAD COMPANY (a Corporation), Plaintiff and Petitioner, v. SUPERIOR COURT OF THE COUNTY OF GLENN, and HONORABLE WM. M. FINCH, Judge Thereof, and CHARLES H. GLENN, Defendants and Respondents.

Eminent Domain—Appeal from Judgment—Stay of Proceedings—Supersedeas.—In an action in eminent domain to secure a railroad right of way, the taking of an appeal by the plaintiff from the judgment of condemnation prior to the expiration of the thirty-day period in which the plaintiff is required by section 1251 of the Code of Civil Procedure to pay the sum of money assessed, has the effect of staying execution on the judgment pending the appeal without the giving of a stay bond, and the appellant is entitled to a writ of *supersedeas* staying such execution.

Id.—Nature of Judgment.—A judgment of condemnation is not, prior to the expiration of the thirty-day period, a judgment for the direct payment of money within the meaning of section 942 of the Code of Civil Procedure requiring the execution of an undertaking to stay the operation of the judgment pending appeal, but amounts to no more than an order fixing the price at which plaintiff may or may not take the property.

Id.—Time of Payment of Damages—Construction of Section 1251, Code of Civil Procedure.—The "final judgment" mentioned in section 1251 of the Code of Civil Procedure relating to the time within which the plaintiff must pay the sum of money assessed as damages, has reference to the preliminary judgment of condemnation entered by the superior court, and not to the final conclusion of the litigation.

APPLICATION for a Writ of Supersedeas upon appeal from a judgment of condemnation of land.

The facts are stated in the opinion of the court.

Frank Freeman, and George R. Freeman, for Petitioner.

Charles L. Donohoe, and W. T. Belieu, for Respondents.

T. T. C. Gregory, Meredith, Landis & Chester, Frank H. Short, and Edward F. Treadwell, as *Amici Curiae.*

BURNETT, J.—In the above-entitled cause a rehearing was ordered by this court. The facts may be stated as follows: Petitioner is a railroad corporation and, as such, it brought in the superior court of Glenn County a suit in eminent domain to secure a right of way over respondent's land. With the assistance of a jury, a trial was had on April 26, 1915, which resulted in a verdict awarding plaintiff (petitioner herein) the 12.18 acres sought to be condemned, fixing the value of said land at the sum of $2,801.40, and assessing the damages, by reason of severance to that portion of the land of defendant not taken, at the sum of $14,130, making a total of $16,931.40 damages. Thereafter, on June 2, 1915, the Honorable Wm. M. Finch, judge of said superior court, made and entered a judgment adopting said verdict and containing the usual formal recitals, and also certain stipulations of the parties as to how the road should be constructed and concluding as follows: "It is further ordered, adjudged, and decreed that upon the payment of the said sum of $2,801.40 and the said sum of $14,130, to wit, the sum of $16,931.40 assessed, the plaintiff shall be entitled to a final order of condemnation which shall describe the property condemned and the purpose of such condemnation, which property shall be as described in the complaint herein, and which purpose shall be as stated in the complaint herein and that said railroad on said right of way shall be constructed in the manner prescribed in this decree, and the said property hereinafter described is hereby taken as a public use for the purposes described and set forth in the complaint, reference to which is hereby made, upon the said payment of the said total sum being made," and then followed a description of the land condemned. On June 11th, the plaintiff filed with the clerk of said court a notice of appeal, and on June 16th, said plaintiff filed a proper undertaking for costs on appeal. The petition for *supersedeas* herein alleged: "That notwithstanding the said perfecting of said appeal . . . defendant has applied to the Superior Court of the State of California, in and for the County of Glenn, and the Hon. Wm. M. Finch, judge of said court, for an order directing and compelling the clerk of said superior court to issue an execution in said action on said judgment for the said sum of $16,931.40 and costs of suit, and the said superior court and the said judge thereof has entertained said motion and said application and threatens to grant the same and order said Clerk of said Court to issue said execution to the end that it may be levied upon the property of your petitioner, the plaintiff in the above entitled action, and the said defendant is not entitled to such order or such execution and your petitioner is entitled to a writ of *supersedeas* for the reason that the appeal taken from said judgment has suspended said judgment and the jurisdiction of said superior court . . . and said judgment has by reason of said appeal been stayed until after the final determination of said appeal. . . . That your petitioner, the plaintiff in the above entitled action, has not taken possession of the land involved in said action or any portion thereof and has not made and is not now making any attempt to take possession of said land.''

In the opinion hereinbefore filed for reasons therein stated, an order was directed denying the writ. The decision was based largely upon our conception of what had been held by our supreme court in certain cases, to which attention was directed. The fundamental principles leading to the conclusion which we reached are manifestly that the judgment rendered in the superior court is ''a money judgment'' in the sense of section 942 of the Code of Civil Procedure and that such judgment is the ''final judgment'' contemplated by section 1251 of said code.

We venture to consider again the various decisions cited and to endeavor to clear up what seems to be a somewhat complicated situation. In doing so, we shall not attempt to segregate these decisions as they bear more directly upon one or the other of these propositions, but it will be more convenient to view them rather indiscriminately as they relate to one or both of these principles.

At the outset, it may be said that of course there is no contention that the judgment has become final in the sense of a ''final conclusion of the litigation.'' It is admitted by both parties that, as said in *Gillmore* v. *American C. I. Co.*, 65 Cal. 63, [2 Pac. 882], ''Until litigation on the merits is ended, there is no finality to the judgment, in the sense of a final determination of the rights of the parties, although it may have become final for the purpose of an appeal from it.'' It is, though, claimed by respondent that section 1251 of the Code of Civil Procedure providing that ''the plaintiff must within thirty days after final judgment pay the sum of money assessed'' does not refer to the end of litigation, but to the judgment as entered or rendered in the superior court and, of course, it is contended that this judgment is one directing "the payment of money" in the sense of section 942 of said code. If it were *res integra*, I should be inclined to the conclusion that said expression used in said section 1251, "after final judgment" has the same signification as "after judgment becomes final." The peculiar form of expression, the definite article *the* being omitted before the word *final* is a significant circumstance in this connection. Respondent's interpretation would be more persuasive if the legislature had provided that the money should be paid within thirty days "after *the* final judgment."

Again, the use of the term "final" is of great importance. Why should the word be used at all if it was intended to make the judgment of the superior court the initial point for computation of the time? Is it not fair to say that if such had been the intention, it would have been provided that the money should be paid within thirty days "after judgment," or "after the judgment," or "after judgment in the superior court?" Any of these expressions or equivalent ones would have placed the matter beyond question, and it seems hardly credible that the deliberate use of the qualifying term "final" was not for the purpose of postponing the declared effect of the judgment until *finality* had attached to it.

Again in section 1254 where the legislature had in mind the judgment as rendered in the superior court, it is interesting to notice the nomenclature used. Therein it is provided: "At any time after trial and *judgment* entered or pending an appeal from the judgment to the supreme court, whenever the plaintiff shall have paid into court, for the defendant, the full amount of the *judgment*, and such further sum . . . the court . . . may . . . authorize the plaintiff . . . to take possession of and use the property during the pendency of and until *the final conclusion of the litigation*. . . . The defendant, who is entitled to the money paid into court for him upon any *judgment*, shall be entitled to . . . receive the same . . . upon obtaining an order therefor from the court. It shall be the duty of the court . . . upon application . . . by such defendant, to order and direct that the money so paid into court for him be delivered to him upon his filing a satisfaction of the *judgment*," etc. It is *the judgment* or *judgment* rendered in the superior court not *final judgment* as in the previous quotation. Herein is also reference to an *appeal* and *the final conclusion of the litigation*. Such contingency, we may reasonably conclude, was also in the mind of the legislature when it used the terminology "final judgment" in said section 1251 and that it contemplated "the final conclusion of the litigation." However, it has been decided otherwise by the supreme court as we shall presently see, and we are bound by that decision.

Moreover, it is not proper to say that the judgment under consideration is one directing the payment of money. It is rather an adjudication that upon payment of a certain sum plaintiff may acquire the property. It did not vest the title to the money in defendant nor the real property in plaintiff. It is rather a conditional award to plaintiff upon the payment of a certain price for the land. It cannot be fairly construed as creating or evidencing a present and unqualified obligation to pay any sum of money. When said judgment was rendered, plaintiff had the right to decline to take the land at the price fixed. No doubt, the payment was purposely made contingent in view of the further proceedings that were open to the parties. Thus it is provided in section 1255a that "plaintiff may abandon the proceedings at any time after filing the complaint and before the expiration of thirty days after final judgment, by serving on defendant and filing in court a written notice of such abandonment." It is therefore plain that plaintiff was not "required to perform the directions of the judgment" at the time it was rendered. It could not, therefore, be enforced by a writ of execution, and it has been held that said section 942 applies only to a judgment which directs the payment of a specific amount of money and which can be directly enforced by a writ of execution. (*Estate of Schedel*, 69 Cal. 241, [10 Pac. 334]; *Born* v. *Horstmann*, 80 Cal. 452, [5 L. R. A. 577, 22 Pac. 169, 338]; *Pennie* v. *Superior Court*, 89 Cal. 31, [26 Pac. 617]; *McCallion* v. *Hibernia Sav. & Loan Soc.*, 98 Cal. 442, [33 Pac. 329]; *Kreling* v. *Kreling*, 116 Cal. 458, [48 Pac. 383]; *Owen* v. *Pomona Land etc. Co.*, 124 Cal. 331, [57 Pac. 71]; *Los Angeles* v. *Pomeroy*, 132 Cal. 340, [64 Pac. 477].)

We may now take up the leading authorities cited by petitioner and respondent as relating directly to the two propositions aforesaid.

In section 785 (third edition) of Lewis on Eminent Domain, it is said as to the character of the judgment: "Some cases hold that it is proper to render a personal judgment upon the verdict of a jury in condemnation cases, and to award execution, the same as in common law suits. If the statute is so far silent upon the subject as to leave the matter open for judicial construction, then the proper judgment to be entered will depend upon the following considerations: If the possession has already been taken of the property, either by consent or otherwise, or if the property has already been taken by virtue of an instrument of appropriation, as it may be in some states, before the compensation is paid, then a personal judgment with all its incidents may properly be entered. But, if the property has not been entered upon and cannot be until compensation is made, and the effect of the proceedings is to fix a price at which the petitioner can take the property if it elects so to do, then a personal judgment is improper and should not be entered." And in section 955, the same learned author says: "The weight of authority undoubtedly is that, in the absence of statutory provisions on the question, the effect of proceedings for condemnation is simply to fix the price at which the party condemning can take the property sought, and that even after confirmation or judgment the purpose of taking the property may be abandoned without incurring any liability to pay the damages awarded."

A large number of cases bearing upon the text is reviewed and an extended quotation made from the opinion of Chief Justice Beasley of the court of errors and appeals of New Jersey in the case of *O'Neill* v. *Freeholders of Hudson*, 41 N. J. L. 161, concluding with the declaration that "the legal effect of the proceedings for condemnation should be held that they compel the landowner to offer the public the required land at the ascertained price, and that when such price has been finally ascertained, the public has a reasonable time within which to make an election either to accept or reject the offer." Judge Beasley's language applies to the situation here. Until thirty days after "final judgment," such election may be exercised, and until the expiration of said period the judgment does not operate as conclusive evidence of an unconditional or absolute obligation to pay the amount assessed. It would seem, therefore, that until said period had expired, it could not be regarded as a "personal

judgment" with all its incidents. It is at least clear that at
the time said appeal was taken no execution could issue on
said judgment, and it could be regarded as simply "fixing the
price at which the condemning party could take the land."

We proceed to other citations. In *California Southern
R. R. Co.* v. *Southern Pac. R. R. Co.*, 67 Cal. 59, [7 Pac. 123],
it is said: "The judgment based in part on the assessment
of damages, and adjudicating that the use is public, and the
taking necessary, etc., is the 'final judgment' from which an
appeal may be taken. The sum of money assessed must be
paid within thirty days after 'final judgment.' (Code Civ.
Proc., sec. 1251.) It may, as suggested, be an inaccurate use
of terms to designate as *final* a judgment, which the court may
set aside (with all the proceedings on which it is based) if
the sum of money assessed is not paid. (Code Civ. Proc.,
sec. 1252.) And ordinarily a judgment is not final when
the law contemplates further and subsequent proceedings in
the same court to precede the absolute determination of the
rights of the parties. But the question is not what is or is
not a final judgment, within the appropriate meaning of the
terms, but what is intended to be designated as the final
judgment in the title treating of eminent domain."

In *Lincoln Northern Ry. Co.* v. *Wiswell*, 8 Cal. App. 578,
[97 Pac. 536], the question was whether the plaintiff could,
within thirty days after the entry of judgment on the verdict, abandon the route set out in the complaint, and in holding that it had such privilege, the court said: "The final
judgment mentioned in section 1251, as to payment of which
reference is made in section 1252, is the judgment fixing the
amount of damages, and is a final judgment in the proceeding
and is an appealable judgment (*California Southern R. R.
Co.* v. *Southern Pac. R. R. Co.*, 67 Cal. 59, [7 Pac. 123]; the
subsequent final order of condemnation (sec. 1253) being
an order after final judgment."

The statutes of Idaho on Eminent Domain seem to be the
same as ours, and in *Big Lost River Irr. Co.* v. *Davidson*,
21 Idaho, 160, [121 Pac. 88], it is said: "The statute does
not provide the form of judgment to be entered for the damages fixed and assessed by either the court, jury or referee,
under the provisions of section 5220; but under that section
of the statute there could be but one form of judgment, and
that would be a common, ordinary form of judgment for the

recovery of money, the amount determined by the court, jury or referee, and is the final judgment mentioned in section 5223 of the Revised Codes, and is a judgment *in personam* against the plaintiff, and upon which an execution may issue as provided by section 5224 of the statute. . . . After a final judgment has been entered the plaintiff has thirty days within which to pay the same, and if payment is not made then execution may issue, as in civil cases. *Glenn County* v. *Johnston*, 129 Cal. 404, [62 Pac. 66]; *County of Madera* v. *Raymond G. Co.*, 139 Cal. 128, [72 Pac. 915]. . . . There would be no reason for the provisions found in section 5224, providing for an execution, if there was to be no judgment entered for the damages assessed, either by the court, jury, or referee. The very fact that an execution is authorized to be issued presupposes and presumes that an entry of a personal judgment for the damages assessed will be entered, upon which such execution is to be issued."

In *Union Ry. Co.* v. *Standard Wheel Co.*, 149 Fed. 698, [79 C. C. A. 386], the question involved was whether, after judgment assessing damages, plaintiff or petitioner was authorized to dismiss the proceedings as to a portion of the land sought to be condemned merely because in its opinion the damages assessed were too high and in holding to the contrary, the court said: "When a party undertakes to subject another's property to his own use, he must be deemed to be willing and intend to pay a fair price for it, and that such fair price shall be fixed by the verdict of a jury to be approved by the court. Good faith requires that he shall not use the power of the court to vex the other party with successive experiments in the effort to get what he wants at his own price. And the public has an interest in the finality of the judgment. It will endure one litigation between parties, but not a repetition of it, to give one of them a chance to get a better result." And as to the judgment fixing the price to be paid for the land, it was declared that the jury was to assess the damages and the court to render judgment and: "The defendant is bound by it, and so is the petitioner; on principle as we think, but also by force of the statute."

Drath v. *Burlington etc. R. R. Co.*, 15 Neb. 367, [18 N W. 717], and *Neal* v. *Pittsburgh etc. R. R. Co.*, 31 Pa. St. 19, declare a similar doctrine.

However, it may be permissible to notice these cases a little more specifically.

In the first, the Southern Pacific Railroad Company, one of the defendants, appealed from the preliminary order, and also from the final order of condemnation, and the real question presented as far as the judgment is concerned was whether the preliminary order or the final order of condemnation was the judgment from which the appeal should be taken. The supreme court held that the preliminary order of condemnation "is the 'final judgment' from which an appeal may be taken," and dismissed the appeal from the final order of condemnation because not taken within sixty days. The question of what is contemplated by "final judgment" as referred to in the first clause of said section 1251, or when the money must be paid, was not discussed in the briefs and had no bearing upon the disputed points involved in the appeal.

In the Lincoln Northern Railway Co. case, *supra*, the court on motion of plaintiff dismissed the proceeding within thirty days after the preliminary order of condemnation and the defendant appealed from that order. It is apparent that under any possible construction of said section 1251, plaintiff was not required to deposit the money before the expiration of thirty days from the preliminary order of condemnation. Hence, it could not be said that plaintiff was in default, or that it did not have the right to abandon the proceedings, whether "after final judgment" as used in said section 1251, has the meaning attributed to it by petitioner or by respondent.

In the Idaho case "the only issue presented by the pleadings" as stated by the court, "was the value of the land to be taken. The right to take the land described in the complaint, and the necessity for such taking, is admitted by the answer and the description of the land as alleged in the complaint is also admitted by the answer, and the allegation in the answer as to the necessity for taking eighty additional acres is not denied or put in issue, and therefore must have been admitted by the appellant, leaving for determination the value of the land described in the pleadings as the only issue to be determined in said cause." The jury returned a verdict "for the defendants" and assessing "defendants' damages in the sum of $55,593." Whereupon the trial court, after reciting the formal and preliminary matters, entered the following judgment: "Wherefore by virtue of the law and by reason of the premises aforesaid, it is ordered, adjudged, and decreed that the said defendants have and recover from said plaintiff the sum of $55,593 with interest thereon at the rate of seven per cent per annum from the date hereof until paid, etc." From that judgment an appeal was taken by plaintiff and the language hereinbefore quoted appears to have been used with reference to the contention of appellant: "That the court erred in entering an unconditional personal judgment against the appellant."

The question as to the import of the phrase, "final judgment," or when the money had to be paid, was not involved, but the court was called upon to determine the character of the judgment to be entered and it did hold that "a judgment *in personam*" was authorized, treating the amount of the award as damages. As to the Idaho case, it may also be said that the judgment in form created a present obligation for the immediate payment of a definite sum of money upon which an execution could issue. It was not conditional and tentative as in the case at bar.

Of the California cases cited in the Idaho decision, the first, *Glenn County* v. *Johnston*, 129 Cal. 404, [62 Pac. 66], involved a motion to dismiss a condemnation proceeding brought by Glenn County for the reason that more than thirty days had elapsed since the entry of the judgment, and payment had not been made to defendants. The court below denied the motion but the supreme court reversed it, thus virtually holding that "after final judgment" refers to the entry of the preliminary order of condemnation in the superior court. It may be admitted, as claimed by petitioner, that there was no discussion in the briefs as to what constituted the "final judgment'" within the purview of said section, the principal subject of controversy being as to whether the sections in question applied to counties, but as stated, the point was necessarily involved in the decision. *County of Madera* v. *Raymond G. Co.*, 138 Cal. 244, [71 Pac. 112], did not call for the determination of the question considered herein, although said first clause of said section 1251 was quoted in the opinion in connection with the discussion of the form of judgment required, the conclusion being reached that "even if the form of the judgment was not as it should be, defendant was not injured thereby and cannot complain, and plaintiff makes no objection to the form of its judgment."

In *Bensley* v. *Mountain Lake Water Co.*, 13 Cal. 306, 317, [73 Am. Dec. 575], it is said: "The right to take on the terms adjudicated—which is a compulsory statutory sale—accrues from the legal proceedings—the petition—the report—the confirmation; then the price becomes fixed. But no right of entry—much less a title—accrues so far. The party condemning, the representative of a state, is then in a condition to be a purchaser; the other party is in a situation of a vendor making an agreement of sale on condition precedent, but retaining his title and possession until payment."

The theory thus presented harmonizes with petitioner's claim that the award constitutes the determination of the price that must be paid for the property, if it be taken, rather than a personal judgment for the direct payment of money.

In *Lamb* v. *Schottler*, 54 Cal. 319, it was held that "the right of the state to take private property for public use in no sense depends upon any contract between the owner and the public, nor is there any vested right to compensation, until the property is taken; nor is the government under any obligation to take the property if the terms, when ascertained, are not satisfactory."

But the case most strongly relied upon by petitioner is *Pool* v. *Butler*, 141 Cal. 46, [74 Pac. 444]. Therein the appeal was from an order dismissing the action made upon plaintiff's motion. The action was to condemn a strip of land for a ferry landing. There was a prior appeal from the judgment condemning the land for said purpose in which the judgment was affirmed. In that case the trial court gave judgment to the plaintiff condemning the land to the burden of the easement, and assessing the damages at $285. The defendants upon the trial reserved several exceptions and moved the court for a new trial upon all the issues and the motion was denied. From this order also an appeal was taken. The plaintiff deposited with the clerk the said sum of $285 and costs, within thirty days after the entry of judgment. The defendants did not accept the money so deposited, but took and perfected their appeal, and did not abandon all defenses except for greater compensation, and could not demand or obtain the money until the appeal should be determined. It is to be observed that in that case the appeal was taken by the defendants, and under section 1254 of the Code of Civil Procedure they could not get the money without abandoning all the defenses they had to the action except as to the sufficiency of the damages awarded; and such defenses were not abandoned, but were pressed upon the motion for new trial and in the supreme court on appeal. As stated in the opinion: "If they had applied to the court for an order directing the clerk to pay over the money, it could not have been granted pending the motion for a new trial, or at any time after the appeal was taken until the judgment was affirmed or the appeal dismissed." It is thus to be seen how different that case is from this in the very important consideration that therein it was not doubted that the appeal operated to suspend or stay the judgment and the persons who were entitled to the money refused to accept it. As the court said: "The court had no power to make the requisite order for the payment of the money, the judgment having been suspended by the appeal, which was a refusal to accept the money, or to treat the judgment as a final determination of the rights of the parties, though it was in form final."

Judgment in the court below was entered June 21, 1898, and the appeal was decided December 3, 1901, and became final, according to the declaration of the supreme court, January 2, 1902, a period of three and a half years after judgment in the court below. Furthermore declared the court: "Such delay may have furnished in this case, and might in many others, sufficient reasons for an abandonment of the enterprise. During all that time defendants were protesting against the judgment, and when plaintiffs finally relieved them from what they insisted was a wrong, oppressive, and erroneous judgment by dismissing the proceeding, now appeal from the order relieving them from it. The ultimate question, however, is whether the court erred in dismissing the action." And it is in view of this situation that the court entered into a learned discussion of the nature of condemnation proceedings and came to the consideration of the question at what stage of such proceedings a plaintiff may abandon an enterprise or decline to take the property. It was clearly right to hold that during the pendency of the motion for a new trial and of the appeal by the defendants, the plaintiffs had the right to abandon the enterprise and refuse to pay the compensation. But it was contended that having deposited

the money with the clerk of the court, they could not withdraw it, and that upon the affirmance of the appeal the defendants were entitled to receive it, and this is the vital point
of the whole case. As to that contention, it was said: "I
think plaintiffs had the right to abandon at any time before
the defendants were willing to receive it, or were in a position to demand it." Thus far it would seem no one could
disagree with the court. Furthermore said the court: "The
deposit under the circumstances was only a tender, and in
such cases the money tendered does not vest in the person
to whom it is tendered unless it is accepted. In this case,
the deposit was not accepted. The defendants persisted in
their contention that the judgment was erroneous and invalid,
and sought to have it reversed and could hardly contend that
the money or the right to it was vested in them so long as
they contended that the plaintiffs had no right to the land."
No such contention is made by the defendant here. On
the contrary, he was satisfied with the judgment and seeks
to obtain the money. He claims, also, that said judgment
was not stayed by the appeal for reasons already stated.
The court proceeded: "The vesting of the title to the deposit in the defendants is coincident with the vesting of the
right to the land for the purposes for which it was sought,
but pending the appeal the plaintiffs could assert no right to
the land or its use under the judgment which had been stayed
and suspended by the appeal, during which time the court
was powerless to enforce it; nor could the defendants say,
'The right to the money is vested in us, but you shall not
have the land.'" The foregoing as applied to the facts of
that case cannot be disputed, but here the defendant asserts
the title to the money for the reason that the judgment has
not been stayed, that he is willing for plaintiff to take the
land at the assessed price, and that by virtue of the express
provisions of the statute he is authorized to reduce the money
to his possession. The opinion proceeds: "The title to the
land does not vest in the plaintiffs until 'the final order of
condemnation' is made by the court and a copy of the order
filed in the office of the county recorder 'and thereupon
the property described therein shall vest in the plaintiff
for the purposes therein specified. (Code Civ. Proc., sec.
1253.)'" After citing certain decisions, the court then
comes to the consideration of the question as to when or

within what time the plaintiff in condemnation proceedings may abandon them and decline to take the property, and it quotes said statement of Lewis as to the weight of authority, and Dillon on Municipal Corporations (fourth edition, section 608) as follows: "Under the language by which the power to open streets and to take private property for that purpose is usually conferred upon municipal corporations, they may at any time before taking possession of the property under completed proceedings, or before the final confirmation, recede from or discontinue the proceedings they have instituted. This may be done, unless it is otherwise provided by legislative enactment, at any time before vested rights in others have attached," and quotation is made from the case of *St. Louis etc. R. R. Co.* v. *Teters*, 68 Ill. 144, to the effect that: "Where the company has not appropriated the land at the time of the trial, it would be improper to render a judgment for the recovery of the money, or to award execution, because it could not be known that the company will ever enter upon the land. It is, under the statute, the payment of the money found by the jury, and not the order of the court alone, that confers the right. Although the petition has been filed, the damages assessed, and the order of the court pronounced and entered, the money must be paid before the right to enter attaches, and until they pay the damages, they have the right to abandon the location of the route thus made, and adopt some other. Hence, it is improper to render a judgment of recovery or award execution, unless the jury find, or it conclusively appears from the record, that the company has entered and is in possession of the land sought to be condemned." The court adds: "Justice requires that where possession has not been taken and the purpose for which condemnation was sought has been abandoned, that the award of damages should not be enforced, especially where the defendants have prevented for an unreasonable time the accomplishment of the purpose."

If this doctrine is to be applied to all cases where the plaintiff has not entered into possession, of course that would end the controversy, and the writ should issue. But the aforesaid statements must be accepted with some qualification. Even where the plaintiff has not entered into possession, he is limited in time within which he must exercise his option to abandon the proceedings. It must be exercised at least within thirty days after the judgment becomes final. (Code Civ. Proc., sec. 1255a.) In construing the language of this interesting decision we must not lose sight of its peculiar facts, or else we may run counter to the plain provisions of the statute.

In *Reed Orchard Co.* v. *Superior Court,* 19 Cal. App. 648, [128 Pac. 9, 18], it was held that "where a railroad company had obtained a judgment in eminent domain and in compliance with section 1254 of the Code of Civil Procedure had made the full amount of the deposits thereby required to secure all demands, the court had jurisdiction under that section to permit the railroad company to take possession of and use the property pending the litigation, and the appellate court will not issue a writ of *supersedeas* of such order for possession pending an appeal from the judgment."

It was in view of that situation that it was declared an appeal would not postpone plaintiff's right to take possession of the property. The decision was grounded upon the peculiar provision of said section 1254 which would, manifestly, be rendered nugatory if its operation was suspended during an appeal. The case really has no application to the facts involved herein.

It is manifest that the different cases cited cover variant aspects of condemnation proceedings, and the peculiar situation of each must be regarded to avoid being misled into a general application of the statements made in the several opinions.

Here, we may reiterate, the situation is this: Plaintiff was dissatisfied with the award, has not taken possession, but has taken an appeal from the judgment. Said appeal has not been determined and, hence, said judgment has not become final. No undertaking was given to stay execution, it being the claim of plaintiff that no such undertaking was required to effect said purpose. The defendant was willing to accept the award, took no appeal, but after the expiration of thirty days from the entry of the preliminary order of condemnation, sought execution.

The determination of the controversy then depends upon the following considerations:

1. Does the phrase "after final judgment" in said section refer to the preliminary judgment of condemnation as entered in the superior court? That has been answered in

the affirmative by the supreme court in *Glenn County* v. *Johnston*, 129 Cal. 404, [62 Pac. 66], where the question was necessarily involved and we must follow it.

2. Was the judgment of such character that execution could issue upon it? This is plainly answered by said section 1242 providing that if the money be not so paid or deposited (that is, paid or deposited within thirty days after the preliminary judgment of condemnation), execution may issue as in civil cases. This is a matter that the authorities hold can be regulated by statute. If execution can issue to enforce the payment of the amount of the award, the judgment must at that time be equivalent to a personal judgment for the payment of money. Prior, however, to this period beginning thirty days "after final judgment," the judgment amounts to no more than an order fixing the price at which plaintiff may or may not take the property. It is, in effect, an adjudication of the amount which plaintiff should pay as a just compensation for it to be entitled to take the property for *the purpose claimed*, but if the status is not changed by some other proceeding, after the expiration of said thirty days, it becomes substantially a personal judgment for the direct payment of money.

3. What, then, was the effect of said appeal? It stayed the operation of the judgment for the reason that the character of said judgment must be determined as of the time when the appeal was taken. It was not then a judgment requiring the payment by plaintiff of a specific amount of money and which could then be enforced by a writ of execution. It was the adjudication of a conditional liability which might or might not become a fixed and absolute obligation. It was not, therefore, within the exception noted in said section 942.

The effect of the appeal being to remove the subject matter of the order from the jurisdiction of the lower court, that court is without power to proceed further as to any matter embraced therein until the appeal is determined. (*Vosburg* v. *Vosburg*, 137 Cal. 493, 496, [70 Pac. 473].)

In conclusion, it may be suggested that even if the appeal bond did not operate to stay proceedings, it would be proper for this court to allow petitioner to file an effective bond for that purpose. The authority for such procedure is found in *Hill* v. *Finnigan*, 54 Cal. 494. Such request is made by petitioner if such action be deemed advisable by the court, but it is believed that the appeal has accomplished that result, and we think the writ should issue, and it is so ordered.

Chipman, P. J., and Hart, J., concurred.

[Crim. No. 638. First Appellate District.—November 1, 1916.]

THE PEOPLE, Respondent, v. EDWARD GORMAN, Appellant.

CRIMINAL LAW—CIRCUMSTANTIAL EVIDENCE—INSTRUCTION.—In a criminal case it is not error to refuse to instruct the jury at the request of the defendant on the law of circumstantial evidence, upon the theory that the case of the prosecution was based upon such evidence alone, where it appears that the prosecution did not rely solely or chiefly upon circumstantial evidence to obtain defendant's conviction.

ID.—MURDER—CONSPIRACY TO COMMIT ROBBERY—INSTRUCTION.—In a prosecution for murder it is not error to refuse to instruct the jury at the request of the defendant upon the subject of conspiracy to commit robbery, where there was little or no evidence offered to support that view of the case.

ID.—LACK OF MOTIVE—CIRCUMSTANCE OF INNOCENCE—INSTRUCTION.—It is not error to refuse to instruct the jury that if the evidence fails to show any motive on the part of the defendant consistent with reason and soundness of mind to commit the crime charged, it is a circumstance in favor of innocence, and should be considered by the jury in connection with the other evidence in the case.

APPEAL from a judgment of the Superior Court of the City and County of San Francisco, and from an order denying a new trial. Frank H. Dunne, Judge.

The facts are stated in the opinion of the court.

J. K. Ross, and John W. Elwell, for Appellant.

U. S. Webb, Attorney-General, and John H. Riordan, Deputy Attorney-General, for Respondent.

THE COURT.—This is an appeal from a judgment of conviction of the defendant of the crime of manslaughter, and from an order denying his motion for a new trial.

The defendant was charged with murder in the killing of one Eugene Kelly in a brawl on Third Street, in the city and county of San Francisco, during the early morning hours of September 8, 1915. It is the first contention of the appellant that the court erred in its refusal to give certain instructions requested by the defendant relating to the law of circumstantial evidence, and presented upon the theory that the case of the prosecution was based upon circumstantial evidence alone; but an inspection of the record discloses that the prosecution did not rely upon circumstantial evidence alone or chiefly to obtain the defendant's conviction, and this being so, it is obvious that the instructions which the defendant requested, however correctly they may have stated the law of circumstantial evidence, had no application to the case, and were therefore properly refused by the trial court.

The same reasoning applies to the instruction asked by the defendant upon the subject of conspiracy. The charge was murder; and while it is true that the prosecuting officer in his opening statement to the jury had something to say about a conspiracy of several of the participants in the embroglio to commit a robbery, there was little or no evidence offered to support this view of the case, while, on the other hand, there was the direct testimony of a police officer to the effect that he saw the defendant strike the fatal blow. Under these conditions the matter of a possible conspiracy between several of the participants in the brawl to rob someone involved in it was not a sufficient factor in the case to warrant the giving of an instruction upon that subject.

The appellant's next contention is that the court erred in refusing to give the jury the following instruction at the defendant's request: "If the evidence fails to show any motive on the part of the defendant consistent with reason and soundness of mind to commit the crime charged, this is a circumstance in favor of his innocence, and should be considered by the jury in connection with the other evidence in the case." The appellant cites no direct authority supporting his contention that this instruction should have been given; while, on the other hand, it has been expressly decided that it is not error in the trial court to refuse to give a requested instruction in substantially the form of that presented by the defendant herein. (*People* v. *Glaze*, 139 Cal. 154, [72 Pac. 965].)

The appellant further contends that the evidence is insufficient to warrant a conviction, and devotes considerable space in the brief of his counsel to certain alleged inconsistencies and uncertainties in the testimony of the witnesses for the prosecution. We are satisfied, however, upon a careful reading of the record that there was sufficient evidence presented which, if believed by the jury, would have warranted a verdict of manslaughter, and this being so, the judgment of conviction will not be disturbed.

The next contention of the appellant is that the court erred in its refusal to grant him a new trial upon the ground of newly discovered evidence. The affidavits offered by the defendant at the hearing of his motion for a new trial were merely cumulative, and besides, were largely negative in their averments, and, in our opinion, the court did not abuse its discretion in denying the defendant's motion upon that ground.

As to the final charge of the appellant, that the court and the prosecuting officer were guilty of certain acts of misconduct which materially and improperly prejudiced the defendant's case before the jury, we find this contention to be entirely without merit.

Judgment and order affirmed.

[Civ. No. 1581. Third Appellate District.—November 1, 1916.]

L. A. HARBAUGH, Appellant, v. LASSEN IRRIGATION COMPANY (a Corporation), Respondent.

EXECUTION—GREATER AMOUNT THAN JUDGMENT—QUASHING OF WRIT.— Where an execution is issued for a greater amount than that for which the judgment was rendered, it may be quashed on motion.

ID.—JURISDICTION—DIFFERENT JUDGES.—The jurisdiction of the court to quash the writ is not affected by the fact that the judge who presided at the hearing of the motion to quash was a different judge from the one who presided when the writ was ordered to issue.

APPEAL from an order of the Superior Court of Lassen County recalling and quashing an execution. H. D. Burroughs, Judge.

The facts are stated in the opinion of the court.

F. A. Kelley, for Appellant.

Pardée & Pardee, for Respondent.

BURNETT, J.—The appeal is from an order granting defendant's motion to recall and quash an execution. The judgment in the cause was rendered October 16, 1907. An attempt was made to have this judgment reviewed by the appellate court, but the appeal was dismissed on August 12. 1914. On May 20, 1915, the superior court of Lassen County, Honorable J. O. Moncur, Judge presiding, made an order directing execution to issue on said judgment and the clerk of said superior court issued an execution under the seal of said court on the twenty-seventh day of November following. A copy of this writ is set out in the transcript. It recites that "$586.95, with interest, is now (at the date of this writ) actually due on said judgment," and contains the usual direction to the sheriff to satisfy said judgment. Then follows in the transcript a copy of the "order granting motion to settle and quash execution." It recites:

"The defendant's motion, issued in the above entitled court and cause, to recall and quash execution, coming on regularly to be heard on Monday, April 3rd, 1916, at two o'clock p. m., Pardee & Pardee for the motion, and no one appearing for plaintiff, the evidence on said motion being presented . . . the said motion was then submitted, and the same being by the court duly considered, it is ordered that the motion be and the same is hereby granted, and the said execution be and the same is hereby recalled and quashed.

"CLARENCE A. RAKER,

"Judge of the Superior Court of the State of California, in and for the County of Modoc, presiding in the above entitled court and cause on the hearing of said motion."

It is apparent that the transcript is quite incomplete, as it does not contain a copy of the notice of said motion or of the papers used on the hearing in the court below as required

by section 951 of the Code of Civil Procedure. Nor is there
any bill of exceptions or other document setting forth in any
way the evidence upon which the court below acted. We
may, therefore, accept as true the statement of other facts by
respondent. Indeed, appellant does not question the accuracy
of said statement. It seems that the only language in said
judgment which purported to be an adjudication of the matters at issue was as follows: ''Wherefore, by virtue of the
law, and by reason of the premises aforesaid, it is ordered,
adjudged and decreed, that the plaintiff do have and recover
from defendant plaintiff's costs and disbursements incurred
in this action, amounting to the sum of Eighty-six and
95/100 Dollars.'' As we have seen, the execution, issued
November 27, 1915, recites that the judgment was for the
sum of $500 and costs $86.95, or a total of $586.95.

In the meantime, L. A. Harbaugh, the plaintiff, died on or
about the twenty-third day of July, 1915, and at the time the
order appealed from was made, no proceedings had been
taken for administration of his estate. The grounds of the
motion were fully stated in the notice and included the following: ''That the writ contained an erroneous statement
that the judgment in the case was for $500, together with
$86.95 costs; whereas, the judgment was for $86.95 costs,
only,'' and ''that owing to the death of the plaintiff prior
to the date when the execution was issued, the attorney for
plaintiff had no authority to cause an execution to be issued
and placed in the hands of the sheriff.''

We must presume that said motion was supported at the
hearing by competent evidence, and we are not required to
go further than to base the decision upon said first ground
mentioned.

It is undoubtedly the rule that an execution issued on a
judgment which does not authorize it may be quashed on
motion. (17 Cyc. 1154.) The judgment being for $86.95,
and the execution for $586.95, the latter, of course, was un-
authorized.

We can see no merit in the contention that the court was
without jurisdiction, for the reason that one judge was presiding when the writ was ordered to be issued and a different
judge when the writ was recalled. It was the same court,
and both judges had the same authority. It is not disputed
that Judge Moncur could have quashed the writ. It must

follow that Judge Raker had power to do the same, since his jurisdiction was coextensive with that of the former. Indeed, in either case, the act was that of the court rather than of the judge.

Section 182 of the Code of Civil Procedure has no application to the condition herein revealed. That section provides: "If an application for an order, made to a judge of a court in which the action or proceeding is pending, is refused in whole or in part, or is granted conditionally, no subsequent application for the same order shall be made to any court commissioner, or any other judge, except of a higher court." The subsequent application here was manifestly not for the same order. The fact is that its purpose was to prevent a violation of the first order. This latter was in effect, of course, to have an execution issued in accordance with the judgment. This was not done, and it was for the correction of this error that the second application was made.

There is nothing in this proceeding, we may state, that would prevent the issuance and operation of a proper writ of execution in accordance with said judgment.

The order is affirmed.

Chipman, P. J., and Hart, J., concurred.

A petition for a rehearing of this cause was denied by the district court of appeal on December 1, 1916, and the following opinion then rendered thereon:

THE COURT.—In his petition for rehearing, appellant calls attention to a certified copy of the judgment entered in the superior court in the above-entitled cause. Said copy was filed herein after our former opinion was rendered and without any suggestion of diminution of the record. Under the recognized practice, we would be justified in disregarding said document. However, we have examined it and we find that the said judgment was radically defective, and through someone's carelessness it utterly failed to determine and decree the amount to which plaintiff was entitled under the verdict of the jury. It does, indeed, recite said verdict, but the judgment is as follows: "Wherefore by virtue of the law and by reason of the premises aforesaid, it is ordered, adjudged and decreed that the plaintiff do have and recover from said defendant plaintiff's costs and disbursements incurred in this action amounting to the sum of eighty-six and 95/100 dollars."

It may be that, upon proper application, the lower court may be warranted in correcting the mistake and making the said judgment conform to the verdict. But there seems no way open to us in this proceeding to accomplish the desired result, although if legally possible, some remedy should be afforded.

The petition for rehearing is denied.

[Civ. No. 1645.   First Appellate District.—November 2, 1916.]

D. A. CURTIN, Appellant, v. B. KATSCHINSKI et al., Respondents.

ATTACHMENT—UNDERTAKING FOR RELEASE—RETURN OF EXECUTION—CONDITION PRECEDENT TO ACTION.—The issuance and return of an execution unsatisfied in whole or in part is required by the provisions of section 552 of the Code of Civil Procedure as a condition precedent to the right to commence an action upon an undertaking given pursuant to section 555 of such code for the release of attached property.

ID.—BANKRUPTCY OF JUDGMENT DEBTORS—RETURN OF EXECUTION NOT EXCUSED BY—NATIONAL BANKRUPTCY ACT.—The issuance and return of an execution unsatisfied in whole or in part as a condition precedent to the maintenance of an action against the sureties on an undertaking given for the release of attached property is not excused by the subsequent bankruptcy of the judgment debtors, where the latter did not obtain a discharge within one year after the adjudication of their bankruptcy, as the National Bankruptcy Act contains no inhibition against the issuance and levy of execution after the lapse of that time.

APPEAL from a judgment of the Superior Court of the City and County of San Francisco, and from an order denying a new trial. George A. Sturtevant, Judge.

The facts are stated in the opinion of the court.

Randolph V. Whiting, for Appellant.

M. H. Wascerwitz, Joseph H. Mayer, and George D. Perry, for Respondents.

RICHARDS, J.—This is an appeal on behalf of the plain-tiff in an action brought to recover the sum of one thousand dollars, alleged to be due upon an undertaking by the defendants as sureties for the release of certain personal property from attachment.

The facts, which are substantially undisputed, are briefly these: The plaintiff and appellant herein commenced an action against the firm of Leipsic Brothers to recover the sum of $3,284.03, and caused to be attached certain personal property owned by said firm. Thereupon the defendants herein, as sureties for Leipsic Bros., executed an undertaking for the release of said attached personal property in the sum of one thousand dollars, and the property was released from the attachment. Subsequently the firm of Leipsic Bros. filed a petition in bankruptcy and were adjudged bankrupts, and the property which had theretofore been under attachment was taken into possession by the trustee, and sold under the order of the referee in bankruptcy for the sum of approximately one thousand dollars and the sale confirmed. Plaintiff presented his claim for the sum of $3,284.03 against said bankrupts, and in due course received dividends thereon aggregating the sum of $2,189.34. He also prosecuted his said action against Leipsic Bros., and recovered judgment against the firm for $3,713.13, upon which nothing was paid except the above dividends. He then began this action against said sureties upon the attachment bond. Leipsic Bros. were not made parties to this action, for the reason that they had not joined in the execution of the attachment bond. The undertaking sued upon was given in conformity with section 555 of the Code of Civil Procedure, and by its terms the respondents herein "undertake in the sum of one thousand dollars and promise that in case the plaintiff recover judgment in said action the defendants (Leipsic Bros.) will upon demand redeliver the attached property so released to the proper officers to be applied to the payment of the judgment, or in default thereof that the defendants and sureties will on demand pay to the plaintiff the full value of the property so released not exceeding the sum of one thousand dollars." Prior to the commencement of the action upon this undertaking the plaintiff demanded of the sureties the sum of one thousand dollars claimed to be due thereon,

but he made no demand upon Leipsic Bros. for the redelivery
of the attached property or the value thereof, nor did the
plaintiff cause to be issued an execution upon the judgment
obtained in the original action against Leipsic Bros., nor
has such execution ever been issued or returned unsatisfied
in whole or in part. It further appears that the firm of
Leipsic Bros. have not obtained their discharge in bankruptcy, and that more than one year had elapsed between
the adjudication of their bankruptcy and the institution of
the present action.

Upon the foregoing facts the trial court gave judgment in
the defendants' favor, and denied the plaintiff's motion for
a new trial, whereupon he prosecutes this appeal.

We are inclined to agree with the contention of the appellant that the fact that as plaintiff in the original action he
presented his claim against Leipsic Bros. to the bankruptcy
court, and received dividends thereon in excess of the sum in
which the undertaking involved in the pending suit was
given, did not operate to discharge the obligation of the sureties upon said undertaking; and also with his contention that
no demand for the return of the released property was necessary in view of the fact that said property had been sold
and the sale confirmed by the bankruptcy court, and hence
that the making of such demand either on Leipsic Bros. or
the defendants herein would have been an idle and useless
act.

But conceding this much to the appellant, the insuperable
objection to the maintenance of this action consists in the admitted fact that no execution was issued or returned unsatisfied in whole or in part prior to the institution of the present
suit. Section 552 of the Code of Civil Procedure, under the
title of "Attachment," reads as follows:

"Sec. 552. When suits may be commenced on the undertaking. If the execution be returned, unsatisfied, in whole
or in part, the plaintiff may prosecute any undertaking given
pursuant to section 540 or section 555, or he may proceed, as in
other cases, upon the return of an execution."

It has been expressly held that under this section of the
code the issuance and return of an execution unsatisfied in
whole or in part is a condition precedent to the maintenance
of an action upon an undertaking given under the terms of
section 555 of the Code of Civil Procedure. (*Brownlee* v.

Riffenburg, 95 Cal. 447, [30 Pac. 587].) It is urged, however, by the appellant that the issuance and return of an execution was rendered unnecessary, and therefore excused, by reason of the fact that Leipsic Bros. had gone into bankruptcy, and that the issuance or attempted levy of an execution would be a fruitless and useless proceeding; and they cite the case of *Rosenthal* v. *Perkins*, 123 Cal. 240, [55 Pac. 804], as sustaining this view. An examination of that case, however, shows that it differs from the case at bar in this essential respect; that in that case the principal debtor, for the release of whose property the undertaking had been given, had taken the benefit of the state insolvent act then in force, by the terms of section 45 of which act the issuance and levy of executions was forbidden against insolvents who had come within its provisions. The supreme court, in distinguishing that case from the case of *Brownlee* v. *Riffenburg*, 95 Cal. 447, [30 Pac. 587], held that this inhibition against the issuance and levy of an execution against insolvent debtors of necessity rendered section 552 of the Code of Civil Procedure inapplicable to such a case; for to hold otherwise would have rendered impossible an action on an undertaking given under section 555 of the Code of Civil Procedure after the principal debtor had taken advantage of the insolvent act. But the National Bankruptcy Act contains no such inhibition against the issuance and levy of executions after the lapse of one year as against debtors who have not obtained their discharge within that time; and this being so, and the entire proceeding being statutory, we are of the opinion that the rule laid down in the case of *Brownlee* v. *Riffenburg*, 95 Cal. 447, [30 Pac. 587], must be given full application to the case at bar.

Judgment and order affirmed.

Lennon, P. J., and Kerrigan, J., concurred.

[Crim. No. 501. Second Appellate District.—November 2, 1916.]

THE PEOPLE, Respondent, v. HARRY DUNCAN, Appellant.

CRIMINAL LAW—MURDER—LACK OF ERROR.—Upon this appeal from a judgment and order denying a new trial in a prosecution for murder, it is held that there was no error committed prejudicial to the rights of the defendant.

APPEAL from a judgment of the Superior Court of Los Angeles County, and from an order denying a new trial. Gavin W. Craig, Judge.

The facts are stated in the opinion of the court.

Arthur E. T. Chapman, for Appellant.

U. S. Webb, Attorney-General, and Robert M. Clarke, Deputy Attorney-General, for Respondent.

CONREY, P. J.—The defendant in this action was accused of the crime of murder and found guilty of manslaughter, for which he has been sentenced to a term of eight years in the state prison at Folsom. He appeals from the judgment and from an order denying his motion for a new trial.

There are no briefs. The present attorney for appellant was substituted in the place of the former attorneys a few weeks before the appeals came on for hearing, and the case has been presented upon his oral argument.

No attack is made upon the sufficiency of the evidence, which shows that one J. F. Toolen, a police officer, came to his death by means of a shot fired from a revolver by the defendant.

Appellant's first proposition is that the defendant was prejudiced by certain alleged misconduct of the district attorney, it being claimed that that officer asked an improper question for the sole purpose of prejudicing the defendant in the minds of the jurors. Defendant's objection to the question was sustained by the court, and we cannot say that the district attorney was not acting in good faith. The record does not show any persistent course of action by the district attorney such as has sometimes been held to constitute prejudicial misconduct.

Appellant next complains of the court's refusal to give two requested instructions. The record does not show by whom those instructions were requested, but we will assume that they were proposed by defendant's counsel. The subject matter of those instructions was covered correctly by the court in other instructions given to the jury, and the refusal to give them in the precise form requested by the defendant did not deprive him of any right.

At the oral argument appellant's counsel suggested that the court erred in giving six of the instructions that were given. As to three of these, he stated no reasons why they were erroneous, and was unable to refer us to the pages of the clerk's transcript where they would be found. Subsequently he sent to us a memorandum of the pages. In two of the three instances there are two instructions on each page, and we do not know to which instruction counsel referred. Solving the doubt in his favor, we have examined all of them without discovering any valid objection thereto.

This leaves for consideration the instructions considered by counsel and designated as points 4, 5, and 6. Under point 5 his claim is that the instruction assumes the defendant to be guilty and thereby invades the province of the jury. In our opinion, the instruction contained no such assumption. Under points 4 and 6 the only objection was that those instructions had no application to the case as presented by the evidence. The point appears to be well taken with respect to one of those instructions, but it related to a minor matter, and the instruction was not at all likely to have affected the verdict.

As none of the points suggested have raised any doubtful question which seems to call for discussion and explanation of the law of the case, we deem it unnecessary to extend this opinion by setting forth the language of the instructions or stating our opinion in detail concerning them. Upon the record in this case, it appears that the defendant is fortunate, in that he was convicted of manslaughter, the lowest degree of the offense charged.

The judgment and order are affirmed.

James, J., and Shaw, J., concurred.

[Crim. No. 512. Second Appellate District.—November 2, 1916.]

THE PEOPLE, Respondent, v. FRANK RENWICK, Appellant.

CRIMINAL LAW—ROBBERY—EVIDENCE—USE OF STOLEN AUTOMOBILE— PREJUDICIAL ERROR.—Where, in a prosecution for robbery, it is shown that the persons engaged in the commission of the crime drove to the scene thereof in a Ford automobile about 7 o'clock in the evening, and the evidence is barely, if at all, sufficient to justify the verdict that the defendant participated in the robbery, it is prejudicial error to permit the owner of a Ford automobile to testify, over objection made by the defendant, that he left his machine at a corner about 4 o'clock in the afternoon, that it was gone when he returned there to get it about 8 o'clock, and that he found it at another place some hours later, in the absence of evidence identifying such machine as the automobile used by the perpetrators of the crime, except that both were Ford machines and the isinglass was out of the back thereof.

ID.—ALIBI—EVIDENCE—MODIFICATION OF TESTIMONY—REFUSAL TO PERMIT—PREJUDICIAL ERROR.—In such a prosecution it is prejudicial error to refuse to permit the defendant to recall a witness for the prosecution in surrebuttal for the purpose of permitting the witness to modify her testimony as to the presence of the defendant at a certain place at the time of the commission of the alleged crime.

APPEAL from a judgment of the Superior Court of Los Angeles County, and from an order denying a new trial. Frank R. Willis, Judge.

The facts are stated in the opinion of the court.

Guy Eddie, for Appellant.

U. S. Webb, Attorney-General, and Robert M. Clarke, Deputy Attorney-General, for Respondent.

CONREY, P. J.—Defendant was convicted of the crime of robbery and now appeals from the judgment and from an order denying his motion for a new trial. The grounds of appeal are that the evidence was insufficient to justify the verdict, and that the court erred in some of its rulings upon objections to offered testimony.

At between 7 and half-past 7 o'clock on the evening of
February 28, 1916, three masked men went into a butcher-
shop on Stephenson Avenue, in the City of Los Angeles, no
other persons being present at the time except the proprietor,
Mrs. Rosenbusch. They locked Mrs. Rosenbusch into a re-
frigerator, took from the till the money (about five dollars)
that was there, and speedily left the place. Mrs. Rosenbusch
testified to these facts and gave some description of the
young men, but the description was not sufficient to identify
any of them. According to the testimony of a police officer
named Raymond, who had been trailing and watching the
defendant and certain other young men, one Burns came to
the corner of Tenth and Los Angeles Streets at 6:35 P. M. in
a Ford automobile. At that place four men, Bill Shank,
Frank Shank, Fleming, and Renwick, got into the car with
Burns, and they drove east on Tenth Street. According to
the testimony of Earl Whitney, employed at a garage on
Stephenson Avenue, about six hundred feet east from the
Rosenbusch shop, a Ford automobile coming from the east
stopped near the garage at between 7 and 7:15 P. M., where
Renwick and Frank Shank got out of the machine and
walked west toward the Rosenbusch shop, and Burns was driving the machine. As they walked along, Renwick signaled
for the machine to follow and the machine passed along
in the same direction. It is in evidence that that is a much
frequented highway, and there is no evidence that these
were the only persons who passed along the street at about
the same time.

Over objections made by the defendant, one Gronsky was
permitted to testify that he was the owner of a Ford
machine which he left at the corner of Ninth and Spring
Streets at 4 o'clock that afternoon; that the machine was
gone when he returned there to get it at about 8 o'clock
P. M., and that he found it at another place some hours
later. There is no evidence identifying Gronsky's automobile with the one in which the defendant was seen by
the other witnesses, except that all three of these witnesses
describe a Ford machine which was not new, and each witness states that the isinglass was out of the back of the
machine which he saw. One Frank Richards testified that
at about a quarter after 7 he passed along Stephenson
Avenue opposite the Rosenbusch shop and his attention was

attracted to two men standing alongside of a building
opposite; that one of them pointed across the street toward
the shop, where Mrs. Rosenbusch was in the act of rolling
up a parcel for a customer. He testified that these men.
whom he afterward saw at the police station, were Burns
and Shank—not stating which one of the Shanks. Mrs.
Rosenbusch stated that immediately before the robbery
she had waited upon a customer, who had just gone out.
Two of the men who robbed the butcher-shop had revolvers
and threatened to shoot Mrs. Rosenbusch if she made resistance. It was proved by the testimony of police officers
that between 8 and half-past 8 o'clock the defendant and
the other men who had been in the automobile at Tenth
and Los Angeles Streets, came in separate groups to the
apartments at 1022 South Hill Street, where the defendant
and his wife were living. These men were arrested separately when they came from the apartment house at separate times during the course of the evening. The officers
found in the Renwick apartment two revolvers, three rifles,
and two shotguns.

While the evidence is sufficient to establish the existence
of suspicious circumstances concerning the defendant, it is
barely, if at all, sufficient to justify the verdict that Renwick participated in the Rosenbusch robbery. Assuming
it to be legally sufficient, the evidence of that fact is purely
circumstantial, and leaves the case in that condition where
errors in the admission or rejection of testimony would
easily turn the scale and be seriously prejudicial to the defendant.

The testimony of Gronsky had no relation to the case,
unless it was introduced for the purpose of showing that
the defendant or some of his associates had stolen Gronsky's
automobile and were using a stolen automobile at the time
of the Rosenbusch robbery. The evidence was insufficient
to establish that fact, and even if it had been sufficient
therefor, the evidence was not admissible for that purpose
in this action. It was not a case wherein the prosecution
was entitled to aid its proof of the charge on which Renwick then was being tried by proving that he had previously committed some other crime. Nevertheless. this
would very probably have the effect of creating prejudice
against the defendant in the minds of the jurors, and

render it easier to obtain from them a verdict that the defendant was guilty of the robbery at the butcher-shop.

On behalf of the defendant, Edward Biehl and his wife, Frances Biehl, testified that Renwick and his wife, some months before the date of this robbery, had occupied rooms in their apartment house at the corner of Washington Street and Maple Avenue; that Renwick came to that apartment house at about a quarter before 7 o'clock on the evening of February 28th and made inquiry to find out whether they would again permit him to occupy an apartment in their house; that Renwick remained there with them until at least as late as half-past 7; that prior to the evening of February 28th Renwick had not been there since the latter part of January. In rebuttal of this testimony the prosecution introduced as a witness Mrs. Gertrude Gorham, who had occupied rooms in the apartment house of the Biehls on February 28th. She stated that she saw Renwick call at Mrs. Biehl's on the morning of February 28th. She also stated that she saw Mr. and Mrs. Biehl that evening at their supper between 6 and 7 o'clock, and that at that time Mrs. Biehl told her that Renwick had been back there to rent rooms. Mr. and Mrs. Biehl had testified that they did not have their dinner that evening until a quarter to 8.

Mrs. Gorham was the last witness at the trial, and her testimony seems to have been given at the close of the day, and the last thing occurring before adjourning was the district attorney's statement, "We rest." On the opening of court the next morning defendant's counsel requested that he be permitted to call back Mrs. Gorham in surrebuttal. The court responded: "I will not open the case for any more evidence." Defendant's attorney replied: "I did not close last night, your Honor; I didn't rest my case, and I have positive information that the jury ought to hear from this witness, Mrs. Gorham, that she does not know within a month's time of the 28th whether the defendant Renwick was at the house there, and she will so testify if I put her on the stand." The court again refused the request and no further evidence was introduced. It can easily be seen that if the testimony of the witnesses Biehl was true, the defendant could not be guilty in this case. The testimony of Mrs. Gorham furnished the only evidence directly contradicting those two witnesses. It may have been the turning point in the case and may have been the controlling reason why the jury determined that the defendant's alibi was not proven. Since the request to call back Mrs Gorham was denied, we must assume that if she had been permitted to testify further, she would have modified her former testimony by admitting that she did not know within a month's time of February 28th whether the defendant Renwick was at that house. If this were so, then the time to which Mrs. Gorham referred might have been on or about the 31st of January, which was the time when Mrs. Biehl testified that Renwick had been there before. We cannot avoid the conclusion that the defendant was entitled to that additional testimony of Mrs. Gorham, and that the refusal to admit it was so prejudicial that the error must be held to constitute a miscarriage of justice by denying the defendant an important and very substantial right in a matter vital to this defense.

The judgment and order are reversed.

James, J., and Shaw, J., concurred.

[Crim. No. 846.   Third Appellate District.—November 2, 1916.]

THE PEOPLE, Respondent, v. HENRY J. BLUNKALL et al., Appellants.

CRIMINAL LAW — ACCOMPLICE — CORROBORATIVE EVIDENCE.—The testimony necessary to corroborate that of an accomplice is sufficient if it, of itself, tends to connect the defendant with the commission of the offense, although it is slight, and entitled, when standing by itself, to but little consideration.

ID.—NATURE OF CORROBORATING EVIDENCE.—The corroboration required may be made by circumstantial as well as by direct evidence.

ID.—QUANTUM OF PROOF OF CORROBORATION—INSTRUCTION.—An instruction that corroborating evidence is sufficient if it tends to connect the defendant with the commission of the offense, though of itself, standing alone, "it would be entitled to little weight," correctly states the rule as to the *quantum* of proof essential to the corroboration of an accomplice.

ID.—CREDIBILITY OF DEFENDANT—INSTRUCTION.—An instruction that a
defendant in any criminal case is a competent witness in his own
behalf, and the fact that he is a defendant is not of itself sufficient
to impeach or discredit his testimony, though the jury are entitled
to take into consideration his interest in the event of the prosecution
in determining his credibility, violates the rule that instructions
which purport to state the rules by which the credibility of witnesses or the weight of evidence is to be determined should be made
applicable to all the witnesses or all the testimony.

APPEAL from a judgment of the Superior Court of
Tehama County, and from an order denying a new trial.
John F. Ellison, Judge.

The facts are stated in the opinion of the court.

James T. Matlock, for Appellants.

U. S. Webb, Attorney-General, and J. Charles Jones,
Deputy Attorney-General, for Respondent.

HART, J.—The defendants were jointly charged by information duly filed in the superior court of Tehama County
with the crime of grand larceny. The defendants Henry
J. Blunkall and Oliver L. Blunkall were convicted of the
crime so charged, and prosecute this appeal from the judgment of conviction and the order denying their motion for
a new trial.

The defendant Scott, who was not on trial in this case,
was made a witness for the people, and as such gave testimony against his codefendants, the Blunkalls, and it is
claimed by the latter: 1. That the verdict is not supported
by the evidence, because the testimony of Scott was not corroborated as required by section 1111 of the Penal Code;
2. That the court committed prejudicial error in its action
in disposing of certain instructions proposed by the respective parties.

The information charges and the evidence shows that the
crime of which the defendants were accused and found guilty
was committed on or about the twenty-seventh day of August, 1915, and that it consisted of the unlawful and felonious
stealing, taking, and driving away of seven head of cattle,
which were the property of one H. W. Purcell.

Purcell owned twelve head of cattle and kept them on an inclosed range near a place called Red Bank, about five miles southwest from Red Bluff, Tehama County. The defendant Scott resided at Burbank, and Purcell's home was about three miles from that place. Scott knew the Purcell herd of cattle, they having ranged up and down near where he resided, and knew that Purcell owned said cattle. Late on the afternoon of August 26, 1915, Purcell went to the range and there saw the cattle. On the last day of August, 1915, he again visited the range and thereupon discovered that seven head of his herd were missing. He proceeded to search for the missing cattle and, on the eighth day of September, 1915, after several days of continuous prosecution of the search, found the seven head on a range in the mountains, in what is generally known as Mill Creek canyon, approximately thirty miles from the range from which they were taken. The defendants, the Blunkalls, had ranged their own cattle on the range on which the missing cattle were found.

The cattle taken from Purcell, before they were driven away, bore the earmarks of Purcell, but did not up to that time carry a brand of any character. When found in the mountains it was discovered that the earmarks upon the cattle had been changed, so that they no longer resembled those of Purcell, and that some of the seven head had been branded with a double "B" brand, viz., "BB," while others. had been branded with the letter "S."

The defendant Scott testified that he and the defendants Henry and Oliver Blunkall stole and drove the cattle off the Purcell range on the night of August 26, 1915, to the range in Mill Creek canyon. Scott's story as he told it on the witness-stand is, briefly, this: "That, prior to the occasion on which the cattle were taken from the Purcell range, he had talked with Henry and Oliver Blunkall, who are brothers, about "picking up" cattle whenever an opportunity for safely taking them presented itself. Thereafter Scott visited Chico and there met the Blunkalls. He told. them that there were grazing near his place several head of unmarked and unbranded cattle. The Blunkalls replied that they would go to the Scott house within a few days and take the cattle referred to by Scott. In pursuance of this understanding, the Blunkalls went to Scott's home on the twenty-sixth day of August, 1915, arriving there in the early morning, long before daybreak. They drove there in a spring-wagon, taking with them saddles and other equipments for horseback riding. On reaching the Scott place they retired to bed, and remained about the place during most of the twenty-sixth day of August. Scott and Oliver Blunkall went out over the range during that day to inspect the cattle and the situation generally. They found that there were only two head of unmarked cattle on the range. Scott expressed the fear that if they took the marked cattle they would readily be detected, but Oliver Blunkall said that they might as well take the marked cattle; that he could so change the marks they then bore that they could not be identified, so far as the marks were concerned. At a late hour of the night of the twenty-sixth day of August, the three defendants, each riding a horse, went to the range, and drove therefrom eight head of cattle, one of the eight being the property of another party. On their way to the Mill Creek canyon with the eight head, they took a calf from a neighboring ranch which belonged to one Barney Bauder. Thus they drove to the mountains nine head of cattle. Scott said that the agreement between the Blunkalls and himself was that the stock should be equally divided, each to take three head; that when they arrived at the canyon the Blunkalls changed the marks on all the marked cattle and branded them. The six which were taken by the Blunkalls as their share were branded with the Blunkall brand, viz., "BB." Scott's three were branded with his brand, viz., the letter "S."

The wife and daughter of Scott testified that the Blunkall brothers were at the Scott house on the twenty-sixth day of August, arriving there in a spring-wagon early in the morning and immediately retiring to bed; that they brought with them their saddles, and remained about the house most of the time during that day. Both testified that they heard Scott and the Blunkalls "planning" the taking of the cattle pasturing "out on the plains." Mrs. Scott said she heard the three defendants say that they intended "to take those cattle on the plains" to Mill Creek canyon. Both mother and daughter testified that a Mrs. Baldwin and a Mr. Eckert, who resided in the neighborhood of the Scotts, visited the house of the latter on August 26th, in the daytime, and that the Blunkalls attempted to avoid being seen by them. The daughter said that Henry Blunkall, upon observing Eckert coming to the Scott home, went into the hou e, whereupon Mrs. Scott asked him, "What is the matter?" to which Henry replied that he did not desire to be seen by anyone, "especially Mr. Eckert, as he would know he was up there doing something, and he did not want him to see him when he was out doing that kind of business." The young woman also testified that a social dance in the district schoolhouse was scheduled for the evening of the 26th of August, and that Oliver Blunkall asked her about the dance and whether she thought there would be a large attendance thereat, and that she replied, expressing the opinion that the affair would be largely attended. "He then said he guessed they wouldn't interfere with the business of taking the cattle." Both the mother and daughter testified that the three defendants left the Scott place on horseback late on the night of the twenty-sixth day of August, and that Scott did not return to his home after that night until the following Sunday, which was the twenty-ninth day of August.

Both Mrs. Scott and her daughter detailed other circumstances connected with the presence of the Blunkalls at the Scott home, which tended to show that those defendants had gone there for the purpose of carrying out the scheme of the three men to take the cattle of Purcell or "the cattle pasturing on the plains"; but we have already presented in substance enough of the testimony of those witnesses to demonstrate that the testimony of Scott was fully corroborated. Indeed, we make bold to say that if there was no other testimony in the case tending to connect the Blunkalls and Scott with the commission of the crime charged but the testimony of Mrs. Scott and that of her daughter, as it is briefly stated above, a reviewing court would go beyond its legitimate function in setting aside a verdict predicated thereon.

Section 1111 of the Penal Code provides, in part: "A conviction cannot be had upon the testimony of an accomplice unless it be corroborated by such other evidence as shall tend to connect the defendant with the commission of the offense; and the corroboration is not sufficient if it merely shows the commission of the offense or the circumstances thereof."

If there be some independent evidence fairly tending to connect the defendant with the commission of the crime, then the testimony of the accomplice is corroborated within the intent of the above section. (*People* v. *Garnett*, 29 Cal. 622; *People* v. *Clough*, 73 Cal. 348, [15 Pac. 5]; *People* v. *Miller*, 65 Iowa, 60, [21 N. W. 181]; *People* v. *Mayhew*, 150 N. Y. 346, [44 N. E. 971].)

In *People* v. *McLean*, 84 Cal. 480, 482, [24 Pac. 32], it is said: "The corroborating evidence is sufficient if it, of itself, tends to connect the defendant with the commission of the offense, although it is slight, and entitled, when standing by itself, to but little consideration. (See *People* v. *Melvane*, 39 Cal. 616.)"

It is true, as is contended, that the "corroborating testimony" in this case consists of circumstantial evidence, but the corroboration required by the section named may properly be made by circumstantial as well as by direct evidence. The circumstances detailed by the corroborating witnesses here are of the most incriminatory character, and, as above stated, sufficient of themselves to fasten guilt upon the accused. They therefore went beyond the requirement of the rule relative to the corroboration of the testimony of an accomplice.

The appellants complain of the following instruction, and declare that it involves an erroneous statement of the rule: "While corroborating evidence must create more than a mere suspicion, it is not required that it be of itself sufficient to convict, nor need it extend to every fact and detail covered by the statements of the accomplice. It is sufficient if, standing alone, it tends to connect the defendants with the crime. It is sufficient if it tends to connect the defendants with the commission of the offense, though of itself, standing alone, it would be entitled to but little weight."

The objection to said instruction may best be stated in counsel's own language as follows: "The words 'it would be entitled to but little weight' is an erroneous instruction. The court should have given the jury the positive instruction that such testimony is not sufficient upon which to convict." We confess that we are not entirely clear regarding the precise point which counsel thus attempts to urge as the ground of his objection to the instruction. If he means to contend that the court should have stated it as a general

proposition to the jury that evidence offered for the purpose
of corroborating the testimony of an accomplice can never
be sufficient to justify a conviction, the obvious reply is that
there is no legal ground or reason upon which such a proposition may be supported.   That evidence corroborative of
the testimony of an accomplice might be sufficient to justify
a conviction, there can be no possible doubt, and no better
illustration of this proposition can be found than in the
present case.   The instruction clearly and correctly states
the rule as to the *quantum* of proof essential to the corroboration of an accomplice, and plainly told the jury, in
effect, that, while corroborative evidence need not, and might
not, when taken alone, be sufficient to warrant the conviction of a person charged with crime, it would meet the test
as corroborative proof if it merely tended to connect the
defendant with the commission of the offense.   This involved
an accurate statement of the rule as the legislature has written it.

The court refused to adopt and read to the jury a number
of instructions proposed by the defendants, and it is insisted
that in its action in so doing it erred to the serious detriment of the defendants' rights at the trial.   One or two only
of the assignments under this head merit special attention.

The following is one of the refused instructions preferred
by the accused: "The jury are instructed that a defendant
in any criminal case is a competent witness on his own behalf, and the fact that he is a defendant is not of itself sufficient to impeach or discredit his testimony, though the
jury are entitled to take into consideration his interest in
the event of the prosecution in determining his credibility."
The instruction was wholly inapplicable to the case, inasmuch as neither of the defendants on trial was called to
testify.   Moreover, the instruction, if pertinent, would be
subject to the objection that it singles out the testimony of
a particular witness, and instructions which purport to state
the tests or rules by which the credibility of witnesses or the
weight of evidence is to be determined should be made applicable, not to a single witness or his testimony only, but
to all the witnesses or all the testimony.

The defendants requested an instruction declaring that the
witness W. A. Scott, one of the defendants, was an accomplice, and the court denied the request.   We perceive in the

court's refusal to so instruct the jury no prejudicial error. It is true that it was established beyond controversy that Scott was an accomplice, if the crime charged was committed as he declared it to have been; still, the court clearly explained to the jury who an accomplice in crime is under our law, and with equal clearness stated that the Blunkalls could not legally be convicted upon the uncorroborated testimony of an accomplice.

We have now considered all the objections to the action of the trial court in disallowing instructions proposed by the accused which we think deserve special notice. It is sufficient to say of the other instructions so proposed and rejected which were pertinent to the issues of the case that they involved the statement of principles which the court, in clear language, announced to the jury in its charge. And, in this connection, it is to be said that the charge of the court contained a full and correct statement of every rule or principle of law applicable to the issues or vital facts developed by the proofs.

The appellants appear to have been accorded a fair and impartial trial, the verdict seems to be supported by ample evidence, and the record is free from prejudicial error.

The judgment and the order are therefore affirmed.

Chipman, P. J., and Burnett, J., concurred.

[Crim. No. 507. Second Appellate District.—November 3, 1916.]

THE PEOPLE, Respondent, v. BRUCE WING, Appellant.

CRIMINAL LAW—BURGLARY—EVIDENCE—CONFESSION.—In a prosecution for the crime of burglary, it is not error to admit in evidence the alleged confession of the defendant, where the *corpus delicti* is established and the confession shown to have been free and voluntary.

ID.—DEFENSE OF ALIBI—TEMPTATION TO RESORT TO—INSTRUCTION.—In such prosecution, it is not an invasion of the province of the jury to give an instruction which contained a statement which suggested to them that the defense of an alibi was occasionally fabricated and that temptation to resort to it might be great in cases of importance.

APPEAL from a judgment of the Superior Court of Los Angeles County, and from an order denying a new trial. Frank R. Willis, Judge.

The facts are stated in the opinion of the court.

C. B. Conlin, for Appellant.

U. S. Webb, Attorney-General, and Robert M. Clarke, Deputy Attorney-General, for Respondent.

JAMES, J.—Appellant was convicted of the crime of burglary of the first degree, and appeals from a judgment of imprisonment and an order denying his motion for a new trial.

The evidence showed that during the month of October, 1915, the appellant visited the salesroom of an automobile dealer in the city of Los Angeles and remained about the place for an hour or so. He made inquiries regarding the purchase of a machine, stating that a physician named McLaughlin desired to buy a car and that if it was purchased that he (appellant) would be employed to drive it. He particularly looked over an "Enger" automobile which was standing on the floor, that machine being painted a cream color; he inquired as to whether it was in running order and ready to be used, and something about the method of operating it. He left the place late in the afternoon and the salesroom was closed up that evening as usual; it being Saturday of the week. On the following day one of the salesmen returned to the place and found that the cream-colored machine at which appellant had been looking was gone. A tire had also been taken from another machine standing in the place. About six months later officers who had been working on the case found an automobile in a closed garage in the lower part of the city which answered the description on the "Enger" automobile. The machine, however, had been painted black, and even the hub caps, which had borne the name "Enger" cut in the metal, had been covered with some substance so as to obliterate the lettering, and the caps, which had been nickel, were also painted black like the rest of the machine. The number had been removed from the automobile and generally it had been disguised as much as could be. The under part of the hood, however, which was not exposed to view, still remained a cream color. The officers watched this garage for a day or so before any one came to take out the machine. Appellant then appeared and, opening the garage, busied himself about the machine. The officers appearing casually to pass by, stopped and inquired of appellant what kind of a machine it was, and he replied that it was a "Pilot." They then asked him to whom it belonged and he said that it belonged to a Dr. McLaughlin, who lived at a certain number on Ditman Street. The officers thereupon disclosed their official identity and requested appellant to take them to the doctor's residence. Appellant replied that he had an engagement with the doctor to meet him there at that time. After waiting a half hour or more, the officers got into the machine with appellant and he drove them to Ditman Street; they searched carefully on both sides of the street in the block containing the number which appellant had given them, but failed to find that any such person as McLaughlin lived in that neighborhood. Thereupon, after having the automobile identified by the owners, they conducted appellant to the jail, where he thereafter remained. Soon after his arrest the appellant was brought into the presence of the detectives and questioned regarding how he had come into possession of the machine. The officers testified that the statement was free and voluntary and not induced by any threats, intimidation, or promises of any sort. While the questions were being asked, one of the officers operating a typewriter took down the questions and answers. In this statement, which was afterward signed by the appellant, the appellant stated that on the day preceding the taking of the automobile he had visited the salesroom where the automobile was kept, and on the same night, at about 11 o'clock, he had returned there, entered through a window, and. after opening the large rear door which was barred, had taken an extra tire from another machine and had driven the "Enger" automobile away and secreted it in a garage, where it remained for some time; that during the time he first had it in the garage he repainted and disguised it; that thereafter he used it in livery service for the purpose of earning money.

It is contended on the part of appellant that the evidence was insufficient to establish the *corpus delicti,* and that therefore the admission of the confession of appellant was error. We do not agree with appellant in this contention, for it seems to us that the facts which we have first briefly stated establish fully that the automobile was unlawfully taken from the possession of the owner and from a building which had been closed and fastened on that night. Three witnesses who were employed about the automobile salesroom all testified to facts from which an irresistible inference would arise that the machine was taken without the consent of any person authorized to give it. The circumstances tended to show also that it was taken during the night-time.

There was no error in the admission of the alleged confession of appellant upon the ground that the confession was not shown to have been voluntary, for the officers testified that no inducement, threat, or other improper influence was exerted upon the appellant to induce him to make the statement. In the statement, which was reduced to writing, defendant was shown to have been asked this question: "All of these statements you have just made have been free and voluntary, have they?" to which the answer was given, "Yes." He was then asked as to whether any threats had been made, or any offers of reward or immunity, and he answered in the negative.

The evidence clearly supports the verdict of the jury.

It is complained that an instruction which the trial judge gave and which contained a statement which suggested to the jury that the defense of an alibi was occasionally fabricated and that temptation to resort to it might be great in cases of importance was erroneous, in that it invaded the province of the jury. The instruction as a whole, a part of which only we have referred to, was copied *verbatim* from one approved by the supreme court in the case of *People* v. *Lee Gam,* 69 Cal. 552, [11 Pac. 183]. In that case the supreme court held that such an instruction did not violate any substantial right of the defendant. No other ground for reversal is urged.

The judgment and order are affirmed.

Conrey, P. J., and Shaw, J., concurred.

[Civ. No. 1587. Third Appellate District.—November 3, 1916.]

M. LEVY, Respondent, v. ORRIN S. HENDERSON, Appellant.

LANDLORD AND TENANT—RECOVERY OF POSSESSION—WITHHOLDING OF PREMISES—SUFFICIENCY OF EVIDENCE.—In an action for rent and for restitution of premises, a finding that the defendant was withholding the possession of the premises at the time of the commencement of the action is sufficiently supported by evidence that he still had a key thereto, that he had not paid the rent, and that his goods were still contained therein.

ID.—DENIAL OF LANDLORD'S TITLE—NOTICE TO QUIT.—If a tenant denies his landlord's title, the denial makes him a trespasser, and he is not entitled to notice to quit before the commencement of an action by the landlord to recover possession of the premises.

APPEAL from a judgment of the Superior Court of San Joaquin County. J. A. Plummer, Judge.

The facts are stated in the opinion of the court.

A. H. Carpenter, for Appellant.

Gordon A. Stewart, for Respondent.

BURNETT, J.—The action was for rent and for restitution of premises.

The court found that on or about the twenty-eighth day of September, 1913, the plaintiff leased to defendant the ground floor of certain premises in Stockton known as the Aurora Flour Mills, from month to month, at the rental of fifteen dollars per month, and that said lease was not in writing; "that by virtue of said lease the defendant went into the possession of said floor space of said premises, and continued to occupy and hold the same as the tenant of the plaintiff until the month of July, 1914, at which time, by the mutual consent and agreement of the plaintiff and defendant, the plaintiff leased and demised to the defendant and the defendant leased from the plaintiff, the annex to the Aurora Flour Mills, which annex is a building annexed to and forming a part of the Aurora Flour Mills upon the same rental, to wit: $15.00 per month . . . and that the said defendant ever since the said month of July,

1914, and up to the present time has been, and he is now, in the exclusive possession and occupancy of said annex" as tenant of said plaintiff and "under said agreement."

Then follows a finding that no part of said rent has been paid and that the amount owing is $405, and that on or about April 25, 1916, plaintiff served upon defendant a written notice that he pay said rent or surrender said premises, but that defendant refused to do either, and that he "still withholds from the plaintiff the possession of said premises and still refuses and neglects to pay the plaintiff said rent or any part thereof as well as the accruing rent."

Judgment followed for plaintiff in acco: lance with the prayer of his complaint.

There is no merit in the contention that the evidence is insufficient to support the finding as to the execution of the lease. Mr. Levy testified: "Mr. Henderson asked me, telling me that he had to leave his place, if I want to rent him the Aurora Flouring Mill; I say I have no objection, but I will rent to him on one proviso, that I don't take any risk regarding fire, theft, destruction, and so on, but he to vacate as soon as I got a permanent tenant or sell the property; and he was satisfied. He said, 'All right.' Then he asked me what I would charge him; I told him I will charge him fifteen dollars per month. I called my man, Mr. Terry, and introduced him to Mr. Henderson. Mr. Terry had the keys, and he gave one of the keys to Mr. Henderson, the key for the front door of the Aurora Flour Mills."

Mr. Terry testified: "Mr. Levy called me and gave me an introduction to Mr. Henderson and said: 'This is our new tenant,' he mentioned the fact, and he said: 'Mr. Henderson was going to take over part of the mill to use as his part.' . . . So I took one of the keys and gave Mr. Henderson one of the keys; one of the keys was supposed to be in Mr. Henderson's possession, and I had this other key for the privilege of going in there and turning the water into the large tank which was there for the purpose of fire, and I did this every two weeks."

There is also testimony to the effect that in July, or at least the summer of 1914, the lease, with the consent of the appellant, was modified so as to give him the use and occupancy of the annex instead of the main building, on the same terms as in the original agreement. Mr. Levy testified that there was no change in the terms of the original agreement, and Mr.

Terry's testimony in reference to a conversation with Mr.
Henderson in the summer of 1914 was: "I went out to Mr.
Henderson's house a couple of times. I couldn't find him,
so I telephoned out and I met Mr. Henderson at the door, and
I told Mr. Henderson in a quiet way, Mr. Levy had requested
us to move the stuff, and Mr. Henderson said he would be
down in the morning. He was to move his stuff and clean the
place out. He moved it into the annex."

Mr. Henderson, the defendant, was asked if his equipment was moved at the time he received from Terry notice
to move it out of the main building into the annex, and he
replied that it was so moved under his supervision, and that
he still had his merchandise there. It is certainly a fair inference from the foregoing that there was an agreement for the
use and occupancy of the premises as claimed by plaintiff, and
that under said contract defendant went into said possession.
There is also evidence, which we need not set out, that defendant's occupancy of said annex was exclusive, he being in the
sole occupancy of the same.

The theory of appellant, it may be said, is that the transaction constituted a bailment, that he never took possession of
the premises, but, on the contrary, delivered his goods to the
respondent, and that the latter from that time on held the
goods in his possession. We need not enter upon a consideration of the principles involved in such bailment, for it is sufficient to say that conceding there is some evidence in support
of such theory, it is clear that the findings of the court to the
contrary were entirely warranted.

It is equally plain that the evidence justified the finding
that defendant was withholding the possession of the premises
at the time of the commencement of the action. He still had
the key to the annex of the building and his goods were even,
to the time of the trial, within the premises. It is also undisputed that the rent was unpaid. The defendant himself so
testified as to his possession and the nonpayment of the rent.

It is objected by appellant that the three-day notice was
ineffectual, for the reason that more than one year had elapsed
since the defendant had been in arrears in the payment of his
rent. This position is taken by virtue of section 1161 of the
Code of Civil Procedure. We deem it unnecessary to attempt
elucidation of that provision, although we venture the suggestion it was not intended to protect a tenant from month to

month in the indefinite withholding of the leased premises. The forbearance of the landlord for more than a year to press his claim for rent or to obtain possession would surely not defeat his action altogether in a proceeding of this kind, but might result in the loss of the rent accruing in the period antedating the twelve months. But this need not be decided, as the notice can be entirely disregarded. This follows from the consideration that the relation of landlord and tenant was denied by defendant, and, hence, no such notice was required. The principle applies that was announced in *Cox* v. *Delmas*, 99 Cal. 104, 121, [33 Pac. 836]. Therein it was said: "When the time has come for the doing of an act which it is the duty of the defendant to do unconditionally, no demand other than the suit itself is necessary; nor is a demand before suit required where it appears that it would have been unavailing, and would not have changed the rights and relations of the parties, or where the answer denies the relation on which the action is founded, although a demand and refusal would otherwise be a condition precedent to the right of the plaintiff to maintain the action."

Moreover, it has been expressly held in this state that notice is waived by a denial of the relation of landlord and tenant. By such denial the tenancy is, in fact, forfeited, and the tenant becomes a trespasser. (*Smith* v. *Ogg Shaw*, 16 Cal. 88; *Dodge* v. *Walley*, 22 Cal. 225, [83 Am. Dec. 61]; *Bolton* v. *Landers*, [No. 1], 27 Cal. 104; *Simpson* v. *Applegate*, 75 Cal. 342, 345, [17 Pac. 237].)

We think the judgment is just and legal, and it is therefore affirmed.

Chipman, P. J., and Hart, J., concurred.

A petition to have the cause heard in the supreme court, after judgment in the district court of appeal, was denied by the supreme court on January 2, 1917.

[Crim. No. 357.   Third Appellate District.—November 3, 1916.]

THE PEOPLE, Respondent, v. J. E. CARRELL, Appellant.

CRIMINAL LAW—FELLATIO—INSUFFICIENT INFORMATION.—An information charging a defendant with the commission of the acts technically known as *fellatio* upon the person of a human being by force and violence and against the will of such person, fails to state a public offense, in the absence of any definition of such term, or of any statement of the particular acts constituting the alleged offense.

ID.—INFORMATION—ESSENTIALS OF.—An information must contain a statement of acts constituting the offense in ordinary and concise language, and in such manner as to enable a person of common understanding to know what is intended.

APPEAL from a judgment of the Superior Court of Sonoma County, and from an order denying a new trial. Emmet Seawell, Judge.

The facts are stated in the opinion of the court.

R. M. Quackenbush, for Appellant.

U. S. Webb, Attorney-General, and J. Charles Jones, Deputy Attorney-General, for Respondent.

CHIPMAN, P. J.—Defendant was convicted of a felony under section 288a of the Penal Code, and was sentenced to imprisonment at San Quentin for the period of seven years. He appeals from the judgment of conviction and from the order denying his motion for a new trial.

The charging part of the information is as follows: "Did willfully, unlawfully and feloniously commit the acts technically known as *fellatio* upon the person of one Ethel Carrell, a human being, by force and violence and against the will of the said Ethel Carrell, contrary," etc.

Section 288a of the Penal Code was passed in 1915 and is as follows: "The acts technically known as *fellatio* and *cunnilingus* are hereby declared to be felonies and any person convicted of the commission of either thereof shall be punished by imprisonment in the state prison for not more than fifteen years."

Defendant demurred to the information on the ground that it "does not contain a statement of the acts constituting the offense, in ordinary and concise language, and in a manner to enable a person of common understanding to know what is intended"; that the information is not direct and certain "as it regards the crime charged therein"; and that the facts stated do not constitute a public offense. The demurrer was overruled. The motion for a new trial was on the grounds that the court misdirected the jury in that the offense defined by the court "is not included in the word *fellatio* as defined in its technical use"; also, on the ground that the prosecuting witness was an accomplice, and her testimony was not corroborated as required by section 1111 of the Penal Code. Upon the denial of defendant's motion for a new trial, he moved in arrest of judgment on the foregoing grounds, which motion was also denied. Neither the statute nor the information defines what is meant by the term "*fellatio.*" No definition of this word have we been able to find in any English dictionary. The particular acts constituting the crime of *fellatio* are not set forth in the information, and as none of the ordinary sources of information would enlighten defendant on the subject, how can it be said that "the acts constituting the offense" were charged in such a manner as to enable "a person of common understanding to know what is intended?" (Pen. Code, sec. 950.) In *People* v. *Ah Sum*, 92 Cal. 648, [28 Pac. 680], the information was held insufficient and judgment arrested because in a portion of the information the lottery ticket involved in the transaction was set out in Chinese characters. The court said: "An indictment or information must contain a statement of acts constituting the offense in ordinary and concise language, and in such manner as to enable a person of common understanding to know what is intended. (Pen. Code, sec. 950.) An information partly in English and partly in Chinese cannot be said to be in ordinary language. The constitution requires judicial proceedings to be conducted, preserved, and published in no other language than the English language. (Const., art. IV, sec. 24.) Mr. Bishop says: 'In some of our states there are statutes expressly excluding all languages but the English, and such is clearly the general American law.' " See, also, *Stevens* v. *Kobayshi*, 20 Cal. App. 153, [128 Pac. 419], where the rule was applied in a civil case for libel.

Unexplained, the word *"fellatio"* would, to a man of common understanding (indeed, we think also to one of uncommon understanding), be as cabalistic as if written in Egyptian or Mexican hieroglyphics or in Japanese or Chinese characters. The attorney for the defendant says in his brief: "The defendant entered into the trial of this case, and so did his attorney, without any knowledge of what the word *'fellatio'* would be defined to mean as used in the statute, or what the elements constituting the offense might be, but rather supposed" the court would instruct in accordance with a definition the attorney found in Andrew's Latin-English Lexicon. In this sense the definition might not meet the act proven but would seem to apply to the woman rather than the man. This is mentioned to emphasize the soundness of the statutory rule that the offense must be so stated as to be intelligible to a person of common understanding. Under no other rule could a defendant safely go to trial. The circumstance is mentioned also for the reason that it is by no means certain what acts the legislature intended to characterize as the crime of *fellatio*. We do not find it spoken of in any work on criminal law, and its introduction into our statutes is of so recent a date that the courts have not been called upon to deal with it so far as we are aware until this case arose.

The exigencies of the case do not seem to require that we should stain the pages of our reports with the definition as given, or to enlighten the profession or the public as to what the learned trial judge found it necessary to inform the jury the legislature meant when it announced *"fellatio"* as a felony.

We are entirely satisfied that the defendant should not have been forced to trial upon this information; that his demurrer should have been sustained, failing in which his motion in arrest of judgment should have been granted and a new trial accorded him.

The judgment and order are reversed.

Hart, J., and Burnett, J., concurred.

A petition to have the cause heard in the supreme court, after judgment in the district court of appeal, was denied by the supreme court on January 2, 1917.

[Civ. No. 1586. Third Appellate District.—November 4, 1916.]

ERNEST A. VICTORS, Respondent, v. E. C. KELSEY, County Treasurer, etc., Appellant.

COUNTIES—EXPENSE INCURRED IN CRIMINAL ACTION—ATTENDANCE OF EXPERT—AUTHORITY OF DISTRICT ATTORNEY—APPROVAL BY SUPERVISORS—DETERMINATION CONCLUSIVE.—That district attorney of a county has authority, under the provisions of subdivision 2 of section 4307 of the Political Code, to incur an expense in procuring the attendance of an expert upon the trial of a criminal action to testify as to the result of certain blood tests made by the witness, and where the incurring of such expense is approved by the board of supervisors, the determination of the board is not subject to review by the courts.

APPEAL from a judgment of the Superior Court of Plumas County. J. O. Moncur, Judge.

The facts are stated in the opinion of the court.

L. N. Peter, and L. H. Hughes, for Appellant.

Frederick L. Berry, for Respondent.

CHIPMAN, P. J.—Mandate. Petitioner is a resident of the city and county of San Francisco, a physician and surgeon of many years' practice. The nature of the action sufficiently appears from the following findings:

"VI.

"That in the determination of the said cause, '*People of the State of California* v. *Frank S. Cook*,' and in preparing said cause for trial in behalf of the plaintiff therein, it became material and important to said plaintiff that certain experimental tests be made to determine whether or not certain specimens were or were not human blood stains; that the said District Attorney of the said County of Plumas duly engaged and duly employed and subpoenaed the petitioner herein to make said experimental tests upon certain specimens then and there submitted to him prior to the trial of said action and for the purpose above stated, and in anticipation of calling the said petitioner as an expert witness at the trial of said cause to testify as to the results of said experimental tests;

that the petitioner herein did make said experimental tests
upon certain specimens duly submitted to him and in pursuance of his employment as aforesaid for the purpose of preparing as a witness in the trial of the said cause, and was
duly and regularly subpoenaed therefor at the City and
County of San Francisco, State of California, to attend and
did attend upon the trial of said cause in the City of Quincy,
County of Plumas, on the 10th and 11th days of February,
1915, and was then and there duly called as a witness in said
cause and testified as an expert witness thereat for the purpose of testifying to the result of said experimental tests
above referred to, and his said testimony then and there
became a part of the record of the trial and proceedings of
said action.

"VII.

"That thereafter, to wit, on February 11; 1915, the petitioner herein filed and presented in due form to the Board of
Supervisors of Plumas County his bill, claim and demand for
payment of his services rendered as referred to above for the
making of said experimental test recited therein and above
referred to, and for testifying in relation as set forth and
referred to above and for his necessary expenses incurred in
attending said trial.   Said bill, demand and claim were filed
in due form with the Board of Supervisors of said Plumas
County on the 11th day of February, 1915; that said Board
of Supervisors received said claim and demand, fully and
duly considered the same and duly acted thereon and approved the same, and allowed the same, and ordered the said
claim be duly paid to the petitioner herein and that the
Auditor of said Plumas County issue his warrant forthwith
for the payment of said claim from the general fund of the
Treasury of said County; that thereupon said bill and demand
was duly audited by said Auditor of said County of Plumas,
was duly allowed and issued his warrant upon the said Treasurer of said County of Plumas on the 2nd day of March, 1915,
payable to the petitioner for the sum of Two Hundred
seventy-two dollars and twenty cents ($272.20) in payment of
said claim, demand and bill, and said warrant provided that
said payment should be made from the general fund of the
Treasury of said County; and that said bill, claim and
demand was in the form and as set forth and alleged in the
first amended petition herein and as set forth and appended

thereto in a copy thereof and marked as Exhibit 'A' and made a part of said first amended petition herein.

"VIII.

"That immediately subsequent to March 2, 1915, and prior to the filing of the petition herein the petitioner duly presented said claim and demand as allowed and as set forth above and in the form alleged herein to the said Treasurer of said Plumas County at the office of said Treasurer during the business hours thereof and that said Treasurer refused to pay the same and still continues to refuse to pay the same, and offered as a reason for said refusal that the item in said claim designated 'February 10th, 11th, one and one-half days' service as witness $150.00' was and is illegal and does not and did not constitute a legal charge against the said County of Plumas. . . .

"X.

"That there was and is at all of the times mentioned in said petition sufficient money in the hands of the County Treasurer, County of Plumas, State of California, in the proper fund in the hand of said Treasurer with which to pay said demand."

No objection is made to the form of the claim. The items were:

"Date.	Items.	'Amount.
Jan. 19.	Examination and Experimental tests of Four specimens for the purpose of determining as to whether the same were Human Blood..................	$100.00
Feb. 10–11.	1½ days' service as witness $150.00 and expenses to Quincy, as a witness and return, $22.20......................	172.00
		$272.20"

Indorsed as follows:

"Expenditures authorized and approved by me.
                                        "M. C. Kerr,
                                        "Dist. Atty."

"Examined. A legal charge.
                                        "M. C. Kerr,
                                        "Dist. Atty."

"Allowed by Board of Supervisors March 2, 1915, for $272.20, payable out of the General Fund.
"Countersigned—H. J. TRELEAVEN,
"Chairman Board of Supervisors.
"Attest: F. R. YOUNG,
"Clerk of Board of Supervisors.
"Warrant No. 577. Allowed March 2, 1915, for $272.20, payable out of the General Fund.
"F. R. YOUNG,
"County Auditor."

As conclusions of law, the court found that petitioner is entitled to a peremptory writ of mandate directed to E. C. Kelsey, treasurer of Plumas County, commanding him to pay said claim to petitioner with interest at seven per cent per annum from March 2, 1915, and judgment was accordingly entered.

The appeal is from said judgment on the judgment-roll alone.

The only item challenged for its illegality is the charge of $150 for per diem services as a witness. And appellant contends that petitioner was entitled only to the usual and ordinary witness fees. (Pol. Code, sec. 4300g; Pen. Code, sec. 1329.)

It must be conceded that unless the district attorney was authorized by law to engage the services of petitioner in an expert capacity and agree to compensate him for his services as such, the contention of appellant must prevail. If, however, the district attorney had such authority and no objection to the claim arising out of the exercise of that authority is made other than want of authority, it was the duty of the treasurer to pay the claim and mandate will lie to compel its performance.

Section 4307 of the Political Code provides as follows: "The following are county charges: . . . 2. The traveling and other personal expenses of the district attorney, incurred in criminal cases arising in the county, . . . and all other expenses necessarily incurred by him in the detection of crime and prosecution of criminal cases, and in civil actions and proceedings and all other matters in which the county is interested." (Same as sec. 228 of the County Government Act of 1897, Stats. 1897, p. 575.)

The board of supervisors are authorized, "To examine, settle, and allow all accounts legally chargeable against the county, except salaries of officers, and such demands as are authorized by law to be allowed by some other person or tribunal, and order warrants to be drawn on the county treasurer therefor." (Pol. Code, sec. 4041, subd. 12. Same as subd. 11, sec. 25, County Government Act of 1897, *supra.*)

These sections as found in the County Government Act were before the supreme court in *County of Yolo* v. *Joyce,* 156 Cal. 429, [105 Pac. 125]. In that case the claim was for the transcription of certain testimony to be used in the prosecution of a criminal case which the district attorney certified was necessary "in the prosecution of Dean McGrew and was necessary in the conduct of the trial of said McGrew." It was contended in that case that the transcription could only be ordered by the judge under section 274 of the Code of Civil Procedure. But the court held that the power was not vested exclusively in the trial court and that the authority could be exercised by the district attorney under the act cited. The court said: "The district attorney is an executive officer charged with the detection of crime and the prosecution of criminal cases. In furtherance of the proper discharge of his duties the legislature has, under the section of the County Government Act, enlarged his power so as to permit him to incur expense necessary to enforce the criminal law. His authority to do so for that purpose is not made subject to the control or supervision of any court or judicial officer, but is a matter for the consideration of the board of supervisors alone to the extent of determining whether the expense was necessarily incurred so as to constitute a county charge. Of course, the right of a district attorney to incur expense is not an arbitrary one. All that the section of the County Government Act permits is to give to the district attorney, in the first instance, the discretion to determine whether it is necessary in the detection of crime, or the prosecution of a criminal case, to incur an expense chargeable against the county. Any such claim, however, must be presented to the board of supervisors for allowance, and that body reviews the action of the district attorney and determines whether the expense was a necessary one and acts accordingly. And as the board of supervisors is vested with the authority to determine the question whether the expense was necessary or not, and is the tribunal to which is committed under the County Government Act the jurisdiction to supervise the action of the district attorney in incurring the expense, its determination that it was a proper and necessary expense is conclusive." (*Colusa County* v. *De Jarnatt*, 55 Cal. 373, 375; *McFarland* v. *McCowen*, 98 Cal. 330, [33 Pac. 113]; *McBride* v. *Newlin*, 129 Cal. 36, [61 Pac. 577]; *County of Santa Cruz* v. *McPherson*, 133 Cal. 282, [65 Pac. 574]; *County of Alameda* v. *Ebers*, 136 Cal. 132, [68 Pac. 475].)

We regard this decision as conclusive of the question here. The district attorney acted under express authority given him by the statute, and the board of supervisors determined that the expense was necessary. We cannot go behind the finding of the supervisors to inquire whether they decided rightly or wrongly. We have nothing before us but the record of official action and the findings of the court. The supervisors might well have concluded that the time of the expert given as a witness was as valuable to him as the time given to his examination of the specimens, and as to this latter item no objection is made. The examination of the specimens submitted to the expert and his conclusion upon such examination would have been of no assistance to the state in the trial of the case without the expert's presence at the trial.

It is suggested in appellant's reply brief that the complaint does not allege that an agreement was made by the district attorney to pay the petitioner for his services in attending as a witness at the trial. There is no direct averment of such agreement, but the claim shows on its face that the expenditure was "authorized and approved by" the district attorney. This was sufficient to meet the objection, for the claim was made part of the complaint.

We do not think that the general law fixing the fees of witnesses is a limitation upon the power given the district attorney and the board of supervisors by the statutes above referred to.

The judgment is affirmed.

Hart, J., and Burnett, J., concurred.

MEMORANDUM CASE.

[Crim. No. 349.   Third Appellate District.—September 2, 1916.]

THE PEOPLE, Respondent, v. C. H. GISH, Appellant.

CRIMINAL LAW.—Appeal dismissed and record stricken from the files.

ATTEMPTED APPEAL from a judgment of the Superior Court of Napa County, and from an order refusing a new trial.   Henry C. Gesford, Judge.

The facts are stated in the opinion of the court.

E. S. Bell, for Appellant.

U. S. Webb, Attorney-General, and J. Charles Jones, Deputy Attorney-General, for Respondent.

BURNETT, J.—The record in the above-entitled cause has been filed in this court.   It contains, however, no notice of appeal either from the judgment or the order denying the motion for a new trial.   Neither has there been any appearance of appellant in this court.   We may say, though, that we have read the record, and there appears to be no doubt of defendant's guilt or that he had a fair trial.

The purported appeal is dismissed, and the record stricken from the files.

Chipman, P. J., and Hart, J., concurred.

INDEX.

(803)

INDEX.

ABATEMENT. **See Husband and Wife, 1, 2.**

ACCOMPLICE. **See Criminal Law, 6-8.**

ACCOUNT STATED.

1. ESSENTIALS OF—NEW CONTRACT.—An account stated is a writing which exhibits the state of account between parties and the balance owing from one to the other; and when assented to, either expressly or impliedly, it becomes a new contract. (Fee v. McPhee Company, 295.)

2. ACTION FOR SERVICES—SUPPORT OF FINDINGS.—In this action to recover an alleged balance due for services in superintending the construction of certain buildings for a contracting company, it is held that the finding that the document upon which the plaintiff relied as an account stated constituted such an account is supported by the evidence. (Id.)

3. OPENING OF ACCOUNT—FRAUD OR MISTAKE.—In the absence of allegation and proof of fraud or mistake which taints the entire contract, the court will not open and unravel it as if no accounting had been made, but the settlement will be binding except for the errors shown. (Id.)

4. EVIDENCE—PROOF OF OMISSIONS AND ERRORS.—In an action upon an account stated it is proper to allow evidence of omissions and errors therein and find in favor of plaintiff in accordance with the facts. (Id.)

5. INTEREST — ALLOWANCE FROM COMMENCEMENT OF ACTION. — In an action on an account stated, interest is allowable from the date of the commencement of the action. (Id.)

6. SUPERINTENDENCY OF BUILDINGS FOR CORPORATION — PERCENTAGE OF PROFITS—STATUS OF PARTIES.—Contracts between a corporation engaged in the general contracting business and an individual who is to superintend the construction of certain buildings for the former for a percentage of the "net profits" do not make the relationship of the parties that of partners. (Id.)

7. CONSTRUCTION OF TERM "NET PROFITS"—EVIDENCE.—Evidence of similar contracts made between the parties is admissible to assist the court in interpreting the term "net profits." (Id.)

ADVERSE POSSESSION.

1. OWNERSHIP OF ADJOINING PATENTED LANDS — INCLOSURE OF BOTH HOLDINGS—LEASING FOR GRAZING PURPOSES—INSUFFICIENT PROOF

ADVERSE POSSESSION (Continued).

OF TITLE.—Where two brothers owned adjoining quarter sections of patented land of little value, and neither lived nor resided upon the land covered by his patent for any long period after obtaining it, and neither had lived on any part of the half section for many years, the fact that one of the brothers inclosed both holdings with a wire fence, and leased the land for short periods for grazing purposes unknown to the other brother, is insufficient to sustain a claim to the whole tract by adverse possession. (Gallo v. Gallo, 189.)

2. HOSTILE CHARACTER OF HOLDING—ESSENTIAL ELEMENT.—In order to make out an adverse possession sufficient to constitute a defense under the statute of limitations, the owner must be notified in some way that the possession is hostile to his claim. (Id.)

3. PAYMENT OF TAXES—REDEMPTION FROM TAX SALES—INSUFFICIENT COMPLIANCE WITH STATUTE.—The payment of taxes required as an element of adverse possession is not complied with by the redemption of the land from tax sales. (Id.)

4. EJECTMENT—FINDINGS—LACK OF INCONSISTENCY.—In an action in ejectment, wherein the plaintiff alleges seisin or right of possession in itself for the period of five years last past, and also alleges possession on the part of the defendants at the time of the commencement of the action, and the answer of the defendants denies the plaintiff's possession and right of possession for the period claimed, and alleges that the defendants have been in the adverse possession of the premises for more than twelve years, there is no inconsistency between the finding of the plaintiff's seisin within five years and of the defendants' adverse possession for the period of twelve years prior to the filing of the complaint, nor is the latter finding sufficient to bar the plaintiff's recovery under section 318 of the Code of Civil Procedure, where it is also found that the defendants had not paid the taxes for the requisite years. (People's Water Company v. Boromeo, 270.)

5. FAILURE TO PAY TAXES—INVALIDITY OF ASSESSMENTS—BURDEN OF PROOF.—Where in such an action it is admitted that the taxes levied and assessed for the years in question were not paid, and it is contended that the assessments were invalid, the burden is upon the defendants to show such invalidity. (Id.)

6. COMPUTATION AND ENTRY OF TAXES BY AUDITOR — OMISSION NOT FATAL.—A tax assessment is not invalid by reason of the failure of the county auditor to comply with section 3731 of the Political Code, which requires him, after receiving from the state board of equalization a statement of whatever changes have been ordered by said board in the assessment-book of the county, and after making the corresponding changes, if any, in said assessment-book, to then compute and enter in a separate money column in the assessment-

ADVERSE POSSESSION (Continued).

book the respective sums to be paid as a tax on the property, and segregate and place in their proper columns of the book the respective amounts due in installments, as such work is no part of the levy, but is merely a step in the process of the collection of taxes. (Id.)

7. QUIETING TITLE — EVIDENCE — BURDEN OF PROOF. — In an action to quiet title to real property in which the defendants claim title by adverse possession and also under a purported tax sale, where the record title to the land is shown to be in the plaintiff, presumptively he was seised of the possession within the time required by law, and the burden is upon the defendants to show that they or either of them, having color of title to the land, had held and possessed the same against the plaintiff for the full statutory period of five years preceding the commencement of the action. (Cory v. Hotchkiss, 443.)

8. ABSENCE OF RECORD TITLE—ESSENTIALS OF ADVERSE POSSESSION.— One who does not connect himself with a record title cannot be said to have had possession of land under color of title, and therefore, in order to establish a claim of adverse possession, it is incumbent upon him to show compliance with the provisions of section 325 of the Code of Civil Procedure, viz., (1) that the land had been protected by a substantial inclosure; or (2) that it had been cultivated and improved during his alleged use and occupation of the same, and, failing in this, his claim fails. (Id.)

9. CLAIM UNDER COLOR OF TITLE—ABSENCE OF POSSESSION.—Where it does not appear that one claiming land under a tax deed at any time personally or otherwise occupied and used the land, or that he did anything with reference to the same after receiving the deed save to pay the taxes thereon, he cannot sustain a claim of adverse possession. (Id.)

10. LEASING OF LAND—FAILURE TO SHOW EXCLUSIVE USE.—The mere fact that one of the defendants assumed the ownership of the land and leased the same to another may be some evidence that it was his intent to claim the land, but where he fails to show that it was occupied by his lessee for the statutory period, or that it was not used by plaintiff or other persons during that time, his mere intent to claim the land is insufficient to support a claim of title by adverse possession. (Id.)

11. JOINT CLAIM OF ADVERSE POSSESSION—INSUFFICIENCY OF EVIDENCE. Where it is alleged in the cross-complaint in an action to quiet title to land that the title was conveyed by the holder of a tax deed to one of the defendants (who the evidence does not show ever had possession of the land), for the benefit of himself and the other defendant (who leased the land for grazing purposes), the latter cannot

ADVERSE POSSESSION (Continued).

be said to have connected himself with the purported title of his codefendant, there being no evidence that he was acting for his codefendant or for himself and the latter jointly. (Id.)

AFFIDAVIT OF MERITS. See Place of Trial.

AGENCY. See Brokers; Sale, 4, 5.

ALIBI. See Criminal Law, 10, 23, 55.

ANTENUPTIAL AGREEMENT. See Insurance, 2-5.
APPEAL.

1. MANDAMUS—ACTION TO COMPEL SHERIFF TO DELIVER PERSONAL PROPERTY—EXECUTION NOT STAYED.—An order of the superior court requiring a sheriff to take into his possession and deliver to the petitioner certain personal property and documents is not stayed by the mere fact of perfecting an appeal from the judgment therein, under the alternative method of appeal, without giving the stay bond provided in section 943 of the Code of Civil Procedure. (Bailey v. Superior Court, 78.)

2. DUTY OF SHERIFF TO COMPLY WITH ORDER—ABILITY TO COMPLY—PROPERTY HELD BY THIRD PARTY.—It is the duty of a sheriff to comply with a judgment against him commanding him to take possession of and deliver to petitioner certain personal property, where the judgment has not been reversed or set aside and no stay bond given; and whether the defendant can comply with the order by reason of the fact that the property is in the possession of another can only be determined by the court upon the showing made by him in response to a citation to show cause why he should not be punished for contempt for failure so to do. (Id.)

3. JUDGMENT AGAINST HOLDER OF PROPERTY—STAY BOND ON APPEAL. The fact that another party having possession of the property in question has appealed from a judgment against it for its recovery and given a stay bond on appeal is not a matter for consideration in the proceedings against the sheriff. (Id.)

4. MOTION TO DISMISS—INSUFFICIENT NOTICE OF MOTION.—A notice of motion to dismiss an appeal on the ground that the appellant had failed to furnish the requisite papers is insufficient where such notice fails to point out and designate the particular papers necessary to the consideration of the appeal which are claimed to have been omitted from the record. (Garrett v. Garrett, 178.)

5. GENERAL ORDER GRANTING NEW TRIAL—CONFLICTING EVIDENCE.—Where the evidence is conflicting as to material matters, an order

APPEAL (Continued).

granting a new trial will be affirmed on appeal, notwithstanding the written order of court contains a statement of what purports to be the reasons influencing the court in granting the motion, where the order is such as to require it to be treated as a general one, the court not having expressly limited it to definite grounds, and the grounds of motion having included the one of the insufficiency of the evidence. (Brode v. Clark, 182.)

6. JUDGMENT-ROLL — ORDERS NOT INCORPORATED IN BILL OF EXCEPTIONS—REVIEW NOT PERMITTED.—Upon an appeal taken from a judgment in an action to quiet title upon the judgment-roll without any bill of exceptions or statement of the case, the appellate court can only consider such papers and orders as are declared by the code to constitute a part of the judgment-roll, notwithstanding included in the transcript there are certain exhibits and orders upon which reliance is made for a reversal of the judgment. (Brown v. Canty, 183.)

7. JUDGMENT IN FAVOR OF STATE—PARTY AGGRIEVED.—The state of California is a party aggrieved and has the right of appeal from a judgment in its favor in an action brought against it to condemn land, notwithstanding the state in its answer denied any ownership in the land, and declared that the United States was the owner thereof. (Pacific Power Company v. State of California, Mono County Irrigation Company v. State of California, 719.)

8. DEFAULT IN FILING OF BRIEF — SUFFICIENCY OF EXCUSE. — An appeal taken by the state from a judgment will not be dismissed for the failure of the appellant to file its points and authorities within the prescribed time, where it is made to appear that the time to file its briefs was inadvertently allowed to expire by reason of misunderstandings between representatives of the attorney-general's office and the deputy attorney-general, who had charge of the litigation, as to the obtaining of an extension of time from the court. (Id.)

See Attachment, 6, 7; Costs, 1–3; Criminal Law, 5, 16, 29; Divorce, 6, 7, 10, 11; Eminent Domain, 15; Illegal Contract; Injunction; Justice's Court, 1, 2, 5–8, 12–17.

ASSAULT AND BATTERY.

1. ASSAULT AND UNLAWFUL IMPRISONMENT — FORCE USED BY DEFENDANT—QUESTION FOR JURY—APPEAL.—In an action for damages for an assault and battery and for an unlawful imprisonment following an altercation concerning the ownership of a ten-dollar bill, it is for the jury to determine from the evidence whether or not excessive and unnecessary force was used upon the person of the plaintiff, and where there is evidence favorable to the plaintiff upon such issue,

ASSAULT AND BATTERY (Continued).

the verdict of the jury is conclusive on the appellate court. (Riffel v. Letts, 426.)

2. Award of Damages—Discretion—Excessive Verdict—Review on Appeal.—As a general rule, what will be a proper and reasonable compensation for the damages occasioned by injuries to the person is a question committed to the sound discretion of the jury. In considering an attack upon a verdict as excessive the appellate court must treat every conflict of the evidence as resolved in favor of the respondent, and must give him the benefit of every inference that can reasonably be drawn in support of his claim. (Id.)

3. Arrest "Without Legal Justification"—Damages—Instruction. An instruction defining an arrest, and then stating that "for a private person to take another into custody, without legal justification, and restrain him of his liberty for a time and then turn him loose without taking him before a magistrate, or to a peace officer, is unlawful, and constitutes a trespass upon the liberty of the one so restrained for which he may be compensated in damages," is not prejudicial, for failure to adequately explain the words "without legal justification," where in other instructions, to which no objection is made, the court gives instructions showing the circumstances under which an arrest or imprisonment is legal or justifiable and also the circumstances under which an arrest or imprisonment is not legal or justifiable. (Id.)

4. Evidence—Verdict not Excessive.—In an action to recover damages for injuries received from an assault and battery and from an unlawful imprisonment, the complaint being in two counts, it cannot be said that a verdict in the sum of two thousand five hundred dollars is excessive, where the jury is instructed that only actual damages are recoverable, and the evidence shows that the plaintiff was an unmarried woman and in good health at the time of the alleged occurrence, that she suffered much humiliation and distress of mind at the time and afterward, caused by being arrested and imprisoned in a caged wagon in a public street and in the presence of her neighbors, and that this caused great nervous excitement and shock, which seriously affected her health for a considerable time after the occurrence. (Id.)

See Criminal Law, 10–15.

ASSIGNMENT. See Pledge, 1, 2.

ATTACHMENT.

1. Defective Affidavit on Undertaking — Amendment. — An undertaking on attachment to which is attached an affidavit of justification of sureties which by inadvertence fails to state whether the sureties are freeholders or householders is subject to amendment, and

ATTACHMENT (Continued).

when amended it has the effect of validating the proceeding from its inception. (Bone v. Trafton, 30.)

2. FILING OF NEW UNDERTAKING — FIRST ATTACHMENT NOT ABANDONED—INTERVENING CHATTEL MORTGAGE—LACK OF PRIORITY.—The filing of a new affidavit and undertaking on attachment and the procuring thereon of a new writ of attachment to correct the omission in the original affidavit accompanying the undertaking to state whether or not the sureties were freeholders or householders, does not constitute an abandonment of the original or first attachment, so as to permit a chattel mortgage executed between the issuance of the two writs to become a first lien, where the attached property was held by the sheriff at all times under the first attachment. (Id.)

3. RELEASE — SUBSEQUENT BANKRUPTCY OF DEFENDANT — ENTRY OF QUALIFIED JUDGMENT—LIABILITY OF SURETIES—RIGHT OF PLAINTIFF. Where in an action for goods sold and delivered the property of the defendant is attached and afterward released upon the giving of an undertaking conditioned that if the plaintiff should recover judgment the sureties upon demand would pay the amount thereof, the plaintiff is entitled, where the defendant by way of supplemental answer sets up his adjudication and discharge in bankruptcy since the commencement of the action, to have a special or qualified judgment entered against the defendant with a perpetual stay of execution, for the purpose of enforcing the liability of the sureties on the undertaking. (Tormey v. Miller, 469.)

4. PROCEDURE—MOTION FOR ENTRY OF QUALIFIED JUDGMENT AT CLOSE OF TRIAL.—Under such circumstances, it is proper procedure to enter such a judgment upon motion made at the conclusion of the trial of the issues raised by the original pleadings and supplemental answer. (Id.)

5. PLEADING — ATTACHMENT AND RELEASE — EVIDENTIARY MATTERS. — Under such circumstances it is not necessary to the entry of the judgment against the defendant, for the special purpose of fixing and enforcing the liability of the sureties on the undertaking, that the plaintiff should plead the issuance of the writ of attachment, its levy, the giving of the undertaking for the release, or the release of the property, as the same are purely evidentiary matters. (Id.)

6. APPEAL FROM JUDGMENT — REVIEW OF ERRORS OCCURRING DURING TRIAL.—In such an action alleged errors in excluding proof of the issuance of the writ of attachment and the execution of the undertaking are reviewable upon appeal taken from the judgment, where the appeal was taken after the abrogation by the legislature of 1915 of the right to appeal from an order denying a new trial (Stats. 1915, p. 209). (Id.)

ATTACHMENT (Continued).

7. ORDER RELEASING LEVY—EXEMPT PROPERTY—CONFLICT OF EVIDENCE
—APPEAL.—Upon an appeal from an order vacating and setting
aside the levy of an attachment, the appellate court is not authorized to review the evidence and make a different finding, where the
trial court upon evidence definitely tending to support the defendant's claim determined that the property attached was exempt from
attachment under subdivision 4 of section 690 of the Code of Civil
Procedure. (Development Building Company v. Woodruff, 732.)

8. UNDERTAKING FOR RELEASE — RETURN OF EXECUTION — CONDITION
PRECEDENT TO ACTION.—The issuance and return of an execution
unsatisfied in whole or in part is required by the provisions of section 553 of the Code of Civil Procedure as a condition precedent to
the right to commence an action upon an undertaking given pursuant
to section 555 of such code for the release of attached property.
(Curtin v. Katschinski, 766.)

9. BANKRUPTCY OF JUDGMENT DEBTORS—RETURN OF EXECUTION NOT
EXCUSED BY—NATIONAL BANKRUPTCY ACT.—The issuance and return
of an execution unsatisfied in whole or in part as a condition precedent
to the maintenance of an action against the sureties on an undertaking given for the release of attached property is not excused by
the subsequent bankruptcy of the judgment debtors, where the latter
did not obtain a discharge within one year after the adjudication of
their bankruptcy, as the National Bankruptcy Act contains no inhibition against the issuance and levy of execution after the lapse of
that time. (Id.)

See Parties.

ATTORNEY AT LAW.

1. DISBARMENT PROCEEDING — VIOLATION OF CONFIDENCE OF CLIENT —
SUFFICIENCY OF EVIDENCE.—In this proceeding for the disbarment
of an attorney at law for violating his oath in certain transactions
involving the property of a client, it is held that on the record the
court was justified in determining that the accused violated such
oath, that the client reposed confidence in him, and that he abused
such confidence. (Matter of Soale, 144.)

2. JUDGMENT OF SUSPENSION—TIME—CONTINGENT UPON PAYMENT OF
CLAIM OF ACCUSER.—A judgment suspending an attorney at law for
one year "and thereafter until the claim of the accuser is fully paid,"
is warranted, if the amount is ascertained, but is too uncertain to be
enforced, except as to the stated period of one year, where the corporate stock wrongfully purchased by the attorney with the money
of his client is not shown to be wholly worthless, and the amount
lost thereby is not determined. (Id.)

3. SUSPENSION OF ATTORNEY FOR UNLIMITED PERIOD.—In a disbarment
proceeding an attorney may be suspended for a period not necessarily

ATTORNEY AT LAW (Continued).

limited as a fixed and determinate period of time, but for an uncertain time, subject to the right of the accused to relieve himself therefrom by making restitution of a stated amount of money which he had improperly obtained by means of his misconduct. (Id.)

See Conservation Commission, 1.

BAIL. See Criminal Law, 3, 4.

BANK.

1. BANKING ACT — SALE OF PROPERTY — LIABILITY FOR TAXES — CONSTRUCTION OF ORDER AUTHORIZING SALE. — An action cannot be maintained against the superintendent of banks to recover of him, as the grantor of certain real property belonging to an insolvent banking corporation, the amount of the taxes which the grantee was required to pay to protect the property from sale on account of delinquency, notwithstanding such taxes were a lien on the property but not due at the time of the conveyance, where such conveyance was made pursuant to an order of court directing such official to make a conveyance of only such right, title, and interest as the insolvent had in the property, and neither the order, nor the deed, made any reference to taxes. (National Bank of Bakersfield v. Williams, 705.)

2. DEED—USE OF TERM "GRANT"—COVENANT AGAINST TAXES—WHEN NOT IMPLIED.—While the use of the word "grant" in a conveyance implies a covenant against encumbrances made or suffered by the grantor, and while taxes which were at the date of the grant a lien upon the property conveyed are embraced therein, nevertheless the covenant implied from the use of the term "grant" must be deemed limited by the subject matter of the conveyance. (Id.)

3. SALE UNDER ORDER OF COURT — JUDICIAL SALE — APPLICABILITY OF DOCTRINE OF CAVEAT EMPTOR.—A sale made by the superintendent of banks under an order of court in accordance with the provisions of the Banking Act is a judicial sale, to which the doctrine of *caveat emptor* applies. (Id.)

4. CONFIRMATION OF SALE—NONESSENTIAL ELEMENT.—A confirmation of such a sale is not required, as the order authorizing the sale is sufficient confirmation. (Id.)

See Joint Owners; Parties.

BANKRUPTCY. See Attachment, 3, 9; Illegal Contract, 6.

BOARD OF CONTROL. See Conservation Commission, 2-5; Public Officers, 1-4.

BROKERS.

1. REAL ESTATE BROKERS—ORAL AGREEMENT TO SHARE COMMISSIONS—STATUTE OF FRAUDS—SECTION 1624, SUBDIVISION 6, CIVIL CODE.—The provision of subdivision 6 of section 1624 of the Civil Code was only designed to protect owners of real estate against unfounded claims of brokers, and does not extend to agreements between brokers to co-operate in making sales for a share of the commissions. (Sellers v. Solway Land Company, 259.)

2. CONTRACT BETWEEN REAL ESTATE BROKERS — AGREEMENT TO PAY SPECIFIC COMPENSATION—AUTHORITY TO EXECUTE CONTRACT—WRITING ESSENTIAL.—A contract made by the manager of the land and loan department of a real estate partnership agreeing to pay a second broker a specific amount of money for the procuring of a purchaser for land for the sale of which the copartnership were the agents, is void, where the authority of the person signing the contract on behalf of the partnership is not in writing. (Id.)

3. ACTION ON CONTRACT—PLEA OF STATUTE OF FRAUDS—KNOWLEDGE OF RENDITION OF SERVICES—LACK OF ESTOPPEL.—In an action to recover upon such a contract the copartnership is not estopped from setting up the statute of frauds, by reason of the fact that it knowingly held the signer of the contract out to the world as having the authority he assumed, and of its knowledge that such employee was dealing with the plaintiff, and had performed services under the invalid contract, where it also appears that the sale was made without knowledge that the plaintiff was interested other than by a verbal notification made some time previously that he was endeavoring to sell the land to the purchasers. (Id.)

4. REAL ESTATE BROKER—EXCHANGE OF PROPERTIES—FAILURE OF CONSUMMATION—COMMISSIONS NOT EARNED.—Under the terms of a contract for an exchange of properties, wherein each party agreed to convey title free of encumbrances and to pay the broker who procured the contract to be executed a commission, the commission is not earned where the exchange was not consummated by reason of the inability of one of the parties to convey title to a portion of his property, and the subsequent mutual abandonment of the contract. (Jennings v. Jordan, 335.)

5. BROKER'S COMMISSIONS—PROCURING LESSEES FOR REAL PROPERTY—PLEADING—SUFFICIENCY OF COMPLAINT.—In an action to recover commissions alleged to have been earned by procuring a lessee for real property, the complaint states a cause of action, where it is alleged that the defendant made and delivered to the plaintiff an instrument in writing by the terms of which the defendant agreed to pay plaintiff a commission if he procured a lease upon the terms specified in the writing, or other terms acceptable to the defendant, and that plaintiff did procure persons and produced them to defendant who were ready, able, and willing to enter into a lease upon

BROKERS (Continued).

terms which by the written acknowledgment of defendant were acceptable, but that defendant thereafter refused, and continues to refuse, to enter into any lease with such proposed lessees and disclaimed and repudiated any liability to plaintiff for commissions. (Merwin v. Shafner, 374.)

6. COMMISSIONS—WHEN EARNED.—Where the agreement to pay commissions upon the sale or leasing of real estate is in writing, the agent, as a condition to the earning of his commissions, need only produce to his principal persons who are ready, able, and willing to contract according to the terms proposed or acceptable to such principal. (Id.)

7. OFFER TO LEASE—TIME OF COMMENCEMENT.—An offer in writing to lease real property is not invalid by reason of the failure to specify any time for the commencement of the lease, as it is implied that the term will commence upon the making thereof. (Id.)

8. REPUDIATION OF LIABILITY TO PAY COMMISSION—RIGHT OF AGENT.—Where a writing authorizing the procuring of a lessee for real property provides for the time of the payment of the commission "along during the first year," and the liability to pay the commission is repudiated after the rendition of all of the consideration required of the agent, he may sue to recover the amount of such commission. (Id.)

9. BROKER'S COMMISSIONS—FINDING OF PURCHASER—CONFLICT OF EVIDENCE—APPEAL.—In an action brought to recover a sum of money alleged to be due as the commission of a real estate agent in securing a purchaser for the property of the defendant pursuant to a written contract of authorization and also an alleged oral agreement as to the amount of the commission to be received in the event of a sale, where it is found on conflicting evidence that the plaintiff procured a purchaser, the finding will not be disturbed on appeal. (Daniel v. Calkins, 514.)

10. AMOUNT OF COMPENSATION—EVIDENCE—PAROL AGREEMENT.—In an action to recover a broker's commission in securing a purchaser of real property pursuant to the terms of a written authorization of sale which designated the "net" amount which the owner was to receive upon the sale and which provided that "no percentage as a commission" was to be paid to the broker, it is not error to permit the plaintiff to introduce evidence of an oral agreement that he was to receive as compensation for his services all over the net sum stated in the writing as the purchase price of the property. (Id.)

11. COMMISSIONS—WHEN EARNED.—Under the terms of such a written authorization, the broker is entitled to his compensation when he produces a purchaser who is ready, able, and willing to buy the

BROKERS (Continued).

property for any sum up to or in excess of the net amount specified in the writing. (Id.)

See Illegal Contract.

BUILDING CONTRACT.

1. INSTALLATION OF ELEVATOR PLANT — UNSATISFACTORY CONTROLLING
DEVICES—UNWARRANTED REMOVAL OF ENTIRE PLANT BY OWNER.—
Under the terms of a contract for the construction and installation of an elevator plant and service in a building, the owner is
not justified in removing the machines installed under the contract
on the ground that the controlling devices furnished for the elevators were unsatisfactory, and in installing a particular type of controllers, which could not be purchased without also purchasing the
machine itself, where the construction of the plant was in every
other way satisfactory to the owner, and it is shown that other controlling devices were obtainable in the open market which could be
used with the installed machines and purchased independent of the
machines themselves. (Bryan Elevator Company v. Law, 204.)

2. SATISFACTORY PERFORMANCE OF CONTRACT — WHAT CONSTITUTES.—
Where a contract requires work to be done to the satisfaction of
the person contracting therefor, only such performance is required
as is satisfactory to the mind of a reasonable person. (Id.)

3. INSTALLATION OF ELEVATOR PLANT—PURCHASE OF OLD MACHINERY—
LIABILITY FOR LOSS.—Under the terms of a contract for the construction and installation of an elevator plant and service, which
provided, among other things, that the owner of the building agreed
to sell for the sum of one dollar in hand paid to the contractor
all old elevator machinery, the contractor must sustain the loss
thereof, where it removed the machinery to its shops, and it was
there destroyed by fire, notwithstanding the contractor made a reduction in its bid in the contract of a certain sum on account of
such old machinery, which was to be reinstalled and used as a freight
elevator in the building in question. (Bryan Elevator Company v.
Law, 216.)

4. ABANDONMENT BY CONTRACTOR — AMOUNT APPLICABLE TO LIENS—
RULE PRIOR TO REVISORY ACT OF 1911.—Under the mechanic's lien
statutes as they existed prior to the Revisory Act of 1911 (Stats.
1911, p. 1313), where a valid building contract was executed and
filed and the work thereunder abandoned by the contractor before
completion, the amount of the contract price applicable to the liens
of other persons than the contractor was to be determined in accordance with section 1200 of the Code of Civil Procedure, and in determining such amount allowance was required to be made for the cost

BUILDING CONTRACT (Continued).

of completing the building. (Pacific Manufacturing Company v. Perry, 274.)

5. DEVIATIONS FROM PLANS — ADDED COST OF BUILDING — RIGHT OF CONTRACTOR — VALIDITY OF CONTRACT. — A building contract is not rendered void by reason of alterations in the plans adding materially to the cost of the building, where the contract was recorded and expressly provided that should the owner at any time during the progress of the building request any alterations, deviations, additions, or omissions from said contract, specifications, or plans, he should be at liberty to do so, and the same should in no way affect or make void the contract, but would be added to or deducted from the amount of said contract price, as the case might be, by a fair and reasonable valuation. (Id.)

6. NOTICE OF NONRESPONSIBILITY — WHEN NOT REQUIRED. — An owner of a building is not required to give notice of nonresponsibility, as provided by section 1192 of the Code of Civil Procedure, in a case where there is a valid recorded contract made on her behalf and with her knowledge and consent, as the contract is the measure of her liability. (Id.)

7. PLUMBING — ABANDONMENT BY OWNER — REMEDY. — Where a contract to furnish and install the plumbing in a building is abandoned by the owner before completion, the contractor is entitled to recover the reasonable value of the materials furnished and the work performed. (Haub v. Coustette, 424.)

See Mechanics' Liens.

BURGLARY. See Criminal Law, 16–23.

COMMUNITY PROPERTY. See Divorce, 1–4.

CONSERVATION COMMISSION.

1. STATE CONSERVATION COMMISSION — COMPILATION OF LAWS — EMPLOYMENT OF ATTORNEY AT LAW — ASSENT OF ATTORNEY-GENERAL NOT REQUIRED. — The State Conservation Commission, under the provisions of the act creating such commission (Stats. 1911, p. 822), is not required to procure the assent of the attorney-general as provided by section 472 of the Political Code, as a condition to its employment of an attorney at law to compile the laws of the different nations, the federal government and the states of the Union affecting conservation, for the use of such commission, as such services are in the main clerical in character and possible of performance by other than a licensed attorney at law. (U'Ren v. State Board of Control, 6.)

31 Cal. App.—52

CONSERVATION COMMISSION (Continued).

2. CLAIM FOR SALARY — MANDAMUS TO AUDIT DEMAND — FORM AND MANNER OF PRESENTATION.—In a proceeding in *mandamus* to compel the State Board of Control to audit and allow the claim of such attorney for his salary for a certain month, it cannot be urged in defense that the claim therefor was not presented in the form and manner provided by law, where the same was presented in the same form and manner in which the salary claims for previous months had been presented under the rules of the board and upon which it had acted approvingly. (Id.)

3. EMPLOYEES OF COMMISSION — APPROVAL OF SALARY CLAIMS — POWERS OF STATE BOARD OF CONTROL.—Under the act creating the State Conservation Commission and authorizing it to employ for the purposes for which the commission was created such expert, technical, professional, and clerical assistants "upon such terms as it may deem proper," and setting apart a specific fund for the payment of such obligations as the commission might thus create, the approval of a claim for such services by the commission is final, and the functions of the State Board of Control relative thereto are merely those of an auditing body, with no discretion or control over the amount for which the claim should be allowed. (Id.)

4. AUDITING OF CLAIMS — MANDAMUS.—Where one official board or body is given authority by statute to create an obligation against a specific fund in the state treasury, and another official board or body is intrusted with the powers of an auditor in respect to claims generally against the state, the powers and duties of the latter in respect to such claims may be controlled by the courts and compelled by writs of mandate. (Id.)

5. AUDITING OF CLAIM FOR SERVICES FOR COMMISSION—MANDAMUS—CONSENT OF STATE NOT REQUIRED.—The principle that the state cannot be sued without its consent has no application to a proceeding in *mandamus* to compel the State Board of Control to audit a claim for services rendered to the State Conservation Commission. (Id.)

CONSIDERATION. See Corporation, 10.

CONSTITUTIONAL LAW. See Criminal Law, 39; Fish and Game; Justice's Court, 3, 4; Office and Officers, 5–7.

CONTRACT.

1. TRUTH OF REPRESENTATIONS—RELIANCE UPON.—A contracting party is entitled to rely on the express statement of an existing fact, the truth of which is known to the opposite party and unknown to him, as the basis of a mutual agreement, and he is under no obligation

CONTRACT (Continued).

to investigate and verify the statements to the truth of which the other party to the contract, with full means of knowledge, has deliberately pledged his faith. (Gleason v. Proud, 123.)

2. EXCHANGE OF REAL PROPERTY FOR BONDS—VALUE OF BONDS—LACK OF MISREPRESENTATION AS TO VALUE.—Such principles, however, are inapplicable to an action to rescind a contract of exchange of real property for bonds of a corporation, on the ground of misrepresentation as to the value of the bonds, where the agent of the defendant furnished the plaintiff with all the information that his principal and himself had concerning the value of the bonds, which consisted of letters written by third parties, and requested the plaintiff to investigate the writers of the letters. (Id.)

3. ACTION FOR PERSONAL SERVICES—AMOUNT OF COMPENSATION—PAYMENT OF EXTRA SALARY OUT OF SECRET FUND—EVIDENCE—SUPPORT OF FINDINGS.—In an action to recover an alleged balance due on account of salary as chief clerk and accountant of a general merchandise business, the amount of such salary entered on the books of the company and the receipted card in full for salary is not conclusive evidence of the amount of the plaintiff's compensation, where it is made to appear from the evidence that the plaintiff had for several years been paid an additional amount out of a "secret fund," and that such fund was a recognized part of the machinery of the company kept for paying extra salaries to good employees. (Breslauer v. McCormick-Saeltzer Company, 284.)

4. LIQUIDATED DAMAGES—PLEADING—INSUFFICIENCY OF COMPLAINT—SUBSTANTIAL BREACH NOT SHOWN.—In an action to recover the sum of money fixed as liquidated damages for the breach of the terms of a contract guaranteeing that in consideration of a loan of a sum of money to a person to permit him to become a member of a retail liquor partnership, the partners would, during the entire period of the leasehold of the premises wherein such business was being conducted, purchase of the lenders "all steam and lager beer and liquors of every kind and character and all incidentals pertaining to the retail liquor business," the complaint fails to state a cause of action, where it is only alleged that on or about a stated date the defendants, contrary to the terms of said agreement and in violation of their obligation thereof, neglected and refused to purchase all lager beer of the plaintiffs as provided in the contract. (Vath v. Hallett, 290.)

5. CONSTRUCTION OF WAGON ROAD—JOINT AND SEVERAL LIABILITY OF SIGNERS.—A contract for the construction of a wagon road which recites that "the parties of the first part" (not named but described as "settlers" of a certain school district) agree to pay a named person, described as party of the second part, a certain sum per rod for the building of the road, creates a joint and several liability. (Shelton v. Michael, 328.)

CONTRACT (Continued).

6. CONDITIONAL EXECUTION OF CONTRACT—SIGNATURE OF CERTAIN NUMBER OF PERSONS — INSUFFICIENCY OF DEFENSE.—In an action to recover the balance due on such a contract, where it is set up as an affirmative defense that it was agreed that the contract was not to be considered executed until at least a certain number of settlers had signed it, it is not error to refuse to instruct the jury that their verdict should be in favor of the "defendants," if they found that the writing was so executed, in the absence of any such limitation contained in the contract, or of any evidence except that of one of the eight signers that such was the understanding of the parties. (Id.)

7. CONTRACT FOR FILLING IN LAND — RECOVERY OF BALANCE DUE— PLEADING — UNWARRANTED VERDICT.—In an action by a dredging company to recover the balance due for material furnished and work performed under a contract for the filling in of a tract of land owned by a railroad company, the jury is not warranted in allowing the plaintiff in addition to the number of cubic yards found to have been deposited multiplied by the contract price per cubic yard, an amount based upon evidence that the hardest part of the work had been done when the plaintiff discontinued the work, in the absence of any averment in the complaint authorizing such additional allowance. (Richmond Dredging Company v. Atchison, Topeka & Santa Fe Railway Company, 399.)

8. NATURE OF WORK—MECHANICS' LIEN LAW INAPPLICABLE.—The filling in of a part of a tract of land of fifty or more acres belonging to a railroad company, having for its principal object the location and opening of an avenue across the land and to provide a roadbed to which the line of another railway company might sometime be removed from its present location between the company's tracks and the proposed avenue, is not within the provisions of section 1183 of the Code of Civil Procedure which gives a lien to "all persons . . . performing labor upon, or furnishing materials to be used in the construction, alteration, addition to, or repair, either in whole or in part, of any building . . . , railroad, wagonroad or other structure," etc. (Id.)

9. NUMBER OF CUBIC YARDS DEPOSITED — ACCEPTANCE OF MONTHLY VOUCHERS.—Monthly vouchers made out by the defendant showing the estimated amount due for work done during the previous month and, as provided by the contract, the installment of seventy-five per cent due and twenty-five per cent retained, are not to be regarded as accounts stated, as to the number of cubic yards actually deposited, in the absence of any evidence other than a receipt signed by the plaintiff at the bottom of each voucher for the amount thereof. (Id.)

10. DELAY IN PAYMENT—ACCEPTANCE OF MONEY ON OVERDUE VOUCHERS — LACK OF ESTOPPEL.— The acceptance of money on such

CONTRACT (Continued).

vouchers at dates later than provided in the contract, without protest, does not estop the plaintiff from denying that payment for a subsequent month was not tendered in time, where the defendant was notified that prompt payment must be made in the future. (Id.)

11. PLEADING—DAMAGES—FAILURE TO MAINTAIN LEVEES—FAILURE TO CONSTRUCT IN TIME—SEPARATE COUNTS—LACK OF PREJUDICE.—In such an action the setting up as separate causes of action alleged damages for failure to maintain the levees necessary to impound the material deposited, and for the failure to have the levees in readiness at the time promised, is not prejudicial, where there was evidence sufficient to support the verdict on both counts. (Id.)

12. EVIDENCE—LETTERS—LACK OF PRELIMINARY PROOF OF AUTHENTICITY—INSUFFICIENT GROUND OF REVERSAL.—In such action, the admission in evidence of certain letters purporting to have been written by defendant's engineer in charge of the work, which to some extent conceded the defendant's default in failing to construct the levees to impound the material, and which were received by the president of the plaintiff company through the mail, without preliminary proof of their authenticity, is error, but not so prejudicial as to justify a reversal, where the genuineness of the letters was not challenged, and the writer and the recipient were both present in court, and the latter testified that he received the letters from the former through the mail. (Id.)

See Account Stated; Building Contract; Employer and Employee; Illegal Contract; Sale; Warehouseman.

CORPORATION.

1. SALE OF STOCK—NATURE OF TRANSACTION.—The acceptance by a corporation of a promissory note given in payment for its stock upon the agreement that the corporation will issue the stock and deliver it to the purchaser upon the execution and delivery of the note, constitutes a present sale of the stock, and the stock becomes *ipso facto* the property of the purchaser, notwithstanding the certificate therefor is not issued and delivered. (Majors v. Girdner, 47.)

2. CERTIFICATE OF STOCK—EVIDENCE OF OWNERSHIP.—A certificate of stock of a corporation is only the evidence of the ownership thereof, and merely constitutes proof of property which may exist without it. (Id.)

3. RESCISSION OF SALE—FRAUD—PLEADING—OFFER OF RESTORATION OF STOCK—ESSENTIAL AVERMENT.—In an action by the assignee of a corporation to recover on a promissory note, assigned to the plaintiff for the purpose of collection only, and accepted by the corporation for the purchase price of stock, where the answer asks for affirmative relief by way of a rescission of the contract of sale upon

CORPORATION (Continued).

the grounds of fraud and misrepresentation, and the surrender and cancellation of the note for want of consideration by reason of such fraud, it is essential that the answer by appropriate averment show an offer to restore the stock, notwithstanding the certificate therefor has not been issued. (Id.)

4. FRAUD OF CORPORATION—INSUFFICIENCY OF EVIDENCE.—The failure of a corporation to keep its agreement, upon a purchase of its stock, that it will contemporaneously with the execution and delivery of the promissory note of the purchaser given therefor, issue the stock to the purchaser, and the failure to keep its agreement to sell the stock upon his demand at a price in advance of that paid therefor, does not involve such misrepresentation and fraud as will work a rescission of the contract of sale, but is merely a breach of the covenants of the contract. (Id.)

5. MORTGAGE BY PRESIDENT — SUBSEQUENT RATIFICATION.—A corporation is estopped from asserting that its president was not authorized by its board of directors to execute a mortgage on the property of the corporation to secure a loan of money to the corporation, where it subsequently made a deed of trust of all its property to a trustee for the purpose of straightening out its affairs, and in such deed made express reference to such mortgage and therein declared that the deed was subject thereto. (Doerr v. Fandango Lumber Company, 318.)

6. CONVEYANCE OF CORPORATE PROPERTY TO TRUSTEE—RECOGNITION OF MORTGAGE—SCOPE OF RESOLUTION.—The estoppel of the corporation to deny the validity of the mortgage under such circumstances is not affected by the fact that the resolution authorizing the execution of the deed of trust did not expressly vest the board of directors with authority to include in the deed of trust the provision that it should be subject to the mortgage, where the resolution did recite that the object of the deed was to place the properties and business of the corporation in the hands of a trustee for the purpose of operating the business and paying off the indebtedness of the corporation. (Id.)

7. RECEIPT AND USE OF MONEY BY CORPORATION—ESTOPPEL.—A corporation which receives and uses money for the purposes of its business, to secure the repayment of which a mortgage on the property of the corporation is given, is estopped from denying the validity of the obligation. (Id.)

8. SUBSCRIPTION FOR STOCK—PAYMENT BY NOTE—RIGHT TO RECALL IN EVENT OF DISSATISFACTION WITH PURCHASE—VALIDITY OF AGREEMENT.—An agreement made by a fully organized corporation with a subscriber for a certain number of shares of its stock that the subscriber should have the right at any time within ten months after the date of the subscription agreement to cancel his

CORPORATION (Continued).

subscription by recalling his note, if dissatisfied with his purchase, is enforceable against the corporation, where it is not shown that any later subscriber was defrauded by reliance upon such subscription, or that any subsequent creditor relied thereon in dealing with the corporation, or that there was any secrecy contemplated or connived at by the subscriber in the making of such agreement. (Tidewater Southern Railway Company v. Vance, 503.)

9. PROMISSORY NOTE SIGNED BY PRESIDENT AND SECRETARY—SUFFICIENCY OF AUTHORIZATION.—A promissory note of a corporation signed by its president and secretary requires no ratification by the directors or stockholders, where the same was so executed in strict conformity to a resolution of the board of directors authorizing the corporation to borrow from a bank an amount of money not to exceed at any one time a certain sum, and empowering the president or vice-president, together with the secretary or treasurer, to execute its promissory note or notes therefor to such bank for all such sums so borrowed upon such terms in respect to amount or rate of interest or otherwise as might be agreed upon. (Western National Bank v. Wittman, 615.)

10. INDORSER AND GUARANTOR — SUFFICIENCY OF CONSIDERATION — —ULTRA VIRES ACT—DEFENSES NOT AVAILABLE.—An indorser and guarantor of the payment of such note cannot be heard to say that it was executed without consideration, or that it was ultra vires, where its genuineness was admitted by the corporation and its validity recognized by numerous payments made thereon and an acquiescence of several years. (Id.)

11. AGREEMENT BETWEEN CORPORATION AND CREDITORS — CONDITION— GUARANTOR NOT RELEASED.—An indorser and guarantor of the payment of such a note is not released by a subsequent agreement made between the corporation and its creditors relating to a settlement of the debts of the corporation, where the agreement expressly provided that it should be void, unless signed by all creditors, and it in fact was not so signed. (Id.)

See Estates of Deceased Persons, 1; Municipal Corporations; Novation.

COSTS.

1. REPORTER'S TRANSCRIPT—APPEAL.—Where a judgment is affirmed on appeal, the respondent is not entitled to recover the amount paid for the reporter's transcript of the testimony taken at the trial, which was obtained solely for the purpose of assisting respondent's counsel in the preparation of amendments to a bill of exceptions proposed by the appellant on its motion for a new trial in the superior court. (Eaton v. Southern Pacific Company, 379.)

2. COST OF PRINTING ANSWER TO PETITION FOR REHEARING—WHEN NOT ALLOWABLE.—Where a judgment affirmed on appeal had become

COSTS (Continued).

final prior to the going into effect of the amendment of 1913 to section 1027 of the Code of Civil Procedure, allowing the costs of printing briefs to a limited amount as part of the costs on appeal, the respondent is not entitled to the cost of printing her brief in answer to the petition of the appellant for a hearing of the appeal in the supreme court after decision by the district court of appeal, notwithstanding the provision of section 1034 of such code that the time for filing a memorandum of costs on appeal is limited to begin after the filing of the *remittitur* in the superior court. (Id.)

3. TIME OF ACCRUAL OF COSTS.—The right of the prevailing party to recover any costs on appeal is obtained by virtue of the judgment as rendered, and this necessarily includes the assumption that he is to have those costs and only those costs to which he is entitled by law at the time of the rendition of such judgment. (Id.)

4. ACTION INVOLVING WATER RIGHTS—RIGHT OF PLAINTIFF.—An action concerning water rights is an action in the nature of a suit to quiet title to real property, and it falls, so far as regards costs, within the provisions of section 1022 of the Code of Civil Procedure, which declares that costs are allowed, of course, to the plaintiff upon a judgment in his favor in an action which involves the title or possession of real estate. (Stimson Canal & Irrigation Co. v. Lemoore Canal & Irrigation Co., 396.)

5. JUDGMENT FOR PART OF DEMAND—RIGHT TO COSTS.—In an action involving water rights, where the plaintiff recovers a judgment for only a part of its demand, it is nevertheless entitled to its costs. (Id.)

COUNTY.

EXPENSE INCURRED IN CRIMINAL ACTION—ATTENDANCE OF EXPERT—AUTHORITY OF DISTRICT ATTORNEY—APPROVAL BY SUPERVISORS—DETERMINATION CONCLUSIVE.—That district attorney of a county has authority, under the provisions of subdivision 2 of section 4307 of the Political Code, to incur an expense in procuring the attendance of an expert upon the trial of a criminal action to testify as to the result of certain blood tests made by the witness, and where the incurring of such expense is approved by the board of supervisors, the determination of the board is not subject to review by the courts. (Victors v. Kelsey, 796.)

COURTS. See Justice's Court.

COVENANTS. See Banks, 2, 3.

CRIMINAL LAW.

1. PRONOUNCEMENT OF JUDGMENT—DELAY—RIGHT TO NEW TRIAL.—Where judgment is not pronounced upon a person convicted of a

CRIMINAL LAW (Continued).

crime, within the time prescribed by section 1191 of the Penal Code. he is entitled to a new trial, although the delay in pronouncing judgment was had with his consent. (People v. Winner, 352.)

2. PREJUDICIAL REMARKS OF COURT TO JURY.—It is reversible error in a criminal case, upon the jury returning into court and reporting their inability to agree, for the court to make such remarks as, "I don't want to decide any question of fact for you; *that question though it seems very plain to me"*; and, "You must try to reconcile the testimony if you can and come to a verdict, gentlemen, if you possibly can. These cases are expensive to try"; and "*How many contrary ones are there"*; and "Questions of fact you must decide: *there oughtn't to be any trouble. It's a case you ought to decide. ought to agree upon and don't make up your minds that you can't agree, don't get contrary but just in a good humor, good natured way work it out."* (People v. Carder, 355.)

3. RELEASE FROM CUSTODY PENDING TRIAL — FALSE AND WORTHLESS BAIL BOND—SUFFICIENCY OF INDICTMENT.—An indictment alleging that the defendant, acting in concert with his three codefendants, "did unlawfully, willfully, and fraudulently conspire, combine, confederate, and agree to obtain the release and discharge from custody" of a prisoner (who was confined in the county jail pending trial upon an indictment which charged him with the commission of a felony), "by presenting to the superior court of the state of California in and for the city and county of San Francisco a fraudulent, worthless, and void bail bond," states facts sufficient to constitute the offense denounced by the terms of subdivision 5 of section 182 of the Penal Code. (People v. Ambrose, 460.)

4. COUNSELING OF CODEFENDANT TO BECOME SURETY—EVIDENCE—UNWARRANTED CONVICTION.—In such a prosecution, where the only evidence adduced which tended in any way to connect the defendant with the alleged conspiracy was that he advised and counseled one of his codefendants to become a surety on the bond, and to swear that he was owner of property which stood of record in his name, but in fact belonged to the defendant, his conviction is unwarranted. (Id.)

5. APPEAL—FAILURE TO APPEAR—AFFIRMANCE OF JUDGMENT.—Where on an appeal taken in a criminal case the appellant's counsel fails to appear at the time set for oral argument, it is proper to move for an affirmance of the judgment under the provisions of section 1253 of the Penal Code. (People v. Andrade, 730.)

6. ACCOMPLICE—CORROBORATIVE EVIDENCE.—The testimony necessary to corroborate that of an accomplice is sufficient if it, of itself, tends to connect the defendant with the commission of the offense, although it is slight, and entitled, when standing by itself, to but little consideration. (People v. Blunkall, 778.)

CRIMINAL LAW (Continued).

7. NATURE OF CORROBORATING EVIDENCE.—The corroboration required may be made by circumstantial as well as by direct evidence. (Id.)

8. QUANTUM OF PROOF OF CORROBORATION—INSTRUCTION.—An instruction that corroborating evidence is sufficient if it tends to connect the defendant with the commission of the offense, though of itself, standing alone, "it would be entitled to little weight," correctly states the rule as to the *quantum* of proof essential to the corroboration of an accomplice. (Id.)

9. CREDIBILITY OF DEFENDANT—INSTRUCTION.—An instruction that a defendant in any criminal case is a competent witness in his own behalf, and the fact that he is a defendant is not of itself sufficient to impeach or discredit his testimony, though the jury are entitled to take into consideration his interest in the event of the prosecution in determining his credibility, violates the rule that instructions which purport to state the rules by which the credibility of witnesses or the weight of evidence is to be determined should be made applicable to all the witnesses or all the testimony. (Id.)

10. ASSAULT WITH DEADLY WEAPON WITH INTENT TO MURDER—DEFENSE OF ALIBI—INSTRUCTION.—In a prosecution for assault with a deadly weapon with intent to murder, where the evidence of the prosecution made out a *prima facie* case, and the defendant offered evidence in support of his claim of an alibi, it was error for the court to refuse to instruct the jury, upon defendant's request, that in making the proof of an alibi defendant was not obliged to establish that defense by a preponderance of evidence or beyond a reasonable doubt, but that it was sufficient to entitle him to a verdict of not guilty if the proof raised in the minds of the jury a reasonable doubt as to the presence of the defendant at the place where the crime was alleged to have been committed and at the time referred to in the information; nor did the fact that the court gave a general instruction to the effect that the jury must believe beyond a reasonable doubt that the defendant committed the crime before they could convict him, relieve the failure to give said instruction from prejudice. (People v. Visconti, 169.)

11. ASSAULT TO MURDER—INSANITY FROM USE OF ALCOHOLIC LIQUORS—REFUSAL OF INSTRUCTION ON LAW OF SETTLED INSANITY—PREJUDICIAL ERROR.—In a prosecution for the crime of assault to commit murder, it is prejudicial error to refuse an instruction proposed by the defendant on the law of insanity brought on by the use of intoxicating liquors that will excuse a criminal act, where it was expressly admitted by the people that the defendant was not intoxicated at the time of the assault, and there was evidence introduced which would support the theory that the alleged insanity of the defendant was the effect of long-continued intoxication prior to the commission of the crime. (People v. Goodrum, 430.)

CRIMINAL LAW (Continued).

12. CHARACTER OF MENTAL DERANGEMENT — ERRONEOUS INSTRUCTION — QUESTIONS OF FACT.—The reading to the jury, as a part of the instructions in the case, of the following language taken from a recent decision of the appellate court, to wit: "Defendant's normal condition was that of a sane man. His alleged mental derangement was not only transient in character, but such condition was the result of his voluntary acts in the use of alcoholic liquors. Under such circumstances, one prosecuted for the commission of a crime cannot urge such condition as a defense thereto,"—is prejudicial error, as the question whether the defendant's mental derangement was only of a transient character, and his condition the result of his voluntary acts in the use of alcoholic liquors, was a question solely and exclusively for the jury. (Id.)

13. TEMPORARY AND SETTLED INSANITY—USE OF INTOXICANTS.—There is a well-recognized distinction in law between temporary insanity or mental aberration brought on by voluntary intoxication and "settled insanity" superinduced by long-continued indulgence in alcoholic liquors. A sane person who voluntarily drinks and becomes intoxicated is not excused; but if one, by reason of long-continued indulgence in intoxicants has reached the stage of chronic alcoholism where the brain is permanently diseased and where permanent general insanity has resulted, he is not legally responsible for his acts. (Id.)

14. TEMPORARY DERANGEMENT FROM USE OF INTOXICANTS—EVIDENCE—MOTIVE OR INTENT.—Mere temporary mental derangement resulting from the use of intoxicants, whether it manifests itself in the form of *delirium tremens* or in some milder form, cannot operate to absolve a person from liability for a criminal act, and testimony disclosing that precise mental state at the time the criminal act was committed is admissible only where the existence of a particular purpose, motive, or intent is a necessary element of the crime charged, and then it may be considered by the jury, not as the predicate for the full exoneration of the accused, but solely to enable or assist them in determining the purpose, motive, or intent with which he committed the act. (Id.)

15. SCOPE OF DEFENSE—OPENING ADDRESS OF COUNSEL.—A defendant in a criminal case, in making a defense and proving his case, is not necessarily required to remain strictly within the literal scope of the defense outlined by his counsel in his opening address to the jury. (Id.)

16. BURGLARY—QUALIFICATION OF JURORS—IMPLIED BIAS—CONTRADICTORY ANSWERS—PROVINCE OF TRIAL COURT—REVIEW UPON APPEAL. Where, on the impaneling of a jury for the trial of a defendant charged with burglary, some of the jurors, in reply to questions by defendant's counsel, stated that the accused would be required to

CRIMINAL LAW (Continued).

produce evidence in his favor to create a reasonable doubt in their mind as to his guilt, but upon being questioned by the district attorney each declared that, if accepted as a juror in the case, he would at all times give the defendant the benefit of the presumption of innocence until his guilt was satisfactorily proved and acquit him if, after a full and fair consideration of the evidence by the light of the court's instructions upon the law, he entertained a reasonable doubt of the defendant's guilt, it was the province of the court, under this state of the record, to determine whether or not such jurors were disqualified for implied bias; and its discretion will not be disturbed on appeal unless it appears that it has been abused. (People v. Martinez, 413.)

17. EVIDENCE—DESCRIPTION OF DEFENDANT AND COMPANION.—In a prosecution for the crime of burglary, there is no error in permitting the people to prove that the defendant and another man, who was shown to have been the defendant's companion, applied for and obtained work together, that the defendant wore a particular kind of cap, that his companion wore a particular kind and size of shoes, that footprints in the snow leading to the burglarized premises corresponded in size with the shoes worn by the two men, and that the remnants of a leather case in which one of the stolen articles was incased were found a few days after the burglary in a town toward which the defendant and his companion were seen hastily going by foot on the night of the crime. (Id.)

18. STATEMENTS CONCERNING POSSESSION OF STOLEN PROPERTY—ADMISSIBILITY OF.—Statements made by the defendant when placed under arrest, involving conflicting or inconsistent explanations concerning the possession of one of the stolen articles, are properly admitted in evidence, without a preliminary showing that they were voluntarily made, as they do not involve a confession of guilt. (Id.)

19. REASONABLE DOUBT AS TO DEGREE OF CRIME—DUTY OF JURY—INSTRUCTION.—An instruction that "under the information in this case you may, *if the evidence warrant it*, find the defendant guilty of burglary of the first degree or burglary of the second degree. Should you entertain a reasonable doubt as to which of the two degrees he is guilty, *if any*, you will give the defendant the benefit of the doubt and acquit him of the higher offense," contains no intimation that the defendant is guilty of the crime of burglary, but obviously means that, if the jury find by the proper degree of proof that the defendant committed the crime charged, but should entertain a reasonable doubt as to which of the degrees of that crime, *if any*, he was, under the evidence, guilty of, then he would be entitled to the benefit of that doubt and in that case should only be convicted of the lower degree of the crime. (Id.)

20. CIRCUMSTANTIAL EVIDENCE—INSTRUCTION.—An instruction explaining that where circumstantial evidence is solely relied upon for the

CRIMINAL LAW (Continued).

proof of an accused's connection with the commission of a crime, "any fact essential to sustain the hypothesis of guilt and exclude the hypothesis of innocence," and any single fact from which the inference of guilt is to be drawn, "must be proved by evidence which satisfies the minds and conscience of the jury to the same extent that they are required to be satisfied of the facts in an issue in cases where the evidence is direct," is not argumentative, but if it were, the defendant cannot complain of it, where the record shows that it was given and read to the jury at his request. (Id.)

21. VERDICT OF CONVICTION—CIRCUMSTANTIAL EVIDENCE—SUFFICIENCY OF.—On appeal from a judgment of conviction of burglary in the first degree, it cannot be said that the verdict was not justified, where the proof showed the presence of the defendant and his companion in the town where the crime was committed just before such commission, the correspondence in size of the footprints on the surface of the snow leading to and from the burglarized building with the shoes worn by the defendant and his companion, the finding at a place in which direction the accused were seen traveling, of a part of the leather case in which one of the stolen watches was incased when taken from the building, a short time after the burglary, the possession by one of the parties of one of the stolen watches, and the contradictory statements made by the defendant and his companion in attempting to explain such possession. (Id.)

22. BURGLARY—EVIDENCE—CONFESSION.—In a prosecution for the crime of burglary, it is not error to admit in evidence the alleged confession of the defendant, where the *corpus delicti* is established and the confession shown to have been free and voluntary. (People v. Wing, 785.)

23. DEFENSE OF ALIBI—TEMPTATION TO RESORT TO—INSTRUCTION.—In such prosecution, it is not an invasion of the province of the jury to give an instruction which contained a statement which suggested to them that the defense of an alibi was occasionally fabricated and that temptation to resort to it might be great in cases of importance. (Id.)

24. EMBEZZLEMENT—LARCENY.—If one honestly receives goods upon trust, and afterward fraudulently converts them to his own use, he is guilty of embezzlement; but if he obtains possession fraudulently, with intent to convert the same to his own use, and the owner does not part with the title, the offense is larceny. (People v. Howard, 358.)

25. WRONGFUL TAKING OF MONEY BY WIFE—HUSBAND AS AIDER AND ABETTOR—EVIDENCE—UNWARRANTED CONVICTION OF GRAND LARCENY.—The conviction of a married man of the crime of grand larceny on the theory that he aided and abetted his wife in the wrongful taking of money by her, cannot be sustained, in the

CRIMINAL LAW (Continued).

absence of any evidence showing that the taking of the money was the result of a fraudulent and felonious design of the defendant and his wife conceived before she obtained employment in the commercial college from which the money was taken, and it is shown by the evidence presented that the money came into her control and care while employed in such college as a stenographer, and that among the duties assigned to her was that of selling small articles of merchandise, receiving the money therefor, and depositing the same in the cash register, to which she was given free access to make change and *permission* to handle the money therein. (Id.)

26. STATEMENT OF DIFFERENT OFFENSES—OMISSION TO CONCLUDE EACH COUNT WITH PHRASE "CONTRARY TO FORM OF STATUTE"—SUFFICIENCY OF INFORMATION.—An information in three counts, each stating a different offense, is not prejudicial to the defendant, because of the omission to conclude each count with the statement that the commission of the offense was "contrary to the form, force and effect of the statute in such case made and provided, and against the peace and dignity of the people of the state," etc., where the information is ended with such statement. (Id.)

27. DIFFERENT OFFENSES—NUMBER OF PEREMPTORY CHALLENGES.— Under an information charging more than one offense, the defendant is entitled to but ten peremptory challenges in all, and not ten as to each offense. (Id.)

28. CHARGE OF DIFFERENT OFFENSES — ELECTION NOT REQUIRED.— Under an information charging more than one offense, the people are not required to make an election, before offering proof, upon which count they intend to rely. (Id.)

29. APPEAL—STATEMENT OF "GROUNDS" AND "POINTS"—CONSTRUCTION OF SECTION 1247, PENAL CODE.—In an application for an appeal, made under section 1247 of the Penal Code, it is sufficient if the application states the *grounds* of the appeal, without specifying the *points* upon which the appellant relies, as there is no substantial distinction intended in the use of the two words. (People v. Preciado, 519.)

30. EMBEZZLEMENT—ESTABLISHMENT OF DEFENSE OF INSANITY—DEGREE OF PROOF—ERRONEOUS INSTRUCTIONS.—In a prosecution for the crime of embezzlement, wherein the principal defense made was that the defendant at the time of the commission of the alleged offense was not responsible, because he was incapable of understanding the nature and quality of the act on account of his then insanity, it is erroneous for the court to instruct the jury in three or four different instructions that the defense of insanity must be "clearly proved," "clearly established," or "satisfactorily established," although the jury was also instructed that the defense of insanity may be established by a preponderance of the evidence. (Id.)

CRIMINAL LAW (Continued).

31. INSANITY—PROOF OF DEFENSE—PREPONDERANCE OF EVIDENCE.—
The defense of insanity may be established by a preponderance of
the evidence, and trial courts are not allowed to qualify the rule by
requiring a higher degree of proof. (Id.)

32. EMBEZZLEMENT OF TAX MONEYS—PLEA OF ONCE IN JEOPARDY—
EVIDENCE—TAKING OF MONEYS AT SAME TIME.—In the prosecution
of a tax collector for the alleged embezzlement of certain moneys
paid to him as such officer by certain persons, wherein he interposed
the plea of once in jeopardy based upon his acquittal of the alleged
embezzlement of moneys paid to him by other parties, it is error
to refuse him permission to show in support of his plea that both
sums were taken at the same time. (Id.)

33. ACQUITTAL—WHEN A BAR.—Where the offense on trial is a necessary element in, and constitutes an essential part of, another
offense, and both are in fact but one transaction, a conviction or
acquittal of one is a bar to the prosecution of the other. (Id.)

34. REFUSAL TO PROVIDE FOR WIFE—IGNORANCE OF PRESENCE WITHIN
STATE—UNWARRANTED CONVICTION.—The conviction of a husband
of willfully neglecting to provide his wife with the necessaries of
life, as provided in section 270a of the Penal Code, is not warranted
where it is shown that he left her in another state, and had no
information of her presence in this state until he was arrested.
(People v. Smith, 736.)

35. LACK OF MEANS OF SUPPORT—PROOF BY WIFE.—In such a prosecution it is necessary that the wife should show that she was without
other sufficient means of support at the time of the alleged offense.
(Id.)

36. FELLATIO—INSUFFICIENT INFORMATION.—An information charging a
defendant with the commission of the acts technically known as
fellatio upon the person of a human being by force and violence
and against the will of such person, fails to state a public offense,
in the absence of any definition of such term, or of any statement
of the particular acts constituting the alleged offense. (People v.
Carrell, 793.)

37. INFORMATION—ESSENTIALS OF.—An information must contain a statement of acts constituting the offense in ordinary and concise language, and in such manner as to enable a person of common
understanding to know what is intended. (Id.)

38. INCEST—ACCOMPLICE—LACK OF CORROBORATION—EVIDENCE—IM-
PROPER ADMISSION OF.—In a prosecution for incest charged against
a father and alleged to have been committed with his eldest
daughter, a conviction cannot be sustained where the only corroboration of the prosecuting witness, who consented to the acts charged
and was therefore an accomplice, was the testimony of the younger
sister, admitted over the objection of the defense, who was called

CRIMINAL LAW (Continued).

by the prosecution as a witness in rebuttal to testify as to trouble between herself and her father about the time of his arrest, and asked by the district attorney whether or not she had trouble with him with regard to his acts of sexual intimacy with her, which question was answered in the affirmative, as evidence of similar acts with a person other than the one named in the information in such a case is not admissible; nor was such evidence admissible as rebuttal testimony, on the theory that the defendant had opened the door for it by testifying that he had had trouble with his two daughters on the subject of their staying out late at night, the latter testimony having been adduced upon cross-examination and under adverse rulings upon his objections thereto, in which he stated that he had not had any trouble with his daughters. (People v. Letoile, 166.)

39. TRIAL BEHIND CLOSED DOORS—VIOLATION OF CONSTITUTION.—While the court has the right to regulate the admission of the public to the courtroom in the trial of a criminal case in any appropriate manner in order to prevent overcrowding or disorder, the right does not exist to wholly exclude the public, as under article I, section 13, of the constitution of this state the party accused in a criminal prosecution is given the right to a public trial. (Id.)

40. MURDER—SELF-DEFENSE—DOCTRINE OF APPARENT DANGER—INCONSISTENT INSTRUCTION.—In a prosecution for the crime of murder, where the plea made by the defendant is that of self-defense, an instruction that there must have been a present ability on the part of the assailant to accomplish his criminal design in order to justify the person assailed in taking his life is inconsistent with the doctrine of apparent danger to one who is assailed, but is not so misleading as to have caused a miscarriage of justice, where the evidence shows whatever real or apparent necessity defendant believed to exist for the killing was created by his own fault. (People v. Finali, 479.)

41. PLEA OF SELF-DEFENSE—WHEN NOT AVAILABLE—SEEKING OF QUARREL.—An instruction that self-defense is not available as a plea to a defendant who has sought a quarrel with a design to force a deadly issue and thus, through his fraud, connivance, or fault, create a real or apparent necessity for the killing, is proper, where the evidence shows that whatever real or apparent necessity the defendant believed to exist for the killing was created by his own fault. (Id.)

42. DOCTRINE OF SELF-DEFENSE.—The doctrine of self-defense presupposes that one who would avail himself of it has, without his fault, found himself in threatened danger of serious bodily injury, to avert which the law gives him the right to resort to extreme measures. But the plea is not available to him where he willfully and without any necessity for his own protection creates the danger with which he is threatened. (Id.)

CRIMINAL LAW (Continued).

43. RETURN OF JURY FOR FURTHER INSTRUCTIONS—RIGHT OF DEFENDANT. Upon the return of the jury for further instructions while deliberating on the verdict, the defendant is not entitled as a matter of right to have read to them instructions not called for, or to have all of the instructions upon a given subject read, when such as are read are stated to be satisfactory to them. (Id.)

44. ARGUMENT OF DISTRICT ATTORNEY—COMMENT UPON FAILURE OF DEFENDANT TO DENY SELF-INCRIMINATORY STATEMENT—LACK OF PREJUDICE.—In such a prosecution, while it is wrong for the district attorney in his argument to the jury to make reference to the fact that the defendant, while on the witness-stand, had failed to make denial of a somewhat self-incriminatory statement which he made at the time of his arrest and which was introduced in evidence, such misconduct is not prejudicially erroneous, under section 4½ of article VI of the constitution, where the jury was fully advised as to the subject matter of such statement through other testimony. (Id.)

45. MISCONDUCT OF DISTRICT ATTORNEY—WHEN GROUND FOR REVERSAL. Where misconduct of the district attorney is claimed as prejudicial, if attention is called to it and the court instructs the jury to disregard it and not allow themselves to be influenced by it, the misconduct must be flagrant and obviously prejudicial to justify a reversal. (Id.)

46. CIRCUMSTANTIAL EVIDENCE—INSTRUCTION.—In a criminal case it is not error to refuse to instruct the jury at the request of the defendant on the law of circumstantial evidence, upon the theory that the case of the prosecution was based upon such evidence alone, where it appears that the prosecution did not rely solely or chiefly upon circumstantial evidence to obtain defendant's conviction. (People v. Gorman, 762.)

47. MURDER—CONSPIRACY TO COMMIT ROBBERY—INSTRUCTION.—In a prosecution for murder it is not error to refuse to instruct the jury at the request of the defendant upon the subject of conspiracy to commit robbery, where there was little or no evidence offered to support that view of the case. (Id.)

48. LACK OF MOTIVE—CIRCUMSTANCE OF INNOCENCE—INSTRUCTION.— It is not error to refuse to instruct the jury that if the evidence fails to show any motive on the part of the defendant consistent with reason and soundness of mind to commit the crime charged, it is a circumstance in favor of innocence, and should be considered by the jury in connection with the other evidence in the case. (Id.)

49. MURDER—LACK OF ERROR.—Upon this appeal from a judgment and order denying a new trial in a prosecution for murder, it is held that there was no error committed prejudicial to the rights of the defendant. (People v. Duncan, 772.)

CRIMINAL LAW (Continued).

50. ROBBERY—EVIDENCE—REGISTRATION AT HOTEL UNDER OTHER THAN TRUE NAME—VERBAL PROOF BY WITNESS.—In a prosecution for the crime of robbery, it is not error to permit a witness, who went with the defendant on the night of the commission of the crime to an adjoining town, to testify that they went to a hotel and that the defendant registered under a name other than his true name. (People v. Ferrara, 1.)

51. STATEMENTS OF DEFENDANT AT PRELIMINARY EXAMINATION— PROOF BY REPORTER—REFERENCE TO NOTES NOT FILED.—In such a prosecution there is no error in allowing the phonographic reporter who acted at the preliminary examination to refer to his original notes to enable him to testify as to certain statements made by the defendant at such hearing, notwithstanding such notes had not been filed. (Id.)

52. CONTRADICTORY TESTIMONY—CONSIDERATION BY JURY—INSTRUCTION.—An instruction that contradictory testimony is admissible only for the purpose of impeaching the credibility of a witness and that the jury might not consider it as evidence of the truth of such statements, is properly refused. (Id.)

53. GUILT OF DEFENDANT—TAKING OF PROPERTY BY FORCE AND FEAR— USE OF DISJUNCTIVE—INSTRUCTION.—An instruction that if the jury found that the taking of the money was accomplished by means of "force or fear," they could find a verdict of guilty, is not erroneous, notwithstanding that the information charged that the taking was accomplished by means of force and fear. (Id.)

54. ROBBERY—EVIDENCE—USE OF STOLEN AUTOMOBILE—PREJUDICIAL ERROR.—Where, in a prosecution for robbery, it is shown that the persons engaged in the commission of the crime drove to the scene thereof in a Ford automobile about 7 o'clock in the evening, and the evidence is barely, if at all, sufficient to justify the verdict that the defendant participated in the robbery, it is prejudicial error to permit the owner of a Ford automobile to testify, over objection made by the defendant, that he left his machine at a corner about 4 o'clock in the afternoon, that it was gone when he returned there to get it about 8 o'clock, and that he found it at another place some hours later, in the absence of evidence identifying such machine as the automobile used by the perpetrators of the crime, except that both were Ford machines and the isinglass was out of the back thereof. (People v. Renwick, 774.)

55. ALIBI—EVIDENCE—MODIFICATION OF TESTIMONY—REFUSAL TO PERMIT—PREJUDICIAL ERROR.—In such a prosecution it is prejudicial error to refuse to permit the defendant to recall a witness for the prosecution in surrebuttal for the purpose of permitting the witness to modify her testimony as to the presence of the defendant at a certain place at the time of the commission of the alleged crime. (Id.)

DAMAGES. See Assault and Battery, 2-4; Contract, 4, 11; Eminent Domain, 14; Negligence, 11; Rape, 3, 4; Sale, 6,

DEED. See Banks; Vendor and Vendee.

DISMISSAL. See Practice, 1, 4.

DIVORCE.

1. ASSIGNMENT OF COMMUNITY PROPERTY—DISCRETION.—In actions for divorce on the ground of adultery or extreme cruelty, subdivision 1 of section 146 of the Civil Code confers upon the trial court a wide latitude for the exercise of its judgment and discretion in assigning the community property to the respective parties, and in every case it will be presumed that such discretion has been wisely and properly exercised. (Thomsen v. Thomsen, 185.)

2. CRUELTY OF WIFE—AWARD OF MORE THAN ONE-HALF OF COMMUNITY PROPERTY TO HUSBAND—DISCRETION NOT ABUSED.—In an action for divorce wherein the decree is granted to the husband on the ground of extreme cruelty, there is no abuse of discretion in awarding to the husband more than one-half of the community property, notwithstanding the wife has been a hard-working woman and by her efforts has assisted in accumulating the property, as her cruelty must be taken into consideration in making the award. (Id.)

3. ANTENUPTIAL HOLDINGS OF HUSBAND—CONSIDERATION IN AWARDING COMMUNITY PROPERTY.—Where a divorce is granted to the husband on the ground of the wife's cruelty, it is proper to take into consideration, in awarding the community property, the antenuptial holdings of the husband used by him after marriage and intermingled with the common holdings, notwithstanding such separate holdings cannot be traced into any specific piece of property. (Id.)

4. AWARD OF PROPERTY IN SEVERALTY TO ONE SPOUSE.—In awarding the community property, the court may consider all of the property as one asset or fund, composed of separate units, and award all of designated and described pieces of property to one party, instead of an undivided interest in all. (Id.)

5. MANDATE—EXECUTION ON ALIMONY ORDER—REVOCATION OF.—An order commanding the clerk of the superior court to issue a writ of execution to enforce an order for the payment of alimony *pendente lite* in an action of divorce, will be reversed on appeal, where it is made to appear that the order granting the alimony had been revoked before the making of the order appealed from. (Machado v. Machado, 378.)

6. DENIAL OF RELIEF—AWARD OF CUSTODY OF CHILDREN—POWER OF COURT.—In an action for divorce, the court has power under section 138 of the Civil Code to make an order affecting the custody of the children of the marriage, although the divorce is denied. (Matter of John E. Saul, 382.)

DIVORCE (Continued).

7. CONSTRUCTION OF SECTION 138, CIVIL CODE.—Section 138 of the Civil Code itself does not state any limitation of its effect to cases in which divorce is denied, and if such limitation be imposed upon the language of the statute it must be a limitation by construction, but such section is designed for the protection of children and should be liberally construed. (Id.)

8. APPLICATION FOR COUNSEL FEES AND COSTS—ALLEGED NONRESIDENCE OF WIFE—RIGHT TO PRIOR HEARING OF APPLICATION.—A wife who is without means to prosecute an action for divorce is entitled to have an application made by her for attorney's fees, court costs, and alimony *pendente lite* heard and determined in advance of the question raised by the defendant as to her alleged nonresidence, and consequent lack of jurisdiction of the court. (Dahne v. Superior Court, 664.)

9. RESIDENCE IN DIVORCE ACTIONS—CONSTRUCTION OF SECTION 128, CIVIL CODE.—Section 128 of the Civil Code relative to residence of the plaintiff in actions for divorce does not impose any limitation on the jurisdiction of the superior court in such actions, but simply prescribes certain facts essential to the making out of a case warranting a divorce, and allegations in regard to residence stand upon the same footing as any other allegation of facts showing the right to a divorce. (Id.)

10. CUSTODY OF CHILDREN—APPEAL—STAY OF PROCEEDINGS.—In an action for divorce an order included in the interlocutory decree awarding the father the custody of the minor children of the parties is stayed by the taking of an appeal from such decree by the wife, and the trial court has no jurisdiction pending the appeal to order that such children be taken from the possession of their mother and given to their father. (Matter of Dupes, 698.)

11. EFFECT OF APPEAL—REMOVAL OF JURISDICTION.—The effect of the perfecting of an appeal is to stay all further proceedings upon the judgment or order appealed from or matters embraced therein in the court below, and to remove the subject matter of the adjudication from the jurisdiction of such court. (Id.)

See Husband and Wife, 3.

EASEMENT. See Eminent Domain, 11.

EJECTMENT. See Adverse Possession, 4.

EMBEZZLEMENT. See Criminal Law, 24-33.

EMINENT DOMAIN.

1. OWNERSHIP—FORMER ADJUDICATION—EVIDENCE—ADMISSIBILITY OF JUDGMENT-ROLL AND FINDINGS—ESTOPPEL.—In an action by a city

EMINENT DOMAIN (Continued).

to condemn land for the purpose of widening a thoroughfare, where defendant pleaded a former adjudication as to the title of the land between the city and his predecessor, the judgment-roll and findings in the former action are admissible in evidence, although uncertain as to the identity of the land, where the pleadings admitted that the precise tract involved was in dispute in the former action, the judgment not being so ambiguous as to be void; and the former judgment estops the plaintiff in the second action. (City of Los Angeles v. Moore; Johnston v. City of Los Angeles, 39.)

2. WIDENING OF CITY THOROUGHFARE—OWNERSHIP OF LAND—BURDEN OF PROOF.—In this action brought by the city of Los Angeles to condemn, for the purpose of widening a certain thoroughfare therein, an irregular plot of ground aligning a portion of the northeasterly boundary of lands patented to the city, and to which the appellant claimed ownership as devisee under the will of a grantee of the city to a large tract of land, which was claimed to include the plot in question, it is held that by reason of the inaccuracies appearing in the surveys of the engineers who gave testimony for the appellant as to the monuments and lines of the land described in the deed of appellant's testate, the appellant had failed to sustain the burden of proof that the plot in dispute was included in the deed. (City of Los Angeles v. Moore; Johnston v. City of Los Angeles, 41.)

3. REPAYMENT OF SEWER ASSESSMENT—REDEMPTION FROM EXECUTION SALE—RIGHT TO REIMBURSEMENT.—The appellant in such action is not entitled, as a condition to a determination against his ownership of the property, to be repaid the amount of a sewer assessment, which he paid upon redeeming the property from an execution sale had on a judgment against him. (Id.)

4. PUBLIC PARK—POWER POLE LINE AND PROPOSED SUBWAY RIGHTS OF ELECTRIC RAILROAD COMPANY—PROTECTION FROM CONDEMNATION—DUTY OF COURT.—In an action brought by a municipal corporation to condemn a large tract of land for the purposes of a public park, where there is included in such tract certain parcels belonging to an electric railway company and used by it for the purposes of a power pole line and certain other parcels which the company had acquired for the purpose of constructing and operating a subway, it is the duty of the court to determine as a matter of fact, both as to the pole line and the subway parcels, whether they had been dedicated to a public use, upon which issue the burden of proof is on the defendant, and if either or both of them were devoted to a public use, then the court should determine as a matter of fact whether that and the proposed park use were consistent, upon which issue the burden of proof is on the plaintiff, and if the respective uses are not in fact wholly inconsistent, then it is the

EMINENT DOMAIN (Continued).

further duty of the court to fix the terms and conditions of condemnation by the city, and the manner and extent of use of the property "for each of such purposes." (City of Los Angeles v. Los Angeles Pacific Company, 100.)

5. TAKING OF PROPERTY ALREADY DEVOTED TO PUBLIC USE—CONSTRUCTION OF STATUTES.—The statutes contemplate the taking of private property for public use, and also that property already devoted to public use may be taken for a more necessary public use, but that in the latter case where the proposed new use is also consistent with the existing public use, the two rights shall be exercised in common, under the terms and conditions appropriate to the case. (Id.)

6. TAKING OF PROPERTY FOR PARK PURPOSES—DETERMINATION OF LEGISLATIVE BODY OF MUNICIPALITY—HOW FAR CONCLUSIVE—CONSTRUCTION OF PARK AND PLAYGROUND ACT AND CODE.—The general rule which is found in section 1241 of the Code of Civil Procedure and in the Park and Playground Act (Stats. 1909, p. 1066 et seq.), and which authorizes the legislative body of a city to finally determine that the public necessity and convenience require that certain land be condemned for park purposes, is modified by subdivision 4 of section 1240 of such code, enacted to meet the specifically designated case where it is proposed to condemn land already subject to an existing public use; and under such a situation, while the court will recognize as final the determination of the legislative body that the taking of the land is necessary for public use, it is required also to recognize the existing public use, and to provide for the terms and conditions upon which the existing use may continue, if in fact the two uses are capable of coexisting on the same premises. (Id.)

7. LOS ANGELES CHARTER—USE OF PART OF PARK FOR POWER POLE LINE.—The provision of section 119b of the charter of the city of Los Angeles, that all property located therein which has been or may be set apart or dedicated for the use of the public as a park or parks shall forever remain inviolate to the use of the public for such purpose, means no more than that when land has been acquired by the city for park uses, such land shall not thereafter be appropriated to other uses, and does not prevent such city from acquiring land for park purposes, subject to the use thereof for another purpose to which it has been dedicated, where the two uses are consistent and capable of existing together. (Id.)

8. LANDS OCCUPIED FOR POWER POLE LINE PURPOSES—PUBLIC USE.—The use of land occupied by an electric railway company for pole line purposes is a public use. (Id.)

9. LANDS ACQUIRED FOR SUBWAY—NONCOMPLETION—PUBLIC USE.—Parcels of land purchased and held by an electric railway company for the purpose of constructing therein a subway are devoted to a public use, notwithstanding that all parcels necessary to the construction of such subway had not been obtained, where about ninety

EMINENT DOMAIN (Continued).

per cent of the parcels had been acquired and it is shown to be the intention of the company to complete the enterprise. (Id.)

10. AMOUNT OF COMPENSATION—ACCRUED TAXES AT TIME OF AWARD.— In awarding damages in an action in eminent domain, section 1249 of the Code of Civil Procedure excludes all consideration other than the value of the property at the date of the issuance of the summons in the action, and therefore no award is permissible for taxes and assessments not accrued at the time of the award. (Id.)

11. EASEMENT FOR POLE LINE—RIGHT TO COMPENSATION FOR TAKING.— An easement over land for a power pole line acquired by a street railroad corporation is a substantial property right, the value of which should be accounted for by any other party seeking to enforce a superior right of eminent domain upon the same premises; and the owners of the fee are not entitled to all the compensation to be allowed for the taking of the land, if the right of way is to be included in the condemnation without any reservation of further right of use by the company. (Id.)

12. CONDEMNATION OF LAND FOR LEVEE—EVIDENCE—OPINION OF VALUE— OTHER SALES—IMPROPER REDIRECT EXAMINATION.—In an action in eminent domain brought by a reclamation district, to condemn a strip of land as a part of a right of way for a levee, it is error to permit the plaintiff upon redirect examination of one of its trustees, who had on direct examination given his opinion as to the market value of the strip, to state that he based his opinion upon what other lands in the district of a similar character as to quality had been sold for to the district, although the defendant on cross-examination brought out the fact of other sales and the prices at which they were made, but such error is without prejudice, where it is obvious from the verdict that the jury did not accept the testimony of the witness as to value. (Reclamation District No. 730 v. Inglin, 495.)

13. OTHER SALES AND PRICES OBTAINED—PROPER CROSS-EXAMINATION —LIMITED PURPOSE.—In such an action it is proper to bring out on the cross-examination of a witness as to value the fact of other sales in the district and the prices at which they were made, for the purpose of testing the witness' knowledge and impeaching his opinion, but not for the purpose of fixing the value of the strip in suit. (Id.)

14. VALUE OF LAND—RIGHT OF OWNER.—The owner of land sought to be condemned is entitled to its actual market value for the most valuable use or uses to which it is adapted or may be put, and the prices at which other lands of like quality and adaptation and similarly situated may have been sold cannot reasonably be accepted as a just criterion for measuring, and finally ascertaining, the actual value of the land sought to be taken. (Id.)

EMINENT DOMAIN (Continued).

15. APPEAL FROM JUDGMENT—STAY OF PROCEEDINGS—SUPERSEDEAS.—
In an action in eminent domain to secure a railroad right of
way, the taking of an appeal by the plaintiff from the judgment
of condemnation prior to the expiration of the thirty-day period
in which the plaintiff is required by section 1251 of the Code
of Civil Procedure to pay the sum of money assessed, has the
effect of staying execution on the judgment pending the appeal
without the giving of a stay bond, and the appellant is entitled to
a writ of *supersedeas* staying such execution. (Colusa and Hamilton Railroad Company v. Superior Court, 746.)

16. NATURE OF JUDGMENT.—A judgment of condemnation is not, prior
to the expiration of the thirty-day period, a judgment for the direct
payment of money within the meaning of section 942 of the Code
of Civil Procedure requiring the execution of an undertaking to
stay the operation of the judgment pending appeal, but amounts
to no more·than an order fixing the price at which plaintiff may
or may not take the property. (Id.)

17. TIME OF PAYMENT OF DAMAGES—CONSTRUCTION OF SECTION 1251,
CODE OF CIVIL PROCEDURE.—The "final judgment" mentioned in section 1251 of the Code of Civil Procedure relating to the time within
which the plaintiff must pay the sum of money assessed as damages,
has reference to the preliminary judgment of condemnation entered
by the superior court, and not to the final conclusion of the litigation.
(Id.)

EMPLOYER AND EMPLOYEE.

1. ACTION FOR DAMAGES—BREACH OF CONTRACT OF EMPLOYMENT—DIS-
CHARGE FROM SERVICE—PLEADING—INSUFFICIENT COMPLAINT.—In an
action for the recovery of damages for the breach of a contract,
wherein the plaintiff assigned to the defendant certain leases and
contracts for the removal of earth and clay materials to be used in
the manufacture of brick and other articles, and agreed to give his
entire time and attention to the business of the defendant for a
period of years, in consideration of the delivery to him of certain
shares of the capital stock of the defendant and the agreement to
employ him for the said period at a stated monthly salary, the complaint fails to state a cause of action for damages for the alleged
violation of the terms of the contract in so far as the wrongful dismissal of the plaintiff by the defendant is alleged, where the only
averment charging such dismissal is that the defendant refused "to
perform the contract any longer or further or in whole or in part
or to any extent," and still so refuses, and that the plaintiff has
been prevented from performing the contract in any respect or at
all by reason of the "aforesaid refusal and continued refusal of said
defendant." (Winsor v. Silica Brick Company, 85.)

2. DISCHARGE OF PLAINTIFF—INSUFFICIENCY OF EVIDENCE.—A letter
written by the defendant to the plaintiff stating that the former

EMPLOYER AND EMPLOYEE (Continued).

"hereby releases you from any further services in its behalf. This will enable you to seek employment elsewhere," does not constitute a clear and unequivocal act of dismissal, and is not sufficient to support a finding of a discharge, when read in connection with the uncontradicted testimony of the secretary of the defendant as to a statement made by the plaintiff a few days before the receipt of the letter that he had an opportunity to obtain employment elsewhere if the defendant would release him from the contract. (Id.)

3. PREVENTION OF PERFORMANCE—INSUFFICIENCY OF EVIDENCE.—In the absence of evidence of any affirmative act on the part of the plaintiff after the receipt of such letter showing a willingness upon his part to proceed with the contract, the allegation in such complaint that the defendant prevented the plaintiff from proceeding with the performance of the contract is not sustained. (Id.)

See Workmen's Compensation Act.

ESTATES OF DECEASED PERSONS.

1. SURRENDER OF STOCK IN LOCAL CORPORATION TO FOREIGN EXECUTOR—RECOVERY BY SUBSEQUENTLY APPOINTED LOCAL ADMINISTRATOR.—The voluntary surrender by a domestic corporation of stock therein owned by a resident of another state at the time of his death to the foreign domiciliary executor of the deceased, and subsequently to the rightful devisee under the will, prior to any local ancillary administration, constitutes a good defense to an action for the stock brought by the local ancillary administrator against the corporation. (Union Trust Company of San Francisco v. Pacific Telephone & Telegraph Company, 64.)

2. PERSONAL PROPERTY OUTSIDE OF STATE—TAKING OF POSSESSION BY LOCAL ADMINISTRATOR.—Although the executor or administrator of the domicile cannot maintain a suit in another state to recover personal property or collect a debt due the estate, yet he may take possession of such property peaceably without suit, or collect a debt if voluntarily paid, and if there is no opposing administration in the state where the property was situated, its courts will recognize his title as rightful, and protect it as fully as if he had taken out letters of administration there; and the voluntary payment of the debt by such debtor under such circumstances would be good, and constitute a defense to a suit by an ancillary administrator subsequently appointed. (Id.)

ESTOPPEL. See Brokers, 3; Contract, 10; Corporation, 5, 7; Eminent Domain, 1; Mechanics' Liens, 5.

EVIDENCE. See Account Stated, 4, 7; Adverse Possession, 7, 11;
    Appeal, 5; Brokers, 10; Contract, 8, 12; Corporation, 4; Crim-
    inal Law, 1–10, 14, 16–22, 25, 31, 38, 46, 50–52, 54, 55; Emi-
    nent Domain, 1, 2, 12–14; Fraud, 4, 5; Illegal Contract, 2, 3;
    Negligence, 1–3, 14, 15, 29, 31–33; Rape; Receipt; Warehouse-
    man.

EXECUTION.

1. STAY OF EXECUTION—RUNNING OF PERIOD OF LIMITATION.—An order
    staying execution of a judgment made on the day a judgment is
    rendered runs from that date, and not from the date of the entry of
    the judgment. (Garrett v. Garrett, 173.)

2. GREATER AMOUNT THAN JUDGMENT—QUASHING OF WRIT.—Where
    an execution is issued for a greater amount than that for which
    the judgment was rendered, it may be quashed on motion. (Har-
    baugh v. Lassen Irrigation Company, 764.)

3. JURISDICTION—DIFFERENT JUDGES.—The jurisdiction of the court to
    quash the writ is not affected by the fact that the judge who pre-
    sided at the hearing of the motion to quash was a different judge
    from the one who presided when the writ was ordered to issue. (Id.)
    See Appeal, 1, 3, 8, 9; Eminent Domain, 15.

EXECUTORS AND ADMINISTRATORS. See Estates of Deceased
    Persons.

FALSE IMPRISONMENT. See Assault and Battery.

FELLATIO. See Criminal Law, 36, 37.

FENCES.

1. RAILROAD CORPORATION—FAILURE TO FENCE TRACK—KILLING OF DO-
    MESTIC ANIMAL—RIGHT OF ACTION—CONSTRUCTION OF CODE.—The
    provisions of section 485 of the Civil Code, as that section existed
    prior to the amendment of 1915, giving a right of action against a
    railroad company for the killing or maiming of a domestic animal
    upon its line of road which passes through or along the property of
    the owner thereof, in case of the company's failure to fence the
    track, are not intended to be for the benefit of the owners of stock
    running at large, but the right of action there given exists only in
    favor of one having some interest in land adjoining the right of way
    of the railroad. (Wills v. Southern Pacific Company, 723.)

2. ACTION BY LESSEE—INTEREST IN LAND—FAILURE OF PROOF.—In
    an action against a railroad corporation for damages on account of
    the loss of certain horses of the plaintiff which were killed by a
    collision with one of the defendant's trains by reason of the negli-
    gence of the defendant in permitting the gate in its fence inclosing
    its right of way to be left open and the animals to stray thereon

FENCES (Continued).

from adjacent land, the right of the plaintiff in or to the land is not established by proof that she leased the land from a third party, without any further proof that such party owned the land, or any interest therein, or that he was in possession of it, or that the plaintiff obtained possession through him. (Id.)

8. CLOSING OF GATES—DUTY OF RAILROAD CORPORATIONS—ERRONEOUS INSTRUCTION.—An instruction declaring it to be the duty of a railroad corporation to keep gates in fences along its tracks closed on all proper occasions to prevent stock from adjoining lands from passing upon its right of way, is erroneous, in that it imposes upon such a corporation the absolute duty of keeping the gates closed, whereas in fact its only duty is to use reasonable care to keep them closed. (Id.)

FINDINGS.

1. ACTION FOR SERVICES—CROSS-COMPLAINT FOR MONEY LOANED AND GOODS SOLD—FAILURE TO FIND ON ISSUE—REVERSAL OF JUDGMENT. Where in an action to recover for services performed in working a mine, the defendant filed a cross-complaint alleging an indebtedness to him for money loaned and goods sold, and the plaintiff in his answer to such pleading denied the indebtedness, and evidence was admitted on such issue, a finding thereon was essential, and where omitted, the judgment must be reversed on appeal. (Math v. Crescent Hill Gold Mines Co. of California, 636.)

2. MATERIAL ISSUE—APPEAL.—A judgment will be reversed on appeal where there is a failure to make a finding on a material issue. (Id.)

See Adverse Possession, 4.

FIRE INSURANCE. See Insurance, 13–15.

FISH AND GAME.

1. POWER OF LEGISLATURE—CONSTITUTIONAL LAW.—By the adoption in the year 1902 of section 25½ of article IV of the constitution, providing that the legislature may provide for the division of the state into fish and game districts and may enact such laws for the protection of fish and game therein as it may deem appropriate to the respective districts, the people expressly vested in the legislature of the state the sole and exclusive power over and control of legislation relating to the fish and game of the state, and withdrew from the local subdivisions of the state whatever power they might have previously exercised over such subject under section 11 of article XI of the constitution, which grants to counties, cities, towns, and townships of the state the right to make and enforce within their respective limits all such local, police,

FISH AND GAME (Continued).

sanitary, and other regulations as are not in conflict with general laws. (Matter of Cancinino, 238.)

2. CONSTITUTIONAL PROVISION MANDATORY.—The provisions of section 25½ of article IV of the constitution are mandatory, notwithstanding the use therein of the word "may." (Id.)

3. STATUTORY CONSTRUCTION—PERMISSIVE LANGUAGE.—Where the purpose of the law is to clothe public officers with power to be exercised for the benefit of the public, language which is permissive in form is to be construed as peremptory. (Id.)

4. WITHDRAWAL OF POLICE POWER.—The people may at any time legally withdraw from local authorities the power of police or any portion thereof which they have by their constitution granted to such authorities. (Id.)

FRAUD.

1. TRANSFER OF CORPORATE STOCK — INTENT TO DEFRAUD CREDITORS—SUPPORT OF FINDING. — In an action by a judgment creditor to have a transfer of corporate stock made by a husband to his wife declared void on the ground that the transfer was made without consideration and at a time when the defendant was indebted to the plaintiff and to others in a large amount, a finding that the gift was made with intent to delay and defraud creditors is supported by evidence that the defendant owned one-third of the stock of the corporation, that the year before the transfer the corporation lost one-third of the amount for which it was capitalized, and that the defendant, fully aware of the financial condition of the corporation, a few months before the transfer offered to plaintiff all his stock if plaintiff would assume his liabilities thereon. (S. E. Slade Lumber Company v. Derby, 155.)

2. TRANSFER WITH INTENT TO DEFRAUD—INSOLVENCY IMMATERIAL.— A solvent person may transfer property with intent to hinder his creditors, as well as one who is insolvent. (Id.)

3. EVIDENCE OF FRAUD.—The question whether a conveyance is in fraud of the rights of a creditor is one of fact, and it can only be inferred in most cases from all the attending facts and circumstances. (Id.)

4. JUDGMENT AND EXECUTION—ADMISSION IN EVIDENCE.—In an action by a judgment creditor to set aside a transfer on the ground of fraud, it is not error to admit in evidence the judgment, and writs of execution in the action in which the judgment was obtained, as it is necessary to enable such a creditor to maintain the action for him to show that he was a judgment creditor and that he had exhausted his legal remedies to obtain satisfaction of the judgment. (Id.)

5. ADMISSION OF EVIDENCE—LIBERAL RULE.—In an action to set aside transfers on the ground of fraud, great latitude should be allowed

FRAUD (Continued).

in the admission of circumstantial evidence, and objections to questions on the ground of irrelevancy are not favored. (Id.)

See Corporation, 3, 4; Mortgage; Pledge, 2.

GRANTOR AND GRANTEE. See Banks; Deed.

GUARANTY. See Corporation, 10.

HOMESTEAD.

1. EXCHANGE OF REAL PROPERTY—REFORMATION AND SPECIFIC ENFORCEMENT.—A husband and wife are not entitled to have a written contract for an exchange of real property reformed and then specifically enforced where the writing consisted of a written offer made and signed only by the husband and accepted in writing by the defendant, and the property of the plaintiffs was encumbered with a homestead declared by the wife. (Ainsworth v. Morrill, 509.)

2. ENCUMBRANCE—STRICT COMPLIANCE WITH STATUTE.—The policy and purpose of section 1242 of the Civil Code is to prevent the destruction or encumbrance of a homestead by either spouse acting alone, and a purported conveyance or encumbrance of the homestead by either spouse not made in strict compliance with the requirements of such section is invalid and inoperative for any purpose. (Id.)

HUSBAND AND WIFE.

1. ACTIONS—ABATEMENT AND SURVIVAL OF CAUSES OF ACTIONS—TORTS. An action arising out of a tort, unconnected with contract and which affects the person only and not the estate, is purely personal, and abates with the death of the wrongdoer, while an action virtually founded upon contract, though nominally in tort, survives against the tort-feasor's legal representatives. (Vragnizan v. Savings Union Bank and Trust Company, 709.)

2. SETTLEMENT OF PROPERTY RIGHTS — RECOVERY OF CONCEALED PROPERTY—ACTION NOT ABATED UPON DEATH.—An action to recover one-half of the value of certain property concealed by a husband from his wife upon the settlement of their property rights during the pendency of an action for divorce, is in the nature of an action for the recovery of an interest in property, and does not abate with the death of the husband. (Id.)

3. MAINTENANCE OF ACTION—DECREE OF DIVORCE NOT A BAR.—The maintenance of such an action is not barred by the decree in the suit for divorce, where such decree dealt only with the status of the parties. (Id.)

4. PLEADING—OFFICIAL CAPACITY OF EXECUTOR.—An allegation in the complaint that on a stated day letters testamentary were duly and regularly issued to the defendant executor, and that such defendant ever since has been and now is the duly qualified and acting ex-

HUSBAND AND WIFE (Continued).

ecutor of the will of the deceased husband, is a sufficient allegation of official capacity, in the absence of a special demurrer. Where such allegation is admitted in the answer, such admission has the effect of a stipulation of the fact, which renders the allegation of more specific facts unnecessary. (Id.)

5. FALSE REPRESENTATIONS — STATEMENT IN DIVORCE PROCEEDINGS— RIGHT OF ACTION NOT AFFECTED BY.—The fact that most of the false representations made by the deceased upon which the plaintiff relied were not made to her personally, but by the testimony of the deceased and in affidavits filed by him in the action for divorce, does not affect the right of the plaintiff to maintain the action. (Id.)

See Criminal Law, 34, 35; Divorce; Trust.

ILLEGAL CONTRACT.

1. CONTRACT FOR PURCHASE OF STOCKS ON MARGIN—PLEDGE TO SECURE BROKERS — ACTION TO RECOVER PLEDGED PROPERTY — PLEADING— SUFFICIENCY OF COMPLAINT.—In an action in replevin to recover certain certificates of stock and a certain bond deposited with a firm of stockbrokers engaged in the business of buying and selling stocks and bonds on margin, and otherwise, as collateral security for any debt that might accrue from the plaintiff to the defendants on account of any loss caused by reason of any contract that plaintiff might make with defendants whereby defendants might purchase of or for, or sell to or for, plaintiff, on margin, shares of the capital stock of various corporations, the complaint states a cause of action where it is alleged that in none of the various contracts entered into was there any intention on the part of either party that there should be delivery of the shares of stock bought or sold, but that only the difference between the contract price and the market price of said shares should be paid, and only such difference was ever paid. (Hartnett v. Wilson, 678.)

2. EVIDENCE — UNLAWFUL CHARACTER OF TRANSACTIONS — GENERAL QUESTIONS—LACK OF PREJUDICE.—In an action to recover the possession of such certificates and bond, the defendants are not prejudiced by the rulings of the court in permitting the plaintiff to show the character of many of the transactions in a general way, where previous thereto a great deal of evidence had been received covering particular details of many of the transactions, showing their unlawful character. (Id.)

3. RULES OF NEW YORK STOCK EXCHANGE — PROOF PROPERLY EXCLUDED.—The rules of the New York Stock Exchange in regard to buying and selling stock are properly excluded in such an action, where there was no evidence that the defendants were members of such exchange, or transacted any of the plaintiff's business through it. (Id.)

ILLEGAL CONTRACT (Continued).

4. VALUE OF PROPERTY—TIME OF DEMAND FOR DELIVERY.—The value of the property involved in such an action is to be computed according to its value at the time when demand for delivery was made, and not as of the date of the original deposit. (Id.)

5. TRIAL—REFUSAL OF CONTINUANCE — DISCRETION NOT ABUSED.—It is not an abuse of discretion to refuse a continuance of the trial at the close of the plaintiff's evidence in order to permit the defendants to obtain evidence to meet the amendment made to the plaintiff's complaint on the day of trial, which showed that the dealings were to include cotton, as well as corporate stock, in the absence of any showing that the witness whose attendance was required would or could testify as to the lawful character of the cotton transactions. (Id.)

6. APPEAL—BANKRUPTCY OF APPELLANTS PENDING DETERMINATION—RIGHTS OF RESPONDENT.—Upon an appeal taken from the judgment and order denying a new trial in such action, the right of the respondent to have the appeal determined is not affected by the bankruptcy of the defendants pending the appeal, and if the appeal be affirmed, the plaintiff is entitled to recover the property or to assert his rights under the appeal bond. (Id.)

INCEST. See Criminal Law, 38, 39.

INJUNCTION.

1. PRELIMINARY INJUNCTION—DISCRETION—APPEAL.—The granting of a preliminary injunction is not a matter of right, but the application is addressed to the sound discretion of the court, which is to be exercised according to the circumstances of the particular case; and its action upon such application will not be reviewed in the appellate court unless it shall clearly appear that there was an abuse of its discretion. (Temple v. Gordon, 127.)

2. SIMILARITY OF BREAD WRAPPERS—DENIAL OF PRELIMINARY INJUNCTION—DISCRETION NOT ABUSED.—Upon this appeal from an order denying a motion for a preliminary injunction restraining the defendant from using a certain wrapper upon bread manufactured and sold by him, on the ground of its similarity to the wrapper used by the plaintiff, it is held that in view of the nature of the relief demanded, and of the conflicting evidence which came before the superior court upon the order to show cause, it cannot be said that the plaintiff's right to such injunction was conclusively established, or that the court abused its discretion in denying the motion. (Id.)

See Pledge, 3.

INSANE PERSONS.

RESTORATION TO CAPACITY—ABSENCE OF GUARDIANSHIP PROCEEDINGS—JURISDICTION OF OFFICERS OF ASYLUM.—The superior court is with-

INSANE PERSONS (Continued).

out jurisdiction, under the provisions of section 1766 of the Code of Civil Procedure, to restore to capacity a person adjudged to be insane and committed to an insane asylum, without having been put under guardianship, as such jurisdiction, in the absence of guardianship proceedings, is vested exclusively in the officers of the hospital. (Knorp v. Board of Police Commissioners, 539.)

See Criminal Law, 11–14, 30, 31.

INSTRUCTION. See Assault and Battery, 33; Criminal Law, 9, 12, 19, 20, 23, 30, 40, 41, 43, 46–48, 52, 53; Fences, 3; Negligence, 5, 11–13, 16, 20; Rape, 1.

INSURANCE.

1. LIFE INSURANCE—ACTION BETWEEN CONFLICTING CLAIMANTS—PAYMENT INTO COURT—PLEADING.—Where, in an action between conflicting claimants to the amount called for in a policy of life insurance, the insurer does not defend the action but deposits the money in court subject to a determination of such conflicting claims, it becomes immaterial as to whether the complaint states a cause of action against such insurer. (Freitas v. Freitas, 16.)

2. ACTION ON POLICY — RIGHTS UNDER ANTENUPTIAL AGREEMENT.—SUFFICIENCY OF COMPLAINT.—The complaint in such an action is sufficient as between the conflicting claimants, where it is alleged that the plaintiff was induced to marry the insured by an antenuptial agreement, wherein he promised the plaintiff that if she would marry him he would make her the beneficiary of the policy, and that upon his marriage with the intent of performing his agreement he caused the plaintiff to be named as beneficiary and delivered the policy to her, and thereafter secured possession thereof and without her knowledge or consent substituted the defendants as beneficiaries. (Id.)

3. ANTENUPTIAL AGREEMENT — REDUCTION TO WRITING—NONESSENTIAL AVERMENT—PRESUMPTION.—The complaint in such an action is not subject to general demurrer for failure to allege that the antenuptial agreement was reduced to writing, as such agreement, as a matter of pleading, will be presumed to be in writing. (Id.)

4. EXECUTION OF ANTENUPTIAL AGREEMENT—WRITING NOT ESSENTIAL. Such an antenuptial agreement is not required to be in writing where the same became fully executed by the act of the insured in procuring his wife to be designated as the beneficiary of the policy. (Id.)

5. LIFE INSURANCE—ACTION TO RECOVER AMOUNT OF POLICY—CLAIM UNDER ANTENUPTIAL AGREEMENT—PAYMENT TO SUBSTITUTED BENEFICIARIES—PLEADING—SUFFICIENCY OF COMPLAINT.—In an action to recover the amount called for by a policy of insurance, the com-

INSURANCE (Continued).

plaint states a cause of action where it is alleged that the plaintiff was made the beneficiary of the policy under the terms of an antenuptial agreement, and that the insured after delivering the policy to the plaintiff secured possession thereof and without her knowledge or consent substituted the defendants as beneficiaries, notwithstanding that the insurer had paid the amount of the policy to the defendants prior to the commencement of the action. (Freitas v. Freitas, 19.)

6. ACTION FOR MONEY HAD AND RECEIVED—LACK OF CONTRACTUAL PRIVITY—WHEN MAINTAINABLE.—An action for money had and received may be successfully maintained even though not founded upon allegations showing an express privity of contract between the parties, upon the theory that if one of the parties has received money due and owing to the other under circumstances which make it his duty to surrender the money to the rightful owner, the law will imply the promise to do so, and thereby create the requisite contractual privity. (Id.)

7. LIFE INSURANCE—ILLNESS OF INSURED BETWEEN DATE OF APPLICATION AND DELIVERY OF POLICY—LACK OF KNOWLEDGE BY INSURER—CANCELLATION OF POLICY.—A life insurance company is entitled to have a policy of insurance canceled upon tender of the amount of premium paid, where the applicant for the policy between the date of her application and the time of acceptance of the application and date of the delivery of the policy had an attack of typhoid fever, and the company was without knowledge or notice of such illness until after the delivery of the policy. (Security Life Insurance Company of America v. Booms, 119.)

8. APPLICATION FOR LIFE INSURANCE—CHANGES IN PHYSICAL CONDITION PENDING NEGOTIATIONS — DUTY OF APPLICANT.—The obligation rests upon an applicant for life insurance to disclose such changes in his physical condition as occur pending the negotiations as would influence the judgment of the company as to the advisability of accepting the risk. (Id.)

9. REPRESENTATIONS IN APPLICATION—TIME.—The representations contained in an application for insurance must be presumed to refer to the time of the completion of the contract of insurance. (Id.)

10. LIFE INSURANCE LAW—CHANGE OF BENEFICIARY—CONSENT OF INSURER—VOID BY-LAW.—A by-law of a life insurance company providing that a change in the beneficiary named in the certificate of membership "shall not be binding until the consent of the association shall be indorsed on the said certificate of membership" must be disregarded as of no force or effect, where it is inconsistent with and restrictive of the right given by the laws of the state under which said company was created to an insured to change his beneficiary at pleasure. (Garrett v. Garrett, 173.)

INSURANCE (Continued).

11. FILING OF COPY OF INDORSEMENT CHANGING BENEFICIARY—PRESENTATION OF ORIGINAL—SUFFICIENT COMPLIANCE WITH BY-LAW.—A by-law of a life insurance company providing that a copy of the indorsement on the certificate of membership changing the beneficiary and signed by the member shall be filed with the company is sufficiently complied with where the original was presented to the company. (Id.)

12. CHANGE OF BENEFICIARY—WHEN EFFECTED.—Where the holder of a life insurance certificate has the right to change the beneficiary named therein at his pleasure, and makes indorsement of the change upon his certificate in the manner and form required by a by-law of the company, and forwards the same to the company, which received it the day before his death, the change is effectually made, notwithstanding his death occurs before the change is indorsed by the company upon his certificate. (Id.)

13. FIRE INSURANCE LAW—OCCUPANCY OF BUILDING—EVIDENCE.—A private dwelling is not vacant or unoccupied within the meaning of a clause in a policy of insurance providing that the company will not be liable for loss or damage from fire occurring while the building is vacant or unoccupied beyond the period of ten days, where, at the time of the fire, the occupant of the premises for the period of one year next preceding the fire was in the act of removing from the premises, but had not completed such removal nor surrendered possession to the landlord, although he had actually removed himself and his family from the premises. (Covey v. National Union Fire Insurance Company of Pittsburgh, 579.)

14. DISAGREEMENT WITH AMOUNT OF LOSS CLAIMED—INSUFFICIENCY OF NOTICE.—Where a policy of fire insurance provides that the company shall be deemed to have assented to the amount of the loss claimed by the insured in his preliminary proof of loss, unless within twenty days after the receipt thereof the company shall notify the insured in writing of its disagreement with the amount claimed, a notice of disagreement given by letter mailed on the twentieth day after the receipt of such proof of loss to the insured residing in a different place, and received two days after the mailing, is not given in time. (Id.)

15. DEMAND FOR APPRAISEMENT—INSUFFICIENCY OF NOTICE.—Where a policy of fire insurance provides that if for any reason not attributable to the insured or to the appraiser appointed by him, an appraisement is not had and completed within ninety days after the preliminary proof of loss is received by the company, the insured is not to be prejudiced by the failure to make an appraisement and may prove the amount of his loss in an action brought without such appraisement, a demand for an appraisement given by letter mailed before the expiration of said ninety-day period but not received until after its expiration is not within time. (Id.)

INTEREST. See Account Stated, 5; Promissory Note, 2–4; School Lands.

INTERVENTION.

1. ACTION TO ESTABLISH TRUST—PLEDGEE OF STOCK — INTERVENTION AFTER JUDGMENT—KNOWLEDGE OF ACTION—LEAVE PROPERLY REFUSED.—In an action to establish a trust in corporate stock, a bank to whom the stock had been pledged as security for a loan is properly denied leave to intervene where such application is not made until after judgment, and it is shown that the president of the bank had knowledge of the pendency of the action long prior to the time of trial and had discussed the case with the defendant. (Mack v. Eummelen, 506.)

2. WHEN NOT ALLOWED.—Any person who has an interest in the matter in litigation, or in the success of either of the parties, or an interest against both, may intervene in the action or proceeding at any time before trial, but the law does not contemplate that a person thus interested may willfully omit to intervene, and then compel a retrial of the case because it has gone against his interests. (Id.)

IRRIGATION DISTRICT.

1. LEVYING OF ASSESSMENT—MANNER AND FORM.—Under the provisions of the act of 1897 (Stats. 1897, p. 254), authorizing the organization and government of irrigation districts, it is not necessary that the levying of an assessment by the board of directors for the purposes of the district shall be by or in the form of a resolution. (Corson v. Crocker, 626.)

2. ASSESSMENT-ROLL AND DELINQUENT LIST—CERTIFICATION NOT ESSENTIAL.—Under the provisions of such act, it is not necessary that the assessment-roll and delinquent list be certified by any person or officer of the irrigation district. (Id.)

3. DESCRIPTION OF PROPERTY ASSESSED — SUFFICIENCY OF.—Under such act, assessed property described as "Modesto Bl'k 123, lots 1 to 5 inclusive," in the assessment-book under the heading "Description of Property," is sufficient. (Id.)

4. SUFFICIENCY OF DESIGNATION OF LAND.—Where the designation of the land in the assessment-book is such as to afford the owner the means whereby the land may readily be identified, or does not mislead or is not calculated to mislead him, it is sufficient. (Id.)

5. PUBLICATION OF DELINQUENT NOTICE—EVIDENCE—SUFFICIENCY OF.— The *prima facie* showing made through proof of the collector's deed that notice of delinquency was duly published is not overcome by testimony that the numbers of a certain newspaper had been examined and that the notice was found in but one issue, where it is not shown that the notice was published in such newspaper. (Id.)

IRRIGATION DISTRICT (Continued).

6. DATE OF CERTIFICATE OF SALE.—Under the provision of such act requiring that the collector must make out in duplicate a certificate of sale of property sold for delinquent assessment "dated on the day of sale," a certificate is not void because dated on a day subsequent to the sale, where it is recited therein that the property may be redeemed within twelve months from the date of sale, which date of sale is stated in the recital. (Id.)

See Office and Officers, 5-7.

JOINT OWNERS.

1. BANK DEPOSIT—JOINT OWNERSHIP—RIGHT OF SURVIVORSHIP—CONSTRUCTION OF DEPOSIT AGREEMENT.—The deposit by two persons of a sum of money in a bank in a joint account and under a written agreement that the same and any additional money deposited, and all accumulations thereof, shall be payable to and collectible by them, or either of them, during their joint lives, and then belong absolutely to and become the absolute property of the survivor, without reference to or consideration of the original or previous ownership of such moneys, creates a joint ownership in the moneys with the right of ownership in the survivor upon the death of the other depositor. (Waters v. Nevis, 511.)

2. COMPETENCY TO EXECUTE AGREEMENT—FINDINGS ON CONFLICTING EVIDENCE—APPEAL.—In an action brought after the death of one of the parties to such a deposit agreement to recover the amount of the deposit, based upon the ground that the deceased was incompetent to execute such an agreement, where the evidence is conflicting, the findings of the trial court as to competency are conclusive on the appellate court. (Id.)

JUDGMENT.

REVERSAL OF JUDGMENT—RESTORATION OF AMOUNT.—A party obtaining through a judgment before reversal any advantage or benefit must restore the amount he got to the other party after the reversal. (Garrett v. Garrett, 173.)

See Appeal, 1-3, 7, 8; Attachment, 6; Criminal Law, 1; Eminent Domain, 1, 15-17; Execution; Findings; Intervention.

JUDICIAL SALE. See Banks, 3, 4.

JURISDICTION. See Divorce, 11; Execution, 2; Insane Persons; Justice's Court, 9-11, 13-17.

JURY AND JURORS. See Criminal Law, 16, 27.

JUSTICE'S COURT.

1. JUSTICE'S COURT APPEAL—DISMISSAL—LACK OF DILIGENCE.—The provision of section 583 of the Code of Civil Procedure that an action shall be dismissed by the court in which the same shall have been commenced, or to which it may be transferred on motion of the defendant, unless brought to trial within five years after the defendant has filed his answer, does not apply to actions pending in the superior court on appeal thereto from a justice's court, but the court possesses inherent power in its discretion to make an order of dismissal. (Long v. Superior Court, 84.)

2. JUSTICE'S COURT APPEAL—BOND ON—JUSTIFICATION OF SURETIES—FAILURE TO GIVE NOTICE OF TIME OF JUSTIFICATION—DISMISSAL.—Where the sureties on a bond on appeal from a justice's court appear and justify without any notice being given to the opposite party, and without circumstances excusing the justification after the time prescribed by law, the bond is ineffectual, and the appeal must be dismissed. (Peters v. Superior Court, 82.)

3. JUSTICES OF THE PEACE—COMPENSATION—INCREASE DURING TERM OF OFFICE—CONSTRUCTION OF CONSTITUTION.—Justices of the peace of townships are included in the officers referred to in section 9 of article XI of the state constitution, which forbids an increase in the compensation paid to them during their terms of office. (Cox v. Jerome, 97.)

4. COUNTY GOVERNMENTS—CREATION OF TOWNSHIPS.—The legislature is required, under section 4 of article XI of the constitution, to establish a system of county governments which shall be uniform throughout the state, and under this section the legislature may provide for township organization, but no such township organization has been established, although the legislature from time to time, by various general laws and statutes known as county government acts, has provided for a uniform government of the counties and subdivisions therein, but the townships mentioned in such acts have no governmental machinery or officers so distinct from the county as to identify such townships as being possessed of functions designed to be possessed by "township organization" referred to in section 4 of article XI of the constitution. (Id.)

5. JUSTICE'S COURT APPEAL—MOTION TO DISMISS—FAILURE OF SURETIES TO JUSTIFY—SERVICE OF NOTICE OF JUSTIFICATION.—Upon a motion made to dismiss a justice's court appeal upon the ground that the sureties on the undertaking on appeal did not justify in the manner and form required by law, the decision of the superior court upon conflicting affidavits as to when the notice of justification of the sureties was served, is not subject to review in the appellate court upon *certiorari* proceedings. (Fletcher Collection Agency v. Superior Court of Los Angeles County, 193.)

JUSTICE'S COURT (Continued).

6. WAIVER OF JUSTIFICATION—FAILURE TO APPEAR.—Justification of sureties on an undertaking given on a justice's court appeal is waived where the party excepting to the sufficiency of the sureties fails to appear at the time and place mentioned in the notice of justification. (Id.)

7. FILING OF NEW UNDERTAKING—PRIMA FACIE JUSTIFICATION.—The filing of a new undertaking on the day fixed for the justifica.ion of sureties, which has attached to it the requisite affidavit sworp to before the justice, establishes a *prima facie* justification. (Id.)

8. APPEAL UPON QUESTION OF LAW—RECORD—STATEMENT OF GROUNDS. Jurisdiction of a justice's court appeal taken on questions of law alone is not lost by reason of the omission to include in the statement on appeal the grounds upon which the party appealing intended to rely. (Id.)

9. CITY OF SACRAMENTO—MISDEMEANORS COMMITTED WITHIN CORPORATE LIMITS—JURISDICTION.—The several justices' courts of the county of Sacramento have jurisdiction over all misdemeanors enumerated by the general laws of the state committed within the municipal limits of the city of Sacramento, as well as those committed outside of such limits and within the territorial boundaries of the county of Sacramento. (Matter of Yee Kim Mah, 196.)

10. JURISDICTION OF MISDEMEANORS—WHITNEY ACT—EFFECT OF CODE AMENDMENT—REPEAL OF ACT AS TO SACRAMENTO.—The provisions of the "Whitney Act" (Stats. 1885, p. 213), giving to police courts of cities having a population of over thirty thousand and under one hundred thousand inhabitants exclusive jurisdiction of all misdemeanors punishable by fine or imprisonment, or both by such fine and imprisonment, committed within the limits of such cities, if ever applicable at any time to the city of Sacramento, have been, so far as such city is concerned, repealed or superseded by the enactment of section 1425 of the Penal Code, in the year 1905 (Stats. 1905, p. 705), which provides, among other things, that justices' courts shall have jurisdiction of all misdemeanors committed within their respective counties punishable by fine not exceeding five hundred dollars, or imprisonment not exceeding six months, or by both such fine and imprisonment. (Id.)

11. JURISDICTION OF POLICE COURT OF SACRAMENTO—EFFECT OF CHARTER.—The provisions of sections 162 and 164 of the freeholders' charter of the city of Sacramento, approved in 1911 (Stats. Ex. Sess. 1911, p. 305), establishing a police court in such city and giving it jurisdiction "of all misdemeanors enumerated by the general laws or by ordinances of the city and of all other crimes cognizable by justices' courts and courts of justices of the peace and police courts under the constitution and laws of the state of

JUSTICE'S COURT (Continued).

California," do not confer upon the police court so established *exclusive* jurisdiction of all simple misdemeanors committed under the general laws of the state within the limits of such city, but give it concurrent jurisdiction with the justices' courts of the county of Sacramento. (Id.)

12. APPEAL—SUFFICIENCY OF UNDERTAKING.—An undertaking on appeal from the justice's court from a judgment for the payment of money in a sum equal to twice the amount of the judgment and costs (an amount in excess of one hundred dollars), and conditioned that if proceedings be stayed the appellant will pay the amount of the judgment appealed from, and all costs if the appeal be withdrawn or dismissed, or the amount of any judgment and all costs that may be recovered against him in the action in the superior court, is sufficient, under section 978 of the Code of Civil Procedure, as an undertaking for the payment of costs on the appeal and to give the superior court jurisdiction of the appeal, regardless of its sufficiency as an undertaking to stay execution. (Rich v. Superior Court of Mendocino County, 689.)

13. DISMISSAL OF APPEAL—INSUFFICIENCY OF UNDERTAKING—JURISDICTION OF SUPERIOR COURT.—The superior court has jurisdiction to hear and determine a motion to dismiss an appeal taken thereto from the justice's court on the ground that a sufficient undertaking had not been filed. (Id.)

14. JURISDICTION—MEANING OF RULE.—The rule that when a court once obtains jurisdiction of the subject matter of an action, it then has jurisdiction to decide a question arising therein erroneously as well as correctly, has no application to a case where the very question to be determined is whether the court has the legal authority to hear and determine the matter before it. The rule simply means that when the court has jurisdiction of the subject matter of the action, and makes error during the course of the trial or in its final decision, such error is correctible, not through a jurisdictional writ, but solely by appeal. (Id.)

15. JUSTICE'S COURT APPEAL—AMENDMENT OF COMPLAINT—LACK OF JURISDICTION.—The superior court is without jurisdiction upon an appeal taken to it from a judgment rendered in an action in a justice's court upon a contract to recover a sum of money less than three hundred dollars, to permit the complaint to be amended so as to state a cause of action for a sum in excess of three hundred dollars. (Tracy v. Sumida, 716.)

16. EXTENT OF JURISDICTION OF SUPERIOR COURT.—Where jurisdiction is derived through an appeal from a judgment rendered in the justice's court, the superior court cannot, by permitting an amendment of the complaint, acquire jurisdiction in excess of that of the justice's court from which the appeal was taken. (Id.)

JUSTICE'S COURT (Continued).

17. APPEAL FROM JUDGMENT OF SUPERIOR COURT—LACK OF JURISDIC-
TION OF DISTRICT COURT OF APPEAL—DISMISSAL.—A judgment
rendered on a justice's court appeal is not within the appellate
jurisdiction of the district court of appeal, and an appeal taken
therefrom must be dismissed. (Id.)

LANDLORD AND TENANT.

1. CONTINUANCE OF TENANCY UPON EXPIRATION OF LEASE—CONSTRUC-
TION OF ORAL AGREEMENT—TIME OF PAYMENT OF RENT.—An oral
agreement made between the parties to a written lease just prior
to its expiration providing that the lessee might remain a tenant
of the premises "from month to month at the same rental" as stipulated in the lease, contemplates that the rental shall be continued
to be paid in the same manner as provided in the lease. (Rosenbaum Estate Company v. Robert Dollar Company, 576.)

2. REMOVAL FROM DEMISED PREMISES—UNFITNESS FOR HABITATION—
NOTICE TO REPAIR.—A tenant is not warranted in removing from
demised premises under the provisions of sections 1941 and 1942
of the Civil Code, where no definite notice to repair is given. (Id.)

3. ABANDONMENT OF PREMISES—UNQUALIFIED TAKING OF POSSESSION
BY LESSOR—ACTION FOR DAMAGES NOT MAINTAINABLE.—Where the
possession of demised premises is vacated by the lessees prior to
the expiration of the term, the lessor cannot maintain an action
for damages in a sum equal to the difference between the rent which
should have been paid under the lease and the amount for which
he was able to rent the property for the period of the unexpired
term, where he, upon being informed by the lessees of their intention to vacate the premises, took possession of the property and
made a new lease thereof, without making any further demand upon
the lessees, or in any manner informing them of the course which
he would pursue. (Rehkopf v. Wirz, 695.)

4. REPUDIATION OF LEASE BY TENANTS—ACCEPTANCE OF POSSESSION
FOR BENEFIT OF LESSEE—DUTY OF LESSOR.—Where a tenant abandons the leased property and repudiates the lease, the landlord
may accept possession of the property for the benefit of the tenant
and relet the same, and thereupon may maintain an action for
damages for the difference between what he was able in good faith
to let the property for and the amount provided to be paid under
the lease agreement. But a lessor who chooses to follow that
course must in some manner give the lessee information that he is
accepting such possession for the benefit of the tenant, and not in
his own right and for his own benefit. (Id.)

5. UNQUALIFIED ACCEPTANCE BY LESSOR — RELEASE OF LESSEE.—An
unqualified taking of possession by the lessor, and reletting of the
premises by him as owner to new tenants, is inconsistent with the

LANDLORD AND TENANT (Continued).

continuing force of the original lease. If done without the consent of the tenant to such interference, it is an eviction, and the tenant will be released. If done pursuant to the tenant's attempted abandonment, it is an acceptance of the surrender and likewise releases the tenant. (Id.)

6. RECOVERY OF POSSESSION—WITHHOLDING OF PREMISES—SUFFICIENCY OF EVIDENCE.—In an action for rent and for restitution of premises, a finding that the defendant was withholding the possession of the premises at the time of the commencement of the action is sufficiently supported by evidence that he still had a key thereto, that he had not paid the rent, and that his goods were still contained therein. (Levy v. Henderson, 789.)

7. DENIAL OF LANDLORD'S TITLE—NOTICE TO QUIT.—If a tenant denies his landlord's title, the denial makes him a trespasser, and he is not entitled to notice to quit before the commencement of an action by the landlord to recover possession of the premises. (Id.)

See Fences, 2; Negligence, 34–37.

LARCENY. See Criminal Law, 24.

LEASE. See Brokers, 5–8; Landlord and Tenant.

LEVEE. See Eminent Domain, 12–14.

LIFE INSURANCE. See Insurance, 1–12.

LOS ANGELES, CITY OF. See Eminent Domain, 4–11.

MANDAMUS. See Conservation Commission, 2–5; Office and Officers, 3, 4, 13.

MASTER AND SERVANT. See Employer and Employee; Negligence, 1–15.

MEASURE OF DAMAGES. See Damages.

MECHANICS' LIENS.

1. EQUITABLE JURISDICTION—APPEAL.—A mechanic's lien is of equitable cognizance, although created by law; and an appeal in an action to foreclose the same lies to the supreme court. (Emigh-Winchell Hardware Company v. Pylman, 46.)

2. FORECLOSURE—PLEADING—DATE OF COMPLETION OF BUILDING—SUFFICIENCY OF COMPLAINT.—In an action to foreclose a mechanic's lien, an allegation that the building was completed "on or about" a specified date, which date was less than thirty days before the

MECHANICS' LIENS (Continued).

alleged date of the filing of the claim of lien, is sufficient to warrant proof of the exact date of completion. (Boscus v. Waldmann, 245.)

3. COMPLETION OF CONTRACT—SUFFICIENCY OF AVERMENT.—An allegation in such an action that the building was completed according to the terms of the contract sufficiently shows that the contract was completed. (Id.)

4. BUILDING CONTRACT — OMISSION TO FILE BOND — LIABILITY OF OWNER.—Under section 1183 of the Code of Civil Procedure, as amended in 1911, it is the duty of the owner to exact from the contractor a bond and file the same in the office of the county recorder, if he would restrict his liability to laborers, materialmen, or subcontractors for their claims to the contract price, and where he fails to make such exaction, there is then imposed upon him the penalty of paying all liens to the extent of the value of the work done and materials furnished. (Id.)

5. COMPLETION OF BUILDING BY OCCUPATION — OMISSION TO FILE NOTICE—ESTOPPEL.—The owner of a building is estopped from claiming that the lien of a claimant other than the original contractor was not filed within thirty days after occupation of the building, where no notice of such occupation was filed, as the requirement of section 1187 of the Code of Civil Procedure as to the filing of notice of completion applies as well to the statutory completion of a building by occupation, acceptance, or cessation of labor, as to actual completion. (Id.)

See Building Contract, 4–6; Contract, 8.

MONEY HAD AND RECEIVED. See Insurance, 6.

MORTGAGE.

1. FRAUD ON CREDITORS OF MORTGAGOR—INSUFFICIENCY OF EVIDENCE—DECISION ON FORMER APPEAL CONCLUSIVE.—In the second trial of an action for the foreclosure of a mortgage, where the court had before it practically the same evidence which was before it upon the first trial and also before the supreme court upon the first appeal, the decision of the supreme court upon such appeal as to the insufficiency of the evidence to support the defense set up by a judgment creditor of the mortgagor that such mortgage was executed with intent to defraud creditors is conclusive upon the second appeal. (Goldner v. Spencer, 13.)

2. RELEASE OF FRACTIONAL ACRE FROM MORTGAGE—ERRONEOUS FINDING—RIGHTS OF REDEMPTIONER NOT PREJUDICED—RELEASED PORTION WITHOUT VALUE.—A judgment creditor of the mortgagor, entitled to be a redemptioner of the property to be sold under the decree of foreclosure and sale, is not injured by an erroneous finding that

MORTGAGE (Continued).

a small fraction of an acre had been released from the operation and effect of the mortgage, where it is expressly found that such fraction of land was of practically no value. (Id.)

See Corporation, 5-7.

MUNICIPAL CORPORATIONS.

LIABILITY FOR ELECTRICITY FOR STREET LIGHTING—FAILURE OF PROOF.— An electric light and power company engaged in furnishing electricity for lighting dwellings, business places, and streets of a municipal corporation, cannot recover in an action against the city for current consumed in the street lights between the hours of 7 o'clock A. M. and 4:30 o'clock P. M., where the complaint alleges that such current was furnished at the instance and request of the municipality, but the evidence shows that the city expressly notified the power company that it would only pay for electricity furnished between the hours of 4:30 o'clock P. M. and 7 o'clock A. M. (Tuolumne County Electric Power and Light Company v. City of Sonora, 655.)

See County; Irrigation District; San Francisco, City and County of.

MURDER AND MANSLAUGHTER. See Criminal Law, 40-49.

NEGLIGENCE.

1. EVIDENCE—PROOF OF FACT BY INFERENCE.—Direct evidence of a fact in dispute is not required in all cases, as the law recognizes the force of indirect evidence which tends to establish such fact by proving another, which, though not in itself conclusive, affords an inference or presumption of the existence of the fact in dispute. (Arundell v. American Oil Fields Company, 218.)

2. PROOF BY INDIRECT EVIDENCE.—Negligence, like any other fact, may be inferred from a preponderance of the evidence, whether it be circumstantial or direct, and the plaintiff is not required to prove his case beyond a reasonable doubt. (Id.)

3. INJURY TO TOOL-DRESSER ON OIL DERRICK—FALLING OF IMPROPERLY HOISTED CASING-PIPE—INFERENCE OF NEGLIGENCE.—In an action for damages for personal injuries sustained by a tool-dresser in a derrick for drilling an oil well from the falling upon his hand of a joint of casing-pipe which he and the driller in charge were endeavoring to hoist from the well, the negligence of the defendant is sufficiently proven by evidence that the driller adopted a plan of handling the pipe, which was testified to by experts as unsafe, and by not using the elevators provided for the purpose. (Id.)

4. MASTER AND SERVANT—RISKS OF INJURY ASSUMED BY SERVANT.— The ordinary risks which a servant assumes as incidental to his

NEGLIGENCE (Continued).

employment are such as may not be avoided by the exercise of reasonable care by the master or by his servant who is superior to the injured servant. (Id.)

5. INSTRUCTION—SYMPATHIES AND PREJUDICES OF JURY—PROPER REFUSAL.—An instruction to the effect that the jury should not be governed by sympathy but by the evidence, and that in considering the evidence the jury should not be influenced by the fact that the plaintiff is a laboring man and the defendant a corporation, is properly refused. (Id.)

6. EMPLOYER AND EMPLOYEE—PERSONAL INJURIES FROM ELECTRIC CURRENT—CHANGING SWITCH WITHOUT NOTICE.—An employee of a corporation who receives personal injuries from a powerful electric current while engaged in replacing a fuse in the electrical apparatus of the company, under the orders of its chief engineer, whose duty it was to make the repair, the accident resulting from the failure of a switch, used to protect the employees while putting in fuses, to perform its functions, the employee having no knowledge or notice of this change of condition in the switch, and having every reason to believe that by manipulating the switch the current would be completely cut off so that the fuse could be inserted without danger, is entitled to recover from his employer damages for the injury sustained. (Earl v. San Francisco Bridge Company, 839.)

7. CONTRIBUTORY NEGLIGENCE—FAILURE TO EXAMINE APPARATUS—WHEN EXCUSED.—Where the proximate cause of the injury was the failure of the switch to disconnect the current, and this resulted from a change made by the company unknown to the employee, it was not negligence for the latter to assume that conditions were as before, and that the switch would disconnect the current; and he was therefore not chargeable with contributory negligence in not examining the apparatus. (Id.)

8. KNOWLEDGE OF DANGER—EMPLOYEE ACTING UNDER ORDERS.—If the employee had full knowledge of the change in such a case he would not be chargeable with contributory negligence in obeying orders of the chief engineer under whose direct supervision he was acting, unless performance thereof was inevitably or imminently dangerous. (Id.)

9. EMPLOYERS' LIABILITY ACT—ASSUMPTION OF RISK.—Under the Employers' Liability Act in force at the time of the accident in question a defense that the employee assumed the risk of the employment was not open to the defendant. (Id.)

10. MEASURE OF DAMAGES—DISCRETION OF JURY.—In actions for damages for personal injuries it must be largely left to the discretion and sense of justice of the jury, subject to the supervision and correction of the trial court, to determine the amount that will be a

NEGLIGENCE (Continued).

fair compensation for the suffering and misery and financial loss endured by the injured party. (Id.)

11. INSTRUCTIONS—MEASURE OF DAMAGES.—In an action for damages for personal injuries, an instruction to the jury that they should assess the damages, if any, in such sum as they believe under all the circumstances and evidence plaintiff ought to recover, if standing alone might be misleading, but where it is supplemented by specific directions as to all the elements of damage that the plaintiff can recover, it cannot be misunderstood. (Id.)

12. STATEMENT OF CLAIM—USING LANGUAGE OF COMPLAINT.—There is no error in the court stating the claim of plaintiff in the language of the complaint. (Id.)

13. AFFIRMATION OF THE ISSUE — PREPONDERANCE OF EVIDENCE— DEFINITIONS OF.—Where the court in the instructions given on behalf of the defendant sufficiently defined the terms "affirmation of the issue," and "preponderance of the evidence," if any further elucidation was desired, it should have been requested. (Id.)

14. EVIDENCE—HOSPITAL CHARGES.—A motion to strike out the testimony on cross-examination of a doctor as to the value of the hospital services incurred by the plaintiff in an action for damages for personal injuries, the motion being made upon the ground that he was testifying as to what the usual charges were, and not the actual charges in the case, is made too late, where he had so testified on direct examination without objection. (Id.)

15. EVIDENCE—INADMISSIBILITY OF WRITTEN REPORT.—Where a witness testified from memory with his written report before him that he was at a certain place at a certain time, the report itself was not admissible as corroboration of this testimony. (Id.)

16. COLLISION OF PEDESTRIAN WITH AUTOMOBILE—ERRONEOUS INSTRUCTION—CONTRIBUTORY NEGLIGENCE.—In an action to recover damages for personal injuries received by a pedestrian as the result of a collision with an automobile while crossing a city street over which a street-car was then passing, it is prejudicial error to instruct the jury, without any qualifications whatever, that "If an automobile driver, not being able to see a street crossing which he is approaching because of a passing street-car, instead of stopping his machine, merely changes its direction so as to go around the car and in doing so comes suddenly upon and runs into and injures a person, he is guilty of gross negligence, and is liable for all damage proximately caused thereby," where the answer alleges contributory negligence, and there is evidence supporting the claim that plaintiff had her eyes turned away from the automobile, the approach of which she had noticed, and that she stepped back to escape collision with a passing motorcycle. (Bellinger v. Hughes, 464.)

NEGLIGENCE (Continued).

17. WHEN QUESTION OF LAW.—It is only where the undisputed facts are such as to leave but one reasonable inference, and that of negligence, that the court is justified in taking the question from the jury. (Id.)

18. COLLISION AT RAILROAD CROSSING—OBSTRUCTIONS—FAILURE TO STOP AND LISTEN—CONTRIBUTORY NEGLIGENCE.—In an action for damages for personal injuries received from a collision between an automobile driven by the plaintiff and a freight train of the defendant at a grade crossing on a public highway, the plaintiff is guilty of such contributory negligence as to preclude recovery, where it is shown by his own testimony that the view of approaching trains at the place of the accident was obstructed by a dense growth of sunflowers and weeds, which was well known to the plaintiff, and that he did not, upon approaching the crossing and while within the lines of the right of way of the railroad company, stop his machine, or look or listen for an approaching train. (Thompson v. Southern Pacific Company, 567.)

19. OBSTRUCTED VIEW AT CROSSINGS—DUTY OF TRAVELERS.—While it is true that the rule requiring the traveler to *stop* at railroad crossings and look and listen for approaching trains is not an absolute one, yet if the view is obstructed he must place himself in a position where he can use his faculties of observation to advantage. (Id.)

20. LACK OF NEGLIGENCE OF TRAIN OPERATIVES—RIGHT TO ASSUME—ERRONEOUS INSTRUCTION.—An instruction advising the jury that the plaintiff had the right to assume that the defendant's employees would observe the law requiring them to ring the bell and sound the whistle when approaching the crossing is erroneous. (Id.)

21. ACTION AGAINST RAILROAD COMPANY AND TRAIN OPERATIVES—JUDGMENT EXONERATING AGENTS—ACQUITTAL OF COMPANY.—In such an action, where recovery is sought against the railroad company and its servants, based upon the acts of the latter in running the train at a high rate of speed without sounding any warning of its approach, an acquittal of the latter of negligence is an acquittal of the company. (Id.)

22. ELECTRIC RAILWAY CROSSING—CAUTION IN APPROACHING.—The rule requiring a person upon approaching a railroad track with intent to cross it to exercise his faculties in order to ascertain whether a train is approaching, is applicable to electric railroads operated under conditions similar to the operation of steam railroads. (Martz v. Pacific Electric Railway Company, 592.)

23. DEATH OF AUTOMOBILE DRIVER—COLLISION WITH ELECTRIC RAILWAY-CAR AT CROSSING—ABILITY TO SEE APPROACHING CAR—FINDING.—In an action for damages for the death of an automobile driver from a collision with a rapidly moving electric railway-car

NEGLIGENCE (Continued).

at a crossing, where the question presented to the jury was whether or not a person traveling, as was the deceased, and using reasonable care in observing, would have seen the approaching car, notwithstanding the obstruction of trees and brush along the highway, and notwithstanding the further obstruction made by poles erected at intervals between the railway tracks and carrying the power wires, the conclusion of the jury must be accepted on appeal. (Id.)

24. APPROACHING RAILROAD CROSSING—FAILURE TO USE FACULTIES——INFERENCE FROM PHYSICAL FACTS—CONTRIBUTORY NEGLIGENCE.—Where the physical facts shown by undisputed evidence raise the inevitable inference that the person approaching a railroad crossing did not look or listen, or that having looked and listened, he endeavored to cross immediately in front of a rapidly approaching train, which was plainly open to view, he was, as matter of law, guilty of contributory negligence. (Id.)

25. EXPLOSION OF GASOLINE—SALE FOR KEROSENE—PROXIMATE CAUSE. In an action for damages against an oil company and a grocer for the death of a patron of the latter from an explosion of gasoline sold to the deceased by the grocer for kerosene, where it is shown that the oil company in filling an order of the grocer for kerosene had mistakenly made a delivery of kerosene and gasoline mixed, and that the grocer upon discovering such mistake, notified the company thereof and the latter agreed to take the oil back, but before the oil was taken back the grocer relying upon his experience in dealing in such oils, and upon a personal test made by him, sold the oil which caused the explosion, the direct and proximate cause of the damage was the intervening act of the grocer, and not the negligence of the oil company. (Catlin v. Union Oil Company of California, 597.)

26. PROXIMATE CAUSE—WHAT CONSTITUTES.—Proximate cause is that cause arising out of a breach of duty which in a natural and continuous sequence produces the damage complained of. (Id.)

27. INTERVENING ACT OF NEGLIGENCE—LIABILITY OF ORIGINAL WRONG-DOER.—If the negligent acts of two or more persons, all being culpable and responsible in law for their acts, do not concur in point of time, and the negligence of one only exposes the injured person to risk of injury in case the other should also be negligent, the liability of the person first in fault will depend upon the question whether the negligent act of the other was one which a man of ordinary experience and sagacity, acquainted with all the circumstances, could reasonably anticipate or not. If such a person could have anticipated that the intervening act of negligence might, in natural and ordinary sequence, follow the original act of negligence, the person first in fault is not released from liability by reason of the intervening negligence of the other. If it could

NEGLIGENCE (Continued).

not have been thus anticipated, then the intervening negligent person alone is responsible. (Id.)

28. WHEN QUESTION OF LAW.—While it is true that questions involving alleged negligent action which turn upon the proposition as to what should be expected of an ordinarily reasonable man under the circumstances, present mixed questions of law and fact which generally should go to the jury under proper instructions as to the law, leaving the deductions of fact to be made by the verdict, yet, on the other hand, where the facts are undisputed and clearly settled, and the dictates of common prudence point to only one reasonable conclusion, the question is then one of law for the court, and a verdict may be either directed or a nonsuit granted. (Id.)

29. EVIDENCE—CHARACTER OF FLUID—STATEMENTS OF DECEASED—INCOMPETENT TESTIMONY.—Statements made by the deceased immediately after the explosion to the effect that the fluid used was gasoline are inadmissible, being self-serving and expressive of the opinion and conclusion of the witness. (Id.)

30. MANNER OF FILLING LAMP—CONTRIBUTORY NEGLIGENCE—QUESTION FOR JURY.—The question whether the deceased was guilty of contributory negligence at the time of the explosion by reason of the fact that he was engaged in filling an oil-lamp with the fluid, while he had a lighted miner's lamp on his cap, is one for the jury, where there was expert testimony that a lamp could be thus filled with reasonable safety, and without great danger, provided the fluid was coal-oil of ordinary quality. (Id.)

31. MALPRACTICE IN SETTING OF FRACTURED ARM—EVIDENCE—PROPER SETTING—EXPERT TESTIMONY.—In an action against a physician and surgeon for damages for alleged malpractice in the setting of a fractured arm, the plaintiff is not prejudiced by the sustaining of an objection to a question asked an expert witness, who caused to be made certain X-ray plates of the bones some two months after the fracture, as to whether a fracture set in the manner shown by the plates was a proper setting, where the witness later in his testimony made the statement that if the fracture had been properly set in the first place, there would have been no angulation at that time, and also testified fully as to how the operation should have been performed. (Barsi v. Simpson, 612.)

32. EVIDENCE—ADMISSION SUBJECT TO MOTION TO STRIKE OUT—ABSENCE OF MOTION—APPEAL.—Where evidence is admitted subject to a motion to be thereafter made to strike it out if certain proof is not supplied, and no such motion is made, the adverse party cannot be heard on appeal to say that the ruling of the court was erroneous. (Id.)

NEGLIGENCE (Continued).

33. PROPER TREATMENT OF ARM—TRAINED NURSE.—A trained nurse, who was superintendent of the operating-room of a large hospital, and who witnessed the performance of the operation on the plaintiff by the defendant, is properly permitted to testify, that from her experience, the treatment was proper. (Id.)

34. FALL IN MAKING EXIT FROM OPERA HOUSE—DANGEROUS AND UNSAFE PASSAGEWAY—LIABILITY OF LESSEES.—In an action against the owners of an opera house and the lessees thereof to recover damages for personal injuries sustained by a spectator at an entertainment held therein, in passing out through a side door, which had been opened during the performance by the manager and agent of the lessees, at the request of spectators, for ventilating purposes, the lessees are liable in damages for such injuries, where it is shown that the door was not used or intended to be used as an exit or entrance, and that it was left open, unguarded, and unlighted at the close of the entertainment and with no step to aid a person in reaching the sidewalk three feet below. (Shellman v. Hershey, 641.)

35. NONLIABILITY OF OWNERS.—The owners of the opera house are not liable in damages for such injuries, where it is shown that such door was not intended to be used and never was used for the convenience of patrons, but was intended for the use of and to be used only by lessees to take in and out stage properties and for the purpose of occasionally sweeping dirt through, or to air the house. (Id.)

36. NUISANCE CREATED BY LESSEES—LESSOR NOT LIABLE.—Where property is demised, and at the time of the demise is not a nuisance, and becomes so only by the act of the tenant while in his possession, and injury happens during such possession, the owner is not liable. (Id.)

37. INJURIES IN MAKING EXIT FROM OPERA HOUSE—PLEADING—SUFFICIENCY OF COMPLAINT AGAINST LESSEES.—In an action against the owners and the lessees of an opera house to recover damages for personal injuries received by a patron in making her exit therefrom, the complaint sufficiently states a cause of action against the lessees, where it is alleged that they were the lessees of the premises on the day of the accident, and the nuisance and the accident are fully described. (Shellman v. Hershey, 654.)

NEGOTIABLE INSTRUMENTS. See Promissory Note.

NEW TRIAL. See Appeal, 5; Criminal Law, 1.

NOVATION.

STATUTE OF FRAUDS—PAYMENT FOR SUPPLIES FURNISHED THIRD PERSON—VERBAL PROMISE OF CORPORATION.—A verbal promise made

NOVATION (Continued).

by the foreman of a corporation engaged in the construction of
a dam that the corporation would pay for certain supplies which
had been furnished to the person who had the contract for the
hauling of the necessary gravel for the work, is binding on the
corporation, and without the statute of frauds, where it is shown
that such foreman had authority to hire and discharge men and
to procure needed supplies, and that the promisee accepted the
new promise and canceled the antecedent obligation. (Baxter v.
Chico Construction Company, 492.)

OFFICE AND OFFICERS.

1. PUBLIC OFFICERS—SERVICES OF SHERIFF IN CONVEYING PRISONERS—
UNWARRANTED DISALLOWANCE OF CLAIM BY BOARD OF CONTROL—
OVERCHARGE FOR PREVIOUS SERVICES.—The State Board of Control is
without power to refuse to allow the claim of the sheriff of a county
for services rendered and expenses necessarily incurred in conveying
persons adjudged by the superior court to be committed to state
prisons and other state institutions, on the ground that such official
was indebted to the state in a certain amount for similar services
rendered in previous years which he had received and which was
in excess of that to which he was justly and legally entitled. (Hammel v. Neylan, 21.)

2. SERVICES IN CONVEYING PERSONS TO STATE INSTITUTIONS—ALLOW-
ANCE OF CLAIM BY STATE BOARD OF CONTROL.—Under the provisions
of section 4290 of the Political Code, the sheriff of a county is entitled to receive and retain for his own use the sum of five dollars
per diem for conveying prisoners to and from the state prisons,
and for conveying persons to and from insane asylums, together
with all expenses necessarily incurred therewith, subject only to
the condition that his claim therefor is properly presented to the
State Board of Control, as provided by section 663 of the Political
Code, for its scrutiny, which scrutiny and examination is limited
by such provision to an inquiry as to whether such officer has rendered the services set forth in his claim and whether the amount
claimed for expenses was necessarily incurred in the performance
thereof. (Id.)

3. REFUSAL TO ALLOW CLAIM—REMEDY OF CLAIMANT.—Upon the refusal of the board of control to allow such a claim upon the ground
of overcharges made in previous years, the remedy of the claimant
is mandamus, and not by appeal to the legislature, as under the
provisions of section 671 of the Political Code the latter remedy
is only applicable where the board finds that the services were not
performed or the expenses not incurred. (Id.)

4. MANDAMUS—ABUSE OF DISCRETION—ENFORCEMENT OF PARTICULAR
ACTION.—While it is the general rule that where an officer, board,
or tribunal is vested with power to determine a question upon

OFFICE AND OFFICERS (Continued).

which a right depends, *mandamus* will not. lie to control the discretion of such officer, board, or tribunal· in the determination thereof, nevertheless the writ will lie to correct abuses of discretion, and to force a particular action by the inferior tribunal or officer, when the law clearly establishes the petitioner's right to such action. (Id.) .

5. PUBLIC OFFICERS—RECALL—IRRIGATION DISTRICT OFFICERS—ACT OF 1911—CONSTITUTIONALITY OF.—The act of 1911 providing that the holder of any elective office of any irrigation district may be removed or recalled at any time by the electors does not violate section 18 of article IV or section 1 of article XXIII of the constitution, and is valid. (Wigley v. South San Joaquin Irrigation District, 162.)

6. POWER OF LEGISLATURE—CONSTRUCTION OF SECTION 18, ARTICLE IV, AND SECTION 1, ARTICLE XXIII, OF CONSTITUTION.—Prior to the adoption of the constitutional provisions upon the subject, the legislature had the power, under its general legislative authority, to pass acts for the recall of public officers; and neither section 18 of article IV nor section 1 of article XXIII of the constitution can be construed to have taken that power from it. (Id.)

7. CONSTRUCTION OF CONSTITUTION — RESTRICTION OF LEGISLATIVE POWERS.—The constitution of this state is not to be considered as a grant of power, but rather as a restriction upon the powers of the legislature, and it is competent for the legislature to exercise all powers not forbidden by the constitution of the state, or delegated to the general government, or prohibited by the constitution of the United States. (Id.)

8. SAN BERNARDINO COUNTY CHARTER — AMENDMENT CONCERNING COUNTY OFFICERS—EFFECT OF.—The amendment to the charter of the county of San Bernardino approved by the electors at the general election held in November, 1914, and approved by the legislature by resolution which was filed with the Secretary of State January 30, 1915 (Stats. 1915, p. 1727), which, without naming any of the seven articles contained in such charter, purported to strike from such instrument "sections 4, 5 and 6 of said charter" and inert in lieu thereof the following amendment to be known as section 4 thereof, to wit: "Section four (4): All county officers other than supervisors of said county shall be elected at each general election by the qualified electors of said county as is now, or may be hereafter provided by general law, and all deputies and assistants to such county officers shall be appointed as is now or may be hereafter provided by general law; and the powers and duties of such officers, deputies and assistants shall be such as are now or may be hereafter provided by general law, and any part of this charter in conflict herewith is hereby repealed," is fatally defective as an attempted direct repeal of any sections of the

OFFICE AND OFFICERS (Continued).

original charter, because it is impossible to determine what sections of the charter are intended to be repealed; but such amendment is effective in that it adds to the charter a new section, and by so doing impliedly repeals those provisions contained in the original charter which relate to the same subject matter as the new section and are in conflict therewith. (More v. Board of Supervisors of the County of San Bernardino, 388.)

9. COUNTY OFFICERS — SHERIFF AND CORONER — CHARTER PROVISIONS NOT REPEALED BY AMENDMENT.—Section 1 of article II of the charter of the county of San Bernardino which provides for certain county officers, including a sheriff and a coroner, and section 2 of the same article which provides that the sheriff shall be *ex-officio* coroner, were not repealed either expressly or impliedly by the charter amendment adopted at the general election held in November, 1914. (Id.)

10. CONSOLIDATION OF OFFICES OF SHERIFF AND CORONER — VALID CHARTER PROVISION.—The office of coroner is a separate office from that of sheriff, with separate duties and powers as provided by law, and when the sheriff is performing the duties of coroner he is in contemplation of law the coroner of the county as distinctly and completely as any other duly appointed or elected person would be when lawfully performing those duties, and therefore, the powers and duties pertaining to the office of coroner are not affected by the charter provision that the person appointed as sheriff shall also be the coroner. (Id.)

11. OFFICERS PROVIDED FOR BY CHARTER NOT ABOLISHED BY AMENDMENT.—Such amendment in providing that all county officers other than the supervisors shall be elected as is now or may be hereafter provided by general law, and that the powers and duties of such officers shall be such as are now or may be hereafter provided by general law, did not intend to refer only to those officers provided for by general law, and thereby eliminate some county officers provided for by the charter and not by general law, so that such offices ceased to exist. (Id.)

12. CHARTER PROVISIONS AS TO CONSOLIDATION OF COUNTY OFFICES— SECTION OF POLITICAL CODE—PROVISIONS NOT SUPERSEDED BY.—The provisions of the charter of the county of San Bernardino with respect to the consolidation of county offices, even under such charter amendment, are not superseded by the terms of section 4017 of the Political Code upon the same subject, and which does not provide for the consolidation of the offices of sheriff and coroner, in view of section 7½ of article XI of the constitution, which provides that county charters shall provide "for the consolidation and segregation of county offices." (Id.)

13. POLICE OFFICER—REINSTATEMENT — MANDAMUS—STATUTE OF LIMITATIONS.—The right of a member of the police department of the

OFFICE AND OFFICERS (Continued).

city and county of San Francisco, whose resignation was accepted on account of collapse due to mental strain, to be reinstated, is barred by laches and the provisions of sections 338 and 343 of the Code of Civil Procedure, where the *mandamus* proceeding to compel such reinstatement was not instituted until some seven years and eight months after the date of his certificate of discharge from the state hospital to which he was committed, although the proceeding was instituted within the statutory period after his restoration to capacity pursuant to the provisions of section 1766 of the Code of Civil Procedure, where the petition for such restoration failed to show that there had been any previous guardianship proceedings. (Knorp v. Board of Police Commissioners, 539.)

See Conservation Commission; County; Justice's Court, 3, 4; San Francisco, City and County of.

PARENT AND CHILD. See Divorce, 6, 7, 10, 11.

PARKS. See Eminent Domain, 4–11.

PARTIES.

1. BANK DEPOSIT—ATTACHMENT OF—SUBSTITUTION OF PARTIES.—Under the provisions of section 386 of the Code of Civil Procedure, in an action brought against a bank by a married woman to recover money on deposit therein in her name, which the bank refused to pay to her because it had been attached for a debt of the husband under the claim that it was his money, the bank has the right, upon payment of the money into court, to have the plaintiff in the attachment suit substituted as party defendant in its place. (Youtz v. Farmers & Merchants' National Bank of Los Angeles, 370.)

2. PURPOSE OF SECTION 386, CODE OF CIVIL PROCEDURE—CONSTRUCTION.—The design of section 386 of the Code of Civil Procedure is to enable a party who has been sued upon a contract as to which he admits full liability as to the amount thereof to show that a third party not named in the action claims some right to the proceeds of the contract either by way of complete ownership or that he possesses a lien against the same; and so showing, to deposit the money due in court and have the third party made defendant in his stead, thus placing in positions of adversaries the real parties at interest. (Id.)

PARTNERSHIP. See Account Stated, 6, 7.

PHYSICIANS AND SURGEONS. See Negligence, 31–33.

PLACE OF TRIAL.

1. CHANGE OF PLACE OF TRIAL—AFFIDAVIT OF MERITS—AFFIDAVIT OF THIRD PARTY—SECTION 396, CODE OF CIVIL PROCEDURE.—An affidavit of merits, under section 396 of the Code of Civil Procedure, on motion for a change of place of trial, may be made by any person on behalf of the defendant who is sufficiently familiar with the facts of the case to make the same. (Gardner v. Steadman, 447.)

2. INSUFFICIENT AFFIDAVIT—AMENDMENT.—An affidavit of merits, on motion for a change of place of trial, made by the defendant's wife, which is insufficient by reason of containing affiant's mere conclusion as to defendant's residence, may be amended, and the affidavit of residence and merits of the attorney for the defendant, which is admittedly sufficient in form, may be considered as an amendment to the prior affidavit. (Id.)

PLEADING. See Attachment, 5; Brokers, 5; Contract, 4, 7, 11; Corporation, 3; Employer and Employee; Husband and Wife, 4; Insurance, 1, 5; Mechanics' Liens, 2, 3; Vendor and Vendee, 5, 7.

PLEDGE.

1. ASSIGNMENT OF PLEDGED COMMERCIAL PAPER—RIGHTS OF ASSIGNEE. A pledgee of commercial paper may assign and deliver the same, and, in the event of such transfer, the assignee holds it in the same capacity as the original pledgee, and may bring suit to collect the collateral note when due. (Pease v. Fitzgerald, 727.)

2. ACTION BY ASSIGNEE—FRAUD IN PROCUREMENT OF NOTE—DEFENSE WHEN NOT AVAILABLE.—In an action brought by the assignee of a pledged promissory note to recover the amount alleged to be due thereon, the maker cannot set up as a defense to the action that the note, which was given as the purchase price of certain corporate stock for which he subscribed, was procured through the false and fraudulent representations of the agent who acted for the corporation, where such defendant at the time of making his subscription, signed a memorandum attached thereto to the effect that his subscription was based upon the printed literature and printed statements of the corporation, and that no representations made by its agents not in accordance therewith should be binding upon the corporation. (Id.)

3. JUDGMENT—SALE OF STOCK BY PLEDGEE—STRIKING OUT OF INJUNCTIVE ORDER—LACK OF JURISDICTION.—Where in an action involving the ownership of certain shares of stock in the possession of the defendant, it is apparent from the pleadings and the findings that the purpose of the action was to have it declared that the defendant held the stock as pledgee, and to prevent him in the meantime from

PLEDGE (Continued).

making an absolute sale of it, the court has no jurisdiction to entirely strike from the judgment rendered the provision enjoining
the defendant from making any sale of the stock to any person
save the plaintiff, but it has the right to modify the phraseology
of the injunctive part of the judgment to the extent of making it
clear that the defendant might sell the stock as pledgee, and in no
other way. (Golden v. Superior Court, 734.)

POLICE POWER. See Fish and Game, 4.

POSSESSION. See Adverse Possession.

PRACTICE.

1. DISMISSAL OF ACTION—FAILURE TO PROSECUTE WITH DUE DILIGENCE
—STIPULATION DROPPING CASE FROM CALENDAR—ACTION PROPERLY
DISMISSED.—An action at issue for over seventeen years and not
in the meantime brought to trial, is properly dismissed under the
provisions of section 583 of the Code of Civil Procedure for failure to prosecute with due diligence, although the parties sixteen
years previous to the service of the notice of the motion to dismiss
entered into a stipulation that the action be dropped from the
calendar to be reset upon notice. (Central Pacific Railroad Company v. Riley, 394.)

2. TIME OF TRIAL—INSUFFICIENT NOTICE—PRESENCE IN COURT—RE-
FUSAL OF CONTINUANCE—DISCRETION NOT ABUSED.—It is not an
abuse of discretion to refuse a motion made by the defendant
for a continuance of the trial of an action, based upon the fact
that he had not received a full five days' notice of the time fixed
for the trial, where he had filed his answer, was present in court
when the case was called for trial, and filed no affidavit setting
forth the reasons why he was unable to proceed, or why his witnesses were not present, or who they were, or what they would
testify to if present. (Handy v. Handy, 590.)

3. NOTICE OF TRIAL—CONSTRUCTION OF SECTION 594, CODE OF CIVIL
PROCEDURE.—The provision of section 594 of the Code of Civil
Procedure, requiring as a condition to proceeding with a trial proof
that the adverse party has had five days' notice of such trial, has
reference only to proceedings taken against a party in his absence,
and has no application to cases in which both parties are represented and present when the case is called for trial. (Id.)

4. DISMISSAL OF ACTION—ORDER SETTING ASIDE—APPEAL—AFFIRMANCE
OF ORDER.—Upon an appeal taken from an order setting aside an
order dismissing an action entered upon the written request of the
attorneys for the plaintiff, the order appealed from must be affirmed, where the record shows that the defendant prior to the

PRACTICE (Continued).

order of dismissal had filed an answer asking for affirmative relief, and no stipulation authorizing the dismissal is furnished. (Dellaringa v. Hooker, 667.)

See Appeal; Attachment; Costs; Evidence; Instructions; New Trial; Parties; Pleading.

PRIORITIES. See Attachment, 2.

PROBATE LAW. See Estates of Deceased Persons.

PROMISSORY NOTE.

1. ACTION ON PROMISSORY NOTE—COUNTERCLAIM FOR MONEY ADVANCED—CONFLICTING EVIDENCE—FINDINGS CONCLUSIVE.—In an action on a promissory note, where the defendant set up a counterclaim based on the claim that defendant had paid a certain joint note of himself and plaintiff's assignor, the proceeds of which had been used by the latter for his personal use instead of on a joint enterprise, the finding of the trial court against the counterclaim, based upon conflicting evidence, is conclusive on appeal. (Clark v. Hotle, 29.)

2. MATURITY OF PAYMENT OF FIRST INSTALLMENT OF INTEREST—CONSTRUCTION OF INSTRUMENT—ACTION NOT PREMATURELY BROUGHT.—Under the terms of a promissory note dated February 13, 1912, "with interest from November 1, 1911, until paid, at the rate of seven per cent per annum, payable semi-annually," the first installment of interest is due May 1, 1912, and where default is made in the payment of such interest, and the note provides that the whole sum of principal and interest shall become due at the option of the holder in such an event, an action commenced on the twenty-fourth day of June, 1912, to foreclose the mortgage given to secure the payment of such note, is not prematurely brought. (Colton v. Anderson, 397.)

3. DEFAULT IN INTEREST—EXERCISE OF OPTION—TENDER—CONFLICTING EVIDENCE—APPEAL.—In an action to recover on a promissory note, which contained a provision that if interest payments were not made when due, the whole sum of principal and interest should become immediately due and payable at the option of the holder, the finding of the trial court, on conflicting evidence, that the option to mature the note had been exercised prior to the alleged tender of the overdue interest is conclusive upon the appellate court. (Copp v. Guaranty Oil Company, 543.)

4. AGREEMENT NOT TO SELL NOTE—KEEPING OF PLEDGED STOCK AVAILABLE FOR VOTING PURPOSES—RIGHT OF PAYEE AFTER DEFAULT.—An agreement made at the time of the execution of a note and as a part of the consideration therefor that the payee would not negotiate or sell or allow the note to go out of his possession

PROMISSORY NOTE (Continued).

other than to deposit it in a bank until the same became due, and that he would keep certain stock delivered to the payee as collateral security at all times available, so that the maker of the note could use or vote the stock in any stockholder's meeting of the corporation, is not, to be construed as an agreement which would hinder the payee from transferring the note after default had been made in the payment of interest, or for the purpose of collecting the debt. (Id.)

See Corporation, 9–11; Pledge.

PUBLIC OFFICERS. See Office and Officers.

PUBLIC USE. See Eminent Domain.

RAILROAD. See Fences; Negligence, 18–24.

RAPE.

1. ACTION FOR RAPE—WEIGHT OF UNCORROBORATED TESTIMONY—QUESTION FOR JURY—APPEAL.—In an action to recover damages for a criminal assault upon a single woman, the weight to be given uncorroborated testimony is a matter solely for the consideration of the jury, unless it is inherently improbable, and its conclusion is conclusive upon the appellate court. (Valencia v. Milliken, 533.)

2. ARGUMENT TO JURY—COMPARISON OF CHILD WITH DEFENDANT—LACK OF PREJUDICIAL ERROR.—In such an action a remark made by plaintiff's counsel in his argument to the jury, requesting them to compare the child to which the plaintiff gave birth with the defendant, is not prejudicial, in the absence of anything in the record showing whether or not it bore any resemblance to the defendant, or that the defendant was prejudiced by the remark. (Id.)

3. PREVIOUS CHASTITY OF PLAINTIFF — EVIDENCE OF DAMAGES—INSTRUCTION LIMITING EVIDENCE—LACK OF PREJUDICE.—The defendant is not prejudiced by the giving of an instruction limiting the purpose of evidence of previous chastity of the plaintiff to the question of damages suffered, where his defense is an alibi, and not that the plaintiff consented to the act. (Id.)

4. COMPENSATORY DAMAGES FOR "ACT COMPLAINED OF"—PROPER INSTRUCTION.—An instruction that compensatory damages should be given in such amount as will fairly compensate the plaintiff for the injury she has received by reason of the "act complained of," "taking into consideration her physical suffering and disability during pregnancy and in childbirth, if the jury should find the pregnancy was the result of defendant's act, also her mental suffering, shame, and disgrace, and her loss of social standing, and all other harm they find she suffered as the natural result of the wrong," is not an in-

RAPE (Continued).

vation of the right of the jury by telling them that damages should be awarded regardless of whether she gave her consent or not. (Id.)

RECEIPT.

EVIDENCE.—A receipt is never conclusive evidence, but is always open to explanation. (Breslauer v. McCormick & Co., 284.)

RESIDENCE. See Divorce, 8, 9.

ROBBERY. See Criminal Law, 50–55.

SACRAMENTO, CITY OF. See Justice's Court, 9–11.

SALE.

1. CONTRACT—SALE OF PORTION OF SALMON PACK ON COMMISSION—SUBSEQUENT NEGOTIATIONS FOR HANDLING OF ENTIRE PACK—EFFECT OF TERMINATION OF NEGOTIATIONS.—An optional agreement entered into between a corporation engaged in the business of packing salmon and a brokerage corporation, whereby the former agreed to deliver to the latter five thousand one hundred cases of certain kinds of canned salmon of the pack of the year 1909, to be sold by the latter at what is conventionally termed the opening price for the pack of that year, thereafter and before delivery to be named, and to be communicated by the former to the latter, and to be by the latter confirmed and assented to within five days after such communication, the latter to receive a brokerage of five per cent upon its sales, is not canceled by negotiations entered into in the early part of the year following the date of the agreement for the handling of the whole pack of the year, amounting to some fifty thousand cases, and the subsequent writing of a letter, referring to the letters by dates containing the proposition as to the handling of the entire pack, and declining the business, as such optional agreement and the subsequent negotiations were separate contracts, and the refusal to make delivery of the cases called for by such agreement constituted a breach of contract. (Williams v. Parrott & Company, 73.)

2. SALE OF PRUNE CROP—ACTION FOR BALANCE DUE—OWNERSHIP—EVIDENCE — PLAINTIFF NOT REAL PARTY IN INTEREST.—Where, in an action to recover a sum of money alleged to be the balance due on a contract for the sale of a crop of dried prunes, the case was tried and decided upon the sole theory that the plaintiff was not the real party in interest, by reason of the fact that the prunes were owned by the individual lessee of the ranch upon which they were grown, and not by the plaintiff corporation, which such lessee organized and of which he owned all the capital stock, except a few shares issued for the working purposes of the corporation, the judgment will not be disturbed upon appeal, even though the evidence upon the ques-

SALE (Continued).

tion of such ownership was not in conflict, where such evidence was of a character that the trial court was warranted in discrediting it. (Pacific Coast Dried Fruit Company v. Sheriffs, 131.)

2. EVIDENCE—REJECTION OF TESTIMONY—RIGHT OF TRIAL COURT.—It is within the legal province or discretion of the trial court to reject *in toto* the testimony of any witness, but such rejection must not be arbitrary. (Id.)

4. SALE OF PRODUCE—PLACE OF DELIVERY AND ACCEPTANCE—EVIDENCE. In an action to recover the price of certain produce alleged to have been sold and delivered to the defendant pursuant to the terms of a written contract, which designated the place of delivery and acceptance as different from the place of shipment, the admission of proof that prior to and at the time of such shipment the authorized agent of the defendant approved and accepted such produce at the point of shipment does not constitute a variance of the terms of the writing by parol, but amounts to evidence of a waiver of such provision of the contract upon the part of the defendant. (Reese v. G. B. Amigo Company, 450.)

5. AUTHORITY OF AGENT—CONFLICT OF EVIDENCE—APPEAL.—Where the evidence is conflicting as to whether the person who acted for the defendant was the duly authorized agent for the purpose of accepting the produce at the point of shipment, the finding of the trial court on such issue is conclusive on the appellate court. (Id.)

6. SALE OF BONDS—PAYMENT OUT OF PROCEEDS OF MARBLE QUARRY—FAILURE TO WORK QUARRY—MEASURE OF DAMAGES.—Where a sale of mortgage bonds of a corporation owning a marble quarry is made upon condition that the purchase price of such bonds, other than the amount paid upon their delivery, should be made by the vendee causing a corporation to be organized for the working of the quarry and having such corporation enter into an agreement with the vendor to pay to the latter such balance out of the proceeds of the quarry, and the vendee thereafter repudiates his agreement to work the mine, the measure of the plaintiff's damage is the full balance due in cash, and not the amount of the royalty that the quarry might have yielded had it been worked. (Grant v. Warren, 453.)

7. CONTRACT FOR PURCHASE AND SALE OF TIRE PROTECTORS—RELATIONSHIP CREATED—UNCERTAINTY OF CONTRACT—FINDINGS CONCLUSIVE. Upon an appeal taken from the judgment in favor of the defendants in an action to recover an alleged balance due on account of a certain quantity of tire protectors shipped to them by the plaintiff, where the single question presented by the appeal is whether the contract upon which the action was founded was one whereby the plaintiff agreed to sell and the defendants agreed to buy the protectors at the prices and upon the conditions specified in the contract, or was one whereby the plaintiff agreed to ship or make

SALE (Continued).

consignments of the protectors to the defendants upon the understanding or condition that the protectors to be so shipped or consigned should be paid for only when they were sold by the defendants, and the contract upon its face is ambiguous and uncertain as
to the nature of the relation which the parties intended thereby to
establish between themselves, the finding of the trial court will not
be disturbed. (Slama Tire Protector Co. v. Ritchie, 555.)

8. RELATIONSHIP CREATED BY CONTRACT — UNCERTAINTY — CONSTRUC-
TION OF TRIAL COURT—APPEAL.—Where a writing is so characterized by ambiguity and uncertainty as to the nature of the relation
which the parties intended thereby to create between themselves
that either of the two constructions of the contract urged by the
respective parties might upon reasons equally cogent be sustained,
it is not within the proper or legal functions of a court of review
to declare that the construction given the writing by the trial court
should be rejected and supplanted by the other construction of
which the instrument is susceptible. (Id.)

9. NATURE OF TRANSACTION — UNCERTAINTY OF CONTRACT — QUESTION
OF FACT.—Where the contract is uncertain or not clear as to its
purpose and effect, the question whether the transaction of which
it purports to be the evidence is a sale or a bailment is to be determined from all the circumstances giving rise to it, and on conflicting evidence a question of fact is presented for the jury's
determination. (Id.)

See Corporation, 1–4.

SAN FRANCISCO, CITY AND COUNTY OF.

CIVIL SERVICE COMMISSION—POWER TO EMPLOY PRIVATE COUNSEL—SAN
FRANCISCO CHARTER.—The civil service commission of the city and
county of San Francisco has no power, express or implied, to
employ private legal counsel at the expense of the city and county
to defend the commission in legal proceedings, when the city attorney is ready and willing to perform such services, as such officer,
by virtue of article V, chapter 2, section 2 of the charter of said
city and county, is alone authorized to conduct the legal business
of the municipality. (Rafael v. Boyle, 623.)

SCHOOL LANDS.

1. SCHOOL LANDS—REDEMPTION FROM DELINQUENT TAX SALES—FAIL-
URE TO PAY INTEREST—EFFECT OF ACT OF MAY 14, 1915.—Purchasers
of school lands sold to the state for delinquent taxes in the year
1907, and for which a deed to the state was made in the year 1912,
are not entitled to redeem, where they did not, prior to the going
into effect of the act of May 14, 1915 (Stats. 1915, p. 605), providing that "the unsold portions of the sixteenth and thirty-sixth

SCHOOL LANDS (Continued).

sections of school lands . . . shall be sold at public auction by the surveyor-general," make a payment of all interest due and unpaid on the land as required by section 3788 of the Political Code under the amendment of March 2, 1909 (Stats. 1909, p. 122), along with their payment of the taxes, penalties, and accruing costs. (Curtin v. Kingsbury, 57.)

2. STATUS OF DEFAULTING PURCHASERS — RESTORATION — COMPLIANCE WITH EXISTING LAWS.—Upon a sale made to the state of school lands for nonpayment of taxes followed by a deed to the state therefor, all rights of defaulting purchasers in such lands are extinguished, and the only method by which they can be restored to their former rights is by compliance with the law existing at the time of making application for such restoration. (Id.)

3. CONDITIONS TO RESTORATION — RIGHT OF STATE TO IMPOSE.—The state under such circumstances has the right, as the absolute owner of the lands, to dictate the terms upon which they may be repurchased by the original or a new purchaser, or the conditions upon which the owners or purchasers or their assigns may be restored to their original state or title. (Id.)

4. PAYMENT OF INTEREST AS CONDITION TO REDEMPTION—REASONABLENESS OF METHOD.—The method provided by the amendment of 1909 to section 3788 of the Political Code (repealed by the act of 1915) of enforcing payment of interest as a condition to the repurchase or redemption of school lands sold for nonpayment of taxes is not more burdensome than the former method of foreclosure. (Id.)

SCHOOLS.

1. SCHOOL LAW—OFFER OF EMPLOYMENT OF LIBRARIAN—FAILURE TO ACCEPT IN TIME—SECTION 1617, POLITICAL CODE.—Even though section 1617 of the Political Code, providing that "any teacher who shall fail to signify his acceptance [of a school position] within twenty days after such election, shall be deemed to have declined the same," be held not to apply to the position of librarian, it is within the right of the board of trustees of a school district to require one seeking such position to give notice of acceptance within the time provided by said section, and where the board in its offer of such position requires acceptance to be made within twenty days, under the belief that said section applies, but the applicant fails to accept within said time, there is no employment, and no salary can be recovered. (Hopkins v. Sanderson, 141.)

2. OFFER OF EMPLOYMENT—EVIDENCE.—Where a written notice of the employment of a party as librarian of a school district stated that it was given under section 1617 of the California school code, and that an acceptance was required under said section within twenty days, and that failure to comply with such provision rendered the

SCHOOLS (Continued).

position vacant, it was sufficiently made to appear that the employment was conditional upon acceptance within the time prescribed,
although no demand was made for the production of the original
notice, where the president of the school board, without objection,
was permitted to testify that the board of trustees elected the plaintiff with the proviso outlined in the notice. (Id.)

3. SCHOOL LAW—PRELIMINARY ELEMENTARY SCHOOL CERTIFICATE—FEE
FOR.—An applicant for a preliminary elementary school certificate
authorizing him to do practice and cadet teaching in any of the
elementary schools of a county is required to pay the fee of two
dollars provided by section 1565 of the Political Code to be paid
by each applicant for a teacher's certificate, "except for a temporary certificate." The term "temporary certificate," is not used
anywhere in the code as applied to any form of certificate issued
by a county board of education. (Blanchard v. Keppel, 351.)

SHERIFF. See Office and Officers, 1–4, 9, 10.

STATE LANDS. See School Lands.

STATUTE OF FRAUDS.

EXECUTED ORAL AGREEMENT.—The statute of frauds has no application
to executed oral agreements. (Freitas v. Freitas, 16.)

See Brokers, 1, 3; Novation.

STATUTE OF LIMITATIONS. See Office and Officers, 13.

STREET ASSESSMENT.

STREET LAW—SECOND IMPROVEMENT—EFFECT OF FILING OF OBJECTIONS
—SANTA ROSA CHARTER.—Under the provisions of the charter of the
city of Santa Rosa relating to the public streets thereof and their
improvement (Stats. 1905, pp. 891 to 898, inclusive), where a street
of that municipality, or any part thereof, has once been improved,
and after such improvement has been made, proceedings are taken
by the governing body of the municipality to again improve the
street, timely written objections filed by the owners of the prescribed amount of the frontage of the property fronting on the
line of the proposed improvement has the effect of barring further
proceedings in relation to the proposed improvement for the period
of six months. (City Street Improvement Company v. Lee, 738.)

SUPERSEDEAS. See Eminent Domain, 15.

SURETIES. See Attachment, 1–3; Justice's Court, 2, 5–7.

TAXATION. See Adverse Possession, 3, 5, 6; Eminent Domain, 10;
School Lands.

TENDER. See Vendor and Vendee, 4.

TORTS. See Assault and Battery; Husband and Wife, 1.

TRIAL. See Practice, 2, 3.

TRUST.

CONVEYANCE BY HUSBAND TO WIFE—CONFLICTING EVIDENCE—FIND-INGS CONCLUSIVE.—In an action by a husband for a decree that his wife holds title to certain real property, conveyed by him to her by gift deed, in trust for his use and benefit, findings based upon conflicting evidence that the wife held an undivided one-half interest in a certain piece of the property in litigation for the use and benefit of plaintiff, but that plaintiff had made a gift of the other property to defendant, cannot be disturbed on appeal. (Hagan v. Hagan, 36.)

See Intervention.

ULTRA VIRES. See Corporation, 10.

UNDERTAKINGS. See Attachment, 1, 2.

VENDOR AND VENDEE.

1. VENDOR AND PURCHASER—EXTENSION OF TIME OF PAYMENT OF IN-STALLMENT OF PURCHASE MONEY—CONSTRUCTION OF AGREEMENT—TIME AS OF THE ESSENCE OF THE CONTRACT INCLUDED.—Where an agreement extending the time for making payment of an installment of the purchase price of real property expressly provided that the agreement was "subject to all of the terms, covenants, and condi-tions" of the original contract of sale, such provision had the effect of carrying into such agreement all of the terms and conditions of the original contract, including the provision that time was of the essence of the contract, and no express declaration in such agree-ment to that effect was essential. (Newhall Land and Farming Company v. Burns, 549.)

2. DEFAULT—TERMINATION OF RIGHTS OF VENDEES.—Under the terms of such an extension agreement, the default in making the payment at the time therein provided, unexcused and not waived, ipso facto terminated the rights of the vendees under the original contract. (Id.)

3. ACTS OF VENDEES AFTER DEFAULT — RIGHT TO DECLARE TIME OF ESSENCE NOT WAIVED.—The right to declare time of the essence of such contract after default in making payment is not waived by the vendor in thereafter making no protest against the efforts of the vendees to sell the property and in the making of surveys, where

VENDOR AND VENDEE (Continued). .

the contract contained no requirements that the vendees should perform such acts. (Id.)

4. TENDER OF DEED — WHEN UNNECESSARY.—Where under the terms of such a contract the deed to the property had been delivered to a third party with instructions to deliver to the grantees upon payment of the price, no further tender of the deed was necessary to declare a forfeiture upon default of the vendees. (Id.)

5. ACTION TO RECOVER MONEY — EXECUTORY CONTRACT TO PURCHASE LAND — RESCISSION — PLEADING.—A complaint to recover a certain sum of money paid under an executory contract for the purchase of land states a cause of action where it alleges that the defendants without cause repudiated the contract, declared it canceled, and denied to plaintiffs any right or interest thereunder, as, this being true, plaintiffs were relieved from the obligation of further performance on their contract and were privileged to accept defendants' renunciation of the contract as a rescission of the same. (McNeil v. Kredo, 76.)

6. RESTORATION OF CONSIDERATION.—In the absence of a special demurrer, such a complaint is sufficiently certain in its allegations to the effect that plaintiffs had not received and retained by virtue of the contract anything of value from the defendants, and it was not essential to the statement of a cause of action to allege that the plaintiff had placed or had offered to place defendants *in statu quo* before electing to accept defendants' alleged rescission of the contract. (Id.)

7. PLEADING AND PROOF — PARTNERSHIP OBLIGATION — INDIVIDUAL LIABILITY.—The allegation of the complaint that the contract in controversy was a partnership obligation does not preclude proof of the fact that it was the individual obligation of one of the defendants. (Id.)

See Brokers.

VENUE. See Place of Trial.

WAREHOUSEMAN.

1. WAREHOUSE—LOSS OF STORED GOODS BY FIRE—STORAGE IN FIREPROOF WAREHOUSE—EXPRESS CONTRACT—EXISTENCE OF IMPLIED CONTRACT IMMATERIAL.—Upon an appeal from a judgment in an action against a warehouse-keeper for the loss of stored goods by fire, the judgment must be sustained irrespective of whether an implied contract arose that the goods were to be stored in a fireproof warehouse, where the evidence amply sustains the finding that there was an express contract to that effect. (Lynch v. Bekins Van & Storage Company, 68.)

WAREHOUSEMAN (Continued).

2. EVIDENCE OF EXPRESS CONTRACT — ADVERTISEMENTS AND PRINTED MATTER.—The admission of evidence showing representations by advertisements and printed matter, to the effect that the defendant had at its disposal fireproof warehouses and offered to customers to furnish storage of that kind, is without error, as it tends to corroborate the evidence of the plaintiff as to the express contract made and found by the court. (Id.)

3. DIFFERENCES IN PRICES BETWEEN FIREPROOF AND NONFIREPROOF STORAGE.—The practice or habit of the defendant in charging a different price for storage, according to whether or not it was fireproof, is not admissible, in the absence of knowledge by plaintiffs of such fact prior to the contract of storage. (Id.)

4. CHARACTER OF STORAGE—BOOK ENTRIES OF DEFENDANT—SELF-SERVING DECLARATIONS.—The entry made by defendant's agent in its order book at the time of the giving of the order to it for storage, not having been seen or known of by the plaintiff when the transaction was closed, is self-serving, and not admissible to corroborate its evidence, consisting of the positive statement of its agent, contradicting plaintiff, that nothing was said in the conversation about fireproof storage, and that the contract was for nonfireproof storage. (Id.)

5. CUSTOM AS TO LIMITATION OF LIABILITY—LACK OF KNOWLEDGE OF PLAINTIFFS—PROOF INADMISSIBLE.—In the absence of any misrepresentation made by plaintiffs as to the character of the stored goods, or that they refused upon demand to truly state that character, a general custom among warehousemen to insert in their receipts a provision limiting their liability for loss by fire to $50 per package, or one of refusing to accept antiques and jewelry of great value, is inadmissible. (Id.)

6. IMPEACHMENT OF DEFENDANT'S AGENT — ADVERTISEMENTS.—Defendant's advertisement of ability to furnish fireproof storage, though unknown to plaintiffs, is admissible, for the purpose of contradicting defendant's agent's testimony that nothing was said about storage in a fireproof building. (Id.)

WATER AND WATER RIGHTS. See Costs, 4, 5.

WORKMEN'S COMPENSATION ACT.

1. SALESMAN OF REAL ESTATE—INJURIES IN HOTEL FIRE.—Injuries and losses by one employed as a salesman of real estate upon commission do not come within the scope of the Workmen's Compensation Act (Stats. 1913, p. 279), where they resulted from a fire in a hotel in which the employee was spending the night in a town to which he had been sent for the purpose of selling real estate and at which he was to remain indefinitely; and the employee is not entitled to

31 Cal. App.—56

WORKMEN'S COMPENSATION ACT (Continued).

recover compensation under said act from his employer. (Forman v. Industrial Accident Commission, 441.)

2. DEATH OF EMPLOYEE OF TEAMING COMPANY—HIRING OUT OF TEAM AND EMPLOYEE TO THIRD PARTY—LIABILITY OF EMPLOYER.—Under the terms of the Workmen's Compensation, Insurance and Safety Act, a person engaged in the business of contract teaming and hauling is liable to the dependent parents of an employee for his accidental death while engaged in hauling lumber for a lumber company, where he, in pursuance of a request made to his employer by the lumber company for a team and driver, was directed by his employer to perform such work. (Kirkpatrick v. Industrial Accident Commission, 668.)

3. MEANING OF TERMS "EMPLOYER" AND "EMPLOYEE."—The Workmen's Compensation, Insurance and Safety Act, in sections 13 and 14 thereof, furnishes its own definition of the terms "employer" and "employee." The former term includes every person who has any person in service under any contract of hire, express or implied, and the latter term includes every person thus in the service of such employer. (Id.)

4. COMPENSATION TO DEPENDANTS OF KILLED EMPLOYEES — CONSTITUTIONALITY OF ACT.—The provisions of the Workmen's Compensation Act authorizing the payment of compensation to dependents of employees whose death has resulted from injuries received in the course of their employment, are constitutional. (Id.)

5. REVIEW OF AWARD—REFERENCE TO EVIDENCE—WHEN PERMISSIBLE.—In a proceeding to review an award made by the Industrial Accident Commission, where the findings are meager in detailing the facts upon which the commission based its conclusion, the evidence may be referred to, not to vary or contradict the findings of fact, but for the purpose of explaining or supplementing the same. (Kramer v. Industrial Accident Commission, 673.)

6. INJURY TO PERSON EMPLOYED AS JANITOR AND GARDENER—PRUNING OF FIG TREE—GARDEN LABOR—COMPENSATION NOT AWARDABLE. A person employed as janitor for a dancing academy in a building which was also used by his employer for the purpose of a residence, the duties of which position were to take charge of the rooms, sweep and dust the same, and in general keep them in order, and also employed as a gardener to look after and care for the grass, flowers, shrubbery, and trees growing upon the lot and upon the adjoining lot, which latter lot the employer used for garage purposes, is not entitled to compensation for injuries received in pruning a fig tree upon the latter lot, as such injury arose in the course of his employment as gardener, and not as janitor, which first-named employment is excluded from the operation of the Workmen's Compensation, Insurance and Safety Act by section 14 thereof, which excepts

WORKMEN'S COMPENSATION ACT (Continued).

employees engaged in farm, agricultural, or horticultural labor, or in household domestic service. (Id.)

7. DEATH OF ERRAND BOY IN ELEVATOR ACCIDENT—DISREGARD OF INSTRUCTIONS—ANNULMENT OF AWARD.—An award of compensation made by the Industrial Accident Commission for the death of an errand boy, who met his death while endeavoring to ascend to the floor of the building upon which his employer had its place of business, by means of a freight elevator operated by himself, is beyond the jurisdiction of the commission, where the undisputed evidence shows that the deceased had been expressly warned not to ride in, or attempt to operate, the freight elevators in the building under penalty of discharge, and that notices were posted at, or near, the entrance of such elevators of similar import, and there is no evidence that the alleged disregard of such instructions and warnings on the part of employees was ever brought to the notice of their employer, or of any negligence from which such knowledge would be chargeable. (Pacific Coast Casualty Company v. Pillsbury, 701.)

Lightning Source UK Ltd.
Milton Keynes UK
UKHW010629010219
336547UK00009B/771/P

9 781528 587525